PROCEEDINGS OF THE SECOND ANNUAL WORKSHOP ON

# Computational Learning Theory

Sponsored by the ACM SIGACT / SIGART

University of California, Santa Cruz

July 31 – August 2, 1989

**RONALD RIVEST**

*(Massachusetts Institute of Technology)*

**DAVID HAUSSLER**

*(University of California, Santa Cruz)*

**MANFRED K. WARMUTH**

*(University of California, Santa Cruz)*

MORGAN KAUFMANN PUBLISHERS, INC.
SAN MATEO, CALIFORNIA

Senior Editor   *Bruce Spatz*
Coordinating Editor   *John Galbraith*
Production Manager   *Shirley Jowell*
Cover Designer   *Jo Jackson*
Production and Composition
    *Kennon-Kelley Graphic Design*

**Library of Congress Cataloging-in-Publication Data**

Workshop on Computational Learning Theory (2nd : 1989 :
    University of California at Santa Cruz)
    Proceedings of the Second Workshop on Computational
Learning Theory.

    1. Machine learning—Congresses.   I. Rivest, Ronald L.
II. Haussler, David.   III. Warmuth, Manfred K.   IV. Title
Q325.5.W67   1989            006.3'1            89-15545
                                                      CIP


ISBN 1-55860-086-8
MORGAN KAUFMANN PUBLISHERS, INC.
*Editorial Office:*
    2929 Campus Drive, Suite 260
    San Mateo, CA  94403
*Order from:*
    P.O. Box 50490
    Palo Alto, CA  94303-9953

93  92  91  90  89   5  4  3  2  1

# Contents

## SHORT ABSTRACTS

# Foreword

The papers in this volume were presented at the Second Workshop on Computational Learning Theory, jointly sponsored by the ACM Special Interest Group on Automata and Computability Theory (SIGACT), and the ACM Special Interest Group on Artificial Intelligence (SIGART). The workshop was held at the University of California at Santa Cruz, July 31 to August 2, 1989. The 31 papers that were presented were selected from among 66 extended abstracts submitted for consideration.

This workshop is the second in a series of annual workshops focusing on theoretical issues in machine learning. The intention of these workshops is to bring together theoretically oriented computer scientists, practitioners of machine learning, and experts in related fields to explore computational models of learning. The first workshop, held last year at MIT, featured a variety of papers on computational learning models and complexity theoretic analysis of machine learning algorithms. The papers covered a wide range of problems in inductive inference, pattern recognition and concept learning. Rather than narrowing the focus, this year's papers offer a still larger variety of learning models and perspectives. A larger number of different learning domains are being explored as well. Included in this volume are papers addressing learning problems for neural nets, several classes of Boolean formulae and first order formulae, automata and formal languages, classes of recursive functions, binary relations and other combinatorial objects, search strategies, prototypical genetic sequences, real-valued functions, and various patterns of correlation in unclassified data. We take this as a healthy sign for a field as young as ours, and look forward to even greater diversity as our work begins to reach a wider audience.

In addition to our technical papers, this year we are especially honored to have Professor V. N. Vapnik of the Soviet Academy of Sciences give an invited lecture at our workshop. His lecture is entitled *Inductive Principles of the Search for Empirical Dependences* (*Methods Based on Weak Convergence of Probability Measures*), and is presented in its entirety in this volume. The work of Professors Vapnik and Chervonenkis on the theoretical foundations of pattern recognition has been extremely influential in the recent development of computational learning theory. In his talk, Prof. Vapnik emphasizes his principle of structural risk minimization as a method of trading simplicity for goodness of fit in pattern recognition, a method that is currently little known among researchers outside the Soviet Union, and potentially very rich in new applications.

In closing, we would like to thank the many individuals responsible for the success of this workshop, including our sponsors at ACM, our publishers at Morgan Kaufmann, and the members of our program committee (Ron Rivest, Dana Angluin, John Cherniavsky, David Haussler, Balas Natarajan, Lenny Pitt, Carl Smith, Leslie Valiant, and Manfred Warmuth). Special thanks also to Jean McKnight and Nancy Furber, who ran the show at Santa Cruz, to Be Hubbard, who handled the program committee affairs at MIT, and to Rob Schapire, who set up the software for the anonymous electronic voting systems we used in conjunction with the program committee deliberations.

Ron Rivest (Program Chair)
David Haussler (Conference Chair)
Manfred Warmuth (Local Arrangements)

# Invited Lecture

# Inductive Principles of the Search for Empirical Dependences
## (Methods Based on Weak Convergence of Probability Measures)

V. N. Vapnik

Institute of Control Sciences

Soviet Academy of Sciences

Moscow 117343

## §I. Introduction

Problems of inductive type, when a general law has to be found on the basis of a finite number of observations, are one of the important trends of analysis.

There are many examples of such problems. It would be sufficient to mention just widely known mathematical problems such as the basic problem of statistics: estimation of a probability density on the basis of random independent observations; the most important applied statistics problem of regression estimation; and finally one of the latest modern problems: the problem of pattern recognition.

For all these problems the appropriate algorithms of estimation have been developed and studied in detail by theoretical scientists. But until lately the question has still been open: "Does the general inductive principle exist that provides success of these algorithms?"

It is the answer to this question to which my lecture is dedicated. Today I shall tell about an inductive principle based on weak convergence of probability measures—the principle of empirical risk minimization. Necessary and sufficient conditions of its consistency will be given and a more general principle will be formulated—the principle of structural risk minimization.

It will be shown that the existing methods of density estimation, regression estimation, and construction of decision rules for pattern recognition are covered by this principle.

The lecture will consist of theorem formulations and comments regarding them. To formulate theorems we need to introduce a few abstract concepts. But these concepts have a good interpretation in simple constructions, and those of you who are acquainted with works on induction by a remarkable English philosopher, K. Popper, will see how nicely the obtained conclusions can be interpreted in terms of his theory of falsifiability.

Thus, the topic of this lecture is inductive principles in problems of dependence estimation.

## §2.  The problem of expected risk minimization

To begin investigations in the field of induction, we should first formulate the general model embracing as broad a class as possible of problems classified as inductive (below we shall consider problems of density estimation, regression estimation, and construction of decision rules).  This model will be the problem of expected risk minimization from empirical data.

Let on the probability space $(X, \Omega, P)$ a set of measurable functions $Q(x, \alpha)$, $\alpha \in \Lambda$ be given.  For convenience, functions are given in parametrical form.  However such notation does not decrease the generality of the statement as the parameter $\alpha \in \Lambda$ may be an abstract element.

It is required to minimize over all $Q(x, \alpha)$, $\alpha \in \Lambda$ the functional of expected risk

$$R(\alpha) = \int Q(x, \alpha) dP(x) \tag{1}$$

if probability measure $P(x)$ is unknown, but a random independent set of observations

$$x_1, \ldots, x_l$$

obtained according to $P(x)$ is given.

It is to this scheme that all the estimation problems named above may be reduced.

### 1.  Density estimation (statement by Fisher-Wald)

Let $p(x, \alpha)$, $\alpha \in \Lambda$ be a set of densities that have Shannon entropy

$$H(\alpha) = -\int p(x, \alpha) \ln p(x, \alpha) \, dx.$$

Consider the functional

$$\hat{H}(\alpha) = -\int \ln p(x, \alpha) \, dP(x).$$

It is known that the functional minimum is attained on the function $p(x, \alpha_0)$ for which

$$p(x, \alpha_0) = \frac{dP(x)}{dx}$$

everywhere except perhaps on a set of zero measure.

In such a way the problem of density estimation from observations on a random independent sample

$$x_1, \ldots, x_l$$

may be treated as a problem of the minimization of the functional (1) on the class of functions $-\ln p(x, \alpha)$, $\alpha \in \Lambda$ in conditions when the probability measure $P(x)$ is unknown, but a random independent sample obtained with respect to the unknown measure is given.

## 2. Regression estimation

Now let $x = (y, t)$, where $t$ is a vector and $y$ is a scalar, and let $Q(x, \alpha) = (y - f(t, \alpha))^2$, where $f(t, \alpha)$, $\alpha \in \Lambda$ is a set of functions that are square integrable. Examine the functional

$$R(\alpha) = \int (y - f(t, \alpha))^2 \, dP(y, t). \tag{2}$$

It is easy to verify that the minimum of this functional is attained on the regression function

$$r(t) = \int y \, dP(y|t)$$

if the regression belongs to $f(t, \alpha)$, $\alpha \in \Lambda$, and on the function closest to the regression in the metric

$$\rho(r(t), f(t, x)) = \sqrt{\int (r(t) - f(t, \alpha))^2 dP(t)}$$

if the regression does not belong to $f(t, \alpha)$, $\alpha \in \Lambda$. Here $P(y|t)$ and $P(t)$ are the functions defined by joint distribution

$$P(y, t) = \int P(y|t) dP(t).$$

Thus, the problem of regression estimation on a random independent sample of observations

$$(y_1, t_1), \ldots, (y_l, t_l) \tag{3}$$

also is reduced to the problem of minimization of the functional of expected risk (2) in conditions when probability measure $P(y, t)$ defined on pairs $(y, t)$ is unknown, but a random independent sample (3) obtained with respect to this measure is given.

### 3. Pattern recognition problem

Let $x$ define the pair $(\omega, t)$ where $t$ is a vector and $\omega$ is an indicator of the class, $\omega \in \{0, 1, \ldots, N\}$. Let $\Phi(t, \alpha)$, $\alpha \in \Lambda$ be a set of decision rules, each of which assigns to each vector t a number of the corresponding class, i.e., $\Phi(t, \alpha)$ also takes one of the $N + 1$ values $0, 1, \ldots, N$.

Let $\Pi(\omega, \Phi(t, \alpha))$ be a function the value of which is chosen from the matrix (error cost matrix)

$$\begin{bmatrix} 0 & a_{12} & \cdots & a_{1N} \\ a_{21} & 0 & \cdots & a_{2N} \\ \cdots & \cdots & \cdots & \cdots \\ a_{N1} & a_{N2} & \cdots & 0 \end{bmatrix}$$

(the value $a_{rp}$ is chosen if $\omega = r$ and $\Phi(t, \alpha) = p$). For simplicity assume $a_{rp} = 1$ if $p \neq r$, the corresponding function is denoted by $\Pi_0(\omega, \Phi(t, \alpha))$.

Consider the functional

$$R(\alpha) = \int \Pi(\omega, \Phi(t, \alpha))\, dP(\omega, t). \tag{4}$$

This attains its minimum on the decision rule $\Phi(t, \alpha_0)$ that provides the minimum value to the expected risk. (For the function $\Pi_0(\omega, \Phi(t, \alpha_0))$, this is the minimum value of error probability.)

Thus, the pattern recognition problem consists of minimization of the expected risk functional (4) on the set of decision rules $\Phi(t, \alpha)$, $\alpha \in \Lambda$ when the probability measure defined on pairs $(\omega, t)$ is unknown, but a random independent sample of pairs

$$(\omega_1, t_1), \ldots, (\omega_l, t_l)$$

is defined.

## §3. The principle of empirical risk minimization

Thus, all three problems can be reduced to the scheme of minimization of the expected risk functional

$$R(\alpha) = \int Q(x, \alpha)\, dP(x) \tag{5}$$

on the basis of empirical data

$$x_1, \ldots, x_l. \tag{6}$$

However, as the measure $P(x)$ is not defined explicitly, direct minimization of the functional (5) is impossible.

There is only one possibility under these conditions: utilize the sample $x_1, \ldots, x_l$ to construct explicitly the functional

$$R^*(\alpha) = \Phi\left(Q(x, \alpha); x_1, \ldots, x_l\right)$$

and take the minimum point of this functional as the minimum point of the initial functional.

There exist two ideas for replacing the functional (5):

1. To use instead of expected risk functional (5) the empirical risk functional

$$R_{emp}(\alpha) = \frac{1}{l} \sum_{i=1}^{l} Q(x_i, \alpha). \tag{7}$$

2. On the basis of the sample $x_1, \ldots, x_l$ to estimate the density $p_0(x) = \dfrac{dP(x)}{dx}$ and use instead of the functional (5) the functional

$$R^*(\alpha) = \int Q(x, \alpha)\, \tilde{p}(x)\, dx,$$

where $\tilde{p}$ is the estimate of $p_0$.

This lecture deals with the induction step connected with the replacement of initial functional $R(\alpha)$ by the empirical risk functional (7).

First we observe that the principle of empirical risk minimization is decisive in solving all three abovementioned problems of function estimation from empirical data.

So, in the problem of density estimation where $Q(x, \alpha) = -\ln p(x, \alpha)$, the principal of empirical risk minimization leads to minimization of the functional

$$L(\alpha) = -\sum_{i=1}^{l} \ln p(x_i, \alpha). \tag{8}$$

In the form with the reversed sign before the functional and the maximum sought instead of the minimum, (8) becomes the principle of maximum likelihood.

In the problem of regression estimation where $Q(x, \alpha) = (y - f(t, \alpha))^2$, the principle of empirical risk minimization leads to minimization of the functional

$$M(\alpha) = \sum_{i=1}^{l} (y_i - f(t_i, \alpha))^2, \tag{9}$$

which is the least squares method.

Finally, in the problem of pattern recognition, algorithms based on the principle of empirical risk minimization are called correct algorithms.

The main problem in investigation of the principle of empirical risk minimization is to find when it is consistent and to estimate the rate of convergence of the risk yielded by the estimate to the true minimum.

## §4. The concept of consistency and strong consistency

<u>Definition</u>. The method of empirical risk minimization is called *consistent* in the class $Q(x, \alpha), \alpha \in \Lambda$ if

$$\inf_{\alpha \in \Lambda} \frac{1}{l} \sum_{i=1}^{l} Q(x_i, \alpha) \xrightarrow[l \to \infty]{p} \inf_{\alpha \in \Lambda} \int Q(x, \alpha) dP(x). \tag{10}$$

Observe that in view of (10)

$$\int Q(x, \alpha_{\text{emp}}) dP(x) \xrightarrow[l \to \infty]{p} \inf_{\alpha \in \Lambda} \int Q(x, \alpha) dP(x),$$

where $Q(x, \alpha_{\text{emp}})$ is a function that yields the minimum of the empirical risk functional. (The reverse statement in general does not hold.)

However, such a definition of consistency is not a good basis for the study of principal conditions for the justification of the induction step. And this is why. Let the method of empirical risk minimization on the set $Q(x, \alpha), \alpha \in \Lambda$ be not consistent. Consider a new set containing the set $Q(x, \alpha), \alpha \in \Lambda$ and one function $\Phi(x)$ more such as

$$\Phi(x) < Q(x, \alpha), \alpha \in \Lambda.$$

For this new set, the method of empirical risk minimization will be consistent for any measure $P(x)$.

It follows from the given example that necessary and sufficient conditions of consistency must be based not only on the characteristics of the set $Q(x, \alpha), \alpha \in \Lambda$ as a whole but on the properties of the functions themselves. To obtain the conditions of consistency solely in terms of the characteristics of the set as a whole, we use a stronger concept of consistency.

Definition. The method of empirical risk minimization is *strongly consistent* if for any subset $\Lambda^* \subset \Lambda$

$$\inf_{\alpha \in \Lambda^*} \frac{1}{l} \sum_{i=1}^{l} Q(x, \alpha) \xrightarrow[l \to \infty]{P} \inf_{\alpha \in \Lambda^*} \int Q(x, \alpha) dP(x)$$

is valid.

## §5. Strong consistency and uniform convergence

We need two more definitions.

Definition. We shall say that uniform two-sided convergence of means to their mathematical expectations takes place if the expression

$$\sup_{\alpha \in \Lambda} \left| \int Q(x, \alpha) dP(x) - \frac{1}{l} \sum_{i=1}^{l} Q(x_i, \alpha) \right| \xrightarrow[l \to \infty]{P} 0 \qquad (11)$$

is valid.

Definition. We shall say that uniform one-sided convergence takes place if the expression

$$\sup_{\alpha \in \Lambda} \left[ \int Q(x, \alpha) dP(x) - \frac{1}{l} \sum_{i=1}^{l} Q(x_i, \alpha) \right]_+ \xrightarrow[l \to \infty]{P} 0 \qquad (12)$$

is valid, where plus at the bottom is defined by

$$(z)_+ = \begin{cases} z, & \text{if } z \geq 0 \\ 0, & \text{if } z < 0. \end{cases}$$

The statement about the existence of one-sided uniform convergence on the set of functions $Q(x, \alpha)$, $\alpha \in \Lambda$ proves to be equivalent to the statement about strong consistency of the method of empirical risk minimization on this set.

<u>Theorem 1</u>. [4] Let

$$-\infty < a < \int Q\,(x,\alpha)dP\,(x) < A < \infty, \alpha \in \Lambda.$$

Then the following two statements are equivalent:

– one-sided uniform convergence takes place on $Q\,(x,\alpha)$, $\alpha \in \Lambda$, and

– the method of empirical risk minimization is strongly consistent on $Q\,(x,\alpha)$, $\alpha \in \Lambda$.

Hence, Theorem 1 reduces the conditions of the strong consistency of the method of empirical risk minimization to conditions of existence of uniform one-sided convergence.

## §6.  Necessary and sufficient conditions of uniform convergence

Consider a class of uniformly bounded functions $Q\,(x,\alpha)$, $\alpha \in \Lambda$. Let $\mid Q(x,\alpha)\mid\ \leq C$. On this class of functions necessary and sufficient conditions of uniform convergence can be found in terms of the *expected entropy* of the set of functions $Q\,(x,\alpha)$, $\alpha \in \Lambda$. This concept is defined as follows.

Let an independent random sample of vectors $x_1, \ldots, x_l$ and the class of functions $Q\,(x,\alpha)$, $\alpha \in \Lambda$ be given. For each $\alpha \in \Lambda$, assign to each function $Q\,(x,\alpha)$ a vector with coordinates

$$\Gamma_\alpha = (Q\,(x_1,\alpha), \ldots, Q\,(x_l,\alpha)).$$

Thus, by means of vectors $x_1, \ldots, x_l$, assign to the set of functions $Q\,(x,\alpha)$, $\alpha \in \Lambda$ the set of $l$-dimensional vectors $\Gamma_\alpha$, $\alpha \in \Lambda$. As the functions $Q\,(x,\alpha)$, $\alpha \in \Lambda$ do not exceed $C$ in absolute value, the set $\Gamma_\alpha$, $\alpha \in \Lambda$ lies inside an $l$-dimensional cube, the edge length of which does not exceed $2C$.

Consequently, there exists a finite $\varepsilon$-net for the set of $\Gamma_\alpha$, $\alpha \in \Lambda$ in the uniform metric, i.e., a set $T$ of vectors such that for all $\alpha \in \Lambda$ there exists a vector $t \in T$ with $\rho(\Gamma_\alpha, t) \leq \varepsilon$, where

$$\rho(\Gamma_\alpha, t) = \max_{1 \leq i \leq l} \mid Q\,(x_i,\alpha) - t_i \mid.$$

Let the number of elements of the smallest such $\varepsilon$-net be equal to $N^\Lambda\,(\varepsilon, x_1, \ldots, x_l)$.

<u>Definition.</u> Call the value

$$H^\Lambda(\varepsilon, x_1, \ldots, x_l) = \log_2 N^\Lambda(\varepsilon, x_1, \ldots, x_l)$$

the random entropy of the set of functions $Q(x, \alpha)$, $\alpha \in \Lambda$ on the sample $x_1, \ldots, x_l$.

Call the value

$$H^\Lambda(\varepsilon, l) = \mathbf{E} H^\Lambda(\varepsilon, x_1, \ldots, x_l),$$

where mathematical expectation is obtained with respect to product measure $P^l(x)$, the expected entropy of the set of functions $Q(x, \alpha)$ on samples of size $l$.

Here and below without special reference we shall assume all the considered functions to be measurable with respect to product measure $P^l(x)$.

<u>Theorem 2.</u> [3] For the uniform two-sided convergence on a set of uniformly bounded functions $Q(x, \alpha)$, $\alpha \in \Lambda$ it is necessary and sufficient that for any $\varepsilon > 0$ the equality

$$\lim_{l \to \infty} \frac{H^\Lambda(\varepsilon, l)}{l} = 0 \qquad (13)$$

holds.

In other words, the value of expected entropy with respect to the number of elements of the sample is required to tend to zero as sample size increases.

<u>Theorem 3.</u> [4]. For the uniform one-sided convergence on a set of uniformly bounded functions $Q(x, \alpha)$, $\alpha \in \Lambda$ it is necessary and sufficient that for any $\varepsilon$, $\rho$ and $\eta > 0$, the set of functions $R(x, \beta)$, $\beta \in B$, be found such that:

1)    for any function $Q(x, \alpha^*)$ the function $R(x, \beta^*)$ can be found satisfying the conditions

$$Q(x, \alpha^*) \geq R(x, \beta^*) \qquad \text{(the condition of minorization)}$$

$$(14)$$

$$\int [Q(x, \alpha^*) - R(x, \beta^*)] dP(x) < \rho \qquad \text{(the condition of closeness in } L_1(P))$$

2)    the expected entropy of the set $R(x, \beta)$, $\beta \in B$, on the samples of the size $l$ satisfied the condition

$$\lim_{l \to \infty} \frac{H^B(\epsilon, l)}{l} < \eta \qquad (15)$$

In other words, one-sided uniform convergence on the set $Q(x, \alpha)$, $\alpha \in \Lambda$ takes place if and only if this set can be approximated (in the sense of (14)) by another set $R(x, \beta)$, $\beta \in B$, for which two-sided uniform convergence takes place.

Thus, strong consistency of the principle of empirical risk minimization (according to Theorems 1 and 2) depends on capacity characteristics of the sets as a whole (i.e., entropy characteristics of the set $Q(x, \alpha)$, $\alpha \in \Lambda$ on samples of the size $l$).

### §7.  The relation to the theory of falsifiability by K. Popper

In the 1920s a philosopher, K. Popper, working on induction theory suggested the principle of falsifiability.  Popper thought that the necessary condition for the justification of the induction method is a possibility of falsifying the method—the existence of such a set of propositions for which a general rule cannot be found.  With respect to the problem of pattern recognition this means that the necessary condition for justification of the algorithm that searches for the decision rule in the class of functions $\Phi(t, \alpha)$, $\alpha \in \Lambda$ is the existence of such a sample

$$(t_1, \omega_1), \ldots, (t_l, \omega_l)$$

for which in the class $\Phi(t, \alpha)$, $\alpha \in \Lambda$ there cannot be found a function $\Phi(t, \alpha^*)$ satisfying the equalities

$$\Phi(t_i, \alpha^*) = \omega_i, \qquad i = 1, 2, \ldots, l.$$

The following statement appeared to be central in the proof of the necessary conditions for the existence of uniform one-sided convergence in a class of uniformly bounded functions $Q(x, \alpha)$, $\alpha \in \Lambda$ (Theorem 3).

<u>Theorem 4</u>. [4].  Let the set of functions $Q(x, \alpha)$, $\alpha \in \Lambda$ be such that $\epsilon = \epsilon_0 > 0$ will be found for which the equality

$$\lim_{l \to \infty} \frac{H^\Lambda(\epsilon_0, l)}{l} = c > 0$$

will be fulfilled.  Then such two functions $\psi_1(x)$ and $\psi_0(x)$ and the constant $d(\epsilon_0)$ satisfying the conditions

$$\psi_1(x) \geq \psi_0(x),$$

$$\int (\psi_1(x) - \psi_0(x)) dP(x) > d(\varepsilon_0)$$

can be found that for any binary sequence $\omega_1, \ldots, \omega_l$ ($\omega_i \in \{0, 1\}$), arbitrary $\rho > 0$ and almost any sample $x_1, \ldots, x_l$, such a function $Q(x, \alpha^*)$ will be found that the inequality

$$|\psi_{\omega_i}(x_i) - Q(x_i, \alpha^*)| < \rho, \qquad i = 1, 2, \ldots, l$$

will be satisfied.

For the problem of pattern recognition this means that if on the set of decision rules $\Phi(x, \alpha)$ the conditions of the uniform convergence are not fulfilled (in this case $\psi_0(x) = 0$, $\psi_1(x) = 1$ and $\psi_{\omega_i}(x) = \omega_i$) there exists such a non-empty subset $X^*$ of the set $X$ on which the method of empirical risk minimization can not be falsified.

## §8.  The capacity of a set of functions

Above we established necessary and sufficient conditions for the consistency of the principle of empirical risk minimization depending upon characteristics of the entropy $H^\Lambda(\varepsilon, l)$. However, it is not always simple to verify these characteristics—the entropy is constructed by means of the probability measure $P(x)$, which by assumption is unknown to us.

That is why it is important to have good justifiable (sufficient) conditions for the consistency of the method of empirical risk minimization (the conditions for uniform convergence) that would be independent of the properties of the probability measure. Below we shall consider such characteristics—the capacity of a set of functions in terms of which we shall state sufficient conditions for uniform convergence and its rate.

Recollect how the entropy of the set $Q(x, \alpha)$, $\alpha \in \Lambda$ was defined. At first we defined a random entropy of the set on the sample

$$H^\Lambda(\varepsilon, x_1, \ldots, x_l) = \log_2 N^\Lambda(\varepsilon, x_1, \ldots, x_l)$$

and then averaged the random entropy with respect to product measure given on samples of the size $l$

$$H^\Lambda(\varepsilon, l) = \mathbf{E}H^\Lambda(\varepsilon, x_1, \ldots, x_l).$$

Now we give up averaging with respect to a measure and consider the upper bound of the random entropy on all possible samples of the size $l$

$$\overline{H}(\varepsilon, l) = \max_{x_1, \ldots, x_l} H^\Lambda(\varepsilon, x_1, \ldots, x_l).$$

We shall realize this idea first for a set of indicator functions $I(x, \alpha)$, $\alpha \in \Lambda$, taking values 0 or 1. Observe that if $\varepsilon < 1$ then for indicator functions the number $N^\Lambda(\varepsilon, x_1, \ldots, x_l)$ of different elements of a minimal $\varepsilon$-net does not depend on $\varepsilon$. Denote it by $N^\Lambda(x_1, \ldots, x_l)$.

Definition. The value

$$m^\Lambda(l) = \max_{x_1, \ldots, x_l} \log_2 N^\Lambda(x_1, \ldots, x_l)$$

is called the growth function.

The following theorem holds.

Theorem 5. [2] The growth function $m^\Lambda(l)$ either is defined by the quality

$$m^\Lambda(l) = l \tag{16}$$

or if such $h$ can be found that $m^\Lambda(h) = h$ and $m^\Lambda(h + 1) \neq h + 1$, the growth function is bounded by the inequality

$$m^\Lambda(l) < h \log_2 l. \tag{17}$$

Thus, the function $m^\Lambda(l)$ grows either linearly or logarithmically. To find the coefficient $h$ it is sufficient to find such a sample size $h + 1$ that the function stops being linear.

Definition. We say that an indicator set $I(x, \alpha)$, $\alpha \in \Lambda$ has a finite capacity $h$ if the inequality (17) is fulfilled. Due to Dudley, a class of functions of bounded capacity is called a Vapnik-Chervonenkis class and the number $h$ its Vapnik-Chervonenkis number.

It is easy to see that if the value $h$ is finite, uniform convergence takes place and hence the method of empirical risk minimization is strongly consistent.

Actually

$$\frac{H^\Lambda(\varepsilon, l)}{l} \leq \frac{h \, \log_2 l}{l} \xrightarrow[l \to \infty]{} 0.$$

We now extend the definition of capacity to an arbitrary set of real-valued functions $Q(x, \alpha)$, $\alpha \in \Lambda$.

Consider the set of indicator functions

$$I(x, \alpha) = \Theta(Q(x, \alpha) - \beta^*), \quad \alpha \in \Lambda$$

where $\beta^*$ is a fixed value and

$$\Theta(z) = \begin{cases} 1, & z \geq 0 \\ 0, & z < 0. \end{cases}$$

Definition. Let the capacity $h$ of the set of functions $Q(x, \alpha)$, $\alpha \in \Lambda$ be the maximum of the capacities of the sets

$$I(x, \alpha) = \Theta(Q(x, \alpha) - \beta), \quad \alpha \in \Lambda$$

over all real $\beta$.

The capacity of the set can be easily bounded. In particular, the capacity of the set of functions

$$Q(x, \alpha) = \sum_{i=1}^{n} \alpha_i \, \phi_i(x), \quad \text{where } \alpha = (\alpha_1, \ldots, \alpha_n)$$

is equal to the value $n$, the number of terms of the expansion.

## §9. Theorems about the rate of uniform convergence

The following theorems establishing the rate of the uniform convergence are valid.

Theorem 6. [2] Let $|Q(x, \alpha)| \leq A$, $\alpha \in \Lambda$ be a set of functions with a capacity $h$. Then the bound

$$P\left\{\sup_{\alpha \in \Lambda} \left| Q(x,\alpha) - \frac{1}{l}\sum_{i=1}^{l} Q(x_i,\alpha)\right| > \varepsilon\right\} < 9\frac{(2l)^h}{h!}\exp\left\{-\frac{\varepsilon^2 l}{4A^2}\right\}$$

is valid.

Theorem 7. [1] Let $Q(x,\alpha) \geq 0$ and let for a certain $1 < p < \infty$ the inequality

$$\sup_{\alpha \in \Lambda}\frac{\left[\int Q^p(x,\alpha)dP(x)\right]^{1/p}}{\int Q(x,\alpha)\,dP(x)} \leq \tau \tag{18}$$

be fulfilled.  Then if $p > 2$ the bound

$$P\left\{\sup_{\alpha \in \Lambda}\frac{\int Q(x,\alpha)\,dP(x) - \frac{1}{l}\sum_{i=1}^{l} Q(x_i,\alpha)}{\int Q(x,\alpha)dP(x)} > \varepsilon\right\} < 12\frac{(2l)^h}{h!}\exp\left\{-\frac{\varepsilon^2 l}{4a_p^2\tau^2}\right\},$$

where

$$a_p = \sqrt{\frac{1}{2}\left[\frac{p-1}{p-2}\right]^{p-1}},$$

is valid.

If $1 < p \leq 2$ the bound

$$P\left\{\sup_{\alpha \in \Lambda}\frac{\int Q(x,\alpha)\,dP(x) - \frac{1}{l}\sum_{i=1}^{l} Q(x_i,\alpha)}{\int Q(x,\alpha)dP(x)} > \tau\varepsilon\left[1 - \frac{\ln\varepsilon}{(p-1)p^{1/(p-1)}}\right]^{1-1/p}\right\}$$

$$< 12\frac{(2l)^h}{h!}\exp\left\{-\frac{\varepsilon^2}{4}l^{2-2/p}\right\}$$

is valid.

Each of these theorems gives an estimate for the expected risk value of the function minimizing the empirical risk that depends on the value of the obtained empirical risk and the capacity of the class of functions.

It follows from the above theorems that the function minimizing the empirical risk $Q(x, \alpha_{emp})$ chosen from a set of functions whose absolute values are uniformly bounded by $A$ which has finite capacity $h$ with probability not less than $1 - \eta$ satisfies the inequality

$$\int Q(x, \alpha_{emp})dP(x) \leq \frac{1}{l} \sum_{i=1}^{l} Q(x_i, \alpha_{emp}) + 2A \sqrt{\frac{h(\ln(2l/h) + 1) - \ln(\eta/9)}{l}} \tag{19}$$

The function minimizing the empirical risk on the set of functions $Q(x, \alpha) \geq 0$, $\alpha \in \Lambda$ of bounded capacity $h$ satisfying (18) with $p > 2$ with probability not less than $1 - \eta$ satisfies the inequality

$$\int Q(x, \alpha_{emp})dP(x) \leq \frac{\dfrac{1}{l} \sum_{i=1}^{l} Q(x_i, \alpha_{emp})}{\left[1 - 2\tau a_p \sqrt{\dfrac{h(\ln(2l/h) + 1) - \ln(\eta/12))}{l}}\right]_+} \tag{20}$$

where

$$(z)_+ = \begin{cases} z, & \text{if } z \geq 0 \\ 0, & \text{if } z < 0. \end{cases}$$

## §10. The principle of structural risk minimization

Now let the set of functions $Q(x, \alpha)$, $\alpha \in \Lambda$ be such that the principle of empirical risk minimization is not consistent.

Introduce on the set $Q(x, \alpha)$, $\alpha \in \Lambda$ the structure

$$S_1 \subset S_2 \subset \cdots \subset S_n \tag{21}$$

of functions $S_n = \{Q(x, \alpha): \alpha \in \Lambda_n\}$ such that

$$\inf_{\alpha \in \Lambda_n} \int Q(x, \alpha)dP(x) \underset{n \to \infty}{\longrightarrow} \inf_{\alpha \in \Lambda} \int Q(x, \alpha)dP(x) \tag{22}$$

and define the law $n = n(l)$ determining the index $n$ of the element $S_n$ of the structure (21) depending on the sample size $l$. Choose as an approximation to the function $Q(x, \alpha_0)$ minimizing the expected risk functional the function $Q(x, \alpha_l)$ which on the element $S_n$ of the structure (21) minimizes the empirical risk, i.e., choose the function

$$Q(x, \alpha_l) = \arg\min_{\alpha \in \Lambda_{n(l)}} \frac{1}{l} \sum_{i=1}^{l} Q(x_i, \alpha).$$

Call this method of expected risk minimization the method of structural risk minimization. This term stresses the priority of finding the proper element of the structure as opposed to finding the function minimizing the empirical risk.

The basic question of the theory of the structural risk minimization is a question of what conditions the elements of the structures and the law $n = n(l)$ should satisfy so that the method of structural risk minimization is consistent, and what the rate of convergence of the estimate to the required function is.

<u>Theorem 8</u>. [4] Let in addition to (22) the elements of the structure satisfy two requirements:

1)    the capacity of the set $S_n = \{Q(x, \alpha) : \alpha \in \Lambda_n\}$ is finite and equal to $h_n$

2)    the functions belonging to $Q(x, \alpha)$ are bounded in absolute value by $A_n$.

Then the estimate of structural risk minimization is such that the value of its expected risk converges almost surely to the minimum possible one with asymptotic rate

$$V(l) = \left[ \inf_{\alpha \in \Lambda_n} \int Q(x, \alpha) dP(x) - \inf_{\alpha \in \Lambda} \int Q(x, \alpha) dP(x) \right] + \sqrt{\frac{h_{n(l)} A_{n(l)}^2 \ln l}{l}}.$$

if the law $n = n(l)$ is such that the equality

$$\lim_{l \to \infty} \frac{h_{n(l)} A_{n(l)}^2 \ln(l)}{l} = 0$$

holds.

<u>Theorem 9</u>. [4] Let $Q(x, \alpha) \geq 0$, $\alpha \in \Lambda$ and let in addition to (22) the elements $S_n$ of the structure satisfy the following two requirements:

1. The capacity of the set $S_n$ is finite and equal to $h_n$

2. For a certain $p > 2$ the inequality

$$\underset{\alpha \in \Lambda_n}{\text{Sup}} \frac{\left[ \int Q^p(x, \alpha) dP(x) \right]^{1/p}}{\int Q(x, \alpha) dP(x)} \le C_n$$

holds.

Then the estimate of structural risk minimization is such that the value of its expected risk converges almost surely to the minimum possible one with asymptotic rate

$$V(l) = \left[ \inf_{\alpha \in \Lambda_n} \int Q(x, \alpha) dP(x) - \inf_{\alpha \in \Lambda} \int Q(x, \alpha) dP(x) \right] + \sqrt{\frac{h_{n(l)} C_{n(l)}^2 \ln l}{l}}$$

if the law $n = n(l)$ is such that the equality

$$\lim_{l \to \infty} \frac{h_{n(l)} C_{n(l)}^2 \ln l}{l} = 0$$

is fulfilled.

In the given theorems the estimate of the rate of convergence consists of two summands. The first one defines the value of the deviation of the risk of the best function in $S_n$ from the minimal risk of any function. It characterizes the approximation properties of the structure.

The second summand defines the deviation of the risk of the discovered function from the minimal risk in the given class. It characterizes the statistical properties of algorithms.

The larger the class $S_n$ the better are its approximation properties and the worse are its statistical ones. In this way the optimal rate of convergence is achieved by a compromise between two conflicting demands on the algorithm.

The law $n = n(l)$ may be defined in view of the requirement of minimization of the expected risk estimate on the elements of the structure (minimization of the guaranteed risk on the elements of the structure).

For this purpose one chooses an element of the structure on which the minimum of the right-hand side of the inequality (19) is attained if the structure satisfies the assumptions of Theorem 6, and the minimum of the right-hand side of the inequality (20) is attained if the structure satisfies the assumptions of Theorem 7.

## §11.  Concluding remarks

By means of the method of structural risk minimization it is easy to construct methods of density estimation consistent for estimates of any density that has Shannon entropy; methods of regression estimation consistent for the estimation of any regression belonging to the space $L_2(P)$; and methods of constructing decision rules consistent for estimation of any rule belonging to the set of measurable functions.

Lately, a great interest has been paid to the problem of estimation of parabolic regression, the essence of which consists in finding the polynomial order to be used for the regression approximation on samples of the size $l$.  Some tests of finding the order of regression (Akaike method, Helms method, etc.) have been suggested.  A test constructed on the basis of the estimate (20) consists in minimizing the value

$$I(p) = \frac{\dfrac{1}{l} \sum_{i=1}^{l} (y_i - f_p(t_i, \alpha_{\text{emp}}))^2}{\left[ 1 - \dfrac{\sqrt{p(\ln(l/p)+1)} - \ln\eta}{l} \right]_+}$$

where $f_p(t, \alpha)$ is a polynomial of order $p$.

Comparisons of this test with already existing tests that were done in different laboratories on different examples showed that it is, at any rate, not worse than any of these other tests.

On the other hand, taking into consideration that the concept of the set capacity is defined for an arbitrary set of functions, we can attach to the principle of structural risk minimization a general meaning in order to use it in construction of any induction system. To provide the justification of the induction step it is necessary to be able to construct a generalizing rule that satisfies the proper correspondence between the complexity of the generalizing rule (the capacity of the element of the structure from which this rule is chosen), the quality of the explanation of the available facts, and the number of these facts.

## REFERENCES

I.    Vapnik V.N. (1982) Estimation of Dependences Based on Empirical Data.  Springer-Verlag, N.Y.

2.    Vapnik V.N., Chervonenkis A.J. (1971)  On Uniform Convergence of Relative Frequencies of Events to Their Probabilities.  Theory of Prob. and Appl., 16, 264-280.

3.    Vapnik V.N., Chervonenkis A.J. (1981)  Necessary and Sufficient Conditions of the Uniform Convergence of Means to their Expectations.  Theory of Prob. and Appl. 26, p. 532-553.

4.    Vapnik V.N., Chervonenkis A.J. (1988)  Minimization of Expected Risk Based on Empirical Data.  Proceeding of the First World Congress of the Bernoulli Society, v.2.  VNU Sciencepress, Utrecht, The Netherlands, p. 821-832.

# Technical Papers

# Polynomial Learnability of Semilinear Sets[*]

Naoki Abe

Department of Computer and Information Science,
University of Pennsylvania, Philadelphia, PA19104.
abe@linc.cis.upenn.edu

### Abstract

We characterize learnability and non-learnability of subsets of $N^m$ called 'semilinear sets', with respect to the distribution-free learning model of Valiant. In formal language terms, semilinear sets are exactly the class of 'letter-counts' (or Parikh-images) of regular sets. We show that the class of semilinear sets of dimensions 1 and 2 is learnable, when the integers are encoded in unary. We complement this result with negative results of several different sorts, relying on hardness assumptions of varying degrees – from $P \neq NP$ and $RP \neq NP$ to the hardness of learning DNF. We show that the minimal consistent concept problem is NP-complete for this class, verifying the non-triviality of our learnability result. We also show that with respect to the binary encoding of integers, the corresponding 'prediction' problem is already as hard as that of DNF, for a class of subsets of $N^m$ much simpler than semilinear sets. The present work represents an interesting class of countably infinite concepts for which the questions of learnability have been nearly completely characterized. In doing so, we demonstrate how various proof techniques developed by Pitt and Valiant [15], Blumer et al. [3], and Pitt and Warmuth [17] can be fruitfully applied in the context of formal languages.

## 1 Introduction

We consider the problem of learning semilinear subsets of $N^m$, with respect to the distribution-free learnability model of Valiant [19]. Semilinear sets are finite unions of linear subsets of $N^m$, where a linear set is the set of values assumed by a linear integral formula of the form:

$$v_0 + c_1 \cdot v_1 + ... + c_k \cdot v_k$$

as the $c_i$'s vary over natural numbers, where the $v_i$'s are constant integral vectors of dimension $m$ ($v_i \in N^m$). The constant vectors $v_1,...,v_k$ are called 'generators' of the linear set, as they are indeed generators of the set $S$ obtained by uniformly subtracting the 'offset vector' $v_0$ from the linear set $L$ (i.e. $S = \{x - v_0 \mid x \in L\}$), when one views the set as the additive semigroup generated by the $v_i$'s.

[*]The work reported herein is supported in part by an IBM graduate fellowship awarded to the author and by the Office of Naval Research under contract number N00014-87-K-0401.

The model of learnability we use is that of 'polynomial learnability' (or 'pac-learnability'), introduced by Valiant [19], [18] in the context of boolean concept learning, and subsequently generalized to arbitrary concepts by Blumer et al. [3]. We consider the learnability of semilinear subsets of $N^m$ with respect to both the unary encoding and the binary encoding of integers both for examples and concept representations.

We settle, up to varying degrees of hardness assumptions ranging from $P \neq NP$ and $RP \neq NP$ to the hardness of learning DNF, a host of learnability questions for these and related classes of subsets of $N^m$. This work provides an interesting class of infinite concepts for which the questions of learnability in Valiant's model have been nearly completely settled, and demonstrates how various proof techniques recently developed by Pitt and Valiant [15], Blumer et al. [3], and Pitt and Warmuth [17] can be fruitfully applied to classes of formal languages.

## 2    Results and Significance

With respect to the unary encoding, we show that the entire class of semilinear sets, for dimensions 1 and 2, is polynomially learnable. Since $m$-dimensional semilinear sets are exactly the sets of "letter counts" (or Parikh-images) of regular sets over an $m$-letter alphabet (see [13]), our result implies that NFA (non-deterministic finite state automata) of alphabet size at most 2 is polynomially learnable *modulo* equivalence under Parikh-mapping, in a certain well-defined sense. This result is particularly interesting, in light of the recent results by Pitt and Warmuth [16] and Kearns and Valiant [11] indicating that learning the entire class of NFA is most likely hard. We show this result by a proof technique due to Blumer et al. [4], namely by exhibiting an 'Occam algorithm', that is, a polynomial time algorithm which reliably compresses a given sample to a consistent hypothesis, which is polynomially approximately minimal and less than linear in the sample size (number of examples).

We complement this result with negative results of varying sorts which, in addition to being of interest on their own, provide specific reasons to suspect that a significantly stronger positive result for this class is difficult to obtain. First, we show that the corresponding 'minimal consistent concept representation' problem (to find a minimal hypothesis consistent with a given sample from the class of concept representations under consideration) is strongly NP-complete. Obtaining an approximately minimal consistent hypothesis, therefore, is the best we can reasonably expect to do in polynomial time. Second, we show that the Vapnik-Chervonenkis dimension[1] of successive subclasses of $m$-dimensional semilinear sets of bounded size $n$, where 'size' is taken to mean the size in unary of the concept representations in question, grows at least as fast as $n^{\frac{m}{m+1}}$, hence it follows that the lower-bound for the number of examples required for pac-learning is also at best order of $n^{\frac{m}{m+1}}$, by a result of Ehrenfeucht et al. [6]. Finally, we show that the 'prediction' problem[2] for linear sets encoded in binary is at least as hard as that for DNF – a long-standing open problem in the field. In fact, the existence of any prediction algorithm for linear sets encoded in *unary*, which runs in time polynomial in the 'domain dimension' ($m$) in addition to other parameters, would also show the predictability of DNF. Furthermore, the analogous results are shown to hold for a class of subsets of $Z^m$ which is significantly simpler than semilinear sets.

Our result on the minimal consistent concept representation problem for semilinear sets in unary is one of non-approximability. More specifically, it cannot be approximated within any guaranteed constant factor

---

[1] Vapnik-Chervonenkis dimension, or VC-dimension for short, is a measure of combinatorial complexity of a concept class. A great many of the performance guarantees for polynomial learnability are stated in terms of the VC-dimension of the concept class in question [3].

[2] The prediction problem for a class of concepts is a slightly relaxed notion of learning where the algorithm need not output any hypothesis concept explicitly. Predictability of a given class is implied by its learnability (cf. [17]).

less than 2 in polynomial time, unless $P = NP$. This result complements the recent result of Pitt and Warmuth [16] that the 'minimal consistent DFA problem' cannot be approximated within any polynomial. On the one hand, we do not have the non-polynomial approximability result that they have. On the other hand, the class under consideration here is a much simpler class which is in fact polynomially learnable (if only for a restricted range of dimensions). We also show a related result using a proof technique due originally to Pitt and Valiant [15]; The class of semilinear sets that are unions of a bounded number, say $k$, of linear sets ('k-fold semilinear sets') is not properly polynomially learnable[3] unless $RP = NP$.

Our results on predictability are shown using the proof technique of 'prediction preserving reducibility' recently developed by Pitt and Warmuth [17]. The result that the class of linear sets encoded in binary is as hard to predict as DNF is not surprising, as we have also shown that even the 'evaluation problem'[4] for linear sets in binary is NP-complete [1]. [5] It was noted by Manfred Warmuth, however, that the prediction-preserving reduction exhibited to prove this result can be extended to show that the prediction problem for linear sets in unary is also as hard as that of DNF, *if* one considers the dimension of the class to be a variable ('variable dimensions'). The class of concepts for which we show the analogous results is the 'submodules' of $Z^m$, the learning problem of which has been extensively investigated by Helmbold, Sloan and Warmuth [10]. They show that not only is the class of submodules of $Z^m$ encoded in binary efficiently learnable, but so is the class of 'nested differences' of members of this class. [6] In contrast, we have shown that the prediction problem for the class of finite unions of modules (or 'semi-modules') is also as hard as that for DNF, for fixed dimensions in binary, or variable dimensions in unary.

These results together draw up a nearly complete characterization of learnability of the concept classes in question, as summarized in the tables in Figures 1 and 2.[7] The positive results for modules are due to Helmbold, Sloan and Warmuth [10], as indicated.

# 3    Learnability Models Used

We are concerned with the question of probably approximately correct(pac) learnability of countably infinite concept classes from randomly generated examples, essentially in the sense of Valiant [19]. In adapting Valiant's original formulation of learnability of boolean concepts to infinitary domains, an interesting question arises as to exactly what parameters quantifying the complexity of the concept class under consideration should be included in the arguments to the polynomial of sample complexity. In Valiant's formulation of learnability of boolean concepts, the sample complexity was allowed to polynomially (and at most polynomially) depend on the number of variables, which could be thought of as either the length of examples (assignments), or the 'dimension' of the domain under consideration. In an infinitary domain such as $\Sigma^*$, it is arguable whether the sample complexity should be allowed to polynomially depend on the (maximum)

---

[3] A class of concept representations $\mathcal{A}$ is said to be learnable *by* another class $\mathcal{B}$, if there exists a learning algorithm which only outputs hypotheses from $\mathcal{B}$ and learns $\mathcal{A}$. $\mathcal{A}$ is *properly* learnable iff $\mathcal{A}$ is learnable by $\mathcal{A}$ (cf. [15]).

[4] The evaluation problem for a class of language representations $\mathcal{G}$ is the language $\{\langle G, w \rangle \mid G \in \mathcal{G} \wedge w \in L(G)\}$ where $L(.)$ denotes the mapping from a representation to the language it represents (cf. [17]).

[5] It has been suggested by several different sources that this result had been known, although no correct reference to the result has been pointed out to the author.

[6] Algebraically these classes are closely related. A linear set is a finitely generated semigroup under addition with a constant offset, while a module is indeed a finitely generated module under addition and subtraction. The former is a much more complicated class of concepts, however, both computationally and learning-theoretically. For the former the evaluation problem (in binary) is NP-complete and the Vapnik-Chervonenkis dimension grows nearly linearly already with respect to the unary encoding, whereas for the latter the evaluation problem is efficiently solvable in polynomial time, and the Vapnik-Chervonenkis dimension grows logarithmically with respect to the unary encoding.

[7] In these tables, 'Thm x.y' indicates that the result is stated in Theorem x.y, and 'Cor x.y' indicates that it follows (essentially) as a corollary of Theorem x.y. '$\triangleright$ DNF' indicates that DNF is prediction-preserving reducible to it. '[10]' indicates a result by Helmbold et al., and '*' an extension by Manfred Warmuth.

| | Linear Sets | Semilinear Sets | Modules | Semi-modules |
|---|---|---|---|---|
| *Fixed Dimensions* | | | | |
| unary | yes $m \leq 2$ (Cor 5.2) | yes $m \leq 2$ (Thm 5.2) | yes [10] | yes (Cor 5.2) |
| binary | ▷ DNF (Thm 5.5) | ▷ DNF (Cor 5.5, 5.6) | yes [10] | ▷ DNF (Thm 5.6) |
| *Variable Dimensions* | | | | |
| unary | ▷ DNF * (Thm 5.7) | ▷ DNF * (Cor 5.7, 5.8) | yes [10] | ▷ DNF (Thm 5.8) |
| binary | ▷ DNF (Cor 5.7) | ▷ DNF (Cor 5.7, 5.8) | yes [10] | ▷ DNF (Cor 5.8) |

Figure 1: Results on pac-learnability and predictability.

| *Semilinear Sets (Proper Pac-learnability, Minimal Consistency)* | | | | |
|---|---|---|---|---|
| | Linear Sets (proper-pac) | K-fold Semilinear Sets (proper-pac) | Minimal Consistent Semilinear Sets | Semilinear Sets (pac) |
| unary | ? | hard ($k \geq 3$) unless $RP = NP$ (Thm 5.4) | NP-hard (Thm 5.3) | yes ($m \leq 2$) (Thm 5.2) |

Figure 2: Results on Semilinear Sets encoded in Unary.

length of examples seen. Subsequent generalizations of Valiant's model to infinitary domains have taken different views on this issue. In this paper we employ different ones among these competing formulations of learnability, depending on whether we are considering the unary encoding or the binary encoding. In particular, we adopt the exact formulation of 'polynomial learnability with respect to concept complexity' by Blumer et al. [3] for the unary case, in which the sample complexity is *not* allowed to depend on the example lengths. For the binary case, we employ the version of polynomial learnability in which sample complexity is allowed to polynomially depend on the length of the longest example seen, following the formulation of 'predictability' by Haussler et al. [9] and Pitt and Warmuth [17]. It is important to note this distinction particularly because the prediction problem with respect to the unary encoding becomes trivial if the sample complexity is allowed to polynomially depend on the length of the longest example seen [14]. With respect to both the unary and binary encodings, we also consider the variant in which the 'domain dimension' is taken to mean the dimension $m$ of $N^m$. We briefly review in the following the definition of 'polynomial learnability'.

We assume the 'functional' model of learning algorithm, as opposed to the 'oracle' model. (See [8].) In other words, a learning algorithm implements a function $f : S_{\mathcal{P}(X)} \to H$, where $S_{\mathcal{P}(X)}$ is the set of all finite labeled samples for concepts over $X$ and $H$ is some class of concept representations.

**Definition 3.1** *A learning algorithm $A$ is said to 'achieve $(\epsilon, \delta)$-performance' for a concept $C$ with respect to distribution $P$ with sample size $m$, if and only if $A$'s output on a labeled sample of size $m$, randomly generated according to $P$, is a representation of an $\epsilon$-approximation of $C$ with probability at least $1 - \delta$. We write '$\Upsilon(f, \epsilon, \delta, m, C, P)$'.*

**Definition 3.2** *Let $X$ be the domain under consideration, and $\mathcal{D}_X$ the set of all distributions over $X$. Let $R$ be a class of concept representations, with the implict representation mapping $c_R : R \to \mathcal{P}(X)$. Let $\mathcal{R} = \{c_R(g) \mid g \in R\}$, and define size $: \mathcal{R} \to N^+$ by $size(C) = min\{length(g) \mid g \in R \wedge c_R(g) = C\}$. Let $\mathcal{R}_s = \{C \mid size(C) \leq s\}$. $R$ is said to be 'polynomially leanable (with respect to concept complexity)' by $H$ if and only if there exists a learning algorithm $A : S_{\mathcal{R}} \to H$ such that*

$$\exists q \ polynomial \ \forall \epsilon > 0 \ \forall \delta > 0 \ \forall s \in N^+ \ \forall C \in \mathcal{R}_s \ \forall m \geq q(\epsilon, \delta, s) \ \forall P \in \mathcal{D}_X \ \Upsilon(A, \epsilon, \delta, m, C, P)$$

**Definition 3.3** *Let $X = \cup_{n \in N+} X_n$ be the domain under consideration. Let $R$ be a class of concept representations, and define $\mathcal{R}$, size and $\mathcal{R}_s$ as before. $R$ is said to be 'polynomially leanable (with respect to concept complexity and domain dimension)' by $H$ if and only if there exists a learning algorithm $A : \mathcal{S}_{\mathcal{R}} \rightarrow H$ such that*

$$\exists q \;\; polynomial \; \forall \epsilon > 0 \; \forall \delta > 0 \; \forall s \in N^+ \; \forall n \in N^+ \; \forall C \in \mathcal{C}_s \; \forall P \in \mathcal{D}_{X_n} \; \forall m \geq q(\epsilon, \delta, s, n) \; \Upsilon(A, \epsilon, \delta, m, C, P)$$

In this paper, we consider the following three 'instantiations' of the above general definitions of polynomial learnability. Since integers are presented to the learning algorithm as strings, all the domains considered in this paper are $(\Sigma^*)^m$ for some dimension $m$, with $\Sigma$ being $\Sigma_2 = \{0,1\}$ in the binary encoding, and $\Sigma_1 = \{0\}$ in the unary encoding. Integers appearing in concept representations are also either encoded in binary, or encoded in unary. In this paper we consider the two cases (out of the four in total), in which the *same* encoding is used for the elements of the domain and for the concept representations.

**I. Unary, With respect to Concept Complexity**
Let the domain $X$ be $\Sigma_1^*$ or $(\Sigma_1^*)^d$ for a constant $d$ in Definition 3.2. Integers in $R$ are encoded in unary.

**II. Binary, With respect to Concept Complexity and Word Length**
We let the domain $X$ be $\Sigma_2^*$ and let $X_n$ be $\Sigma_2^{[n]} = \{x \in \Sigma_2^* \mid length(x) \leq n\}$ in Definition 3.3. In other words, at each run, examples are assumed to be drawn from a subdomain $\Sigma_2^{[n]}$ for some fixed $n$. Integers in $R$ are encoded in binary.

**III. Unary/Binary, With respect to Concept Complexity and Variable Dimension**
We let the domain $X$ be $(\Sigma^*)^*$ and let $X_n$ be $(\Sigma^*)^n$ in Definition 3.3. $\Sigma$ is either $\Sigma_1$ or $\Sigma_2$.

# 4    Classes of Concepts Considered

We define the class of concept representations considered in this paper. Throughout, $b_0, .., b_n$ are integral vectors in $N^m$.

**Linear Bases (LB) for Linear Sets**
$B = \langle b_0, \{b_1, ..., b_n\} \rangle$ is called the *linear basis* of the linear set $L(B) = \{b_0 + \sum_{i=1}^n x_i b_i \mid \forall i \leq n \; x_i \in N\}$.

**Semilinear Basis Sets (SLB) for Semilinear Sets**
If $B_1, ..., B_n$ are linear bases, then $\{B_1, ..., B_n\}$ is called the *semilinear basis set* of the set $\cup_{i=1}^n L(B_i)$.

**Module Bases (MB) for Modules**
The set $B = \{b_1, ..., b_n\}$ is called the *module basis* of the module $L(B) = \{\sum_{i=1}^n x_i b_i \mid \forall i \leq n \; x_i \in Z\}$.

**Semi-module Basis Sets (SMB) for Finite Unions of Modules**
If $B_1, ..., B_n$ are module bases, then $\{B_1, ..., B_n\}$ is called the *module basis set* of the set $\cup_{i=1}^n L(B_i)$.

We define '*size*' in binary of a concept representation to be the sum of the log of all the integers appearing as components of vectors in it, and the '*size*' in unary to be the sum of all the component integers themselves. For any concept representation class $A$ we denote by $A_n$ the subclass of $A$ of bounded size $n$, that is, $A_n = \{B \in A \mid size(B) \leq n\}$. We explicitly quantify all our results in this paper with the encodings used, the dimension of the domain, and whether the dimension is variable or fixed: For example, $SLB(m, binary)$ denotes the $m$-dimensional SLB in binary, and $LB(variable, unary)$ denotes the variable-dimensional LB in unary. Thus, in any statement concerning learnability of a concept representation class $R$, $R(m, unary)$ indicates that the learnability model used is the version **I**, $R(m, binary)$ the version **II**, and $R(variable, binary)$ or $R(variable, unary)$ the version **III**.

# 5   Technical Details

## 5.1   Vapnik-Chervonenkis Dimensions of Semilinear Sets in Unary

We characterize the VC-dimension of $LB_n$ of dimension 1 up to a constant factor, and those of $LB_n$ and $SLB_n$ of arbitrary dimensions within at most $\sqrt{n}$ factor, and thereby establish a lowerbound for the sample complexity of any learning algorithm for these classes by a result of Ehrenfeucht et al. [6].

**Theorem 5.1** *If we let $VCdim(C)$ denote the VC-dimension of the concept class represented by $C$,*

*(1) $VCdim(LB(1, unary)_n) = \Theta(\sqrt{n})$*
*(2) $VCdim(LB(m, unary)_n) = \Omega(\sqrt{n})$*
            $= O(n)$
*(3) $\forall m \in N^+ \; VCdim(SLB(m, unary)_n) = \Omega(n^{\frac{m}{m+1}})$*
            $= O(n)$

**Corollary 5.1** *Any learning algorithm for $SLB(m, unary)$ requires at least $\Omega(\epsilon^{-1} \cdot \log \delta^{-1} + \epsilon^{-1} \cdot n^{\frac{m}{m+1}})$ many examples to achieve $\epsilon$ accuracy with $1 - \delta$ confidence.*

In both cases, the upperbound of $O(n)$ trivially follows from the fact that a string of length $n$ can represent at most $O(2^n)$ different concepts.

**Proof of Theorem 5.1(1)**
**Lowerbound:** Let $S_n = \{n, n+1, ..., 2n-1\}$. Then, for an arbitrary subset $T \subseteq S_n$, if we let $B_T = \langle 0, T \rangle$, then, $L(B_T) \cap S_n = T$. Also, $size(T) = \sum_{x \in T} x \leq \sum_{x \in S_n} x \leq 2 \cdot n^2$. Hence, $S_n$ is shattered by $LB(1, unary)_{2n^2}$ for an arbitrary $n$. It follows therefore that for some constant $c$, $\forall n \in N \; VCdim(LB(1, unary)_n) \geq c \cdot \sqrt{n}$.

**Upperbound:** This is shown by a counting argument. If we let $P(n)$ denote the number of 'partitions' of $n$, that is, the number of multisets of positive integers whose sum equal $n$, then we have $card(LB(1, unary)_n) = O(\sum_{i=1}^n P(n))$. By a result by Hardy and Ramanujan (See for example [2].), we have $P(n) = \Theta(2^{\sqrt{n}})$. So, $\sum_{i=1}^n P(i) = \Theta(\sum_{i=1}^n 2^{\sqrt{i}}) = \Theta(2^{\sqrt{n}})$. Hence, $VCdim(LB(1, unary)_n) \leq \log(card(LB(1, unary)_n)) = \Theta(\sqrt{n})$.

**Proof of Theorem 5.1(3)**
We prove the lowerbound. Let $S_{n,m} = \{1, 2, .., n^{\frac{1}{m}}\}^m$, where we assume that $n$ is a perfect $m$-th power. Note the following:[8]
(1) $card(S_{n,m}) = n$.
(2) $size(S_{n,m}) = m \cdot n^{\frac{m-1}{m}} \cdot \sum_{i=1}^{n^{\frac{1}{m}}} i = O(m \cdot n^{\frac{m-1}{m}} \cdot n^{\frac{2}{m}}) = O(n^{\frac{m+1}{m}})$.
Now, for an arbitrary $T \subseteq S_{n,m}$, define $B_T = \{\langle b, \phi \rangle \mid b \in T\}$. Then for any $T$, it is clear that $L(B_T) \cap S_{n,m} = T$, and $size(B_T) \leq size(S_{n,m}) = O(n^{\frac{m+1}{m}})$. thus, $S_{n,m}$ is shattered by $SLB(m, unary)_{n^{\frac{m+1}{m}}}$: Hence, $VCdim(LB(m, unary)_n) = \Omega(n^{\frac{m}{m+1}})$.

---

[8] For any set $S$ of vectors, we define $size(S)$ to be the sum of all the components of vectors in it.

## 5.2   Learnability Result for Semilinear Sets

**Theorem 5.2** *SLB(m, unary) is Properly Polynomially Learnable for m = 1, 2.*

We prove this theorem (for the 2 dimensional case only) by exhibiting an Occam Algorithm with a range dimension (cf. [4]) logarithmic in the sample size, and polynomial in the size of a minimal basis set.

### 5.2.1   Proof Sketch of Theorem 5.2

We exhibit a normal form for semilinear bases, with a 'polynomial blow-up',[9] such that each semilinear basis set in this normal form is a finite union of linear bases each of which has at most two generators. Now, for a given positive sample, we can generate all such linear bases that are *relevant* to that sample and eliminate the ones that are inconsistent with the negative sample in time polynomial in the total sample length. This leaves us with a polynomially bounded set of linear bases of *varying* sizes all consistent with the input sample, of which the 'relevant' part of a minimal consistent semilinear basis set in the normal form is guaranteed to be a subset. We can then apply the polynomial time approximation algorithm of Chvatal [5] to the instance of Weighted Set Cover obtained by taking the positive sample to be the set to be covered, its subsets defined by the relevant linear bases and the sizes of these bases to be the weighted legal subsets. As Chvatal's algorithm always outputs a cover whose total weight is polynomially bounded in the total weight of a minimal weight cover and logarithmic in the number of points to be covered, this will give us an Occam algorithm.

The main significance of this result lies in the fact that via the 'poly-blowup' normal form, we are able to show the entire class of semilinear sets of dimensions 1 and 2 to be learnable, without having to put an explicit bound on the number of generators, as is necessary, for example, in the case of k-DNF. It is worth noting that our proof in some sense uses a special case of the notion of 'prediction preserving reduction'. Namely, we have reduced the learning problem of unrestricted SLB to that of '2-SLB', by a reduction with the concept mapping being the 'poly-blowup' normal form, and the example mapping being the identity function.

### 5.2.2   The Normal Form Lemma

As it is clear from the proof sketch we just gave, the key step in the proof is the poly-blowup normal form lemma. We now state the normal form theorem for (2-dimensional) semilinear bases formally.

**Lemma 5.1** *There is a polynomial p such that for every semilinear basis set $\mathcal{B}_1$ in SLB(2), there is another semilinear basis set $\mathcal{B}_2$ such that*

*(1) $size(\mathcal{B}_2) \leq p(size(\mathcal{B}_1))$*
*(2) $\forall B \in \mathcal{B}_2 \; card(generators(B)) = 2$*
*(3) $L(\mathcal{B}_1) = L(\mathcal{B}_2)$*

The intuitive reason why the above holds is that a linear set is ultimately periodic. For analogy let us first consider the 1-dimensional case. A 1-dimensional linear set looks very complicated close to 0. However, past a certain point called the conductor [12], it becomes very simple, i.e. an integer is in the set if and only if it is expressible as the sum of the offset and some multiple of the greatest common divisor of all the generators of its basis. (See Figure 3(a).) Furthermore, the conductor of any linear set is polynomially bounded in the size of its basis.

---

[9] That is, for each semilinear basis set there exists a language equivalent one in the normal form whose size is only polynomially larger, for some fixed polynomial.

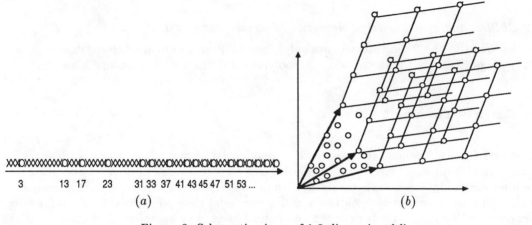

Figure 3: Schematic views of 1,2-dimensional linear sets.

In the 2-dimensional case, the exact analogue of the 'conducting' phenomenon does not happen. A slightly weaker phenomenon does happen, however, which suffices for our present purpose. A 2-dimensional linear set is also complicated around the origin (0,0), but if one goes sufficiently (polynomially) far from it, then a point is in the set if and only if it is expressible as the sum of a linear combination of some *fixed* pair of vectors and one of a polynomially bounded set of polynomially small offset vectors. In other words, each linear set is equivalent to a semilinear set consisting of polynomially many linear sets, each of which has a basis with two generator vectors. Hence, so does each semilinear set. (See Figure 3(b).)

The first key fact for showing this is the following. Given an arbitrary pair of vectors, say $v_1$ and $v_2$, and any vector, say $v$, in between[10] them, there is a multiple of $v$, which is at most the determiner of the matrix $A = [v_1, v_2]$, which is expressible as a linear integral combination of $v_1$ and $v_2$. The determiner of $A$ is, in turn, bounded by a fixed polynomial $a^m$ where $a$ is the maximum component in $A$ – a quadratic function for the case $m = 2$. Thus, given an arbitrary set of generator vectors, the two vectors that are 'rightmost' and 'leftmost' among them can express every sufficiently large multiple of every other vector in the set as their linear combination.

Given this fact, it is easy to see that the normal form lemma holds. Given an arbitrary set of *two-dimensional* generator vectors, say $V = \{v_1, ..., v_n\}$, one can always pick the 'rightmost' one and the 'leftmost' one, say $v_1$ and $v_2$.[11] Then any linear combination $w$ of vectors in $V$ is expressible as $\Sigma_{i=1}^n c_i \cdot v_i$, where all of integral constants $c_i$'s, except for $c_1$ and $c_2$, are less than or equal to some integer, say $d$, which is at most order of $(size(v))^2$. Hence given an arbitrary linear basis $B = \langle v_0, \{v_1, ..., v_k\}\rangle \in LB(2)$ (where we assume without loss of generality that $v_1$ is the "rightmost" one, and $v_2$ is the "leftmost" one among $v_1$ through $v_k$), if we take the set of linear bases $\mathcal{B} = \{\langle(v_0 + y_3 \cdot v_3 + ... + y_k \cdot v_k), \{v_1, v_2\}\rangle \mid y_3, ..., y_k \leq d\}$ then $L(B) = L(\mathcal{B})$. Furthermore, if we let $n = size(B)$, then the size of $\mathcal{B}$ is seen to of order $n^9$, because each of the offset vectors in $\mathcal{B}$ has size order of $n^3$, and there are at most $o(n^6)$ many different offsets of the form $v_0 + y_3 \cdot v_3 + ... + y_k \cdot v_k$. That the size of each offset is of order $n^3$ follows because each multiple $y_i$ is of order $n^2$, and there are $k$ offsets: Clearly $k \leq n$. To obtain the bound on the number of distinct offsets, we observe that each offset is a 2-dimensional vector with both of its coordinates bounded by $n^3$, and hence there can be $n^6$ such vectors at the most. Hence $\mathcal{B}$ satisfies all the conditions of Theorem 5.1.

---

[10] In other words, cosine of $v$ is in between those of $v_1$ and $v_2$.

[11] The corresponding statement for the 3-dimensional case is false, and this is why the above lemma in the 3-dimensional case does not give rise to the analogue of the next lemma. The same technique does not yield an Occam Algorithm for the 3-dimensional and higher dimensional cases.

## 5.3   NP-completeness of the Minimal Consistent Concept Problem

The results in this section concern the problem of finding a consistent concept (representation) for a given labeled sample, satisfying a certain minimality constraint. We define this as an optimization problem below, and state our results in terms of it.

$MCC(\mathcal{G}, measure)$
for a class $\mathcal{G}$ of concept representations with associated measure $measure$ on them to be minimized;
INSTANCE: A finite labeled sample $S$.
PROBLEM: Find $G$ in $\mathcal{G}$ which is consistent with $S$, and $measure(G) = min\{measure(F) \mid consistent(F, S)\}$.

**Theorem 5.3** *MCC(SLB(unary), size) cannot be approximated within any constant less than 2 in polynomial time unless $P = NP$.*

**Theorem 5.4** *MCC(SLB(unary), cardinality) cannot be approximated within any constant less than 2 in polynomial time unless $P = NP$.*

By a lemma (Lemma 5.2) which is essentially due to Pitt and Valiant [15], our proof of Theorem 5.4 implies that the subclasses of SLB with a bounded 'cardinality' ($k$-fold-SLB) are not properly polynomially learnable (for $k \geq 3$), provided that $RP \neq NP$.

**Lemma 5.2** *Let $A$ be a class of concept representations, and $L$ an NP-hard language. If there exists a polynomial time transformation $\tau$ from $L$ to finite samples and a polynomial $p$ such that all of the following conditions are equivalent, then $A$ is not properly polynomially learnable, unless $RP = NP$.*

*(1) $x \in L$*
*(2) There exists $G \in A$ which is consistent with $\tau(x)$.*
*(3) There exists $G \in A$ which is consistent with $\tau(x)$, and $size(G) \leq p(size(x))$.*

**Corollary 5.2** *$k$-fold-SLB(unary) is not properly polynomially learnable for $k \geq 3$, unless $RP = NP$.*

We give a sketch of the proof of Theorem 5.4, and then explain how it can be modified to prove Theorem 5.3.

### 5.3.1   Proof Sketch of Theorem 5.4

We exhibit a polynomial time transformation from instances of Graph-k-Colorability (GkC) [7] to finite samples such that there exists a (1-dimensional) k-fold semilinear set consistent with the resulting sample, just in case the original graph is k-colorable. We give a rough outline of this transformation.

Given an arbitrary graph, we 'represent' each vertex in the graph by a unique integer (call them 'vertex numbers') and put them in the positive sample. We then put, for each edge in the graph, the sum of the numbers representing the two end vertices of the edge in the negative sample. Further, by means of additional negative examples, we enforce that any linear basis that generates a vertex number must include that very number either in its generators or as its offset, and hence if it generates any two vertex numbers, it must also generate their sum. First, we add all the integers between 0 and the maximum vertex number, which have not already been put into the sample, to our negative sample. We then add for each pair of vertex numbers, say $a < b$, the integer $a + 2(b - a)$ into our negative sample thereby ensuring that no vertex number could be generated as a linear combination of another vertex number and the difference between the two.

**The Transformation**
$G = \langle V, E \rangle$ where $V = \{v_i \mid 1 \leq i \leq n\}$ and $E \subseteq \{(v_i, v_j) \mid v_i, v_j \in V\}$ is transformed to $S = S^+ \cup S^-$, where

$T_n$ is the set of $n$ vertex numbers to be specified later (in Lemma 5.4).

$$S^+ = \{\langle t_i, + \rangle \mid t_i \in T_n\}$$
$$S^- = \{\langle t_i + t_j, - \rangle \mid (v_i, v_j) \in E\}$$
$$\cup \ \{\langle x, - \rangle \mid 0 < x < max(T_n) \ \wedge \ x \notin T_n\}$$
$$\cup \ \{\langle t_j + (t_j - t_i), - \rangle \mid i, j \leq n \ \& \ t_i < t_j\}$$

Since we make sure that each vertex number must be 'colored', but no two vertex numbers are to be 'colored' by the same linear set if there is an edge between them, the resulting sample should have a consistent k-fold-semilinear set if and only if the original graph is k-colorable. Note further that when there is a k-fold semilinear basis set consistent with a sample generated in the above manner, there is one that has as its offsets and periods all and only the vertex numbers of the transformation. Thus the size of a minimal consistent semilinear basis set is predictably small. We summarize this in the following lemma, which by Lemma 5.2 implies Corollary 5.2.

**Lemma 5.3** *If $G$ is any graph of $n$ vertices, and $S$ is the sample that the above transformation maps $G$ to, then all of the following conditions are equivalent.*

*(1) $G$ is k-colorable.*

*(2) There exists a k-fold-semilinear basis set consistent with $S$.*

*(3) There exists a k-fold-semilinear basis set consistent with $S$, and is of size $\sum_{i=1}^{n} t_i$.*

In order to verify Lemma 5.3, we must demonstrate that the outlined transformation can be carried out without either accidentally 'putting an edge' where there is none, or making the resulting sample inconsistent.[12] We specify a certain set of conditions for the vertex numbers ($T_n$) which suffice for this purpose, and show that for an arbitrary number of vertices ($n$), a set of vertex numbers $T_n$ satisfying such conditions can be quickly computed. This is formalized in the following lemma.

**Lemma 5.4** *There is an algorithm, which on input $n \in N$, computes in time polynomial in $n$, a set $T_n$ of $n$ integers with the following properties.*

1. $\sum_{x \in T_n} x \leq q(n)$ *for a fixed polynomial $q$.*
2.    (a) $\forall u, v, w, x \in T_n \ [(\{u, v\} \neq \{w, x\}) \rightarrow (u + v \neq w + x)]$
   (b) $\forall x, y, z \in T_n \ [x + y > z]$
3.    (a) $\forall x, y, z \in T_n[(x < y) \rightarrow (y + (y - x) \neq z)]$
   (b) $\forall x, y, z_1, z_2 \in T_n[(x < y) \rightarrow (y + (y - x) < z_1 + z_2)]$

**Proof Sketch of Lemma 5.4**

First note that *3(a)* in fact follows from *2(a)*, because if there were $x, y, z \in T_n$ such that $y + (y - x) = z$, then we would have $x + z = y + y$, which contradicts *2(a)*. Note also that *2(b)* follows from *3(b)*. Thus, we need only be concerned with *1*, *2(a)*, and *3(b)*. Furthermore, if we can show that a set of $n$ integers, say $S_n$, with properties *1* and *2(a)* can be generated in polynomial time, then we can obtain $T_n$ by adding $2 \cdot max(S_n) + 1$ to each member of $S_n$ so that *3(b)* is satisfied. We can do this because property *2(a)* is preserved under any "translation" of the set by a constant offset.

We are left to verify that $S_n$ can indeed be computed from $n$ in polynomial time. We define $S_n = \{s_1, ..., s_n\}$ in stages (iterations).

**Stage 1**

Let $S_1 = \{0\}$ and $S_1^2 = \{0\}$.

**Stage i**

Let $S_i = \{s_i\} \cup S_{i-1}$ where $s_i = min\{x \in N \mid x > max(S_{i-1}) \ \wedge \ (\forall y \in S_{i-1} \forall z \in S_{i-1}^2 \ [x + y \neq z])\}$.

---

[12] That is, the same integer is never put both to the positive and negative sample.

Let $S_i^2 = \{s_i + s_j \mid s_i, s_j \in S_i\}$.

It is easy to see that for each $n$, $S_n$ satisfies property $2(a)$. For suppose otherwise, then for some $s_i, s_j, s_k, s_l \in S_n$ such that $\{s_i, s_j\} \neq \{s_k, s_l\}$ we have $s_i + s_j = s_k + s_l$. Pick the maximum index among $i, j, k$ and $l$, say $l$. Then all of $i, j, k$ are strictly less than $l$, for if $i = l$ then, that would imply $j = k$ and the two sets are identical, and if $k = l$ then we would have to have $i = j = k = l$ for the equality to hold because $s_l$ is maximal. Thus, at stage $l$, $s_k \in S_{l-1}$, and $s_i + s_j \in S_{l-1}^2$. So, letting $y = s_k$ and $z = s_i + s_j$ in the minimization clause, this would have rejected $s_l$ as an $x$ satisfying the condition. This is a contradiction. It is straightforward to verify that all the members of $S_n$ are bounded by a fixed polynomial in $n$ (in fact $n^4$), and that $S_n$ can be computed in time polynomial in $n$ (at most $O(n^4 \cdot \log n)$).

### 5.3.2   Proof Sketch of Theorem 5.3

We modify the above transformation to prove Theorem 5.3 as follows: We add to every example in the sample some constant offset $a > max(T_n)$, chosen depending on the constant of non-approximability and $n$, add $a$ in the positive sample and all the integers less than $a$ in the negative sample. More precisely, the new sample $S_a$ is defined as $S_a = S_a^+ \cup S_a^-$ where:

$$S_a^+ = \{\langle x + a, + \rangle \mid \langle x, + \rangle \in S^+\} \cup \{\langle a, + \rangle\}$$

$$S_a^- = \cup\{\langle x + a, - \rangle \mid \langle x, - \rangle \in S^-\} \cup \{\langle 2a, - \rangle\} \cup \{\langle x, - \rangle \mid x \in N \wedge 0 \leq x < a\}$$

First we note that if some linear basis $B$ consistent with $S_a$ generates $\{a + x \mid x \in A\}$ for some subset $A$ of $T_n$ then we must have either of the following two cases.
(i) $B$'s offset equals $a$. Its generators must contain $A$. We say that such a $B$ is of 'type 1' and write $type(B, 1)$.
(ii) $B$'s offset does not equal $a$. If its offset is 0 then its generators contain $\{a + x \mid x \in A\}$ because it cannot contain $a$ as a generator to respect $\langle 2a, - \rangle$ in $S_a^-$. Otherwise, $A$ must be a singleton, and $B$'s offset must equal that one member in $A$. We say that such a $B$ is of 'type 2', and write $type(B, 2)$.

The crucial fact is that since all the required properties of $T_n$ of Lemma 5.4 are preserved under positive 'translation', by $a$ in this case, essentially the same argument as before applies, *if* all of the linear bases in question are of type 1: Namely, there is a k-fold-SLB all of whose bases are of type 1 consistent with $S_a$ if and only if the original graph $G$ is k-colorable. Using this fact, we can verify the following 'gap' lemma.

**Lemma 5.5** *Let $S_a$ be the sample obtained as above from an arbitrary graph $G$, and $\mathcal{B}$ a minimal consistent SLB for it. Then we have:*

*(1) If $G$ is k-colorable, then $size(\mathcal{B}) = (\sum_{x \in T_n} x) + k \cdot a$.*
*(2) If $G$ is not k-colorable, then $size(\mathcal{B}) \geq (\sum_{x \in T_n} x) + (k + 1) \cdot a$.*

**Proof of Lemma 5.5**
If the graph $G$ is k-colorable, then there is a k-fold semilinear basis set consistent with $S_a$, such that each of its linear basis is of type 1, and hence has size $k \cdot a + \sum_{i=1}^n t_i$. Suppose on the other hand that $G$ is not k-colorable, and let $\mathcal{B} = \{B_i \mid i = 1, ..., l\}$ be a minimal consistent SLB for $S_a$ and let $Q_i = L(B_i) \cap \{a + t_i \mid t_i \in T_n\}$. Now let $I = \{i \leq l \mid type(B_i, 1)\}$, $J = \{i \leq l \mid type(B_i, 2)\}$, and $R = \cup_{i \in J} Q_i$. Then, note that:

$$size(\mathcal{B}) \geq \sum_{x \in T_n} x + a \cdot (card(I) + card(R))$$

We claim that we must have $card(I) + card(R) \geq k + 1$. For suppose otherwise, i.e. $card(I) + card(R) \leq k$. Then define $\mathcal{B}' = \{B_i \mid i \in I\} \cup \{\langle a, \{x - a\} \rangle \mid x \in R\}$. Note that (i) all of the bases in $\mathcal{B}'$ are of type 1, (ii)

$card(\mathcal{B}') \leq k$, and (iii) $\mathcal{B}'$ is consistent with $S_a$. Hence it follows that $G$ must be k-colorable, contradicting our hypothesis. Thus, we have shown that $card(I) + card(R) \geq k+1$, and hence $size(\mathcal{B}) \geq \sum_{x \in T_n} x + a \cdot (k+1)$. $\square$

By appropriately setting $a$ as a polynomial function of $\sum_{i=1}^{n} t_i$ and $\epsilon^{-1}$, we can show that any approximation algorithm for MCC($SLB(unary), size$) with a guaranteed constant factor $2 - \epsilon$ can be used to approximate GkC within $2 - \frac{\epsilon}{2}$, which is known to be NP-hard [7].

## 5.4  Prediction Preserving Reductions from DNF

The results in this section are all stated in terms of the notion of 'prediction preserving reducibility' due to Pitt and Warmuth [17]. We note that if a class of concepts $A$ is prediction-preserving reducible to $B$ (written $A \trianglelefteq B$), then the predictability of $B$ implies that of $A$.

**Theorem 5.5** $\forall m \in N^+$  $DNF \trianglelefteq LB(m, binary)$.

**Theorem 5.6** $\forall m \in N^+$  $DNF \trianglelefteq SMB(m, binary)$, and $DNF \trianglelefteq SLB(m, binary)$.

**Theorem 5.7** $DNF \trianglelefteq LB(variable, unary)$.

**Theorem 5.8** $DNF \trianglelefteq SMB(variable, unary)$, and $DNF \trianglelefteq SLB(variable, unary)$.

To show that DNF $\trianglelefteq$ R, for a class of representations for concepts over $N$, we must exhibit the following two mappings [17] : the 'example mapping' $f : \{0,1\}^* \times N \times N \to N$, mapping any assignment to an integer, and the 'concept mapping' $g : DNF \times N \to R$ mapping any DNF-formula $A$ to a semilinear basis set, satisfying the following conditions.[13]
(1) $\forall s, n \in N \; \forall w \in \{0,1\}^n \; \forall A \in DNF^{[s]} \; f(w, s, n) \in L(g(A, n))$ if and only if $w$ satisfies $A$.
(2) $f$ is computable in time polynomial in $n$ and $s$.
(3) $g$ is 'poly-blowup', that is, for some fixed polynomial $q$, $\forall n, s \in N \; \forall A \in DNF^{[s]} \; size(g(A, n)) \leq q(n, s)$.

In each of the reductions to be exhibited in the sections to follow, no use is made of the variable 'offset' (available for LB and SLB only), i.e. it is always the zero vector. We therefore abbreviate the linear basis $\langle \vec{0}, B \rangle$ by the set of generators $B$ for readability, in the expositions below.

### 5.4.1  Proof Sketch of Theorem 5.5

We use the idea of 'bit maps' in our transformation. The integers that are yielded by the example mapping or the concept mapping all have a bit-map representation of the form in Figure 4(a). This map has $2n$ fields each of $q(n)$-bits, where $q$ is some polynomial, plus the most significant field (MSF). The $2n$ fields are to correspond to the $2n$ literals, say; $X_1, ..., X_n, \neg X_1, ..., \neg X_n$, in that order from right. We make use of the following notation: If $w$ is an assignment of $n$ variables: $IND(w) = \{i \mid w_i = 1\} \cup \{n + i \mid w_i = 0\}$. If $T$ is a term, then $IND(T) = \{i \mid X_i \in T\} \cup \{n + i \mid \neg X_i \in T\}$. $I_{IND(x)}$ denotes the characteristic function for $IND(x)$, i.e. $I_{IND(x)}(i) = 1$ if $i \in IND(x)$ and 0 otherwise.

$f$ maps an assignment $w$ to an integer whose bit representation is as in Figure 4 (b); It contains $I_{IND(w)}$ in its first $2n$ fields, and $2n - 1$ in its most significant field. $g$ maps a DNF $A$ to the union of the set

---

[13] $DNF^{[s]}$ denotes the subclass of $DNF$ with at most $s$ terms.

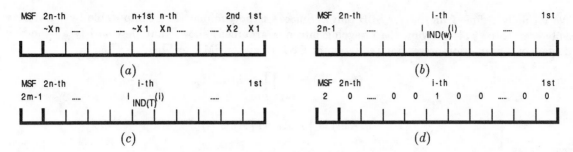

Figure 4: Bit-maps for $f(w, s, n)$, $g'(T, n)$, and $e_i$.

$\{g'(T) \mid T \in A\}$, and the 'extra' numbers, $E(n) = \{e_1, ..., e_{2n}\}$, which will serve the role of 'stuffings'. $g'$ maps a term $T$ to an integer whose bit representation is as in Figure 4 (c) ; Each $i$-th field contains $I_{IND(T)}(i)$, and the MSF is $2m - 1$, where $m$ is the number of literals in $T$. The 'extra' generators also have the same format: $E(n)$ is the set of $2n$ integers $e_1, ..., e_{2n}$ where each $e_i$ has the bit representation in Figure 4 (d); $e_i$ has 2 in its MSF, and 0's everywhere except in the $i$-th field where it has 1.

The claim is that $f(w, s, n)$ is generated by $g(A, n)$ just in case $w$ satisfies $A$. We give a brief, informal explanation of why this claim holds. The first crucial fact is that $IND(T) \subseteq IND(w)$ if and only if $w \models T$, for any term $T$. The next crucial fact is that *if any linear combination of $g(A, n)$ generates $f(w, s, n)$, then there can be no 'carries'.* Therefore, if for any term $T$, $g'(T)$ is in some linear combination generating $f(w, s, n)$, then $T$ must be satisfied by $w$. Finally, the fact that MSF's of $f(w, s, n), g'(T)$ and $e_i$ are $2n - 1$, $2m - 1$, and 2, respectively, ensures that if any linear combination is to equal $f(w, s, n)$, then it must contain a non-zero multiple of $g'(T)$ for some term $T$. This $T$ must be satisfied by $w$. It is easily seen, on the other hand, that if there is a term $T$ in $A$ that is satisfied by $w$, then the sum of $g'(T)$ and the appropriate stuffings; $\{e_i \mid i \in IND(w) \setminus IND(T)\}$, equals $f(w, s, n)$.

It is easy to check that $f$ can be computed in time polynomial in $n$ and $s$, and that $g$ is 'poly-blowup'.

### 5.4.2   Proof Sketch of Theorem 5.6

First, we note the following fact, which is essentially a corollary to the Prime Number Theorem.[14]

**Fact 5.1** *There exists an algorithm which takes an integer $n$ as input and outputs $2n$ distinct primes in time polynomial in $n$. We let $h$ denote the function computed by one such algorithm, and let $h(n)$ denote the output of $h$ on $n$, and $h(n, i)$ the $i$-th smallest element in $h(n)$.*

These $2n$ primes are then associated with the $2n$ literals there are for $n$ variables: We map any assignment $w$ to the product of the associated primes for those $n$ literals made true by the assignment, say $f(w)$. (For simplicity, we ommit other parameters to $f$ for now.) We then map any term $T$ to the product of the associated primes for all the literals in it, $g'(T)$. The simple but crucial observation is that $g'(T)$ divides $f(w)$ if and only if $T$ is a subset of the set of literals made true by $w$. Thus, $f(w)$ is in the linear set (module) generated by $\{g'(T)\}$, if and only if $w$ satisfies $T$. It follows immediately then, that if $A$ is a DNF formula, then $f(w)$ is in the semilinear set (semi-module) generated by $g(A) = \{\{g'(T)\} \mid T \in A\}$ if and only if $w$ satisfies $A$.

---

[14] The prime number theorem states that the number of primes less than or equal to n is of order $\frac{n}{\log n}$ – in fact $\Theta(\frac{n}{\log n})$. This, together with the fact that primality checking is performable in pseudo polynomial time, implies the claimed fact.

We formally define $f$ and $g$ (for SLB only). Since $f$ is polynomial time computable by Fact 5.1 and $g$ is easily seen to be poly-blowup, the foregoing informal argument shows that they satisfy all the required conditions of a prediction-preserving reduction of DNF to either SMB or SLB.

$$f(w, s, n) = \prod_{i \in IND(w)} h(n, i)$$

$$g(A, n) = \{g'(A_j, n) \mid A_j \in A\}$$

where

$$g'(T, n) = \{ \prod_{i \in IND(T)} h(n, i) \}$$

### 5.4.3    Proof Sketch of Theorem 5.7

The reduction is identical to the one in the proof of Theorem 5.5, except for the fact that the $2n$ fields and MSF of bit maps in the previous case are replaced by $2n$ independent dimensions. Namely, we define our $f$ and $g$ as follows.

$$f(w, s, n) = \langle 2n - 1, I_{IND(w)}(2n), ..., I_{IND(w)}(i), ..., I_{IND(w)}(1) \rangle$$

$$g(A, n) = \{g'(T) \mid T \in A\} \cup E(n)$$

where

$$g'(T) = \langle 2m - 1, I_{IND(T)}(2n), ..., I_{IND(T)}(i), ..., I_{IND(T)}(1) \rangle$$

$$E(n) = \{e_i \mid 1 \le i \le 2n\}$$

$$e_i = \langle 2, 0, ..., 0, 1, 0, ..., 0 \rangle$$

An essentially identical argument as before shows that this gives us a prediction preserving reduction from DNF to LB(variable-dimension, unary).

### 5.4.4    Proof Sketch of Theorem 5.8

The reduction is similar to the one in the proof of Theorem 5.6 with some twist. Here, instead of the $2n$ primes that were associated with the $2n$ literals for $n$ variables in the previous case, we use $2n$-dimensional unit vectors for the same purpose. In essence, we use the variable dimension at hand to express $2n$ independent components which, in the previous case, we used primes for.

We map any assignment $w$ to the sum of the unit vectors associated with exactly those $n$ literals made *false* by the assignment, and call this $f(w)$. (Again for simplicity, we ommit other parameters to $f$ for now.) Recall that, in the previous reduction, we mapped $w$ to the product of all the primes for those literals made *true* by the assignment. We then map any term $T$ to the basis (with 0 offset) and the set of generators consisting of the associated unit vectors for all the literals *not* in it, denoted $g'(T)$. The crucial fact is that $g'(T)$ can generate $f(w)$ as an integral linear combination of its elments if and only if $T$ contains no literals that are made false by $w$. Thus, $f(w)$ is in the linear set (module) generated by $g'(T)$ if and only if $w$ satisfies $T$. Hence if $A$ is a DNF formula, then $f(w)$ is in the semilinear set (semi-module) generated by $\{g'(T) \mid T \in A\}$ if and only if $w$ satisfies at least one of the terms in $A$.

We formally define the mappings $f$ and $g$ in the following (for SLB only). We introduce the notation '$NIND(.)$' as a short hand for the 'complement' of $IND(.)$, i.e. if $w$ is an assignment then $NIND(w) = \{i \mid w_i = 0\} \cup \{n + i \mid w_i = 1\}$.

$$f(w, s, n) = \langle I_{NIND(w)}(2n), ..., I_{NIND(w)}(i), ..., I_{NIND(w)}(1) \rangle$$

$$g(A, n) = \{g'(T, n) \mid T \in A\}$$

where

$$g'(T, n) = \{e_i \mid i \in NIND(T)\}$$

and $e_i$ is the unit vector whose only non-zero component is its $i$-th component.

# 6    Open Problems

Our characterization of learnability is complete, up to various degrees of hardness assumptions, except the learnability question for semilinear sets in unary for dimensions 3 and higher which is an open problem. Also, the question of proper-learnability of linear sets for any dimension is open, though they are clearly learnable by semilinear sets for dimensions up to 2.

# Acknowledgments

The author gratefully acknowledges his advisor, Scott Weinstein, for guiding him to the learnability questions of semilinear sets. Thanks are also due to Herbert S. Wilf for his generous help in my understanding of properties of additive semigroups and the theory of partitions, and to Sanguthevar Rajasekaran for pointing out to the author some facts of number theory. Finally, the author has greatly benefited from valuable discussions with Leonard Pitt and Manfred Warmuth, particularly in regard to the subject of 'prediction preserving reducibility', and the learnability results on modules.

# References

[1] Naoki Abe. *Money Changing Problem is NP-Complete*. Technical Report MS-CIS-87-45, University of Pennsylvania, June 1987.

[2] George Andrews. *The Theory of Partitions*. Addison-Wesley, 1976.

[3] A. Blumer, A. Ehrenfeucht, D. Haussler, and M. Warmuth. Classifying learnable geometric concepts with the vapnik-chervonenkis dimension. In *Proc. 18th ACM Symp. on Theory of Computation*, pages 243 – 282, 1986.

[4] A. Blumer, A. Ehrenfeucht, D. Haussler, and M. Warmuth. Occam's razor. *Information Processing Letters*, 24:377 – 380, 1987.

[5] V. Chvatal. A greedy heuristic for the set-covering problem. *Mathematics of Operations Research*, 4(3):233 – 235, 1979.

[6] A. Ehrenfeucht, D. Haussler, M. Kearns, and Leslie G. Valiant. A general lower bound on the number of examples needed for learning. In *Proceedings of the 1988 Workshop on Computational Learning Theory*, pages 139 – 154, 1988. Also to appear in Information and Computation.

[7] Michael A. Garey and David S. Johnson. *Computers and Intractability – A Guide to the Theory of NP-Completeness*. Freeman, 1979.

[8] D. Haussler, M. Kearns, N. Littlestone, and M. Warmuth. Equivalence of models for polynomial learnability. In *Proceedings of the 1st Workshop on Computational Learning Theory*, 1988.

[9] D. Haussler, N. Littlestone, and M. K. Warmuth. Predicting $\{0,1\}$ functions on randomly drawn points. In *Proceedings of 1988 IEEE Symposium on the Foundations of Computer Science*, 1988. Also in Proceedings of the 1988 Workshop on Computational Learning Theory.

[10] D. Helmbold, R. Sloan, and M. Warmuth. Learning nested differences of intersection closed concept classes. In *Proceedings of the 1989 Workshop on Computational Learning Theory*, July 1989.

[11] Michael Kearns and Leslie G. Valiant. *Learning Boolean Formulae or Finite Automata is as Hard as Factoring*. Technical Report TR-14-88, Aiken Computation Laboratory, Harvard University, 1988.

[12] Albert Nijenhuis and Herbert S. Wilf. Representation of integers by linear forms in nonnegative integers. *Journal of Number Theory*, 4:98–106, 1972.

[13] R. J. Parikh. Language generating devices. *M.I.T. Res. Lab. Electron. Quart. Prog. Rep.*, 60:199–212, 1961.

[14] Leonard Pitt. personal communication.

[15] Leonard Pitt and Leslie G. Valiant. Computational limitations on learning from examples. *Journal of the ACM*, 35(4):965–984, 1988.

[16] Leonard Pitt and Manfred Warmuth. *The minimum consistent DFA problem cannot be approximated within any polynomial*. Technical Report UIUCDCS-R-89-1499, University of Illinois at Urbana-Champaign, February 1989.

[17] Leonard Pitt and Manfred Warmuth. Prediction preserving reducibility. 1989. To appear in Journal of Computer and System Sciences.

[18] Leslie G. Valiant. Learning disjunctions of conjunctions. In *The 9th IJCAI*, 1985.

[19] Leslie G. Valiant. A theory of the learnable. *Communications of A.C.M.*, 27:1134–1142, 1984.

# LEARNING NESTED DIFFERENCES OF INTERSECTION-CLOSED CONCEPT CLASSES

David Helmbold*
Dep. of Computer Sc.
U. C. Santa Cruz

Robert Sloan†
MIT Lab. for Computer Sc.
Cambridge, MA 02139

Manfred K. Warmuth‡
Dep. of Computer Sc.
U. C. Santa Cruz

## ABSTRACT

This paper introduces a new framework for constructing learning algorithms. Our methods involve a master algorithm which uses learning algorithms for intersection closed concept classes as subroutines. For example, we give master algorithm capable of learning any concept class whose members can be expressed as nested differences (e.g. $c_1 - (c_2 - (c_3 - (c_4 - c_5)))$) of concepts from an intersection closed class.

We show that our algorithms are optimal or nearly optimal with respect to several different criteria. These criteria include: the number of examples needed to produce a good hypothesis with high confidence, the worst case total number of mistakes made, and the expected number of mistakes made in the first $t$ trials.

## 1 Introduction

We are interested in efficient algorithms for learning concepts from examples. Formally, *concepts* are subsets of some *instance domain* $X$ from which instances are drawn and a *concept class* is a subset of $2^X$, the power set over $X$. The instances are labeled *consistently* with a fixed *target concept* $t$ which is in the *concept class* $C$ to be learned, i.e. an instance is labeled "+" if it lies in the target concept and "−" otherwise. Labeled instances are called *examples*.

There has been a surge of interest in learning from examples sparked by the introduction of a model of learning by Valiant [Val84]. This model accounts for both the performance of the learning algorithm as well as the computational resources and the number of examples used. Even though some practical learning algorithms have been

*Supported by ONR grant N00014-86-K-0454.
†Supported by an NSF graduate fellowship and by ONR grant N00014-86-K-0454.
‡Supported by ONR grants N00014-85-K-0445 and N00014-86-K-0454.

found [Val84,BEHW89,Shv88,Riv87,Lit88,Hau89], and learnability of concept classes has been characterized [BEHW89] using the Vapnik-Chervonenkis (VC) dimension [VC71], no practical algorithms have been found for many natural classes, such as DNF's, DFAs, and general decision trees. Recently strong evidence has been found that classes such as boolean functions and DFAs are actually not efficiently learnable [PW88,KV88,PW89].

In this paper we give various schemes for composing known efficient learning algorithms to create provably efficient learning algorithms for more complicated problems. Thus we give *constructive* results for learning new classes of concepts for which efficient learning algorithms were not previously known. The composition technique consists of new master algorithms that use the algorithms for the "simpler" classes as subroutines. The master algorithms learn nontrivially more complicated classes which can be defined in terms of the simpler classes. The master algorithms do not need to know the specific simpler classes, since they only pass information among the various algorithms for the simpler classes.

The "simple" classes considered here are usually intersection closed concept classes and the master algorithms learn various compositions of intersection closed concept classes. (A concept class is *intersection closed*[1] if the non-empty intersection of any subclass is also in the class.) There is a canonical algorithm for learning intersection closed classes which we call here the *Closure* algorithm: The hypothesis of this algorithm is always the smallest concept containing all of the positive examples (POS) seen so far [Nat87]. We denote this concept as CLOSURE(POS). Given an unlabeled instance the Closure algorithm predicts using this concept as its hypothesis.

The simplest composition scheme we consider learns the concept class DIFF($C$), which consists of all concepts of the form $c_1 - (c_2 - (c_3 - \cdots - (c_{p-1} - c_p)\cdots))$, where all $c_i$ are in $C$, and $p$ is a positive integer called the *depth* of the concept. It is easy to see that an instance $x$ is in the concept $c_1 - (c_2 - (c_3 - \cdots - (c_{p-1} - c_p)\cdots))$ iff the lowest indexed $c_i$ that does not contain $x$ has an even index (Assume for convenience that $c_{p+1} = \emptyset$).

A more involved scheme efficiently learns the class DIFF($C_1 \cup C_2 \cup \cdots \cup C_s$); i.e. each $c_i$ may be in any $C_j$, for $1 \leq j \leq s$. This scheme assumes that all the $C_j$ are intersection closed and that their Closure algorithms can be implemented efficiently.

Examples of intersection closed classes with efficient Closure algorithms include orthogonal rectangles in $R^n$, monomials (i.e. orthogonal sub-rectangles of the boolean hypercube), vector sub-spaces of $R^n$ [Shv88], and so forth. In Figures 1 and 2 we give examples of DIFF($C$), when $C$ is the class of orthogonal rectangles in $R^2$. In this case DIFF($C$) contains staircase type objects and some restricted unions of orthogonal rectangles. If $C$ is the class of initial segments on the real line (orthogonal rectangles in dimension one with the same left endpoint), then DIFF($C$) is the class of unions of inter-

---

[1]The following weaker definition of intersection closed suffices: for any finite set contained in some concept the intersection of all concepts containing the finite set is also a concept in the class.

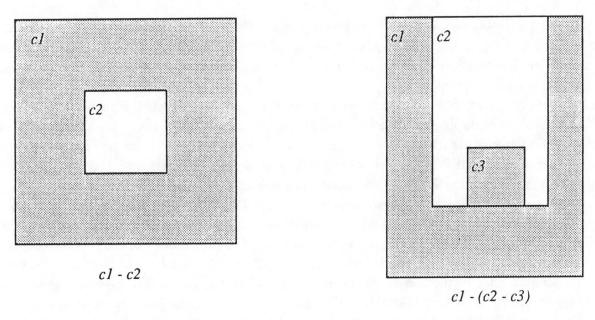

Figure 1:  Two concepts in DIFF(orthogonal rectangles).

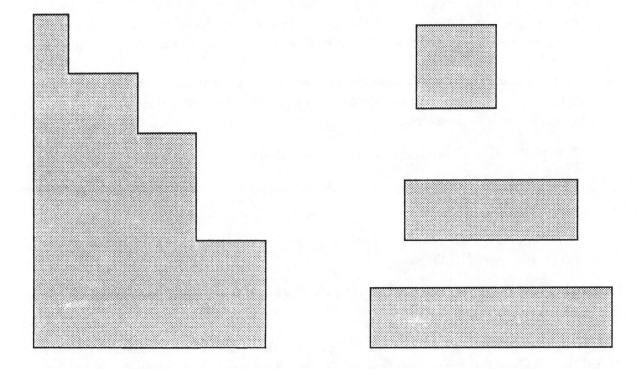

Figure 2: Another two concepts in DIFF(orthogoal rectangles).

vals. In the finite case, it has been shown [Nat87] that a concept class is learnable with one-sided error (i.e. the error with respect to the negative distribution is zero)[2] if and only if it is intersection closed and the VC dimension of the class grows polynomially in the relevant parameters.

If a concept class $B$ is not intersection closed one can always embed it into a larger class $C$ that is. However, the VC dimension of $C$ may be much larger than the VC dimension of $B$. The Closure algorithm learns an intersection closed class $C$ from positive examples only. Note that DIFF($C$) is not necessarily intersection closed, and thus our master algorithms for learning DIFF($C$) will use both positive and negative examples.

One can generalize the composition scheme for DIFF($C$) by allowing the innermost concept, $c_p$, to be in an *arbitrary* polynomially learnable (using both positive and negative examples) class $B$. Let DIFF($C, B$) be all concepts of the form $c_1 - (c_2 - (c_3 - \cdots - (c_{p-1} - b) \cdots))$ where the $c_j$ are in the intersection closed class $C$ and $b$ is in $B$. The $c_j$ are in some sense a filter formed with special concepts, while $b$ is allowed to be more general.

Concepts in DIFF($C$) and DIFF($C, B$) of depth two were previously shown to be learnable in [KLPV87]. In this paper, we consider the case of unbounded depth. Observe the following closure properties: for two intersection closed classes $C_1$ and $C_2$ the class $C_1 \wedge C_2 = \{c_1 \cap c_2 : c_1 \in C_1 \wedge c_2 \in C_2\}$ is intersection closed as well; the same holds for the class $C_1 \cap C_2$, and dual results hold if intersection is replaced by union.

Note also that $C$ is intersection closed iff $\bar{C}$ which consists of the complements of the concepts of $C$ is "union closed".

There are many ways to evaluate learning algorithms, such as the run time and space required by the algorithm, and the performance criteria (how well the algorithm learns). The performance criteria we consider include the following:

1. The probability of producing a hypothesis of unacceptably large error [Val84].

2. The probability of making a mistake on predicting the label of the last instance [HLW88].

3. The expected total number of mistakes for on-line prediction of the labels of the first $t$ instances [HLW88].

4. The worst case total number of mistakes for on-line prediction of the labels of any sequence of instances [Lit88].

We have developed two master algorithms, one that remembers all examples seen (the Total Recall algorithm), and one that remembers a number of examples bounded by the VC dimension (the Space Efficient algorithm). The Total Recall algorithm for DIFF($C$) is

---

[2]Learnability with one-sided error implies learnability from positive examples [KLPV87]. The opposite is not quite true.

nearly optimal for the first three performance criteria. If the Closure algorithm for $C$ can be implemented in polynomial time then the Total Recall algorithm is computationally efficient as well. Similarly, if the learning algorithm for $B$ is efficient and has optimal performance, then the same holds for learning DIFF$(C, B)$ under the first and third performance criteria.

When learning DIFF$(C)$ and DIFF$(C, B)$ with either of our algorithms, we have tight bounds with respect to the last performance measure (assuming that good algorithms for $C$ and $B$ are available).[3] Despite the simplicity of the Space Efficient algorithm, its hypothesis is neither consistent with all of the examples previously seen, nor independent of their order. Therefore the standard techniques for proving probabilistic performance are not applicable. Proving distribution independent bounds for the Space Efficient algorithm with respect to the three probabilistic measures are open problems.

We recently discovered that Steven Salzberg [Sal88] has independently developed a space efficient algorithm similar to ours for DIFF$(C)$ (where $C$ consists of orthogonal rectangles in $R^n$) as a subroutine in his algorithm for predicting, among other things, breast cancer data. In some cases, his algorithms outperform the best previously known prediction algorithms. However those results are only empirical. The crux of the type of research presented here is that using the methodology of computational learning theory [Val84,HLW88] (which is rooted in the earlier works of Vapnik and others in the area of pattern recognition [VC71,Vap82]), we can give efficient algorithms and *prove* their optimality.

In a companion paper [HSW89] we present an interesting application of our methods. We give a time and space efficient implementation of the Closure algorithm for a non-trivial intersection closed class: the class $C$ of subsets of $\mathbf{Z}^k$ that are closed under addition and subtraction. In algebraic terms $C$ consists of all submodules of the free $\mathbf{Z}$-module of rank $k$. In the following $n$ denotes the absolute value of the largest component in any positive example seen.

The standard Closure algorithm keeps a minimal set of up to $\frac{k \log n}{\log \log n}$ positive examples. Our improved algorithm stores only $k$ derived examples which have the same closure as the positive examples seen. Thus our algorithm has the advantages of space efficiency (and faster prediction). Furthermore, we can prove an absolute mistake bound of $k + k \log n$ for our algorithm.

Basically the same algorithm for learning submodules of $\mathbf{Z}^k$ can be used to learn zero-reversible commutative[4] regular languages [HSW89]. A trivial subfamily of the above class is the class of "counter languages": For a subset $\Delta$ of the alphabet and a number $p$, the corresponding counter language contains all words over the alphabet where the

---

[3] A similar space efficient algorithm for DIFF$(C)$ with the same worst case mistake bound was given in [Lit89a] for the special case where $C$ is the class of monomials.

[4] A language $L$ is *commutative* if for every word $x \in L$ all permutations of the word $x$ are also in $L$. In [Abe89] the learning of more complex commutative languages is investigated.

total number of letters in $\Delta$ is zero mod $p$. Recently it has been shown that for any polynomial $Q$, the problem: "given a set of examples consistent with some counter language accepted by a DFA with $p$ states, find a consistent DFA or a consistent NFA with fewer than $Q(p)$ states," is $NP$-hard [PW89]. Surprisingly we can bypass that hardness result by representing the hypothesis not as a DFA, but as the submodule defined by a set of derived examples. Indeed, we show in [HSW89] that zero-reversible commutative regular languages (which contain counter languages) are not only predictable but are even predictable with a small absolute mistake bound.

In [HSW89] we also show how the submodule algorithm can be used to learn a version of the word problem for finitely generated abelian groups. Furthermore, by "subtracting off" the first positive example, we can learn arbitrary cosets of submodules. Finally, the submodule algorithm itself is appropriate for use as a subroutine in either of our master algorithms. This allows us to learn (for example) the nested differences of zero-reversible commutative regular languages with good mistake bounds.

## 2    The Inclusion-Exclusion Algorithms

We first present a basic composition algorithm that assumes "total recall", i.e. sufficient space is available to store all of the examples. Then we show how the Total Recall algorithm can be modified for space efficiency (so that only a few examples are memorized) and analyze the two versions. Finally we generalize the composition procedure to handle the concepts $\text{DIFF}(C_1 \cup C_2 \cup \cdots \cup C_s)$ and $\text{DIFF}(C, B)$.

A very important combinatorial parameter used to estimate the complexity of learning a concept class is its Vapnik-Chervonenkis dimension (See [VC71,Pea78,Hau86]).

DEFINITION. A set $S$ is *shattered* (by the concept class $C$) if for each subset $S' \subseteq S$, there is a concept $c \in C$ which contains all of $S'$, but none of the points in $S - S'$. The *Vapnik-Chervonenkis dimension* of a concept class, denoted by $VCdim(C)$, is the cardinality of the largest set shattered by the concept class.

For any intersection closed class $C$ the algorithm shown in Figure 3 learns $\text{DIFF}(C)$ assuming an efficient implementation of the Closure algorithm. The functions POS (NEG) takes a set of examples and returns those which are labeled positive (negative).

The concept $h = h_1 - (h_2 - \cdots - (h_{p-1} - h_p) \cdots)$ is called the hypothesis of the algorithm (Note that $h_p \neq \emptyset$ and $h_{p+1} := \emptyset$).

When given a new instance $x$, the algorithm predicts its label according to $h$ as follows. Let $l$ be the least index such that $h_l$ does not contain $x$. If $l$ is even then $h(x) = +$, and if $l$ is odd then $h(x) = -$. If the prediction was wrong on $x$ then update $h$ by adding $x$ to $\text{EX}_l$ and executing the Total Recall loop starting with $i = l$.

The Space Efficient algorithm differs from the Total Recall algorithm in that it keeps only a "minimal" number of instances for each $h_i$.

```
EX₁ := all examples; i := 0
repeat
        increment i
        if i is odd then hᵢ := CLOSURE(POS(EXᵢ))
                   else hᵢ := CLOSURE(NEG(EXᵢ))
        EXᵢ₊₁ := hᵢ ∩ EXᵢ
until EXᵢ₊₁ = ∅
p := i; hₚ₊₁ := ∅
```

**Figure 3**: Total Recall Algorithm

DEFINITION. Let $S$ be a set of instances. A *spanning set* of $S$ (with respect to some intersection closed concept class $C$) is any minimal $S' \subseteq S$ for which CLOSURE$(S') = $ CLOSURE$(S)$. If no concept in $C$ contains $S$ then CLOSURE$(S)$ is not defined and $S$ has no spanning set.

The *Space Efficient* algorithm represents each $h_i$ by a spanning set, $S_i$, and the hypothesis $h = h_1 - (h_2 - \cdots - h_p) \cdots)$ by a sequence of spanning sets, $S_1, \ldots, S_p$. Predicting is done as in the Total Recall algorithm. However, if there was a mistake made on an instance $x$ and $l$ is the least index such that $x \notin h_l$, then $S_l$ is updated to a spanning set of $S_l \cup \{x\}$ and thus $h$ is modified by changing $h_l$ to CLOSURE$(S_l \cup \{x\})$. An example of the functioning of the Space Efficient algorithm with domain $R^2$ and concept class DIFF(orthogonal rectangles) is given in Figures 4a and 4b.

In order to get a good bound on the number of points stored by the Space Efficient algorithm we use the following.

**Theorem 1** *Given an intersection closed concept class $C$ and subset $S$ of the domain, every spanning set of $S$ is shattered by $C$.*

*Proof* Let $S'$ be a spanning set of $S$. Since $C$ is intersection closed, it suffices to show that some concept contains all of $S'$ (by definition of spanning set), and for each $x \in S'$, some concept of $C$ contains $S' - \{x\}$ but not $x$. Since $S'$ is minimal, if $x \in S'$ then CLOSURE$(S') \neq$ CLOSURE$(S' - \{x\})$. Therefore, the closure of $S' - \{x\}$ contains $S' - \{x\}$ but not $x$. $\square$

Theorem 1 or statements equivalent to it have appeared in several places, including [Nat87,HLW88,Bou88]. A trivial consequence of it is that any spanning set (with respect to $C$) has cardinality at most $VCdim(C)$, the VC-dimension of $C$. Also, any shattered set is its own spanning set. Therefore the Space Efficient algorithm requires that at most $p \cdot VCdim(C)$ examples be stored while learning a concept with depth $p$.

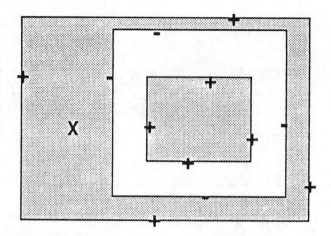

**Figure 4a:** The minimal hypothesis stored by the space efficient algorithm and the corresponding hypothesis. Point X is predicted to be positve.

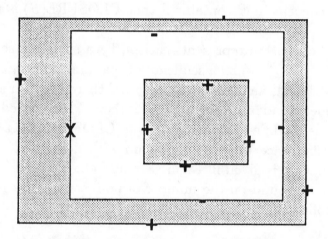

**Figure 4b:** If a mistake was made on point X, then the space efficient algorithm updates to the pictured hypothesis.

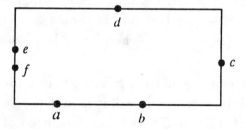

**Figure 5:** Only points *c* and *d* are corners. Both {*a*,*c*,*d*,*e*} and {*a*,*c*,*d*,*f*} are among the spanning sets.

An important fact about our algorithms is that in some sense they converge to the target concept from below. This idea is made more precise in the following lemma.

**Lemma 1** *Let* EX *be a set of examples consistent with some target concept,* $c_1 - (c_2 - \cdots (c_{p-1} - c_p) \cdots)$, *and let* $h = h_1 - (h_2 - \cdots - (h_{p'-1} - h_{p'}) \cdots)$ *be the current hypothesis of either the Total Recall algorithm or the Space Efficient algorithm generated by* EX. *Then* $p' \leq p$ *and for all* $1 \leq i \leq p'$, $c_i \supseteq h_i$. *In the case of the Total Recall algorithm,* $h$ *is consistent with* EX.

*Proof*   By induction on $p'$ for the Total Recall algorithm and by induction on the number of mistakes made by the Space Efficient algorithm.                                        □

Often we will want to focus our attention on concepts in $\mathrm{DIFF}(C)$ of restricted depth. To meet this need we define the concept class $\mathrm{DIFF}^p(C)$ as all concepts in $\mathrm{DIFF}(C)$ whose depth is at most $p$. The classes $\mathrm{DIFF}^p(\cup_j^s C_j)$ and $\mathrm{DIFF}^p(C, B)$ are defined analogously.

It is easy to see that the VC-dimension of $\mathrm{DIFF}^p(C) = p \cdot VCdim(C)$ for at least some concept classes (for example, orthogonal rectangles). The following lemma shows that this is also a general upper bound on the VC-dimension of $\mathrm{DIFF}^p(C)$.

**Lemma 2** *If* $C$ *is intersection closed and* $p \geq 1$, *then* $\mathrm{VCdim}(\mathrm{DIFF}^p(C)) \leq p\mathrm{VCdim}(C)$.

*Proof*   By induction on $p$. Let $d = VCdim(C)$. The Lemma trivially holds when $p = 1$ since $\mathrm{DIFF}^1(C) = C$.

Assume to the contrary that $\mathrm{DIFF}^p(C)$ shatters at most $pd$ elements, but $\mathrm{DIFF}^{p+1}(C)$ shatters a set $S$ of size $(p+1)d + 1$. This means that for every assignment of labels to points in $S$, there is a concept $c_1 - (c_2 - (c_3 - \cdots - (c_{l-1} - c_l) \cdots)) \in \mathrm{DIFF}^{p+1}(C)$ (i.e. $l \leq p + 1$) agreeing with the label assignment.

Let $S'$ be a spanning set of $S$ (with respect to $C$), so $|S'| \leq d$ (by Theorem 1). Consider a labeling of the points in $S$ where every point in $S'$ is labeled positive. If the concept $c = c_1 - (c_2 - (c_3 - \ldots - (c_{l-1} - c_l) \cdots)) \in \mathrm{DIFF}^{p+1}(C)$ is consistent with this labeling, then $c_1$ must contain all of $S'$ (and thus all of $S$). Therefore, for $S$ to be shattered, the remaining $c_i$'s (which form concepts in $\mathrm{DIFF}^p(C)$) must shatter the remaining $pd + 1$ points in $S - S'$, contradiction.                                        □

Since (a) the hypothesis of the Total Recall algorithm is always consistent with the examples seen and (b) the hypothesis produced does not depend on the order in which the examples are seen, we can get bounds on the first three performance criteria given in the introduction. Note that the Space Efficient algorithm satisfies neither (a) nor (b); however we are still able to prove a worst case mistake bound for the Space Efficient algorithm (deferred to later) expressed as a function of the worst case mistake bound of the Closure algorithm for $C$.

Since (a) holds for the Total Recall algorithm, we can apply the following result of [BEHW89]:

**Theorem 2** *Let $B$ be a well-behaved[5] concept class over some instance domain $X$, and let $P$ be an arbitrary but fixed probability distribution on $X$. Then for a sample $S$ of size at least $\max(\frac{4}{\epsilon}\log\frac{4}{\delta}, \frac{8\text{VCdim}(B)}{\epsilon}\log\frac{13}{\epsilon})$, drawn independently at random according to $P$ which is labeled consistently with some target concept $c \in B$, the probability that all $b \in B$ that are consistent with $S$ have error at most $\epsilon$ is at least $1 - \delta$. This holds for any $\epsilon$ and $\delta$ between 0 and 1.*

Applying the above theorem with $B = \text{DIFF}^p(C)$ together with the previous lemmas we get the following bound on the number of samples required by the Total Recall algorithm.

**Theorem 3** *After $\max(\frac{4}{\epsilon}\log\frac{4}{\delta}, \frac{8pd}{\epsilon}\log\frac{13}{\epsilon})$ examples, the Total Recall algorithm produces a hypothesis whose error is at most $\epsilon$ with probability at least $1 - \delta$ where $p$ is the depth of the target concept in $\text{DIFF}(C)$.*

To bound both the probability of making a prediction mistake on the $t^{\text{th}}$ instance and the expected total number of mistakes on the first $t$ instances, we use the methodology developed in [HLW88], which bounds the probability of a mistake by averaging over all permutations of the input.

DEFINITION. Let $S$ be a subset of the domain and $x \in S$. The point $x$ is a *corner* of $S$ (with respect to some Closure algorithm) if and only if $x \notin \text{CLOSURE}(S - \{x\})$.

Thus the corners of a set are in some sense the extremal points of the set. Notice that some spanning sets of $S$ may contain points that are not corners of $S$, and that the closure of the corners of $S$ may not be equal to $S$ (see Figure 5 for examples). However, the following lemma points out an important relationship between spanning sets and the corners.

**Lemma 3** *Let $S$ be a set of points in the domain. The set of corners of $S$ is the intersection of all the spanning sets of $S$.*

*Proof* Let $x$ be a corner of $S$. Since $x$ is not in the closure of $S - \{x\}$, $x$ must be in every $S' \subseteq S$ for which $\text{CLOSURE}(S') = \text{CLOSURE}(S)$. Therefore $x$ is in all spanning sets of $S$. Conversely, if $x$ is in every spanning set of $S$, then no subset of $S - \{x\}$ (including $S - \{x\}$ itself) can have the same closure as $S$. Hence $x$ must be a corner. $\square$

It follows from Lemma 3 that the number of corners of a set of positive instances of a concept is no greater than the VC-dimension of the concept class. The canonical Closure algorithm for learning intersection closed concept classes makes a mistake on the $t^{\text{th}}$ instance, $x_t$, only when $x_t$ is one of the corners of the set of all positive examples seen in the first $t$ trials. Since the $x_i$'s are drawn independently at random, each one is equally

---

[5]Some relatively benign measure-theoretic assumptions are required [BEHW89].

likely to be the last. Therefore, the probability that the standard prediction algorithm makes a mistake on the $t^{\text{th}}$ trial is at most $\frac{\text{\# of corners}}{t} \leq \frac{VCdim}{t}$, and the expected total number of mistakes in the first $t$ trials is thus bounded by $VCdim \cdot H_t$ (where $H_t$ is the $t^{\text{th}}$ harmonic number).

**Theorem 4** *The probability that the Total Recall algorithm makes an error on $x_t$ is bounded by $\frac{p \cdot \text{VCdim}(C)}{t}$, and the expected total number of mistakes over the first $t$ trials is at most $p \cdot \text{VCdim}(C) \cdot H_t$, where the $p$ is the depth of the target concept in $\text{DIFF}(C)$.*

*Proof*   The Total Recall algorithm for learning $\text{DIFF}(C)$ makes a mistake on $x_t$ only when $x_t$ is a corner (with respect to $C$) of some $EX_i$. Since each $EX_i$ has at most $VCdim(C)$ corners, the probability that we make a mistake on the $t^{\text{th}}$ trial is at most $\frac{p\,VCdim(C)}{t}$. The remaining part of the theorem is obtained by summing up the probabilities of making an error on each trial.                                                                       □

We follow [Lit88] in defining mistake-based performance criteria for learning algorithms. In particular, for target concept $c$ define $M(c)$ to be the maximum number of mistakes made by the Closure algorithm on any possible sequence of instances consistent with $c$. For any non-empty concept class $C$, define $M(C) = \max_{c \in C} M(c)$.

Note that if the Closure algorithm is used when learning an intersection closed class, no mistakes are made on the negative examples. Furthermore, negative examples do not cause changes to the hypothesis. Each mistake is caused by a positive example which increases the closure of all positive examples seen. Thus $M(c)$ is the maximum number of mistakes made by the Closure algorithm on any sequence of *positive* instances of $c$.

Using $M(C)$ we can obtain an absolute bound on the the number of mistakes made by our master algorithms.

**Theorem 5** *Both the Total Recall and the Space Efficient Algorithm make at most $pM(C)$ mistakes on any sequence of examples consistent with a concept in $\text{DIFF}^p(C)$.*

*Proof*   Each time a master algorithm makes a prediction error, one of the $h_i$'s is updated. All updates on the $i^{\text{th}}$ level are caused by positive examples if $i$ is odd, and by negative examples if $i$ is even. At the $i^{\text{th}}$ level a concept of the original class $C$ is learned based on the examples that reach that level. The number of update/mistakes at level $i$ is at most $M(C)$. Therefore, if $p$ is the depth of the target concept, the total number of mistakes made by our algorithms on any sequence of examples is at most $pM(C)$.                      □

We now consider the problem of learning $\text{DIFF}(\cup_{j=1}^{s} C_j)$. The target concept is of the form $c = c_1 - (c_2 - (c_3 - \cdots - (c_{p-1} - c_p) \cdots))$ where each $c_i$ is in one of the $s$ $C_j$'s. If we assume that the availability of a function $f$ that for each nesting depth $i$ returns an index $j$, such that $c_i \in C_j$, then a simple variant of the Total Recall algorithm learns $\text{DIFF}(\cup_{j=1}^{s} C_j)$. At each iteration $i$, simply use the Closure algorithm for the concept class $C_{f(i)}$. We call $f$ a *spectra* of $c$.

The main problem with learning $\mathrm{DIFF}(\cup_{j=1}^s C_j)$ is that we may not know ahead of time which $c_i$'s belong to which $C_j$'s. Since there are $s^p$ choices for the spectra of the target concept, any algorithm which tries all choices will have a running time that is exponential in $p$. However, the following shows that every concept in $\mathrm{DIFF}(\cup_{j=1}^s C_j)$ can be written in a normal form, assuming that each concept class $C_j$ contains the entire domain, which we call the universal concept.

The class $\mathrm{NDIFF}^{2ps}(\cup_{j=1}^s C_j)$ consists of all nested differences having depth at most $2ps$ and the pattern:

$$
\begin{aligned}
c = \quad & c_{1,1} - (c'_{1,1} - (c_{1,2} - (c'_{1,2} \cdots - (c_{1,s} - (c'_{1,s} \\
-( \quad & c_{2,1} - (c'_{2,1} - (c_{2,2} - (c'_{2,2} \cdots - (c_{2,s} - (c'_{2,s} \\
& \cdots \\
-( \quad & c_{p,1} - (c'_{p,1} - (c_{p,2} - (c'_{p,2} \cdots - (c_{p,s} - (c'_{p,s}) \cdots)
\end{aligned}
$$

where each $c_{\star,j}$ and $c'_{\star,j}$ are members of $C_j$. (Note that if the depth of $c$ is less than $2ps$ then pattern will be truncated at the appropriate depth.)

**Lemma 4** *If each $C_j$ contains the universal concept, then $\mathrm{NDIFF}^{2ps}(\cup_{j=1}^s C_j)$ contains every concept of depth $p$ in $\mathrm{DIFF}(\cup_{j=1}^s C_j)$.*

*Proof* By construction. Let $c = c_1 - (c_2 - (\cdots - (c_{p-1} - c_p)) \cdots)$ be a concept in $\mathrm{DIFF}^p(\cup_{j=1}^s C_j)$, and let $f$ be a spectra of $c$. Consider the concept $\hat{c}$ in $\mathrm{NDIFF}^{2ps}(\cup_{j=1}^s C_j)$ defined as follows:

- If $i$ is odd then $c_{i,f(c_i)} = c_i$.

- If $i$ is even then $c'_{i,f(c_i)} = c_i$.

- If $p$ is odd, the pattern is truncated with $c_{p,f(c_p)}$; otherwise the pattern is truncated with $c'_{p,f(c_p)}$.

- All other $c_{i,j}$'s in the (truncated) pattern are the universal concept.

We again use the convention that $c_{p+1} = \emptyset$, and if $p$ is odd then $c'_{p,f(c_p)} = \emptyset$. Thus an instance $x$ is in $\hat{c}$ iff there is an unprimed $c_{i,j}$ such that $x \in c_{i,j}$ and $x \notin c'_{i,j}$.

Assume first that $x \in c$, i.e. there is an even $k$ such that $x \in c_i$ for all $1 \le i < k$ and $x \notin c_k$. Therefore, $x$ is in each $c_{x,y}$ and $c'_{x,y}$ up to and including $c_{k,f(c_k)}$, but $x$ is not in $c'_{k,f(c_k)}$, establishing that $x \in \hat{c}$. A symmetric argument shows that if $x \notin c$ then $x \notin c'$. $\square$

Observe that the concepts of $\mathrm{NDIFF}(\cup_{j=1}^s C_j)$ have a fixed spectra function $\hat{f}$: the sequence $\hat{f}(1), \hat{f}(2), \cdots$ is simply the sequence $1, 1, 2, 2, \cdots, s, s, 1, 1, 2, 2, \cdots s, s, 1, 1, 2, 2, \cdots$.

Thus the normal forms give us a way of expressing concepts so that there is a fixed spectra function $\hat{f}$. However, the depth of an equivalent concept in $\text{NDIFF}^{2ps}(\cup_{j=1}^{s} C_j)$ for a concept in $\text{DIFF}^p(\cup_{j=1}^{s} C_j)$ can increase by a factor of up to $2s$. This increase in depth is reflected in our performance bounds for learning $\text{DIFF}(\cup_{j=1}^{s} C_j)$. An interesting question is whether $\text{DIFF}(\cup_{j=1}^{s} C_j)$ can be learned significantly more efficiently using either more concise normal forms or some sort of voting strategy to determine which concept class is associated with each $c_i$.

The argument in Lemma 2 shows $VCdim(\text{NDIFF}^{2ps}(\cup_{j=1}^{s} C_j)) \leq 2p \sum_{j=1}^{s} VCdim(C_j)$. Based on this, we can extend the above theorems developed for learning $\text{DIFF}(C)$, showing that an arbitrary concept in $\text{DIFF}(\cup_{j=1}^{s} C_j)$ of depth $p$ can be learned by the Total Recall algorithm (using the spectra $\hat{f}$) with the following bounds (assuming that each $C_j$ contains the universal concept):

- After $\max(\frac{4}{\epsilon} \log \frac{4}{\delta}, \frac{16p \sum_{j=1}^{s} VCdim(C_j)}{\epsilon} \log \frac{13}{\epsilon})$ examples, it produces a hypothesis whose error is at most $\epsilon$ with probability at least $1 - \delta$.

- The probability that it makes an error on $x_t$ is bounded by $\frac{2p \sum_{j=1}^{s} VCdim(C_j)}{t}$.

- The expected total number of mistakes made by the algorithm, over $t$ trials, is bounded by $2pH_t \sum_{j=1}^{s} VCdim(C_j)$.

In addition, for both the Total Recall *and* Space Efficient algorithms we get:

- The total number of mistakes is bounded by $2p \sum_{j=1}^{s} M(C_j)$.

Another variant of our Total Recall algorithms can learn $\text{DIFF}(C, B)$. This variant iterates $p$ times, stopping when $EX_p$ is consistent with some concept $h_p \in B$. The hypothesis will then be $h_1 - (h_2 - (h_3 - \cdots - (h_{p-1} - h_p) \cdots))$, where $h_1$ through $h_{p-1}$ are concepts in $C$.

By the same argument as in Lemma 2, the VC-dimension of $\text{DIFF}^p(C, B)$ is at most $(p-1)VCdim(C) + VCdim(B)$. Thus applying Theorem 2, we can generalize Theorem 3 to:

**Theorem 6** *After* $\max(\frac{4}{\epsilon} \log \frac{4}{\delta}, \frac{8((p-1)\text{VCdim}(C) + \text{VCdim}(B))}{\epsilon} \log \frac{13}{\epsilon})$ *examples, the modified Total Recall algorithm produces a hypothesis whose error is at most $\epsilon$ with probability at least $1 - \delta$ where $p$ is the depth of the target concept in* $\text{DIFF}(C, B)$.

In the complete paper we show that Theorem 4 can be refined to:

**Theorem 7** *Given a consistent algorithm for $B$ whose (distribution independent) probability for making a mistake at trial $t$ is at most $e(t)$ and where $t \cdot e(t)$ is non-decreasing, then the expected total number of mistakes of the Total Recall algorithm for $\text{DIFF}(C, B)$ (where the target concept has depth $p$) is at most $(p-1)\text{VCdim}(C)H_t + \sum_{i=1}^{t} e(i) + p$.*

If there is an algorithm $A$ which makes at most $M_A(B)$ mistakes learning a concept in $B$ then we can bound the total number of mistakes made by the Space Efficient algorithm when learning a concept of depth $p$ in $\mathrm{DIFF}(C, B)$. If the depth $p$ is given to the algorithm then the mistake bound is $(p-1)M(C) + M_A(B)$. If $p$ is not known, then the algorithms have to guess $p$. By trying $p$ incrementally and attempting to learn $B$ at each level (until $M_A(B)$ is exceeded) we get a mistake bound of $O(p(M(C) + M_A(B)))$.

If $C$ contains the universal concept then we can do better by using a doubling trick: use the sequence $1, 2, 3, 4, 7, 8, \ldots, 2^k - 1, 2^k, \ldots$ of guesses for $p$, and each time $M_A(B)$ is exceeded go on to the next value of $p$. The reason for trying a pair of consecutive guesses at each power of two is that $p$ must have the proper parity with respect to the depth of the target concept. The doubling trick improves the bound to $O(p \cdot M(C) + \log p \cdot M_A(B))$.

Our algorithms generalize to other cases as well. For example, by combining the analysis of the $\mathrm{DIFF}(\cup_{j=1}^s C_j)$ case with that for $\mathrm{DIFF}(C, B)$, we see that our algorithms can learn concepts of the form $c = c_1 - (c_2 - (c_3 - \cdots - (c_{p-1} - b) \ldots))$ where each $c_i$, $1 \le i \le p - 1$, is in some intersection closed $C_j$, $1 \le j \le s$, and $b$ is in some arbitrary learnable concept class $B$.

# 3     Conclusions and Open Problems

Previous work in this area includes general lower bounds on the number of examples required to produce, with high confidence, a hypothesis with small error [EHKV88,HLW88]. These general bounds show that our Total Recall Algorithm uses at most a log factor more examples than the minimum required to produce good hypothesis with high probability for concepts in $\mathrm{DIFF}(C)$ and $\mathrm{DIFF}(C, B)$. When the learning criteria is the probability of a mistake on the last trial our Total Recall Algorithm's performance for $\mathrm{DIFF}(C)$ is within a constant factor of optimal. Similarly, for the case of $\mathrm{DIFF}(C, B)$ the expected total number of mistakes made by our algorithm over the first $t$ trials is optimal up to a constant factor (assuming that we have a good subroutine for learning $B$).

The VC-dimension is a trivial lower bound on the total number of mistakes made in the worst case [Lit88]. Thus if $M(C) = VCdim(C)$, then under this performance measure our Space Efficient and Total Recall algorithms optimally learn $\mathrm{DIFF}(C)$ since they make at most $pM(C) = VCdim(\mathrm{DIFF}^p(C))$ many mistakes[6]. The class $\mathrm{DIFF}(C, B)$ is also learned optimally by these algorithms if the algorithm for $B$ is optimal and the depth, $p$, is known in advance. If the algorithm for $B$ is optimal, but $p$ is not known in advance, then our bounds are off by a factor of $\log p$. The bounds can be greatly improved (to within a constant factor and an additive term of $\log \log p$) by running multiple copies of

---

[6]Note that [Lit89b] gives an optimal transformation from an algorithm making at most $M$ mistakes to an algorithm producing with probability at least $1 - \delta$ a hypothesis of error at most $\epsilon$ from $O(\frac{M}{\epsilon} + \frac{1}{\epsilon} \log \frac{1}{\delta})$ random examples.

the Space Efficient algorithm with different values of $p$ and predicting with the Weighted Majority Algorithm [LW89]. It remains unclear if some kind of voting scheme can be used to improve the performance bounds for learning $\text{DIFF}(\cup_{j=1}^{s} C_j)$.

The major intriguing open problem is to analyze the space efficient algorithm with respect to the probabilistic performance measures. Although the Space Efficient algorithm is simple, its hypothesis is neither consistent with all of the examples previously seen, nor independent of their order. Therefore additional analysis techniques are needed to determine whether or not it is necessary to remember all previous examples for good probabilistic performance.

# 4    Acknowledgements

We thank David Haussler for valuable discussions.

# References

[Abe89]   Naoki Abe. Polynomial learnability of semilinear sets. In *Second Workshop on Computational Learning Theory*, Morgan Kaufmann, Santa Cruz, Cal., July 1989.

[BEHW89]   Anselm Blumer, Andrzej Ehrenfeucht, David Haussler, and Manfred K. Warmuth. Learnability and the Vapnik-Chervonenkis dimension. *Journal of the ACM*, 1989. To appear.

[Bou88]   Stéphane Boucheron. Learnability from positive examples in the Valiant framework. 1988. Unpublished manuscript.

[EHKV88]   Andrzej Ehrenfeucht, David Haussler, Michael Kearns, and Leslie Valiant. A general lower bound on the number of examples needed for learning. In *First Workshop on Computatinal Learning Theory*, pages 139–154, Morgan Kaufmann, Cambridge, Mass., August 1988.

[Hau86]   David Haussler. Quantifying the inductive bias in concept learning. In *Proceedings AAAI-86*, pages 485–489, American Association for Artificial Intelligence, August 1986.

[Hau89]   David Haussler. Learning conjunctive concepts in structural domains. *Machine Learning*, 1989. To appear.

[HLW88]   David Haussler, Nick Littlestone, and Manfred K. Warmuth. Predicting $\{0,1\}$-functions on randomly drawn points. In *29th Annual Symposium on Foundations of Computer Science*, pages 100–109, IEEE, White Plains, NY, 1988. Tech. Report, U. C. Santa Cruz. To appear (longer version).

[HSW89]   David Helmbold, Robert Sloan, and Manfred K. Warmuth. *Learning submodules and reversible, commutative regular languages*. Technical Report, U. C. Santa Cruz Computer Research Laboratory, 1989. To appear.

[KLPV87]   Michael Kearns, Ming Li, Leonard Pitt, and Leslie Valiant. On the learnability of boolean formulae. In *Proceedings of the Nineteenth Annual ACM Symposium on Theory of Computing*, pages 285–295, New York, New York, May 1987.

[KV88]    Michael Kearns and Leslie G. Valiant. *Learning Boolean Formulae or Finite Automata is as hard as factoring*. Technical Report TR 14-88, Harvard University Aiken Computation Laboratory, 1988.

[Lit88]    Nick Littlestone. Learning when irrelevant attributes abound: a new linear-threshold algorithm. *Machine Learning*, 2:285–318, 1988.

[Lit89a]   Nick Littlestone. 1989. private communication.

[Lit89b]   Nick Littlestone. From on-line to batch learning. In *Second Workshop on Computatinal Learning Theory*, Morgan Kaufmann, Santa Cruz, Calif., July 1989.

[LW89]    Nick Littlestone and Manfred K. Warmuth. The weighted majority algorithm. In *Second Workshop on Computatinal Learning Theory*, Morgan Kaufmann, Santa Cruz, Calif., July 1989.

[Nat87]    B. K. Natarajan. On learning boolean functions. In *Proceedings of the Nineteenth Annual ACM Symposium on Theory of Computing*, pages 296–304, New York, New York, May 1987.

[Pea78]    Judea Pearl. On the connection between the complexity and credibility of inferred models. *Journal of General Systems*, 4:255–264, 1978.

[PW88]    Leonard Pitt and Manfred K. Warmuth. Reductions among prediction problems: on the difficulty of predicting automata. In *3rd IEEE Conference on Structure in Commplexity Theory*, pages 60–69, Washington, DC, June 1988.

[PW89]    Leonard Pitt and Manfred K. Warmuth. The minimum DFA consistency problem cannot be approximated within any polynomial. In *Proceedings of the Twenty-First Annual ACM Symposium on Theory of Computing*, pages 421–432, Seattle, Washington, May 1989. Also in the *Fourth Annual Conference on Structure in Complexity Theory*, Eugene, Oregon, June 1989.

[Riv87]    Ronald L. Rivest. Learning decision lists. *Machine Learning*, 2(3):229–246, 1987.

[Sal88]    Steven Salzberg. *Exemplar-based learning: theory and implementation*. Center for Research in Computing Technology TR-10-88, Harvard University, Cambridge, Mass., October 1988.

[Shv88]    Haim Shvaytser. Linear manifolds are learnable from positive examples. April 1988. Unpublished manuscript.

[Val84]    Leslie G. Valiant. A theory of the learnable. *Communications of the ACM*, 27(11):1134–1142, November 1984.

[Vap82]    V. N. Vapnik. *Estimation of Dependences Based on Empirical Data*. Springer-Verlag, New York, 1982.

[VC71]    V. N. Vapnik and A. Ya. Chervonenkis. On the uniform convergence of relative frequencies of events to their probabilities. *Theory of Probability and its Applications*, XVI(2):264–280, 1971.

# A Polynomial-time Algorithm for Learning
# $k$-variable Pattern Languages from Examples

(extended abstract)

Michael Kearns*
Laboratory for Computer Science
Massachusetts Institute of Technology
Cambridge, Massachusetts

Leonard Pitt[†]
Department of Computer Science
University of Illinois
Urbana, Illinois

## 1   Introduction

In this paper we give, for each constant $k$, a polynomial-time algorithm for learning the class of $k$-variable *pattern languages* in the learning model introduced by Valiant [16]. A *pattern* is a string of constant and variable symbols, for instance the 3-variable pattern $p = 10x_1x_2x_21x_300x_1$. The associated language $L(p)$ is obtained by substituting for each variable in the pattern any constant string. Thus, the string 1011011011110110011 is contained in $L(p)$, since it can be obtained from $p$ by the substitutions $x_1 = 11, x_2 = 011, x_3 = 1011$.

For any constant $k$, our algorithm learns a $k$-variable target pattern $p$ by producing a polynomial-sized disjunction of patterns, each of between 0 and $k$ variables. (See below for a discussion of the potential difficulty of learning *general* patterns — where the number of variables is not bounded by a constant.) We assume the algorithm has access to a random source of negative examples, generated according to an arbitrary distribution, and a random source of positive examples of the target pattern $p$ in which the $k$-tuple of substitution strings (which entirely determines the positive example generated) is drawn not from an *arbitrary* distribution, but from any product distribution $D = D_1 \times \cdots \times D_k$, where each $D_i$ is an arbitrary distribution on substitution strings for variable $x_i$. This appears to be a natural and very general class of distributions.

Our algorithm runs in time polynomial in parameters $|\Sigma|, n, s, \frac{1}{\epsilon}$, and $\frac{1}{\delta}$ (and in time doubly exponential in the constant $k$), where $\Sigma$ is the alphabet of constant symbols, $n$ is the length of the target pattern, $s$ is the maximum length substitution string for any variable, and $\epsilon$ and $\delta$ are "accuracy" and "confidence" parameters. The algorithm outputs a disjunction of patterns, each over $k$ or fewer variables, that with probability at least $1 - \delta$, has accuracy of classification at least $1 - \epsilon$ on future positive and negative examples generated randomly from the distributions on which the algorithm was run. Thus the algorithm *PAC*-learns (*Probably Approximately Correctly* learns) the class of $k$-variable patterns *in terms of* the class of disjunctions of $k$ or fewer variable patterns.

*Supported by an A.T. & T. Bell Laboratories Ph.D. Scholarship, ONR grant N00014-85-K-0445, and by a grant from the Siemens Corporation.

†Supported in part by NSF grant IRI-8809570, and by the Department of Computer Science, University of Illinois at Urbana-Champaign.

The algorithm presented here is a positive result in a model that has recently seen a number of strongly negative results. In particular, the work of [8, 13] suggests that for language classes in the Chomsky hierarchy (e.g., regular languages), distribution-free learning is too ambitious a goal to be accomplished in polynomial time. For this reason it is heartening to discover a natural and general class of languages that is learnable in polynomial time under a wide class of distributions. The pattern languages are particularly interesting in light of the results in [8, 13], since they are incomparable to the classes discussed there. For example, it is shown in [8] that learning regular languages is hard under certain cryptographic assumptions. However, Angluin [1] shows that pattern languages and context-free languages are incomparable. Thus, our results suggest that perhaps there are large classes of languages that are efficiently learnable from examples, but that these classes constitute a "cut" of the complexity hierarchy other than the standard Chomsky classification.

It should be noted that our algorithm works when the empty string $\lambda$ is allowed as a substitution for a variable; thus each variable may be viewed as a "placeholder" for a substitution that may or may not be present in any given positive example of $p$. Previous results on pattern languages (discussed below) typically do not allow $\lambda$-substitutions.

We can also extend our techniques to learn a wider class of patterns, where restricted homomorphisms of the original variables may also appear in the target pattern. In particular, let $t = t(n, s, |\Sigma|)$ be any polynomial, and $h_1, \ldots, h_t$ a collection of bijective maps $h_i : \Sigma \to \Sigma$ such that for each $1 \leq i \leq t$, $h_i(a) \neq a$. Extend $h_i$ to strings in the usual way: If $a = a_1 \cdots a_l$, then $h_i(a) = h_i(a_1) \cdots h_i(a_l)$. An example of such a homomorphism (over $\Sigma = \{0, 1\}$) is $h(0) = 1$, and $h(1) = 0$. Thus $h(a) = \overline{a}$, the complement of $a$. A target pattern including such homomorphisms might be $x_1 10 x_2 h_2(x_1) 0 h_1(x_2) 110$, and positive examples are obtained by substituting constant strings for the variables $x_1$ and $x_2$, and applying the homomorphisms as indicated.

Given our initial requirement that the positive distribution be a product distribution, the allowance of the maps $h_i(x_j)$ in the target pattern is important in that it reintroduces a natural form of dependence within the example strings. While we still require that the substitution for variable $x_1$ is drawn independent of the substitution for $x_2$, we may regard the transformations $h_1(x_1), \ldots, h_t(x_1)$ as a polynomial-sized collection of "variables" whose substitution is strongly dependent on the substitution for $x_1$. The additional running time is a small polynomial increase depending on $t$, in particular, there is no increase in the exponent of the running time. Thus in some sense, the algorithm can handle a polynomial number of variables, as long as all but a constant number $k$ are highly dependent, and the remaining $k$ variables are independent. In this extended abstract, we will restrict our attention to basic patterns (without homomorphisms). The modified algorithm and analysis for the homomorphisms described above will be given in the full paper.

A brief comment on the potential difficulty of learning general patterns from examples is now in order. Previous algorithms for learning patterns either limit their attention to a constant number of variables, place strong restrictions on the order of the appearance of the variables, or allow various types of queries. While the problem of learning general patterns from examples by some hypothesis space in polynomial time remains open, there appear to be significant obstacles to overcome in this direction. First, Angluin [1] showed that for general patterns, deciding membership in the corresponding language is $NP$-complete. This suggests difficulties in the design of an algorithm that learns $k$-variable patterns in time *polynomial* in $k$. In particular, such an algorithm would not be able to use a general membership test to determine the consistency of a candidate pattern with a set of examples, a tool commonly used in the $PAC$-learning model. Second, it has recently been shown by Ko, Marron and Tzeng [9] that the problem of finding any pattern consistent with a set of positive and negative examples is $NP$-hard; the results of [12] (see also [4]) can be applied to show that the problem of learning general patterns by an algorithm outputting a single pattern in the $PAC$-learning model is $NP$-hard.

Our work in this area was motivated by the results of Angluin [1], Marron and Ko [11], and Marron [10]. Angluin's main result is a polynomial-time algorithm for finding a *descriptive pattern* for a positive sample $S$ of an unknown 1-variable target pattern: a pattern $p$ such that $S \subseteq L(p)$, and for any 1-variable pattern $p'$, $L(p') \not\subseteq L(p)$. Angluin's algorithm has no obvious application to the $PAC$-learning model, and there appear to be significant obstacles in extending her approach to finding descriptive $k$-variable patterns for constant $k > 1$ [1, 5]. Shinohara [14, 15] gives a polynomial-time algorithm for finding a descriptive pattern when there is at most one occurrence of each variable, and when $\lambda$-substitutions are allowed as well. He also gives an algorithm for patterns where all occurrences of variable $x_i$ appear before any occurrence of $x_{i+1}$. These results also do not have obvious applications in the $PAC$-learning model, where negative examples are present as well as positive, and the source of examples is an arbitrary distribution.

Ibarra and Jiang [6] give a polynomial-time algorithm for exact identification of general patterns in a model where the algorithm may conjecture an hypothesis pattern, and is provided with a *shortest* counterexample to the equivalence of the conjectured pattern and the target pattern (or is told they are equivalent). Angluin [2] shows that if each equivalence query may be answered by an *arbitrary* counterexample, but the algorithm is also provided with membership queries (access to an oracle deciding membership in the target pattern language) and subset queries (access to an oracle deciding if an hypothesis pattern accepts a subset of the target pattern language), exact identification must take exponential time. Again, these query results have no clear application to learning pattern languages in the $PAC$-learning model.

Marron and Ko [11] considered necessary and sufficient conditions on a finite positive initial sample that would allow *exact* identification of a target $k$-variable pattern from the initial sample and from polynomially many *membership queries*. Subsequently, Marron [10] considered the learnability of $k$-variable patterns in the same model, but where the initial sample consisted of only a single positive example of the target pattern. In both of these papers, a greedy learning algorithm (used as a subroutine here) was proposed. For the case of 1-variable and 2-variable patterns, Marron gave a careful analysis of the structural properties of initial examples that can cause this algorithm to fail. He also showed that only a small fraction of strings possess these properties.

We study the learnability of pattern languages in a model where the examples are generated randomly according to an unknown product distribution. Thus, the fact that the number of strings causing the greedy algorithm to fail is small compared to the total number of strings is no guarantee of success, since the underlying distribution may give large weight to these bad strings. We tackle this problem with a careful probabilistic analysis of the failures of the greedy algorithm together with a new algorithm that avoids these pitfalls with high probability. More precisely, we show that the "bad" portion of the target distribution that causes the greedy algorithm to fail in learning the $k$-variable target pattern can in fact be covered (within any $\epsilon$) by a polynomial number of $k - 1$ variable patterns (the exact number depending on $\epsilon$, and the probability of the bad portion of the distribution). However, the greedy algorithm may of course also fail to learn these covering patterns, and some of them may cover a fraction of the distribution that is too small to notice in polynomial time.

Our algorithm works by repeatedly running the greedy algorithm in an attempt, for each $0 \leq$

$d \leq k$, to learn all patterns of $d$ variables that cover a significant portion of the positive distribution. The main tool introduced in the analysis is a data structure called an *event tree*. The event tree has depth at most $k$, and its nodes consist of subsets of possible $k$-tuples of substitution strings (any such subset is called an *event*.) Thus each node represents a set of positive examples of the target pattern. The root of the tree represents the set of all positive examples, and the children of any node represent disjoint subevents of the parent.

The correctness of our algorithm essentially hinges on a proof that the algorithm will learn the leaves of the event tree with high probability. To ensure that our algorithm runs in polynomial time, we define the event tree so as to simultaneously provide an upper bound on the branching factor at any node, and a lower bound on the probability associated with the node. We then show that the leaves of the event tree represent disjoint subevents of the root covering an overwhelming fraction of the positive distribution. Furthermore, for each leaf at depth $d$, $0 \leq d \leq k$, there is a corresponding pattern over at most $d$ variables that is a subpattern of the target pattern, obtained by replacing $k - d$ of the variables with particular constant substitutions, and whose positive examples include all positive examples of the target pattern that can be obtained from substitution $k$-tuples corresponding to the leaf.

These leaf patterns are shown to be contained in a larger pool of patterns constructed by repeated application of the greedy algorithm. Our main algorithm then eliminates patterns in this pool whose inclusion would incur too much error on the negative distribution. It then applies an approximation algorithm for the partial set cover problem [7] to find a disjunction of the remaining patterns, whose size exceeds the number of leaves in the event tree by at most a logarithmic factor. This disjunction is shown to be small enough to be a $(1 - \epsilon)$-accurate hypothesis by applying a generalization of the technique known as Occam's Razor [3, 7].

## 2    Definitions and Notation

Let $\Sigma$ be a finite alphabet. A *k-variable pattern* is an element of $(\Sigma \cup \{x_1, \ldots, x_k\})^*$. For any $k$-variable pattern $p$, and any set of $k$ strings $u_1, \ldots, u_k \in \Sigma^*$, let $p[x_1 : u_1, \ldots, x_k : u_k]$ denote the string $w \in \Sigma^*$ obtained by substituting $u_i$ for each occurrence of $x_i$ in the pattern $p$. The *language generated by* $p$ is defined by $L(p) = \{p[x_1 : u_1, \ldots, x_k : u_k] : u_1 \ldots u_k \in \Sigma^*\}$. Let $P_k$ consist of all $k$-variable patterns.

For this abstract, we will assume that all substitution strings for variables have maximum length $s$, where $s$ will typically be polynomially related to the length $n$ of the *target pattern* to be learned. See [13] for the justification and motivation of such an assumption. Also, without loss of generality [4, 13] we assume that $n$ and $s$ are given as input to the learning algorithm. Let $\Sigma^{[s]}$ denote strings of any length between 0 and $s$. Call any such string a *substitution string*.

A *binding* is a list $x_{i_1} : u_1, \ldots, x_{i_d} : u_d$, where $1 \leq d \leq k$, the $x_{i_j}$'s are distinct variables, and each $u_i$ is a substitution string. The pattern $p[x_{i_1} : u_1, \ldots, x_{i_d} : u_d]$ is the pattern $p$ with strings $u_1, \ldots u_d$ substituted in for variables $x_{i_1}, \ldots x_{i_d}$, respectively. Thus $p[x_{i_1} : u_1, \ldots, x_{i_d} : u_d]$ is a $k - d$ variable pattern over variable set $\{x_1, \ldots, x_k\} - \{x_{i_1}, \ldots x_{i_d}\}$. Such a pattern is called a *subpattern* of $p$. Note that if $d = k$ then a binding of (all $k$) variables produces a "subpattern" that is a constant string.

For any string $w$, let $w(i, j)$ denote the substring of $w$ beginning at position $i$, and having length $j$.

For each variable $x_i$ $(1 \leq i \leq k)$, we assume an arbitrary probability distribution $D_i$ on substitution strings. Let $\mathbf{Pr} : (\Sigma^{[s]})^k \to [0,1]$ be the product distribution $D_1 \times \cdots \times D_k$, thus $\mathbf{Pr}(\langle u_1, \ldots, u_k \rangle) = \Pi_{i=1}^k D_i(u_i)$. Positive examples of the target pattern are generated according to distribution $\mathbf{Pr}$. That is, the $k$-tuple $\langle u_1, \ldots, u_k \rangle$ is generated with probability $\mathbf{Pr}(\langle u_1, \ldots, u_k \rangle)$, and for each $i$, the string $u_i$ is substituted in place of variable $x_i$ in $p$ to obtain an example string $p[x_1 : u_1, \ldots, x_k : u_k]$. Let the distribution on positive examples of $p$ induced by probability measure $\mathbf{Pr}$ be denoted by $D_s^+$.

We assume an arbitrary probability distribution $D_s^-$ on negative examples of target pattern $p$ of length at most $ns$. Note that a positive example has length at most $ns$, since each substitution string has length at most $s$.

**Definition 1** *The class $P_k$ of $k$-variable patterns is* PAC-learnable *(with respect to a positive product distribution and an arbitrary negative distribution) in terms of hypothesis space $H$ iff there exists an algorithm $A$ such that on input of any parameters $n, s, \epsilon,$ and $\delta$, for any pattern $p$ of $P_k$ of length at most $n$, and for any product distribution $D_s^+$ on positive examples of $p$, and any distribution $D_s^-$ on negative examples of $p$, if $A$ has access to $D_s^+$ and $D_s^-$, then $A$ produces an element $h \in H$ such that, with probability at least $1 - \delta$, $\sum_{h(w)=0} D_s^+(w) \leq \epsilon$ and $\sum_{h(w)=1} D_s^-(w) \leq \epsilon$. The run time of $A$ is required to be polynomial in $n, s, \frac{1}{\epsilon}, \frac{1}{\delta},$ and $|\Sigma|$.*

Let $SUB = (\Sigma^{[s]})^k$, the set of all possible $k$-tuples of substitution strings. An *event $E$* is a subset of $SUB$. For any event $E$, let $E[x_{i_1} : u_1, \ldots, x_{i_d} : u_d]$ be the subset of elements of $E$ where the $i_j$th component is the string $u_j$, for $1 \leq j \leq d$.

A variable $x_i$ is *bound* in event $E$ if there exists a substitution string $u$ such that $E = E[x_i : u]$. In this case, we say that $x_i$ is bound to $u$. (There can be at most one such $u$.) Define $bound(E) = \{i : 1 \leq i \leq k$ and $x_i$ is bound in $E\}$. Define $free(E) = \{1, 2, \ldots, k\} - bound(E)$. Define $bindings(E)$ to be the list of bindings for each bound variable of $E$. That is, if $bound(E) = \{i_1, \ldots, i_d\}$, and for each $j, 1 \leq j \leq d$, variable $x_{i_j}$ is bound to substitution string $u_j$, then $bindings(E) = x_{i_1} : u_1, \ldots, x_{i_d} : u_d$. Given an event $E$, there is a subpattern of the target pattern $p$ that is induced by the bound variables of $E$. This induced subpattern is the pattern $p[bindings(E)]$, hereafter written $p_E$. Notice that if $bound(E) = \{1, 2, \ldots, k\}$ (i.e., all variables are bound), then $p_E$ is a string of $\Sigma^+$, which is also interpreted as a 0-variable pattern.

The key property of $p_E$ that we will exploit is that for any event $E$, and for any $\langle u_1, \ldots, u_k \rangle \in E$, $p[x_1 : u_1, \ldots, x_k : u_k] \in L(p_E)$. In other words, the pattern $p_E$ "covers" the portion of the language $L(p)$ when we consider only substitution $k$-tuples $\langle u_1, \ldots, u_k \rangle$ drawn from the set $E$.

## 3    The Algorithm COVER

We describe an algorithm COVER, that *PAC*-learns (with respect to an arbitrary product distribution on positive examples, and an arbitrary distribution on negative examples) the class of $k$-variable patterns in terms of the union of at most $poly(n, s, \frac{1}{\epsilon}, \frac{1}{\delta}, |\Sigma|)$ of patterns over $k$ or fewer variables.

Before describing algorithm COVER, we describe a simple variant of a greedy algorithm that was used in [10, 11]. GREEDY (Figure 1 – last page) takes a string $w$ and a list of $d$ variable bindings of $(1 \leq d \leq k)$. On input $w$ and list $x_{i_1} : u_1, \ldots, x_{i_d} : u_d$, GREEDY attempts to find, one symbol at a time, a $d$-variable pattern $p_d$ (over variables $\{x_{i_1}, x_{i_2}, \ldots, x_{i_d}\}$) such that $p_d[x_{i_1} : u_1, \ldots, x_{i_d} : u_d] = w$. Initially, GREEDY looks for the first match in $w$ of any substitution string $u_j$ (breaking ties in favor of shorter strings). If $u_j$ is the first match at some position of $w$, GREEDY assumes that all prior characters of $w$ are constants of $p_d$, and that the substring $u_j$ found was generated by $x_{i_j}$. It outputs $x_{i_j}$, and continues in this fashion, iteratively finding the next matching substitution that does not overlap with the portion of the input string "parsed" so far.

Algorithm COVER uses GREEDY as a subroutine. COVER, on input parameters $n, s, \epsilon, \delta$, and $\Sigma$, first computes the values $m_P = m_1 + m_2$ and $m_N$, described later, each bounded above by a polynomial in the parameters $n$, $s$, $\frac{1}{\epsilon}$, $\frac{1}{\delta}$, and $|\Sigma|$. Then COVER executes the code in Figure 2 (last page). Briefly, COVER takes the first $m_1$ positive examples, and from each generates many candidate patterns by guessing a binding (of $d$ between 1 and $k$ variables), and calling GREEDY to produce a pattern (of $d$ variables). The candidate set is then pruned so that all remaining candidate patterns are consistent with all $m_N$ negative examples obtained, and finally, a small collection of patterns from the remaining candidate set is produced that accepts most of the remaining $m_2$ positive examples. This last step is achieved by using a greedy heuristic for the partial set cover problem [7]. It is easily argued that COVER runs in polynomial time for constant $k$.

# 4    Good Things and Bad Things

The greedy algorithm takes as input a string $w$ and a binding $x_{i_1}:u_1, \ldots, x_{i_d}:u_d$ of variables to substrings of $w$, and outputs a pattern $GREEDY(w, x_{i_1}:u_1, \ldots, x_{i_d}:u_d)$. For any event $E$, the event $GOOD(E)$, will consist of $k$-tuples $\langle u_1, \ldots, u_k \rangle \in E$ such that if the set POS contains $w = p[x_1:u_1, \ldots, x_k:u_k]$, then in step 3 of algorithm COVER, the pattern $p_E$ is produced by GREEDY when supplied with the correct bindings.

**Definition 2** *Let $E$ be any event with $d$ free variables. If $d = 0$, then define $GOOD(E) = E$. (Note that there exists at most one element $\langle u_1, \ldots, u_k \rangle \in E$ if $d = 0$.) Otherwise, if $x_{i_1}, \ldots x_{i_d}$ are the $d$ free variables of $E$, then*

$$GOOD(E) = \{\langle u_1, \ldots, u_k \rangle \in E : \text{GREEDY}(p[x_1:u_1, \ldots, x_k:u_k], x_{i_1}:u_{i_1}, \ldots, x_{i_d}:u_{i_d}) = p_E\}.$$

Let $BAD(E) = E - GOOD(E)$. Suppose for some event $E$, a GOOD thing does not happen for the $k$-tuple $\langle u_1, \ldots, u_k \rangle$ of $E$. That is, the positive example string induced by the $k$-tuple does not result in the pattern $p_E$ being included in $C$ during the run of COVER. It can be argued that there are at most a polynomial number of reasons that $\langle u_1, \ldots, u_k \rangle \in BAD(E)$. For example, suppose that GREEDY is called with example string $p[x_1:u_1, \ldots, x_k:u_k]$, and binding $x_1:u_1, \ldots, x_d:u_d$ (i.e., the bindings given to GREEDY are correct). If the pattern begins with $x_j$, but in fact the supplied substitution string $u_i$ is a proper prefix of $u_j$, then GREEDY will incorrectly output $x_i$ as the first symbol of the pattern. Thus, substitution tuples $\langle u_1, \ldots, u_k \rangle$ such that for some $i$ and $j$, $u_i$ is a prefix of $u_j$, may cause GREEDY to fail to output the correct pattern when given the correct bindings. Thus if for all $i, j$, we define

$$B(E, i, j) = \{\langle u_1, \ldots, u_k \rangle : \langle u_1, \ldots, u_k \rangle \in E \text{ and } u_i \text{ is a prefix of } u_j\},$$

we obtain at most $k^2$ subevents of $E$ that cover part of $BAD(E)$. For our purposes, we can define the events $B(E, i, j)$ to be disjoint.

A careful analysis of all additional ways that the GREEDY algorithm might fail when given a string and the correct bindings that produced that string yields a collection of at most $3k^2 + 3k$

reasons for failure, and corresponding subevents $B_l(E)$ (after appropriate renaming — e.g., each event $B(E, i, j)$ above is renamed as some $B_l(E)$ for a subscript $l$ based on $i$ and $j$). We can then prove that these subevents satisfy the following lemma, whose statement is implicit in [10]:

**Lemma 1** *For any event $E$, there are at most $c = 3k^2 + 3k$ sets $\{B_l(E)\}_{l=1}^{c}$ such that the sets $B_l(E)$ are pairwise disjoint, each is a subset of $E$, and such that $BAD(E) \subseteq \bigcup_{l=1}^{c} B_l(E)$.*

We next show that for each of these bad subevents $B_l(E)$ of any event $E$, we can restrict one of the variables of $free(E)$ to polynomially many substitution strings, and still cover most of the bad event $B_l(E)$. The size of the restricted set of substitution strings depends inversely on $\mathbf{Pr}(B_l(E))$; for this reason in the subsequent analysis it will be necessary to avoid events $E$ such that $\mathbf{Pr}(B_l(E))$ is too small. As an example, consider the bad event $B(E, i, j)$ above, consisting of $k$-tuples of $E$ such that the substitution string $u_i$ is a prefix of $u_j$. In this case, we have the following lemma:

**Lemma 2** *Let $E \subseteq SUB$ be an event, and let $i, j \in free(E)$. Let $q = \mathbf{Pr}(B(E, i, j))$. Then for any $0 < \gamma < 1$ there is a set of strings $U_i$ of size at most $\frac{s}{\gamma q}$ such that*

$$\mathbf{Pr}(\{\langle u_1, \ldots, u_k \rangle : \langle u_1, \ldots, u_k \rangle \in B(E, i, j) \text{ and } u_i \notin U_i\}) \leq \gamma q.$$

**Proof:**     The set $U_i$ will be given as a union of recursively defined subsets $U_i^r$. Let $U_i^0 = \emptyset$. Then for $t \geq 1$, let

$$B(E, i, j)_t = \{\langle u_1, \ldots, u_k \rangle : \langle u_1, \ldots, u_k \rangle \in B(E, i, j) \text{ and } u_i \notin \bigcup_{r=0}^{t-1} U_i^r\}.$$

Thus $B(E, i, j)_t$ is the set of all $k$-tuples $\langle u_1, \ldots, u_k \rangle$ in the set $B(E, i, j)$ whose coordinate $u_i$ is not already contained in one of the previous $U_i^r$. Let

$$q_t = \mathbf{Pr}(B(E, i, j)_t).$$

Note that $B(E, i, j)_1 = B(E, i, j)$ and $q_1 = q$. For any substitution string $v$, define the set

$$S_t(v) = \{\langle u_1, \ldots, u_k \rangle : u_i \text{ is a prefix of } v \text{ and } u_i \notin \bigcup_{r=0}^{t-1} U_i^r\}.$$

This is the set of all $k$-tuples $\langle u_1, \ldots, u_k \rangle$ with a coordinate $u_i$ that is a prefix of $v$ and is not contained in one of the previous $U_i^r$. Now

$$\mathbf{Pr}(\{\langle u_1, \ldots, u_k \rangle : u_i \text{ is a prefix of } u_j \text{ and } u_i \notin \bigcup_{r=0}^{t-1} U_i^r\}) \geq \mathbf{Pr}(B(E, i, j)_t) = q_t.$$

But we also have

$$\mathbf{Pr}(\{\langle u_1, \ldots, u_k \rangle : u_i \text{ is a prefix of } u_j \text{ and } u_i \notin \bigcup_{r=0}^{t-1} U_i^r\})$$

$$= \sum_v \mathbf{Pr}(\{\langle u_1, \ldots, u_k \rangle : u_j = v\})\mathbf{Pr}(S_t(v)).$$

Thus, for some fixed string $v_t$ we must have $\mathbf{Pr}(S_t(v_t)) \geq q_t$. We then let

$$U_i^t = \{u : u \text{ is a prefix of } v_t\}.$$

We now establish two claims we need to prove the lemma.

**Claim 1.** For all $t \geq 0$, $q_{t+1} \leq q_t$. This follows from the fact that $B(E, i, j)_t \supseteq B(E, i, j)_{t+1}$.

**Claim 2.** For all $t \geq 1$, $q_t \leq \frac{1}{t}$. Suppose for contradiction that $q_t > \frac{1}{t}$. Then by Claim 1, $q_1, \ldots, q_{t-1} > \frac{1}{t}$. Thus, $q_1 + \cdots + q_t > 1$. This implies that $\mathbf{Pr}(S_1(v_1)) + \cdots + \mathbf{Pr}(S_t(v_t)) > 1$. This is a contradiction, since the sets $S_r(v_r)$ are disjoint (for $r_2 > r_1$, the definition of $S_{r_2}(v_{r_2})$ explicitly excludes all $\langle u_1, \ldots, u_k \rangle$ whose component $u_i$ is a prefix of $v_{r_1}$, and $S_{r_1}(v_{r_1})$ contains only such $\langle u_1, \ldots, u_k \rangle$). Thus we must have $q_t \leq \frac{1}{t}$.

We now complete the proof of the lemma. Let

$$U_i = \bigcup_{t=0}^{\frac{1}{\gamma q}} U_i^t.$$

Since $|U_i^r| \leq s$ we have $|U_i| \leq \frac{s}{\gamma q}$. Furthermore,

$$\mathbf{Pr}(\{\langle u_1, \ldots, u_k \rangle : \langle u_1, \ldots, u_k \rangle \in B(E, i, j) \text{ and } u_i \notin U_i\})$$

$$= \mathbf{Pr}(B(E, i, j)_{\frac{1}{\gamma q + 1}}) = q_{\frac{1}{\gamma q + 1}} \leq \gamma q$$

by Claim 2.    □

Similar lemmas corresponding to each of the sets $B_j(E)$ can be proved. In the above example lemma, we obtained the bound $|U_i| \leq \frac{s}{\gamma q}$. The upper bounds we obtain for the lemmas corresponding to other sets $B_j(E)$ is at worst $|U_i| \leq \frac{2ns^4}{\gamma q}$. Each such lemma implies that if we restrict the pattern $p_E$ to one of a polynomial number of substitution strings for one of the free variables, then the resulting patterns cover all but $\gamma$ of the examples induced by $k$-tuples of $B_j(E)$. This follows because in all but $\gamma$ of $B_j(E)$, some particular (free) variable $x_i$ always receives a substitution $u_i$ from a polynomially sized set $U_i$ of possibilities. In particular, we have:

**Lemma 3** *For each $j \leq c$, for any $\gamma$, $0 < \gamma < 1$, and for all events $E$, if $B_j(E)$ is nonempty, then there exists an index $i_j$ between 1 and $k$ such that $i_j \in \text{free}(E)$, and a set $U_{i_j}$ of size at most $\frac{2ns^4}{\gamma \mathbf{Pr}(B_j(E))}$ such that the events in the collection $\{B_j(E)[x_{i_j} : u]\}_{u \in U_{i_j}}$ of subevents of $E$ are disjoint, and satisfy*

$$\sum_{u \in U_{i_j}} \mathbf{Pr}(B_j(E)[x_{i_j} : u]) \geq (1 - \gamma)\mathbf{Pr}(B_j(E)).$$

**Proof:**    Omitted from this abstract.

## 5    The Event Tree

We define an *event tree* $T$ with the following properties: (1) The root (depth 0) of $T$ is the set $SUB$ of all possible $k$-tuples; (2) Each node in the tree will be an event, and the children of an event/node will be disjoint subevents of the node; (3) If $E'$ is a child of event $E$ in the tree, then

$|bound(E')| \geq |bound(E)| + 1$. Thus for any event $E$ in the tree, $|bound(E)| \geq depth(E)$, and the maximum depth will be $k$.

$T$ will have other properties that we discuss later. $T$ is defined inductively. Let the root be $SUB$, the set of all $k$-tuples. If $E$ is an event/node at depth $d \leq k$, then, inductively, $|bound(E)| = l \geq d$. Let $bound(E) = \{i_1, \ldots i_l\}$, and let $bindings(E) = x_{i_1} : u_1, \ldots, x_{i_l} : u_l$. Let $\gamma$ be a number $(0 < \gamma < 1)$ to be specified later. If $\mathbf{Pr}(GOOD(E)) \geq \gamma\mathbf{Pr}(E)$, then $E$ is a leaf of the tree. Intuitively, if $\mathbf{Pr}(GOOD(E))$ is large enough, we'll have a reasonable chance of including $p_E$ in the candidate set $C$. However, if $\mathbf{Pr}(GOOD(E))$ is small, then it may be ignored (since $BAD(E)$ accounts for most of the event $E$), and we will cover most of the event $BAD(E)$ with a polynomial number of leaves.

Note that if $d = k$, then since $bound(E)$ increases by at least one as the depth increases by one (this is inductively implicit in our construction), we have $GOOD(E) = E$. Thus if $d = k$, $E$ is a leaf by the criterion just given. Thus all leaves are at depth $k$ or less.

Otherwise, $\mathbf{Pr}(GOOD(E)) < \gamma\mathbf{Pr}(E)$. Now by Lemma 1, the event $BAD(E)$ is covered by events $B_1(E), \ldots B_c(E)$, where $c = 3k^2 + 3k$. The children of event $E$ will be chosen by obtaining, from *some* of the events $B_j(E)$, a polynomial number of subevents of $B_j(E)$.

For each $j$ between 1 and $c$, if $\mathbf{Pr}(B_j(E)) < \frac{\gamma\mathbf{Pr}(E)}{c}$, then ignore $B_j(E)$ entirely, and obtain no children from it.

For each $j$ between 1 and $c$ such that $\mathbf{Pr}(B_j(E)) \geq \frac{\gamma\mathbf{Pr}(E)}{c}$, we obtain at most $\frac{2ns^4}{\gamma\mathbf{Pr}(B_j(E))} \leq \frac{2ns^4c}{\gamma^2\mathbf{Pr}(E)}$ subevents of $B_j(E)$ that are children of the node/event $E$ as follows. Let $i_j \in free(B_j(E)) \subseteq free(E)$ be such that the sets $\{B_j(E)[x_{i_j} : u]\}_{u \in U_{i_j}}$ are disjoint subevents of $B_j(E)$, as guaranteed by Lemma 3, where

$$\sum_{u \in U_{i_j}} \mathbf{Pr}(B_j(E)[x_{i_j} : u]) \geq (1 - \gamma)\mathbf{Pr}(B_j(E)),$$

and such that

$$|U_{i_j}| \leq \frac{2ns^4}{\gamma\mathbf{Pr}(B_j(E))} \leq \frac{2ns^4c}{\gamma^2\mathbf{Pr}(E)},$$

the latter inequality following from the lower bound on $\mathbf{Pr}(B_j(E))$.

Further note that each event of the form $B_j(E)[x_{i_j} : u]$ is disjoint from any other event $B_{j'}(E)[x_{i_{j'}} : u']$ for any $j' \neq j$, and for any $x_{i_{j'}}$ and $u'$, since $B_j(E)$ and $B_{j'}(E)$ are disjoint.

Now, for any $u \in U_{i_j}$, let $B_j(E)[x_{i_j} : u]$ be a child of $E$ only if

$$\mathbf{Pr}(B_j(E)[x_{i_j} : u]) \geq \frac{\gamma^3(\mathbf{Pr}(E))^2}{2ns^4c^2}.$$

**Lemma 4** *If event $E$ in event tree $T$ is not a leaf, then the children $\{E_i\}_{i=1}^r$ of $E$ are disjoint events, $|bound(E_i)| > |bound(E)|$, and $\mathbf{Pr}(\bigcup_{i=1}^r E_i) \geq (1 - 4\gamma)\mathbf{Pr}(E)$.*

**Proof:** That the children are disjoint, and that each child has at least one more bound variable than its parent, follows immediately from the construction of the event tree.

We can categorize the portion of event $E$ that is not covered by any child of $E$ into the following groups:

1. $GOOD(E)$ is not covered, which has probability at most $\gamma(\mathbf{Pr}(E))$.

2. If event $B_j(E)$ is such that $\mathbf{Pr}(B_j(E)) < \frac{\gamma\mathbf{Pr}(E)}{c}$, then $B_j(E)$ is ignored completely. There are at most $c$ sets $B_j(E)$ (and hence at most as many ignored), thus the total fraction of $E$ that is uncovered due to the ignored events $B_j(E)$ is at most $\gamma\mathbf{Pr}(E)$.

3. For each $B_j(E)$ that was not ignored, the sets $B_j(E)[x_{i_j} : u]$ do not completely cover all of the event $B_j(E)$. But we do have the bound

$$\mathbf{Pr}(\bigcup_{u \in U_{i_j}} B_j(E)[x_{i_j} : u]) \geq (1 - \gamma)\mathbf{Pr}(B_j(E)).$$

Since the sets $B_j(E)$ are mutually disjoint, taking the union of each side over all unignored sets $B_j(E)$, we obtain

$$\mathbf{Pr}\left(\bigcup_{j : B_j(E) \text{ was not ignored}} \bigcup_{u \in U_{i_j}} B_j(E)[x_{i_j} : u]\right) \geq (1 - \gamma)\mathbf{Pr}(\bigcup_{j : B_j(E) \text{ was not ignored}} B_j(E)).$$

Thus the children induced by the sets $B_j(E)$ cover all but at most $\gamma\mathbf{Pr}(\cup B_j(E))$ of the events $\cup B_j(E)$. Thus the amount uncovered is at most $\gamma\mathbf{Pr}(E)$.

4. Finally, for any unignored $B_j(E)$, some of the elements of $\{B_j(E)[x_{i_j} : u]\}_{u \in U_{i_j}}$ are not necessarily included as children of $E$. For each element not included, a subset of event $E$ of probability at most $\frac{\gamma^3(\mathbf{Pr}(E))^2}{2ns^4c^2}$ is not covered. The number of such sets is at most the product of the number of sets $B_j(E)$ and the number of possible $u$'s in any set $U_{i_j}$. Thus we fail to cover at most $\frac{2ns^4c^2}{\gamma^2\mathbf{Pr}(E)}$ sets, each of probability at most $\frac{\gamma^3(\mathbf{Pr}(E))^2}{2ns^4c^2}$, a total loss of at most $\gamma\mathbf{Pr}(E)$.

By the above analysis, the disjoint events consisting of the children of $E$ have total probability at least $(1 - 4\gamma)\mathbf{Pr}(E)$. $\qquad\square$

For any event $E$ in the tree, define *leaves*$(E)$ to be the set of events that are leaves in the subtree rooted at $E$. Note that if $E$ is itself a leaf, then *leaves*$(E) = \{E\}$. Let the *height* of a node in the tree be the length of the longest path from it to one of its leaves, and let the *depth* of a node in the tree be the length of the path from the root to the node.

**Lemma 5** *If $E$ is an event in $T$ at height $h$, then $\sum_{L \in leaves(E)} \mathbf{Pr}(L) \geq (1 - 4\gamma)^h \mathbf{Pr}(E)$.*

**Proof:**    The proof is by induction on $h$. If $h = 0$, then $E$ is a leaf, and the lemma follows trivially. Assume inductively that the lemma is true for events at a height $h - 1 \leq k - 1$, and consider any event $E$ at height $h \leq k$. By the construction of the event tree $T$, we know that if $E_1, \ldots, E_t$ are the children of event $E$, then $\sum_{i=1}^{t} \mathbf{Pr}(E_i) \geq (1 - 4\gamma)\mathbf{Pr}(E)$. The children of $E$ are mutually disjoint events, and each is at height at most $h - 1$. Further, each leaf of the tree rooted at $E$ must be a leaf of a tree rooted at one of the children $E_i$ of $E$. Then, applying the inductive hypothesis and the above observations, we have

$$\sum_{i=1}^{t} \sum_{L \in leaves(E_i)} \mathbf{Pr}(L) \geq \sum_{i=1}^{t} (1 - 4\gamma)^{h-1}\mathbf{Pr}(E_i) \geq (1 - 4\gamma)^{h-1} \sum_{i=1}^{t} \mathbf{Pr}(E_i) \geq (1 - 4\gamma)^h \mathbf{Pr}(E).$$

$\qquad\square$

**Lemma 6** *If $E$ is an event in the tree at depth $d \geq 0$ then*

$$\mathbf{Pr}(E) \geq \left(\frac{\gamma^3}{2ns^4(3k^2 + 3k)^2}\right)^{2^d - 1}.$$

**Proof:** We prove the lemma by induction on $d$. If $d = 0$, then the event $E$ is at the root, and $\mathbf{Pr}(E) = 1$, which satisfies the bound required by the lemma. Assume inductively that the lemma holds for events $E$ at depth $d - 1 < k$. Let $E$ be an event at depth $d$ in the tree. Let $E'$ be the parent of $E$ in the tree, where $E'$ has depth $d - 1$. Then by construction, $E$ would not have been included as a child of $E'$ unless $\mathbf{Pr}(E) \geq \frac{\gamma^3(\mathbf{Pr}(E'))^2}{2ns^4(3k^2=3k)^2}$. Applying the inductive hypothesis to $\mathbf{Pr}(E')$, we obtain

$$\mathbf{Pr}(E) \geq \frac{\gamma^3}{2ns^4(3k^2 + 3k)^2}\left(\left(\frac{\gamma^3}{2ns^4(3k^2 + 3k)^2}\right)^{2^{d-1}-1}\right)^2 \geq \left(\frac{\gamma^3}{2ns^4(3k^2 + 3k)^2}\right)^{2^d-1}.$$

$\square$

# 6   Putting it All Together

We have now defined the event tree $T$ rooted at $SUB$, and obtained lower bounds on the probability of events in $T$ and the portion of the distribution they cover in terms of the unspecified parameter $\gamma$. We now argue that for appropriate $\gamma$, $T$ has polynomial size, and its leaves cover almost all of the distribution.

**Lemma 7** *Let $\gamma$ be such that $(1 - 4\gamma)^k \geq 1 - \frac{\epsilon}{4}$. Then $\sum_{E \in leaves(SUB)} \mathbf{Pr}(E) \geq 1 - \frac{\epsilon}{4}$ and*

$$|leaves(SUB)| \leq l = \left(\frac{2ns^4(3k^2 + 3k)^2}{\gamma^3}\right)^{2^k-1}.$$

*Furthermore, for any $E \in leaves(SUB)$, $\mathbf{Pr}(GOOD(E)) \geq \frac{\gamma}{l}$.*

**Proof:** Follows from Lemmas 5, 6 and the disjointness of the leaf events. Note that $\frac{1}{\gamma}$ is polynomial in $\frac{1}{\epsilon}$, and that $l$ (and hence $\frac{\gamma}{l}$) is polynomial in the relevant parameters. $\square$

Thus, we have shown that the event tree $T$ has a polynomial number of leaves, each of significant probability. We now use these facts to argue that the set $C$ of candidate patterns constructed by COVER contains a subset whose disjunction has error at most $\frac{\epsilon}{4}$ on distribution $D_s^+$, and no error on $D_s^-$.

**Lemma 8** *Let $m_1 \geq \lceil \frac{l}{\gamma} \ln \frac{4l}{\delta} \rceil$ and $C = \{p_1, \ldots, p_r\}$ be the pool of candidate patterns constructed by calls to GREEDY in step 3 of COVER. Then with probability at least $1 - \frac{\delta}{4}$ there are $l$ patterns $\{p_{i_1}, \ldots, p_{i_l}\} \subseteq C$ satisfying*

$$\mathbf{Pr}(\langle u_1, \ldots, u_k \rangle : p[x_1 : u_1, \ldots, x_k : u_k] \in L(p_{i_1}) \cup \cdots \cup L(p_{i_l})) \geq 1 - \frac{\epsilon}{4} \tag{1}$$

$$L(p_{i_1}) \cup \cdots \cup L(p_{i_l}) \subseteq L(p). \tag{2}$$

**Proof:** The $l$ patterns are the patterns $p_E$ for each $E \in leaves(SUB)$. If $m_1 \geq \lceil \frac{l}{\gamma} \ln \frac{4l}{\delta} \rceil$, then with probability at least $1 - \frac{\delta}{4}$ a sample of $m_1$ positive examples contains for each leaf $E$ at least one element of $GOOD(E)$. This follows from the lower bound on $\mathbf{Pr}(GOOD(E))$ given in Lemma 7 and Chernoff bounds. By definition of $GOOD(E)$ we have that with probability at least $1 - \frac{\delta}{4}$, $C$ contains, for each leaf $E$, the pattern $p_E$. By Lemma 7 and our choice of $\gamma$, the probability that a random $\langle u_1, \ldots, u_k \rangle \in SUB$ is contained in some leaf $E$ is at least $1 - \frac{\epsilon}{4}$. Thus the example $p[x_1 : u_1, \ldots, x_k : u_k]$ is also a positive example of $p_E$, proving Equation (1). Equation (2) follows immediately from the fact that $p_E$ is a subpattern of $p$, and thus $L(p_E) \subseteq L(p)$. It can be shown that the size $r$ of the candidate set $C$ satisfies $r \leq m_1 (ns^2)^k k^{k+1}$, so $r$ is bounded above by a polynomial in $n$, $s$, $\frac{1}{\epsilon}$, and $\frac{1}{\delta}$.     □

In addition to the $l$ patterns satisfying Equations (1) and (2), the pattern pool $C$ may initially contain some patterns $p_i$ such that $L(p_i) \not\subseteq L(p)$. To eliminate the most offensive of these, in step 4 COVER discards any pattern $p_i \in C$ such that one of the $m_N$ negative examples is contained in $L(p_i)$. There is a constant $c_1$ such that if $m_N$ is chosen so that $m_N \geq c_1 \frac{r}{\epsilon} \ln \frac{r}{\delta}$, then with probability at least $1 - \frac{\delta}{4}$, any $p_i$ that has probability at least $\frac{\epsilon}{r}$ of accepting a negative example will in fact accept one of the $m_N$ negative examples drawn. Thus *any* disjunction of patterns from $C$ has probability at most $r \frac{\epsilon}{r} = \epsilon$ of accepting a negative example. In other words, with high probability any disjunction of remaining patterns has error at most $\epsilon$ with respect to the negative distribution. Without loss of generality, let $C' = \{p_1, \ldots, p_{r'}\}$ be the set of remaining patterns.

The goal of COVER in step 5 is to discover among the remaining patterns a good approximation to the disjunction of $l$ patterns satisfying Equations (1) and (2). Note that Equation (1) is a probabilistic statement; in order to apply the partial cover algorithm of [7], we need the following:

**Lemma 9** *Let $m_2 \geq c_2 \frac{1}{\epsilon} \ln \frac{1}{\delta}$ for some constant $c_2$. Let $R$ be a multiset of $m_2$ random positive examples. Then for $\{p_{i_1}, \ldots, p_{i_l}\}$ satisfying Equation (1) above, with probability at least $1 - \frac{\delta}{4}$ we have that*
$$|R \cap (L(p_{i_1}) \cup \cdots \cup L(p_{i_l}))| \geq (1 - \frac{\epsilon}{2})|R|, \text{ where the cardinalities are multiset cardinalities.}$$

**Proof:**     Follows from Equation (1) and application of Chernoff bounds.     □

For each $p_i \in C'$, let the multiset $S_i$ be defined by $S_i = L(p_i) \cap R$. Then by Lemma 9, with probability at least $1 - \frac{\delta}{4}$, among the multisets $S_1, \ldots, S_{r'}$ there is a collection of $l$ of the $S_i$ that collectively cover a fraction $1 - \frac{\epsilon}{2}$ of the multiset $R$.

The results of [7] give a polynomial-time algorithm that will find at most $c_3 l \ln m_2$ of the $S_i$ that cover $1 - \frac{\epsilon}{2}$ of $R$ for some constant $c_3$. Without loss of generality, let $C_{cover} = \{p_1, \ldots, p_{c_3 l \ln m_2}\}$ be the corresponding patterns obtained in step 5 of COVER. Then the hypothesis $L(C_{cover}) = L(p_1) \cup \cdots \cup L(p_{c_3 l \ln m_2})$ is consistent with a fraction $1 - \frac{\epsilon}{2}$ of the positive sample $R$. We now argue that with high probability, the error of this hypothesis is at most $\epsilon$.

**Theorem 10** *Let $C_{cover} = \{p_1, \ldots, p_{c_3 l \ln m_2}\}$ be the the set of patterns output by algorithm COVER in step 5. Then with probability at least $1 - \delta$,*

$$L(C_{cover}) = L(p_1) \cup \cdots \cup L(p_{c_3 l \ln m_2})$$

*has error at most $\epsilon$ with respect to both the positive and negative distributions.*

**Proof:**     The probability that $L(C_{cover})$ has error greater than $\epsilon$ on the negative distribution $D_s^-$ is at most $\frac{\delta}{4}$; this follows immediately from the removal of patterns from $C$ in step 4 discussed above. By Lemma 8, the probability that the collection $C$ produced in step 3 of COVER fails to contain a subcollection $\{p_{i_1}, \ldots, p_{i_l}\}$ satisfying equation (1) is at most $\frac{\delta}{4}$. By Lemma 9, the probability that the set $\{p_{i_1}, \ldots, p_{i_l}\}$ fails to cover at least $1 - \frac{\epsilon}{2}$ of $R$ is at most $\frac{\delta}{4}$. We invoke a generalization of Occam's Razor from [7] to argue that $L(C_{cover})$ in fact has error at most $\epsilon$ with respect to the positive distribution. Note that the total number of symbols needed to represent the patterns in $C_{cover}$ is at most $(c_3 l \ln m_2) ns$; thus the *effective hypothesis space* $H = H(n, s, \epsilon, \delta)$ satisfies $|H| \leq (k + |\Sigma|)^{(c_3 l \ln m_2) ns}$. (If $A$ is a $PAC$-learning algorithm for $P_k$ with hypothesis space $H$, then the *effective hypothesis space* of $A$ on target patterns of length $n$ is denoted by $H(n, s, \epsilon, \delta)$, and consists of that subset of $H$ that $A$ might ever output when run with input parameters $n, s, \epsilon, \delta$.) By the results of [7] there is a constant $c_4$ such that if $m_2 \geq c_4(\frac{1}{\epsilon} \ln \frac{1}{\delta} + \frac{1}{\epsilon} \ln(k + |\Sigma|)^{(c_3 l \ln m_2) ns})$ then with probability at least $1 - \frac{\delta}{4}$, $L(C_{cover})$ has error at most $\epsilon$ with respect to the positive distribution $D_s^+$.

In summary, the probability that $L(C_{cover})$ has error greater than $\epsilon$ on the negative distribution is at most $\frac{\delta}{4}$, and the probability that $L(C_{cover})$ has error greater than $\epsilon$ on the positive distribution is at most $\frac{\delta}{4} + \frac{\delta}{4} + \frac{\delta}{4} = \frac{3\delta}{4}$. Thus with probability at least $1 - \delta$, $L(C_{cover})$ has error at most $\epsilon$ on both positive and negative distributions. Note that the total number of positive examples $m_P = m_1 + m_2$ and the total number of negative examples $m_N$ are polynomial in $n, s, \frac{1}{\epsilon}, \frac{1}{\delta}$, and $|\Sigma|$. □

# 7   Conclusions and Future Research

We have given a polynomial-time algorithm for learning the class of $k$-variable pattern languages from positive and negative examples under a wide and natural class of distributions on the examples. Our algorithm allows empty substitutions and can be extended to handle restricted homomorphisms on the substitution strings, to be discussed in the full paper.

The algorithm and analysis presented here immediately suggest a number of interesting areas for further research. Perhaps the most obvious of these is that of finding either positive or negative results for learning $k$-variable patterns in the $PAC$-learning model under *arbitrary* distributions on the positive examples (here we considered only product distributions).

It would also be nice to have results for learning general patterns in polynomial time. While the results mentioned in the Introduction seem to suggest that this is computationally difficult, the problem of learning general patterns by an hypothesis space other than single patterns in the $PAC$-learning model in polynomial time remains open.

Another interesting question concerns the performance of the algorithm presented here. For instance, it is possible that a tighter analysis of the event tree might yield considerably improved sample and time complexity bounds for our algorithm. The algorithm may also demonstrate performance better than the worst-case analysis on more restrictive classes of distributions. Finally, extensions to our algorithm might be found by investigating larger classes of homomorphisms and other operations on the substitution strings.

# References

[1] D. Angluin. Finding patterns common to a set of strings. *Journal of Computer and System Sciences*, 21:46–62, 1980.

[2] D. Angluin. Queries and concept learning. *Machine Learning*, 2:319–342, 1988.

[3] A. Blumer, A. Ehrenfeucht, D. Haussler, and M. Warmuth. Occam's razor. *Information Processing Letters*, 24:377–380, 1987.

[4] D. Haussler, M. Kearns, N. Littlestone, and M. K. Warmuth. Equivalence of Models for Polynomial Learnability. In *Proceedings of the 1st Workshop on Computational Learning Theory*, pages 42–55, Morgan Kaufmann, San Mateo, CA, August 1988.

[5] C. Hua and K. Ko. A note on the Pattern-finding Problem. Technical Report UH-CS-84-4, Department of Computer Science, University of Houston, 1984.

[6] O. Ibarra and T. Jiang. Learning regular languages from counterexamples. In *Proceedings of the 1st Workshop on Computational Learning Theory*, pages 371–385, Morgan Kaufmann, San Mateo, CA, August 1988.

[7] M. Kearns and M. Li. Learning in the presence of malicious errors. In *Proceedings of the 20th Annual ACM Symposium on Theory of Computing*, pages 267–280, Assoc. Comp. Mach., New York, May 1988.

[8] M. Kearns and L. G. Valiant. Cryptographic limitations on learning Boolean formulae and finite automata. In *Proceedings of the 21st Annual ACM Symposium on Theory of Computing*, pages 433–444, Assoc. Comp. Mach., New York, May 1989.

[9] K. Ko, A. Marron, and W. Tzeng. Learning string patterns and tree patterns from examples. Abstract, State University of New York at Stony Brook, 1989.

[10] A. Marron. Learning pattern languages from a single initial example and from queries. In *Proceedings of the 1988 Workshop on Computational Learning Theory*, pages 345–358, Morgan Kaufmann, San Mateo, CA, August 1988.

[11] A. Marron and K. Ko. Identification of pattern languages from examples and queries. *Information and Computation*, 74(2), 1987.

[12] L. Pitt and L. G. Valiant. Computational limitations on learning from examples. *Journal of the ACM*, 35(4), pages 965–984, 1988.

[13] L. Pitt and M. K. Warmuth. Reductions among prediction problems: On the difficulty of predicting automata. In *Proceedings of the 3rd Annual IEEE Conference on Structure in Complexity Theory*, pages 60–69, IEEE Computer Society Press, Washington, D.C., June 1988.

[14] T. Shinohara. Polynomial time inference of extended regular pattern languages. In *Proceedings, Software Science and Engineering*, Kyoto, Japan, 1982.

[15] T. Shinohara. Polynomial time inference of pattern languages and its applications. In *Proceedings of the 7th IBM Symposium on Mathematical Foundations of Computer Science*, 1982.

[16] L. G. Valiant. A theory of the learnable. *Communications of the ACM*, 27(11):1134–1142, 1984.

$$\text{GREEDY}(w, x_{i_1} : u_1, \ldots, x_{i_d} : u_d):$$

1. $a \leftarrow 1$. (Initialize pointer into string $w$.)

2. If $a \geq |w| + 1$ then HALT.

3. Let MATCH $= \{j : u_j = w(a, |u_j|)\}$. (MATCH contains indices of supplied substitution strings that appear as substrings of $w$ starting at the current position $a$ of $w$.)

4. If MATCH $= \emptyset$ then (the next symbol of the pattern is a constant)

    (a) Output $w(a, 1)$. (Output the constant.)

    (b) $a \leftarrow a + 1$. (Move the pointer.)

    (c) Return to step 2.

5. (Else MATCH $\neq \emptyset$.) Choose an arbitrary element $j$ of the set $\{j : j \in \text{MATCH} \text{ and for all } l \in \text{MATCH}, |u_j| \leq |u_l|\}$. (Pick a shortest matching substring.)

6. Output $x_{i_j}$. (Hopefully, $x_{i_j}$ is what produced $u_j$.)

7. $a \leftarrow a + |u_j|$. (Move the pointer to the next unparsed character of the input.)

8. Return to step 2.

Figure 1: Algorithm GREEDY

$$\text{COVER}(n, s, \epsilon, \delta, \Sigma):$$

1. From distributions $D_s^+$ and $D_s^-$, obtain sets POS of $m_P = m_1 + m_2$ positive examples, and NEG of $m_N$ negative examples.

2. $C \leftarrow \emptyset$. ($C$ will be a set of candidate patterns).

3. For each of the first $m_1$ elements $w$ of POS do:

    (a) For each $d$ between 1 and $k$, and for each list $x_{i_1} : u_1, \ldots, x_{i_d} : u_d$ of bindings of some subset of $d$ variables of $\{x_1, \ldots, x_k\}$ to $d$ substrings $u_1, \ldots, u_d$ of $w$, each of length at most $s$, add the pattern GREEDY$(w, x_{i_1} : u_1, \ldots, x_{i_d} : u_d)$ to $C$

    (b) Add the (0-variable) pattern $w$ to $C$

4. Eliminate from $C$ any pattern $q$ such that $L(q) \cap \text{NEG} \neq \emptyset$.

5. Run the greedy partial set cover algorithm of [7] to obtain, with high probability, a subcollection $C_{cover}$ of elements of $C$ that are consistent with $1 - \frac{\epsilon}{4}$ of the remaining $m_2$ positive examples.

Figure 2: Algorithm COVER

# ON LEARNING FROM EXERCISES

B.K. Natarajan
The Robotics Institute
Carnegie Mellon University
Pittsburgh, PA 15232

## ABSTRACT

This paper explores a new direction in the formal theory of learning – learning in the sense of improving computational efficiency as opposed to concept learning in the sense of Valiant. Specifically, the paper concerns algorithms that learn to solve problems from sample instances of the problems. We develop a general framework for such learning and study the framework over two distinct random sources of sample instances. The first source provides sample instances together with their solutions, while the second source provides unsolved instances or "exercises". We prove two theorems identifying conditions sufficient for learning over the two sources, our proofs being constructive in that they exhibit learning algorithms. To illustrate the scope of our results, we discuss their application to a program that learns to solve restricted classes of symbolic integrals.

## 1. INTRODUCTION

In [1], Valiant introduced a rich framework for the analysis of algorithms that learn to approximate sets from randomly chosen elements within and without the sets. This framework and its extensions has been analyzed by a number of authors, [2, 3, 4, 5] amongst others. In this paper, we present a new framework concerning algorithms that learn to solve problems approximately. instances. Early steps in this direction were taken in [4]. In a sense, this can be viewed as learning to improve computational efficiency as opposed to concept learning in the sense of Valiant. We believe that this is an important new direction in the formal theory of learning.

Consider the problem of symbolic integration. Given the definition of the problem and a standard table of integrals, we have complete information on how to solve the problem. Yet, although we are capable of solving instances of symbolic integration immediately, we are by no means efficient in our methods. It appears that we need to examine sample instances, study solutions to these instances, and based on these solutions build up a set of heuristics that will enable us to solve the problem fast. In this sense, the learning process has helped improve our computational efficiency. Similarly, given some other problem, say Rubik's cube, and the instructions concerning its solution, we would like to become proficient at it just as quickly. In essence, we would like to behave in the following manner: given the specification of a problem, we quickly learn to be efficient at solving the problem. Stated more abstractly: Consider a class of problems, such that each problem in the class is known to possess an efficient algorithm. We are interested in a meta-algorithm for the class – an algorithm that takes as input the specification of a problem drawn from the class as well as sample instances of the problem, and produces as output an efficient algorithm for the problem. As we will see, the sample instances play a crucial role in the process, as in their absence, constructing an algorithm for the input problem can be computationally intractable. In this paper, we are interested in examining learning in the aforementioned sense. Specifically, we inquire into the conditions under which such learning is possible. Our methods of analysis are probabilistic in flavour, akin to those of Valiant [1].

In Section 2, we present a formal definition of the learning framework. The framework formalizes learning in the above sense, demanding that the learner learn to solve a problem, given a source of randomly chosen <u>solved</u> instances of the problem. (This framework is more general than that defined in [4], with respect to the choice of the solutions of the instances made by the source. Specifically, each instance may have many solutions and in [4], the source must choose from amongst these in a predictable and deterministic manner. Here, the solutions may be picked at random.) We prove a theorem identifying conditions sufficient to allow such learning. In Section 3, we consider an application of our theorem to a restricted version of symbolic integration. In particular, we show how to construct an algorithm that is capable of learning to solve such restricted classes of integrals from randomly chosen examples. In Section 4, we change the source of sample instances to one that provides unsolved instances that are chosen in a random but slightly benevolent manner. Specifically, rather than present the learning algorithm with randomly chosen solved instances of the problem, the learning algorithm is only allowed randomly chosen "exercises" on the problem – <u>unsolved</u> instances of the problem, chosen according to a probability distribution measuring their importance to the learner. This is very much the same as the exercises in a work-book, such as one might find at the end of a book dealing with say symbolic integration or differential equations. We are able to prove that the conditions sufficient for learning from solved instances are sufficient for learning here as well. The proof is constructive in that we give a general learning algorithm that learns by solving the exercises, solving them in order of least difficult to most difficult. This theorem constitutes our main result.

## 2. LEARNING FROM SOLVED INSTANCES

Let $\Sigma$ be the $\{0,1\}$ boolean alphabet.

**Defn:** A *problem D* is the pair $(G, O)$, where

(a) The *goal* $G:\Sigma^* \to \{0,1\}$ is function from $\Sigma^*$ to $(0,1)$ computable in polynomial time.

(b) $O$ is a finite set of *operators* $\{o_1, o_2,...\}$ where each $o_i:\Sigma^* \to \Sigma^*$ is a function computable in polynomial time.

A *specification* of a problem $D = (G,O)$ is a set of programs for $G$ and $O$ that run in polynomial time.

**Defn:** We say an instance $x \in \Sigma^*$ of a problem $D =(G,O)$ is *solvable* if there exists a sequence of operators $\sigma$ such that $G(\sigma(x)) = 1$. The sequence $\sigma$ is a *solution sequence* for $x$. The *sequence length* of a solution sequence is the number of operator applications in it, i.e., the length of $\sigma = |\sigma|$. Unless demanded by context, we use the term length to refer to the sequence length of a solution sequence. A solution sequence $\sigma$ is *optimal* for $x$ if its length is as short as that of any solution sequence for $x$.

**Defn:** Let $\sigma = p_1 p_2 p_3 ... p_t$ be a solution sequence to $x$, where the $p_i$ are operators in $O$. We say $x$, $p_t(x)$, $P_{t-1}p_t(x),...$ are *steps* in the solution of $x$ and that $p_t(x)$, $P_{t-1}p_t(x),...$ are *intermediate steps* in the solution of $x$. The *step-length* of $\sigma$ with respect to $x$ is the maximum of $\{|x|, |p_t(x)|, |P_{t-1}p_t(x)|, ....\}$, i.e., it is the length of the longest instance encountered in using $\sigma$ to solve $x$.

**Defn:** An algorithm for a problem $D$ is a program that takes as input a string $x \in \Sigma^*$ and produces as output a solution sequence for $x$, if such exists.

A *family* of problems $M$ is simply any set of problems. We are interested in an algorithm that is useful over a family of problems, in that it is capable of learning to solve any of the problems in the family. To this end, we define the notion of a meta-algorithm for a family. Loosely speaking, a *meta-algorithm* for a family $M$ is an algorithm that takes as input the specification of a problem $D$ in $M$ and attempts to construct an algorithm for $D$. Given the scope of our definition of a family of problems, it is easy to see that the task of the meta-algorithm will be $NP$-hard for most non-trivial families. See [4]. This is true, even if we guarantee that every problem in the family has a polynomial-time algorithm – the difficulty lies in finding such an algorithm, given the specification of the problem. In order to reduce this complexity and thereby aid the meta-algorithm in its task, we provide the meta-algorithm with sample instances of the problem specified in its input. Specifically, we consider two distinct sources of such sample instances, one providing the meta-algorithm with randomly chosen solved instances, and the other providing unsolved instances that are randomly chosen, although in a slightly more benevolent manner than the first source. The first source is the simpler to analyze and will be the subject of the remainder of this section. The second source is considered in Section 4.

We place at the disposal of the mera-algorithm a subroutine INSTANCE which acts as a random source of solved instances. We may view INSTANCE as a black box with a button, such that at each push of the button, INSTANCE outputs a randomly chosen solved instance of the input problem $D$. Specifically, at each call, INSTANCE returns a pair $(x,\sigma)$. The string $x \in \Sigma^*$ is randomly drawn according to an arbitrary and unknown probability distribution $P$ on $\Sigma^*$. The operator sequence $\sigma$ is a randomly chosen optimal solution sequence for $x$, being the null-sequence if $x$ is not solvable or if $x$ is solved as it is. By randomly chosen, we mean that at any stage in the solution of $x$, the next operator used by INSTANCE is picked randomly from among those that are useful. In order to make this precise, we need the following definition.

**Defn:** Let $D=(G,O)$ be a problem. For each operator $o \in O$, consider the set

$U(o) = \{x| \exists$ an optimal solution of form $\sigma \cdot o$ for $x\}$

We call $U(o)$ the *projection* of $o$, and $U(D) = \{U(o)|o \in D\}$ the *projections* of $D$.

For any $x$ in $\Sigma^*$, let $O_x$ be the set of operators useful on $x$, i.e.,

$O_x = \{o| o \in O, x \in U(o)\}$.

When solving $x$, the first operator used by INSTANCE is picked at random from $O_x$. Specifically, if there are $p$ operators in $O_x$, each is picked with probability $1/p^1$. Similarly, the second operator is picked at random from $O_y$, where $y$ is the result of applying the first operator to $x$. And so on.

With these definitions in hand, we attempt to make precise our notion of a meta-algorithm. In essence, a meta-algorithm $A$ for a family of problems $M$ will take as input an *error parameter* $h$ and the specification of a problem $D$ in $M$. $A$ will then compute for time polynomial in various parameters and output a program $H$ that efficiently approximates an algorithm for $D$. By this we mean that we mean that $H$ will behave like an algorithm for $D$ with probability $(1-1/h)$. A formal definition follows.

**Defn:** An algorithm $A$ is a *meta-algorithm* for a family of problems $M$ if there exists an integer $k$ such that

(a)$A$ takes as input an integer $h$ and the specification of a problem $D \in M$. Let $l$ be the string length of this input.

---

[1]It is sufficient if each is picked with probability at least $1/poly(n)$, where $n = |x|$ and $poly(n)$ denotes a polynomial in $n$.

(b) *A* may call INSTANCE. INSTANCE returns examples for *D*, chosen according to some unknown distribution *P* over $\Sigma^*$. Let *n* be the longest step-length and *m* the longest sequence length of the solutions so provided by INSTANCE. For inputs of length *n*, let $t(n)$ be the sum of the running times of the programs in the specification of *D*. *A* computes in time $(lhmt(n))^k$, i.e., in time polynomial in the length of its input *l*, the error parameter *h* and the time required to evaluate the programs in the specification of *D* on the examples seen. *A* may be a randomized algorithm.

(c) For all $D \in M$ and all distributions *P* over $\Sigma^*$, with probability $(1-1/h)$ *A* outputs a (possibly randomized) program *H* that runs in time $t(n)^k$ on inputs of length *n* and approximates an algorithm for *D* in the sense that

$$\sum_{x \in C} P(x) \leq 1/h$$

where $C = \{x \mid H \text{ is correct on } x\}$.

Since *H* may be randomized, by "*H* is correct on *x*", we mean that *H* soloves *x* with probability greater than 1/2, if *x* is solvable.

We now inquire into the conditions under which a family of problems posseses a meta-algorithm. Theorem 1 identifies conditions sufficient to guarantee the existence of a meta-algorithm. Necessary conditions appear to be much harder to obtain, perhaps requiring a greater understanding of learning with "advice" as explored in [4]. The statement and proof of Theorem 1 are based on previous results on learning sets with one-sided error [3]. These results are reviewed briefly in Appendix A. We refer the unfamiliar reader to that section before proceeding to the theorem.

**Theorem 1:** A family of problems *M* possesses a meta-algorithm if there exists a family of sets *F* such that

(a) *F* contains the projections of every problem *D* in *M*.

(b) *F* is polynomial-time learnable with one-sided error. (See Appendix A for details.)

**Proof:** (sketch) For a given problem *D*, if we can test membership in the projections of *D* efficiently, then we can construct an efficient algorithm for *D*. The following is such an algorithm.

**input** *x*: string;
**begin**
    $\sigma \leftarrow$ null-sequence ;
    **While** $G(x) \neq 1$ **do**
        pick $o \in O$ such that $x \in U(o)$;
        if no such exists, halt; ---*x* is not solvable---
        $x \leftarrow o(x)$;
        $\sigma \leftarrow o \cdot \sigma$;
    **end**
    output $\sigma$ as solution for *x*;
**end**

The key idea in the proof is as follows: Given a problem *D*, the meta-algorithm will construct approximations to the projections of *D* using the solved instances. It will then substitute these approximations in the above algorithm to obtain an approximate algorithm for *D*. If the conditions of the theorem are satisfied, this can be carried out in random polynomial-time, yielding a good approximation of an algorithm for *D*.

The rest of the proof deals with the details. Specifically, we will exhibit a meta-algorithm for *M*. We need the following definition. Let *D* be a problem in *M*. We define the quantity $I_D(n)$ to be the set of all instances in $D$ that possess optimal solutions of step-length less than $n$.

$$I_D(n) =$$
$$\{x | \text{optimal solution of } x \text{ has step-length} \leq n\}$$

When the problem $D$ is clear from the context, we will simply write $I(n)$. Also, for $\delta \in (0,1)$ define the quantity $n_\delta$ as the least integer $n$ such that

$$\sum_{x \in I(n)} P(x) \geq 1-\delta$$

That is, $n_\delta$ is the least integer such that the probability of occurrence of an optimal solution of step-length greater than $n_\delta$ is less than $\delta$. In what follows, we will arrange for the meta-algorithm to learn approximations to the projections of $D$ that are good for strings of length $n_\delta$ or less, for a value of $\delta$ that will be appropriately chosen.

Let $F$ be a family as in the statement of the theorem. By Theorem A of Appendix A, $F$ must possess a polynomial-time ordering $Q$. We use $Q$ to construct a meta-algorithm $A$ for $M$ as shown below. The algorithm uses $Q$ to construct good approximations for the projections of $D$ and then uses these projections to build an algorithm for $D$.

**Meta-Algorithm $A_1$**
**input** $h, D=(G,O)$
Let $F$ be of dimension $d(n)$;
Let $O = \{o_i | i= 1..k\}$;
Let $S(o_1),...S(o_k), V(o_1),...V(o_k)$ be sets, initially empty;
**begin**
Section 1:
---Estimate $n_{1/3h}$ with confidence $(1-1/3h)$---
call INSTANCE $3h \cdot log(3h)$ times.
Let $n$ be the longest step-length amongst those seen.
Section 2:
---Generate examples for projections -----
**repeat** $3h(kd(n))+log(3h))$ **times**
    call INSTANCE to obtain $(x,\sigma)$;
    let $\sigma$ be the sequence $o_{x_1} o_{x_2}...o_{x_r}$;
    $S(o_{x_1}) \leftarrow S(o_{x_1}) \cup \{x\}$
    $S(o_{x_2}) \leftarrow S(o_{x_2}) \cup \{o_{x_1}(x)\}$
    ......
    $S(o_{x_r}) \leftarrow S(o_{x_r}) \cup \{o_{x_{r-1}}...o_{x_1}(x)\}$
**end**
Section 3:
---Construct approximations of projections---
**repeat** $i=1..k$ **times**
    $V(o_i) \leftarrow Q(S(o_i))$;
    if $Q$ is randomized, repeat to confidence $1-1/3h$;
**end**

Section 4:
Output the following as approximate algorithm for $D$
**Algorithm** $H$
**input** $x$: string;
**begin**
      $\sigma \leftarrow$ null-sequence ;
      **While** $G(x) \neq 1$ **do**
          let $O_x = \{o | x \in V(o)\}$;
          **if** $O_x$ is empty **then** halt
               **else** pick $o$ in $O_x$ uniformly randomly.
          $x \leftarrow o(x)$;
          $\sigma \leftarrow o \cdot \sigma$;
      **end**
      output $\sigma$ as solution for $x$;
**end**

**end**

We now show that the above is indeed a meta-algorithm for $M$. Consider Section 1 of the algorithm. We need to show that drawing $3h \cdot log(3h)$ instances will produce a step-length $m$ such that $n_{1/3h} \leq n$. For any single call of INSTANCE, the probability of a step-length of less than $n_{1/3h}$ occurring is $(1 - 1/3h)$ by definition. In $t$ calls of INSTANCE, the probability of all the step-lengths being less than $n_{1/3h}$ is hence $(1 - 1/3h)^t$. We only need pick $t$ such that

$(1 - 1/3h)^t \leq 1/3h$

Which inequality is satisfied by choosing $t = 3h \cdot log(3h)$.

We will consider Sections 2, 3, and 4 of the algorithm simultaneously. With respect to strings of length $n$ or less, each set $V(o)$ can be chosen in $|F_n|$ ways in Section 3 of the algorithm. Hence, the number of distinct algorithms that can be constructed in Section 4 is $|F_n|^k$. Let $S$ be the set of algorithms so constructible. If $n \geq n_{1/3h}$, at least one of these algorithms will approximate an algorithm for $D$ within $1/3h$. This is because the statement of the theorem demands that $F$ contains the projections of $D$. Now, the aim of Sections 2 and 3 is to eliminate those algorithms in $S$ that are bad approximations. Consider algorithms in $S$ that do not approximate an algorithm for $D$ within $1/3h$. Call such algorithms "bad". The probability that a particular bad algorithm will correctly solve a randomly chosen instance is $(1 - 1/3h)$, and the probability that the algorithm will correctly solve all of $r$ randomly chosen instances is $(1 - 1/3h)^r$. The probability that any bad algorithm in $S$ will correctly solve $r$ random instances is at most $|S|(1 - 1/3h)^r$. To eliminate all bad algorithms in $S$ with confidence $(1 - 1/3h)$, we only need to make the above quantity less than $1/3h$. That is,

$|S|(1 - 1/3h)^r \leq 1/3h$

Since, $|S| \leq |F_n|^k$ and $|F_n| \leq 2^{d(m)}$, we have,

$2^{kd(n)}(1 - 1/3h)^t \leq 1/3h$

or

$r \geq 3h(kd(m) + log(3h))$.

This is exactly the number of instances employed by Sections 2 and 3 to eliminate the bad algorithms in $S$. Since Sections 1, 2 and 3 are each carried out to a confidence of $(1 - 1/3h)$, the overall confidence is $(1 - 1/h)$. Furthermore, the elimination of bad algorithms from $S$ constructs an algorithm that approximates an algorithm for $D$ within $(2/3h)$. This is so because the best approximation within $S$ need only be within $1/3h$ owing to our choice of $m$, and the elimination process will construct an algorithm within $1/3h$ of this best algorithm.

In all, with probability $(1-1/h)$ the meta-algorithm constructs an algorithm for the input problem $D$ that is within $2/3h$ in accuracy.  Hence, $A$ is a meta-algorithm for $M$ and the theorem is proved.  •

# 3. AN APPLICATION

In this section we discuss an application of Theorem 1 to the domain of symbolic integration.  There have been reports in the AI literature of programs that learn to carry out restricted forms of symbolic integration.  See [6] for instance. We will show how this can be achieved by a straightforward application of Theorem 1.

Consider the class of integrals that can be solved by the following standard integrals.

$$\int kf(x)dx = k\int f(x)dx$$

$$\int f(x)-g(x)dx = \int f(x)dx - \int g(x)dx$$

$$\int f(x)+g(x)dx = \int f(x)dx + \int g(x)dx$$

$$\int x^n dx = \frac{x^{n+1}}{n+1}$$

$$\int sinxdx = -cosx$$

$$\int cosxdx = -sinx$$

$$\int ud(v) = uv - \int vd(u)$$

Suppose we wish to construct an algorithm that can solve this class of integrals.

Consider the following grammar $\Gamma$.

$$prob \quad \rightarrow \int exp\ var \mid d(exp)$$

$$exp \qquad \rightarrow term \mid term + exp \mid term - exp$$
$$\qquad\qquad \mid term\ /\ term \mid$$
$$term \quad \rightarrow p\text{-}term \mid p\text{-}term * term$$
$$p\text{-}term \rightarrow const\ var \mid -term$$
$$\qquad\qquad \mid trig\ power\ prob \mid exp$$
$$power \rightarrow var ** term$$
$$trig \quad \rightarrow SIN\ var \mid COS\ var$$
$$const \rightarrow int \mid a \mid k$$
$$var \qquad \rightarrow x \mid y \mid z$$
$$int \qquad \rightarrow 1 \mid 2 \mid 3 \mid 4 \mid 5 \mid 6 \mid 7 \mid 8 \mid 9 \mid 0$$

This grammar generates a superset of the strings that will be seen as input to the integration algorithm. Let $\alpha$ be any sentential form in the grammar $\Gamma$. Define $L(\alpha)$ to be the set of strings derivable in $\Gamma$ from $\alpha$. That is,

$L(\alpha) = \{x | \alpha \rightarrow_\Gamma x\}$.

Let $F$ be the family of all such sets, i.e.,

$F = \{L(\alpha) | \alpha$ is a sentential form in $\Gamma\}$.


It is easy to see that $F$ is polynomial-time learnable with one sided error. To do so, we only need invoke Theorem A of Appendix A and check that (a) $F$ is closed under intersection. We show the equivalent condition [3] that for any set of strings, there exists a "least" sentential form that generates them. By least, we mean that any other sentential form that generates these strings will be a super set of the least sentential form. To see this, given a set of strings we can efficiently compute the least sentential form that generates them as follows. Construct the parse trees for these strings in $\Gamma$, and then march up these parse trees simultaneously to pick off points common to all of them. Since the parse trees are unique in $\Gamma$, the claim follows. (b) $F$ posseses a polynomial-time ordering. Indeed, we will exhibit a deterministic linear time ordering for $F$. For any set of strings, compute the least sentential form that generates them as described above. Once we have this least sentential form, it is a simple matter to output a program that recognizes strings that can be generated from it. (c) Since the number of sentential forms of length $n$ is at most $c^n$ for some constant $c$, $F$ is of dimension $n \cdot log(c)$.


We now hope that $F$ contains the projections of all the standard integrals listed earlier. (To be honest, it does contain them.) We can then invoke the meta-algorithm of Theorem 1, and provide it with randomly chosen solved instances of these integrals. By Theorem 1, the output of the meta-algorithm will indeed be a good algorithm for the class of integrals in question. Tadepalli, in [4] implemented this algorithm and verified this to be the case.


## 4. LEARNING FROM EXERCISES

In the foregoing, we considered a model of learning wherein the external agent INSTANCE provided solved instances of the problem of interest. In this section, we consider a model of learning wherein the external agent provides unsolved instances of the problem of interest, although these instances are chosen a little more carefully than in the previous model. The unsolved instances are exercises, in much the same sense as those that may be found at the end of a text book on symbolic integration. Note that the exercises in the back of the book are not representative of the "natural" distribution of problem instances, but are chosen to reinforce the techniques required to solve them. In this section, we formalize the notion of learning from exercises and prove a theorem similar to that of Theorem 1.


We now replace the routine INSTANCE of the previous section with a routine EX. The key idea is to provide the learning algorithm with a source of unsolved instances of varying difficulty. This will permit the learning algorithm to consider increasingly difficult instances, improving its capabilities as it progresses. Let $P$ be a probability distribution on $\Sigma^*$, and let INSTANCE be defined according to $P$ as described earlier. We can best describe EX in terms of INSTANCE, as shown below. In essence, EX takes as argument an integer $l$ and returns an instance $x$ such that the optimal solution of $x$ has length $l$. The probability that a particular instance $x$ will be returned by any call of EX is the probability that $x$ will be used in a solution by INSTANCE. This is a measure of the importance of knowing how to solve $x$, with respect to the natural distribution $P$.

**function** EX($l$)
**begin**
        call INSTANCE to obtain $(x, \sigma)$;

**if** |σ| < *l*, output the null instance.
**else**
let σ = σ₁σ₂, where |σ₁| = *l*
output σ₂(*x*).
**end**

We now define the notion of a meta-algorithm for a family of problems in this setting. This definition is largely identical to that of Section 2, except for the use of EX instead of INSTANCE.

**Defn:** An algorithm *A* is a *meta-algorithm* for a family of problems *M* if there exists an integer *k* such that

(a) *A* takes as input integer *h* and the specification of a problem *D* ∈ *M*. Let *l* be the string length of this input.

(b) *A* may call EX. EX returns instances of *D* drawn according to some unknown distribution *P* over Σ*. Let *n* be the least integer such that all the instances so produced by EX are in *I*(*n*), and let *m* be the largest integer used as argument to EX. For inputs of length *n*, let the sum of the running times of the programs in the specification of *D* be *t*(*n*). *A* computes for time less than $(lhmt(n))^k$, i.e., in time polynomial in the length of its input *l*, the error parameter *h*, the length *m* of the optimal solutions of the instances seen, and the time required to evaluate the programs in the specification of *D* on the instances seen. *A* may be a randomized algorithm.

(c) For all *D* ∈ *M* and all distributions *P* over Σ*, with probability (1−1/*h*) *A* outputs a (possibly randomized) program *H* that runs in time $(t(r))^k$ on inputs of length *r* and approximates an algorithm for *D* in the sense that

$$\sum_{x \in S} P(x) \le 1/h$$

where *S* = {*x*| *H* fails on *x*}

Since *H* may be randomized, by "*H* fails on *x*", we mean that *H* fails to solve *x* with probability greater than 1/2, although *x* is solvable.

We now inquire into the conditions under which a family of problems possesses a meta-algorithm in this model. As it happens, the theorem we prove for this model is identical in its statement to Theorem 1.

**Theorem 2:** A family of problems *M* possesses a meta-algorithm if there exists a family of sets *F* such that

(a) *F* contains the projections of every problem *D* in *M*.

(b) *F* is polynomial-time learnable with one-sided error. (See Appendix A for details.)
Note that this pertains to the model wherein the meta-algorithm seeks unsolved instances from EX.

**Proof:** (Sketch) The key idea in this proof is similar to that of Theorem 1 − the meta-algorithm constructs approximations to the projections of *D*. The catch is that it must provide solutions to the instances on its own. To do so, the meta-algorithm iteratively learns to solve problems with increasingly longer solution sequences. Specifically, the meta-algorithm first learns to solve problems with solution sequences of length one. Knowing how to solve problems with solution sequences of length *i*, it learns to solve problems with solutions of length *i*+1. In order to describe such an algorithm, we need the following definition.

**Defn:** For $D \in M$ and $\delta \in (0,1)$ define the quantity $m_\delta$ to be the least integer such that

$$\sum_{x \in S} P(x) \geq 1-\delta$$

where $S = \{x | x$ has a solution of length $m$ or less in $D\}$.

**Meta-Algorithm A$_2$**
**input** $h$, $D=(G,O)$
Let $F$ be of dimension $d(n)$;
Let $O = \{o_i | i = 1..k\}$;
Let $S(o_1),...S(o_k)$, $V(o_1),...V(o_k)$ be sets, initially empty;
**begin**
Section 1:
let $\alpha = 1/4h$.
Estimate $m \geq m_\alpha$ to a confidence of $(1-\alpha)$.
Let $\varepsilon = 1/(2hm^2)$.
Estimate $n \geq n_\varepsilon$ to a confidence of $(1-\varepsilon)$.
Substitute the null sets for the $V(o)$'s in the algorithm
of Section 3 to obtain the algorithm $H_0$.
Section 2:
**for** $l = 1, 2, ...,m$ **do**
    pick $t$, such that
    $t/ln(t) \geq 1/\varepsilon(kd(n) + ln(1/\varepsilon)) + ln(1/\varepsilon)$
    call EX($l$) $t$ times
    let $E$ be the set of instances so obtained;
    **for** each $o \in O$ and each $x \in E$ **do**
        run $H_{l-1}$ on $o(x)$, repeating to a confidence
        of $(1-\varepsilon/kt)$.
        **if** $H_{l-1}$ solves $o(x)$ in $l-1$ steps **then**
            $S(o) = S(o) \cup \{x\}$
    **od**
    **for** each $o \in O$ **do**
        $V(o) = Q(S(o))$;
        if $Q$ is randomized, repeat to
        confidence of $(1-\varepsilon)$
    **od**
    construct the algorithm $H_l$ by
    substituting the $V_o$)'s in Section 3.
**od**

Section 3:
**Algorithm** $H$
**input** $x$: string;
**begin**
    $\sigma \leftarrow$ null-sequence ;
    **While** $G(x) \neq 1$ **do**
        let $O_x = \{o | x \in V(o)\}$;
        **if** $O_x$ is empty **then** halt and report failure.
        **else** pick $o$ in $O_x$ uniformly randomly.
        $x \leftarrow o(x)$;
        $\sigma \leftarrow o \cdot \sigma$;
    **end**
    output $\sigma$ as solution for $x$;
**end**

Output $H_m$ as an approximate algorithm for $D$
**end**

We will prove the above meta-algorithm correct in stages. First we consider Section 1. The estimation here is to be done exactly as in Section 1 of Meta-Algorithm 1, and the corresponding proof holds.

We now consider Sections 2 and 3 simultanously. We proceed by induction, with the following being our inductive hypothesis. To simpify the proof, let us assume that our estimate $n$ for $n_\varepsilon$ is to a confidence of unity. We will account for this at a later stage.

<u>Inductive Hypothesis:</u> In any run of the meta algorithm, with probability $(1-\varepsilon)^{4l}$

$$\sum_{x \in C_l} P_l(x) \geq (1-\varepsilon)^l \tag{1}$$

where $C_l = \{x | H_l \text{ is correct on } x\}$ and $P_l$ is the conditional distribution given by
$P_l(x) =$
$Pr\{x \text{ is produced by any call of } EX(l) \mid x \in I(n)\}.$

<u>Basis:</u> For $l = 0$: $H_0$ produces the empty sequence as solution for the set $\{x|, G(x) = 1\}$ and fails on all other inputs. Hence $\sum_{x \in C_0} P_0(x) = 1$, and the inductive hypothesis is satisfied for $l = 0$.

<u>Induction:</u> Assume that the inductive hypothesis is true for $(l-1)$ and prove true for $l$.

Let $S_l(o)$, $S_{l-1}(o)$, $V_l(o)$, $V_{l-1}(o)$ represent the sets $S(o)$ and $V(o)$ for operator $o$ at the end of iterations $l$ and $l-1$ respectively of the outer **for** loop in the meta-algorithm. Now, consider the following algorithm.

**Algorithm** $H^*_l$.
**input** $x$: string;
**begin**
    let $O_x = \{o | x \in V_l(o)\}$;
    **if** $O_x$ is empty **then** halt and report failure.
    **else** pick $o$ in $O_x$ uniformly randomly.
        $x \leftarrow o(x)$.
        run $H_{l-1}$ on $x$.
        **if** $H_{l-1}$ solves $x$ with solution $\sigma$
            output $\sigma o$ and halt.
        **else** report failure.
        **end**

$H^*$ is different from $H_l$ in that it uses the $V_l$'s for deciding only on the first operator in the solution of an input instance $x$. After that it runs $H_{l-1}$. By the inductive hypothesis, $H_{l-1}$ can be as inaccurate as $(1-\varepsilon)^l$. Hence, $H^*$ cannot do better than that. The important thing is that it is possible to choose the $V_l(o)$'s from $F$ so that this accuracy is attained. To see this, recall that $F$ contains the projection of $O$ - the $U(o)$'s. And choosing $V(o) = U(o)$ for each $o$ will satisfy our demands. Furthermore, since the probability distribution $P_l$ is non-zero only on instances of length $n$ (and the null instance), it follows that we could just as well pick $V(o) = U(o) \cap \Sigma^n$. That is, we could pick $V(o)$ from $F_n$ rather than from $F$.

We will now show how to construct good approximations to the $U(o) \cap \Sigma^n$'s so that the inductive hypothesis may stand. Consider $H^*$. For a given $H_{l-1}$, there are $|F_n|$ ways to choose each of the $k$ sets $V_i(o)$, and hence there are at most $|F_n|^k$ choices for $H^*$. Call a choice "bad" if it does not satisfy equation (1) of the inductive hypothesis. We wish to eliminate the bad choices. To do so, we will call EX($l$), so that if our current choice is bad, EX($l$) will produce a witness to this with high probability. That is, EX($l$) will produce an instance $x$ such that $x$ is not in $V_i(o)$ for any $o$, and yet there exists $o_i$ such that $o_i(x)$ can be solved by $H_{l-1}$ in $l-1$ steps. Now, at any call of EX($l$), given that the call resulted in an instance $x \in I(n)$, the probability that a bad choice of $H^*$ will be correct on the instance produced is at most $(1-\varepsilon)^l$. If we make $s$ calls of EX($l$), given that all of them resulted in instances from $I(n)$, the probability that a bad choice of $H^*$ will be correct on all $s$ instances is at most $(1-\varepsilon)^{ls}$. Hence, the probability that any bad choice of $H^*$ will be correct on all $s$ instances is bounded by $(1-\varepsilon)^{ls}|F_n|^k>$. We choose $s$ so that the probability of the above event is at most $\varepsilon$. That is, we choose $s$ so that

$(1-\varepsilon)^{ls}|F_n|^k \leq \varepsilon.$

It certainly suffices to pick $s$ to satisfy

$s \geq 1/(\varepsilon)(kd(n) + ln(1/\varepsilon)),$

where d(n) is the dimension of F. But by our choice of $n$, the probability that any call of EX($l$) will result in an instance from $I(n)$ is only $(1-\varepsilon$. Hence, we will call EX($l$) $t$ times, for some $t > s$ so that with probability $(1-\varepsilon)$, these $t$ calls will result in at least $s$ instances from $I(n)$. A simple Chernoff estimate yields that if $t$ should satisfy $t/ln(t) \geq s + ln(1/\varepsilon)$. Such a choice would imply that with probability $(1-\varepsilon)^2$, we have eliminated the bad choices for $H^*$, i.e, with probability $(1-\varepsilon)^2$, $H^*$ satisfies inequality (1), given that $H_{l-1}$ satisfies (1).

We also have to account for verifying these witnesses. That is, given an instance $x$, for each operator $o$, we must run $H_{l-1}$ on $o(x)$. Since $H_{l-1}$ is randomized, it has a certain probability of failure and this must be accounted for. To do so, we run $H_{l-1}$ sufficiently many times so that our confidence in the result is $(1-\varepsilon/kt)$. This will require $O(ln(kt/\varepsilon))$ repetitions. Since we must run $H_{l-1}$ on $kt$ inputs, our simultaneous confidence in the results of all the $kt$ computations is $(1-\varepsilon/kt)^{kt}$, which is bounded by $(1-\varepsilon)$. Finally, we note that picking a candidate $V(o)$ from $F_n$ is done with the ordering $Q$, which may be randomized. We carry out this computation to a confidence of $(1-\varepsilon/k)$ for each operator $O$, leading to a confidence of $(1-\varepsilon/k)^k \geq (1-\varepsilon)$ for all the $k$ operators. Combining the above estimates with the result of the last paragraph, we conclude that with probability $(1-\varepsilon)^4$, $H^*$ satisfies inequality (1), given that $H_{l-1}$ satisfies (1). By the inductive hypothesis, $H_{l-1}$ satisfies (1) with probability $(1-\varepsilon)^{4(l-1)}$. Therefore, $H^*$ satisfies (1) with probability

$(1-\varepsilon)^{4(l-1)}(1-\varepsilon)^4 = (1-\varepsilon)^{4l}.$

Then, since $S_{l-1}(o) \subseteq S_l(o)$ for each $o$, it follows from the definitions of Appendix A[2] that $V_{l-1}(o) \subseteq V_l(o)$. This directly implies that the set of instances solved by $H^*$ is a subset of the set of problems solved by $H_l$. Therefore, $H_l$ satisfies the inductive hypothesis as well.

We now seek to bound the error of $H_m$ with respect to the natural distribution $P$. Specifically, we seek a lower bound on the following quantity.

---

[2]Condition (b) of the definition of ordering $Q$, Appendix A.

$$\sum_{x \in C_m} P(x)$$

where, as earlier, $C_m = \{x | H_m \text{ is correct on } x\}$.

Let $N$ be the set of instances that are not solvable.

$N = \{x | x \text{ is not solvable}\}$.

We define the following sets, parametric in $l$, with respect to $H_l$.

$X_l = \{x | x \in I(n), \text{ optimal solution of } x \text{ has } l \text{ steps},$

$\qquad\qquad H_l \text{ solves } x\}$

$Y_l = \{x | x \text{ is solvable in fewer than } l \text{ steps}$

$\qquad\qquad \text{or } x \text{ is not solvable}\}$.

$Z_l = \{x | x \text{ is solvable and optimal solution of}$

$\qquad\qquad x \text{ has more than } l \text{ steps}\}$.

Also, for an instance $x$, define the event $B(x)$ as follows.

$B(x) = \{x \text{ is an intermediate step in}$

$\qquad\qquad \text{the solution produced by INSTANCE}\}$

Now consider the sum $\sum_{x \in C_l} P_l(x)$. We can decompose this sum as follows.

$$\sum_{x \in C_l} cP_l(x) = \sum_{x \in X_l} P(x) + \sum_{x \in X_l} Pr\{B(x)\} + \sum_{x \in Y_l} P(x).$$

In the above, $c$ is a normalization factor to account for the fact that $P_l$ is conditional on those instances that are in $I(n)$. By our choice of $n \geq n_\varepsilon$, (recall that we are still under the assumption that our estimate of $n_\varepsilon$ is of confidence unity), this normalization factor satisfies $c \leq (1-\varepsilon)$. To see this, simply note that $\sum_{x \in I(n_\varepsilon)} P(x) \geq 1-\varepsilon$, by the definition of $n_\varepsilon$. By the definitions of $B(x)$, $X_l$ and $Z_l$,

$$\sum_{x \in X_{l-1}} Pr\{B(x)\} \leq \sum_{x \in Z_l} P(x) \qquad\qquad (2)$$

Therefore,

$$\sum_{x \in X_{l-1}} Pr\{B(x)\} + \sum_{x \in Y_l} P(x) \leq \sum_{x \in Z_l} P(x) + \sum_{x \in Y_l} P(x) \leq 1. \qquad (3)$$

Summing $\sum_{x \in C_l} cP_l(x)$ over $l = 0,1,2...m$ and substituting (3) in the sum $(m-1)$ times we obtain,

$$\sum_{l=0}^{l=m} \sum_{x \in C_l} cP_l(x) \leq \sum_{l=0}^{l=m} \sum_{x \in X_l} P(x) + \sum_{x \in X_m} Pr\{B(x)\} + (m-1) + \sum_{x \in N} P(x)$$

Using (2) to replace the second term on the right, we get

$$\sum_{x \in C_l} cP_l(x) \leq \sum_{l=0}^{l=m} \sum_{x \in X_l} P(x) + \sum_{x \in Z_{m+1}} P(x) + (m-1) + \sum_{x \in N} P(x)$$

But by our choice of $m$, with probability $(1-\alpha)$, $\sum_{x \in Z_{m+1}} P(x) \leq \alpha$. Therefore we can rewrite our inequality thus, to hold with probability $(1-\varepsilon)$.

$$\sum_{l=0}^{l=m} \sum_{x \in C_l} cP_l(x) \;\leq\; \sum_{l=0}^{l=m} \sum_{x \in X_l} P(x) + \alpha + (m-1) + \sum_{x \in N} P(x) \tag{4}$$

Now, by the inductive hypothesis, with probability $(1-\varepsilon)^{4l}$

$$\sum_{x \in C_l} P_l(x) \;\geq\; (1-\varepsilon)^l$$

Hence,

$$\sum_{l=0}^{l=m} \sum_{x \in C_l} P_l(x) \;\geq\; m(1-\varepsilon)^m \tag{5}$$

Noting that (4) and (5) hold with probability $(1-\alpha)$ and probability $(1-\varepsilon)^{4m}$ respectively, we can substitute (5) in (4) to write: With probability $(1-\varepsilon)^{4m}(1-\alpha)$

$$cm(1-\varepsilon)^m \;\leq\; \sum_{l=0}^{l=m} \sum_{x \in X_l} P(x) + \alpha + (m-1) + \sum_{x \in N} P(x) \tag{6}$$

Grouping the first and last terms on the right hand side and substituting $c \geq (1-\varepsilon)$, we get,

$$\sum_{x \in S} P(x) \;\geq\; m(1-\varepsilon)(1-\varepsilon)^m - \alpha - (m-1) \tag{7}$$

Where $S = \{x | H_m$ is correct on $x\}$. We desire the quantity on the right hand side to be greater than $(1-1/h)$. Simplifying, we find that $\varepsilon \leq 1/(2hm^2)$ suffices.

Finally, we estimate our confidence that (7) holds. Under the assumption that our estimate $n$ for $n_\varepsilon$ was to unit confidence, we obtained the confidence estimate of $(1-\alpha)(1-\varepsilon)^{4m}$ as noted with (6). Since the confidence in our estimate of $n_\varepsilon$ is only $(1-\varepsilon)$, the overall confidence that (7) holds is $(1-\varepsilon)^{4m+2}$. We need to check whether our choice of $\varepsilon \leq 1/(2hm^2)$ is sufficient to ensure that this confidence level exceeds $(1-1/h)$. As it happens, this is the case.

We have therefore proved that $A$ is indeed a meta-algorithm for $M$. •

# 5. CONCLUSION

This paper explored a new direction in the formal theory learning – algorithms that learn to solve problems from sample instances of the problems. Two random sources of sample instances are considered, one providing solved instances and the other providing unsolved instances or exercises. For both sources, general theorems are proved identifying conditions sufficient to permit learning. To illustrate the scope of these results, the are applied to the construction of an algorithm that learns to perform a restricted versions of symbolic integration.

We also note here that the frameworks discused in this paper can be viewed as formal models for the paradigm of "explanation based learning" [6].

## Acknowledgements

I thank T. Mitchell and P. Tadepalli for the interesting discussions.

## References

[1] Valiant, L., "A Theory of the Learnable", Symposium on Theory of Computing, 1984.

[2] Blumer, Ehrenfeucht, Haussler and Warmuth ,"Learning Geometric Concepts and the Vapnik-Chervonenkis Dimension", Symposium on Theory of Computing, 1986.

[3] Natarajan, B.K., "On Learning Boolean Functions", Symposium on Theory of Computing, 1987.

[4] Natarajan and Tadepalli, "Two New Frameworks for Learning", Int. Conf on Machine Learning, 1988.

[5] Kearns, Li, Pitt and Valiant, "On Learning Boolean Formulae", Symposium on Theory of Computing", 1987.

[6] Mitchell, Keller, Kedar-Cabelli, Machine Learning, Vol1, 1986.

# Appendix A

This section reviews some necessary definitions and results on learning families of sets with one-sided error as presented in [3].

Let $f$ denote a subset of $\Sigma^*$ and $F$ be a family (a set) of such sets.

**Defn:** A family of set $F$ is polynomial-time learnable with one-sided error if there exists an algorithm $A$ and an integer $k$ such that

(a) $A$ takes as input integer $h$, the error parameter.

(b) $A$ may call EXAMPLE, where EXAMPLE returns randomly drawn elements of some set $f$ in $F$. These elements are drawn according to an arbitrary and unknown probability distribution $P$ on $f$. $A$ computes in time $(hl)^k$, where $l$ is the length of the longest example produced by EXAMPLE. $A$ may be randomized.

(c) For all $f$ in $F$ and all probability distributions $P$ on these sets $f$, with probability $(1-1/h)$ $A$ outputs a program $C$ that runs in time $n^k$ on inputs of length $n$ and accepts a set $g$ in $F$ such that $g \subseteq f$ and

$Prob\{f-g\} \le 1/h$.

**Defn:** Let $f \subseteq \Sigma^*$. For natural number $n$, the induced set $f_n$ is defined by $f_n = \{x | x \in f, |x| \le n\}$. Similarly $F_n = \{f_n | f \in F\}$.

**Defn:** The *dimension* of a family $F$ is $d(n)$ if for all $n$, $|F_n| \le 2^{d(n)}$. If $d(n)$ is a polynomial in $n$, we say $F$ is of polynomial dimension.

**Defn:** An algorithm $Q$ is said to be a *polynomial-time ordering* for family $F$ if there exists an integer $k$ such that

(a) $Q$ takes as input a set of strings $S$. $Q$ outputs a program $C$ such that $C$ accepts a set $f$ in $F$, $S \subseteq f$. Also, for all $g$ in $F$, $S \subseteq g$ implies $f \subseteq g$.

(b) Both $Q$ and $C$ run in (possibly randomized) time $l^k$ on inputs of length $l$.

**Theorem A:**   A family $F$ is polynomial-time learnable with one-sided error if and only if $F$ is of polynomial dimension, $F$ is closed under intersection, and $F$ possesses a polynomial-time ordering.

**Proof:** See [3] for details.  •

# On Approximate Truth*

Daniel N. Osherson       Michael Stob       Scott Weinstein
M. I. T.              Calvin College       University of Pennsylvania

May 26, 1989

## Abstract

We propose a definition for the relation: structure $\mathcal{U}$ approximates structure $\mathcal{S}$. A first order sentence is then defined to be approximately true in a structure just in case it is true (standardly) in an approximating structure. The deductive and inductive logic of approximate truth in this sense is discussed. Regarding deduction, we consider a modal language where $\lozenge\theta$ is true in a structure $\mathcal{S}$ just in case $\theta$ is approximately true in $\mathcal{S}$, and show that the set of theorems of this language is not recursively enumerable. Regarding induction, we define a paradigm of probably approximately correct truth detection, and show that successful induction is possible in this paradigm with respect to a wide class of sentences.

# 1  Introduction

A claim may be wrong but "almost" right; a theory may be false but "truer" than another. Since at least Pierce (1958) and Popper (1963) it has been recognized that giving precise meaning to these ideas is central to understanding the nature of scientific progress. The importance of approximate truth to the semantic analysis of natural language, and to the development of artificially intelligent systems has similarly been stressed by a variety of investigators (e.g., Rescher, 1969; Zadeh, 1965; Lakoff, 1987). The present paper offers a definition of the concept "first order sentence $\theta$ is approximately true in structure $\mathcal{S}$." The deductive and inductive logic of the defined concept is subsequently examined. Our theory starts from consideration of the degree to which one structure approximates another. Approximate truth in a structure is then construed as (exact) truth in an approximating structure. It is not claimed that this approach illuminates every aspect of the problem of approximate truth. Rather, our theory is designed for situations of the following kind.

*Research support was provided by the Office of Naval Research under contract No. N00014-87-K-0401 to Osherson and Weinstein, and by NSF grants DMS-85-21712 and DMS-88-00030 to Stob. Correspondence to D. Osherson, E10-006, M.I.T., Cambridge, MA 02139; e-mail: dan@psyche.mit.edu

Imagine a long, narrow strip of land (e.g., a coastline) undergoing mineral exploration. A point along the strip is to be designated randomly according to some unknown probability distribution. Once the site is designated, it will be decided whether to drill at that location. Let $p$ be a variable for points along the strip, and consider the following predicates and hypothesis (1).

$Lp$  $\equiv$  a lode exists within 1000 feet of the surface at point $p$.

$Rp$  $\equiv$  there is superficial igneous rock at point $p$.

(1)  $(\forall p)(Lp \to Rp)$

Even if false about the actual strip under exploration, (1) might be useful if true about a fictitious strip that approximates it. In this case, (1) can be considered to be approximately true about the actual strip.

To give substance to the foregoing idea, let the actual and fictitious strips be represented by the same, real interval $I$. Let $\mathbf{L}$, $\mathbf{R}$ be the extensions of $L$ and $R$ in the actual strip, and $\mathbf{L'}$, $\mathbf{R'}$ be their extensions in the fictitious strip. For the fictitious strip to approximate the actual one we require that every point in $\mathbf{L'}$ be near to some point in $\mathbf{L}$, and that every point in the complement of $\mathbf{L'}$ be near to some point in the complement of $\mathbf{L}$; similarly for $\mathbf{R'}$ and $\mathbf{R}$. It is natural, however, to ask for greater nearness in high probability subregions than in low probability subregions since our judgment about drilling is more likely to be put to the test in the former than in the latter. We thus define the "probability distance" of two points to be the probability mass of the interval that separates them. It can be seen that two points separated by a small probability distance are either metrically close in a high mass interval or else common members of a low mass interval.

Now fix $b \in (0,1)$. The fictitious strip is called a "$b$-variant" of the actual strip just in case for every point $p'$ there is a point $p$ such that $p'$ is within probability distance $b$ of $p$, and $p' \in \mathbf{L'}$ iff $p \in \mathbf{L}$; likewise for $\mathbf{R'}$ and $\mathbf{R}$. Thus, for the fictitious strip to be a $b$-variant of the actual one, every point $p' \in \mathbf{L'}$ must be justified by a nearby point $p \in \mathbf{L}$; likewise, every point $p' \notin \mathbf{L'}$ must be justified by a nearby point $p \notin \mathbf{L}$ —and similarly for $\mathbf{R'}$ and $\mathbf{R}$. In this case, we consider the fictitious strip to approximate the actual one, up to the parameter $b$.

Our theory is a generalization of the foregoing illustration. We rely on the following notation. $N$ denotes the set of positive integers. $\Re$ denotes the reals. Given any set $S$ and $m \in N$, $S^m$ denotes the set of $m$-tuples over $S$. The set of infinite sequences over $S$ is denoted by $S^\omega$. The complement of $S$ is denoted by $S^c$. For variables over tuples of arbitrary length we use barred letters such as $\bar{q}$.

In what follows, by "language" is meant a first-order, relational language with $=$. It is the sentences of such languages for which approximate truth in a structure will be defined.

# 2   Approximate Truth

This section advances a definition of approximate truth for an arbitrary, relational first-order language with $=$. As a first step, structures are equipped with probability distributions, and probability-distance is formally introduced. A parameterized approximation relation over structures is then defined.

Let nonempty set $D$ and metric $d$ over $D$ be given. A set of the form $\{x \in D \mid d(x,e) \leq r\}$ for fixed $e \in D$ and nonnegative $r \in \Re$ is called a ball (for $D$ and $d$), and denoted $B(e,r)$. (In discussing balls, the underlying $D$ and $d$ will be clear from context.) Probability set-function $P$ over $D$ is called a *distribution over* $(D,d)$ just in case $P(B)$ is defined for all balls $B$.

(2) DEFINITION: An *augmented structure for language* $\mathcal{L}$ is a quadruple $(D, d, P, \alpha)$ where

   (a) $(D, d)$ is a metric space;

   (b) $P$ is a distribution over $(D, d)$;

   (c) $\alpha$ is a mapping of the relation symbols of $\mathcal{L}$ into relations over $D$ such that for all $n \in N$, $n$-ary relation symbols are mapped to $n$-ary relations, and $=$ is mapped to identity.

In the remainder of this section we fix a language $\mathcal{L}$ and assume that all augmented structures are for $\mathcal{L}$. In addition, "augmented structure for $\mathcal{L}$" is abbreviated to "structure."

Let $\mathcal{S}=(D, d, P, \alpha_\mathcal{S})$ be a structure. Given $n \in N$, $P$ is extended to $D^n$ and to $D^\omega$ in the usual way (via the product probability, see Halmos, 1950, Ch. 7). Given sentence $\theta \in \mathcal{L}$ we write $\mathcal{S} \models \theta$ just in case $(D, \alpha_\mathcal{S})$ satisfies $\theta$ in the standard sense.

Let structure $\mathcal{S}=(D, d, P, \alpha_\mathcal{S})$ be given. We define function $\delta_\mathcal{S} : D \times D \to [0,1]$ by the condition: For all $e, f \in D$, $\delta_\mathcal{S}(e,f) = \text{glb}\{P(B) \mid B \text{ is a ball and } e, f \in B\} - P(\{e,f\})$. Observe that $P(\{e,f\})$ is defined because $P(B(e,0))$ and $P(B(f,0))$ are defined. In the illustration discussed in Section 1, $P(\{e,f\}) = 0$ for all $e, f \in D$. When $D$ is countable, $P(\{e,f\})$ is typically positive and may be construed as a continuity correction. Intuitively, $\delta_\mathcal{S}(e,f)$ is the weight of the gap that separates $e$ from $f$. $\delta_\mathcal{S}$ is extended to $\bigcup\{D^n \times D^n \mid n \in N\}$ as follows. Let $\bar{e}, \bar{f} \in D^n$ be given. We define:

$$\delta_\mathcal{S}(\bar{e}, \bar{f}) = \sqrt{\delta_\mathcal{S}(e_1, f_1)^2 + \cdots + \delta_\mathcal{S}(e_n, f_n)^2}.$$

$\delta_\mathcal{S}$ need not be a metric over $D$ or $D^n$. However, the definition implies:

(3) For all $\bar{e}, \bar{f} \in D^n$, $\delta_\mathcal{S}(\bar{e}, \bar{f}) = \delta_\mathcal{S}(\bar{f}, \bar{e})$.

(4) For all $\bar{e} \in D^n$, $\delta_\mathcal{S}(\bar{e}, \bar{e}) = 0$.

We now define the approximation relation between structures.

(5) DEFINITION: Let $b \in (0, 1)$ and structures $\mathcal{S}$ and $\mathcal{U}$ be given. $\mathcal{U}$ is a *b-variant of* $\mathcal{S}$ just in case

   (a) $\mathcal{S}$ and $\mathcal{U}$ have the forms $\mathcal{S}=(D, d, P, \alpha_\mathcal{S})$, $\mathcal{U}=(D, d, P, \alpha_\mathcal{U})$ (hence $\delta_\mathcal{S} = \delta_\mathcal{U}$);

   (b) for every relation symbol $A$ in $\mathcal{L}$ other than $=$, and every $\bar{u} \in D^{\text{arity}(A)}$ there is $\bar{s} \in D^{\text{arity}(A)}$ such that

    i. $\delta_S(\bar{u}, \bar{s}) < b$

    ii. $\bar{u} \in \alpha_{\mathcal{U}}(A)$ iff $\bar{s} \in \alpha_S(A)$.

By (4), Definition (5) implies:

(6) For all $b \in (0,1)$ and structures $S$, $S$ is a $b$-variant of $S$.

On the other hand, symmetry does not hold: $\mathcal{U}$ can be a $b$-variant of $S$ without $S$ being a $b$-variant of $\mathcal{U}$. This is shown by the following example.

(7) EXAMPLE: Suppose that $\mathcal{L}$ contains but a single relation symbol $A$ (other than $=$). Let $S = (\Re, d, P, \alpha_S)$ and $\mathcal{U} = (\Re, d, P, \alpha_{\mathcal{U}})$ be such that d is euclidean distance, P is any continuous distribution over $\Re$, $\alpha_{\mathcal{U}}(A) = \emptyset$ and $\alpha_S(A) = \{e\}$. By continuity, for any $b \in (0,1)$, there is $f \neq e$ with $\delta_S(e, f) < b$. Hence, $\mathcal{U}$ is a $b$-variant of $S$ for any $b \in (0,1)$. However, $S$ is not a $b$-variant of $\mathcal{U}$ for any $b \in (0,1)$.

Approximate truth may now be formally defined.

(8) DEFINITION: Let $\theta \in \mathcal{L}$, $\Theta \subseteq \mathcal{L}$, $b \in (0,1)$, and structure $S$ be given.

    (a) $\theta$ is $b$-*true in* $S$ just in case there is a $b$-variant $\mathcal{U}$ of $S$ such that $\mathcal{U} \models \theta$. $\theta$ is $b$-*false in* $S$ just in case there is a $b$-variant $\mathcal{U}$ of $S$ such that $\mathcal{U} \not\models \theta$.

    (b) $\Theta$ is $b$-*true in* $S$ just in case there is a $b$-variant $\mathcal{U}$ of $S$ such that $\mathcal{U} \models \Theta$.

From (6) and (8) we have the following:

(9) If $S \models \theta$ then $\theta$ is $b$-true in $S$. If $S \not\models \theta$ then $\theta$ is $b$-false in $S$.

(10) If $\theta$ is not $b$-true in $S$ then $\theta$ is $b$-false in $S$. If $\theta$ is not $b$-false in $S$ then $\theta$ is $b$-true in $S$.

The following example illustrates the potential usefulness of $b$-true sentences.

(11) EXAMPLE: Let $I$, $\mathbf{L}$, and $\mathbf{R}$ be as described in the introductory illustration. We imagine that $I$ has been partitioned into ten regions. A point will be drawn randomly from $I$ according to unknown, continuous probability distribution $P$, and the following question will be posed.

    (12) $p \in \mathbf{L}$ for all $p$ in the region from which the sampled point was drawn?

Suppose that inspection reveals there to be no superficial igneous rock in the region actually sampled, and that hypothesis (1) is known to be .01-true in the structure $S = (I, d, P, (\mathbf{L}, \mathbf{R}))$ (where $d$ is euclidean distance). Then, (12) is false with probability at least .80.

PROOF: Let $X$ be the sampled region. It is easy to see that with probability .8, $P(X) \geq .02$. It thus suffices to deduce a contradiction from the following assumptions:

(13)  (a) $X \subseteq \mathbf{L}$

(b) $P(X) \geq .02$

(c) $X \subseteq \overline{\mathbf{R}}$

(d) (1) is .01-true in $\mathcal{S}$.

By (13)b, we choose $m \in X$ with:

(14)  $\delta_{\mathcal{S}}(m, p) \geq .01$ for all $p \notin X$.

($m$ may be taken to be the "probability midpoint" of $X$.)  By (14) and (13)c, $\delta_{\mathcal{S}}(m, p) \geq .01$ for all $p \in \mathbf{R}$. Hence, by Definition (5):

(15)  In every .01-variant $\mathcal{U}$ of $\mathcal{S}$, $m \notin \alpha_{\mathcal{U}}(R)$.

By (13)a and (14), $\delta_{\mathcal{S}}(m, p) \geq .01$ for all $p \in \overline{\mathbf{L}}$. Hence:

(16)  In every .01-variant $\mathcal{U}$ of $\mathcal{S}$, $m \in \alpha_{\mathcal{U}}(L)$.

By (13)d, let $\mathcal{U}$ by an .01-variant of $\mathcal{S}$ satisfying (1). Then, (16) implies $m \in \alpha_{\mathcal{U}}(R)$, contradicting (15). ■

Other uses of $b$-true sentences depend somewhat on the underlying probability distribution. To illustrate, let $\mathcal{S} = (\Re, d, P, \alpha_{\mathcal{S}})$, where $d$ is euclidean distance and $P$ is a continuous distribution given by probability density function $g$.

(17)  EXAMPLE: Let $\theta$ be $\forall x A x$. Call interval $I$ a "gap" if $I \subseteq (\alpha_{\mathcal{S}}(A))^c$. Then the $b$-truth of $\theta$ in $\mathcal{S}$ implies that long gaps have low density. For example, if $\theta$ is .01-true in $\mathcal{S}$ then for no gap $I$ of length 1 is $g(r) \geq .02$ for all $r \in I$.

(18)  EXAMPLE: Let $\theta$ be $\forall x \exists y A x y$. Call $r \in \Re$ a "$\theta$-counterexample" if there is no $s \in \Re$ with $(r, s) \in \alpha_{\mathcal{S}}(A)$. Call interval $I$ a "gap" if every $r \in I$ is a $\theta$-counterexample. Then (parallel to Example (17)), the $b$-truth of $\theta$ in $\mathcal{S}$ implies that long gaps have low density. For example, if $\theta$ is .02-true in $\mathcal{S}$ then for no gap $I$ of length 1 is $g(r) \geq .02$ for all $r \in I$.

Examples (17) and (18) can be verified by easy calculus. The final example underscores the "pointwise" conception of approximation that animates our theory.

(19)  EXAMPLE: Suppose that $\alpha_{\mathcal{S}}(A)$ is the set of rationals. Then, for any $b \in (0, 1)$, both $\forall x A x$ and $\forall x \sim A x$ are $b$-true in $\mathcal{S}$.

# 3    Some deductive logic of approximate truth

In this section we consider the deductive closure of approximately true sentences, and the formalizability of deductive calculi for approximate truth.

## 3.1   Closure

Let $b \in (0,1)$ and language $\mathcal{L}$ be given. A sentence can be both $b$-true and $b$-false in the same structure. To see this, let $\mathcal{S}$ and $\mathcal{U}$ be as specified in Example (7). Then $\exists \bar{x} A \bar{x}$ is true in $\mathcal{S}$, hence $b$-true in $\mathcal{S}$. On the other hand, $\exists \bar{x} A \bar{x}$ is false in $\mathcal{U}$ (for any $b \in (0,1)$), hence $b$-false in $\mathcal{S}$. A related fact is that—unlike truth—$b$-truth is not closed under conjunction. Refering again to Example (7), $\exists \bar{x} A \bar{x}$ is $b$-true in $\mathcal{S}$, $\sim\exists \bar{x} A \bar{x}$ is $b$-true in $\mathcal{S}$, but their conjunction (a contradiction) is not $b$-true in $\mathcal{S}$. Thus, every member of $\Theta \subseteq \mathcal{L}$ can be $b$-true in a structure $\mathcal{S}$ without $\Theta$ being $b$-true in $\mathcal{S}$ (compare Definition (8)). Approximate truth does enjoy a restricted kind of closure under conjunction, however, as revealed by the following theorem. To state it, a definition is needed. Recall that a quantifier-free formula is called a "matrix".

(20)   DEFINITION: A matrix $M$ is *monotone* just in case:

   (a)   $M$ is in disjunctive normal form;

   (b)   no relation symbol occurs both negated and nonnegated in $M$;

   (c)   = does not occur in $M$.

Sentence $\theta \in \mathcal{L}$ is *monotone* just in case $\theta$ is logically equivalent to a sentence in prenex normal form with monotone matrix. A set $\Theta$ of $\mathcal{L}$-sentences is *monotone* just in case every finite conjunction of sentences drawn from $\Theta$ is monotone.

(21)   THEOREM: Let $\Theta$ be a monotone set of $\mathcal{L}$-sentences, and let $\mathcal{S}$ be a structure. If every member of $\Theta$ is $b$-true in $\mathcal{S}$, then $\Theta$ is $b$-true in $\mathcal{S}$, and hence every logical consequence of $\Theta$ is $b$-true in $\mathcal{S}$.

PROOF: Let $\mathcal{S}=(D, d, P, \alpha_{\mathcal{S}})$. Define $\mathcal{W}=(D, d, P, \alpha_{\mathcal{W}})$ by the conditions:

- If relation symbol $A$ occurs positively in $\Theta$, then

$$\alpha_{\mathcal{W}}(A) \ = \ \{\bar{e} \in D^{\mathrm{arity}(A)} \,|\, \exists \bar{f} \in \alpha_{\mathcal{S}}(A)[\delta_{\mathcal{S}}(\bar{e}, \bar{f}) < b]\}$$

- If relation symbol $A$ occurs negatively in $\Theta$, then

$$\alpha_{\mathcal{W}}(A^c) \ = \ \{\bar{e} \in D^{\mathrm{arity}(A)} \,|\, \exists \bar{f} \in \alpha_{\mathcal{S}}(A^c)[\delta_{\mathcal{S}}(\bar{e}, \bar{f}) < b]\}$$

Now suppose that $\theta \in \Theta$ is $b$-true in $\mathcal{S}$. Then, because = does not occur in $\theta$, $\mathcal{W} \models \theta$. So $\mathcal{W} \models \Theta$. Moreover, $\mathcal{W}$ is a $b$-variant of $\mathcal{S}$ by construction. ∎

Theorem (21) shows that piecemeal discovery is possible for approximately true, monotone theories. If the axioms of a monotone theory are each shown to be approximately true in the actual world, then the entire theory is approximately true in the actual world.

Finally, the reader may verify the following statements:

- $\exists \bar{x} A \bar{x}$ is $b$-true in $\mathcal{S}$ iff $\exists \bar{x} A \bar{x}$ is true in $\mathcal{S}$.

- $\exists \bar{x} A \bar{x}$ may be $b$-false in $\mathcal{S}$ even though $\exists \bar{x} A \bar{x}$ is true in $\mathcal{S}$.

- $\forall \bar{x} A \bar{x}$ is $b$-false in $\mathcal{S}$ iff $\forall \bar{x} A \bar{x}$ is false in $\mathcal{S}$.

- $\forall \bar{x} A \bar{x}$ may be $b$-true in $\mathcal{S}$ even though $\forall \bar{x} A \bar{x}$ is false in $\mathcal{S}$.

## 3.2    Formalizability

Given an arbitrary language $\mathcal{L}$, we extend $\mathcal{L}$ to $\mathcal{L}^+$ by adding the following condition to the formation rules for $\mathcal{L}$. For any sentence $\theta \in \mathcal{L}$, $\Diamond \theta \in \mathcal{L}^+$. Observe that $\mathcal{L}^+$ is a decidable subset of the usual modal language built from $\mathcal{L}$; in the usual case, $\Diamond$ may apply to open formulas, and iteration of $\Diamond$ is possible. For each $b \in (0,1)$ we fix the semantics of $\mathcal{L}^+$ by adding the following clause to the definition of $\models$ for $\mathcal{L}$. Given structure $\mathcal{S}$ and sentence $\theta \in \mathcal{L}$, $\mathcal{S} \models \Diamond \theta$ iff $\theta$ is $b$-true in $\mathcal{S}$. To indicate the dependence of $\models$ on the choice of $b$, we write $\models_b$ for $\models$. $\theta \in \mathcal{L}^+$ is $b$-*valid* iff $\mathcal{S} \models_b \theta$ for all structures $\mathcal{S}$. Given $\theta \in \mathcal{L}$ we abbreviate $\sim \Diamond \sim \theta$ by $\Box \theta$. Thus, $\mathcal{S} \models_b \Box \theta$ just in case $\theta$ is true in every $b$-variant of $\mathcal{S}$.

The next theorem shows that the deductive logic just defined admits of no mechanical proof procedure.

(22) THEOREM: There is a finite language $\mathcal{L}$ such that for every $b \in (0,1)$, the $b$-valid subset of $\mathcal{L}^+$ is not recursively enumerable.

PROOF: Assume that $\mathcal{L}$ contains the binary relation symbol $R$, and let $\Omega$ be the conjunction of the following sentences.

(23) $\exists x \forall y \forall z (\sim Ryz \leftrightarrow (y = x \wedge z = x))$

(24) $\Diamond \forall x \forall y \sim Rxy$

(25) $\Box [(\forall x \forall y \forall z ((Rxy \wedge Rxz \rightarrow y = z) \wedge (Rxz \wedge Ryz \rightarrow x = y)) \wedge \forall x \exists y Rxy) \rightarrow \forall x \exists y Ryx]$

Note that (25) says that if $R$ represents a total injective function, then the function is surjective.

(26) LEMMA: For all $b \in (0,1)$ and all structures $\mathcal{S} = (D, d, P, \alpha_{\mathcal{S}})$ for $\mathcal{L}$:

  (a) if $\mathcal{S} \models_b \Omega$ then $D$ is finite.

  (b) if $D$ is finite then there is a structure $\mathcal{U} = (D, d, P', \alpha_{\mathcal{U}})$ such that $\mathcal{U} \models_b \Omega$, and for all relation symbols $Q$ in $\mathcal{L}$ other than $R$, $\alpha_{\mathcal{U}}(Q) = \alpha_{\mathcal{S}}(Q)$.

PROOF OF LEMMA (26): Let $b \in (0,1)$ and $\mathcal{S} = (D, d, P, \alpha_{\mathcal{S}})$ for $\mathcal{L}$ be given. For (26)a, suppose that $\mathcal{S} \models_b (23) \wedge (24)$ and that $D$ is infinite. We show that $\mathcal{S} \not\models_b (25)$. By (23), there is $s \in D$ such that $\alpha_{\mathcal{S}}(R) = D^2 - (s,s)$. By (24), for every $u, v \in D, \delta_{\mathcal{S}}((s,s),(u,v)) < b$. Hence, by Definition (5), for every $Y \subseteq \alpha_{\mathcal{S}}(R)$ there is a $b$-variant $\mathcal{U}$ of $\mathcal{S}$ such that

$\alpha_\mathcal{U}(R) = Y$. But since $D$ is infinite, there is $Y \subseteq \alpha_\mathcal{S}(R)$ such that $Y$ is the graph of a total injection on $D$ that is not surjective. Let $\mathcal{U}$ be a $b$-variant of $\mathcal{S}$ such that $\alpha_\mathcal{U}(R) = Y$. Then $\mathcal{U}$ witnesses that $\mathcal{S} \not\models_b (25)$.

Now suppose that $D$ is finite and let $s \in D$ be given. To define the needed witness $\mathcal{U}$ for (26)b, let $\alpha_\mathcal{U}(R) = D^2 - (s, s)$; hence, $\mathcal{U} \models_b (23)$. Let $P'$ be a probability distribution with $P'(\{s\}) = 1$. Then, by the definition of probability distance, $\delta_\mathcal{U}(u, s) = 0$ for all $u \in D$; hence $\delta_\mathcal{U}((u, v), (s, s)) = 0 < b$ for all $u, v \in D$. Hence, $\mathcal{U} \models_b (24)$. $\mathcal{U} \models_b (25)$ because $D$ is finite. Thus, $\mathcal{U} \models_b \Omega$. Finally, we define $\alpha_\mathcal{U}(Q) = \alpha_\mathcal{S}(Q)$ for all $Q \neq R$. ∎

Returning to the proof of Theorem (22), recall that a (nonmodal) first-order sentence is called "finitely valid" just in case it is true in every relational structure with finite domain. Let $\theta$ be an $R$-free sentence of $\mathcal{L}$. If $\theta$ is finitely valid, then $\Omega \to \theta$ is $b$-valid by Lemma (26)a. If $\theta$ is not finitely valid, then by Lemma (26)b (since $R$ does not occur in $\theta$) there is a countermodel to $\Omega \to \theta$, hence $\Omega \to \theta$ is not $b$-valid. This proves:

(27) For all $b \in (0, 1)$ and any language $\mathcal{L}$ containing the binary relation symbol $R$, if the $b$-valid subset of $\mathcal{L}^+$ is recursively enumerable, then so is the set of finitely-valid, $R$-free sentences of $\mathcal{L}$.

By Trahtenbrot's Theorem (see Ebbinghaus, Flum and Thomas, 1984, X.5.4), there is a finite language $\mathcal{L}_0$ not containing $R$ such that the set of finitely valid sentences of $\mathcal{L}_0$ is not recursively enumerable. Let $\mathcal{L}$ have the vocabulary of $\mathcal{L}_0$ along with $R$. It follows from (27) that the $b$-valid subset of $\mathcal{L}^+$ is not recursively enumerable. ∎

(28) COROLLARY: Let language $\mathcal{L}$ contain at least one binary relation symbol. Then for every $b \in (0, 1)$ the relation $\models_b$ is not compact for $\mathcal{L}^+$.

PROOF: Let $\Omega$ be the conjunction of (23) – (25). Define:

$$\varphi_n = \exists x_1 \ldots \exists x_n \bigwedge_{1 \leq i < j \leq n} x_i \neq x_j$$

Let $\Sigma = \{\Omega\} \cup \{\varphi_n | n \in N\}$. By Lemma (26)b, for all $b \in (0, 1)$, every finite subset of $\Sigma$ is $b$-satisfiable. But by Lemma (26)a, $\Sigma$ is $b$-satisfiable for no $b \in (0, 1)$. ∎

# 4   Some inductive logic of approximate truth

The present section is devoted to a paradigm of empirical inquiry that may be called "probably approximately correct truth detection." Within this paradigm scientists convert a given first-order sentence $\theta$ along with accuracy and reliability parameters $b$,$c$ into a set of queries. The queries bear on the interpretation of predicates within a fixed but unknown structure $\mathcal{S}$. Illustrating with a unary predicate $A$, these queries take the form:

Does the $n$th randomly sampled point from the domain of $\mathcal{S}$ fall into the $\mathcal{S}$-extension of $A$?

The scientist has no knowledge of the probability distribution that governs random sampling from $\mathcal{S}$'s domain. On the basis of a set of queries whose size grows no faster than polynomially in $\frac{1}{b}$ and $\frac{1}{c}$ the scientist must emit, with reliability at least $1-c$, a $b$-truth-value for $\theta$ in $\mathcal{S}$. In Osherson, Stob & Weinstein (1988) we show that there are formal scientists who succeed in this task with respect to a wide class of first-order sentences and structures.

Our paradigm is inspired by the research of Valiant (1984) and Blumer et al. (1987). However, the present model differs from earlier ones inasmuch as scientists are here required to judge the approximate truth of a given sentence, rather than to hypothesize a set that approximately matches some unknown target.

Before giving details, it might be helpful to describe informally the *dramatis personae* of our paradigm. Scientists are conceived as comprising a pair of agents, namely:

- an experimenter, who reacts to a research question by proposing an experimental design;

- a theorist, who interprets the results of the experiment.

The interaction between scientists and their environments may be described in the following terms. Nature fixes the external environment in the form of an unknown structure $\mathcal{S}=(D,d,P,\alpha_{\mathcal{S}})$. A research objective is then defined, of the form: determine with reliability $1-c$ whether a given sentence $\theta$ is $b$-true in $\mathcal{S}$. Next, an experimenter and a theorist are selected. The experimenter proposes a research design in which a finite number of tuples are drawn randomly from $D$ according to $P$. Each tuple $\sigma$ is associated with a question of the form: "Is $\sigma$ a member of $\alpha_{\mathcal{S}}(A)$?" where $A$ occurs in $\theta$. On the basis of the answers that the environment provides to these queries, the theorist claims either that $\theta$ is $b$-true or that $\theta$ is $b$-false in $\mathcal{S}$.

After formally specifying this paradigm, we present a result about the class of sentences that can be successfully investigated. For the remainder of this section let (nonmodal) language $\mathcal{L}$ be fixed.

## 4.1   Probably approximately correct truth detection

(29) DEFINITION: Let $\theta \in \mathcal{L}$ and $b,c \in (0,1)$ be given. By a *design for $\theta,b,c$* is meant a finite set of quintuples of the form $(\theta,b,c,A,\sigma)$ where $A$ is a relation symbol occurring in $\theta$ and $\sigma \in N^{\text{arity}(A)}$. By a *design* is meant a design for some $\theta,b,c$.

To see the motivation behind the definition, suppose that structure $\mathcal{S}=(D,d,P,\alpha_{\mathcal{S}})$ is the situation under investigation, and conceive of $h \in D^\omega$ as an infinite sequence of independent random draws from $D$ according to $P$. Then, an element $(\theta,b,c,A,(i_1\ldots i_n))$ of a design breaks into two parts: $\theta,b,c$ and $A,(i_1\ldots i_n)$. $\theta,b,c$ represents a research objective, namely, to determine with reliability greater than $1-c$ whether $\theta$ is $b$-true or $b$-false in $\mathcal{S}$. $A,(i_1\ldots i_n)$ represents the query "$(h(i_1)\ldots h(i_n)) \in \alpha_{\mathcal{S}}(A)$?"

(30) DEFINITION: An *experimenter* is any mapping $E$ of $\mathcal{L} \times (0,1)^2$ into the class of designs such that for all $\theta, b, c \in \mathcal{L} \times (0,1)^2$, $E(\theta, b, c)$ is a design for $\theta, b, c$.

The number of quintuples in a design $\Delta$ is a reasonable measure of its "cost." This number will be denoted by $|\Delta|$.

We now consider the environment's response to the design proposed by an experimenter.

(31) DEFINITION: Let $\theta \in \mathcal{L}$ and $b, c \in (0,1)$ be given. By a *completed design for* $\theta, b, c$ is meant a finite set of sextuples of the form $(\theta, b, c, A, \sigma, Z)$, where $A$ is a relation symbol occurring in $\theta$, $\sigma \in N^{\mathrm{arity}(A)}$, and $Z \in \{\mathrm{yes, no}\}$. By a *completed design* is meant a completed design for some $\theta, b, c$.

Member $(\theta, b, c, A, \sigma, Z)$ of a completed design is just a design element $(\theta, b, c, A, \sigma)$ paired with the answer $Z$ to the query represented by $A, \sigma$. Given design $\Delta$ and structure $\mathcal{S}$ with associated random sequence $h$, there is exactly one completed design that represents the responses provided by $\mathcal{S}$ and $h$ to the queries in $\Delta$. To state this idea precisely, we rely on the following notation. Given $\sigma = (i_1 \ldots i_n) \in N^n$ and $h \in D^\omega$, we denote $(h(i_1) \ldots h(i_n)) \in D^m$ by $h(\sigma)$.

(32) DEFINITION: Let $\mathcal{S} = (D, d, P, \alpha_\mathcal{S})$ be a structure. Let $h \in D^\omega$ be given. We denote by $\mathcal{S}_h$ the following mapping of the class of designs into the class of completed designs. Given design $\Delta$, $\mathcal{S}_h(\Delta)$ is the set of sextuples of form $(\theta, b, c, A, \sigma, Z)$, where

(a) $(\theta, b, c, A, \sigma) \in \Delta$,

(b) $Z = $ yes if $h(\sigma) \in \alpha_\mathcal{S}(A)$; $= $ no otherwise.

The function $\mathcal{S}_h$ represents the environment that provides data to the scientist.

(33) DEFINITION: A *theorist* is any mapping of the class of completed designs into the set $\{\mathrm{true, false}\}$. A *scientist* is any pair $(T, E)$ where $T$ is a theorist and $E$ is an experimenter.

Thus, given scientist $(T, E)$, structure $\mathcal{S}$, random sequence $h$, and research objective $\theta, b, c$, the expression $T(\mathcal{S}_h(E(\theta, b, c)))$ may be understood as denoting the approximate truth-value that $T$ hypothesizes upon examining the response given by the environment $\mathcal{S}_h$ to the design that $E$ proposes for the research objective $\theta, b, c$.

Having characterized scientists, environments, and their interaction, we turn now to the sense in which a scientist can be credited with the ability to infer the approximate truth-value of a sentence.

(34) DEFINITION: Let scientist $(T, E)$, sentence $\theta \in \mathcal{L}$, and collection **K** of structures be given.

(a) $(T, E)$ *infers* $\theta$ *in* **K** just in case for all $\mathcal{S} = (D, d, P, \alpha_\mathcal{S}) \in$ **K** and all $b, c \in (0,1)$, there is measurable $H \subseteq D^\omega$ such that:

i. $P(H) > 1 - c$;

ii. for every $h \in H$, if $T(\mathcal{S}_h(E(\theta, b, c))) =$ true then $\theta$ is $b$-true in $\mathcal{S}$, and if $T(\mathcal{S}_h(E(\theta, b, c))) =$ false then $\theta$ is $b$-false in $\mathcal{S}$.

(b) $(T, E)$ *polynomially infers* $\theta$ *in* **K** just in case:

i. $(T, E)$ infers $\theta$ in **K**;

ii. there is a polynomial function $p : \Re^2 \to \Re$ such that for all $b, c \in (0, 1)$, $|E(\theta, b, c)| \leq p(\frac{1}{b}, \frac{1}{c})$.

(c) Let $\Sigma$ be a set of $\mathcal{L}$-sentences. $\Sigma$ is *polynomially inferable in* **K** just in case there is a scientist $(T, E)$ that polynomially infers every $\theta \in \Sigma$ in **K**.

Note that clause (a)ii is not equivalent to: $T(\mathcal{S}_h(E(\theta, b, c))) =$ true iff $\theta$ is $b$-true in $\mathcal{S}$. In the special case where $\theta$ is both $b$-true and $b$-false in $\mathcal{S}$, clause (a)ii is satisfied whether $T(\mathcal{S}_h(E(\theta, b, c))) =$ true or $T(\mathcal{S}_h(E(\theta, b, c))) =$ false.

## 4.2   A theorem about inferability

We now state a theorem affirming that the monotone sentences (see Definition (20)) are polynomially inferable in a wide class of structures. The structures in question meet both clauses of the following definition.

(35) DEFINITION: Let structure $\mathcal{S} = (D, d, P, \alpha_{\mathcal{S}})$ be given.

(a) $\mathcal{S}$ is *continuous* just in case for all $e \in D$ and $p \in [0, 1)$ there is a ball $B(e, r)$ such that $P(B(e, r)) = p$.

(b) $\mathcal{S}$ is *measurable* just in case for all relation symbols $A$ in $\mathcal{L}$, $\alpha_{\mathcal{S}}(A)$ is measurable (with respect to $P$).

(36) THEOREM: The set of monotone sentences is polynomially inferable in the class of continuous, measurable structures.

Theorem (36) is proved in Osherson, Stob & Weinstein (1988) by exhibiting a scientist $(T, E)$ that witnesses it. $T$ and $E$ are constructed in a natural way, which we illustrate with the sentence $\theta = \forall x \exists y A x y$. In response to $\theta, b, c$, $E$ proposes a design which amounts to the following procedure. Draw points $x_1 \ldots x_n$ (independently from the unknown structure $\mathcal{S} = (D, d, P, \alpha_{\mathcal{S}})$ according to the probability distribution $P$); to each sampled point $x_i$ associate newly sampled points $y_{i1} \ldots y_{im}$. The completed design resulting from $E(\theta, b, c)$ thus consists of the answers to the queries "$(x_i, y_{ij}) \in \alpha_{\mathcal{S}}(A)$". The theorist $T$ returns "true" in response to such a completed design just in case for every $x_i$ there is a $y_{ij}$ with $(x_i, y_{ij}) \in \alpha_{\mathcal{S}}(A)$; $T$ returns "false" otherwise. The delicate part of the proof is showing that $n$ and $m$ (and hence the number $nm$ of queries) can be chosen polynomially in $\frac{1}{b}$ and $\frac{1}{c}$. The proof is by induction on the quantifier complexity of $\theta$. We show also that $T$ and $E$ are computable in their arguments, that $T$ can be programmed to run in time linear in the size of its input, and that $E$ can be programmed to run in time polynomial in $\frac{1}{b}$ and $\frac{1}{c}$. Though the number of queries is polynomial in $\frac{1}{b}$ and $\frac{1}{c}$ for fixed $\theta$, the number of queries required by the $E$ of our proof grows exponentially in the quantifier-complexity of the sentence under examination.

# 5    Stable predicates

In certain applications, approximation is tolerable with respect to some predicates but not others. For example, in a chemical setting, we might take a sentence involving the predicate "is an acid" to be $b$-true in a structure $\mathcal{S}$ only if there is a $b$-variant of $\mathcal{S}$ in which this predicate has the same extension as in $\mathcal{S}$. More generally, we may distinguish "stable" from "varying" subsets of the vocabulary of $\mathcal{L}$, and define $b$-variance between structures in such a way as to preserve the extensions of all stable predicates. Note that our present definitions already ensure that $=$ counts as stable (see Definition (2)).

To investigate stability, we partition the vocabulary of $\mathcal{L}$ into three sets:

$\mathcal{L}_V$: the varying relation symbols, whose extensions may shift in an approximating structure;

$\mathcal{L}_S$: the stable relation symbols, whose extensions do not change in approximating structures;

$\{=\}$: the equals sign, which is always interpreted as identity.

In the context of stable vocabulary, $b$-approximation between structures is defined as follows.

(37)  DEFINITION: Let $b \in (0, 1)$ and structures $\mathcal{S}$ and $\mathcal{U}$ be given. $\mathcal{U}$ is a *b-variant of* $\mathcal{S}$ just in case

   (a)  $\mathcal{S}$ and $\mathcal{U}$ have the forms $\mathcal{S}=(D, d, P, \alpha_{\mathcal{S}})$, $\mathcal{U}=(D, d, P, \alpha_{\mathcal{U}})$ (hence $\delta_{\mathcal{S}} = \delta_{\mathcal{U}}$);

   (b)  for every relation symbol $A \in \mathcal{L}_V$ and every $\bar{u} \in D^{\mathrm{arity}(A)}$ there is $\bar{s} \in D^{\mathrm{arity}(A)}$ such that

      i.  $\delta_{\mathcal{S}}(\bar{u}, \bar{s}) < b$

      ii.  $\bar{u} \in \alpha_{\mathcal{U}}(A)$ iff $\bar{s} \in \alpha_{\mathcal{S}}(A)$.

   (c)  for every relation symbol $C \in \mathcal{L}_S$, $\alpha_{\mathcal{U}}(C) = \alpha_{\mathcal{S}}(C)$.

It is easy to see that no result about inductive inference as general as Theorem (36) is possible in the presence of stable vocabulary. Rather, additional assumptions must be made about the structures serving as environments. One kind of assumption is embodied in the following definition. To state the definition we henceforth assume that $C$ is a distinguished, unary relation symbol belonging to $\mathcal{L}_S$.

(38) DEFINITION: Let $a \in (0,1)$, and structure $S$ be given.

(a) $S$ is *a-round* just in case for all $e \in D$ there is a ball $B$ such that:

    i. $e \in B$;

    ii. $P(B) \geq a$;

    iii. if $e \in \alpha_S(C)$ then $B \subseteq \alpha_S(C)$;

    iv. if $e \in \alpha_S(C)^c$ then $B \subseteq \alpha_S(C)^c$.

(b) A collection **K** of structures is *round* just in case there is $a \in (0,1)$ such that every $S \in \mathbf{K}$ is $a$-round.

Thus, a structure is round if every member of $C$'s extension is contained in a ball within the extension, and likewise for the extension's complement. Call $\theta \in \mathcal{L}$ *regular* just in case $\theta$ contains a single occurrence of $C$ and a single occurence of just one relation symbol in $\mathcal{L}_V$. By adapting the proof of Theorem (36), the following result is obtained.

(39) THEOREM: The set of regular sentences is polynomially inferable in any round collection of continuous, measurable structures.

# 6    Concluding remarks

The foregoing definitions may be modified in several directions, yielding alternative theories of approximate truth and new theorems about their deductive and inductive logic. To illustrate, for some applications of the theory, Example (19) might prompt a revision in the definition of $b$-variance, to ensure that $\forall x A x$ does not count as $b$-true in a structure in which the extension of $A$ is sparse but dense in the domain. A straightforward means to this end is to require the extensions of predicates in an approximating structure to largely overlap the orginal extension. The following, two-parameter version of the variance concept formalizes this idea. Given sets $X$ and $Y$ of the same arity, we use $X \oplus Y$ to denote the symmetric difference of $X$ and $Y$, i.e., $(X - Y) \cup (Y - X)$.

(40) DEFINITION: Let $a,b \in (0,1)$ and structures $S$ and $\mathcal{U}$ be given. $\mathcal{U}$ is an *a, b-variant of* $S$ just in case

(a) $\mathcal{U}$ is a $b$-variant of $S$ (hence, $\mathcal{U}$ and $S$ have common probability distribution P);

(b) for every relation symbol $A$ in $\mathcal{L}$, $P(\alpha_{\mathcal{U}}(A) \oplus \alpha_S(A)) < a$.

Sentence $\theta \in \mathcal{L}$ is *a, b-true* in structure $S$ just in case $\theta$ is true in some $a, b$-variant of $S$; similarly for $a, b$-falsity. It is straightforward to reformulate the definition of polynomial inferability so that it incorporates both the weight parameter $a$ and the distance parameter $b$. A polynomial inferability result parallel to Theorem (36) can be demonstrated within this extended theory (we do not provide details).

Other modifications of the theory involve:

- changes in the questions that experimenters are allowed to ask of the environment;

- alternative measures of the cost of a design;

- different definitions of probability distance; and

- introduction of vocabulary with fixed interpretation in all structures (as $=$ is fixed).

Such modifications can be considered separately or in combinations.

# 7 References

Blumer, A., A. Ehrenfeucht, D. Haussler, M. Warmuth (1987) "Learnability and the Vapnik-Chervonenkis dimension", Technical Report UCSC-CRL-87-20, U. C. Santa Cruz.

Ebbinghaus, H., Flum, J. and Thomas, W. (1984) *Mathematical Logic*, New York: Springer-Verlag.

Halmos, P. (1950) *Measure Theory*, Van Nostrand.

Lakoff, G. (1987) *Women, Fire, and Dangerous Things*, Chicago: University of Chicago Press.

Osherson, D., M. Stob, S. Weinstein (1988) "A theory of approximate truth", manuscript.

Peirce, C. (1958) *Selected Writings*, New York: Dover.

Popper, K. (1963) *Conjectures and Refutations*, London: Routledge and Kegan Paul.

Rescher, N. (1960) *Many-valued Logic*, New York: McGraw-Hill.

Valiant, L. (1984) "A theory of the learnable", *Comm. ACM*, 27(11), pp. 1134–1142.

Zadeh, L. (1965) "Fuzzy sets", *Information and Control* 8:338-53.

# Informed parsimonious inference
# of prototypical genetic sequences

Aleksandar Milosavljević
Baskin Center for Computer Engineering and Information Sciences
University of California at Santa Cruz, CA 95064

David Haussler
Baskin Center for Computer Engineering and Information Sciences
University of California at Santa Cruz, CA 95064

Jerzy Jurka
Linus Pauling Institute of Science and Medicine
440 Page Mill Rd., Palo Alto, CA 94306

### Abstract

Informed Parsimonious inference (IP) generalizes the *compatibility* and *weighted parsimony* methods, which are most often applied in biology. IP is successfully applied to infer classes of genetic sequences that are accepted by biologists. IP falls into the categories of Bayesian and Minimum Description Length methods. The biological assumptions that underly inductive inference are expressed in the form of an encoding scheme. A local search strategy is then applied to find a theory that minimizes the number of bits that are needed to encode the observations under the encoding scheme.

## 1 Introduction

Inductive assumptions (background knowledge, inductive bias) are necessary for inductive inference in biology. There are at least two practical reasons for making them explicit in our learning programs. (1) Consistency. If two programs infer two different theories from the same sample, the difference should be traceable to the different assumptions that are built into these programs; otherwise a biologist would not have any rational basis to decide between them. (2) Decoupling. The work of the biologist and that of the computer scientist should be decoupled. One way to achieve this is to have an engine for inductive inference that has two inputs: the first, biological data, and the second, biological assumptions that underly inference. The goal of the computer scientist is then to make the inference engine that could accommodate the largest possible range of data and assumptions within the computational constraints. This allows the biologist to run the program on the same data under different assumptions.

Parsimony methods have been used in biology for decades [8]. Many kinds of ad-hoc parsimony criteria have been proposed by biologists; they are typically based on a set of implicit biological assumptions and they perform well on the data for which the assumptions are valid.

The Informed Parsimony (IP) method introduced here generalizes the two most widely used biological parsimony methods, the compatibility method and the weighted parsimony method [7]. IP provides means for using, in an explicit way, a variety of very specific inductive assumptions about genetic sequences. The assumptions are expressed in the form of an encoding scheme for sets of sequences. This encoding scheme incorporates a theory about prototypical ancestors from which the sequences are derived by a mutation or noise process. The most plausible theory can be defined as the theory that achieves the minimum length encoding of a given set of sequences under the encoding scheme.

IP falls into the categories of Minimum Description Length (MDL) and Bayesian methods. MDL methods were pioneered by Solomonoff [21]. Solomonoff also pointed out the relation between Bayesian and MDL methods. Kolmogorov [14] proposes description length as a measure of quantity of information; he suggests the application of this principle to genetics. Wallace and Boulton [23] apply the MDL method to the classification problem. Rissanen [18] and Hart [10] apply description length as a universal criterion for estimation; MDL methods are used not only to estimate the parameters of a model with predefined structure but to infer the structure itself; they are also used to infer the optimal precision for quoting the estimates of real-valued parameters [22]. Several approaches to image analysis are based on the MDL principle [10] [20]. Quinlan and Rivest [17] apply this principle to obtain the best "pruning" of a decision tree. Georgeff and Wallace [9] propose description length as the selection criterion for inductive inference. Cheeseman [3] and Rivest [19] discuss the relation of the MDL method to Bayesian inference.

## 2    Model of sequence generation

A *sample* $S$ consists of $m$ aligned sequences $(S_1, \ldots, S_i, \ldots, S_m)$. Each sequence $S_i$ consists of $n$ letters. Since the sequences are aligned, a position in a sequence can be regarded as an attribute and the letter in that position can be regarded as the value of that attribute. However, in this paper we will use the term "position" instead of "attribute" because the order in which the letters appear does play a role in inference; for example, whether a letter in a certain position is likely to be "noisy" may depend on the adjacent letters. The letters come from a finite alphabet $\Gamma$ of size $|\Gamma| = g$. In the case of DNA-sequences, the alphabet is $\{A, G, C, T\}$, representing the four nucleotides that form DNA, while in the case of proteins the alphabet contains twenty letters representing amino acids. By $\mathcal{S}(m, n, \Gamma)$ we denote the set of all samples of $m$ sequences of length $n$ over the alphabet $\Gamma$.

A *pool of prototypes* $\theta$ consists of prototypical sequences $(\theta_1, \ldots, \theta_i, \ldots, \theta_k)$, where each $\theta_i$ is a sequence of $n$ letters from $\Gamma$. While a pool of prototypes has the same form as a sample, its meaning is different; a prototype is used to represent the common ancestor of the sequences from a particular class.

The basic assumptions that underly inference of prototypical sequences are represented by the randomized procedures Creator and Nature in Figure 1. A pool of prototypes is produced by the procedure Creator; a sample is then produced from the pool by the procedure Nature.

Procedures Creator and Nature contain independent random steps (A), (B), (C), (D), and (E), each beginning with the word "pick". We assume that each of these steps represents

Procedure Creator()
    pick the number of prototypes $k$ from $\{1, \ldots, m\}$;               (A)
    for $j := 1, \ldots, k$
        for $l := 1, \ldots, n$
            $\text{pick}_{j,l}$ the $l$-th letter of the $j$-th prototype $\theta_{j,l}$ from $\Gamma$;    (B)
        $\theta_j := (\theta_{j,1}, \ldots, \theta_{j,n})$;
    $\theta := (\theta_1, \ldots, \theta_k)$;
    return $(k, \theta)$.


Procedure Nature$_i(k, \theta)$
    pick the index $c(i)$ of the ancestral prototype
        of the $i$-th sequence from $\{1, \ldots, k\}$;              (C)
    for $l := 1, \ldots, n$
        $\text{pick}_{c(i),l}$ the mutation flag $p$ for the $l$-th position
            of the $i$-th sequence from $\{noisy, not\_noisy\}$;    (D)
        if $(p = noisy)$ then
            $\text{pick}_{c(i),l}$ the replacement letter $S_{i,l}$ for the $l$-th position
                of the $i$-th sequence from $\Gamma - \{\theta_{c(i),l}\}$ ;    (E)
        else
            $S_{i,l} := \theta_{c(i),l}$;
    $S_i := (S_{i,1}, \ldots, S_{i,n})$;
    return $(S_i)$.


$(k, \theta) := \text{Creator}()$;
for $i := 1, \ldots, m$
    $S_i := \text{Nature}_i (k, \theta)$;
$S := (S_1, \ldots, S_m)$;
return $(S)$.

Figure 1: Model of sequence generation

independent random draws from underlying distributions $P^{(A)}$, $P^{(B)}$, $P^{(C)}$, $P^{(D)}$, and $P^{(E)}$, respectively. However, in the steps (B), (D), and (E) there is a (possibly) different distribution associated with each position in each prototype. Hence $P^{(B)}$ actually represents a two dimensional array of distributions $P_{j,l}^{(B)}$, $1 \leq j \leq k$ and $1 \leq l \leq n$, and similarly for $P^{(D)}$ and $P^{(E)}$. The notation "pick$_{j,l}$" in step (B) indicates an independent random draw from $P_{j,l}^{(B)}$; similar notation is used in steps (D) and (E).

Procedure Creator first chooses the number $k$ of prototypes by drawing from the distribution $P^{(A)}$ over the numbers $\{1, \ldots, m\}$. The upper bound $m$ is equal to the number of sequences in our sample, i.e. we assume *a priori* that the number of prototypes is less than or equal the number of sequences in the sample. Next, a pool of prototypes $\theta$ is chosen, letter by letter. Here pick$_{j,l}$ chooses the l-th letter of the j-th prototype, denoted $\theta_{j,l}$, using the distribution $P_{j,l}^{(B)}$ over $\Gamma$.

Procedure Nature then generates the sample from the pool produced by Creator. To generate a sequence in the sample, an ancestral prototype is chosen from the pool of prototypes using the distribution $P^{(C)}$ over the numbers $\{1, \ldots, k\}$. Then a mutational process is applied to this prototype. For each position in the prototype a coin is flipped to determine if the letter in this position will be replaced. If it is the $j$-th prototype, the decision for the $l$-th position is made according to the distribution $P_{j,l}^{(D)}$ over the two values $\{noisy, not - noisy\}$. If *noisy* is chosen, then the replacement letter is chosen from the distribution $P_{j,l}^{(E)}$ over the possible replacement letters.

For a given sample $S$ from $\mathcal{S}(m, n, \Gamma)$ that is produced by procedure Nature the task is to infer the input to Nature, which consists of the number of prototypes $k$ and a pool $\theta$ of $k$ prototypes $(\theta_1, \ldots, \theta_i, \ldots, \theta_k)$. Unless they are specified in advance, the probability distributions $P^{(C)}, P^{(D)}$, and $P^{(E)}$ that govern the random steps of Nature are also to be inferred from the sample. A *theory* $T$ consists of an input to procedure Nature and the probability distributions that govern its random steps; formally, a theory $T = (k, \theta, P^{(C)}, P^{(D)}, P^{(E)})$. By $\mathcal{T}(m, n, \Gamma)$ we denote the set of all such theories.

Consider a theory that has $m$ prototypes that are identical to the sequences from the sample. While such a theory does eliminate noise from observations, the explanation it offers may be too complex for the data at hand. In the other extreme case, a theory may propose a single prototype. While such a theory is the simplest possible, it may not explain the data well; i.e., many sequences may differ greatly from the prototype. Clearly, a tradeoff occurs between the complexity of the inferred theory and its accuracy in describing the data.

# 3　Bayes model

We now formalize the tradeoff between the complexity of the inferred theory and its accuracy in describing the data. Let the function $I(.) : \mathcal{T}(m, n, \Gamma) \to R^+$, where $R^+$ denotes the positive real numbers, measure the complexity of a theory. Let the function $I(S|.) : \mathcal{T}(m, n, \Gamma) \to R^+$ measure the complexity of the description of a sample $S$ by a theory. To describe the whole sample, we first describe the theory and then describe the sample, given the theory. Thus the total complexity of a sample $S$, as described by theory $T$, is the sum

$$I(S,T) = I(T) + I(S|T) \qquad (1)$$

Given sample $S$ from $\mathcal{S}(m,n,\Gamma)$, a *parsimonious learning function* $L$ returns a theory $T$ from $\mathcal{T}(m,n,\Gamma)$ that minimizes $I(S,T)$. Any particular definition of the measures $I(T)$ and $I(S|T)$ yields a particular parsimonious learning function.

One way to define $I(T)$ and $I(S|T)$ is to fix a binary encoding scheme for theories, and for each theory, a binary encoding scheme for samples relative to that theory. We then define $I(T)$ to be the number of bits in the (shortest) encoding of $T$ and $I(S|T)$ to be the number of bits in the (shortest) encoding of $S$ relative to $T$.

Another way to define $I(T)$ and $I(S|T)$ is to postulate two probabilistic processes; the first process selects a "law of Nature" while the second generates a sample, given the "law of Nature"; e.g. procedures Creator and Nature that are described above. For a theory $T$ and a sample $S$, let $P(T)$ denote the a priori probability of the "law of Nature" that is described by the theory $T$ and $P(S|T)$ denote the probability of $S$ given $T$. Now, let

$$I(T) = -\log P(T) \qquad (2)$$

and

$$I(S|T) = -\log P(S|T). \qquad (3)$$

From (2) it follows that the lower the complexity $I(T)$ of a theory $T$, the higher its a priori probability $P(T)$; this is a formal version of the principle of Occam's Razor. From (3) it follows that the smaller the complexity $I(S|T)$ the larger the likelihood $P(S|T)$ of the theory $T$; in other words, the theory that fits the data better has higher likelihood.

By substituting (2) and (3) into (1) we obtain

$$I(S,T) = -\log(P(T)P(S|T)) = -\log P(S,T), \qquad (4)$$

where $P(S,T)$ is the joint probability of $S$ and $T$. Hence, the theory that minimizes the total complexity $I(S,T)$ is the same one that maximizes the joint probability $P(S,T)$. Since $P(S,T) = P(T|S)P(S)$, where $P(S)$ is fixed, the same theory also maximizes $P(T|S)$, the a posteriori probability of $T$ given $S$. Hence, this method of defining $I(T)$ and $I(S|T)$ reduces the parsimony method to the standard Bayesian method [3]. If we define $I(T) = 0$ then parsimony method reduces to the maximum likelihood method [4].

Since it is most convenient for a biologist to represent certain assumptions about how sequences are generated directly in a probabilistic model, we will derive $I(T)$ and $I(S|T)$ from $P(T)$ and $P(S|T)$, respectively, rather than defining them by postulating an encoding scheme. The form of the resulting measures $I(T)$ and $I(S|T)$ sheds further light on the nature of the assumptions being made, and is very convenient from a computational point of view. In essence, we "compile" a Bayesian-style probabilistic model into an encoding scheme for samples, which will then be the basis for our IP method.

## 4  Expressing the inductive assumptions

Our basic assumption is that procedures Creator and Nature (Figure 1) define the probabilities $P(T)$ and $P(S|T)$ and, by (2) and (3), the complexities $I(T)$ and $I(S|T)$. (We will later see that the structure of the randomized procedure Nature may have to be changed to account for some more specific biological assumptions.) While the structure of the randomized procedures must be specified in advance, the distributions that govern the random steps may be either specified in advance or they may be inferred from data.

Recall that a theory consists of five parts, $T = (k, \theta, P^{(C)}, P^{(D)}, P^{(E)})$. The probability $P(T)$ of a theory $T$ is then given by

$$P(T) = P^{(A)}(k) \prod_{j=1}^{k} \prod_{l=1}^{n} [P_{j,l}^{(B)}(\theta_{j,l})] P(P^{(C)}, P^{(D)}, P^{(E)}) \tag{5}$$

where $P(P^{(C)}, P^{(D)}, P^{(E)})$ denotes the probability that the distributions $P^{(C)}, P^{(D)}$, and $P^{(E)}$ govern the random steps in the procedure Nature.

We assume that any number of prototypes is equally likely, i.e. $P^{(A)}(k) = 1/m$ for any k, where $1 \leq k \leq m$ and that the probability distributions $P_{j,l}^{(B)}$ that govern the choice of the letters in prototypes are identical for $1 \leq j \leq k$ and $1 \leq l \leq n$. By applying (2), we then obtain

$$I(T) = \log m + kn \sum_{x \in \Gamma} -\frac{n(x)}{kn} \log P^{(B)}(x) - \log P(P^{(C)}, P^{(D)}, P^{(E)}) \tag{6}$$

where by $n(x)$ we denote the number of occurrences of the letter $x$ in the pool $\theta$. We note that the sum in the middle term represents the cross entropy between the empirical distribution $(\frac{n(x_1)}{kn}, ..., \frac{n(x_g)}{kn})$, where $x_i, 1 \leq i \leq g$ are the letters from the alphabet $\Gamma$, and the distribution $P^{(B)}$.

One way to define this term is to specify the distribution $P^{(B)}$ in advance; for example letter "T" is known to be less likely to occur than "A", "C", or "G" in Alu sequences. Another way is to estimate $P^{(B)}(x)$ by empirical frequencies $\frac{n(x)}{kn}$; the middle term of (6) then becomes $kn\hat{H}^{(B)}$, where by $\hat{H}^{(B)} = \sum_{x \in \Gamma} -\frac{n(x)}{kn} \log \frac{n(x)}{kn}$ we denote the empirical estimate of entropy. For simplicity, in this paper we assume that $P^{(B)}$ is specified in advance to be uniform, which is equivalent to specifying $\hat{H}^{(B)} = \log g$, where $g$ is the size of the alphabet. Then we obtain

$$\hat{I}(T) = \log m + kn \log g + h(m, n, g, k) \tag{7}$$

This expression has a simple direct interpretation as a code length; the first term is the number of bits to encode the number of prototypes; the second term is the number of bits to encode, letter by letter, the pool of prototypes $\theta$. The last term, $h(m, n, g, k) = -\log P(P^{(C)}, P^{(D)}, P^{(E)})$, represents the number of bits to encode the distributions $P^{(C)}, P^{(D)}$, and $P^{(E)}$.

To derive the formula for $\hat{I}(S|T)$ by (3), we first need to derive a formula for the estimate $\hat{P}(S|T)$. Given a theory $T$, the probability $P(S_i|T)$ of a sequence $S_i$ from $S$ is given by

$$
\begin{aligned}
P(S_i|T) &= \sum_{j=1}^{k} P(S_i|S_i \text{ is derived from } \theta_j) P^{(C)}(j) \\
&= \sum_{j=1}^{k} [\prod_{l=1}^{n} P(S_{i,l}|S_i \text{ is derived from } \theta_j)] P^{(C)}(j)
\end{aligned} \tag{8}
$$

Let $p_{j,l} = P_{j,l}^{(D)}(noisy)$ be the probability that there is a mutation in the $l$-th position of the $j$-th prototype. Then

$$P(S_{i,l}|S_i \text{ is derived from } \theta_j) = \begin{cases} 1 - p_{j,l} & if\ S_{i,l} = \theta_{j,l} \\ p_{j,l}P^{(E)}(S_{i,l}) & otherwise \end{cases} \tag{9}$$

To write this in a more concise form we introduce the following function that indicates mutations. For all $1 \le i \le m$, $1 \le j \le k$, and $1 \le l \le n$ let

$$\Delta_{i,j,l} = \begin{cases} 0 & if\ S_{i,l} = \theta_{j,l} \\ 1 & otherwise \end{cases} \tag{10}$$

Then

$$P(S_{i,l}|S_i \text{ is derived from } \theta_j) = (1 - p_{j,l})^{1-\Delta_{i,j,l}}(p_{j,l}P_{j,l}^{(E)}(S_{i,l}))^{\Delta_{i,j,l}} \tag{11}$$

Hence

$$P(S_i|T) = \sum_{j=1}^{k} [\prod_{l=1}^{n} (1 - p_{j,l})^{1-\Delta_{i,j,l}}(p_{j,l}P_{j,l}^{(E)}(S_{i,l}))^{\Delta_{i,j,l}} P^{(C)}(j)] \tag{12}$$

Typically, this sum contains a single dominant term; in other words, for each sequence there is a prototype that is much more likely to have generated it than any other prototype from the pool. Let $c(i)$, where $1 \le i \le m$, denote the index of the prototype that is the most likely ancestor of $S_i$. Then we can write

$$P(S_i|T) \approx \prod_{l=1}^{m} (1 - p_{c(i),l})^{1-\Delta_{i,c(i),l}}(p_{c(i),l}P_{c(i),l}^{(E)}(S_{i,l}))^{\Delta_{i,c(i),l}} P^{(C)}(c(i)) \tag{13}$$

Finally, we have

$$P(S|T) = \prod_{i=1}^{m} P(S_i|T) \tag{14}$$

By substituting (13) into (14) and by applying (3), we obtain

$$\begin{aligned} I(S|T) \approx\ & \sum_{i=1}^{m} -log(P^{(C)}(c(i))) + \\ & \sum_{i=1}^{m}\sum_{l=1}^{n}[-\Delta_{i,c(i),l}\log p_{c(i),l} - (1 - \Delta_{i,c(i),l})\log(1 - p_{c(i),l})] + \\ & \sum_{i=1}^{m}\sum_{l=1}^{n}[-\Delta_{i,c(i),l}\log P_{c(i),l}^{(E)}(S_{i,l})] \end{aligned} \tag{15}$$

We now discuss the three terms of this expression in more detail. The result will be a much simpler formula with a straightforward interpretation.

Towards that goal, let $m_j$ denote the number of sequences that are assigned to the $j-th$ prototype by the classification $c(i)$. Then the first term of (15) can be rewritten as

$$m \sum_{j=1}^{k} -\frac{m_j}{m} \log P^{(C)}(j) \qquad (16)$$

We note that the sum represents the cross entropy between the empirical distribution $(\frac{m_1}{m}, ..., \frac{m_k}{m})$ and the distribution $P^{(C)}$. One way is to define this term is to specify the distribution $P^{(C)}$ in advance; for example, we may specify in advance that the ancestral prototypes are picked uniformly at random. However, in this paper we estimate the distribution $P^{(C)}$ by empirical frequencies $\frac{m_j}{m}$; in this case, (16) becomes $m\hat{H}^{(C)}$, where by $\hat{H}^{(C)} = -\sum_{j=1}^{k}(\frac{m_j}{m})\log(\frac{m_j}{m})$, we denote the empirical estimate of entropy.

Now let $\Delta_{j,l}$ be the total number of mutations of the $l$-th letter of the $j$-th prototype and let $f_{j,l} = \frac{\Delta_{j,l}}{m_j}$ be the frequency of mutations. Then the second term of (15) can be rewritten as

$$\sum_{j=1}^{k} m_j \sum_{l=1}^{n}[-f_{j,l} \log p_{j,l} - (1 - f_{j,l}) \log(1 - p_{j,l})] \qquad (17)$$

We note that each element of the inner sum represents the cross entropy between the empirical distribution $(f_{j,l}, (1 - f_{j,l}))$ and the distribution $P_{j,l}^{(D)}$. One way to define this term is to specify the distributions $P_{j,l}^{(D)}$ in advance; for example we may know in advance the positions that are noisy and the ones that are well preserved within the classes. However, in this paper we estimate the distribution $P_{j,l}^{(D)}$ by using empirical frequencies $f_{j,l}$; in this case, (17) becomes $\sum_{j=1}^{k} m_j \sum_{l=1}^{n} \hat{H}_{j,l}^{(D)}$, where by $\hat{H}_{j,l}^{(D)} = -f_{j,l} \log f_{j,l} - (1 - f_{j,l}) \log(1 - f_{j,l})$ we denote the empirical estimate of entropy.

Now let $\Delta_{j,l}(x)$ be the total number of mutations in which the replacement letter for the $l$-th letter of the $j$-the prototype is the letter $x$. Then the third term of (15) can be rewritten as

$$\sum_{j=1}^{k} \sum_{l=1}^{n} \Delta_{j,l} \sum_{x \neq \theta_{j,l}} -\frac{\Delta_{j,l}(x)}{\Delta_{j,l}} \log P_{j,l}^{(E)}(x) \qquad (18)$$

We note that the innermost sum represents the cross entropy between the empirical distribution of frequencies $\frac{\Delta_{j,l}(x)}{\Delta_{j,l}}$, where $x \neq \theta_{j,l}$, and the distribution of probabilities $P_{j,l}^{(E)}(x)$. One way to define this term is to specify the distributions $P_{j,l}^{(E)}$ in advance; for example, for biochemical reasons, the mutations between "A" and "G" and the ones between "T" and "C", taken together, are two times more likely than all the other mutations in DNA sequences. However, in this paper we estimate the probabilities $P_{j,l}^{(E)}(x)$ by empirical frequencies $\frac{\Delta_{j,l}(x)}{\Delta_{j,l}}$; in this case, (18) becomes $\sum_{j=1}^{k} \sum_{l=1}^{n}[\hat{H}_{j,l}^{(E)} \Delta_{j,l}]$, where by $\hat{H}_{j,l}^{(E)} = \sum_{x \neq \theta_{j,l}} -\frac{\Delta_{j,l}(x)}{\Delta_{j,l}} \log \frac{\Delta_{j,l}(x)}{\Delta_{j,l}}$ we denote the empirical estimate of entropy.

Thus (15) may be rewritten as the sum of the terms (16,17,18). Each of these terms involves the cross entropy between the distributions $P^{(C)}$, $P^{(D)}$, and $P^{(E)}$ of the theory and the corresponding empirically observed frequencies. If the distributions of the theory are fixed then these terms are minimized by assignments to prototypes such that the empirical frequencies are the same as the probabilities in the given distributions. However, if the distributions are not specified in advance then these terms are minimized by the theory in which the probabilities in the distributions are the same as the empirically observed frequencies. For this choice of the distributions in the theory $T$, (15) reduces to

$$\hat{I}(S|T) \approx m\hat{H}^{(C)} + \sum_{j=1}^{k} m_j \sum_{l=1}^{n} \hat{H}_{j,l}^{(D)} + \sum_{j=1}^{k}\sum_{l=1}^{n} \hat{H}_{j,l}^{(E)}\Delta_{j,l}. \tag{19}$$

This expression has a simple direct interpretation as a code length. The entropy function $\hat{H}^{(C)}$ represents the estimated average number of bits needed to specify the index of the ancestral prototype. Since there are $m$ sequences, the total number of bits to specify the indices of all the ancestors is equal to the first term in (19). The entropy function $\hat{H}_{j,l}^{(D)}$ represents the estimated average number of bits needed to encode the information as to whether or not a letter in the $l$−th position of a sequence that comes from the $j$−th prototype is different from the corresponding letter in the prototype. The second term in (19) is then the number of bits needed to encode this information for all the positions of all the sequences. The entropy function $\hat{H}_{j,l}^{(E)}$ represents the estimated average number of bits needed to specify a replacement letter in the $l$-th position of a sequence that comes from the $j$-th prototype. There are $\Delta_{j,l}$ mismatches in the $l$-th position between the $j$-th prototype and the sequences that originate from it; the total number of bits to encode all the mismatching letters is then equal to the last term in (19).

Experiments indicate that our model of noise, as expressed by the procedure Nature, is too weak for the repetitive genetic sequences (e.g. Alu and L1); the correct inference depends critically on the knowledge about the process of "CpG noise", a biological process that causes mutation of the letters "C" if they are followed by a "G". If we wanted to express this assumption, we would have to modify procedure Nature so that $\hat{H}_{j,l}^{(D)}$ becomes dependent on the letter in the $(l+1)$−st position. The development of this more specific model is still in progress.

## 5    Computing the optimal theory

As indicated above, given a suitable encoding scheme the estimate of encoding length $\hat{I}(S,T)$ can be efficiently computed for any sample $S$ and theory $T$. In contrast, the problem of finding the theory $T$ that minimizes the estimate $\hat{I}(S,T)$ seems to be hard, so we apply a local-search strategy (Figure 5). To improve the chances of finding the globally optimal theory, we repeat local search several times, each time selecting at random a new starting point; at the end, the algorithm returns the best among the locally optimal theories. More sophisticated strategies are possible, e.g. based on simulated annealing, but our experimental results so far indicate that simple local search is often sufficient (see the next section).

To begin the local search for a theory with $k$ prototypes, we initially partition the $m$ sequences in the sample into $k$ classes at random. This defines a classification function $c : \{1,\ldots,m\} \to \{1,\ldots,k\}$. Then we repeatedly apply a local transformation to this classification in an attempt to improve it under the measure $\hat{I}(S,T)$. The local transformation in the local search consists of a move of one sequence from one class into the other. Cycling repeatedly through the sequences in the sample, the first move found that brings an improvement in $\hat{I}(S,T)$ is performed. The

Procedure MASC (sample S)
    for $k = 1, \ldots, K$        /* $k$ is the number of prototypes */
      repeat many times     /* search from many different starting points */
          pick a random initial classification $c$;
          find a locally optimal theory $T$ by local search;
    return the best locally optimal theory found.

Figure 2: Multiple Aligned Sequence Classification (MASC)

search ends in a local minimum when none of the moves in an entire cycle brings an improvement.

In order to be able to use this simple strategy, it is essential that we can recover an optimal theory $T$ given a number $k$ of prototypes and a classification $c : \{1, \ldots, m\} \to \{1, \ldots, k\}$ for a given sample of $m$ sequences. For the measure $\hat{I}(S, T)$ that we have used in our experiments, it can be shown that the protypes in $T$ can be constructed by a majority vote of the sequences in each of the classes, and that the distributions $\hat{P}^{(C)}$, $\hat{P}^{(D)}$ and $\hat{P}^{(E)}$ can then be taken from the empirical estimates in the sample.

Our algorithm is similar to the standard Basic Minimum Squared Error clustering algorithm that is described by Duda and Hart [4]. We list the main differences. (1) Our sample consists of sequences of letters as opposed to vectors of real-valued parameters. (2) Our measure that is to be optimized is not fixed; it depends on the inductive assumptions. (3) In our case, the number of classes $k$ does not have to be specified in advance; it is inferred from the sample and from the inductive assumptions.

# 6   Experimental results

The goal of our experiments was to get an indication of the adequacy of our model of inference and an indication of the success rate of our local search algorithm. The sum of the measures $I(T)$ and $I(S|T)$, as defined in (7) and (19) was used as the parsimony criterion; there were only two modifications. First, the term $h(m, n, g, k)$ was set to 0; this is because there are many ways to encode probability distributions and we have not come to any definite conclusion about what kind of assumptions are implicit in the particular choices. Second, the number of prototypes was limited to at most two; in all the experiments the local search procedure MASC (Figure 5) was used with $K = 2$. Local search was repeated 10 times, each time starting from a new random classification. If the best theory discovered in these 10 trials split the samples into two classes, then the procedure was repeated on each of these two subclasses, and so forth until no further splitting was found. In this fashion one obtains a hierarchical decomposition of the sample into classes, subclasses, sub-subclasses, etc., commonly called a *taxonomy*. We applied this procedure to a class of proteins, Cytochromes P450, and to the two classes of repetitive genetic sequences, *Alu* and L1. The results were then compared to the classifications that were independently obtained by biologists.

| Cytochromes | 0% (1/10),   10% (5/10) |
|---|---|
| Alu sequences | 1%          (6/10) |
| L1 sequences | no split |

Figure 3: The main subclasses

The Cytochrome P450 sample consists of 124 sequences, each about 600 letters long; the alphabet contains 20 letters, each denoting an amino acid. In case of *Alu* and L1 sequences, the alphabet contains 4 letters, each denoting a nucleotide. The *Alu* sample consists of 126 sequences, each about 400 letters long; the L1 sample consists of 20 fragments, each about 600 letters long.

The results obtained by MASC for the main split are summarized in Figure 3. The percentages denote the percentage of sequences in the sample for which the classification produced by MASC disagrees with that accepted by biologists. The parenthesized ratios represent the fraction of runs that found the best local minimum. (Two sets of values are given for Cytochromes, as explained below.) The notation "no split" indicates that the best minimum for the two prototype case did not have an encoding length shorter than the best encoding of the entire sample with one prototype.

The best among the local minima that was found for Cytochromes agrees completely with biologist's classification; however, it was found only once in 10 trials; on the other hand, 5 other local minima were also found that disagree with the biologist's split only on 10 % of the sample. This suggests a "rough bottom" of the main "basin of attraction" of the surface that is explored by local search. In contrast, the best local minimum found for *Alu* sequences appears to be very easy to find; it was found in 6 out of 10 trials and it disagrees with the accepted biological clsssification [13] on only 1 out of the 126 sequences. Non-split was preferred for the sample of 20 L1 sequences; however, 8 out of 10 trials ended up in a local minimum that was dominated only by the non-split minimum; moreover, this split exactly identifies the two main classes of L1 sequences [12]. Unfortunately, in this small sample there is not enough data to justify the introduction of two classes under our current assumptions.

To further examine the effect of sample size on inference, we halved the samples of Cytochromes and *Alu* sequences by taking only every second sequence. Repeating this process, we obtained progressively smaller subsamples. MASC was then applied to find the main split from the subsamples; the results are sumarized in Figure 4. The experiment with the 1/4 of the Cytochromes resulted in an unexpected 10 % disagreement with the accepted biological classification. To increase our chances of finding the global minimum we performed 100 trials for this case; as suspected, the best local minmum this time agreeed completely with the biological classification; however, it was first found only in the 30-th trial (and 11 more times within the 100 trials).

By recursively applying MASC to the newly inferred subclasses we then generated taxonomies of Cytochromes and *Alu* sequences. The taxonomic tree of Cytochromes that was inferred by MASC is given in Figure 5. The leaves of the tree identify exactly the families and subfamilies of Cytochromes that are named by Nebert et al. [15]; the roman numerals denote

|              | 1/2 sample | 1/4 sample              | 1/8 sample | 1/16 sample |
|--------------|------------|-------------------------|------------|-------------|
| Cytochromes  | 0% (1/10)  | 10% (1/10), 0% (12/100) | 0% (6/10)  | no split    |
| Alu sequences| 0% (5/10)  | no split                | no split   | no split    |

Figure 4: Halving the sample size

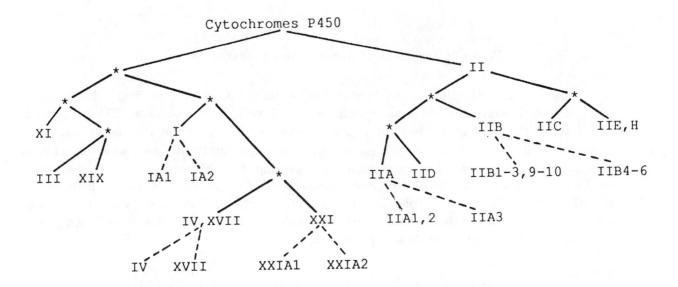

Figure 5: Taxonomy of Cytochromes P450 produced by MASC

gene families, the uppercase letters denote gene subfamilies, and the arabic numerals denote individual genes (several nonidentical sequences may belong to the same gene). Some of the gene families were absent from the sample; this was because the aligned sequences were not available for our experiments. The dotted branches in the figure denote best splits that were frequently found during local search but, for which a non-split is still preferred to a split. With more sequences available, these splits may also be inferred.

The intermediate classes of Cytochromes that are not labeled may have implications for molecular evolution. Moreover, biochemical experiments indicate that the positions that are highly preserved within the intermediate classes play important biochemical roles. However, the biological implications of these results are beyond the scope of this paper and will be discussed in the forthcoming biological paper [11].

The taxonomic tree for *Alu* sequences that was inferred by MASC is in Figure 6. The main split identifies families J and S that were proposed by Jurka and Smith [13] with disagreement on only one sequence. However, the subfamilies S/a and S/bc were identified with an accuracy of only 10 % even after 100 local search trials. Also, no subfamilies of J have been inferred, although they have been proposed by some biologists [16].

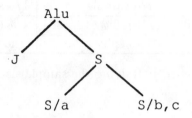

Figure 6: Taxonomy of *Alu* sequences produced by MASC

It appears that to improve inference of classes of *Alu* and L1 sequences, we need to encode more biological assumptions that are specific to repetitive genetic sequences. The process of "CpG noise" that we have discussed in previous sections seems to be the most important such assumption. The development of this more refined model is still in progress, however, ad-hoc simulations indicate that it may greatly help in classifying *Alu* sequences.

Finally, we tried a number of experiments on variants of the IP model presented here. Most of these involved fixing the distributions $P^{(C)}$, $P^{(D)}$ and $P^{(E)}$ in natural ways to simplify the model. However, none of these variants performed as well as the more general formulation given here, so we omit the details of these experiments.

## 7　Comparison to the biological parsimony methods

The parsimony criteria that are applied in biology are based on the maximum likelihood method [8]. We recall that our method reduces to the maximum likelihood method if we define $I(T) = 0$, i.e., $I(S,T) = I(S|T)$. It follows that the complexity of the theory has to be specified in advance; otherwise, since $I(T) = 0$, the most complex theory is always inferred. A good example for this is the failure of the Wagner tree method [5] on *Alu* sequences [1]; a complex evolutionary tree was inferred while the data could support only a few distiguishable classes of sequences. The complete branching pattern was hard to justify by the observed sequences and the whole tree was dismissed as unreliable; the result reported in [1] was that "there are no significant subgroups of *Alu* sequences". However, a year later, four independent groups of researchers correctly identified major *Alu* subfamilies [24], [2], [16], [13].

In order to reduce our method to the standard methods of genetic taxonomy we assume that replacement letters for any position of any prototype are equally likely; in other words, we fix $\hat{H}_{j,l}^{(E)} = \log(g-1)$ for $j = 1, \ldots, k$ and $l = 1, \ldots, n$. Now we can rewrite (19) in the following form.

$$\hat{I}(S|T) = m\hat{H}^{(C)} + \sum_{j=1}^{k}\sum_{l=1}^{n} \Delta_{j,l} \log \alpha_{j,l} + \sum_{j=1}^{k} m_j \sum_{l=1}^{n} \log \beta_{j,l}, \qquad (20)$$

where by $\Delta_{j,l}$ for $j = 1, \ldots, k$ and $l = 1, \ldots, n$ we denote the number of mismatches in the $l$-th position between the sequences in the $j$-th class and the prototype of that class, and $\alpha_{j,l} = (1/f_{j,l} - 1)(g - 1)$, $\beta_{j,l} = 1/(1 - f_{j,l})$, where $g$ is the alphabet size and $f_{j,l}$ denotes the frequency of mismatches in the $l$-th position in the $j$-th class. In other words, $f_{j,l} = \Delta_{j,l}/m_j$.

The two last terms of (20) correspond to the two standard interpretations of the principle of parsimony in biology. The standard *weighted parsimony method* (e.g. [6]) minimizes only the second term while the *compatibility method* (which can also be viewed as a parsimony method [8]) minimizes only the third term. The "weights" log $\alpha_{j,l}$ are concave and unbounded in $f_{j,l}$; this is in complete agreement with the experimental results of Farris [6] that suggest that concave and unbounded weighting functions give the best classification in practice.

Thus, our formula generalizes previous formulae that were derived by biologists. More importantly, our method provides a general way of directly translating biological assumptions into parsimony principles, so a variety of models can be derived, as appropriate. Finally, our experiments indicate that the theoretically derived formulae result in biologically meaningful results.

# 8    Acknowledgements

The authors gratefully acknowledge the support provided by the ONR grant N 00014-86-K-0454.

We thank Ela Holsztynska for making her aligned Cytochrome sequences available to us. Peter Cheeseman and Wray Buntine gave many useful comments on this work. We thank Robert Levinson and the organizers of the Workshop on the Matrix of Biological Knowledge '87 for their support of our initial efforts to bridge biology and computer science. We also thank Emile Zuckerkandl and the Linus Pauling Institute of Science and Medicine for their current support.

# References

[1] W. Bains. The multiple origins of human *Alu* sequences. *Journal of Molecular Evolution*, 23:189–199, 1986.

[2] R.J. Britten, W.F. Baron, D. Stout, and E.H. Davidson. Sources and evolution of human *Alu* repeated sequences. *Proceedings of the National Academy of Sciences of the United States of America*, 85:4770–4774, 1988.

[3] P. Cheeseman, M. Self, J. Kelly, W. Taylor, D. Freeman, and J. Stutz. Bayesian classification. In *Proceedings of the Conference of the American Association for Artificial Intelligence*, 1988.

[4] R.O. Duda and P.E. Hart. *Pattern recognition and scene analysis*. 1973.

[5] J. Farris. Estimating phylogenetic trees from distance matrices. *American Naturalist*, 106:645–668, 1972.

[6] J.S. Farris. A successive approximations approach to character weighting. *Systematics and Zoology*, 18:374–385, 1969.

[7] J. Felsenstein. A likelihood approach to character weighting and what it tells us about parsimony and compatibility. *Biological Journal of the Linnean Society*, 16:183–196, 1981.

[8] J. Felsenstein. Numerical methods for inferring evolutionary trees. *Quarterly Review of Biology*, 57(4):379–404, 1982.

[9] M.P. Georgeff and C.S. Wallace. *Advances in Artificial Intelligence*, chapter A general selection criterion for inductive inference. 1985.

[10] G.W. Hart. *Minimum information estimation of structure*. Technical Report LIDS-TH-1664, MIT, 1987.

[11] E. Holsztynska, A. Milosavljevic, and J. Jurka. in preparation.

[12] J. Jurka. Subfamily structure and evolution of the human L1 family of repetitive sequences. *Journal of Molecular Evolution*. to appear.

[13] J. Jurka and T. Smith. A fundamental division in the *Alu* family of repeated sequences. *Proceedings of the National Academy of Sciences of the United States of America*, 85:4775–4778, 1988.

[14] A.N. Kolmogorov. Three approaches to the quantitative definition of information. *International Journal for Computer Mathematics*, 2:157–168, 1968.

[15] D.W. Nebert, M. Adesnik, M.J Coon, R.W. Estabrook, F.J. Gonzales, F.P. Guengerich, I.C. Gunsalus, E.F. Johnson, B. Kemper, W Levin, I.R. Phillips, R. Sato, and M. Waterman. The p450 gene superfamily: recommended nomenclature. *DNA*, 6:1–11, 1987.

[16] Y. Quentin. The *Alu* family developed through successive waves of fixation closely connected with primate lineage history. *Journal of Molecular Evolution*, 27:194–202, 1988.

[17] J.R. Quinlan and R.L. Rivest. Inferring decision trees using the minimum description length principle. *Information and Computation*. to appear.

[18] J. Rissanen. Stochastic complexity. *Journal of the Royal Statistical Society, Series B*, 49:223–239, 1987.

[19] R.L. Rivest. Machine learning. 1988. class notes.

[20] J. Segen. Conceptual clumping of binary vectors with Occam's razor. In *Proceedings of the Fifth International Conference on Machine Learning*, 1988.

[21] R.J. Solomonoff. A formal theory of inductive inference, Part I. *Information and Control*, 7:1–22, 1964.

[22] C.S. Wallace and D.M. Boulton. Estimation and inference by compact coding. *Journal of the Royal Statistical Society, Series B*, 49:240–252, 1987.

[23] C.S. Wallace and D.M. Boulton. An information measure for classification. *Computer Journal*, 11:185–195, 1968.

[24] C. Willard, H.T. Nguyen, and C.W. Schmid. Existence of at least three distinct *Alu* sub-families. *Journal of Molecular Evolution*, 26:180–186, 1988.

# COMPLEXITY ISSUES IN
# LEARNING BY NEURAL NETS*

(extended abstract)

*Jyh-Han Lin* and *Jeffrey Scott Vitter*

Department of Computer Science
Brown University
Providence, R. I. 02912–1910

## Abstract

We consider the computational complexity of learning by neural nets. We are interested in how hard it is to design appropriate neural net architectures and to train neural nets for general and specialized learning tasks. We introduce a neural net learning model and classify several neural net design and optimization problems within the polynomial-time hierarchy. We also investigate how much easier the problems become if the class of concepts to be learned is known *a priori*. We show that the training problem for 2-cascade neural nets (which have only one hidden unit) is $\mathcal{NP}$-complete, which implies that finding an optimum net to load a set of examples is also $\mathcal{NP}$-complete. We conjecture that training a $k$-cascade neural net, which is a classical threshold network training problem, is also $\mathcal{NP}$-complete, for each $k \geq 2$.

## 1 INTRODUCTION

Neural nets are often used to learn functions, in either a supervised or unsupervised mode. They are enticing because in some instances they can be *self-programming*, in that they can adjust their parameters by using general procedures based solely on examples of input-output pairs. In this paper we consider the computational complexity of learning by neural nets, building upon the work of Judd [1987, 1988] and Blum and Rivest [1988]. We are interested in how hard it is to design appropriate neural net architectures and to train neural nets for general and specialized learning tasks.

---

*Support was provided in part by an NSF Presidential Young Investigator Award with matching funds from IBM and by an NSF research grant. The authors can also be reached by electronic mail at the addresses jhl@cs.brown.edu and jsv@cs.brown.edu, respectively. Correspondence can be addressed to the second author.

In the next section we introduce our neural net model and related definitions. We define the size of a neural net or net architecture to be the number of non-input nodes. In Section 3 we prove that several neural net design and optimization problems are $\mathcal{NP}$-complete or $\mathcal{NP}$-hard and classify them more precisely within the polynomial-time hierarchy. In Section 4 we investigate how hard it is to train a net for a set of examples, both for the case when the net is unconstrained and for when the net is constrained to be in some architecture for learning a particular concept class. In the latter case, it is sometimes easier to train a net that is sufficiently non-optimal, so that there is some "play" in setting its parameters. In Section 5 we prove that the training problem for a simple net architecture with only one hidden unit, called a 2-cascade neural net, is $\mathcal{NP}$-complete. We conjecture that the training of $k$-cascade neural nets, which is a well-known threshold network training problem (see, for example, [Dertouzos 1965]), is also $\mathcal{NP}$-complete, for each $k \geq 2$.

# 2    DEFINITIONS

In this paper, we restrict ourselves to feedforward neural nets of linear threshold elements. In particular, we are mainly concerned with neural nets for classification tasks. Formal definitions are as follows:

**Definition 1** A linear threshold unit $f_v = [\vec{w}; \theta]$ with input $\vec{x}$ is characterized by a weight vector $\vec{w}$ and a threshold $\theta$:

$$f_v(\vec{x}) = \begin{cases} 1 & \text{if } \vec{w} \cdot \vec{x} \geq \theta; \\ 0 & \text{otherwise.} \end{cases}$$

For convenience, we identify the positive region defined by $f_v$ as $f_v$ and the negative region as $\overline{f_v}$.

The inputs to the feedforward net will be from $X^n$, where $X$ is either $\{0, 1\}$ or $\Re$. The nets produce one binary output.

**Definition 2** A *(feedforward) neural net architecture* $F$ is a directed acyclic graph $G$ with $n$ designated input nodes and one output node. Nodes of $G$ that are neither input nor output nodes are called *hidden units*. Each non-input node $v$ in $G$ either is associated with a linear threshold function $f_v$ with *indegree*$(v)$ inputs or is left undefined (denoted by $\perp$). A neural net $f$ is a neural net architecture with no undefined nodes. Thus, $F$ can be identified with a set of functions computable by nets where each undefined node $v$ in $F$ is replaced by some linear threshold function $f_v$. We say that $f \in F$ if the function that $f$ represents is computable by $F$. The *sizes* of $f$ and $F$, which we denote $|f|$ and $|F|$, are the numbers of non-input nodes in $f$ and $F$, respectively.

The motivation for this definition of net architecture is that we may investigate modular or hierarchical neural net design and training problems within the same framework. Other possible definitions of size include height, number of edges, number of nonzero weights, and number of bits in the representation, but for simplicity we restrict ourselves in this paper to the above definition.

**Definition 3** Given two neural net architectures $F$ and $F'$, we write $F \equiv F'$ if they compute the same set of functions and $F \subseteq F'$ if the functions computable by $F$ are also computable by $F'$. We call a neural net architecture $F$ optimal if for all $F' \supseteq F$ we have $|F| \leq |F'|$. These definitions can be extended to particular neural nets as well. We also call a neural net architecture $F$ optimal for a concept class $C_{n,s}$ if $C_{n,s} \subseteq F$ and for all $F' \supseteq C_{n,s}$ we have $|F| \leq |F'|$.

An easy construction gives us the following lemma:

**Lemma 1** *Given two net architectures $F_1$ and $F_2$, we may construct a net architecture $F$ such that $F \equiv F_1 \cup F_2$.*

Let $C_{n,s} \subseteq 2^{X^n}$ be a concept class. Given a set of nonlabeled examples $S \subseteq X^n$, we denote by $\Pi_{C_{n,s}}(S)$ the set of all subsets $P \subseteq S$ such that there is some concept $c \in C_{n,s}$ for which $P \subseteq c$ and $(S - P) \subseteq \bar{c}$. If $\Pi_{C_{n,s}}(S) = 2^S$, we say that $S$ *is shattered by $C_{n,s}$*. The *Vapnik-Chervonenkis dimension* (VC dimension) of $C_{n,s}$ is the cardinality of the largest finite set of examples that is shattered by $C_{n,s}$; it is infinite if arbitrarily large sets can be shattered.

We use log to denote the logarithm base 2 and ln to denote the natural logarithm. The following corollary from [Baum and Haussler 1988] bounds the VC dimension of a net architecture:

**Corollary 1** *Let $F$ be a net architecture with $s \geq 2$ non-input nodes and $E$ edges, then*

$$VCdim(F) \leq 2(E + s)\log(es),$$

*where $e$ is the base of natural logarithm.*

Let $\mathcal{F}_s$ be a net architecture with $s$ noninput nodes and with all possible edges; that is, the $s$ non-input nodes are numbered from 1 to $s$, and each noninput node has inputs from the $n$ input nodes and from all previous noninput nodes. Clearly, $\mathcal{F}_s = \bigcup_{|f| \leq s} f$. The following lemma bounds the VC dimension of $\mathcal{F}_s$.

**Lemma 2** *The VC dimension of $\mathcal{F}_s$ can be bounded as follows:*

*1. $VCdim(\mathcal{F}_0) \leq \log n$,*

*2. $VCdim(\mathcal{F}_1) = n + 1$,*

*3. $VCdim(\mathcal{F}_s) \leq s(2n + s + 1)\log(es)$ for all $s \geq 2$.*

*Proof Sketch*: Bounds 1 and 2 are straightforward. For bound 3, note that the number of edges in $\mathcal{F}_s$ is $ns + s(s - 1)/2$. The proof then follows directly from Corollary 1. $\square$

The next lemma gives a bound on the size of a net architecture that contains some concept class:

**Lemma 3** *Let $C_{n,s}$ be a concept class, where $VCdim(C_{n,s}) \geq 2n$, and let $F$ be a net architecture such that $C_{n,s} \subseteq F$. We have*

$$|F| = \Omega \left( \sqrt{\frac{VCdim(C_{n,s})}{n} \bigg/ \log\left(\frac{VCdim(C_{n,s})}{n}\right)} \right).$$

*Proof Sketch*: The proof follows simply from Lemma 2 and the fact that $VCdim(\mathcal{F}_{|F|}) \geq VCdim(F) \geq VCdim(C_{n,s})$. $\qquad\square$

Since many problems discussed in this paper are $\mathcal{NP}$-hard, it is of theoretical interest to classify these $\mathcal{NP}$-hard problems in the polynomial-time hierarchy [Stockmeyer 1977] [Garey and Johnson 1979]:

$$\Sigma_0^p = \Pi_0^p = \Delta_0^p = \mathcal{P};$$

and for $k \geq 0$,

$$
\begin{aligned}
\Sigma_{k+1}^p &= \mathcal{NP}(\Sigma_k^p), \\
\Pi_{k+1}^p &= \text{co-}\mathcal{NP}(\Sigma_k^p), \\
\Delta_{k+1}^p &= \mathcal{P}(\Sigma_k^p).
\end{aligned}
$$

A natural complete set for $\Sigma_k^p$ is the set $B_k$ of true boolean formulas with $k$ alternating quantifiers.

We shall use the following theorem from [Stockmeyer and Meyer 1973] and [Wrathall 1977] to establish the upper bounds for the problems investigated in next section:

**Theorem 1** *Let $L \subseteq \Gamma^*$ be a language. For any $k \geq 1$, $L \in \Sigma_k^p$ if and only if there exist polynomials $p_1, \ldots, p_k$ and a polynomial time recognizable relation $R$ of dimension $k+1$ over $\Gamma^*$ such that for all $x \in \Gamma^*$ we have $x \in L$ if and only if*

$$(\exists y_1)(\forall y_2) \ldots (Q y_k) \left[ \langle x, y_1, \ldots, y_k \rangle \in R \right],$$

*where $|y_i| \leq p_i(|x|)$ and $Q$ is "$\exists$" if $k$ is odd and "$\forall$" if $k$ is even.*

# 3    NEURAL NET DESIGN PROBLEMS

In typical real-world neural net design problems, we start with a set of training examples, choose (or guess) an appropriate net architecture, and then use some procedure (such as back propagation) to train the neural net (that is, to set the parameters of the net so that we can load (or correctly classify) as many examples as possible). It is shown in [Baum and Haussler 1988] that if enough random examples can be loaded onto the neural net, as a function of the net's size, then the net will "generalize" in Valiant's sense [Valiant 1984] and probably answer future queries with low error. By the principle of Occam's razor, it is desirable to optimize the size of the net architecture or of the particular net. In this section we restrict ourselves to the corresponding decision problems and show their intractability in general.

Before we attack this general problem, we shall first show the infeasibility of comparing the power of different neural net architectures or even just answering whether the function performed by one neural net can be realized by another neural net architecture. The first problem considers the optimality of a neural net architecture:

OPTIMAL NET ARCHITECTURE
Instance: Neural net architecture $F$ and positive integer $K$.
Question: Is there a neural net architecture $F'$ such that $F' \supseteq F$ and $|F'| \leq K$?

**Theorem 2** *The OPTIMAL NET ARCHITECTURE problem is in $\Pi_3^p$ and is $\mathcal{NP}$-hard.*

*Proof Sketch*: The upper bound is established by the fact that $(F, K) \in$ OPTIMAL NET ARCHITECTURE if and only if

$$(\forall f \in F)(\exists f' \in \mathcal{F}_K)(\forall \vec{x})\left[f(\vec{x}) = f'(\vec{x})\right],$$

where $\mathcal{F}_K$ is defined as in Section 2. This problem is $\mathcal{NP}$-hard since it contains the OPTIMAL EQUIVALENT NET problem (see below), which is $\mathcal{NP}$-hard, as a special case. □

We are currently working on showing that the problem is $\Pi_2^p$-hard. The next two problems are concerned with comparing the powers of different architectures.

NET ARCHITECTURE INEQUIVALENCE
Instance: Neural net architectures $F_1$ and $F_2$.
Question: Is $F_1 \not\equiv F_2$?

**Theorem 3** *The NET ARCHITECTURE INEQUIVALENCE problem is in $\Sigma_3^p$ and is $\Sigma_2^p$-hard.*

*Proof Sketch*: The upper bound follows from the fact that $F_1 \not\equiv F_2$ if and only if

$$(\exists f_1 \in F_1)(\forall f_2 \in F_2)(\exists \vec{x})\left[f_1(\vec{x}) \neq f_2(\vec{x})\right].$$

We reduce the NET ARCHITECTURE NONCONTAINMENT problem (see below), which is $\Sigma_2^p$-hard, to this problem. From Lemma 1 we can construct a net architecture that computes exactly $F_1 \cup F_2$. The proof follows from the fact that $F_1 \not\subseteq F_2$ if and only if $(F_1 \cup F_2) \not\equiv F_2$. □

## NET ARCHITECTURE NONCONTAINMENT

Instance: Neural net architectures $F_1$ and $F_2$.
Question: Is $F_1 \not\subseteq F_2$?

**Theorem 4** *NET ARCHITECTURE NONCONTAINMENT is in $\Sigma_3^p$ and is $\Sigma_2^p$-hard.*

*Proof Sketch*: The upper bound follows from the fact that $F_1 \not\subseteq F_2$ if and only if

$$(\exists f_1 \in F_1)(\forall f_2 \in F_2)(\exists \vec{x})\left[f_1(\vec{x}) \neq f_2(\vec{x})\right].$$

We reduce the NET MEMBERSHIP problem (see below), which is $\Sigma_2^p$-complete, to this problem. This is easy to see since $f \in F$ if and only if it is not the case that $f \not\subseteq F$. $\square$

The next problem asks whether a neural net can also be realized by another architecture.

## NET MEMBERSHIP

Instance: Neural net $f$ and neural net architecture $F$.
Question: Is $f \in F$.

**Theorem 5** *The NET MEMBERSHIP problem is $\Sigma_2^p$-complete.*

*Proof Sketch*: The upper bound follows from the fact that $f \in F$ if and only if

$$(\exists f' \in F)(\forall \vec{x})\left[f'(\vec{x}) = f(\vec{x})\right].$$

To establish the lower bound, we reduce $B_2$ QBF SATISFIABILITY to this problem. Given an instance of $B_2$ formula $(\exists \vec{x})(\forall \vec{y})B(\vec{x}, \vec{y})$, we construct a net architecture $F_B$ as shown in Figure 1. We can show that the given $B_2$ QBF formula is satisfiable if and only if $1 \in F_B$. $\square$

The next problem is concerned with the optimality of neural nets.

## OPTIMAL EQUIVALENT NET

Instance: Neural net $f$ and positive integer $K$.
Question: Is there a neural net $f'$ such that $f' \equiv f$ and $|f'| \leq K$?

**Theorem 6** *The OPTIMAL EQUIVALENT NET problem is in $\Sigma_2^p$ and is $\mathcal{NP}$-hard.*

*Proof Sketch*: The upper bound follows from the fact that $(f, K) \in$ OPTIMAL EQUIVALENT NET if and only if

$$(\exists f')(\forall \vec{x})\left[|f'| \leq K \text{ and } f'(\vec{x}) = f(\vec{x})\right].$$

The $\mathcal{NP}$-hardness is obtained by reducing NON-ZERO NET (see below), which is $\mathcal{NP}$-complete, to this problem. Give an instance $f$ of NON-ZERO NET, we construct a neural net $z \vee f$, where $z$ is a new variable. It is not hard to see that $f \not\equiv 0$ if and only if

$$(z \vee f, 0) \notin \text{OPTIMAL EQUIVALENT NET}.$$

$\square$

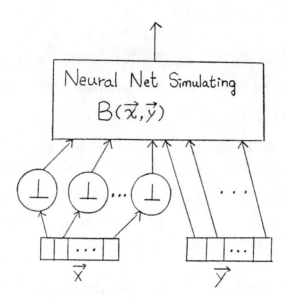

Figure 1: Net architecture for the NET MEMBERSHIP problem.

The next problem asks whether a neural net outputs anything other than 0.

NON-ZERO NET
Instance: A neural net $f$.
Question: Is $f \not\equiv 0$?

**Theorem 7** *The NON-ZERO NET problem is $\mathcal{NP}$-complete.*

*Proof Sketch*: This problem is clearly in $\mathcal{NP}$. To prove completeness, we reduce SATIS-FIABILITY to this problem. Given a boolean formula $\phi$, we construct a neural net $f_\phi$ simulating $\phi$. Clearly, $\phi$ is satisfiable if and only if $f_\phi$ is a non-zero net. □

The next problem asks whether two given nets differ on some input.

NET INEQUIVALENCE
Instance: Neural nets $f_1$ and $f_2$.
Question: Is $f_1 \not\equiv f_2$?

**Theorem 8** *The NET INEQUIVALENCE problem is $\mathcal{NP}$-complete.*

*Proof Sketch*: This problem is clearly in $\mathcal{NP}$. The completeness follows directly from the fact that this problem includes NON-ZERO NET as a special case. □

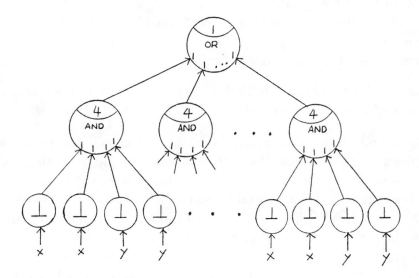

Figure 2: Net architecture for the unions of $s$ isothetic rectangles.

# 4   TRAINING NEURAL NETS

The results of last section indicate that optimizing the neural net architecture for general functions is intractable, assuming the usual conjectures about polynomial-time hierarchy. Judd [1987, 1988] shows that determining whether a neural net architecture can be trained for a set of training examples is $\mathcal{NP}$-complete. This is extended in [Blum and Rivest 1988] to a simple two-layer architecture with only two hidden units. (We shall extend their result further in the next section by showing that for a 2-cascade neural net (with only one hidden unit) the training problem is also $\mathcal{NP}$-complete.) However, these results are mainly concerned with particular fixed architectures. It is conceivable that learning may be easier if the architecture is allowed to be more general. The following problem formalizes the problem at hand:

OPTIMAL CONSISTENT NET
Instance: A set $S$ of training examples and a positive integer $K$.
Question: Is there a neural net $f$ that can load $S$ such that $|f| \leq K$?

This problem is clearly in $\mathcal{NP}$. We show in the next section that this problem is $\mathcal{NP}$-complete by showing $\mathcal{NP}$-completeness for the particular case $K = 2$.

In the remainder of this section we investigate how the complexity of training is affected by restricting the problem's domain to learning a specific concept class $C_{n,s}$. In the problem statements of this section, $C_{n,s}$ is an implicitly known concept class (such as the union of $s$ isothetic rectangles or symmetric boolean functions) and is not a part of the input.

## NET ARCHITECTURE TRAINING

Instance:  A set $S$ of training examples for a concept from $C_{n,s}$ and a neural net architecture $F$
   for $C_{n,s}$ (that is, $C_{n,s} \subseteq F$).

Question:  Is there some $f \in F$ such that $f$ can load $S$?

**Theorem 9** *The NET ARCHITECTURE TRAINING problem is $\mathcal{NP}$-complete if $C_{n,s} = C_s$ is the set of unions of $s$ isothetic rectangles.*

*Proof Sketch*:  It is well known that it is $\mathcal{NP}$-hard to decide if the minimum numbers of isothetic rectangles needed to cover all positive training examples in the plane is less than or equal to $s$. To solve this problem, we construct a three-layer net architecture $F$ as shown in Figure 2. The output node is hardwired to be the OR of the $s$ second-layer hidden units, which are all ANDs. Each AND has inputs from 4 hidden units under it. Among these four hidden units, two have single inputs from $x$ and the other two have single inputs from $y$.

We can show that there exists a neural net $f \in F$ consistent with all training examples if and only if the minimum numbers of isothetic rectangles needed is less than or equal to $s$.   $\square$

This theorem also gives a result similar to that in [Judd 1987] for our model of net architecture. The reason this problem is difficult is that some net architectures are harder to train than others. In practice, neural net researchers often design their nets and net architectures to be slightly nonoptimal so as to allow some "play" in constructing the weights during the training. In some cases, we can show that this makes the training problem tractable. This motivates the notion of Occam nets:

**Definition 4** Let $F^{\text{opt}}$ be an optimal net architecture for $C_{n,s}$. An $(\alpha, j, k)$-*Occam net finder* $A$ for $C_{n,s}$, where $0 \leq \alpha < 1$ and $j, k \geq 0$, is a polynomial-time algorithm that maps each set of training examples $S$ to some consistent *Occam net* $f \in H$, where $H$ is a net architecture, such that $VCdim(H) \leq |S|^{\alpha} n^j |F^{\text{opt}}|^k$.

We can show by modifying the analysis of [Blumer et al 1989] that an Occam net will generalize if it can be trained on an appropriate number of random examples.

**Theorem 10** *If there is an $(\alpha, j, k)$-Occam net finder $A$ for $C_{n,s}$, where $0 \leq \alpha < 1$ and $j, k \geq 0$, and if the number $S$ of random examples satisfies*

$$|S| \geq \max\left\{\frac{4}{\epsilon}\log\frac{2}{\delta}, \left(\frac{8n^j|F^{\text{opt}}|^k}{\epsilon}\log\frac{13}{\epsilon}\right)^{1/(1-\alpha)}\right\},$$

*where $F^{\text{opt}}$ is an optimal net architecture for $C_{n,s}$, then the neural net $f$ output by $A$ is a pac-learning network. That is, with probability at least $1 - \delta$, the neural net $f$ will predict correctly at least a faction $1 - \epsilon$ of future random examples drawn from the same distribution.*

*Proof Sketch*:  The proof is a simple application of Theorem 3.2.1 in [Blumer et al].   $\square$

**Lemma 4** *If $|F^{\text{opt}}| = \Omega(s^\beta)$ for some $\beta > 0$, then the upper bound on $VCdim(H)$ in Definition 4 can be replaced by $|S|^\alpha n^j s^k$, and $|F^{\text{opt}}|^k$ in Theorem 10 can be replaced by $s^k$.*

The next theorem shows an example of Occam net finders:

**Theorem 11** *There is an $(\alpha, j, k)$-Occam net finder for the the concept class $C_{n,s} = C_s$ of the set of unions of $s$ isothetic rectangles.*

*Proof Sketch*: There is a well-known simple greedy algorithm for $C_s$, which is optimal within a factor of $\ln(|S|) + 1$. The output of the greedy algorithm can be transformed easily into a neural net $f \in H$, where $H$ is a net architecture of size $O(s \log |S|)$ and with $O(s \log |S|)$ edges. From Corollary 1 we have

$$VCdim(H) = O((s \log |S|)(\log s + \log \log |S|)).$$

Clearly, $VCdim(C_s) = \Omega(s)$. Now from Lemma 3, we have $|F^{\text{opt}}| = \Omega(\sqrt{s/\log s})$. Thus, from Lemma 4 there is an $(\alpha, j, k)$-Occam net finder for $C_s$.    □

By Theorem 10, the resulting Occam net is a pac-learning network. By Theorem 3.2.4 in [Blumer et al] and Lemma 4, we may generalize Theorem 11 and prove the following:

**Theorem 12** *Let $C$ be a concept class with finite VC dimension $d$, let $C_s = \{\bigcup_{i=1}^{s} c_i \mid c_i \in C, 1 \leq i \leq s\}$, and let $F^{\text{opt}}$ be an optimal net architecture for $C_s$. If there exists a polynomial-time hypothesis finder for $C$ and $|F^{\text{opt}}| = \Omega(s^\beta)$ for some $\beta > 0$, then there also exists an $(\alpha, j, k)$-Occam net finder for $C_s$.*

We can also allow some errors in the training, so that only some portion of the examples are loaded. The recent results of [Kearns and Valiant 1988] show under some cryptographic assumptions that some concept classes do not have pac-learning networks.

# 5   CASCADE NEURAL NETS

A $k$-cascade neural net (see Figure 3), where $k \geq 2$, has $k-1$ hidden units $N_1, N_2, \ldots, N_{k-1}$ and one output node $N_k$. All $n$ inputs are boolean and are connected to nodes $N_1, \ldots, N_k$. In addition, each $N_i$ is connected to $N_{i+1}$; we designate the weight of this edge by $g_i$. Each node has $n + 1$ inputs except for $N_1$, which has only $n$ inputs. We adopt the convention that $g_i$ is the last weight to $N_{i+1}$. Cascade neural nets are more powerful and economical in terms of their size (the number of noninput nodes) than the class of neural nets considered in [Blum and Rivest 1988]. Let us consider the following problem, for any $k \geq 2$:

$k$-CASCADE NEURAL NET TRAINING
Instance: A set $S = S^+ \cup S^-$ of training examples of $n$ boolean inputs, where $S^+$ is the set of positive examples and $S^-$ is the set of negative examples.
Question: Is there a $k$-cascade neural net $f$ consistent with all training examples?

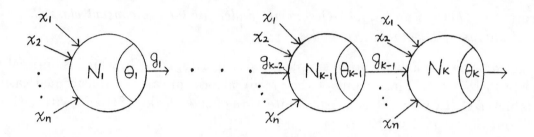

Figure 3: Cascade neural net.

We shall show that this problem is $\mathcal{NP}$-complete for $k = 2$ by reducing the QUAD-RANT problem to it. The QUADRANT problem asks if the positive examples $S^+$ can be confined to a single quadrant, defined by the intersection of two halfspaces, with the negative examples $S^-$ confined to the other three quadrants.

QUADRANT
Instance: A set $S = S^+ \cup S^-$ of training examples of $n$ boolean inputs, where $S^+$ is the set of positive examples and $S^-$ is the set of negative examples.
Question: Are there two halfspaces $N_1$ and $N_2$ such that $S^+ \subseteq N_1 \cap N_2$ and $S^- \subseteq \overline{N_1} \cup \overline{N_2}$?

**Theorem 13** [Blum and Rivest 1988]   *QUADRANT is $\mathcal{NP}$-complete.*

We use this to prove the following:

**Theorem 14** *2-CASCADE NEURAL NET TRAINING is $\mathcal{NP}$-complete.*

*Proof Sketch*: Training a 2-cascade neural net is clearly in $\mathcal{NP}$. To prove $\mathcal{NP}$-hardness, we reduce QUADRANT to it. Given a set of training examples $S = S^+ \cup S^-$ for QUADRANT, we add two new dimensions and create the following set of augmented examples $T = T^+ \cup T^-$ for training a 2-cascade neural net:

$$T^+ = \{\vec{x}00 \mid \vec{x} \in S^+\} \cup \{\vec{x}11 \mid \vec{x} \in S\},$$
$$T^- = \{\vec{x}00 \mid \vec{x} \in S^-\} \cup \{\vec{x}01, \vec{x}10 \mid \vec{x} \in S\}.$$

This is illustrated pictorially in Figure 4. The points $\vec{x}00$ in the $n$-dimensional hypercube

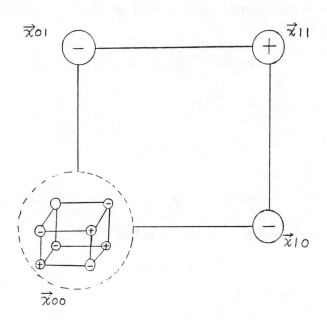

Figure 4: Examples used to show that 2-CASCADE NEURAL NET TRAINING is $\mathcal{NP}$-complete.

on the first $n$ dimensions retain their former sign.

The positive region induced by a 2-cascade net is bordered by a "zig-zag" of hyperplanes, in which the two outer (semi-infinite) hyperplanes are parallel. The basic idea of the proof is that the extra two dimensions of the examples in $T$ force one of the semi-infinite hyperplanes to "miss" the $n$-dimensional hypercube, so that there is a 2-cascade neural net $f$ consistent with $T$ if and only if there is a quadrant solution to $S$.

($\Longrightarrow$) Suppose the quadrant solution to $S$ is

$$[\vec{a}; \theta_1] \wedge [\vec{b}; \theta_2].$$

We construct a 2-cascade neural net $f$ consistent with $T$ as follows:

$$
\begin{aligned}
N_1 &= [\vec{a}, -A - |\theta_1|, -A - |\theta_1|; \theta_1], \\
N_2 &= [\vec{b}, 2B, 2B, 3B - \theta_2; 3B],
\end{aligned}
$$

where $A > \sum_{i=1}^{n} |a_i|$ and $B > \sum_{i=1}^{n} |b_i|$. It is interesting to note that there is also a quadrant solution to $T$:

$$[\vec{a}, 2A + 2|\theta_1|, -A - |\theta_1|; \theta_1] \wedge [\vec{b}, -B - |\theta_2|, 2B + 2|\theta_2|; \theta_2].$$

This is surprising on first glance, given the second-half of the proof, immediately below.

($\Longleftarrow$) Suppose the 2-cascade neural net $f$ consistent with $T$ is as follows:

$$N_1 = [\vec{a}, A_1, A_2; \theta_1],$$
$$N_2 = [\vec{b}, B_1, B_2, g_1; \theta_2].$$

In the following, let

$$N_2{}^{N_1=0} = [\vec{b}, B_1, B_2; \theta_2],$$
$$N_2{}^{N_1=1} = [\vec{b}, B_1, B_2; \theta_2 - g_1].$$

Case 1. Suppose $g_1 \geq 0$. This implies that all examples in $N_2{}^{N_1=0}$ are positive examples and all examples not in $N_2{}^{N_1=1}$ are negative examples. Also note that all positive examples belong either to $N_2{}^{N_1=0}$ or to $N_1 \cap N_2{}^{N_1=1}$. If for all $\vec{x} \in S^+$ we have $\vec{x}00 \in N_2{}^{N_1=0}$, then clearly $S$ is linearly separable and has a trivial quadrant solution:

$$[\vec{b}; \theta_2] \wedge [\vec{b}; \theta_2].$$

Otherwise, we claim for all $\vec{x} \in S^+$ that

$$\vec{x}00 \in N_1 \cap N_2{}^{N_1=1}.$$

There exists at least one example $\vec{x} \in S^+$ such that $\vec{x}00 \in N_1 \cap N_2{}^{N_1=1}$ but $\vec{x}00 \notin N_2{}^{N_1=0}$. Suppose there also exists some $\vec{y} \in S^+$ such that $\vec{y}00 \in N_2{}^{N_1=0}$. Since $\vec{y}00 \in N_2{}^{N_1=0}$ and since $\vec{y}01, \vec{y}10$ are negative examples, we must have $B_1, B_2 < 0$ and $\vec{y}11 \notin N_2{}^{N_1=0}$. But $\vec{y}11$ is a positive example, and so $\vec{y}11 \in N_1 \cap N_2{}^{N_1=1}$. From $B_1, B_2 < 0$, we have $\vec{y}01, \vec{y}10 \in N_2{}^{N_1=1}$. Since $\vec{y}01$ and $\vec{y}10$ are negative examples, it follows that $\vec{y}01, \vec{y}10 \notin N_1$ and $A_1, A_2 > 0$.

From the fact that $\vec{x}00 \notin N_2{}^{N_1=0}$ and $B_1, B_2 < 0$, we have $\vec{x}11 \notin N_2{}^{N_1=0}$. Since $\vec{x}11$ is a positive example, we must have $\vec{x}11 \in N_1 \cap N_2{}^{N_1=1}$. From $B_1, B_2 < 0$, we know that $\vec{x}01, \vec{x}10 \in N_2{}^{N_1=1}$. Since $\vec{x}00 \in N_1 \cap N_2{}^{N_1=1}$ and $A_1, A_2 > 0$, it follows that $\vec{x}01, \vec{x}10 \in N_1$. Thus, we have to conclude that $\vec{x}01, \vec{x}10 \in N_1 \cap N_2{}^{N_1=1}$. But this implies that $\vec{x}01$ and $\vec{x}10$ are positive examples, a contradiction! This proves our claim and shows that the quadrant solution to $S$ is

$$[\vec{a}; \theta_1] \wedge [\vec{b}; \theta_2 - g_1].$$

Case 2. The case when $g_1 < 0$ can be proved similarly, except the trivial quadrant solution is

$$[\vec{b}; \theta_2 - g_1] \wedge [\vec{b}; \theta_2 - g_1].$$

Otherwise we claim for all $\vec{x} \in S^+$ that

$$\vec{x}00 \in \overline{N_1} \cap N_2{}^{N_1=0}.$$

This shows that the quadrant solution to $S$ is

$$[-\vec{a}; -\theta_1 + \eta] \wedge [\vec{b}; \theta_2],$$

where $0 < \eta \leq \min_{\vec{x} \in S^+}\{\theta_1 - \vec{a}\vec{x}\}$. $\qquad\square$

**Corollary 2** *The OPTIMAL CONSISTENT NET problem defined in the last section is $\mathcal{NP}$-complete, even if the inputs are boolean.*

*Proof Sketch*: This result holds, even for the special case of $K = 2$, as a consequence of Theorem 14. □

Blum and Rivest [1988] have shown that the problem of whether $S^+$ can be isolated by two parallel planes is also $\mathcal{NP}$-complete. Since our proof can be modified to cover this restricted case, we have also proved the following theorem:

**Theorem 15** *It is $\mathcal{NP}$-complete to decide whether there is a restricted 2-cascade neural net $f$, where $\vec{b} = -\vec{a}$, consistent with a set of training examples.*

*Proof Sketch*: The only modification needed is as follows: Suppose the quadrant solution to $S$ is

$$[\vec{a}; \theta_1] \wedge [-\vec{a}; \theta_2].$$

Since the inputs are binary vectors, we may assume that $|\theta_1|, |\theta_2| \leq \sum_{i=1}^{n} |a_i|$ without loss of generality. Now it is easy to see that the following restricted 2-cascade neural net is consistent with $T$:

$$
\begin{aligned}
N_1 &= [\vec{a}, -2A, -2A; \theta_1], \\
N_2 &= [-\vec{a}, 2A, 2A, 3A - \theta_2; 3A],
\end{aligned}
$$

where $A > \sum_{i=1}^{n} |a_i|$. □

We are hopeful that our reduction for 2-cascade neural nets can be extended to handle $k$-cascade neural nets, for each $k \geq 3$, by adding new dimensions and creating an augmented training set in a similar manner. We make the following conjecture:

**Conjecture 1** *Training a $k$-cascade neural net is $\mathcal{NP}$-complete for each $k \geq 2$.*

# 6   CONCLUSIONS

Neural nets offer the potential of learning a wide variety of concepts in a simple, uniform way. To fully evaluate this potential, we must determine how difficult it is to construct a neural net that learns a particular class of concepts as a function of the concept complexity, the size of the net architecture, and so on. Difficult concepts cannot be learned efficiently for any net architecture, while simple concepts can be learned quickly (perhaps by specialized learning algorithms) if the architecture is appropriately sized and properly interconnected.

Back propagation [Rumelhart et al 1986] [Hinton 1989] is a method for self-programming neural nets with differentiable node functions. Surprisingly little is known about the conditions under which back propagation works well and efficiently. Although we may show by counting arguments that back propagation works efficiently in learning constant functions, little can be proved beyond that. It is also of interest to show that back propagation works better given non-optimal rather than optimal net architectures.

Self-programming methods are constrained by the network architecture, in that the computation done during training must be local in nature and each example is processed somewhat in parallel, depending upon the topology of the network. This lies somewhat between unconstrained algorithms for training and the parallel algorithms considered in [Vitter and Lin 1988], in which all examples are considered in parallel.

There are other ways to measure the size of a net architecture besides the number of non-input units. For example, we might consider the number of weights or the total number of bits to represent the weights. Corresponding results for other size measures will be reported in the full version of this paper.

# REFERENCES

E. Baum and D. Haussler [1988]. "What Size Net Gives Valid Generalization?", *Proceedings of the IEEE Conference on Neural Information Processing Systems,* Denver, CO (November 1988).

A. Blum and R. L. Rivest [1988]. "Training a 3-Node Neural Network is $\mathcal{NP}$-Complete," *Proceedings of the First ACM Workshop on the Computational Learning Theory,* Cambridge, MA (August 1988), 9–18.

A. Blumer, A. Ehrenfeucht, D. Haussler, and M. K. Warmuth [1989]. "Learnability and the Vapnik-Chervonenkis Dimension," *Journal of the Association for Computing Machinery,* to appear.

M. L. Dertouzos [1965]. *Threshold Logic: A Synthesis Approach,* MIT Press, Cambridge, MA (1965).

M. R. Garey and D. S. Johnson [1979]. *Computers and intractability: A Guide to the Theory of $\mathcal{NP}$-completeness,* W. H. Freeman and Co., San Francisco, CA (1979).

G. E. Hinton [1989]. "Connectionist Learning Procedures," *Artificial Intelligence,* to appear.

J. S. Judd [1987]. "Complexity of Connectionist Learning with Various Node Functions," COINS Technical Report No. 87–60, University of Massachusetts (July 1987).

J. S. Judd [1988]. "On the Complexity of Loading Shallow Neural Networks," *Journal of Complexity,* 4 (1988), 177–192.

M. Kearns and L. G. Valiant [1988]. "Learning Boolean Formulæ or Finite Automata is as Hard as Factoring," Technical Report No. TR–14–88, Aiken Computational Laboratory, Harvard University, Cambridge, MA (November 1988).

D. E. Rumelhart, G. E. Hinton, and R. J. Williams [1986]. "Learning Internal Representations by Error Propagation," *Parallel Distributed Processing,* edited by D. E. Rumelhart and J. E. McClelland, MIT Press, Cambridge, MA (1986), 318–362.

L. J. Stockmeyer [1977]. "The Polynomial-Time Hierarchy," *Theoretical Computer Science,* **3** (1977), 1–22.

L. J. Stockmeyer and A. R. Meyer [1973]. "Word Problems Requiring Exponential Time: Preliminary Report," *Proceedings of the Fifth Annual Symposium on the Theory of Computing* (1973), 1–9.

L. G. Valiant [1984]. "A Theory of the Learnable," *Communications of the ACM*, **27**(11) (November 1984), 1134–1142.

J. S. Vitter and J. H. Lin [1988]. "Learning in Parallel," *Proceedings of the First ACM Workshop on the Computational Learning Theory*, Cambridge, MA (August 1988), 106–124.

C. Wrathall [1977]. "Complete Sets and the Polynomial-Time Hierarchy," *Theoretical Computer Science*, **3** (1977), 23–33.

# Equivalence Queries
# and
# Approximate Fingerprints

Dana Angluin *
Yale University

## Abstract

We report results showing that there is no polynomial time algorithm using only equivalence queries that exactly identifies deterministic finite state acceptors, nondeterministic finite state acceptors, context free grammars, disjunctive or conjunctive normal form boolean formulas, or $\mu$-formulas.

## 1 Introduction

Consider the problem of exactly identifying deterministic finite state acceptors (dfas) in polynomial time using various types of queries. In [2] there is a solution that uses equivalence and membership queries. There is an easy argument ("passwords") that shows that there is no solution to this problem using only membership queries even if we are given a bound on the size of the unknown dfa. However, [2] left open the question of whether there might be a solution using equivalence queries only. Recently we have been able to prove that there is no solution that uses equivalence queries only [5].

Similar techniques show that there is no polynomial time algorithm to exactly identify nondeterministic finite state acceptors (nfas) or context free grammars (cfgs) [5], disjunctive normal form (DNF) formulas [4], or $\mu$-formulas [6]. These results are not conditioned on unproven complexity theoretic assumptions, but they depend critically on the form of the representation of hypotheses as inputs to the equivalence queries. They do not imply negative results for the polynomial-time pac-identifiability or the polynomial time

---

*Supported by NSF grant IRI-8718975. Author's address: Computer Science Dept., Yale University, New Haven, CT 06520, USA.

predictability of these classes. The purpose of this paper is to illustrate the techniques and discuss the meaning of the results; full proofs may be found in the references cited.

## 2    The basic idea

The basic idea of the method is to exhibit a phenomenon we term "approximate fingerprints" in the class $H$ of hypotheses being considered. That is, we exhibit some target set $T$ of hypotheses such that for each hypothesis $h$ from $H$, there is is an example $x_h$ such that "very few" hypotheses in $T$ classify $x_h$ the same way that $h$ does. Although the behavior of $h$ in classifying $x_h$ does not uniquely identify an element of $T$, it narrows the possibilities to a superpolynomially small fraction of $T$.

These approximate fingerprints can be used by an adversary to generate counterexamples to equivalence queries – if a hypothesis $h$ is proposed, then answering the equivalence query with "no" and the counterexample $x_h$ means that the adversary has eliminated only a superpolynomially small fraction of the target set $T$ as candidates for the correct hypothesis. This can be repeated by the adversary a polynomial number of times without exhausting the set of consistent candidates.

## 3    Representations of concepts

We are interested in representations of concepts, which we take to be specified by a quadruple

$$\mathcal{R} = \langle \Sigma, \Delta, R, c \rangle$$

where $\Sigma$ and $\Delta$ are finite alphabets, $R$ is a subset of $\Delta^*$, and $c$ is a map from $R$ to subsets of $\Sigma^*$. $\Sigma$ is the alphabet of examples, and a *concept* is any subset of $\Sigma^*$. $R$ is the set of representations, and $c$ is the map that specifies which concept is represented by a given representation. The class of concepts represented by $\mathcal{R}$ is just $\{c(r) : r \in R\}$. For any concept $c$, $\chi_c$ denotes the characteristic function of $c$.

As an example, for dfas the strings in $R$ represent deterministic finite state acceptors over the input alphabet $\Sigma$ in some straightforward way, and for each $r \in R$, $c(r)$ denotes the set of strings accepted by the dfa represented by $r$. The class of concepts represented in this case is the class of all regular sets over the alphabet $\Sigma$. We use a similar representation for nfas. For cfgs, we may assume that each grammar is in Chomsky normal form, since there is a polynomial time algorithm to convert an arbitrary context free grammar into Chomsky normal form.

For propositional formulas we assume that $\Sigma = \{0, 1\}$. Each $r \in R$ will represent a boolean formula over the variables $X_1, X_2, \ldots$, together with an integer $n$ such that if $X_i$

occurs in the formula then $n \geq i$. The value of $c(r)$ is the set of all binary strings $w$ of length $n$ such that the formula represented by $r$ is assigned 1 by the assignment $X_i = w[i]$ for all $i = 1, \ldots, n$.

## 3.1    Exact identification with equivalence queries

Fix a representation of concepts $\mathcal{R} = \langle \Sigma, \Delta, R, c \rangle$. For the exact identification problem there is an unknown concept $c_*$, and information may be gathered about $c_*$ by asking equivalence queries. The input to an equivalence query is any $r \in R$ and the response is "yes" if $c(r) = c_*$ and "no" otherwise. In addition to the answer "no", a *counterexample* is supplied, that is, a string $w \in \Sigma^*$ such that $w \in c_* \oplus c(r)$. The choice of a counterexample is assumed to be arbitrary.

A deterministic algorithm $A$ exactly identifies $\mathcal{R}$ using only equivalence queries if and only if for every $c_*$ represented by $\mathcal{R}$, when $A$ is run with an oracle for equivalence queries for $c_*$, it eventually halts and outputs some $r$ such that $c(r) = c_*$. Such an algorithm runs in polynomial time if and only if there is a polynomial $p(n, m)$ such that for every $c_*$ represented by $\mathcal{R}$, if $n$ is the minimum length of any $r \in R$ such that $c(r) = c_*$ then when $A$ is run with an oracle for equivalence queries for $c_*$, at any point in the run the time used by $A$ is bounded by $p(n, m)$, where $m$ is the maximum length of any counterexample returned by equivalence queries so far in the run, or $m = 0$ if no equivalence queries have been used. (Note: this definition corrects a loophole in the definition used in [2]. For further discussion, see [5].)

## 3.2    Approximate fingerprints

Let $T$ denote a class of concepts, $w$ a string from $\Sigma^*$, $b$ an element of $\{0, 1\}$, and $\alpha > 0$ a real number. We say that the pair $\langle w, b \rangle$ is an *$\alpha$-approximate fingerprint with respect to $T$* provided that

$$|\{c \in T : \chi_c(w) = b\}| < \alpha |T|.$$

That is, the number of concepts in $T$ that agree with the classification $b$ of $w$ is strictly less than the fraction $\alpha$ of the total number of concepts in $T$.

A *sequence of concept classes* is a sequence

$$C_1, C_2, C_3, \ldots$$

such that each $C_i$ is a class of concepts. Such a sequence is *polynomially bounded* (with respect to a given representation $\mathcal{R}$) provided that there exists a polynomial $p(n)$ such that for all $c \in C_n$, there is a representation $r \in R$ such that $c(r) = c$ and $|r| \leq p(n)$. That is, the shortest representation of every concept in $C_n$ is bounded by a polynomial in $n$.

A representation of concepts $\mathcal{R}$ is said to have the *approximate fingerprint property* if there exists a polynomially bounded sequence of concept classes $T_1, T_2, T_3, \ldots$, and a polynomial $p(n)$ such that for any polynomial $q(n)$, for all sufficiently large $n$, $T_n$ contains at least two concepts and if $r \in R$ and $|r| \leq q(n)$ then there exists a string $w \in \Sigma^*$ of length at most $p(n)$ such that $\langle w, \chi_{c(r)}(w) \rangle$ is a $1/q(n)$-approximate fingerprint with respect to $T_n$. That is,

$$|\{c \in T_n : \chi_c(w) = \chi_{c(r)}(w)\}| < |T_n|/q(n).$$

The use of the approximate fingerprint property by an adversary is captured in the following theorem.

**Theorem 1** *Let $\mathcal{R}$ be a representation of concepts with the approximate fingerprint property. Then there is no polynomial time algorithm for exact identification of $\mathcal{R}$ using only equivalence queries.*

*Proof.* Suppose to the contrary that $A$ is an algorithm that exactly identifies $\mathcal{R}$ using only equivalence queries, and $A$ runs in time bounded by the polynomial $p(n, m)$.

Since $\mathcal{R}$ has the approximate fingerprint property, we may assume that $T_1, T_2, \ldots$ is a polynomially bounded sequence of concept classes (bounded by the polynomial $p_1(n)$), and $p_2(n)$ is a polynomial such that for any polynomial $q(n)$ and for all sufficiently large $n$, $T_n$ contains at least two concepts and for any $r \in R$ with $|r| \leq q(n)$ there exists a string $w \in \Sigma^*$ such that $|w| \leq p_2(n)$ and $\langle w, \chi_{c(r)}(w) \rangle$ is a $1/q(n)$-approximate fingerprint with respect to $T_n$.

We may assume that the polynomials $p(n, m)$, $p_1(n)$ and $p_2(n)$ are all positive and nondecreasing over the natural numbers. Let $q(n) = 2p(p_1(n), p_2(n))$. Let $n$ be sufficiently large with respect to $q(n)$ that the consequence in the previous paragraph follows. Consider the adversary that answers an equivalence query with input $r \in R$ as follows. If $|r| \leq q(n)$ then the reply is "no" and the counterexample is some string $w \in \Sigma^*$ such that $|w| \leq p_2(n)$ and $\langle w, \chi_{c(r)}(w) \rangle$ is a $1/q(n)$-approximate fingerprint with respect to $T_n$. If $|r| > q(n)$, then the adversary answers "yes".

Run the algorithm $A$ with this adversary answering each equivalence query. We claim that for each $1 \leq i \leq q(n)/2$, at least $i$ equivalence queries are made, and after $i$ equivalence queries have been answered, more than $(1 - i/q(n))|T_n|$ concepts in $T_n$ are consistent with the answers given so far, and all the counterexamples given so far are of length at most $p_2(n)$. We prove this by induction on $i$.

Since $A$ exactly identifies $\mathcal{R}$, it must identify each element of $T_n$, and since each element of $T_n$ can be represented by an $r \in R$ of length at most $p_1(n)$, the running time of $A$ at each point must be bounded by $p(p_1(n), m)$, where $m$ is the maximum length of any counterexample seen to that point, or $m = 0$ if no counterexamples have been seen.

Since $|T_n| \geq 2$, $A$ must ask at least one equivalence query. Consider the first equivalence query asked by $A$, say with $r$. Clearly, $|r| \leq p(p_1(n), 0) \leq q(n)$, so the adversary answers with "no" and a counterexample $w$ such that $|w| \leq p_1(n)$ and

$$|\{c \in T_n : \chi_c(w) = \chi_{c(r)}(w)\}| < |T_n|/q(n).$$

The number of elements of $T_n$ consistent with this answer is greater than $(1 - 1/q(n))|T_n|$.

Suppose the claim is true for some $1 \leq i < q(n)/2$. Since more than $(1 - i/q(n))|T_n| \geq (1/2)|T_n|$ elements of $T_n$ are consistent with the answers given so far, and since $|T_n| \geq 2$, at least two distinct concepts in $T_n$ are consistent with the answers given so far. Hence, $A$ must ask another equivalence query, say with input $r \in R$. Then since all the counterexamples so far have been of length at most $p_2(n)$, the running time of $A$, and therefore the length of $r$, must be bounded by $p(p_1(n), p_2(n)) \leq q(n)$. Thus, the adversary answers with "no" and a counterexample $w$ of length at most $p_2(n)$ such that

$$|\{c \in T_n : \chi_c(w) = \chi_{c(r)}(w)\}| < |T_n|/q(n).$$

This answer is inconsistent with fewer than $|T_n|/q(n)$ elements of $T_n$, so more than $(1 - (i + 1)/q(n))|T_n|$ elements of $T_n$ are consistent with the replies to the first $i + 1$ queries.

This completes the induction. Now consider the situation after the first $q(n)/2$ queries have been answered. More than $(1/2)|T_n|$ elements of $T_n$ are consistent with all the replies that have been given, and since $|T_n| \geq 2$, this means that at least two distinct concepts from $T_n$ are consistent with all the replies so far. Moreover, all the counterexamples that have been given are of length at most $p_2(n)$, which means that the running time permitted to $A$ is bounded by $p(p_1(n), p_2(n)) = q(n)/2$. Hence, if $A$ does not ask another query, it will give an incorrect answer for at least one element of $T_n$. But if $A$ asks another query, it will exceed its time bound. This contradiction shows that no such algorithm $A$ is possible. Q.E.D.

Note that the running time of $A$ is only used to give a bound on the input size and number of equivalence queries. Thus in fact there is no algorithm to exactly identify $\mathcal{R}$ that uses a polynomially bounded number of equivalence queries of polynomially bounded size. In subsequent sections we illustrate the approximate fingerprint property for some concrete classes of interest.

# 4    Some examples of approximate fingerprints

## 4.1    dfas

Let $\Sigma$ be the finite alphabet $\{0, 1\}$. Let $\Sigma^k$ denote the set of all strings over $\Sigma$ of length $k$. If $x, y \in \Sigma^k$, let $d(x, y)$ denote the Hamming distance between $x$ and $y$, that is, the number of bit positions $1 \leq i \leq k$ such that $x$ and $y$ are different in the $i^{th}$ bit.

For any $n \geq 1$ and $1 \leq i \leq n$ define the language

$$L(i,n) = \{ubvbw : u \in \Sigma^{i-1}, b \in \Sigma, v \in \Sigma^{n-1}, w \in \Sigma^{n-i}\}.$$

That is, $L(i,n)$ is the set of all strings of length $2n$ such that the $i^{th}$ bit is equal to the $(n+i)^{th}$ bit. Note that $L(i,n)$ is accepted by a dfa with $3n+2$ states.

The target class $T_n$ will consist of all languages $L$ that can be obtained as a concatenation

$$L(i_1,n) \cdot L(i_2,n) \cdots L(i_n,n)$$

such that $1 \leq i_j \leq n$ for each $j$. Thus there are $n^n$ distinct languages in the class $T_n$. Each one can be accepted by a dfa of $3n^2 + 2$ states, so this sequence of concept classes is polynomially bounded.

Now we consider two further sets of strings:

$$A_n = \{x_1 x_1 x_2 x_2 \cdots x_n x_n : \text{ for each } i, x_i \in \Sigma^n\},$$

and

$$B_n = \{x_1 y_1 x_2 y_2 \cdots x_n y_n : \text{ for each } i, x_i \in \Sigma^n, y_i \in \Sigma^n, d(x_i, y_i) > n/4\}.$$

Note that $A_n$ is the intersection of all the languages in $T_n$, and the smallest dfa to accept $A_n$ has a number of states that grows exponentially in $n$.

For every string $w \in B_n$, there are no more than $(3n/4)^n$ languages $L \in T(n)$ that contain $w$. This is an exponentially small fraction of the languages in $T$ since $(3n/4)^n$ divided by $n^n$ is $(3/4)^n$.

Now consider some fixed polynomial $q(n)$. We prove that for all sufficiently large $n$, if $M$ is any dfa with at most $q(n)$ states, then either $M$ rejects a string $w$ in $A_n$ or accepts a string $w$ in $B_n$. In either case, if $n$ is sufficiently large then $\langle w, M(w) \rangle$ is a $1/q(n)$-approximate fingerprint with respect to $T_n$, since in the first case no elements of $T_n$ agree with $M$'s classification of $w$, and in the second case, an exponentially small fraction of the elements of $T_n$ do. The argument is reproduced here from [5].

**Lemma 2** *There exists a constant $c_0$, $0 < c_0 < 1$, such that for all sufficiently large positive integers $n$,*

$$\sum_{i=0}^{\lceil n/4 \rceil} \binom{n}{i} < 2^{c_0 n}.$$

The proof is by straightforward application of Stirling's approximation for $n!$. An immediate consequence is the following.

**Lemma 3** *For the constant $c_0$ of Lemma 2 and all sufficiently large $n$, if $x \in \Sigma^n$ then there are fewer than $2^{c_0 n}$ strings $y \in \Sigma^n$ such that $d(x, y) \leq n/4$.*

*Proof.* Let $c_0$ and $n$ be as indicated, and let $x$ be any element of $\Sigma^n$. Then a string $y \in \Sigma^n$ is such that $d(x, y) \leq n/4$ if and only if $y$ may be obtained from $x$ by complementing at most $n/4$ of the bits of $x$. Hence, any such $y$ can be obtained by selecting a subset of $i \leq n/4$ bits of $x$ and complementing them. Thus, there are at most

$$\sum_{i=0}^{\lceil n/4 \rceil} \binom{n}{i}$$

such strings $y$, and this is less than $2^{c_0 n}$ by Lemma 2. Q.E.D.

**Lemma 4** *Let $q(n)$ be any increasing polynomial in $n$. For all sufficiently large $n$, if $M$ is any dfa of size at most $q(n)$ and $q_i$ is any state of $M$, then there exist two strings $x$ and $y$ of length $n$ such that $d(x, y) > n/4$ and $\delta(q_i, x) = \delta(q_i, y)$, where $\delta$ is the transition function of $M$.*

*Proof.* Consider $\delta(q_i, x)$ for all $x \in \Sigma^n$. There are at most $q(n)$ states in $M$, so there is at least one state, say $q_j$, such that $\delta(q_i, x) = q_j$ for at least $2^n/q(n)$ values of $x \in \Sigma^n$.

Choose any $x \in \Sigma^n$ such that $\delta(q_i, x) = q_j$. By Lemma 3, there are fewer than $2^{c_0 n}$ strings $x' \in \Sigma^n$ such that $d(x, x') \leq n/4$.

Since for all sufficiently large $n$,

$$2^n/q(n) > 2^{c_0 n},$$

there must be at least one string $y \in \Sigma^n$ such that $\delta(q_i, y) = q_j$ and $d(x, y) > n/4$. Q.E.D.

**Lemma 5** *Let $q(n)$ be any increasing polynomial in $n$. Then for all sufficiently large $n$, if $M$ is any dfa of size at most $q(n)$ that accepts all the strings in $A_n$, then $M$ accepts some string in $B_n$.*

*Proof.* Let $n$ be sufficiently large that the conclusion of Lemma 4 holds for $q(n)$ and $n$. Assume that $M$ is any dfa of size at most $q(n)$ and $A_n \subseteq L(M)$. Let $\delta$ denote the transition function of $M$ and let $q_0$ denote the initial state of $M$. We construct a string in $B_n$ accepted by $M$ by induction.

By Lemma 4 there are two strings $x_1$ and $y_1$ in $\Sigma^n$ such that $\delta(q_0, x_1) = \delta(q_0, y_1)$ and $d(x_1, y_1) > n/4$. Let $q_1 = \delta(q_0, x_1 x_1)$. Note that

$$\delta(q_0, x_1 x_1) = \delta(q_0, y_1 x_1) = q_1.$$

Assume that for some $k$, $1 \leq k < n$, and for all $i$, $1 \leq i \leq k$, there exist states $q_i$ and strings $x_i$ and $y_i$ in $\Sigma^n$ such that

$$\delta(q_{i-1}, x_i x_i) = \delta(q_{i-1}, y_i x_i) = q_i$$

and $d(x_i, y_i) > n/4$. Then, by Lemma 4, there exist strings $x_{k+1}$ and $y_{k+1}$ in $\Sigma^n$ such that

$$\delta(q_k, x_{k+1}) = \delta(q_k, y_{k+1})$$

and $d(x_{k+1}, y_{k+1}) > n/4$. Let

$$q_{k+1} = \delta(q_k, x_{k+1} x_{k+1}) = \delta(q_k, y_{k+1} x_{k+1})$$

and the induction hypothesis is satisfied for $k + 1$.

Thus for $i = 1, \ldots, n$, there exist states $q_i$ and strings $x_i$ and $y_i$ in $\Sigma^n$ such that

$$\delta(q_{i-1}, x_i x_i) = \delta(q_{i-1}, y_i x_i) = q_i$$

and $d(x_i, y_i) > n/4$. Thus,

$$x_1 x_1 x_2 x_2 \cdots x_n x_n \in A_n$$

and

$$y_1 x_1 y_2 x_2 \cdots y_n x_n \in B_n.$$

Moreover,

$$\delta(q_0, x_1 x_1 x_2 x_2 \cdots x_n x_n) = \delta(q_0, y_1 x_1 y_2 x_2 \cdots y_n x_n) = q_n.$$

Since $M$ accepts every string in $A_n$ by hypothesis, the state $q_n$ must be accepting, so $M$ accepts the string

$$y_1 x_1 y_2 x_2 \cdots y_n x_n \in B_n.$$

Q.E.D.

## 4.2    nfas and cfgs

The result for dfas does not directly imply the corresponding result for nfas or cfgs since the definition of approximate fingerprints is representation-dependent.

For the case of nfas, we use the same target class $T_n$ and the same set $A_n$ but replace the set $B_n$ by the following. The set $B'_n$ consists of all strings

$$x_1 y_1 x_2 y_2 \cdots x_n y_n$$

such that for each $i$, $x_i \in \Sigma^n$ and $y_i \in \Sigma^n$, and for at least half the values of $j$ between 1 and $n$, $d(x_j, y_j) > n/4$. For any string $w \in B'_n$ there are at most $n^{n/2}(3n/4)^{n/2}$ languages

$L \in T_n$ that contain $w$. This is an exponentially small $((3/4)^{n/2})$ fraction of the elements of $T_n$.

In the full paper [5] we prove that for any polynomial $q(n)$, for all sufficiently large $n$, any nfa of at most $q(n)$ states must either reject a string from $A_n$ or accept a string from $B_n'$, which provides an approximate fingerprint for the nfa with respect to $T_n$. Note that since we have a target class describable by small dfas, this construction implies that even if we are allowed to ask equivalence queries with nfas, there is still no polynomial time exact identification algorithm for dfas using equivalence queries.

For the case of cfgs the techniques become rather involved, but the target class and the approximate fingerprints are easy to understand. For each $n \geq 1$ let

$$C_{1,n} = \{xx^r y : x \in \Sigma^n, y \in \Sigma^n\},$$

where $x^r$ denotes the reverse of the string $x$, and let

$$C_{2,n} = \{yx^r x : x \in \Sigma^n, y \in \Sigma^n\}.$$

Each of $C_{1,n}$ and $C_{2,n}$ can be generated by a Chomsky normal form cfg with $4n+1$ nonterminals. Let

$$I_n = C_{1,n} \cap C_{2,n} = \{xx^r x : x \in \Sigma^n\}.$$

Note that the smallest cfg to generate $I_n$ has size exponential in $n$.

The target class $T_n^{cfg}$ contains each language of the form

$$C_{i_1,n} \cdot C_{i_2,n} \cdots C_{i_n,n}$$

where $i_j \in \{1,2\}$ for each $j$. Thus, there are $2^n$ distinct languages in $T_n^{cfg}$. Each of them can be generated by a Chomsky normal form grammar with $6n$ nonterminals. Thus, this sequence of concept classes is polynomially bounded.

The set of strings corresponding to $A_n$ is just the intersection of all the sets in $T_n^{cfg}$, that is,

$$A_n^{cfg} = (I_n)^n = \{x_1 x_1^r x_1 x_2 x_2^r x_2 \cdots x_n x_n^r x_n : \text{ for each } i, x_i \in \Sigma^n\}.$$

Clearly, $A_n^{cfg}$ is a subset of every language in $T_n^{cfg}$.

For any constant $0 < c < 1$, let $B_{c,n}^{cfg}$ consist of all string of the form

$$w_1 w_2 \cdots w_n$$

such that each $w_i \in \Sigma^{3n}$ and for at least $cn$ values of $j$, $w_j \notin I_n$. Note that for each string $w \in B_{c,n}^{cfg}$, there are at most $2^{n-cn}$ languages $L \in T_n^{cfg}$ that contain $w$. This is an exponentially small $(2^{-cn})$ fraction of $T_n^{cfg}$.

The report [5] proves that there is a constant $c > 0$ such that for any polynomial $q(n)$ and all sufficiently large $n$, any Chomsky normal form context free grammar with at most $q(n)$ nonterminals must either reject a string in $A_n^{cfg}$ or accept a string in $B_{c,n}^{cfg}$, which provides an approximate fingerprint for cfgs with respect to the target class $T_n^{cfg}$.

## 4.3   DNF formulas and $\mu$-formulas

For DNF formulas, the property that we use in the proof is that every DNF formula is satisfied by an assignment with "few" 1's or is falsified by an assignment with "many" 1's. If $a$ is an arbitrary assignment to $X_1, X_2, \ldots X_n$, let $p(a)$ denote the number of variables assigned 1 by $a$, that is,

$$p(a) = |\{i : a(X_i) = 1\}|.$$

Then the fact we use is the following.

**Lemma 6** *Let $n \geq 4$ be an integer, and let $\phi$ be any DNF formula with $t \geq 1$ terms over $V_n$. If $\phi$ contains some term with fewer than $\sqrt{n}$ positive occurrences of literals, then there is an assignment $a_1$ such that $p(a_1) < \sqrt{n}$ and $a_1(\phi) = 1$. If every term of $\phi$ contains at least $\sqrt{n}$ positive occurrences of literals, then there is an assignment $a_0$ such that $p(a_0) \geq n - 1 - (\sqrt{n} - 1) \log t$ and $a_0(\phi) = 0$.*

Thus, a DNF formula with no more than $p(n)$ terms either is satisfied by an assignment with fewer than $\sqrt{n}$ ones or is falsified by an assignment with fewer than about $(\sqrt{n}) \log p(n)$ zeroes. A particular sequence of target classes of concepts is exhibited for which this fact guarantees approximate fingerprints [4].

We also consider $\mu$-formulas, that is, boolean formulas that contain at most one occurrence of every variable. These are also called "read once" formulas. The size of such a formula is just the number of occurrences of variables that it contains. The following fact provides approximate fingerprints in this case [6].

**Lemma 7** *If $\phi$ is any non-constant $\mu$-formula of size $n$, then either there is an assignment with at most $\sqrt{n}$ ones that satisfies $\phi$ or there is an assignment with at most $\sqrt{n}$ zeroes that falsifies $\phi$.*

# 5   Comments

Since the "hard classes" $T_n$ are finite and fixed-length, our proofs also show that dfas, nfas, and cfgs for finite and fixed-length languages cannot be learned in polynomial time using only equivalence queries. See also Ibarra and Jiang's reduction of the general case to the finite and fixed-length case for dfas [10]. In the case of dfas and nfas the target classes $T_n$ are also zero-reversible [1], thus the zero-reversible languages cannot be learned in polynomial time using only equivalence queries, even if those queries are allowed to use nfas to represent the hypotheses.

The results for DNF formulas hold also for CNF formulas. The proof in [4] shows that a polynomial time algorithm for CNF formulas using only equivalence queries can be correct for all $k$-CNF formulas (CNF formulas with at most $k$ literals per clause) for only a finite number of values of $k$. This is the behavior achieved by the equivalence query algorithm for $k$-CNF formulas in [3], adapted from the corresponding algorithm given by Valiant [15].

In [3] there is a polynomial time algorithm that exactly identifies monotone DNF formulas using equivalence queries and membership queries. The target classes used in [4] are representable by monotone DNF formulas, which shows that membership queries are essential to that result.

These arguments do NOT show that these classes are not polynomial-time learnable in Valiant's model of *pac*-identification [15] or in the prediction model [8, 9, 12, 13]. Polynomial-time identification using only equivalence queries implies polynomial-time *pac*-identification, but not conversely. In particular, with an oracle for NP each of these classes becomes *pac*-learnable, by the Occam's razor technique [7], so proving one of these classes cannot be *pac*-identified in polynomial time involves proving or assuming $P \neq NP$, whereas our results do neither. Kearns and Valiant [11] have shown that dfas, nfas, cfgs, and boolean formulas are as hard to predict modulo a polynomial time transformation as certain cryptographic predicates are to compute.

It is interesting to note that identification of dfas with equivalence queries seems to be "harder" than successful prediction. If efficient prediction of dfas in the *pac*-identification sense is required, an oracle for an NP-complete problem is sufficient. With an oracle for a #P-complete problem we can implement an efficient majority-vote prediction strategy for dfas which has a polynomial bound on the worst case number of errors of prediction. However, even an oracle for a PSPACE-complete problem doesn't help in the case of identification of dfas with equivalence queries.

# 6    Acknowledgments

This research was funded by the National Science Foundation, under grant number IRI-8718975. Thanks to Lenny Pitt for helpful suggestions.

# References

[1] D. Angluin. Inference of reversible languages. *J. ACM*, 29:741–765, 1982.

[2] D. Angluin. Learning regular sets from queries and counterexamples. *Information and Computation*, 75:87–106, 1987.

[3] D. Angluin. Queries and concept learning. *Machine Learning*, 2:319–342, 1987.

[4] D. Angluin. Equivalence queries and DNF formulas. Technical report, Yale University, YALE/DCS/RR-659, 1988.

[5] D. Angluin. Negative results for equivalence queries. Technical report, Yale University, YALE/DCS/RR-648, 1988.

[6] D. Angluin. Using queries to identify $\mu$-formulas. Technical report, Yale University, YALE/DCS/RR-694, 1989.

[7] A. Blumer, A. Ehrenfeucht, D. Haussler, and M. Warmuth. Occam's razor. *Information Processing Letters*, 24:377–380, 1987.

[8] D. Haussler, M. Kearns, N. Littlestone, and M. Warmuth. Equivalence of models for polynomial learnability. In *Proc. of the 1988 Workshop on Computational Learning Theory*, pages 42–55. Morgan Kaufmann Publishers, 1988.

[9] D. Haussler, N. Littlestone, and M. Warmuth. Predicting $\{0,1\}$-functions on randomly drawn points. In *Proc. 29th Symposium on Foundations of Computer Science*, pages 100–109. IEEE, 1988.

[10] O. Ibarra and T. Jiang. Learning regular languages from counterexamples. In *Proc. of the 1988 Workshop on Computational Learning Theory*, pages 371–385. Morgan Kaufmann Publishers, 1988.

[11] M. Kearns and L. Valiant. Cryptographic limitations on learning boolean formulae and finite automata. In *Proc. 21st ACM Symposium on Theory of Computing*, pages 433–444. ACM, 1989.

[12] N. Littlestone. Learning quickly when irrelevant attributes abound: a new linear-threshold algorithm. *Machine Learning*, 2:285–318, 1988.

[13] L. Pitt and M. Warmuth. Reductions among prediction problems: On the difficulty of predicting automata. In *Proceedings of the Third Annual Structure in Complexity Theory Conference*, pages 60–69. IEEE Computer Society Press, 1988.

[14] S. Porat and J. Feldman. Learning automata from ordered examples. In *Proc. of the 1988 Workshop on Computational Learning Theory*, pages 386–396. Morgan Kaufmann Publishers, 1988.

[15] L. G. Valiant. A theory of the learnable. *C. ACM*, 27:1134–1142, 1984.

# LEARNING READ-ONCE FORMULAS USING MEMBERSHIP QUERIES

Lisa Hellerstein*
Computer Science Division
University of California
Berkeley, CA 94720
hstein@ernie.berkeley.edu

Marek Karpinski**
International Computer Science Institute
Berkeley, CA 94704
marek@icsi.berkeley.edu

## ABSTRACT

In this paper we examine the problem of exact learning (and inferring) of read-once formulas (also called μ-formulas or boolean trees) using membership queries. An simple argument on the cardinality of the set of all (read-once) 1-term DNF formulas implies an exponential lower bound on the number of membership queries necessary to learn read-once formulas. We prove that it is possible to learn *monotone* read-once formulas in polynomial time using membership queries.† We present an algorithm that runs in time $O(n^3)$ and makes $O(n^3)$ queries to the oracle. We introduce a new oracle, the *projective equivalence oracle*. We show that our membership query algorithm can be adapted to learn arbitrary read-once formulas in polynomial time using a projective equivalence oracle (or, by an observation of Angluin, using superset and subset queries). Our algorithms are based on a combinatorial characterization of read-once formulas developed by Karchmer et. al. [KLNSW88]. We use this combinatorial characterization to prove two other results. We show that read-once formulas can be learned in polynomial time using only one of the three oracles used in Valiant's polynomial-time algorithm. In addition, we show that given an arbitrary boolean formula $f$, the problem of deciding whether $f$ defines a read-once function is complete in the class $D^P$ under randomized $NC^1$-reductions. The main results of this paper can also be interpreted in terms of efficient input oracle algorithms for boolean function interpolation (cf. [KUW85], [GKS]).

## 1. INTRODUCTION

Let $g : \{0,1\}^V \rightarrow \{0,1\}$ and let $|V| = n$. $g$ is called a *read-once function* if $g$ can be written as a *read-once formula,* that is, as a Boolean formula (with $\wedge$, $\vee$, $\neg$ as a basis) in which every variable in $V$ appears at most once. Read-once formulas are also called μ-formulas. Every read-once formula can be represented as a tree in which the internal nodes of the tree contain $\wedge$ and $\vee$ in alternating levels, and the leaves contain the variables (possibly in negated form). We consider two read-once formulas to be identical if their tree representations are isomorphic. There is a unique read-once formula for every read-once function.

---

* Supported by NSF Grant CCR-8411954, and an AT&T GRPW grant.
**On leave from the University of Bonn. Research partially supported by DFG Grant KA 673/2-1, and by SERC Grant GR-E 68297.
† This result was independently discovered by Dana Angluin [A89] using different methods.

How hard is it to learn read-once formulas? Valiant defined three powerful oracles and showed that there exists an algorithm for exactly learning read-once formulas that makes $O(n^3)$ calls to the oracles [V84]. Pitt and Valiant proved that if RP $\neq$ NP, it is not possible to learn read-once formulas by example in polynomial time [PV85,KLPV87]. Their result also applies to learning monotone read-once formulas.

In this paper we consider the complexity of exact learning of both monotone read-once formulas and arbitrary (not necessarily monotone) read-once formulas using a membership oracle. A membership oracle is an oracle which takes as input an assignment to the variables of the formula, and outputs the value of the formula on that assignment. The power of the membership oracle in learning various classes of formulas was studied by Angluin [A88]. We note that the results of this paper can also be interpreted in terms of efficient input oracle algorithms for boolean function interpolation (cf. [KUW85], [GKS]). The algorithm developed here gives an efficient interpolation algorithms for a monotone read-once boolean function given by a (black box) input oracle (for the corresponding results using field extensions and $(\oplus, \wedge)$ formulas cf. [GKS]).

In Section 2 we note that it takes time $\Omega(2^n)$ to learn arbitrary *read-once* formulas using membership queries. We also show that given explicitly a boolean formula $f$ defining a read-once function, if $RP \neq NP$, then there does not exist a polynomial time algorithm for inferring an equivalent read-once formula. Angluin proved that it takes time $2^{\Omega(n)}$ to learn *monotone* n-term DNF formulas using membership queries [A88]. We prove that, in contrast, *monotone read-once* formulas can be learned in polynomial time using membership queries. In Section 5 we present an algorithm for learning monotone read-once formulas using membership queries that takes time $O(n^3)$ and makes $O(n^3)$ queries.† In Section 6 we introduce a new oracle, the *projective equivalence oracle*. We show how our membership query algorithm can be adapted to learn arbitrary read-once formulas using a projective equivalence oracle. By an observation of Angluin, the calls to the projective equivalence oracle in our algorithm can be replaced by subset and superset queries [A89a]. This yields an algorithm for learning arbitrary read-once formulas using subset and superset queries that runs in time $O(n^3)$ and makes $O(n^3)$ queries, answering a question raised in [A89]. Recently, Angluin has shown that equivalence queries alone are not sufficient for learning read-once formulas, even if the formulas are known to be monotone and in disjunctive normal form [A89].

Our algorithms are based on a combinatorial characterization of read-once formulas developed by Karchmer, Linial, Saks, and Wigderson [KLNSW88]. In Section 4 we discuss an algorithm for learning arbitrary read-once formulas using a *relevant possibility oracle* that is easily derived from this characterization. This algorithm is an improvement over Valiant's polynomial-time algorithm because it uses only one of the three oracles that Valiant uses, and it makes fewer oracle calls. In Section 2, we use the combinatorial characterization to show that given an arbitrary boolean formula $f$, the problem of deciding whether $f$ defines a read-one function is complete in the class $D^P$ under randomized $NC^1$-reductions.

---

† Angluin's algorithm achieves the same bounds.

## 2. LEARNING EQUIVALENT READ-ONCE FORMULAS
## FROM EXPLICITLY GIVEN FORMULAS

An easy argument on the cardinality of the set of all (read-once) 1-term DNF formulas implies an $\Omega(2^n)$ lower bound on the number of membership queries necessary to learn arbitrary read-once formulas. The computational difficulty of inferring an equivalent read-once formula from an explicitly given boolean formula is characterized by the following theorem.

**Theorem 1:** Given a boolean formula $f$ defining a read-once function, if $RP \neq NP$, then there does not exist a polynomial time algorithm for inferring an equivalent read-once formula.

**Proof:** A boolean formula with a unique satisfying assignment can be rewritten as a read-once formula consisting of one term corresponding to the satisfying assignment. Valiant and Vazirani proved that if $RP \neq NP$, there is no polynomial time algorithm for finding solutions to instances of SAT having unique solutions [VV85]. $\square$

We define now the complexity class $D^P$ (cf. [PY84]).

$$D^P = \{ L_1 - L_2 \mid L_1, L_2 \in NP \}$$

The proof of the next theorem relies on the development of Section 3. For the definition of randomized $NC$-reductions, see [C85], [KR88].

**Theorem 2:** Given an arbitrary boolean formula $f$, the problem of deciding whether $f$ defines a read-once function is complete for $D^P$ under randomized $NC^1$-reductions.

**Proof:** Suppose $f$ is a boolean formula on the variables $x_1,...,x_n$. Suppose that $f$ either defines the constant function 0, or $f$ has a unique satisfying assignment. Construct a new formula $F = f \vee (y \wedge x_1) \vee (y \wedge x_2) \vee \cdots \vee (y \wedge x_n)$ for $y \notin \{ x_1,...,x_n \}$. We prove that $f$ is satisfiable iff $F$ does not define a read-once function.

Case 1: $f = 0$. In this case, $F$ is easily seen to be read-once.

Case 2: $f$ has the unique satisfying assignment $x_1 = x_2 = \cdots = x_n = 1$. In this case, $\{ x_1, x_2,...x_n \}$ is a minterm of $F$, but $\{ x_1, x_2,...,x_n \}$ is not a maximal clique in the minterm graph of $F$. Hence $F$ is not read-once. (cf. Section 3)

Case 3: $f$ has a unique satisfying assignment different from Case 2. In this case, the satisfying assignment contains a zero at a certain variable $x_k$. From the construction of $F$, any equivalent boolean formula must contain the variable $x_k$ in negated and non-negated form. Therefore $F$ is not a read-once function.

The general problem of checking satisfiability of the function $f$ (UNIQUE SAT restricted to 0 or 1 solutions) is complete for $D^P$ using randomized $NC^1$-reductions ([VV85]). $\square$

## 3. PRELIMINARIES

In a read-once formula, each variable in the formula appears exactly once, either negated, or not negated. In this section, we describe properties of monotone read-once functions. The properties can be applied to an arbitrary read-once function $f$ by replacing every variable that appears in negated form in the read-once formula for $f$ with a new variable that represents the negation of the original variable.

One difficulty in learning arbitrary read-once formulas is to determine for each variable whether it appears in the read-once formula in its negated, or non-negated form. If this can be determined, the problem of learning arbitrary read-once formulas can usually be reduced to the monotone case (depending on which oracles are used).

Let $f : 2^V \rightarrow \{0,1\}$.

A subset $S$ of negated and non-negated variables of $V$ (no variable occuring both in negated and non-negated form) is called a *minterm* of $f$ if setting all the non-negated variables of $S$ to 1 and setting the negated variables of $S$ to 0 forces the value of $f$ to 1, and this property does not hold for any $S' \subset S$. A subset $T$ of negated and non-negated variables of $V$ is called a *maxterm* of $f$ if setting all the negated variables of $T$ to 1 and setting all the non-negated variables of $T$ to 0 forces the value of $f$ to 0, and this property does not hold for any $T' \subset T$. If $f$ is monotone, every minterm is a set of non-negated variables of $V$, and every maxterm is a set of non-negated variables of $V$.

Assume that $f$ is a monotone read-once function.

Let $V'$ denote the subset of variables of $V$ on which the value of $f$ depends. We define the *minterm graph* of $f$ to be the graph whose vertex set is $V'$, and whose edge set consists of all $\{x,y\} \subseteq V'$ such that there exists a minterm $S$ of $f$ such that $\{x,y\} \subseteq S$. We define the *maxterm graph* of $f$ to be the graph whose vertex set is $V'$, and whose edge set consists of all $\{x,y\} \subseteq V'$ such that there exists a maxterm $T$ of $f$ such that $\{x,y\} \subseteq T$.

*P4* is the chordless path on four vertices. A graph is said to be *P4-free* if it does not contain P4 as an induced subgraph.

Karchmer, Linial, Newman, Saks, and Wigderson, developed a combinatorial characterization of read-once functions. Their results include the following.

**Lemma 1 [KLNSW88]:** If $f$ is a monotone read-once function, and $G$ is its minterm graph, then the minterms of $f$ are the sets of vertices composing the maximal cliques of $G$, and the maxterms of $f$ are the sets of vertices composing the maximal independent sets of $G$. Furthermore, $G$ is P4-free.

Lemma 1 can be proved by induction on the read-once formula for $f$.

The following proposition follows directly from Lemma 1.

**Proposition 1:** If $f$ is a monotone read-once function, and $V'$ is the set of variables on which $f$ depends, then for every $\{x,y\} \subseteq V'$, either there exists a minterm $S$ of $f$ such that $\{x,y\} \subseteq S$, or there exists a maxterm $T$ of $f$ such that $\{x,y\} \subseteq T$.

**Theorem 3 [KLNSW88]:** $f$ is read-once iff for all minterms $S$ of $f$, and for all maxterms $T$ of $f$, $|S \cap T| = 1$.

We will use only the easier direction of this theorem, that is, if $f$ is read-once, then $|S \cap T| = 1$. Like Lemma 1, this direction of the theorem can be proved by induction on the read-once formula for $f$.

Karchmer et. al. also showed that given the minterm graph of $f$, it is easy to construct the read-once formula for $f$. Their construction makes use of the following lemma.

**Lemma 2 [S74]:** If a P4-free graph containing more than one vertex is connected, then its complement is disconnected.

The construction of the read-once formula for $f$ from the minterm graph is recursive. Let $G$ be the minterm graph of $f$. If $G$ contains one vertex, then the construction is trivial. Assume $G$ contains more than one vertex. Suppose $G$ is disconnected. Let $V_1', V_2', \cdots V_q'$, be the sets of vertices in the $q$ connected components of $G$. For $i \in \{1,2,...,q\}$, let $f_i$ be the monotone boolean function whose minterm set consists of all minterms $S$ of $f$ such that $S \subset V_i'$. $f_i$ is the function induced from $f$ by setting all variables in $V' - V_i'$ to 0. Since $f$ is expressible by a read-once formula, $f_i$ is expressible by a read-once formula. Recursively construct read-once formulas $F_1,...,F_q$ for $f_1,...,f_q$. $F_1 \vee F_2 \cdots \vee F_q$ is a read-once formula for $f$.

Suppose now that $G$ is connected. Then by Lemma 2 the complement of $G$ is disconnected. By Lemma 1 the complement of $G$ is the maxterm graph of $f$. Therefore, the maxterm graph of $f$ is disconnected. A dual construction to the one above produces a read-once formula for $f$.

It follows from the above construction that given the minterm graph for a read-once function $f$, the read-once formula for $f$ can be constructed in time $O(n^3)$ by repeatedly applying depth first search to find connected components.

## 4. LEARNING READ-ONCE FORMULAS WITH A RELEVANT POSSIBILITY ORACLE

*Relevant possibility oracles* are one of the three types of oracles used in Valiant's algorithm for learning read-once formulas ([V84]). A relevant possibility oracle takes as input a subset $S'$ of negated and non-negated variables of $f$, and outputs 1 if and only if there exists a minterm $S$ of $f$ such that $S' \subseteq S$.

It follows from the previous section that if $F$ is a read-once monotone formula expressing the function $f$, and we have enough information to construct the minterm graph of $f$, then we have enough information to construct $F$. To construct the minterm graph, we need the following information. For every variable $x$ in $V$, we must know whether $f$ depends on $x$ (i.e. is $x$ a vertex in the minterm graph?). For every pair of variables $\{x,y\}$ of $V$ such that $f$ depends on $x$ and $y$, we must know whether $x$ and $y$ appear together in a minterm of $f$ (i.e. is there an edge between $x$ and $y$ in the minterm graph?). Each of these questions can be answered with a query to a relevant possibility oracle. In the case where $F$ is not necessarily monotone, we can use the relevant possibility oracle to determine whether a variable appears in its negated or non-negated form in $F$. This implies that the minterm graph can be constructed in time $O(n^2)$. The read-once formula can then be constructed in time $O(n^3)$. This gives us the following theorem, which improves Valiant's result [V84].

**Theorem 4:** There exists an algorithm for learning read-once formulas with a relevant possibility oracle that runs in time $O(n^3)$ and makes $O(n^2)$ oracle calls.

## 5. LEARNING MONOTONE READ-ONCE FORMULAS USING MEMBERSHIP QUERIES

In this section we present two polynomial time algorithms for learning *monotone* read-once formulas using membership queries. The first algorithm is presented for its conceptual transparency. The second algorithm improves the complexity to time $O(n^3)$ by introducing a more efficient termination condition. (The reader is advised to read Algorithm 1 first.)

Our algorithms work by constructing an exact minterm graph. Constructing a minterm graph using membership queries is much more difficult than constructing one using a relevant possibility oracle.

Let $F$ be a monotone read-once formula expressing a function $f$ of the variables $V$. We use the following proposition, which follows from Lemma 1.

**Proposition 2:** To construct the minterm graph of $f$, it is sufficient to determine a subset MIN of the minterms of $f$, and a subset MAX of the maxterms of $f$, with the following two properties:

Property 1: Every variable on which $f$ depends (i.e. every variable that appears in $F$) is contained in a minterm in MIN, and in a maxterm in MAX.

Property 2: Every pair of variables $\{x,y\}$ on which $f$ depends is contained either in a common minterm in MIN, or a common maxterm in MAX.

## THE ALGORITHMS

We present two algorithms to construct MIN and MAX. Given MIN and MAX, we can construct the minterm graph of $f$ and use it to determine $F$.

To construct MIN and MAX we want to produce minterms and maxterms that help satisfy Properties 1 and 2 above. Our algorithms rely on the procedures *Findmin, Findmax, Xmin, Xmax*, and *XYpair*, to generate these minterms and maxterms. The most basic of these procedures are *Findmin* and *Findmax*.

### Findmin and Findmax
Let $Query(A)$ denote the output of the membership oracle on the string in which all members of $A$ are set to 1, and all members of $V-A$ are set to 0. On input $W$ such that $W$ contains a minterm of $f$, *Findmin*$(W)$ returns a minterm of $f$ contained in $W$.

```
Findmin(W)
{  S := W
   for each w ∈ W {
      if Query(S - {w}) = 1 then
             S:= S - {w} }
   return(S)
}
```

The dual procedure, *Findmax(W)*, finds a maxterm in $W$ provided one exists.

The Findmin (Findmax) procedure produces an arbitrary minterm (maxterm) contained in the input set $W$. To construct MIN and MAX, we need to find "useful" minterms and maxterms--those that help satisfy Properties 1 and 2. For instance, we might like to produce a minterm that contains a particular variable $x$. There is a difficulty in using Findmin to do this. The difficulty is that if the input to Findmin is a set $Q$ which contains a minterm $S_1$ containing $x$, and a minterm $S_2$ not containing $x$, there is no guarantee that Findmin will return $S_1$ instead of $S_2$. However, if the input $Q$ to Findmin has the property that all minterms in $Q$ contain $x$, then Findmin is forced to return a minterm containing $x$ no matter which of the minterms in $Q$ it returns. We exploit this fact in the procedures *Xmin, Xmax,* and *XYpair*.

### Xmin and Xmax

Xmin is a procedure that takes as input a variable $x$ and a maxterm $T$ of $f$ containing $x$, and outputs a minterm of $f$ containing $x$. Because $f$ has a maxterm containing $x$, $f$ must also have a minterm containing $x$. Let $S$ be such a minterm. By Theorem 1, $|S \cap T| = 1$. $S$ and $T$ both contain $x$, and therefore $S \cap T = \{ x \}$. $S \subseteq (V-T) \cup \{ x \}$, and therefore $(V-T) \cup \{ x \}$ contains at least one minterm of $f$. Furthermore, since $(V-T) \cup \{ x \}$ contains only one element of $T$, and every minterm of $f$ must intersect $T$ in exactly one element, it follows that every minterm in $(V-T) \cup \{ x \}$ must contain $x$. This observation gives us the procedure Xmin.

```
Xmin(T, x)
{
      return(Findmin((V-T) ∪ { x }))
}
```

The dual procedure, Xmax, takes as input a variable $x$ and a minterm $S$ of $f$ containing $x$, and outputs a maxterm of $f$ containing $x$.

```
Xmax(T, x)
{
      return(Findmax((V-S) ∪ { x }))
}
```

### XYpair

The procedure XYpair takes as input two variables $x$ and $y$, two minterms $S_1$ and $S_2$, and two maxterms $T_1$ and $T_2$. $S_1, S_2, T_1,$ and $T_2$, have the following properties:

1. $x \in S_1, x \in T_1, y \notin S_1, y \notin T_1$.

2. $y \in S_2, y \in T_2, x \notin S_2, x \notin T_2$.

The output of XYpair is a pair <"Minterm", S> where $S$ is a minterm containing $\{x,y\}$, or a pair <"Maxterm", T> where $T$ is a maxterm containing $\{x,y\}$. Such a minterm or maxterm must exist by Proposition 1. Proposition 1 says that every pair of variables on which $f$ depends appear together in either a common minterm or a common maxterm. The variables $x$ and $y$ are contained in $S_1$ and $S_2$ respectively, and therefore $f$ depends on $x$ and $y$.

We present the procedure XYpair, and then explain why it works.

XYpair($x$ ,$y$,$S_1$ ,$S_2$ ,$T_1$ ,$T_2$ )
{
    if Query(($V$ - ($T_1 \cup T_2$)) $\cup$ $\{x,y\}$) = 1 then
            return( < "Minterm", Xmin(($V$ - ($T_1 \cup T_2$)) $\cup$ $\{x,y\}$, $x$)> ) )
            else return( < "Maxterm", Xmax(($V$ - ($S_1 \cup S_2$)) $\cup$ $\{x,y\}$, $x$)> ) )
}

Suppose $x$ and $y$ appear together in a common minterm $S$ of $f$. By Theorem 1, $|S \cap T_1|=1$, and $|S \cap T_2|=1$. Therefore, $S \cap T_1 = \{x\}$, and $S \cap T_2 = \{y\}$. $S \subseteq (V - (T_1 \cup T_2)) \cup \{x,y\}$. It follows that if $f$ has a minterm that contains $\{x,y\}$, then $Query(V-(T_1 \cup T_2)) \cup \{x,y\}=1$.

The set $(V-(T_1 \cup T_2)) \cup \{x,y\}$ contains exactly one element of $T_1$ (that is, $x$), and exactly one element of $T_2$ (that is, $y$). Thus if $(V-(T_1 \cup T_2)) \cup \{x,y\}$ contains at least one minterm of $f$ (i.e. if $Query((V-(T_1 \cup T_2)) \cup \{x,y\}=1)$, then $x$ and $y$ appear in all minterms of $f$ contained in $V-(T_1 \cup T_2)) \cup \{x,y\}$. It follows that $Query((V-(T_1 \cup T_2)) \cup \{x,y\})=1$ if and only if $f$ has a minterm that contains both $x$ and $y$. Furthermore, if $f$ does have a minterm containing $x$ and $y$, then $Findmin((V-(T_1 \cup T_2)) \cup \{x,y\})$ returns such a minterm.

If $Query((V-(T_1 \cup T_2)) \cup \{x,y\}=0$, then $x$ and $y$ do not appear in a common minterm of $f$, and hence they must apppear in a common maxterm of $f$. By a similar argument to the one above, if $x$ and $y$ appear in a common maxterm of $f$, then $Findmax((V-(S_2 \cup S_2)) \cup \{x,y\})$ returns such a maxterm.

## Algorithm 1

Algorithm 1 constructs the sets MIN and MAX. The algorithm works by using the minterms and maxterms already in MIN and MAX to help generate new minterms and maxterms (as described above in the procedures Xmin, Xmax, and XYpair). We present the algorithm, followed by a proof of its correctness.

## Algorithm 1:

1. MIN := $\varnothing$          /initialize/
   MAX := $\varnothing$

2. if Query($V$) = 0 then terminate      /check if $f$ is identically 0/

3. MIN := MIN $\cup$ {Findmin($V$)}    /put one minterm into MIN/

4. CONTINUE := True.

```
    while CONTINUE = True do {
        if there exists an x ∈ V such that x is contained in a maxterm T of MAX,
            but not in a minterm of MIN, then {
4a.         MIN := MIN ∪ {Xmin(x, T)}
            }                              /add to MIN a minterm containing x/
        else if there exists an x in V such that x is contained in a minterm S of MIN
        but not in a maxterm of MAX, then {
4b.         MAX := MAX ∪ {Xmax(x, S)}
            }                              /add to MAX a maxterm containing x/
        else if there exist { x,y } in V such that
            x is contained in a minterm S₁ of MIN, and a maxterm T₁ of MAX,
            and y is contained in a minterm S₂ of MIN, and a maxterm T₂ of MAX,
            but x and y do not occur in a common minterm of MIN or maxterm of MAX
            then {
4c.         <TYPE, R> := XYpair(x,y, S₁, S₂, T₁, T₂)
            if TYPE = "Minterm" then MIN := MIN ∪ { R }
                else MAX := MAX ∪ { R }
            }                  /adds to MIN or MAX a minterm or maxterm containing x and y/
4d.     else CONTINUE := False
    }
```

We must prove that upon termination of the algorithm, MIN and MAX actually have Properties 1 and 2. Let $V'$ denote the set of variables that appear in minterms in MIN or maxterms in MAX. Steps 4a and 4b guarantee that if $x$ is in $V'$, then $x$ appears in both a minterm of MIN and a maxterm of MAX. Step 4c guarantees that if $x$ and $y$ are variables in $V'$, then $x$ and $y$ either appear together in a minterm of MIN or in a maxterm of MAX. Therefore, Properties 1 and 2 hold for MIN and MAX provided that $V'$ is the set of variables on which $f$ depends.

Let $G$ be the minterm graph of $f$. Let $G'$ be the subgraph of $G$ induced by $V'$. We will show that $G'=G$, and hence $V'$ is the set of variables on which $f$ depends. Assume for purposes of contradiction that $G'\neq G$. Then $G$, $G'$, MAX and MIN have the following properties. The properties follow from Lemma 1, and the correctness of Step 4 of the algorithm.

$1'$. The minterms in MIN are maximal cliques of $G$.
$2'$. The maxterms in MAX are maximal independent sets of $G$.
$3'$. $G'$ is a proper induced subgraph of $G$.
$4'$. $G$ is P4-free.
$5'$. The minterms in MIN are maximal cliques of $G'$, and cover the vertices and edges of $G'$.
$6'$. The maxterms in MAX are maximal independent sets of $G'$, and cover the vertices and non-edges of $G'$.

In the following lemma we show a contradiction. We prove that if $G'$, $G$, MAX, and MIN have Properties $3'$ through $6'$, then they cannot have both Properties $1'$ and $2'$. Therefore, our assumption that $G'\neq G$ must be false. It follows that $G'=G$, and therefore Properties 1 and 2 hold for MIN and MAX upon termination of the algorithm.

**Lemma 3:** Let $G$ be a P4-free graph. If $G'$ is a proper induced subgraph of $G$, MIN is a set of maximal cliques of $G'$ covering the vertices and edges of $G'$, and MAX is a set of maximal independent sets of $G'$ covering the vertices and non-edges of $G'$, then either MIN contains a clique that is not a maximal clique of $G$, or MAX contains an independent set that is not a maximal independent set of $G$.

**Proof:** By induction on the number of vertices in $G$. In the base case, $G$ contains two vertices. $G'$ must consist of one vertex. MIN must contain one maximal clique consisting of that one vertex, and MAX must contain one maximal independent set consisting of that one vertex. If $G$ has an edge, then MIN contains a clique that is not maximal in $G$. If $G$ doesn't have an edge, then MAX contains an independent set that is not maximal in $G$. Therefore, the lemma is true when $G$ has two vertices.

Inductive Step: Let $k > 2$. Assume the lemma is true when $G$ has fewer than $k$ vertices. Show it is true when $G$ has $k$ vertices.

Assume the lemma is false for some P4-free graph $G$ with $k$ vertices. Let $G'$ be a subgraph of $G$ for which the lemma is false. Let MAX and MIN be the associated sets. The cliques of MIN cover the vertices and edges of $G'$. The independent sets of MAX cover the vertices and non-edges of $G'$. We have assumed that the lemma is false for $G$, $G'$, MAX, and MIN, so MAX consists of maximal independent sets of $G$, and MIN consists of maximal cliques of $G$. Let $V$ be the vertices of $G$. Let $V'$ be the vertices of $G'$. Let $x$ be a vertex of $V - V'$.

Consider the subgraph of $G$ induced by $V' \cup \{ x \}$. Call it $G''$. $G$ is P4-free, and hence $G'$ and $G''$ are P4-free. The cliques of MIN are maximal in $G''$, and the independent sets of MAX are maximal in $G''$. If $|V' \cup \{ x \}| < k$, then $G'$, $G''$, MIN, and MAX contradict the inductive assumption that the lemma is true when the graph has fewer than $k$ vertices. Therefore, $|V' \cup \{ x \}| = k$, and hence $V' \cup \{ x \} = V$ and $G'' = G$.

By Lemma 2, either $G'$ is disconnected, or the complement of $G'$ is disconnected.

Case 1: Suppose $G'$ is disconnected, and $G$ is also disconnected. Let $C$ denote the vertices in the connected component of $G$ that contains $x$. Let $G_1$ denote the subgraph of $G$ induced by $C$. Let $G_1'$ denote the subgraph of $G$ induced by $C - \{ x \}$. $|C| < |V| = k$. Let $MAX' = \{ T \cap (C - \{ x \}) | T \in MAX \}$. Let $MIN' = \{ S | S \in MIN, S \subseteq C - \{ x \} \}$. The independent sets in MAX cover all the vertices and non-edges of $G'$, and hence $MAX'$ covers all the vertices and non-edges of $G_1'$. The cliques in $MIN'$ cover all the vertices and edges of $G_1'$. MIN contains maximal cliques of $G'$ and therefore the cliques in $MIN'$ are maximal in both $G_1$ and $G_1'$. The independent sets of MAX are maximal in both $G'$ and $G$. Let $T$ be an independent set in MAX. Because $G$ is disconnected, $T = T_1 \cup T_2$, where $T_1$ is a maximal independent set of $G_1$, and $T_2$ is a maximal independent set of the subgraph of $G$ induced by $V - C$. $G'$ does not contain $x$, and therefore $T_1 \subseteq C - \{ x \}$. Hence, $T \cap (C - \{ x \}) = T_1$, and $T \cap (C - \{ x \})$ is a maximal independent set of both $G_1$ and $G_1'$. It follows that the independent sets in $MAX'$ are maximal in both $G_1$ and $G_1'$. $G_1$, $G_1'$, $MIN'$, and $MAX'$ contradict the inductive assumption that the lemma is true for graphs with fewer than $k$ vertices.

Case 1a: Suppose $G'$ is disconnected and $G$ is connected. Then, in $G$, $x$ is adjacent to a vertex in each of the connected components of $G'$. It follows from the fact that $G$ is P4-free that $x$ must be connected to all the vertices in $G'$. Therefore, every maximal clique of $G$ contains $x$. Let $S$ be a clique in $MIN$. $S$ is maximal in $G'$. $S$ does not contain $\{x\}$. Therefore, $S$ is not maximal in $G$. This contradicts the assumption that the cliques in MIN are maximal in both $G$ and $G'$.

Case 2: A dual argument proves the inductive step when the complement of $G'$ is disconnected. $\square$

Each call to Findmin or Findmax makes $O(n)$ calls to the membership oracle. Therefore, each call to Xmin, Xmax or XYpair makes $O(n)$ calls to the membership oracle. The loop in Step 4 is executed at most $n + \binom{n}{2}$ times--once for each $x \in V$, and once for each pair $\{x,y\} \subseteq V$. Therefore, Algorithm 1 makes $O(n^3)$ queries, and runs in polynomial time.

We now present Algorithm 2, which runs in time $O(n^3)$. Algorithm 2 explicitly constructs the minterm graph by constructing a set VERTICES containing the vertices of the minterm graph, and a set EDGES containing the edges of the minterm graph. The main difference between Algorithms 1 and 2 is that in Algorithm 2, we may (intentionally) produce more minterms and maxterms than actually necessary to determine the minterm graph. In particular, in Step 4c of Algorithm 2 (in contrast to Step 4c of Algorithm 1), we may produce a minterm or a maxterm containing $\{x,y\}$ even if such a minterm or maxterm already appears in MIN or MAX. In our presentation of Algorithm 2, we omit the description of the simple data structures needed to efficiently access needed sets in MIN and MAX.

## Algorithm 2

1. EDGES := $\emptyset$          /initialize/
   MIN := $\emptyset$
   MAX := $\emptyset$

2. if Query($V$) = 0 then terminate     /check if $f$ is identically 0/
3. $S$ := Findmin($V$)
   OLDSET := $\emptyset$   /The following invariants are maintained for OLDSET:
                            For all $x$ in OLDSET, there exists
                            a minterm in MIN containing $x$, and a maxterm in MAX
                            containing $x$. For all pairs of variables $\{x,y\}$ in
                            OLDSET, there exists either a minterm in MIN
                            or a maxterm in MAX containing $\{x,y\}$/
   GROUNDSET := $S$      /GROUNDSET consists of all variables $x$ such that
                            there exists a minterm in MIN containing $x$, or a
                            maxterm in MAX containing $x$ (or both)/
   VARSET := $S$
   MIN := MIN $\cup$ $\{S\}$

4. while (VARSET $\neq \emptyset$) do {
      while (VARSET $\neq \emptyset$) do {
         choose some $x$ in VARSET
4a.      if $x$ is contained in a maxterm $T$ of MAX, but not in a minterm of MIN, then {
            $S$ := Xmin($T, x$)     /$S$ is a minterm containing $x$/
            VARSET := VARSET $\cup$ $S$
            GROUNDSET := GROUNDSET $\cup$ $S$

$$\text{MIN} := \text{MIN} \cup \{ S \}$$

}

4b.       else if $x$ is contained in a minterm $S$ of MIN, but not in a maxterm of MAX, then {

          $T := \text{Xmax}(S, x)$     /$T$ is a maxterm containing $x$/

          $\text{VARSET} := \text{VARSET} \cup T$

          $\text{GROUNDSET} := \text{GROUNDSET} \cup T$

          $\text{MAX} := \text{MAX} \cup \{ T \}$

       }

       $\text{VARSET} := \text{VARSET} - \{x\}$

}   /upon termination of this loop, all variables in GROUNDSET are contained

       in a minterm of MIN, and in a maxterm of MAX/

$\text{NEWSET} := \text{GROUNDSET} - \text{OLDSET}$

for all pairs $\{x,y\}$ such that $x \in \text{NEWSET}, y \in \text{NEWSET} \cup \text{OLDSET}$ do {

       Let $T_1$ and $T_2$ be maxterms in MAX containing $x$ and $y$ respectively.

       Let $S_1$ and $S_2$ be minterms in MIN containing $x$ and $y$ respectively.

       if $\{x,y\} \subseteq S_1$ or $\{x,y\} \subseteq S_2$ then

          $\text{EDGES} := \text{EDGES} \cup \{ (x,y) \}$

       else if $\{x,y\} \subseteq T_1$ or $\{x,y\} \subseteq T_2$ then

          do nothing

       else {

             /Find a minterm or maxterm containing $x$ and $y$/

4c.             $<\text{TYPE}, R> = \text{XYpair}(x, y, S_1, S_2, T_1, T_2)$

          if TYPE = "Minterm" then {

             $\text{EDGES} := \text{EDGES} \cup \{ (x,y) \}$

             $\text{MIN} := \text{MIN} \cup \{ R \}$

          }

          else $\text{MAX} := \text{MAX} \cup \{ R \}$

          $\text{VARSET} := \text{VARSET} \cup R$

          $\text{GROUNDSET} := \text{GROUNDSET} \cup R$

       }

} /upon termination of this loop, all pairs of variables in OLDSET $\cup$ NEWSET are

       contained in either a minterm of MIN or a maxterm of MAX/

$\text{OLDSET} := \text{OLDSET} \cup \text{NEWSET};$

}

5. VERTICES := OLDSET

Note that the proof of correctness of Algorithm 1 is not affected by the production of "redundant" minterms and maxterms, and therefore the proof can be applied to Algorithm 2.

Each variable $x \in V$ contributes at most one minterm or maxterm to the variables in VARSET, and each pair of variable $\{x,y\} \subseteq V$ contributes at most one minterm or maxterm to the variables in VARSET. Each minterm and maxterm contain $O(n)$ variables, and so the total number of variables added to VARSET over the course of the algorithm is $O(n^3)$. Therefore, the while loop in Step 4 is executed at most $O(n^3)$ times. Each variable $x \in V$ is responsible for at most one call to Xmin or Xmax, and each pair of variables $\{x,y\} \subseteq V$ is responsible for at most one call to XYpair. Each call to Xmin, Xmax, or

XYpair makes $O(n)$ membership queries, and takes time $O(n)$. Therefore, the calls to Xmin, Xmax, and XYpair take a total of $O(n^3)$ time. Theorem 5 follows.

**Theorem 5:** There exists an algorithm for learning monotone read-once formulas using membership queries that runs in time $O(n^3)$ and makes $O(n^3)$ queries.

## 6. LEARNING READ-ONCE FORMULAS USING A PROJECTIVE EQUIVALENCE ORACLE

Let $A$ be a boolean assignment of a (possibly improper) subset of the variables of a boolean function $f$. We define $f_A$ to be the function induced on $f$ by the assignment $A$. The input variables to $f_A$ are considered to be those variables of $f$ not fixed by $A$.

We introduce a new oracle, the *projective equivalence* oracle. This oracle is a generalization of the equivalence oracle (cf. [A88]). The projective equivalence oracle for a function $f$ takes two inputs. The first input is a boolean assignment $A$ of a (possibly improper) subset of the variables of $f$. The second input is a formula $F'$. The oracle returns "yes" if $F'$ expresses the function $f_A$. Otherwise, the oracle returns "no" and a counterexample. The counterexample is an assignment $B$ to the variables of $f_A$ such that $F'$ and $f_A$ have different values on the input defined by $B$. The fast interpolation algorithms of [GKS88] for $(\oplus, \wedge)$ formulas use a subroutine that implements a projective equivalence oracle over the extension fields.

The projective equivalence oracle is similar to the EXPERIMENT oracle of John Amsterdam [Am88], which was defined in a randomized setting.

Our algorithms for learning monotone read-once formulas with membership queries (section 5) can be adapted to learn *arbitrary* read-once formulas with a projective equivalence oracle. We sketch the adaptation of the membership query algorithms. Remember that in arbitrary read-once formulas, each variable appears exactly once in the formula, either in negated or non-negated form.

Let $F$ be a read-once formula to be learned, and let $f$ be the read-once function expressed by $F$.

The procedures Findmin and Findmax are central to the execution of the membership query algorithms. Modified versions of Findmin and Findmax are used in the projective equivalence oracle algorithms. Let *Findmin1* denote the version of Findmin used in the projective equivalence oracle algorithms. The input to Findmin1 is a set $Q$ of negated and non-negated variables (no variable appearing in both negated and non-negated form) that contains a minterm of $f$. The output of Findmin1 is a minterm of $f$ contained in $Q$. Because the input $Q$ contains a minterm of $f$, setting all the negated variables in $Q$ to 0, and all the non-negated variables in $Q$ to 1, forces the value of $f$ to 1.

We present Findmin1. *ProjQuery*$(A, F')$ is a call to the projective equivalence oracle.

Findmin1$(Q)$
{   S := Q
   for each literal $q \in Q$ {
    Let $A$ be the assignment in which every negated variable in $Q - \{ q \}$

is set to 0, and every non-negated variable in $Q - \{ s \}$ is set to 1.
    if ProjQuery(A,1) = "yes" then
          S:= S - {q}
  }
  return(S)
}

Xmin, Xmax, and XYpair are also modified for use in the projective equivalence oracle algorithms. We present *Xmin1*, the modified version of Xmin. Xmin1 takes as input a literal $q$ and a maxterm $T$ containing $q$, and outputs a minterm of $f$ containing $q$. The proof of correctness of Xmin1 is similar to the proof of correctness of Xmin.

Xmin1(T, q)
{
    Let $A$ denote the assignment in which all non-negated
    variables in $T - \{ q \}$ are set to 0,
    and all negated variables in $T - \{ q \}$ are set to 1.

    B := Counterexample returned by ProjQuery(A, 0)
    $Q := \{ y \mid y \text{ set to 1 in } B \} \cup \{ \neg y \mid y \text{ set to 0 in } B \}$

    return(Findmin1(Q))
}

We omit descriptions of *Findmax1* and *XYpair1*.

The projective equivalence oracle algorithms begin, like the membership query algorithms, by finding one minterm of $f$. This is done by querying the projective equivalence oracle on the input pair (empty assignment, 0). The output of this query can be transformed in the natural way to a set of literals guaranteed to contain a minterm of $f$. The projective equivalence algorithms then continue in essentially the same manner as the membership query algorithms, repeatedly calling Xmin1, Xmax1, and XYpair1, to generate minterms and maxterms. This gives us Theorem 6.

**Theorem 6:** There exists an algorithm for learning arbitrary read-once formulas with a projective equivalence oracle that runs in time $O(n^3)$ and makes $O(n^3)$ oracle calls.

The projective equivalence algorithms make limited use of the power of the projected equivalence oracle. Specifically, they only test equivalence to the constant functions $F' = 1$ and $F' = 0$. Dana Angluin has observed that subset and superset queries may be substituted for these restricted projected equivalence queries [A89a]. A subset oracle takes as input a formula $F'$, and returns the answer "yes" if the satisfying assignments to $F'$ are a subset of the satisfying assignments to $f$. Otherwise, it returns "no" and a counterexample. Superset oracles are defined analogously. Let $A$ be a partial assignment to the variables of $f$. Let $R$ be the monomial formed by taking the conjunction of the variables set to 1 by $A$ and the negation of the variables set to 0 by $A$. The projective equivalence oracle will return "yes" on input $(A, 1)$ if and only if the subset oracle returns "yes" on input $R$. Similarly, let $R'$ be the disjunction of the variables set to 0 by $A$ and the negation of the variables set to 1 by $A$. The projective equivalence oracle will return "yes" on input $(A, 0)$ if and only if the superset oracle returns "yes" on input $R'$. Using this observation, Angluin noted the the following corollary to Theorem 6.

**Corollary 6.1 [A89a]:** There exists an algorithm for learning arbitrary read-once formulas using subset and superset queries that runs in time $O(n^3)$ and makes $O(n^3)$ oracle calls.

## 7. EXTENSIONS AND OPEN PROBLEMS

Using an extension of the algorithm in Section 5, we are able to prove the following:

**Theorem 7:** There exists an algorithm for learning the number of satisfying assignments of a monotone read-once formula using a membership oracle that runs in time $O(n^3)$ and makes $O(n^3)$ queries.

**Proof (Sketch):** Apply the learning algorithm of Section 5 to produce a boolean tree corresponding to a read-once formula. This takes time $O(n^3)$. Then, starting from the leaves of the tree, for every node in the tree, compute the number of satisfying assignments to the formula rooted at that node. This procedure can be carried out in $O(n^2)$ time. $\square$

One open question is whether it is possible to speed up our algorithms by using randomness and parallelism. This question connects in an interesting way to the problem of finding upper and lower bounds on random and parallel algorithms for learning a minterm of a monotone read-once function using membership queries. Lower bounds on random and parallel algorithms for learning a minterm of an arbitrary monotone function using membership queries can be derived from the [KUW85] lower bounds for independence system oracles.

## 8. SUMMARY

The results of this paper, combined with [PV85], [KLPV87], and [A89], characterize the computational difficulty of learning read-once formulas as follows (Table 1).

Table 1: Existence of Polynomial Time Learning Algorithms

| Learning Protocol | By Example | Relevant Possibility Oracle | Membership Oracle | Equivalence Oracle | Projective Equivalence Oracle | Subset and Superset Oracles |
|---|---|---|---|---|---|---|
| Arbitrary Read-Once Formulas | No (if NP ≠ RP) | Yes ($O(n^3)$ time, $O(n^2)$ queries) | No | No | Yes ($O(n^3)$ time, $O(n^3)$ queries) | Yes ($O(n^3)$ time, $O(n^3)$ queries) |
| Monotone Read-Once Formulas | No (if NP ≠ RP) | Yes ($O(n^3)$ time, $O(n^2)$ queries) | Yes ($O(n^3)$ time, $O(n^3)$ queries) | No | Yes ($O(n^3)$ time, $O(n^3)$ queries) | Yes ($O(n^3)$ time, $O(n^3)$ queries) |

# References

[Am87]      Amsterdam, J., *Extending the Valiant Learning Model*, Proceedings of the Fifth International Conference on Machine Learning (1988), pp. 381-394.

[A88]       Angluin, D., *Queries and Concept Learning*, Machine Learning 2 (1988), pp. 319-342.

[A89]       Angluin, D., *Using Queries to Identify μ-formulas*, Yale University Tech Report Yale/DCS/RR-694, March 1989.

[A89a]      Angluin, D., personal communication.

[C85]       Cook, S.A., *A Taxonomy of Problems with Fast Parallel Algorithms*, Information and Control 64 (1985), pp. 2-22.

[GKS88]     Grigoriev, D.Yu., Karpinski, M., and Singer, M. F., *Fast Parallel Algorithms for Sparse Multivariate Polynomial Interpolation Over Finite Fields*, Research Report No. 8523-C5, University of Bonn (1988), submitted to SIAM J. Comput., 1988.

[KLNSW88]   Karchmer, M., Linial, N., Newman, I., Saks, M., and Wigderson, A., *Combinatorial Characterization of Read Once Formulae*, Presented at the Joint French-Israeli Binational Symposium on Combinatorics and Algorithms (1988). Submitted to a special issue of Discrete Math.

[KR88]      Karp, R.M., Ramachandran, V., *A Survey of Parallel Algorithms for Shared Memory Machines*, Research Report No. UCB/CSD 88/407, University of California, Berkeley (1988). To appear in Handbook of Theoretical Computer Science, North Holland (1989).

[KUW85]     Karp, R.M., Upfal, E., and Wigderson A., *Are Search and Decision Problems Computationally Equivalent?*, Proc. 17th ACM STOC (1985), pp. 464-475

[KLPV87]    Kearns, M., Li, M., Pitt, L., Valiant, L.G., *On the learnability of Boolean Formulae*, Proc. 19th ACM STOC (1987), pp. 285-295.

[PV85]      Pitt, L., and Valiant, L.G., *Computational Limitations on Learning from Examples*, J. ACM 35 (1985), pp. 965-984.

[PY84]      Papadimitriou, C.H. and Yannakakis, M., *The Complexity of Facets (and some Facets of Complexity)*, JCSS 28 (1984), pp. 244-259.

[S74]       Seinsche, D., *On a Property of the Class of n-Colorable Graphs*, Journal of Combinatorial Theory (B) 16 (1974), pp. 191-193.

[V84]       Valiant, L.G., *A Theory of the Learnable*, Communications of the ACM 27 (1984), pp. 1134-1142.

[VV85]      Valiant, L.G., and Vazirani, V.V., *NP is as Easy as Detecting Unique Solutions*, Proc. 17th ACM STOC (1985), pp. 458-463.

# LEARNING SIMPLE DETERMINISTIC LANGUAGES

## Hiroki Ishizaka

ICOT Research Center

21F, Mita Kokusai Bldg.

1-4-28 Mita, Minato-ku, Tokyo, 108, Japan

E-mail: ishizaka%icot.jp@relay.cs.net

## ABSTRACT

This paper is concerned with the problem of learning simple deterministic languages. The algorithm described in this paper is essentially based on the theory of model inference given by Shapiro. In our setting, however, nonterminal membership queries, for nonterminals except the start symbol, are not used. Instead of them, extended equivalence queries are used. Nonterminals that are necessary for a correct grammar and their meanings are introduced automatically.

We show an algorithm that, for any simple deterministic language $L$, outputs a grammar $G$ in 2-standard form, such that $L = L(G)$, using membership and extended equivalence queries. We also show that the algorithm runs in time polynomial in the length of the longest counterexample and the minimum number of nonterminals of a correct grammar.

## INTRODUCTION

We consider the problem of learning simple deterministic languages using membership and extended equivalence queries. A simple deterministic language (SDL) is characterized as the language that is accepted by a 1-state deterministic push-down automaton by empty store. The class of SDLs is a proper sub-class of deterministic languages. Another characterization of SDL is as the language that is generated by a context-free grammar in a special form of Greibach normal form, called a simple deterministic grammar (SDG).

Angluin [Ang87a] shows that the class of $k$-bounded context-free grammars is learnable in polynomial time using equivalence and nonterminal membership queries. The algorithm described in this paper is based on her algorithm. Both algorithms are essentially based on the theory of model inference given by Shapiro [Sha81]. Our setting, however, differs from Angluin's and Shapiro's in available types of queries, that is, in our setting, the learning algorithm is allowed to use membership queries but not nonterminal membership queries. This difference leads to a problem of introducing new nonterminals that are not observed in interaction between a teacher and a learner.

This problem relates to the problem of introducing theoretical terms in learning of first order theories from facts. Recently, there have been several approaches to the problem [Ban88, MB88]. However, in such settings that the algorithm learns not only a concept but also a language for describing the concept, it becomes difficult to ensure the convergence of a learning process. Of course, if the concept is described by a sufficiently restricted language, then we can expect an algorithm that learns the concept even in such a setting. The result of this paper gives one such learning algorithm.

Another feature of our setting is that the algorithm is allowed to use extended equivalence queries. An equivalence query defined in [Ang88] is allowed to propose only element of an original hypothesis space. For example, if the target class of learning is a set of concepts $\{L_1, L_2, \ldots\}$, then the learning algorithm must make each equivalence query with $L_i$ in the set. We do not assume this restriction. Thus, the learning algorithm described in this paper makes each equivalence query proposing a grammar which is simply in 2-standard form but may not necessarily be simple deterministic.

Yokomori [Yok88] gives another algorithm for learning SDLs in polynomial time. Our setting also differs from his. The difference will be described in the last section.

## PRELIMINARIES

We shall give some basic notions and the notation needed in this paper. Most of them are from [Ang87a] and [Yok88].

## CONTEXT-FREE GRAMMARS AND LANGUAGES

An *alphabet* is a finite non-empty set of distinct symbols. For a given alphabet $X$, the set of all finite strings of symbols from $X$ is denoted $X^*$. The empty string is denoted $\varepsilon$. $X^+$ denotes the set $X^* - \{\varepsilon\}$. For a string $x$, $|x|$ denotes the length of $x$. If $S$ is a finite set, then $|S|$ denotes the cardinality of $S$.

Let $\Sigma$ be an alphabet. A *language* $L$ over $\Sigma$ is a subset of $\Sigma^*$. For a string $x$ in $\Sigma^*$ and a language $L$ over $\Sigma$, let $\overline{x}L = \{y \mid xy \in L\}$ ($L\overline{x} = \{y \mid yx \in L\}$). The set $\overline{x}L$ ($L\overline{x}$) is called the *left(right)-derivative of $L$ with respect to $x$*. For a string $x = a_1 a_2 \cdots a_n$, $Pre_i(x)$ denotes the string $a_1 a_2 \cdots a_i$, and $Suf_i(x)$ denotes the string $a_{i+1} a_{i+2} \cdots a_n$.

A *context-free grammar* (CFG) is a 4-tuple $G = (N, \Sigma, P, S)$, where $N$ is an alphabet of *nonterminals*, $\Sigma$ is an alphabet of *terminals* such that $N \cap \Sigma = \emptyset$, $S \in N$ is the *start symbol*, and $P$ is a finite set of *production rules* of the form $A \to \alpha$ $(A \in N, \alpha \in (N \cup \Sigma)^*)$. The *size* of a grammar $G$ is the sum of $|N|$, $|\Sigma|$, $|P|$, and the sum of the lengths of the right-hand sides of all the productions in $P$.

For $\beta, \gamma \in (N \cup \Sigma)^*$, a binary relation $\Rightarrow$ is defined as follows: $\beta \Rightarrow \gamma$ if and only if there exist $\delta_1, \delta_2 \in (N \cup \Sigma)^*$ and there exists a production rule $A \to \alpha \in P$ such that $\beta = \delta_1 A \delta_2$ and $\gamma = \delta_1 \alpha \delta_2$. A *derivation from $\beta$ to $\gamma$* is a finite sequence of strings $\beta = \beta_0, \beta_1, \cdots, \beta_n = \gamma$ such that, for each $i$, $\beta_i \Rightarrow \beta_{i+1}$. If there is a derivation from $\beta$ to $\gamma$, then we denote $\beta \Rightarrow^* \gamma$, that is, the relation $\Rightarrow^*$ is the reflexive, transitive closure of $\Rightarrow$. In each step of the derivation, if the left-most occurrence of a nonterminal in $\beta_i$ is replaced, then it is called the *left-most derivation*. In what follows, unless otherwise stated, a derivation $\beta \Rightarrow^* \gamma$ always means the left-most one.

The language of a nonterminal $A$, denoted $L(A)$, is the set of all $x \in \Sigma^*$ such that $A \Rightarrow^* x$. Similarly, for $\alpha \in N^*$, $L(\alpha)$ denotes the set of all $x \in \Sigma^*$ such that $\alpha \Rightarrow^* x$. (To emphasize the grammar being used, we use the subscript $G$, e.g., $S \Rightarrow_G x$ or $L_G(A)$.) The *language* of the grammar $G$, denoted $L(G)$, is just $L(S)$, where $S$ is the start symbol in grammar $G$.

## SDG AND SDL

A context-free grammar in Greibach normal form $G$ is *simple deterministic* if, for any $A \in N, a \in \Sigma, \alpha, \beta \in N^*$, there exist productions $A \to a\alpha$ and $A \to a\beta$ in $P$, then $\alpha = \beta$. Note that the definition does not imply that SDGs generate only $\varepsilon$-free languages. In this paper, however, our attention focuses on only $\varepsilon$-free SDGs. A language $L$ is *simple deterministic* if there exists an SDG $G$ such that $L(G) = L$.

For example, the grammar $G = (\{S, A, B, C\}, \{a, b\}, P, S)$, where

$$P = \{S \to aA, A \to b, A \to aB, B \to aBC, B \to bC, C \to b\},$$

is one of the SDGs that generate an SDL $\{a^m b^m | 1 \le m\}$.

The following propositions provide the features of SDGs and SDLs desired for our purpose (see, e.g., [Har79]).

**Proposition 1** *Let $G = (N, \Sigma, P, S)$ be an SDG. For any $A \in N, x \in \Sigma^+$ and $\alpha \in N^*$, if there exists a derivation $A \Rightarrow^* x\alpha$, then $L(\alpha) = \overline{x}L(A)$.*

**Proposition 2** *Let $G = (N, \Sigma, P, S)$ be an SDG. For any $A \in N$, $L(A)$ is prefix-free, that is, if $x \in L(A)$, then, for any $y \in \Sigma^+$, $xy \notin L(A)$.*

**Proposition 3** *For any SDG $G$, there exists an equivalent SDG $G'$ that is in 2-standard form, i.e., there exists an SDG $G' = (N', \Sigma, P', S)$ such that*

(1) $L(G) = L(G')$;

(2) *Each production in $P'$ is of one of the following forms: $A \to a$, $A \to aB$, $A \to aBC$, where $A, B, C \in N', a \in \Sigma$.*

Proposition 3 allows us to consider only ($\varepsilon$-free) context-free grammars in 2-standard form.

## MODELS AND INCORRECTNESS/CORRECTNESS

Our algorithm for learning SDL is based on Shapiro's model inference algorithm [Sha81] and Angluin's learning algorithm [Ang87a]. The most important component of these algorithms is the diagnosis routine. The diagnosis routine finds an incorrect element in a hypothesis that implies a negative example, so we need to define notions for incorrectness (or correctness) of the elements of a grammar, that is, incorrectness of productions. In order to do this, we shall introduce some model theoretical notions for grammars.

Let $G = (N, \Sigma, P, S)$ be a context-free grammar. For each nonterminal $A \in N$, a *model* of $A$, denoted $M(A)$, is a subset of $\Sigma^+$. A *model* $M$ for the grammar $G$ consists of the model of each nonterminal.

$$M = \{M(A_1), M(A_2), \ldots, M(A_{|N|})\}.$$

A *replacement* is a finite tuple $\langle (y_1, A_1), \ldots, (y_n, A_n) \rangle$, where $y_i \in \Sigma^*, A_i \in N$. Let $\rho = \langle (y_1, A_1), \ldots, (y_n, A_n) \rangle$ and $\beta \in (N \cup \Sigma)^*$. $\rho$ is *compatible* with $\beta$ if and only if there are finite strings $x_0, \ldots, x_n \in \Sigma^*$ such that $\beta = x_0 A_1 x_1 A_2 \cdots A_n x_n$. If $\rho$ is compatible with $\beta$, then an *instance* of $\beta$ by $\rho$, denoted $\rho[\beta]$, is the terminal string obtained from $\beta$ by replacing each occurrence of $A_i$ in $\beta$ by the terminal string $y_i$.

Let $M$ be a model for a grammar $G$. A production $A \to \alpha$ is *incorrect* for $M$ if and only if there exists a replacement $\rho = \langle (y_1, A_1), \ldots, (y_n, A_n) \rangle$ that is compatible with $\alpha$ such that, for each $i$, $y_i \in M(A_i)$, but $\rho[\alpha] \notin M(A)$. A production is *correct* for $M$ if and only if it is not incorrect for $M$.

**Proposition 4** *Let $G = (N, \Sigma, P, S)$ be a CFG. Suppose a model $M$ for $G$ such that, for each nonterminal $A \in N$, $M(A) = L(A)$. Then every production in $P$ is correct for $M$.*

## TYPES OF QUERIES

Let $L$ be the unknown SDL that is intended to be learned by a learning algorithm. We assume a teacher who knows $L$ and can answer the queries below. The algorithm is allowed to make two types of queries as follows.

A *membership query* proposes a string $x \in \Sigma^+$ and asks whether $x \in L$ or not. The reply is either *yes* or *no*.

An *extended equivalence query* proposes a grammar $G$ in 2-standard form and asks whether $L = L(G)$. The reply is *yes* or *no*. If it is *no*, then a *counterexample* is also provided. A counterexample is a string $x$ in the symmetric difference of $L$ and $L(G)$. If $x \in L - L(G)$, $x$ is called a *positive* counterexample, and if $x \in L(G) - L$, $x$ is called a *negative* counterexample. The choice of a counterexample is assumed to be arbitrary.

Note the difference between extended equivalence queries and equivalence queries defined in [Ang88]. The equivalence query is allowed to propose only element of the original hypothesis space. Thus, in learning SDLs, the hypothesis proposed by an equivalence query is restricted to a grammar that generates an SDL. However, the hypothesis proposed by an extended equivalence query does not have to exactly generate an SDL. A teacher who answers equivalence queries and membership queries is called a *minimally adequate Teacher* [Ang87b], so we call a teacher who answers extended equivalence queries and membership queries an *extended minimally adequate Teacher*.

## THE LEARNING ALGORITHM

In what follows, unless otherwise stated, a grammar is in 2-standard form. Let $L$ be the unknown SDL which should be learned by the algorithm and $G_0 = (N_0, \Sigma, P_0, S)$ be an SDG such that $L(G_0) = L$ and with the minimum number of nonterminals, that is, for any SDG $G' = (N', \Sigma, P', S')$ such that $L(G') = L$, $|N_0| \leq |N'|$. We assume that the terminal alphabet $\Sigma$ and start symbol $S$ are known to the learning algorithm, but that $N - \{S\}$, the set of nonterminals except $S$, and $P$, the set of productions, are unknown.

The main result of this paper is as follows.

**Theorem 5** *There is an algorithm that, for any SDL $L$, learns a grammar $G$ in 2-standard form such that $L(G) = L$ using extended equivalence queries and membership queries that runs in time polynomial in $|N_0|$ and the length of the longest counterexample.*

Note that the grammar learned by the algorithm may not be SDG. The grammar is simply in 2-standard form.

The Learning Algorithm

**Given:** An extended minimally adequate Teacher for $L$ and a terminal alphabet $\Sigma$.

**Output:** A grammar $G = (N, \Sigma, P, S)$ in 2-standard form such that $L(G) = L$.

**Procedure:**

$N := \{S\}$. $P := \{S \to aSS, S \to aS, S \to a | a \in \Sigma\}$. $G := (N, \Sigma, P, S)$.

*repeat*

    Make an extended equivalence query with $G$.

    *If* the reply is positive counterexample, *then*

        introduce new nonterminals with their models.

        Put all candidate productions into $P$.

    *Else if* the reply is negative counterexample, *then*

        diagnose $G$.

        Remove the incorrect production replied by the diagnosis routine from $P$.

*until* the reply is *yes*.

Output $G$.

## AN OUTLINE OF THE ALGORITHM

First, the algorithm initializes nonterminals $N$ to $\{S\}$, and initializes productions $P$ to the set of all productions consisting of only $S$. As a model $M$ for $G$, we initially consider $\{M(S) = L\}$. Models for any other nonterminals that are introduced by the algorithm are defined in the next section. Then it iterates the following loop. An equivalence query is made, proposing $G$. If the reply is *yes*, then the algorithm outputs $G$ and halts. Otherwise, a counterexample $w$ is returned. The algorithm tries to parse $w$ on $G$. If $w$ can be parsed, that is, when $w$ is negative, the algorithm diagnoses $G$ on the parse-tree of $w$ and finds an incorrect production for $M$. The incorrect production is removed from $P$. Otherwise, that is, when $w$ is positive, new nonterminals are introduced and all new productions constructed from them are added to $P$.

We assume a parsing sub-procedure that runs in time polynomial in the size of a grammar $G$ and $w$, e.g., Angluin's parsing procedure [Ang87a][1].

The diagnosis routine finds an incorrect production for $M$ on the input parse-tree that

---

[1]Since $G$ is in 2-standard form, Lemma 3 and Lemma 4 in [Ang87a] hold. In fact, the procedure returns a parse-DAG (directed acyclic graph) instead of a parse-tree. Our discussion, however, is not affected by the difference.

generates a string $w$ and has its root node $A$ such that $w \notin M(A)^2$. For example, consider the following parse-tree for a negative counterexample $abbb$.

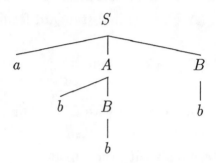

Initially, $abbb \notin M(S) = L$ is known. Then the diagnosis routine considers in turn each child of $S$ which is labeled with a nonterminal. In the example, first, the child labeled with $A$ and generating the string $bb$ is considered. The diagnosis routine inquires whether $bb \in M(A)$ or not. If $bb \notin M(A)$, then it calls itself recursively with the sub-tree rooted $A$. If $bb \in M(A)$, then it goes to the next child labeled with $B$ and makes the same inquiry. If $b \notin M(B)$, then it returns the production $B \to b$. Otherwise, it returns the production $S \to aAB$.

In [Ang87a], such an inquiry is made through nonterminal membership queries. In our approach, however, it is made by using only membership queries. The next section shows how to introduce new nonterminals and replace nonterminal membership queries by membership queries.

Suppose that $New$ is a set of all nonterminals that are newly introduced at a stage of learning. $N$ is set to $N \cup New$. Let $P_{New}$ be a set of all productions in 2-standard form constructed from $N$ that have never appeared in $P$, that is, for each $a \in \Sigma$, $P_{New}$ contains productions $A \to a\alpha$ such that $A\alpha \in N^+$, $|\alpha| \le 2$ and $A\alpha$ contains at least one element of $New$. Then $P$ is set to $P \cup P_{New}$.

**Claim 1** *The set $P_{New}$ is easily computed in time polynomial in $|N|$ and, at any stage of learning, $P$ contains at most $|N| \times |\Sigma| \times (|N| + 1)^2$ productions.*

## GENERATING NONTERMINALS WITH THEIR MODELS

The key idea of the generating nonterminals routine has its roots in an extension of a model described in [Ish89].

---

[2]See [Ang87a] for the precise definition of the diagnosis routine.

First, we show an important feature of SDGs for describing the generating nonterminals routine.

**Lemma 6** *Let $G = (N, \Sigma, P, S)$ be an SDG. Suppose that $A \Rightarrow^* rB\alpha$ for $A, B \in N, \alpha \in N^*, r \in \Sigma^+$, and that $t$ is a string in $L(\alpha)$ such that $Suf_j(t) \notin L(\alpha)$ for any $j$ $(1 \leq j \leq |t| - 1)$ (if $\alpha = \varepsilon$ then $t = \varepsilon$). Then, for any $x \in \Sigma^+$, $x \in L(B)$ if and only if (i) $rxt \in L(A)$ and (ii) $rPre_i(x)t \notin L(A)$ for any $i$ $(1 \leq i \leq |x| - 1)$.*

**Proof:** Suppose $x \in L(B)$. Then $A \Rightarrow^* rB\alpha \Rightarrow^* rx\alpha \Rightarrow^* rxt$. Thus, $rxt \in L(A)$. Since $L(B)$ is prefix-free, $Pre_i(x) \notin L(B)$ for any $i$ $(1 \leq i \leq |x| - 1)$. Hence, if $rPre_i(x)t \in L(A)$, that is, $Pre_i(x)t \in \bar{r}L(A) = L(B\alpha)$, then there exists $j$ $(1 \leq j \leq |t| - 1)$ such that $Pre_i(x)Pre_j(t) \in L(B)$ and $Suf_j(t) \in L(\alpha)$. This contradicts the fact that $Suf_j(t) \notin L(\alpha)$ for any $j$ $(1 \leq j \leq |t| - 1)$. Thus, $rPre_i(x)t \notin L(A)$ for any $i$ $(1 \leq i \leq |x| - 1)$.

Conversely, assume that (i) and (ii) hold. From assumption (i), it holds that $xt \in \bar{r}L(A) = L(B\alpha)$. Since there is no strict suffix of $t$ in $L(\alpha)$, there exists $j$ $(1 \leq j \leq |x|)$ such that $Pre_j(x) \in L(B)$ and $Suf_j(x)t \in L(\alpha)$. On the other hand, from assumption (ii), $Pre_i(x)t \notin L(B\alpha)$ for any $i$ $(1 \leq i \leq |x| - 1)$. Hence, for any $i$ $(1 \leq i \leq |x| - 1)$, $Pre_i(x) \notin L(B)$. Thus, $j = |x|$. This concludes that $Pre_{|x|}(x) = x \in L(B)$. $\qquad\square$

In the learning algorithm, whenever new nonterminals are introduced, there is a positive counterexample $w$. The generating nonterminals routine constructs nonterminals with their appropriate models from $w$.

Let $w$ be a positive counterexample such that $|w| \geq 2$. *Nonterminals generated from a positive counterexample $w$*, denoted $N(w)$, are defined as follows:

$$N(w) = \{(r, s, t) | r, s \in \Sigma^+, t \in \Sigma^* \text{ and } rst = w\}.$$

**Claim 2** *There are at most $|w|(|w| - 1)/2$ elements of $N(w)$, and $N(w)$ is easily computed in time polynomial in $|w|$.*

For example, let $w = aabb$, then

$$N(w) = \{(a, abb, \varepsilon), (a, ab, b), (a, a, bb), (aa, bb, \varepsilon), (aa, b, b), (aab, b, \varepsilon)\}$$

For each triple $(r, s, t) \in N(w)$, let $\varphi(r, s, t)$ be the shortest suffix of $t$ in $\bar{rs}L$, i.e.,

$$\varphi(r, s, t) = Suf_i(t) \text{ where } i = \max_{0 \leq j \leq |t| - 1} \{j \mid Suf_j(t) \in \bar{rs}L\}.$$

**Claim 3** *The string $\varphi(r,s,t)$ can be computed by making $|t|$ membership queries proposing $rsSuf_j(t)$ $(0 \leq j \leq |t| - 1)$.*

The intended model of each nonterminal in $N(w)$ is defined as follows. For each triple $(r,s,t) \in N(w)$, define

$$M((r,s,t)) = \{x \in \Sigma^+ \mid rx\varphi(r,s,t) \in L \text{ and}$$
$$rPre_i(x)\varphi(r,s,t) \notin L \text{ for any } i \ (1 \leq i \leq |x| - 1)\}.$$

**Lemma 7** *Let $N$ be the set of known nonterminals. Suppose that $w$ is a new positive counterexample. Then the time required for generating nonterminals and computing new productions is bounded by a non-decreasing polynomial in $|N|$ and $|w|$.*

**Proof:** By Claim 1, 2 and 3, it is straightforwardly implied.     □

**Lemma 8** *Let $L$ be an SDL, $w$ be a string in $L$, and $G = (N, \Sigma, P, S)$ be an SDG such that $L(G) = L$. For any $A \in N - \{S\}$ that appears in the derivation $S \Rightarrow^* w$, there exists a nonterminal $(r,s,t) \in N(w)$ such that $L(A) = M((r,s,t))$.*

**Proof:** Suppose that $S \Rightarrow^* rA\alpha \Rightarrow^* rs\alpha \Rightarrow^* rst = w$. Then, from the definition of $N(w)$, the triple $(r,s,t)$ is in $N(w)$. (Since $G$ is an SDG and $A \neq S$, neither $r$ nor $s$ is $\varepsilon$.) Since $L(S) = L(G) = L$, by Proposition 1, $L(\alpha) = \overline{rs}L(S) = \overline{rs}L$. By the definition of $\varphi(r,s,t)$, $\varphi(r,s,t) \in L(\alpha)$ and $Suf_j(\varphi(r,s,t)) \notin L(\alpha)$ for any $j$ $(1 \leq j \leq |\varphi(r,s,t)| - 1)$. Hence, by Lemma 6 and the definition of $M((r,s,t))$, $L(A) = M((r,s,t))$.     □

The above lemma ensures that if the learning algorithm is given a positive counterexample $w$, then it can make all nonterminals with appropriate models that are necessary for generating $w$. In the result, nonterminal membership queries used in [Ang87a] can be replaced by membership queries. For any $x \in \Sigma^*$ and $A \in N(w)$, the diagnosis routine can accomplish each inquiry as to whether $x \in M(A)$ or not by making $|x|$ membership queries.

## CORRECTNESS AND COMPLEXITY

In what follows, let $L$ be the target language, $G_0 = (N_0, \Sigma, P_0, S)$ be an SDG such that $L(G_0) = L$ and with the minimum number of nonterminals, $G = (N, \Sigma, P, S)$ be the grammar in the algorithm and $M = \{M(S), M((r_1, s_1, t_1)), \ldots, M((r_{|N|-1}, s_{|N|-1}, t_{|N|-1}))\}$ be the model for $G$ defined in the previous section.

**Lemma 9** *Suppose that the diagnosis routine is given as input a parse-tree that generates a string $x$ and has its root node labeled with $A \in N$ such that $x \notin M(A)$. Then it returns a production in $P$ that is incorrect for $M$.*

**Proof:** The lemma can be proved along the same line of argument as the proof of Lemma 5 in [Ang87a]. □

**Lemma 10** *The time required by the diagnosis routine on an input parse-tree for a negative counterexample $w$ is bounded by a non-decreasing polynomial in $|w|$ and $\ell$, the length of the longest counterexample.*

**Proof:** Since $G$ is in 2-standard form, there are at most $|w|$ occurrences of nonterminals in the parse-tree. Thus, the number of inquiries made by the diagnosis routine is at most $|w|$. For each inquiry as to whether $x \in M(A)$ or not, if $A = S$, then only one membership query "$x \in L$ ?" is made. Otherwise, that is, if $A = (r, s, t)$, the routine makes at most $|x|$ membership queries "$rPre_i(x)\varphi(r, s, t) \in L$ ?" for $1 \leq i \leq |x|$. Since $x$ is a sub-string of $w$, the total number of queries made in a diagnosing process is at most $|w|^2$. Since the main operations made in the diagnosis routine are making strings $rPre_i(x)\varphi(r, s, t)$ and making membership queries, it is clear that the claim of the lemma holds. □

**Lemma 11** *The total number of given positive counterexamples is bounded by $|N_0|$.*

**Proof:** Let $w_n$ be the $n$th given positive counterexample. We define $N_0(w_n)$ and $P_0(w_n)$ as follows:

$$N_0(w_n) = \{A \in N_0 \mid S \Rightarrow^*_{G_0} uA\alpha \Rightarrow^*_{G_0} w_n\},$$

$$P_0(w_n) = \{A \rightarrow a\alpha \in P_0 \mid a \in \Sigma, A\alpha \in (\bigcup_{i=1}^{n} N_0(w_i))^+\}.$$

When $w_n$ is given, the learning algorithm computes $N(w_n)$ and sets $N$ to $N \cup N(w_n)$. Then it computes all new candidate productions and adds them to $P$ as described before.

By Lemma 8, for each nonterminal $A \in N_0(w_n)$, there exists a nonterminal $A' \in N(w_n)$ such that $L(A) = M(A')$. Under this correspondence of $A$ and $A'$, for every production in $P_0(w_n)$, a corresponding production is added to $P$ at least once. By Proposition 4, these corresponding productions are correct for $M$. Since correct productions are never removed from $P$, whenever the $n + 1$st positive counterexample is given, there exists at least one nonterminal $A \in N_0$ such that

$$A \in N_0(w_{n+1}) \quad \text{and} \quad A \notin \bigcup_{i=1}^{n} N_0(w_i).$$

Thus, the number of given positive counterexamples is at most $|N_0|$.    □

**Lemma 12** *The number of nonterminals introduced by the learning algorithm is bounded by $|N_0|\ell_p(\ell_p - 1)/2$, where $\ell_p$ is the length of the longest positive counterexample.*

**Proof:**   For each positive counterexample $w_i$, $|N(w_i)|$ is at most $|w_i|(|w_i| - 1)/2$ as stated in the previous section. By Lemma 11, the total number of nonterminals introduced by the algorithm is bounded by $|N_0|\ell_p(\ell_p - 1)/2$.    □

**Proof of Theorem 5:**   From the way to introduce new productions and Lemma 12, the total number $m$ of productions introduced into $P$ is at most

$$ m = \frac{|N_0|\ell_p(\ell_p - 1)}{2} \times |\Sigma| \times \left( \frac{|N_0|\ell_p(\ell_p - 1)}{2} + 1 \right)^2 . $$

By Lemma 9, for each given negative counterexample, at least one incorrect production is found and it is removed from $P$. With Lemma 11, this implies that, after giving at most $|N_0|$ positive counterexamples and at most $m$ negative ones, the learning algorithm outputs a grammar $G$ such that $L(G) = L$.

Let $\ell$ be the length of the longest counterexample. By Lemma 12, at any stage of learning, the size of $G$ is bounded by a non-decreasing polynomial in $|N_0|$ and $\ell$. From the assumption on the parsing sub-procedure, the algorithm can determine whether a given counterexample is positive or negative in time polynomial in $|N_0|$ and $\ell$. The total number of given counterexamples is at most $|N_0| + m$. With Lemma 7 and Lemma 10, this implies the claim for the complexity of the algorithm.    □

## CONCLUSION

We have discussed the problem of learning SDLs. The main idea presented in this paper was how to introduce necessary nonterminals with their appropriate models (or meanings). The problem introducing new sub-concepts that are useful for representing a target concept but not observed is one of the most important and difficult problems in machine learning. Recently, there have been several approaches to this problem, e.g., [Ban88, MB88]. It seems, however, that we have no sufficient result yet. Of course, our result is also for a class that is too restricted, so we need to try to find more general and useful approaches to the problem.

For the given algorithm, there is a problem of efficiency. As shown in the proof of Theorem 5, it is ensured that the algorithm runs in time polynomial in $|N_0|$ and $\ell$. However, the polynomial has a rather high degree. If we can set each intermediate hypothetical grammar to an SDG, we will be able to decrease the degree. Of course, such a restriction on hypothetical grammars also results in the development of an algorithm that produces an SDG as its output using pure equivalence queries.

Yokomori [Yok88] gives another algorithm for learning SDLs in polynomial time. His algorithm exactly constructs an SDG. In his setting, however, a very powerful teacher is assumed. The teacher can answer the special two types of queries: prefix membership queries and derivatives equivalence queries. A prefix membership query is an extension of the membership query. A derivatives equivalence query proposes two pairs of strings $(u_1, w_1), (u_2, w_2)$ and asks whether $\overline{u_1} L \overline{w_1} = \overline{u_2} L \overline{w_2}$, where $L$ is the target language. It is clear that derivatives equivalence queries can be used, in our algorithm, to test whether two candidate nonterminals are identical. For example, for two nonterminals $(u_1, v_1, w_1)$ and $(u_2, v_2, w_2)$, if $\overline{u_1} L \overline{w_1} = \overline{u_2} L \overline{w_2}$, then they are identical. Thus, the number of nonterminals generated by our algorithm will be reduced. Unfortunately, we have not sufficiently discussed the problem of such relations between the ability of the teacher and the efficiency of the algorithm.

## Acknowledgements

I wish to thank Dr. K. Furukawa and Dr. R. Hasegawa for their continuous support and advice. I am also deeply grateful to Dr. T. Yokomori for his many valuable comments. Mr. Y. Sakakibara pointed out my misunderstanding about equivalence queries in the draft. Discussions with the members of the Learning and Non-monotonic Reasoning Research Group at ICOT have also been very fruitful. Finally, I wish to thank Dr. K. Fuchi, the director of ICOT Research Center, for providing the opportunity to conduct this research in the Fifth Generation Computer Systems Project.

## References

[Ang87a]  Dana Angluin. Learning k-bounded context-free grammars. Research Report 557, Yale University Computer Science Dept., 1987.

[Ang87b]  Dana Angluin. Learning regular sets from queries and counterexamples. *Information and Computation*, 75:87–106, 1987.

[Ang88]  Dana Angluin. Queries and concept learning. *Machine Learning*, 2(4):319–342, 1988.

[Ban88]   Ranan B. Banerji. Learning theories in a subset of a polyadic logic. In *Proc. Computational Learning Theory '88*, pp. 281–295, 1988.

[Har79]   Michael A. Harrison. *Introduction to Formal Language Theory*. Addison-Wesley, 1979.

[Ish89]   Hiroki Ishizaka. Inductive inference of regular languages based on model inference. To appear in IJCM, 1989.

[MB88]    Stephen Muggleton and Wray Buntine. Machine invention of first-order predicates by inverting resolution. In *Proc. 5th International Conference on Machine Learning*, pp. 339–352, 1988.

[Sha81]   Ehud Y. Shapiro. Inductive inference of theories from facts. Technical Report 192, Yale University Computer Science Dept., 1981.

[Yok88]   Takashi Yokomori. Learning simple languages in polynomial time. In *Proc. of SIG-FAI*, pp. 21–30. Japanese Society for Artificial Intelligence, June 1988.

# Learning in the Presence of Inaccurate Information

Mark Fulk      Sanjay Jain
Department of Computer Science
University of Rochester
Rochester, New York 14627

## ABSTRACT

In this paper we discuss the effects of errors in input data on recursion theoretic learning. We consider three types of inaccuracy in input data depending on the presence of extra data (noise), missing data (incompleteness) or both (imperfection). We show that for function learning incompleteness harms strictly more than noise. However for language learning, identification from incomplete text and identification from noisy text are incomparable. We also prove hierarchies based on the number of inaccuracies present in the input.

## INTRODUCTION

In this paper we discuss the effect of inaccuracies in the text on learning in Gold's model. For an introduction to Gold's notion of learning see [CS83] [OSW86] [Gol67]. The study is motivated by the fact that in the real world we rarely have perfect input. We often have the presence of noise and absence of data. We consider three types of inaccuracies in the input data. (a) Extra (noisy) data, (b) missing (incomplete) data and (c) both extra and missing (imperfect) data. In this paper we only consider cases in which the inaccuracies are bounded by a constant or are unbounded but finite. Unbounded but finite inaccuracy was also considered in [OSW86]. Schafer [SR86] independently considered function learning on noisy input. We show that the presence of inaccuracy in the data restricts learning power. We also get a hierarchy based on the bound on the number of inaccuracies allowed. Moreover we show that the language classes learnable from noisy text and and the language classes learnable from incomplete text are incomparable. However for function learning, the class of functions that can be learned from noisy data are a strict superset of the class of functions that can be learned from incomplete data.

## NOTATION

$N$ is the set of natural numbers. The primed, unprimed, subscripted, and unsubscripted versions of $i, j, l, m, n$ range over natural numbers unless otherwise specified. $a, b, c$ range over $N \cup \{*\}$ where $*$ stands for finitely many.

$\emptyset$ denotes the null set. $Card(S)$ denotes the cardinality of the set $S$. $max, min$ denote the maximum and minimum of a set respectively. $\mu x[Q(x)]$ is the least natural number $x$ such that the predicate $Q(x)$ is true (if such exists). We say that something is $\leq *$ to mean it is finite.

$L$ denotes an recursively enumerable subset of $N$. $\oplus$ denotes symmetric difference. $L_1 =^a L_2$ means $card(L_1 \oplus L_2) \leq a$. $f =^a g$ means $card(\{x | f(x) \neq g(x)\}) \leq a$. $\mathcal{L}$ denotes a set of recursively enumerable (r.e.) languages. $\mathcal{E}$ denotes the class of all recursively enumerable languages. $\mathcal{R}$ denotes the set of total recursive functions. $\varphi$ denotes an standard acceptable numbering [Rog58], [Rog67]. $\Phi$ denotes an arbitrary Blum complexity measure [Blu67] for $\varphi$.

$W_i$ denotes the r.e. set $\{x | x \in \delta\varphi_i\}$. $W_i|^n$ denotes the set $\{x | (x \leq n) \wedge (\Phi(x) \leq n)\}$.

$\langle i, j \rangle$ stands for an arbitrary computable one to one encoding of all pairs of natural numbers onto $N$ [Rog67]. Corresponding projection functions are $\pi_1$ and $\pi_2$. $(\forall i, j \in N)$ $[\pi_1(\langle i, j \rangle) = i$ and $\pi_2(\langle i, j \rangle) = j$ and $\langle \pi_1(x), \pi_2(x) \rangle = x$ $]$. Similarly $\langle i_1, i_2, .., i_n \rangle$ denotes a computable one to one encoding of all $n$-tuples onto $N$.

Sequences are functions with domain an initial segment of $N$. An information sequence is an infinite sequence; a segment is a finite sequence. $t$ denotes an information sequence. $\sigma, \sigma_0, ..$ range over segments. $\overline{t_n}$ denotes the initial segment of $t$ with length $n$. $content(t) = \rho t - \{*\}$; intuitively it is a set of meaningful things presented in $t$. Similarly, $content(\sigma) = \rho\sigma - \{*\}$. A *text* $t$ for a language $L$ is a mapping $t$ from $N \to N \cup \{*\}$ such that $content(t) = L$. Note that $\overline{t_n}$ can be encoded as a natural number. $length(\sigma)$ denotes the length of $\sigma$. $\sigma_1 \diamond \sigma_2$ denotes the concatenation of $\sigma_1$ and $\sigma_2$. For all recursive functions $f$, $f|^n$ denotes the finite segment $((\langle 0, f(0) \rangle), (\langle 1, f(1) \rangle), (\langle 2, f(2) \rangle), ....(\langle n, f(n) \rangle))$.

## IDENTIFICATION WITH INACCURATE INPUT

In the real world the data we get are seldom free of error. We consider three types of error in input data.

1) The input text may contain elements not in the language (noisy text).

2) Some elements of the language may be absent from the text (incomplete text).

3) A combination of (1) and (2) may occur(imperfect text).

The definitions below make the notion precise.

Let $a, b \in N \bigcup \{*\}$

## Definition 1

*1) We say that a text $t$ is $a$-noisy for $L \in \mathcal{E}$ iff*

*a) $(\forall x)[[x \in L] \Rightarrow [x \in content(t)]]$,*

*b) $card(\{x | (x \notin L) \wedge (x \in content(t))\}) \leq a$.*

*2) We say that a text $t$ is $a$-incomplete for $L \in \mathcal{E}$ iff*

*a) $(\forall x)[[x \notin L] \Rightarrow [x \notin content(t)]]$,*

*b) $card(\{x | (x \in L) \wedge (x \notin content(t))\}) \leq a$.*

*3) We say that a text $t$ is $a$-imperfect for $L \in \mathcal{E}$ iff $card(\{x | (x \in (L \oplus content(t)))\}) \leq a$.*

We now consider the criteria for identification with respect to noisy, incomplete or imperfect text.

**Definition 2** *We say that $M$ $N^a TxtEX^b(In^a TxtEX^b, Im^a TxtEX^b)$ identifies $\mathcal{L} \subseteq \mathcal{E}$ iff for all $L \in \mathcal{L}$, on all $a$-noisy ($a$-incomplete, $a$-imperfect) text for $L$, $M$ converges to a grammar $i$ such that $W_i =^b L$.*

*We say that $M$ $N^a EX^b(In^a EX^b, Im^a EX^b)$ identifies $\mathcal{C} \subseteq \mathcal{R}$ iff for all $f \in \mathcal{C}$, on all $a$-noisy ($a$-incomplete, $a$-imperfect) text for $L_f = \{\langle x, y \rangle | f(x) = y\}$, $M$ converges to a program $i$ such that $\varphi_i =^b f$.*

This definition can be extended to BC learning in the obvious way.

## HIERARCHY RESULTS

We first show that allowing extra errors in the final program helps even in presence of inaccuracies.

**Theorem 1** *For all $i \in N$*

*1. $Im^* EX^{i+1} - EX^i \neq \emptyset$*

*2. $Im^* EX^* - \bigcup_i EX^i \neq \emptyset$*

*3. $Im^* BC - EX^* \neq \emptyset$*

*4. $Im^* BC^{i+1} - BC^i \neq \emptyset$.*

## Proof:

1) Let $\mathcal{C} = \{f | \varphi_{f(0)} =^{i+1} f \wedge (\forall x)[f(2x) = f(0)]\}$. It is easy to see that $\mathcal{C} \in Im^* EX^{i+1}$. However an easy modification of the proof of $EX^{i+1} - EX^i \neq \emptyset$ in [CS83] shows that $\mathcal{C} \notin EX^i$.

2-4 can be proved by similar extension of the proofs in [CS83]. □

Now we consider the effects of having noise, incompleteness or imperfection in the text bounded by some constant. We show that additional inaccuracy harms. This along with the above theorem gives a two-dimensional hierarchy for each of the three inaccuracy discussed. For simplicity we first consider single inaccuracies.

**Theorem 2** $Im^0 EX - N^1 EX^* \neq \emptyset$.

**Proof:** Consider the following class of functions:

$$\mathcal{C} = \{f | f \in R \text{ and}$$
$$\quad 1) \ (\forall j, x)[f(\langle 0, x \rangle + 1) = f(\langle j, x \rangle + 1)]$$
$$\quad 2) \ f(0) = 0 \Rightarrow card(\{x | f(\langle 0, x \rangle + 1) \neq 0\}) = finite.$$
$$\quad 3) \ f(0) \neq 0 \Rightarrow \varphi_{f(1)} = \lambda x[f(\langle 0, x \rangle + 1)].$$
$$\}$$

It is easy to see that $\mathcal{C} \in EX = Im^0 EX$. Consider the following function classes
$\mathcal{C}_a = \{f | \varphi_{f(0)} = f\}$;
$\mathcal{C}_b = \{f | card(\{x | f(x) \neq 0\}) = finite\}$.

In [CS83] it was shown that $\mathcal{C}_a \bigcup \mathcal{C}_b \notin EX^*$. Suppose by way of contradiction that $\mathcal{C} \in N^1 EX^*$ by machine $M$. We show how to modify $M$ to $EX^*$ *identify* $\mathcal{C}_a \bigcup \mathcal{C}_b$.

Let $M'(\sigma) = F(M(\sigma'))$

where $\langle 0, 0 \rangle \in \sigma'$, $\langle 0, 1 \rangle \in \sigma'$, $\langle x, y \rangle \in \sigma \Rightarrow (\forall i \leq length(\sigma))[\langle \langle i, x \rangle + 1, y \rangle \in \sigma']$ and $F(i)$ is the index of a program $j$ such that $\varphi_j = \lambda x[\varphi_i(\langle 0, x \rangle + 1)]$.

It is easy to see that $M'$ $EX^*$ *identifies* $\mathcal{C}_a \bigcup \mathcal{C}_b$ if $M$ $N^1 EX^*$ *identifies* $\mathcal{C}$. But no such $M'$ can exist. $\Rightarrow\Leftarrow$. Thus $\mathcal{C} \notin N^1 EX^*$.

□

Similar proof shows that $\mathcal{C} \notin In^1 EX$.

**Theorem 3** $Im^0 EX - In^1 EX^* \neq \emptyset$.

**Corollary 1** $Im^0 EX - Im^1 EX^* \neq \emptyset$.

In [CS83] it was shown that $\mathcal{C}_a \bigcup \mathcal{C}_b$ was not in $BC^i$. Thus we also have
For all $i \in N$,

**Theorem 4** $Im^0 EX - In^1 BC^i \neq \emptyset$.

**Theorem 5** $Im^0 EX - N^1 BC^i \neq \emptyset$

We now extend the above results to higher number of permissible errors in input. Consider the function classes

$$C_j = \{f \mid$$

    1) $(\forall i)[f(\langle i, x \rangle + j + 1) = f(\langle 0, x \rangle + j + 1)]$

    2) $[(\forall x \le j)f(x) = 0] \Rightarrow card(\{x \mid f(\langle 0, x \rangle + j + 1) \ne 0\}) = finite.$

    3) $[(\forall x \le j)f(x) = 1] \Rightarrow \varphi_{f(1)} = \lambda x[f(\langle 0, x \rangle + j + 1)].$

    4) $[(\forall x \le j)f(x) = 0] \vee [(\forall x \le j)f(x) = 1].$

$\}$

Easy modification of the proof of the theorem 2 shows that

1) $C_j \in Im^j EX,$

2) $C_j \notin N^{j+1} EX^*.$

3) $C_j \notin In^{j+1} EX^*.$

and for all $i \in N$

4) $C_j \notin N^{j+1} BC^i.$

5) $C_j \notin In^{j+1} BC^i.$

Thus

**Theorem 6** *For all $j$, $Im^j - [N^{j+1} EX^* \cup In^{j+1} EX^* \cup (\bigcup_i In^{j+1} BC^i) \cup (\bigcup_i N^{j+1} BC^i)] \ne \emptyset$*

Also note that for all $j$ if $L_1, L_2 \in C_j$, $L_1 \ne L_2$ then $card(L_1 \oplus L_2) = \infty$. Note that to prove theorem 6, there was no need for the cylindrification done in clause (1) of the definition. We have done so only to show that the above results can be obtained even if we are restricted to classes of languages such that any two languages in a class are infinitely different.

We now show that there exists a class of languages which can be identified with $j$ errors in the text for any constant $j$, but cannot be identified with finite but unbounded error in the text.

**Theorem 7** $(\exists C)[[(\forall i)[C \in N^i EX]] \wedge [C \notin N^* EX^*]]$

**Proof:**

Let $C = \{f \mid f \in R$ and

    1) $(\forall i \ge 1)[f(\langle i, x \rangle) = f(\langle 1, x \rangle)].$

    2) $(\forall x > f(\langle 1, 0 \rangle))[f(\langle 0, x \rangle) = 0].$

    3) $[(\forall x \le f(\langle 1, 0 \rangle))[f(\langle 0, x \rangle) = 0]] \Leftrightarrow [card(\{x \mid f(\langle 1, x \rangle) \ne 0\}) = finite]$

    4) $[(\forall x \le f(\langle 1, 0 \rangle))[f(\langle 0, x \rangle) = 1]] \Leftrightarrow$

            $[[\varphi_{f(0)} = \lambda y.f(\langle 1, y \rangle)] \wedge card\{y \mid f(\langle 1, y \rangle) \ne 0\}) = \infty]$

    5) $[(\forall x \le f(\langle 1, 0 \rangle))[f(\langle 0, x \rangle) = 0]] \vee [(\forall x \le f(\langle 1, 0 \rangle))[f(\langle 0, x \rangle) = 1]].$

$\}$

$\mathcal{C} \notin N^*EX^*$, $In^*EX^*$, $N^*BC^i$ or $In^*BC^i$; we omit the proof which is similar to the proof used in theorem 2. Given any $i$ we show that $\mathcal{C} \in N^iEX$. Let $S_i = \{j|(j \leq i) \land \varphi_j(0) = j \land \varphi_j \in R \land card(\{x|\varphi_j(x) \neq 0\}) = \infty\}$. We describe a machine $M$ $N^iEX^*$-identifying $\mathcal{C}$.

$M(\sigma)$

1. Let $i_m = max(\{i|\exists y \langle\langle i, 0\rangle, y\rangle \in \sigma\})$
2. $e_0 = min\{y|\langle\langle i_m, 0\rangle, y\rangle \in \sigma\}$
3. Let $T = \{\langle x, y\rangle|[\langle\langle i_x, x\rangle, y\rangle \in \sigma] \land$
   $\qquad\qquad \forall z[\langle\langle i_x, x\rangle, z\rangle \in \sigma] \Rightarrow [z \geq y]\}$
   where $i_x = max\{i|\exists y \langle\langle i, x\rangle, y\rangle \in \sigma\}$
4. If $e_0 \leq max(S_i)$ *then* execute step 5a.
   *else* execute step 5b.
5a. If $[e_0 \in S_i \land (\forall\langle x, y\rangle \in T)[\varphi_{e_0}(x) = y]]$ *then* output $F_1(e_0)$.
   *else* output $F_0(T)$
5b. If $[(\forall j \leq e_0)[\langle\langle 0, j\rangle, 0\rangle \in \sigma]]$ *then* output $F_0(T)$
   *else* output $F_1(e_0)$
End

where

$\varphi_{F_0(T)}$ is as follows
$\qquad (\forall x)[\varphi_{F_0(T)}(\langle 0, x\rangle) = 0]$.
$\qquad (\forall i \geq 1)(\forall x)$
$\qquad\qquad$ If there exists $y$ such that $\langle x, y\rangle \in T$ then $\varphi_{F_0(T)}(\langle i, x\rangle) = y]$
$\qquad\qquad$ Else $\varphi_{F_0(T)}(\langle i, x\rangle) = 0$
End

and

$\varphi_{F_1(e_0)}$ is as follows
$\qquad (\forall i \geq 1)(\forall x)[\varphi_{F_1(e_0)}(\langle i, x\rangle) = \varphi_{e_0}(x)]$
$\qquad (\forall x > e_0)[\varphi_{F_1(e_0)}(\langle 0, x\rangle) = 0]$
$\qquad (\forall x \leq e_0)[\varphi_{F_1(e_0)}(\langle 0, x\rangle) = 1]$
End

Now for large enough initial segment $\sigma$ for any *i-noisy text* for $f \in \mathcal{C}$,
$e_0$ found in step 2 is such that $f(\langle 1, 0\rangle) = e_0$.
$T$ found in step 3 is such that $\langle x, y\rangle \in T \Rightarrow f(\langle 1, x\rangle) = y$.
$(\forall x \leq f(\langle 1, 0\rangle)) [\langle\langle 0, x\rangle, f(\langle 0, x\rangle)\rangle \in \sigma]$
Now

*If* $e_0 \leq i$

then If $\varphi_{e_0} = f \wedge card\{y | f(\langle 1, y \rangle) \neq 0\}) = \infty$

then "if clause of step 5a" will succeed and thus $M$ outputs $F_1(e_0)$ in the limit which is a program for $f$.

Else, "if clause of step 5a" will eventually fail and $M$ outputs $F_0(T)$ in the limit, where $T = \{\langle x, y \rangle | f(\langle 1, x \rangle) = y\}$, which is a program for $f$.

Else (i.e. $e_0 > i$) 5b would output either $F_0(T)$ (where $T = \{\langle x, y \rangle | f(\langle 1, x \rangle) = y\}$) or $F_1(e_0)$ in the limit depending on whether $(\forall j \leq e_0)[\langle \langle 0, j \rangle, 0 \rangle \in \sigma]$ or not.

Since the number of noisy data is at most $e_0 - 1$

If $(\forall j \leq e_0)[\langle \langle 0, j \rangle, 0 \rangle \in \sigma]$ then by clause 3 of the definition of $\mathcal{C}$, $F_0(T)$ is a program for $f$.

Similarly if $\neg(\forall j \leq e_0)[\langle \langle 0, j \rangle, 0 \rangle \in \sigma]$ then by clause 4 of the definition of $\mathcal{C}$, $F_1(e_0)$ is a program for $f$.

From the above cases we have that $M$ $N^i EX$-identifies $\mathcal{C}$.
It can be similarly shown that

**Theorem 8** $\exists \mathcal{C}[[\forall i \mathcal{C} \in In^i EX] \wedge [\mathcal{C} \notin In^* EX^*]]$

**Theorem 9** $\exists \mathcal{C}[[\forall i \mathcal{C} \in Im^i EX] \wedge [\mathcal{C} \notin Im^* EX^*]]$

## RELATIVE EFFECTS OF DIFFERENT TYPES OF INACCURACIES

We now consider the relative powers of identification in presence of different types of inaccuracies in text.

**Theorem 10** $N^* EX - In^1 EX^* \neq \emptyset$

As a corollary we obtain.

**Corollary 2** $N^* TxtEX - In^* TxtEX \neq \emptyset$

This solves an open problem in [OSW86].
**Proof:**

We give a class of functions that is in $N^* EX$ but not in $In^1 EX^*$. Note that any two functions in the class differ at infinitely many points. This is necessary for this theorem since we want to identify the class even in presence of finite noise.

We say that $f$ satisfies property $P$ if

a) $f \in \mathcal{R}$,
    Let $f(0) = p$; Let $f(\langle 0, p \rangle + 1) = e$ then
b) $(\forall i, x)[f(\langle i, x \rangle + 1) = f(\langle 0, x \rangle + 1)]$.
c) $(\forall x)[\varphi_e(x) = f(\langle 0, x \rangle + 1)]$
d) $(\forall x)(\forall z)\, [f(\langle 0, x \rangle + 1) = f(\langle 0, z \rangle + 1) \Rightarrow x = z]$
e) $[[y \in range(\varphi_e)] \wedge [y \neq e]] \Rightarrow \varphi_e \neq \varphi_y$

Let $\mathcal{C} = \{f \mid f \text{ satisfies property } P\}$.

The above class of functions can be viewed as the cylindrifications of functions $f$ such that $f$ is 1-1 and a unique element in the range of $f$ computes $f$. $p$ above can be viewed as a pointer to that element.

**Claim 1** $\mathcal{C} \in N^* EX$.

**Proof:** We first define an IIM M that may diverge on some inputs. $M$ will converge for almost all initial segments of any noisy text for $f \in \mathcal{C}$. The IIM can easily be modified so that it converges on all inputs (see $M'$ at the end of the proof, this is a common trick used to convert a partial learning function to a total learning function). $M$ collects all the pointers in the data and using the property $P$ of the function, tries to find the unique pointer that belongs to the function being learned.

Let $M$ be defined as follows

on input $\sigma$
1) Let $PTRS = \{p \mid \langle 0, p \rangle \in \sigma\}$.
2) Let $S = \{\langle x, y \rangle \mid \langle \langle m_x, x \rangle + 1, y \rangle \in \sigma\}$, where
   $$m_x = max\{i \mid (\exists z)[\,\langle \langle i, x \rangle + 1, z \rangle \in \sigma]\}$$
3) For all p in $PTRS$ let $E(p)$ be least $y$ such that $\langle p, y \rangle \in S$, if such a $y$ exists; $E(p)$ is undefined otherwise.
4) Search for a $p \in PTRS$ such that $(\forall \langle x, y \rangle \in S)[\varphi_{E(p)}(x) = y]$.
5) Output the program $PRG(E(p), p)$ (given below) for first such $E(p)$ found in (4) above (output 0 if $PTRS = \emptyset$ or $E(p)$ undefined for all $p \in PTRS$).
End M.

Program $PRG(e, p)$
    $\varphi_{PRG(e,p)}(0) = p$;
    $\varphi_{PRG(e,p)}(\langle i, x \rangle + 1) = \varphi_e(x)$
End $PRG(e, p)$

Clearly, for any $f \in \mathcal{C}$, $PRG(e, p)$ (where $e, p$ are as in property $P$) is a program for $f$. Thus it suffices to show that $M$ on any noisy text for $f \in \mathcal{C}$ converges to $PRG(e, p)$.

By definition of $\mathcal{C}$ and the fact that the errors in the noisy-input text $t$ are finite we have that for sufficiently large initial segment $\sigma$ of $t$, $PTRS$, $S$ constructed in steps 1,2 of the algorithm above is such that

1) $p \in PTRS$
2) $S \subset \{\langle x,y\rangle | f(\langle 0,x\rangle + 1) = y\}$
3) $\langle p,e\rangle \in S$ where $p,e$ are as in property $P$.
4) for all $p' \neq p$ such that $\langle 0,p'\rangle \in rng(t)$ $(\exists \langle x,y\rangle \in S)[\varphi_{E(p')}(x) \neq y]$

Thus the program output by $M$ on $\sigma$ is $PRG(e,p)$.

The above M can be modified to $M'$ which halts on all inputs and identifies $\mathcal{C}$ on noisy text as follows.

$M'$ on input $\sigma$
    let $l$=length $(\sigma)$.
    output $M(\sigma')$ where $\sigma'$ is the largest initial
    segment of $\sigma$ such that $M(\sigma')$ halts in $l$ steps
    (output 0 if no such $\sigma'$ exists).
End $M'$

   $\square$ claim 1.
Before proving that $\mathcal{C} \notin In^1 EX^*$ we prove the following interesting lemma.

**Lemma 1** *Let $\mathcal{C}' = \{f | f$ is 1-1 and there exists exactly one $e \in range(f)$ such that $\varphi_e = f\}$.*
   *Then $\mathcal{C}' \notin EX^*$*

**Proof:** Suppose by way of contradiction that $M$ $EX^*$-identifies $\mathcal{C}'$. Then by *Operator Recursion Theorem* (ORT) [Cas74] there exists a 1-1 increasing recursive function $p$ such that the following holds:

Below let $\varphi_e^s$ denote $\varphi_e$ defined upto stage s. We define $\varphi_{p(i)}$ in stages. $\varphi_{p(i)}$ would be 1-1 (may not be total).

Let $\varphi_{p(0)}(0) = p(0)$. Let $i^0 = 1$. ($i^s$ denotes the least $i$ such that for all $j \geq i$, $p(j)$ has not been considered or output at any stage before s). Let $x^s$ be least $x$ such that $\varphi_{p(0)}^s(x^s)$ is not defined.

   Stage $s$.
      1) Let $\varphi_{p(i^s)}(x) = \varphi_{p(0)}(x)$ for $x < x^s$. Let $\varphi_{p(i^s)}(x^s) = p(i^s)$;
      2) Let $x = x^s+1$ and $i = i^s+1$. Let $\sigma = \varphi_{p(i^s)}|^{i^s+1}$
      3) Repeat the following until $M(\sigma) \neq M(\varphi_{p(0)}^s) \vee \varphi_{M(\varphi_{p(0)}^s)}(z) = y$
          for some $z \geq x^s$.
          $\varphi_{p(i^s)}(x) = p(i)$; $\sigma = \sigma.\langle x,p(i)\rangle$; $i = i+1; x = x+1$;

4) If and when 3 above halts do the following

Let $i_m$ denote the last $i$ considered in step 3.

*case 1* ) If a mind change was found *then*

let $\varphi_{p(0)}^{s+1}(x) = \varphi_{p(i^s)}(x)$ for $x$ such that $\varphi_{p(i^s)}(x)$ defined till now. Let $i^{s+1} = i_m + 1$.

*case 2)* If $\varphi_{f(\varphi_{p(0)}^s)}(z) = y$ for some $z \geq x^s$ *then* let

$$\varphi_{p(0)}(z) = p(j)$$

where $p(j) \neq y$ and $j > i_m + 1$.

Let $\varphi_{p(0)}(x) = p(j_x) | x^s \leq x < z\}$,

where $j_x$ are such that $j_x > j$ and $x \neq x' \Rightarrow j_x \neq j_{x'}$

let $i^{s+1} = 1 + max(j, \{j_x | x^s \leq x \leq z\})$.

From now on $\varphi_{p(i^s)}$ does not converge on any more inputs.

End stage s.


Note that in the above construction only one of $\varphi_{p(i)}$'s is total.


*Case 1*: There exists a stage $s$ such that stage $s$ never halts.

Then let $f = \varphi_{p(i^s)}$. Clearly $\varphi_{p(i^s)}$ is 1-1 and total. Also exactly one element in the range of $\varphi_{p(i^s)}$ calculates $f$. Thus $f \in \mathcal{C}'$. $M(\varphi_{p(i^s)} = f)$ converges to $M(\varphi_{p(0)}^s)$, and $\varphi_{M(\varphi_{p(0)}^s)}$ does not halt on infinitely many inputs.

Thus $M$ does not $EX^*$-identify $f$.

Case 2: all stages halt.

In this case let $f = \varphi_{p(0)}$. Clearly $f \in \mathcal{C}'$.

Case 2a: $M$ on $f$ diverges.

In this case $M$ does not identify $f$.

Case 2b: $M$ on $f$ converges to $e_0$ at stage $s_0$.

In this case by construction there are infinitely many errors.


Thus such a $M$ ($EX^*$-identifying $\mathcal{C}'$) cannot exist. $\square$.

## Claim 2 $\mathcal{C} \notin In^1 EX^*$.

**Proof:** Suppose by way of contradiction $\mathcal{C} \in In^1 EX^*$ by some IIM $M$. Then $M$ on any text for $f \in \mathcal{C}$ without $\langle 0, p \rangle$ converges to a program $i$ such that $\varphi_i =^* f$: A straight forward modification of $M$ would give us $\mathcal{C}'$ ( of lemma 1) $\in EX^*$ contradicting lemma 1. $\square$

A slight modification of the proof in lemma 1 shows that $\mathcal{C}'$ cannot be $BC^i$ identified. This gives us the following

**Theorem 11** *For all $i \in N$,*
$N^*EX - In^1BC^i \neq \emptyset$.
$N^*TxtEX - In^1TxtBC^i \neq \emptyset$.

In contrast to above theorem we show that

**Theorem 12** *For all $a, b \in N \cup \{*\}$, $In^aEX^b \subseteq N^aEX^b$.*

**Proof:** Let $\mathcal{C} \in In^aEX^b$ by machine $M$. We construct $M'$ $N^aEX^b$ identifying $\mathcal{C}$.

Let $M'(\sigma) = M(\sigma')$, where $\sigma'$ is obtained from $\sigma$ by deleting all $\langle x, y \rangle$ from $\sigma$ for which there exists a $\langle x, y' \rangle$ in $\sigma$, $y' \neq y$.

Clearly, on a text $t$ $M'$ outputs $M(t')$ where $t'$ is obtained from $t$ by deleting all elements $\langle x, y \rangle$ from $t$ such that $\langle x, y' \rangle$ ($y' \neq y$) is also in $t$. If $t$ is an *a-noisy* text of $f \in \mathcal{C}$ then $t'$ does not contain any noisy data. Moreover the number of elements $\langle x, y \rangle$, $f(x) = y$ missing from $t'$ is atmost $a$. Therefore $M(t')$, and thus $M'(t)$ converges to a program for $f$.
□

# LANGUAGE LEARNING

We now consider the results in language learning which differ from the corresponding results in function learning.

**Theorem 13** $In^*TxtEX - N^*TxtBC^* \neq \emptyset$

**Proof:** Consider the class of languages:

Let $\mathcal{L} = \{L | (\exists m)$
    1. $[(\forall x > m)[\langle x, 0 \rangle \in L]] \wedge$
    2. $[(\forall x \leq m)[\langle x, 0 \rangle \notin L]] \wedge$
    3. $[(\forall i, j > 0)[(\forall x)\langle x, i \rangle \in L \Leftrightarrow \langle x, j \rangle \in L]] \wedge$
    4. $[max(\{x | \langle x, 1 \rangle \in L\}) = m \vee \{x | \langle x, 1 \rangle \notin L\} = N - \{m\}]\}$

It is easy to see that $\mathcal{L} \in In^*TxtEX$ ($min(\{x | \langle x, 0 \rangle \in content(t)\})$ bounds the value of $m$. $m$ can now be easily calculated (in the limit) using the other elements in the text). Suppose by way of contradiction that $M$ $N^*TxtBC^*$ identifies $\mathcal{L}$. Then $M$ can be easily modified to $TxtBC^*$ identify $\{L | L$ is finite or $L = $ co-singleton $\}$. But this is not true. Thus no such $M$ can exist. This proves the theorem.
□.

**Theorem 14** *For all $i \in N$, $Im^*TxtEX^{2i+1} - TxtBC^i \neq \emptyset$*

**Proof:** Let $\mathcal{L} = \{L | L =^{2i+1} N\}$. Clearly $\mathcal{L} \in Im^*TxtEX^{2i+1}$. It was shown in [CL82] that $\mathcal{L} \notin TxtBC^i$. This proves the theorem.

Case in [Cas88] introduced the notion of TxtFEX learning. Definitions for identification on inaccurate information can be extended to TxtFEX learning in an obvious way.

**Theorem 15** *For all $i \in N$, $Im^*TxtEX^{i+1} - TxtFEX_*^i \neq \emptyset$*

**Proof:** Follows from the corresponding theorem in function learning (since $FEX_*^a = EX^a$ [CS83]).

**Theorem 16** $Im^iTxtEX - [N^{i+1}TxtBC^* \bigcup In^{i+1}TxtBC^*] \neq \emptyset$

**Proof:**

Let $\mathcal{L} = \{L|$

    1. $(\forall j > 1)(\forall x)[\langle j, x \rangle \in L \Leftrightarrow \langle 1, x \rangle \in L]$

    2. $(\forall j > 2i + 1)[\langle 0, j \rangle \notin L]$

    Let $L' = \{x | \langle 1, x \rangle \in L\}$ then

    3. $L'$ is finite or $L' = N$

    4. $L' = N \Rightarrow (\forall j \leq i)[\langle 0, j \rangle \in L \wedge \langle 0, i + j + 1 \rangle \notin L]$

    5. $L'$ is finite $\Rightarrow (\forall j \leq i)[\langle 0, j \rangle \notin L \wedge \langle 0, i + j + 1 \rangle \in L]$

It is easy to see that $\mathcal{L} \in Im^iTxtEX$. Also $[\mathcal{L} \in N^{i+1}TxtBC^* \bigvee \mathcal{L} \in In^{i+1}TxtBC^*] \Rightarrow \{L | L$ is finite or $L = N\} \in TxtBC^*$. But this is not true.

Thus $\mathcal{L} \notin [N^{i+1}TxtBC^* \bigcup In^{i+1}TxtBC^*]$.

$\square$.

**Theorem 17** $N^jTxtEX - In^1TxtBC^* \neq \emptyset$

**Proof:**

Let $\mathcal{L} = \{L|$

    1. $(\forall j > 1)(\forall x)[\langle j, x \rangle \in L \Leftrightarrow \langle 1, x \rangle \in L]$

    2. $Card(\{x | \langle 0, x \rangle \in L\}) = 1$

    Let $L' = \{x | \langle 1, x \rangle \in L\}$ then

    3. $(\exists n)[L' = \{1..n\}] \bigvee L' = N$

    4. $L' = N \Rightarrow [\langle 0, 0 \rangle \in L]$

    5. $L'$ is finite $\Rightarrow [\langle 0, Card(L') + 1 \rangle \in L]$

It is easy to see that $\mathcal{L} \in N^jTxtEX$. Also $[\mathcal{L} \in In^1TxtBC^* \bigvee \mathcal{L} \in In^1TxtBC^*] \Rightarrow \{L | (\exists n)[L = \{1..n\}] \bigvee L = N\} \in TxtBC^*$. But this is not true. Thus $\mathcal{L} \notin In^1TxtBC^*$.

$\square$.

It is open at present if the above theorem can be extended to the case when $j$ is replaced by $*$.

**Theorem 18** $Im^*TxtFEX^0_{i+1} - TxtFEX^*_i \neq \emptyset$

**Proof:** Follows from easy modification of the proof of $TxtFEX^0_{i+1} - TxtFEX^*_i \neq \emptyset$ in [Cas88].

The following theorem gives some advantages of learning on incomplete text compared to noisy text. We have not been able to fully characterize the relationsship between language learning on incomplete text versus language learning on noisy text.

**Theorem 19** *For all* $i \in N$, $In^{2i-1}TxtEX^i - N^iTxtEX^* \neq \emptyset$.

We omit the proof of the theorem.

### CONCLUDING REMARKS

In the previous sections we proved the relationship between different identification classes defined using inaccurate input. One of the open problems is to determine if there exists a class of languages which can be identified on *-incomplete text but not on 1-noisy text. Another open problem is to determine if the containment $Im^aEX^b \subseteq In^aEX^b$ is proper for $a > 1$.

### Acknowledgements

We thank Prof. John Case, Arun Sharma, Rajeev Raman and Lata Narayanan for helpful discussions. The authors were supported by NSF grant CER 5-285-25 to the University of Rochester.

# References

[AL87]    D. Angluin and P. Laird. Learning from noisy examples. *Machine Learning*, 2:343–370, 1987.

[Blu67]   M. Blum. A machine independent theory of the complexity of recursive functions. *Journal of the ACM*, 14:322–336, 1967.

[Cas74]   J. Case. Periodicity in generations of automata. *Mathematical Systems Theory*, 8:15–32, 1974.

[Cas88]   J. Case. The power of vacillation. In *COLT'88*, pages 133–142, 1988.

[CL82]    J. Case and C. Lynes. Machine inductive inference and language identification. *Lecture Notes in Computer Science, Springer-Verlag, Berlin*, 140, 1982.

[CS83]    J. Case and C. Smith. Comparision of identification criteria for machine inductive inference. *Theoretical Computer Science*, 25:193–220, 1983.

[FJ89a]   M.A. Fulk and S. Jain. Learning in presence of inaccurate information. Technical Report 279, University of Rochester, 1989.

[FJ89b]   M.A. Fulk and S. Jain. Open problems in systems that learn. Technical Report 285, University of Rochester, 1989.

[Ful85]   M. Fulk. *A Study of Inductive Inference machines*. PhD thesis, SUNY/ Buffalo, 1985.

[Gol67]   E.M. Gold. Language identification in the limit. *Information and Control*, 10:447–474, 1967.

[JF88]    S. Jain and M. Fulk. Open problems in systems that learn. In *Proceedings of the Workshop on Computational Learning Theory*, pages 425–426, 1988.

[Lai87]   P. Laird. *Learning from Good Data and Bad*. PhD thesis, Yale University, 1987.

[OSW86]   D. Osherson, M. Stob, and S. Weinstein. *Systems that Learn, An Introduction to Learning Theory for Cognitive and Computer Scientists*. MIT Press, Cambridge, Mass., 1986.

[Rog58]   H. Rogers. Godel numberings of partial recursive functions. *Journal of Symbolic Logic*, 23:331–341, 1958.

[Rog67]   H. Rogers. *Theory of Recursive Functions and Effective Computability*. McGraw Hill, New York, 1967.

[SR86]    G Schafer-Richter. Some results in the theory of effective program synthesis - learning by defective information. *Lecture Notes in Computer Science, Springer-Verlag, Berlin*, 215:219–225, 1986.

# Convergence to Nearly Minimal Size Grammars by Vacillating Learning Machines (Extended Abstract)

Sanjay Jain
Dept. of Computer Science
University of Rochester
Rochester, New York 14627

Arun Sharma and John Case*
Dept. of Computer Science
SUNY at Buffalo
Buffalo, New York 14260

## ABSTRACT

In Gold's influential language learning paradigm a learning machine converges in the limit to *one* correct grammar. In an attempt to improve Gold's paradigm, Case considered the question whether people might converge to vacillating between up to (some integer) $n > 1$ distinct, but equivalent, correct grammars. He showed that larger classes of languages can be algorithmically learned (in the limit) by converging to *up to* $n + 1$ rather than up to $n$ correct grammars. He also argued that, for "small" $n > 1$, it is plausible that people might sometimes converge to vacillating between up to $n$ grammars. The insistence on *small* $n$ was motivated by the consideration that, for "large" $n$, at least one of $n$ grammars would be too large to fit in peoples' heads. This latter assumes, of course, that human brain storage is not magic, admitting of infinite regress, etc. Of course, even for Gold's $n = 1$ case, the single grammar converged to in the limit may be infeasibly large. An interesting *complexity restriction* to make, then, on the final grammar(s) converged to in the limit is that they all have small size. In this paper we study some of the tradeoffs in learning power involved in making a well-defined version of this restriction.

We show *and exploit as a tool* the desirable property that the learning power under our size-restricted criteria (for successful learning) is independent of the underlying

*The research was supported in part by NSF grants CER 5-285-25 at the University of Rochester and CCR 871-3846 at the University at Buffalo. Equipment support was provided by the Xerox University Grants Program at the University of Rochester and the Department of Computer Science at the University at Buffalo.

acceptable programming systems. We characterize the power of our size-restricted criteria and use this characterization to prove that *some* classes of languages, which can be learned by converging in the limit to up to $n + 1$ *nearly minimal size* correct grammars, *cannot* be learned by converging to up to $n$ unrestricted grammars even if these latter grammars are allowed to have a finite number of anomalies (i.e., mistakes) per grammar.

We also show that there is *no* loss of learning power in demanding that the final grammars be nearly minimal size *iff* one is willing to tolerate an *unbounded*, finite number of anomalies in the final grammars *and* there is a *constant* bound on the number of different grammars converged to in the limit. Hence, if we allow an unbounded, finite number of anomalies in the final grammars *and* the number of different grammars converged to in the limit is *unbounded* but finite (or if there is a *constant* bound on the number of anomalies allowed in the final grammars), then there *is* a loss of learning power in requiring that the final grammars be nearly minimal size.

These results do not always match what might be expected from the cases, previously examined by Freivalds, Kinber, and Chen, of learning nearly minimal size programs for functions, and, in many cases, our proofs are considerably more difficult.

## Preliminaries

Recursion-theoretic concepts not explained below are treated in [Rog67]. $N$ denotes the set of natural numbers, $\{0, 1, 2, 3, \ldots\}$, and $I^+$ denotes the set of positive integers. Conventions (to follow) as to the range of variables apply to these variables with or without decorations. $a$ and $b$ range over $(N \cup \{*\})$ and $(I^+ \cup \{*\})$, respectively. $f$, $g$, $h$, and $v$ range over (total) functions with arguments and values from $N$. Other lower case letters near the front and rear of the alphabet range over $N$. $L$ ranges over subsets of $N$ which subsets are usually construed as codings of formal languages. $\subseteq$ denotes the subset relation, and $\subset$ denotes proper subset. $L_1 \triangle L_2$ denotes $(L_1 - L_2) \cup (L_1 - L_2)$, the symmetric difference of $L_1$ and $L_2$. We let $\varphi$ range over acceptable programming systems (numberings) for the partial recursive functions: $N \to N$ [Rog58, Blu67, MY78, Ric80, Ric81, Roy87]. $W_p$ denotes the domain of $\varphi_p$. $W_p$ is, then, the r.e. set/language ($\subseteq N$) accepted by $\varphi$-program $p$. We can (and do) also think of $p$ as (coding) a (type 0 [HU79]) grammar for generating $W_p$. We let $P$ range over subsets of $N$ usually construed as sets of $\varphi$-programs/grammars. $\mathrm{card}(P)$ denotes the cardinality of $P$. Let $\lambda x, y . \langle x, y \rangle$ denote a fixed pairing function (a recursive, bijective mapping: $N \times N \to N$ [Rog67]). $\lambda x, y . \langle x, y \rangle$ and its inverses are useful to simulate the effect of having multiple argument functions in the systems $\varphi$. $\mathrm{mingrammar}_\varphi(L)$ denotes $\min(\{p \mid W_p = L\})$. We say that something is $\leq *$ to mean it is finite. $L_1 =^a L_2$ means that $\mathrm{card}(L_1 \triangle L_2) \leq a$, and $f_1 =^a f_2$ means that $\mathrm{card}(\{x \mid f_1(x) \neq f_2(x)\}) \leq a$

$\mathcal{E}$ denotes the class of all *recursively enumerable* languages $\subseteq N$. We let $\mathcal{L}$ range over subsets of $\mathcal{E}$.

**Definition 1** *A text $T$ for a language $L$ is a mapping from $N$ into $(N \cup \{*\})$ such that $L$ is the set of natural numbers in the range of $T$. The content of a sequence, of natural numbers and $*$'s, is the set of natural numbers in its range, where a text is just the infinite case of such a sequence.*

Intuitively, a text for a language is an enumeration or sequential presentation of all the objects in the language with the $*$'s representing pauses in the listing or presentation of such objects. For example, the only text for the empty language is just an infinite sequence of $*$'s.

We let $T$ range over texts, and $\sigma$ and $\tau$ range over *finite* sequences (of natural numbers and $*$'s), i.e., over finite initial segments of texts. $T_s$ denotes the finite initial segment of $T$ with length $s$. Hence, domain$(T_s) = \{z \mid z < s\}$.

**Definition 2** *A learning function is a computable mapping from the set of all finite sequences, of natural numbers and $*$'s, into $N$.*

We let $\mathbf{F}$ range over learning functions, and we think of $\mathbf{F}(\sigma)$ as the (Gödel number of) a grammar (based on some fixed acceptable programming system $\varphi$). We take $\mathbf{F}(\sigma)$ to be $\mathbf{F}$'s conjecture based on the finitely much data in $\sigma$. Suppose $T$ is any text for a language $L$. We are interested in the extent to which, *for sufficiently large $s$*, the grammars $\mathbf{F}(T_s)$ generate $L$.

We consider more specifically what it means for a learning function to be successful on a language. Gold [Gol67] essentially proposed the following criterion of success (Definition 3) which we call **TxtEx**-*identification* after [CL82, Cas86, Cas88] (the nomenclature in which was based on that in [CS83]). The quantifiers '$\forall^{\infty}$' and '$\exists^{\infty}$' from [Blu67] mean 'for all but finitely many' and 'there exists infinitely many', respectively. The concepts introduced in Definitions 3, 5, and 6 below are *implicitly* parameterized by the choice of acceptable programming system $\varphi$ and the corresponding programs and grammars. We take $\varphi$ to be fixed for these definitions.

**Definition 3** $\mathbf{F}$ **TxtEx**-identifies $L \Leftrightarrow (\forall$ *texts $T$ for $L$*$)(\exists p \mid W_p = L)(\forall^{\infty} s)[\mathbf{F}(T_s) = p]$.

Essentially the concepts from Definitions 1, 2, and 3 constitute Gold's influential language learning paradigm discussed, for example, in [OSW86, Pin79, WC80, Wex82]. In an attempt to improve Gold's paradigm, Case in [Cas88] considered the question whether people converge to vacillating between up to (some integer) $n > 1$ distinct, but equivalent, correct grammars. It was shown there that larger classes of languages can be algorithmically learned (in the limit) by converging to *up to $n+1$* rather than up to

$n$ equivalent, correct grammars. He argued that, for "small" $n > 1$, it is plausible that people might sometimes converge to vacillating between up to $n$ grammars. Gold's paradigm allows for convergence to only *one* grammar in the limit.

In the next section, we define appropriate notions from [Cas88] and state some important results.

## Language Learning by Vacillating Machines

In Definition 4 just below we spell out what it means for a learning function on a text to converge in the limit to a finite set of grammars.

**Definition 4** *Suppose* **F** *is a learning function and* $T$ *is a text.* $\mathbf{F}(T)\Downarrow$ *(read:* $\mathbf{F}(T)$ *finitely-converges)* $\Leftrightarrow \{\mathbf{F}(\tau) \mid \tau \subset T\}$ *is finite. If* $\mathbf{F}(T)\Downarrow$, *then* $\mathbf{F}(T)$ *is defined* $= \{p \mid (\exists^{\infty}\tau \subset T)[\mathbf{F}(\tau) = p]\}$; *otherwise,* $\mathbf{F}(T)$ *is undefined.*

**Definition 5** *A language learning function,* **F**, *is said to* $\mathbf{TxtFex}_b^a$-*identify a language* $L \Leftrightarrow (\forall \text{ texts } T \text{ for } L)[\mathbf{F}(T)\Downarrow = \text{ a set of cardinality } \leq b \text{ and } (\forall p \in \mathbf{F}(T))[W_p =^a L]]$.

In $\mathbf{TxtFex}_b^a$-*identification* the $b$ is a "bound" on the number of final grammars and the $a$ is a "bound" on the number of anomalies allowed in these final grammars. A "bound" of $*$ just means unbounded, but finite.

**Definition 6** $\mathbf{TxtFex}_b^a$ *denotes the class of all sets* $\mathcal{L}$ *of languages such that some learning function* $\mathbf{TxtFex}_b^a$-*identifies each language in* $\mathcal{L}$.

$\mathbf{TxtFex}_b^a$ provides a set-theoretic summary of the power of individual learning functions to $\mathbf{TxtFex}_b^a$-identify entire classes of languages. It is easy to show that it does *not* depend on the particular choice of acceptable system $\varphi$ on which it is based.

We proceed (Definitions 7 and 8) to describe an interesting and useful restriction on learning functions which generalizes notions of *order independence* from [BB75, OSW86, Ful85, Ful89].

**Definition 7** *A text* $T$ *stabilizes* $\mathbf{F} \Leftrightarrow \mathbf{F}(T)\Downarrow$.

**Definition 8 ([Cas88])** *A learning function,* **F**, *is $b$-ary order independent* $\Leftrightarrow (\forall L \mid \text{some text for } L \text{ stabilizes } \mathbf{F})(\exists P \text{ of cardinality } \leq b)(\forall \text{ texts } T \text{ for } L)[\mathbf{F}(T)\Downarrow = P]$.

The following result of Case and Fulk [Cas88, Cas89] is an intellectually satisfying, difficult to prove generalization of results from [BB75, OSW86, Ful85, Ful89]. It is also an ostensibly indispensable tool for proving Theorems 4 and 7.

**Theorem 1 (Case and Fulk)** *There is an algorithm for transforming any $b$ and $a$ program for a learning function* **F** *into a corresponding program for a learning function* $\mathbf{F}'$ *such that* $\mathbf{F}'$ *is $b$-ary order independent and* $(\forall a)(\forall L)[\mathbf{F} \ \mathbf{TxtFex}_b^a$-*identifies* $L \Rightarrow \mathbf{F}' \ \mathbf{TxtFex}_b^a$-*identifies* $L]$.

## Convergence to Nearly Minimal Size Grammars

As noted above Case [Cas88] argued that, for "small" $n$, it is plausible that people might sometimes converge to vacillating between up to $n$ grammars. The insistence on *small $n$* was motivated by the consideration that, for "large" $n$, at least one of $n$ grammars would be too large to fit in our heads. This latter assumes, of course, that human brain storage is not magic, admitting of infinite regress, etc. Of course, even for Gold's $n = 1$ case, the single grammar converged to in the limit may be infeasibly large. An interesting *complexity restriction* to make, then, on the final grammar(s) converged to in the limit is that they all have small size. In this paper we study some of the tradeoffs in learning power involved in making such a reasonable restriction on the **TxtFex$_b^a$** criteria.

Freivalds [Fre75], and later Kinber [Kin77] and Chen [Che81, Che82], considered the case of learning small size programs for computable functions. Case and Chi [CC86] consider the case of inferring small size grammars within the context of Gold's paradigm. Jain and Sharma [JS88, JS89] show that within this latter context the severe restriction of requiring the final grammar to be absolutely minimal size produces a learning criterion *dependent* on the choice of acceptable programming system $\varphi$. Freivalds previously [Fre75] obtained a similar result in the context of learning minimal size programs for computable functions. Generally, *strictly* minimal size programs or grammars are hard to deal with, and information-theoretic considerations suggest that such objects may be so deficient in information content [RC89] as to be difficult to understand (even subconsciously). Frievalds [Fre75] invented a mathematically elegant, precise notion of *nearly* minimal size programs—again in the context of learning programs for functions. Kinber [Kin77] and Chen [Che81, Che82] extended this work, and Case and Chi [CC86] consider the extension to the context of Gold's language learning paradigm. In this paper we study the extension to vacillatory learning, i.e., to the **TxtFex$_b^a$** learning criteria. This extension turns out to be non-trivial, its study ostensibly requiring the invention of new tools. Furthermore, the results surprisingly do not always match what might be expected from the case of learning programs for functions. For convenience the concepts introduced in Definitions 9 and 10 below are *explicitly* parameterized by the choice of acceptable system $\varphi$.

**Definition 9** *A language learning function,* **F**, **TxtMfex$_b^a$**-*identifies a class of languages* $\mathcal{L}$ *in the* $\varphi$-*programming system* $\Leftrightarrow$ "$(\exists$ *recursive* $h)(\forall L \in \mathcal{L})$[**F** **TxtFex$_b^a$**-*identifies* $L \wedge (\forall$ *texts* $T$ *for* $L)(\forall P \mid \mathbf{F}(T)\Downarrow = P)(\forall p \in P)[p \leq h(\mathrm{mingrammar}_\varphi(L))]$]".

$h$ in Definition 9 plays the role of a *computable* amount by which the final programs can be larger than minimal size. This size restriction of course does not hold in general, but it is not as severe as requiring that the final programs be strictly minimal size. Mathematically $\mathbf{TxtMfex}_b^a$-identification is well-behaved. For example, Theorem 2 below asserts that it is *independent* of the choice acceptable programming system $\varphi$. First we provide in Definition 10 a notation (analogous to that of Definition 6) providing a set-theoretic summary of the power of individual learning functions to $\mathbf{TxtMfex}_b^a$-identify entire classes of languages *in the $\varphi$ programming system*.

**Definition 10** $\mathbf{TxtMfex}_b^a(\varphi) =$

$\{\mathcal{L} \mid (\exists \mathbf{F})(\forall L \in \mathcal{L})[\mathbf{F} \; \mathbf{TxtMfex}_b^a - identifies \; L \; in \; the \; \varphi - programming \; system]\}.$

Theorem 2 just below says that the power of $\mathbf{TxtMfex}_b^a$-identification is independent of the choice of acceptable programming system. This is a desirable result in its own right *and* is a useful tool to prove other results. There is an analogous result regarding the learning of nearly minimal size programs for functions in [Fre75, Che81, Che82].

**Theorem 2** $(\forall \varphi, \varphi')[\mathbf{TxtMfex}_b^a(\varphi) = \mathbf{TxtMfex}_b^a(\varphi')].$

From now on it is permissible to write $\mathbf{TxtMfex}_b^a$ for $\mathbf{TxtMfex}_b^a(\varphi)$, and we do so.

## A Characterization of $\mathbf{TxtMfex}_b^a$ Criteria

We introduce below (Definition 12) an intrinsically interesting and technically useful notion that will help us formulate a characterization of $\mathbf{TxtMfex}_b^a$. To that end, it is useful to first introduce Definition 11 which provides an interesting new extension of the ordinary notion of limit.

**Definition 11** *Suppose $g$ is a recursive function in two variables. Then we say $b\text{-}\lim_s g(i,s)\Downarrow$ (read: $b\text{-}\lim_s g(i,s)$ finitely-converges)* $\Leftrightarrow$ *($\exists P$ of cardinality $\leq b$)$[(\forall^\infty s)[g(i,s) \in P] \wedge (\forall p \in P)(\exists^\infty s)[g(i,s) = p]]$. If $b\text{-}\lim_s g(i,s)\Downarrow$, we define $b\text{-}\lim_s g(i,s) = \{p \mid (\exists^\infty s)[g(i,s) = p]\}$; otherwise, $b\text{-}\lim_s g(i,s)$ is undefined.*

Definition 12 provides a nice extension of a concept originating with Freivalds [Fre75] (and later studied and extended by Chen [Che81, Che82]) in the context of the learning of nearly minimal size programs for functions.

**Definition 12** $\mathcal{L}$ *is text $b$-limiting $a$-standardizable with a recursive estimate (abbreviated: $\mathcal{L} \in \mathbf{TxtFlsr}_b^a$)* $\Leftrightarrow$ *there exist recursive functions $g$ and $v$ such that, for all $L \in \mathcal{L}$ and $i \in N$, if $W_i = L$, then* *(a)* $b\text{-lim}_s\, g(i,s)\Downarrow$ *and* $(\forall p \in b\text{-lim}_s\, g(i,s))[W_p =^a L]$;

*(b)* *for all* $j$, *if* $W_j = L$, *then* $b\text{-lim}_s\, g(i,s) = b\text{-lim}_s\, g(j,s)$;

*(c)* $\text{card}(\{g(i,s) \mid s \in N\}) \le v(i)$.

We write $\mathcal{L} \subseteq \mathbf{TxtFlsr}_b^a(g,v) \Leftrightarrow$ the recursive functions $g$ and $v$ witness as above that $\mathcal{L} \in \mathbf{TxtFlsr}_b^a$. It is easy to verify that $\mathbf{TxtFlsr}_b^a$ is acceptable programming system independent.

We give some intuitive insight into $\mathbf{TxtFlsr}_b^a$. It will suffice to consider the $a = 0$ and $b = 1$ cases. The *grammar equivalence problem* $(\{\langle x,y \rangle \mid W_x = W_y\})$ is well-known to be $\Pi_1^0$-complete [Rog67]; hence, it cannot be *accepted* by a *limiting* recursive procedure. The role of $g$ in the definition of $\mathbf{TxtFlsr}_1^0$ is to indirectly provide a limiting recursive solution to this problem for the special cases where the grammars generate languages in $\mathcal{L}$: $g$ finds (in the limit) *canonical* grammars. Also $v$ places some extra constraint on how $g$ reaches its limits.

For the rest of the paper we take $\varphi$ to be a fixed acceptable programming system. From now on we write 'mingrammar' for 'mingrammar$_\varphi$'.

Theorem 4 below is a characterization of $\mathbf{TxtMfex}_b^a$. Our proof of this theorem ostensibly requires, in addition to Theorem 1, the following variant of Theorem 1.

**Theorem 3 ([Cas89])** *There is an algorithm for transforming any $b$ and a program for a learning function* $\mathbf{F}$ *into a corresponding program for a learning function* $\mathbf{F}'$ *such that* $\mathbf{F}'$ *is $b$-ary order independent and* $(\forall a)(\forall L)[\mathbf{F}\ \mathbf{TxtMfex}_b^a\text{-}identifies\ L \Rightarrow \mathbf{F}'\ \mathbf{TxtMfex}_b^a\text{-}identifies\ L]$.

The following theorem has analogs [Fre75, Che81, Che82] for the learning of programs for functions.

**Theorem 4** *The following three statements are equivalent.*

*(1)* $\mathcal{L} \in \mathbf{TxtMfex}_b^a$.

*(2)* *There exist recursive functions $g$ and $v$ such that* $\mathcal{L} \subseteq \mathbf{TxtFlsr}_b^a(g,v)$ *and there exists a language learning function* $\mathbf{F}$ *such that* $\mathbf{F}\ \mathbf{TxtFex}_b^a\text{-}identifies\ \mathcal{L}$ *and* $(\forall i \mid W_i \in \mathcal{L})(\forall\ texts\ T\ for\ W_i)[\mathbf{F}(T) = b\text{-lim}_s\, g(i,s)]$.

*(3)* *There exist recursive functions $g$ and $v$ and a language learning function* $\mathbf{F}$ *such that* $\mathbf{F}\ \mathbf{TxtFex}_b^a\text{-}identifies\ \mathcal{L}$ *and* $(\forall L \in \mathcal{L})[(\forall\ texts\ T\ for\ L)[b\text{-lim}_s\, g(\text{mingrammar}(L),s) = \mathbf{F}(T)] \wedge [\text{card}(\{g(\text{mingrammar}(L),s) \mid s \in N\}) \le v(\text{mingrammar}(L))]]$.

The following useful corollary to Theorem 4 involves a variant of a self-referential class from [Cas88]. We could not make it go for the self-referential class from [Cas88]. Chen [Che81, Che82] made direct use of simpler self-referential classes from [CS83] to obtain a useful analog of Corollary 1—but for the problem of learning programs for functions.

**Corollary 1** *Suppose $n > 0$. Let $\mathcal{L}_n = \{L \mid L$ is $\infty \wedge (\exists e_1, e_2, \ldots, e_n)[W_{e_1} = W_{e_2} = \cdots = W_{e_n} = L \wedge (\forall^\infty \langle x, y \rangle \in L)[y \in \{e_1, e_2, \ldots, e_n\}]] \wedge (\forall x)[\mathrm{card}(\{y \mid \langle x, y \rangle \in L\}) \leq n]\}$. Then $\mathcal{L}_n \in \mathbf{TxtMfex}_n^0$.*

## Comparison of Learning with and without Size Restrictions

Using Corollary 1 and a modification of a multiple recursion theorem argument from [Cas88], we show the following result which implies that some classes of languages can be algorithmically learned (in the limit) by converging to *up to $n + 1$ nearly minimal size* grammars but *cannot* be learned by converging to up to $n$ *unrestricted* grammars even if these latter grammars are allowed to have a finite number of anomalies per grammar.

**Theorem 5** *Suppose $n > 0$. Then $\mathcal{L}_{n+1} \in (\mathbf{TxtMfex}_{n+1}^0 - \mathbf{TxtFex}_n^*)$.*

**Corollary 2** $\mathbf{TxtMfex}_1^a \subset \mathbf{TxtMfex}_2^a \subset \cdots \subset \mathbf{TxtMfex}_*^a$.

We can show that in the context of the learning of nearly minimal size programs for functions the analog of the hierarchy of Corollary 2 totally collapses. This complements results in [BP73, CS83] and answers an open problem in [Che81].

We exploit our characterization theorem (Theorem 4 above) and adapt anomaly hierarchy results from [CS78, CS83] to obtain Theorem 6 immediately below.

**Theorem 6** $(\mathbf{TxtMfex}_1^{m+1} - \mathbf{TxtFex}_*^m) \neq \emptyset$.

**Corollary 3** $\mathbf{TxtMfex}_b^1 \subset \mathbf{TxtMfex}_b^2 \subset \cdots \subset \mathbf{TxtMfex}_b^*$.

Theorem 7 to follow says that *if* we are willing to tolerate an *unbounded* finite number of anomalies in final grammars, then, as long as there is a *constant* bound on the number of different grammars converged to in the limit, there is *no* loss of learning power in demanding that the final grammars be nearly minimal size. This theorem is possibly the technically hardest to prove in the paper. Although Chen [Che81, Che82] has an analogous result regarding the problem of learning programs for functions, his proof depends on exploiting totality and single-valuedness of recursive functions. We applied Theorems 1 and 2 and employed a new combinatorial trick.

**Theorem 7** *Suppose $n > 0$. Then $\mathbf{TxtMfex}_n^* = \mathbf{TxtFex}_n^*$.*

Our next theorem (Theorem 8) contrasts sharply and surprisingly with both Theorem 7 just above and the situation regarding the learning of programs for functions [Che81, Che82]. Theorem 8 says that, if we allow an unbounded finite number of anomalies in final grammars and if the number of different grammars converged to in the limit is *unbounded* but finite, there *is* a loss of learning power in requiring that the final grammars be nearly minimal size.

**Theorem 8** $(\mathbf{TxtFex}_*^0 - \mathbf{TxtMfex}_*^*) \neq \emptyset$.

Our proof of Theorem 8 employs Case's operator recursion theorem [Cas74], an infinitary recursion theorem. The construction uses only a finite number of self-other referential grammars, but the finite number is not determined in advance as it is with finitary multiple recursion theorems.

We generalize recursion theorem arguments from [Kin77, Che81, Che82, CC86] to show Theorem 9 immediately below.

**Theorem 9** $(\mathbf{TxtFex}_1^0 - \mathbf{TxtMfex}_*^n) \neq \emptyset$.

Corollary 4 just below follows from Theorems 7 and 9 above.

**Corollary 4** $\mathbf{TxtMfex}_b^m \subset \mathbf{TxtFex}_b^m \subset \mathbf{TxtMfex}_b^*$.

In summary: there is *no* loss of learning power in demanding that the final grammars be nearly minimal size *iff* one is willing to tolerate an *unbounded*, finite number of anomalies in the final grammars *and* there is a *constant* bound on the number of different grammars converged to in the limit. Hence, if we allow an unbounded, finite number of anomalies in the final grammars *and* the number of different grammars converged to in the limit is *unbounded* but finite (or if there is a *constant* bound on the number of anomalies allowed in the final grammars), then there *is* a loss of learning power in requiring that the final grammars be nearly minimal size.

# References

[BB75]    L. Blum and M. Blum. Toward a mathematical theory of inductive inference. *Information and Control*, 28:125–155, 1975.

[Blu67]   M. Blum. A machine-independent theory of the complexity of recursive functions. *J. ACM*, 14:322–336, 1967.

[BP73]    J. Barzdin and K. Podnieks. The theory of inductive inference. In *Proceedings of the Mathematical Foundations for Computer Science*, pages 9–15, 1973.

[Cas74]   J. Case. Periodicity in generations of automata. *Math. Syst. Theory*, 8:15–32, 1974.

[Cas86]  J. Case. Learning machines. In W. Demopoulos and A. Marras, editors, *Language Learning and Concept Acquisition: Foundational Issues*. Ablex Publishing Company, Norwood, NJ, 1986.

[Cas88]  J. Case. The power of vacillation. In D. Haussler and L. Pitt, editors, *Proceedings of the Workshop on Computational Learning Theory*, pages 196–205. Morgan Kaufmann Publishers, Inc., 1988.

[Cas89]  J. Case. Topological constraints of vacillatory learning. 1989. In preparation.

[CC86]  J. Case and H. Chi. Machine learning of nearly minimal size grammars. Unpublished rough manuscript, 1986.

[Che81]  K. Chen. *Tradeoffs in Machine Inductive Inference*. PhD thesis, Computer Science Department, SUNY at Buffalo, Buffalo, NY, 1981.

[Che82]  K. Chen. Tradeoffs in the inductive inference of nearly minimal size programs. *Information and Control*, 52:68–86, 1982.

[CL82]  J. Case and C. Lynes. Machine inductive inference and language identification. In *Proceedings of the 9-th Annual Colloquium on Automata, Languages, and Programming*, Lecture Notes in Computer Science, 140, pages 107–115. Springer–Verlag, Berlin, July 1982.

[CS78]  J. Case and C. Smith. Anomaly hierarchies of mechanized inductive inference. In *Proceedings of the 10-th Annual Symposium on the Theory of Computing*, pages 314–319, July 1978.

[CS83]  J. Case and C. Smith. Comparison of identification criteria for machine inductive inference. *Theor. Comp. Sci.*, 25:193–220, 1983.

[Fre75]  Rūsiņš Freivalds. Minimal Gödel numbers and their identification in the limit. Lecture Notes in Computer Science, 32, pages 219–225. Springer-Verlag, Berlin, 1975.

[Ful85]  M. Fulk. *A Study of Inductive Inference Machines*. PhD thesis, Computer Science Department, SUNY at Buffalo, Buffalo, NY, 1985.

[Ful89]  M. Fulk. Prudence and other restrictions on formal language learning. *Information and Computation*, to appear, 1989.

[Gol67]  M. Gold. Language identification in the limit. *Information and Control*, 10:447–474, 1967.

[HU79]  J. Hopcroft and J. Ullman. *Introduction to Automata Theory, Languages, and Computation*. Addison-Wesley, 1979.

[JS88]  S. Jain and A. Sharma. Study of minimal size restrictions in machine learning. In D. Haussler and L. Pitt, editors, *Proceedings of the Workshop on Computational Learning Theory*, pages 429–430. Morgan Kaufmann Publishers, Inc., 1988. Abstract of work in progress.

[JS89]  S. Jain and A. Sharma. Study of minimal size restrictions in machine learning. 1989. In preparation.

[Kin77]    E. Kinber. On a theory of inductive inference. Lecture Notes in Computer Science, 56, pages 435–440. Springer-Verlag, Berlin, 1977.

[MY78]    M. Machtey and P. Young. *An Introduction to the General Theory of Algorithms*. North-Holland, 1978.

[OSW86]    D. Osherson, M. Stob, and S. Weinstein. *Systems That Learn: An Introduction to Learning Theory for Cognitive and Computer Scientists*. MIT Press, Cambridge, Mass, 1986.

[Pin79]    S. Pinker. Formal models of language learning. *Cognition*, 7:217–283, 1979.

[RC89]    J. Royer and J. Case. *Intensional Subrecursion and Complexity Theory*. Research Notes in Theoretical Science. Pitman Press, being revised for publication, 1989.

[Ric80]    G. Riccardi. *The Independence of Control Structures in Abstract Programming Systems*. PhD thesis, State University of New York at Buffalo, 1980.

[Ric81]    G. Riccardi. The independence of control structures in abstract programming systems. *J. Comput. Syst. Sci.*, 22:107–143, 1981.

[Rog58]    H. Rogers. Gödel numberings of the partial recursive functions. *J. Symbolic Logic*, 23:331–341, 1958.

[Rog67]    H. Rogers. *Theory of Recursive Functions and Effective Computability*. McGraw-Hill, 1967. Reprinted. MIT Press. 1987.

[Roy87]    J. Royer. *A Connotational Theory of Program Structure*. Lecture Notes in Computer Science 273. Springer-Verlag, 1987.

[WC80]    K. Wexler and P. Culicover. *Formal Principles of Language Acquisition*. MIT Press, Cambridge, Mass, 1980.

[Wex82]    K. Wexler. On extensional learnability. *Cognition*, 11:89–95, 1982.

# Inductive Inference with
# Bounded Number of Mind Changes

Mahendran Velauthapillai
Department of Computer Science
Georgetown University
Washington, D.C. 20057, USA
mvp@mimsy.umd.edu

## ABSTRACT

Inductive inference machines (IIMs) synthesize programs, given their intended input-output behavior. The program synthesis is viewed as a potentially infinite process of learning by example. Smith [20] studied team learning and obtained results that characterized trade-offs between the number of machines and resources in the learning process. Pitt [16] defined probabilistic learning and showed that 'probabilistic learning' is the same as 'team learning'. Later [17] introduced probabilistic team learning and compared probabilistic team learning and team learning. However, for any given team when we restrict amount of resources allotted for each IIM, then most of the above results fail to hold. This paper studies the relationships between team learning, probabilistic learning and probabilistic team learning when limited resources are available. Some preliminary results obtained indicates a very interesting relationship between them. The proofs for some of the preliminary results, used n-ary recursion theorems, and some complex diagonalization.

## OVERVIEW

This paper describes a theoretical investigation of how computers learn by example. Essentially there are two types of learning. One introduced by Gold [10], which is recursion theoretic and the other by Valiant [22] which is probabilistic. Here we are interested in the recursion theoretic learning, which is called inductive inference. A mathematically tractable formalization of inductive inference yields a model where an algorithmic device inputs, over time, the graph of a recursive function. While doing so, device outputs programs intended to compute the the function from which it is receiving its input. This paper further motivates the study of inductive inference as a process used by computers to synthesize programs given examples of their intended input/output behavior. Our accomplishments to date are described, along with related work. The proposed extension of research in this area contains several well formalized problems with emphasis on multiple machine learning situations.

## NOTATIONS, DEFINITIOS AND PRIOR RESULTS

Herein we will investigate the inference of programs, which we assume to come from some acceptable programming system [13]. $\varphi_0, \varphi_1 \ldots$ denotes the arbitrary, but fixed, acceptable programming system. $N$ denotes the set of natural numbers, $f$ a total recursive function and $\psi$'s the partial recursive functions. $\subseteq$ and $\subset$ denotes subset and proper subsets respectively. The learning will be performed by inductive inference machines (IIM's) that take the graph of a function as input and outputs programs intended to compute the function generating the input. Suppose an IIM $M$ is given a graph of $f$ as input, (we may suppose without loss of generality that $f$ is given in its natural order $f(0)$, $f(1), \ldots$ to $M$) it will output (possibly infinite) sequence of programs $p_0$, $p_1, \ldots$, each of which may or may not compute $f$. $M$ is said to converge on input from $f$ to $p_n$ (written: $M(f) \downarrow p_n$) if either the sequence of output programs is finite with length $n + 1$ or all the programs output after the first $n$ programs in the sequence are precisely $p_n$. Gold [10] introduced criterion of successful inference called "identification in the limit". This notion will be called $EX$ identification. An IIM $M$ $EX$-infers $f$ (written: $f \in EX(M)$) if and only if $M(f) \downarrow p$ and $\varphi_p = f$. Each IIM will $EX$ infer some recursive set of recursive functions. We will denote this collection of sets by $EX$, e.g. $EX = \{S \,|\, (\exists M)[S \subseteq EX(M)]\}$. $EX$ stands for *explains*, see [5].

For $EX$ inference, the machine must produce a program that is correct on all the values of the function from which it receives its input. This makes the inference more difficult, or perhaps as suggested in [22], impractical. A partial recursive function $\psi$ is an $n$ variant of $f$ (written: $\psi =^n f$) if the cardinality of the number of points at which $\psi$ differs from $f$ is less than or equal to $n$. $\psi$ is an $\star$ variant of $f$ (written: $\psi =^\star f$) if the cardinality of the number of points at which $\psi$ differs from $f$ is finite. For any $a \in N \cup \{\star\}$, an IIM $EX^a$ identifies $f$ (written: $f \in EX^a(M)$) if and only if $M(f) \downarrow p$ and $\varphi_p =^a f$. Here we say that the program $p$ computes $f$ with up to $a$ anomalies; i.e. the learning protocol is allowed to make $a$ mistakes. Making mistakes in learning does not necessarily mean that the conclusion that the learning protocol makes is of no use [5,21]. In fact Newtonian mechanics cannot explain the dispersion in the X ray region, but it is accurate in explaining phenomena in classical mechanics. For any $a \in N \cup \{\star\}$, the collection of all the sets that can be $EX^a$ inferred will be denoted $EX^a$. Note that $EX^0 = EX$. $EX^\star$ was introduced in [2] and $EX^a$ inference, for $a \neq \star$ was introduced in [5].

Although counting the number of times the IIM changes its mind before converging is not an abstract measure of the complexity of inference [6], it does provide a reasonable estimate. Consequently, the number of mind changes made by IIMs has received considerable attention [1,7,4,5,11,12,20,23,24]. For practical inference systems, it is not possible to have unlimited amount of resources. Clearly an IIM with unbounded number of mind changes is bound to use an extensive amount of resources. Therefore it is reasonable to bound the number of mind changes allowed for each IIM. A subscript $b$ on the class name indicates a success criterion where the IIM converges after no more than $b$ changes of conjecture (if the IIM outputs $p_1$, and then $p_2$, we say IIM has changed its conjecture if and only if $p_1 \neq p_2$). Formally, for $a, b \in N \cup \{\star\}$, an IIM $M$ $EX_b^a$-infers $f$ (written: $f \in EX_b^a(M)$) if and only if $M(f) \downarrow p$ with at most $b$ changes of conjecture and $\phi_b =^a f$. For $a, b \in N \cup \{\star\}$, the collection of all the sets that can be $EX_b^a$ inferred will be denoted $EX_b^a$. Observe that for all $a \in N$, $EX_\star^a$ is denoted by $EX^a$. We will use the term "mind changes" interchangeably with the term "changes of conjecture".

For inference using single machines, a fundamental relationship between anomalies and mind changes is given by:

THEOREM 1. $EX_b^a \subseteq EX_d^c$ if and only if $a \leq c$ and $b \leq d$ [5].

This results gives a necessary and sufficient condition for characterizing two inference classes. This also shows that the mind changes and the anomalies are independent entities and you cannot trade mind changes for anomalies or vice versa. Intuitively the above results says the following:

When given two IIMs $M_1$ and $M_2$, $M_1$ can learn more than $M_2$ if and only if $M_1$ has more resources and is also is allowed to make more mistakes about what it learns.

Smith [20] went on to study inductive inference using multiple machines. There are situations in which the notion of team learning is practical. Suppose we wish to send a collection of robots to investigate an alien planet. Each robot is equipped with identical data gathering and transmission equipment. The robots are distinguished by the particular learning program used as subroutine to analyze the data collected to infer a program which is then used to predict the events in the alien environment. It is plausible that a robot which successfully infers a reasonably accurate prediction program has a better chance surviving when faced with a new situation which may be fatal to its existence (landslide, floods, etc.) than does a robot which is using a program which almost always makes inaccurate predictions. It has been shown [20], in general the larger the collection of robots you send, larger the class of phenomena that can be correctly identified.

Formally given a collection of $n$ IIMs (team), we say the team infers a set $S$ of recursive functions if and only if for any $f \in S$ there is at least one IIM in the team that will infer $f$. Also note that, for different $f$'s in the set $S$, the IIM in the team which infers $f$ could be different. Each team of size $n$ will infer a set of recursive functions. Denote the collection of these sets by $[1, n]EX$. This definition can be extended to:

1. Restricting the number of mind changes allowed for each IIM in the team.
2. Allowing anomalies in the output produced by the team on the function from which it is receiving its input.

The following result [20] establishes a hierarchy based on team inference.

THEOREM 2. For all $m, n \geq 1$ for all $a, b \in N \cup \{\star\}$, $[1, m]EX_\star^a \subseteq [1, n]EX_\star^b$ if and only if

$$(m \leq n \text{ and } a \leq b) \text{ or } \left( a, b, m, n \in N \text{ and } n \geq m \cdot \left( 1 + \left\lfloor \frac{a}{b+1} \right\rfloor \right) \right).$$

The above result does not hold in the case when the IIMs are allowed bounded number of mind changes. As noted before for practical inference the number of mind changes for each IIM must be bounded.

Velauthapillai [23] considered the case where, the IIMs were allowed bounded number of mind changes, and was able to obtain a result that established a complete hierarchy for the case $m = 1$.

THEOREM 3. $(\forall n > 1)$ $(a, b, c, d \in N)$, $[1, n]EX_b^a \subseteq [1, 1]EX_d^c$ if and only if $(c \geq a)$ and

$$d \geq \left\lceil \left\lfloor \frac{a(m-1)}{(c-a+1)} \right\rfloor (b + 1) + 2mb + \left\lfloor \frac{a}{(c-a+1)} \right\rfloor b + 2(m - 1) \right\rceil.$$

The above theorem gives a precise bound on the number of mind changes and anomalies necessary for a single machine to simulate a team with some fixed number of mind changes and anomalies. The number of mind changes required depends on the amount of anomalies the single machine was allowed to tolerate. The proof of the theorem required the use of the n-ary recursion theorem, sophisticated diagonalization, some counting techniques and program amalgamation. Also note the complexity of this result comes from the fact the number of parameters in the problem is five.

Pitt [16] investigated and characterized probabilistic inductive inference. Suppose that $M$ is an IIM that has a fair coin to toss while trying to learn a program for the function $f$. For a fixed enumeration of the graph of $f$, the outcome of $M$ applied to $f$ depends only on the results of the coin tosses. Using the standard Borel measure on the possible sequences of coin tosses, the set of sequences for which $M(f) \downarrow$ to a program for $f$ is measurable. Let $M$ be an IIM, $a \in N$ and $0 \leq p \leq 1$, we say that $f \in EX^a \langle p \rangle (M)$ if and only if $M$ $EX^a$ infers $f$ with probability $p$. The classes $EX^a \langle p \rangle$ is defined analogously.

The following theorem is due to Pitt [16]. It establishes the relationship between team inference and probabilistic inference. It also shows that probabilistic inference is discrete [8,9,18,19,24].

THEOREM 4. $a \in N$ and for $n \geq 1$, if $\frac{1}{n+1} < p \leq \frac{1}{n}$ then $EX^a \langle p \rangle = [1, n]EX^a$

The above result shows that given a team inference class there is a probabilistic inference class which is identical to it and vice versa. Most importantly it agrees with our intuition, "**being correct 1 out on $n$ is the same as being correct with probability $\frac{1}{n}$.**"

Recently [15,17] generalized the above concept by considering the case where, given $n$ IIMs, instead of requiring at least one of the $n$ IIM to be correct, require at least $m$ out of $n$ IIMs to be correct. Formally, for $m, n \geq 1$ and $a, b \in N$, a set of functions $S$ is in the class $[m, n]EX_b^a$ if and only if $m \leq n$ and there exists IIMs $M_1, M_2, \ldots, M_n$ such that for each function $f \in S$ there are $1 \leq i_1 < i_2, \ldots, < i_m \leq n$ such that for all $1 \leq j \leq m$, $f \in EX_b^a(M_{i_j})$. The above definition is motivated by the fact that, its better to have many machines trying to learn a concept than just one. We will call this notion multiple team inference. Note that team inference is a special case of multiple team inference.

A natural combination of the notions of team inference and probabilistic inference results in the definition of some new classes of functions [17]. We will call this inference probabilistic team inference.

For $m, n \geq 1$, $a \in N$ and $0 \leq p \leq 1$, a set of functions $S$ is in the class $[m,n]EX^a\langle p\rangle$ if and only if $m \leq n$ and there exists probabilistic IIMs $M_1, M_2, \ldots, M_n$ such that for each function $f \in S$ there are $1 \leq i_1 < i_2 < \ldots < i_m \leq n$ such that for all $1 \leq j \leq m$, $f \in EX^a\langle p\rangle(M_{i_j})$. Here we require at least $m$ out of the $n$ machines in the team, to infer $f$ with probability at least $p$. Note that probabilistic inference is a special case of probabilistic team inference, the case where $m = 1$.

The following theorem was proved by Pitt and Smith [17] which establishes a relationship between team inference, probabilistic team inference and probabilistic inference.

THEOREM 5. For all $a \in N$, $m, n \geq 1$ and $m \leq n$, $[m,n]EX^a = \left[1, \left\lfloor \frac{n}{m} \right\rfloor\right]EX^a = EX^a\left\langle \frac{1}{\left\lfloor \frac{n}{m} \right\rfloor} \right\rangle$.

The above theorem answers the question [14] when a team of IIMs could be combined in to a single machine. Moreover in agrees with intuition that, **being correct $m$ out of $n$ is the same as being correct 1 out of $m/n$ times, or being correct with probability $m/n$**. The following result is a special case of the above theorem:

COROLLARY 6. $[1,2]EX_\star^0 = [2,4]EX_\star^0 = [4,6]EX_\star^0 \cdots$.

COROLLARY 7. $[1,2]EX_\star^0 = [3,6]EX_\star^0 = [6,12]EX_\star^0 \cdots$.

Although these two corollaries' can be combined in to one, the reason for keeping them separate will become clear in the next section. Observe that the above corollaries prove that the classes of sets that can be inferred with any team such that half the members of the team are required to be correct, is the same as the classes of sets that can be inferred using team of size two with one of them being correct. The intuitive reason for it is that, **being correct half the time is the same being correct with probability one half.**

## INFERENCE WITH BOUNDED NUMBER OF MIND CHANGES

In this section we will show that the Theorem 5 does not hold when the IIMs are only allowed bounded number of mind changes. We will do so by disproving the first equality in Corollary 6 which is a special case of Theorem 5.

THEOREM 8. $(\forall n \geq 1)$ $[n, 2n]EX_0^0 \subset [2n, 4n]EX_0^0$.

Proof: Let $n > 1$ be given. First we will prove the containment by simulation. Suppose IIMs $M_1, M_2, \cdots, M_{2n}$ are given, we will construct $M_1', M_2', \cdots, M_{4n}'$ IIMs such that $M_1', M_2', \cdots, M_{4n}'$ will simulate $M_1, M_2, \ldots, M_{2n}$. For $1 \leq i \leq n$ Make $M_i'$ and $M_{2i}'$ output the same as $M_i$'s output. Clearly $[n, 2n]EX_0^0 \subseteq [2n, 4n]EX_0^0$.

The strict containment can be proved by showing $[2n, 4n]EX_0^0 - [n, 2n]EX_0^0 \neq \emptyset$. The proof of this part uses n-ary recursion theorem. We will display a set $S$ of recursive functions such that $S \in [2n, 4n]EX_0^0$ and $S \notin [n, 2n]EX_0^0$. The following is an intuitive description of S. Given a $f \in S$ there will be at most $4n - 1$ other recursive functions in $S$ which will have some same initial segment as $f$. In the longest such initial segment there will be at most $4n$ special integers and $2n$ of which will describe $f$. We will choose special integers to be odd integers. Formally, $f \in S$ if and only if the following two conditions hold.

1. $f(x)$ is odd for no more than $4n$ distinct values of $x$.
2. There exists $x_1, \cdots, x_{2n}$ and $j_1, \cdots, j_{2n}$ such that $f(x_1) = 2j_1 + 1, \cdots, f(x_{2n}) = 2j_{2n} + 1$ and $\varphi_{j_1} = f, \cdots, \varphi_{j_{2n}} = f$.

First we will show that $S \in [2n, 4n]EX_0^0$. We will construct $4n$ IIMs such that for any $f \in S$ there will be at least $2n$ IIMs which will infer $f$. For any $f \in S$, the $i^{\text{th}}$ member $(1 \leq i \leq 4n)$ of the team on input from $f$ will execute the following algorithm.

Begin $M_i$
1. Wait for the $i^{\text{th}}$ odd integer, say $k$.
2. Output $(k - 1)/2$.
End $M_i$

By the definition of $S$, $2n$ of the $4n$ odd integers will describe $f$, therefore $S \in [2n, 4n]EX_0^0$. We will construct a recursive function $f$ such that $f \in S$ and for any $M_1, \cdots, M_{2n}$, $f \notin EX_0^0(M_1, \cdots, M_{2n})$. Let $M_1, \cdots, M_{2n}$ be given. To construct $f$ we will use kleene's n-ary recursion theorem. The following is an intuitive description of the theorem. We construct $6n$ programs $e_1, \ldots, e_{6n}$ such that any program in the sequence can use every program in the sequence as explicit extra parameter including itself. This recursion theorem is a special case of operator recursion theorem [3]. Using $6n$-ary recursion theorem and finite extension argument we construct functions $\varphi_{e_1}, \cdots, \varphi_{e_{6n}}$. For $1 \leq i \leq 6n$, let $\sigma_i$ denote the largest initial segment of $\varphi_{e_i}$ constructed so far and $x_i$ denote the largest value in the domain of $\sigma_i$.

**Phase 0.** Initialize.
1. $x_1 = 0, \cdots, x_{6n} = 0$.
2. $\sigma_1 = \emptyset, \cdots, \sigma_{6n} = \emptyset$.
3. $M_1(\emptyset) = \emptyset, \cdots, M_{2n}(\emptyset) = \emptyset$.
4. $\sigma_1(x_1) = 2e_1 + 1$, $\sigma_1(x_1 + 1) = 2e_2 + 1 \cdots$, $\sigma_1(x_1 + 2n) = 2e_{2n} + 1$. (place special integers)
5. $\sigma_2 = \sigma_1, \sigma_3 = \sigma_1, \cdots, \sigma_{2n} = \sigma_1$. ($2n$ identical initial segments)
**End Phase 0.**

Now we will extend $\sigma_1, \cdots, \sigma_{2n}$ simultaneously with more and more 0's until $n$ out of the $2n$ IIM's $(M_1, \cdots, M_{2n})$ converge on $\sigma_1$. Note that $\sigma_1, \cdots, \sigma_{2n}$ are identical initial segments. If $n$ out of the $2n$ IIM's do not converge then $\sigma_1, \cdots, \sigma_{2n}$ are total functions. Let $f = \sigma_1$, since $2e_1 + 1, \cdots, 2e_{2n} + 1$ are in the range of $f$, and $\varphi_{e_1} = f, \cdots, \varphi_{e_{2n}} = f$ implies that $f \in S$. Now $S \notin [n, 2n]EX_0^0$, since the IIMs $M_1, \cdots, M_{2n}$ have not output $n$ programs. With no loss of generality assume that $n$ out of the $2n$ IIMs have output $n$ programs on some finite initial segment $\sigma_1$.

**Phase 1.** Halt construction of segments $\sigma_1, \cdots, \sigma_{2n}$ temporarily. Construct segments $\sigma_{2n+1}, \cdots, \sigma_{3n}$ such that it will be identical to $\sigma_1$. Now we look for the team to output $n$

new programs or find $n$ distinct programs, from the programs output by the team so far so that, the $n$ programs will converge on some value of $\sigma_1$ defined past phase 0.

1. Set $\sigma_{2n+1} = \sigma_1$.
2. Set $\sigma_{2n+1}(x_{2n+1}+1) = 2e_{2n+1}+1$, $\sigma_{2n+1}(x_{2n+1}+2) = 2e_{2n+2}+1, \cdots, \sigma_{2n+1}(x_{2n+1}+n) = 2e_{3n}+1$ (place special integers).
3. $\sigma_{2n+2} = \sigma_{2n+1}, \cdots, \sigma_{3n} = \sigma_{2n+1}$ and $\sigma_1(x) = \sigma_{2n+1}(x), \cdots, \sigma_n(x) = \sigma_{2n+1}(x)$ for $x_1 \leq x \leq x_{2n+1}$. (make $\sigma_1$ up to $\sigma_n$ and $\sigma_{2n+1}$ up to $\sigma_{3n}$ identical segments).
4. Now simultaneously execute steps (a), (b) and (c) until Condition (B) or (C) is satisfied.
   a) Extend $\sigma_1, \cdots, \sigma_n$ and $\sigma_{2n+1}, \cdots, \sigma_{3n}$ with more and more values of 0's.
   b) See if the team outputs $n$ new programs on $\sigma_1$.
   c) Dove tail all the programs output so far by the team on all the points in the domain of $\sigma_1$ defined in sub step (a).

Condition B. If the team outputs $n$ new programs then do *Case 1*.

Condition C. If there are $n$ programs that converge on points $y_1, y_2, \cdots, y_n$ where $y_1, \cdots, y_n$ are points in the domain of $\sigma_1$ defined in sub step (a) then do *Case 2*.

**End Phase 1.**

If substep(b) and (c) is not satisfied in step (4) then team has not output $n$ programs which compute total recursive functions. But $\sigma_1, \cdots, \sigma_n$ and $\sigma_{2n+1}, \cdots, \sigma_{3n}$ are total recursive functions. Let $f = \sigma_1$, now $2e_1+1, \cdots, 2e_n+1$ and $2e_{2n+1}+1, \cdots, 2e_{3n}+1$ are in the range of $f$, also $\varphi_{e_1} = f, \cdots, \varphi_{e_n} = f$ and $\varphi_{e_{2n+1}} = f, \cdots, \varphi_{e_{3n}} = f$, therefore $f \in S$. Now $S \notin [n, 2n]EX_0^0$, since the team has not output $n$ total recursive functions, otherwise sub step (c) in step (4) would have found $n$ programs which converge at some points in the domain of $\sigma_1$ defined in sub step (a).

*Case 1*. Suppose the team outputs $n$ new programs, then do the following in order. (Note that each team member has output its allotted guess.)

1. Set $\sigma_{n+1}(y) = \sigma_1(y), \cdots, \sigma_{2n}(y) = \sigma_1(y)$ for $x_{n+1} < y \leq x_1$. ($\sigma_1, \cdots \sigma_{3n}$ are $3n$ identical initial segments, on which the team outputs $2n$ programs)
2. Set $\sigma_1(x_1+1) = 2e_{3n+1}+1, \cdots, \sigma_1(x_1+n) = 2e_{4n}+1$. (place special integers)
3. Set $\sigma_{n+1}(x_{n+1}+1) = 2e_{4n+1}+1, \cdots, \sigma_{n+1}(x_{n+1}+n) = 2e_{5n}+1$. (place special integers)
4. Set $\sigma_{2n+1}(x_{2n+1}+1) = 2e_{5n+1}+1, \cdots, \sigma_{2n+1}(x_{2n+1}+n) = 2e_{6n}+1$. (place special integers)
5. Set $\sigma_2(y) = \sigma_1(y), \cdots, \sigma_n(y) = \sigma_1(y)$ for $x_2 < y \leq x_1$ and $\sigma_{3n+1} = \sigma_1, \cdots, \sigma_{4n} = \sigma_1$. ($\sigma_1$ up to $\sigma_n$ and $\sigma_{3n+1}$ up to $\sigma_{4n}$ are identical initial segments.)
6. Set $\sigma_{n+2}(y) = \sigma_{n+1}(y), \cdots, \sigma_{2n}(y) = \sigma_{n+1}(y)$ for $x_{n+2} < y \leq x_{n+1}$ and $\sigma_{4n+1} = \sigma_{n+1}, \cdots, \sigma_{5n} = \sigma_{n+1}$. ($\sigma_{n+1}$ up to $\sigma_{2n}$ and $\sigma_{4n+1}$ up to $\sigma_{5n}$ are identical initial segments.)
7. Set $\sigma_{2n+2}(y) = \sigma_{2n+1}(y), \cdots, \sigma_{3n}(y) = \sigma_{2n+1}(y)$ for $x_{2n+2} < y \leq x_{2n+1}$ and $\sigma_{5n+1} = \sigma_{2n+1}, \cdots, \sigma_{6n} = \sigma_{2n+1}$. ($\sigma_{2n+1}$ up to $\sigma_{3n}$ and $\sigma_{5n+1}$ up to $\sigma_{6n}$ are identical initial segments.)
8. Now do (a) (b) and (c) simultaneously.
   a). Extend $\sigma_1, \cdots, \sigma_n$ and $\sigma_{3n+1}, \cdots, \sigma_{4n}$ with more and more 0's.

b). Extend $\sigma_{n+1},\cdots,\sigma_{2n}$ and $\sigma_{4n+1},\cdots,\sigma_{5n}$ with more and more 2's.

c). Extend $\sigma_{2n+1},\cdots,\sigma_{3n}$ and $\sigma_{5n+1},\cdots,\sigma_{6n}$ with more and more 4's.

Now $\sigma_1,\cdots,\sigma_n$ and $\sigma_{3n+1},\cdots,\sigma_{4n}$ are total functions and are identical. Similarly $\sigma_{n+1},\cdots,\sigma_{2n}$ and $\sigma_{4n+1},\cdots,\sigma_{5n}$ are total functions and are identical. Also $\sigma_{2n+1},\cdots,\sigma_{3n}$ and $\sigma_{5n+1},\cdots,\sigma_{6n}$ are total functions are identical. Clearly $\sigma_1$, $\sigma_{n+1}$ and $\sigma_{2n+1}$ are pairwise distinct. Since the team has output $2n$ programs, (team is only allowed to output $2n$ programs) there cannot be $n$ programs out of the $2n$ programs computing one of the above three functions. Let $f$ be that function. By construction, there are $2n$ distinct odd integers in the range of $f$ and all of which will describe $f$, hence $f \in S$. Since the team has not output $n$ programs to compute $f$, $S \notin [n, 2n]EX_0^0$.

*End Case 1.*

*Case 2.* Suppose $n$ programs converged at some points $y_1, \cdots, y_n$ (Some of the points could be the same). where $y_i > x_{n+1}$ for $1 \le i \le n$. Without loss of generality assume that the programs are $p_1, \cdots, p_n$ and they converged at $y_1, \cdots, y_n$ respectively. Do the following in order. (Here you discard programs $e_1,\cdots,e_n$ and $e_{2n+1},\cdots, e_{3n}$ and use the functions computed by programs $e_{n+1},\cdots, e_{2n}$ to diagonalize against the $n$ programs output by the team.)

1. Set $\sigma_{n+1}(y_j) = 2 + 2\times \text{Max}\{\varphi_{p_i}(y_i)\mid 1 \le i \le n\}$ for $1 \le j \le n$. (range must only have even numbers, and some of the points could be the same.)

2. Set $\sigma_{n+1}(x) = 0$ for $x_{n+2} < x \le x_1$ and $x \notin \{y_1,\cdots,y_n\}$.

3. Set $\sigma_{n+2}(x) = \sigma_{n+1}(x),\cdots, \sigma_{2n}(x) = \sigma_{n+1}(x)$ for $x_{n+2} < x \le x_1$ .

4. Set $\sigma_{n+1}(x_{n+1} + 1) = 2e_{3n+1} + 1,\cdots, \sigma_{n+1}(x_{n+1} + n) = 2e_{4n} + 1$.

5. Set $\sigma_{n+2}(x) = \sigma_{n+1}(x),\cdots, \sigma_{2n}(x) = \sigma_{n+1}(x)$ for $x_{n+2} < x \le x_{n+1}$.

6. Set $\sigma_{3n+1} = \sigma_{n+1},\cdots,\sigma_{4n} = \sigma_{n+1}$. ($\sigma_{n+1},\cdots,\sigma_{2n}$ and $\sigma_{3n+1},\cdots, \sigma_{4n}$ are all identical initial segments)

7. Simultaneously extend $\sigma_{n+1},\cdots,\sigma_{2n}$ and $\sigma_{3n+1},\cdots, \sigma_{4n}$ with more and more values of 0's until the team outputs $n$ new programs. (If the team does not output $n$ new programs, then $\sigma_{n+1},\cdots,\sigma_{2n}$ and $\sigma_{3n+1},\cdots, \sigma_{4n}$ are all total functions and the programs output by the team does not compute any one of the above functions. Hence the desired $f$ would be $\sigma_{n+1}$.)

8. Set $\sigma_{n+1}(x_{n+1} + 1) = 2e_{4n+1} + 1,\cdots, \sigma_{n+1}(x_{n+1} + n) = 2e_{5n} + 1$.

9. Set $\sigma_{n+2}(x) = \sigma_{n+1}(x),\cdots, \sigma_{2n}(x) = \sigma_{n+1}(x)$ for $x_{n+2} < x \le x_{n+1}$.

10. Set $\sigma_{4n+1} = \sigma_{n+1},\cdots,\sigma_{5n} = \sigma_{n+1}$. ($\sigma_{n+1},\cdots,\sigma_{2n}$ and $\sigma_{4n+1},\cdots, \sigma_{5n}$ are all identical initial segments)

11. Set $\sigma_{3n+1}(x_{3n+1} + 1) = 2e_{5n+1} + 1,\cdots, \sigma_{3n+1}(x_{3n+1} + n) = 2e_{6n} + 1$.

12. Set $\sigma_{3n+2}(x) = \sigma_{3n+1}(x),\cdots, \sigma_{4n}(x) = \sigma_{3n+1}(x)$ for $x_{3n+2} < x \le x_{3n+1}$.

13. Set $\sigma_{5n+1} = \sigma_{3n+1},\cdots, \sigma_{6n} = \sigma_{3n+1}$. ($\sigma_{3n+1},\cdots,\sigma_{4n}$ and $\sigma_{5n+1},\cdots, \sigma_{6n}$ are all identical initial segments)

14. Now extend $\sigma_{n+1},\cdots,\sigma_{2n}$ and $\sigma_{4n+1},\cdots,\sigma_{5n}$ with value 0's. and $\sigma_{3n+1},\cdots,\sigma_{4n}$ and $\sigma_{5n+1}, \cdots,\sigma_{6n}$ with value 2's.

Clearly $\sigma_{n+1}$ and $\sigma_{3n+1}$ are two distinct functions. There are only $n$ valid programs remaining out of the $2n$ programs output by the team. Hence one of these functions is the desired $f$. By construction, $f \in S$ and $S \notin EX_0^0$. $\blacksquare$

The above theorem confirms, that with bounded number of mind changes, being correct one half the time is not the same as being correct with probability one half. From this we can conclude that, the probability model introduced by [16] does not hold for IIM's with finite number of mind changes.

COROLLARY 9. $[1,2]EX_0^0 \subset [2,4]EX_0^0 \subset [4,8]EX_0^0 \subset [8,16]EX_0^0 \cdots$

COROLLARY 10. $[1,2]EX_0^0 \subseteq [3,6]EX_0^0 \subset [6,12]EX_0^0 \subset [12,24]EX_0^0 \cdots$

Notice that there are several chains with $[1,2]EX_0^0$ as lower bound. This raises the following question; Given two classes of sets do they belong to the same chain. Formally:

PROBLEM 11. Given $m_1, n_1, n_2, m_2 \geq 1$ such that $n_1 \leq m_1$ and $n_2 \leq m_2$ find a predicate $P$ such that $[n_1, m_1]EX_0^0 \subseteq [n_2, m_2]EX_0^0$ if and only if $P(n_1, m_1, n_2, m_2)$.

This paper does not give a complete solution for the above problem. However, we have some interesting results which we feel will eventually help us solve this problem.

THEOREM 12. $(\forall m, n, r \in N - \{0\})$ such that $m \leq n$, if $r > \lfloor \frac{n}{m} \rfloor$ then $[1,r]EX_0^0 - [m,n]EX_0^0 \neq \emptyset$.

Proof: Let $(m, n, r \in N - \{0\})$ be given. We will display a set $S$ of recursive functions such that $S \in [1,r]EX_0^0$ and $S \notin [m,n]EX_0^0$. The following is an intuitive description of S. Given a $f \in S$ there will be at most 1 other recursive function in $S$ which will have the same initial segment as $f$. In the longest such initial segment there will be at most $r$ special integers one of which will describe $f$. We will choose special integers to be odd integers. Formally, $f \in S$ if and only if the following two conditions hold.

1. $f(x)$ is odd for no more than $r$ distinct values of $x$.
2. There exists $x_1$ and $j_1$ such that $f(x_1) = 2j_1 + 1$ and $\varphi_{j_1} = f$.

First we will show that $S \in [1,r]EX_0^0$. We will construct $r$ IIMs such that for any $f \in S$ there will be at least one IIMs which will infer $f$. For any $f \in S$, the $i^{th}$ member $(1 \leq i \leq r)$ of the team on input from $f$ will execute the following algorithm.

Begin $M_i$
1. Wait for the $i^{th}$ odd integer, say $k$.
2. Output $(k-1)/2$.
End $M_i$

By the definition of $S$, one of the $r$ odd integers will describe $f$, therefore $S \in [1,r]EX_0^0$. We will construct an $f \in S$ such that, for any $M_1, M_2, \ldots, M_n$ $f$ cannot be $EX_0^0$ inferred by any $m$ out of the $n$ IIMs. Let IIMs $M_1, M_2, \ldots, M_n$ be given. To construct $f$ we will use kleene's n-ary recursion theorem. Using $r$-ary recursion theorem and finite extension argument we construct functions $f_1, f_2, \ldots, f_r$. For $i \in \{1, \ldots, r\}$, let $\sigma_i$ denote the largest initial segment of $\varphi_i$, constructed so far and $x_i$ denote the largest value in the domain of $\sigma_i$.

Phase 0. Initialize.
1. $x_0 = 0, x_1 = 0$.
2. $\sigma_1 = \emptyset$.
3. $M_i(\emptyset) = \emptyset$ for $1 \leq i \leq n$.
4. $\sigma_1(x_1) = 2\alpha_1 + 1$ (place special integer).

**End Phase 0.**

Now extend $\sigma_1$ with more and more values of 0's until $m$ members of the team output one guess each (note one member is allowed only one guess). If the team does not output $m$ programs then $\sigma_1$ will be a total function. Let $f = \sigma_1$, $f \in S$ and clearly $m$ member of the team cannot identify $f$. Hence assume that the team has output $m$ programs, say $p_1^1,\ldots,p_m^1$. Also mark these $m$ programs as valid.

**Phase 1.** Here we will construct at most $r - 1$ new functions. The construction of a function begins only after the team $M_1,\ldots,M_n$ outputs $m$ new conjectures on the current function thats being constructed. To obtain the mind changes we first diagonalize against any valid $m$ programs that the team has output. If the diagonalization fails we would have the desired $f$.

*For $i = 1$ to $r - 1$ do Begin step $i$*
Do steps (a), (b) and (c) in order.
a) Now simultaneously execute steps (1) and (2) below until condition (II) is satisfied.
   1. Extend $\sigma_i$ with more and more values 0's.
   2. Dovetail the $m$ valid programs on the extension done in step (1).

Condition II. There exists $y_1,\ldots,y_m$, in the domain of $\sigma_i$ such that $(\forall j)\ 1 \le j \le m$ $\varphi_{p_j^i}(y_j)\downarrow$. Let $v = \text{Max}\{\varphi_{p_1^i}(y_1),\ldots,\varphi_{p_m^i}(y_m)\}$. Mark $p_1^i, p_2^i,\ldots,p_m^i$ as in valid. Set

$$\sigma_{i+1}(x) = \begin{cases} 2 + 2v, & \text{if } x \in \{y_1,\ldots,y_m\}; \\ \sigma_i(x), & \text{if } x \notin \{y_1,\ldots,y_m\} \wedge x_{i-1} \le x \le x_i; \end{cases}$$

b) Set $\sigma_{i+1}(x_{i+1}) = 2\alpha_{i+1} + 1$ (Place special integer).
c) Extend $\sigma_{i+1}$ with more and more values of 0's until the team $M_1,\ldots,M_n$ outputs $m$ new valid programs.
*End Step $i$*

**End Phase 1.**

If the loop does not terminate then, the sub step (2) in step (a) was not completed or step (c) was not completed.

*Case 1.* Step (c) was not completed.
Then the team does not output $m$ new programs then $\sigma_{i+1}$ will be a total function. Then the desired $f$ would be $\sigma_{i+1}$, since Condition (II) was satisfied, the programs $p_1^i,\ldots,p_m^i$ does not compute $f$ and by construction $f \in S$.

*Case 2.* Sub step (2) in step (a) was not completed.
This implies that the programs output by the team compute finite functions. By sub step (2) $\sigma_i$ is a total function. Let $f = \sigma_i$, by construction $\varphi_{\alpha_i} = f$, hence $f \in S$. The programs output by team compute finite functions, hence $S \notin [m,n]EX_0^0$.

If the loop terminates, then set $f = \sigma_r \cup \{(x,0)\mid x > x_r\}$. The team on $f$ can output at most $n$ programs. By Condition (II) $(r-1)m$ of them are invalid. Hence there are

$n - (r - 1)m$ valid programs remaining. If $m$ members of the team $M_1,\ldots,M_n$ correctly infers $f$ then $n - (r - 1)m \geq m$. This implies that $n \geq mr$, which in turn implies that $r \leq \lfloor \frac{n}{m} \rfloor$ which contradicts the initial assumption. Hence $m$ out of the $n$ members of the team cannot infer $f$.

☒

**THEOREM 13.** $(\forall m, n, r \in N - \{0\})$ such that $m \leq n$ then $[1, r]EX_0^0 \subseteq [m, n]EX_0^0$ if and only if $r \leq \lfloor \frac{n}{m} \rfloor$.

**Proof:** $\Longleftarrow$ Let $(m, n, r \in N - \{0\})$ such that $m \leq n$ be given. Suppose $r \leq \lfloor \frac{n}{m} \rfloor$ then we will show that $[1, r] \subseteq [m, n]EX_0^0$. Let $M_1,\ldots,M_r$ be any $r$ IIMs. We will construct $M_1',\ldots,M_n'$ $n$ IIMs such that for any set $S$ of recursive functions, if $S \in [1, r]EX_0^0$ then $S \in [m, n]EX_0^0$.

Let $n = m * t + s$ where $t, s \in N$, $m > s$. Now $\frac{n}{m} = t + \frac{s}{m}$. Which implies $\lfloor \frac{n}{m} \rfloor \leq t + \frac{s}{m}$. But $r \leq \lfloor \frac{n}{m} \rfloor$ and $m > s$, we have $t \geq r$. If $r = 1$ then the $n$ IIM's will output what ever $M_1$ outputs, hence the result. If $r > 1$ then divide the $n$ teams into $t$ groups $G_1,\ldots,G_t$ with each group having at least $m$ IIM's. Now let each member of $G_i$ simulate $M_i$ for $1 \leq i \leq r$ (since $r \leq t$ this is possible). Clearly since there are $m$ IIMs in each group there will be at least $m$ IIMs correct out of the $n$ IIMs.

$\Longrightarrow$ Suppose $(m, n, r \in N - \{0\})$ such that $m \leq n$ are given. Suppose $[1, r]EX_0^0 \subseteq [m, n]EX_0^0$ and $r \geq \lfloor \frac{n}{m} \rfloor$. This contradicts Theorem 12.

☒

**THEOREM 14.** $(\forall n \in N)$ $[n + 2, 2n + 3]EX_0^0 - [n + 1, 2n + 1]EX_0^0 \neq \emptyset$

**Proof:** Let $n > 1$ be given. We will construct a set $S$ of recursive functions such that $S \in [n + 2, 2n + 3]EX_0^0$ and $S \notin [n + 1, 2n + 1]EX_0^0$. The following is an intuitive description of S. Given a $f \in S$ there will be at most $n + 1$ other recursive functions in $S$ which will have some same initial segment as $f$. In the longest such initial segment there will be at most $2n + 3$ special integers and $n + 2$ of which will describe $f$. We will choose special integers to be odd integers. Formally, $f \in S$ if and only if the following two conditions hold.

1. $f(x)$ is odd for no more than $2n + 3$ distinct values of $x$.
2. There exists $x_1,\cdots,x_{n+2}$ and $j_1,\cdots,j_{n+2}$ such that $f(x_1) = 2j_1 + 1,\cdots,f(x_{n+2}) = 2j_{n+2} + 1$ and $\varphi_{j_1} = f,\cdots, \varphi_{j_{n+2}} = f$.

First we will show that $S \in [n + 2, 2n + 3]EX_0^0$. We will construct $2n + 3$ IIMs such that for any $f \in S$ there will be at least $n + 2$ IIMs which will infer $f$. For any $f \in S$, the $i^{\text{th}}$ member $(1 \leq i \leq 2n + 3)$ of the team on input from $f$ will execute the following algorithm.

*Begin $M_i$*
1. Wait for the $i^{\text{th}}$ odd integer, say $k$.
2. Output $(k - 1)/2$.
*End $M_i$*

By the definition of $S$, $n + 2$ of the $2n + 3$ odd integers will describe $f$, therefore $S \in [n + 2, 2n + 3]EX_0^0$. We will construct a recursive function $f$ such that $f \in S$ and for any $M_1,\cdots,M_{2n+1}$, $f \notin EX_0^0(M_1,\cdots,M_{2n+1})$. Let $M_1,\cdots,M_{2n+1}$ be given. To construct

$f$ we will use kleene's n-ary recursion theorem. Using $(2n+3)$-ary recursion theorem and finite extension argument we construct functions $\varphi_{e_1}, \cdots, \varphi_{e_{(n+2)}}, \varphi_{e_{1,1}}, \cdots, \varphi_{e_{1,(n+1)}}, \varphi_{e_{2,1}}, \cdots, \varphi_{e_{2,(n+1)}}, \cdots, \varphi_{e_{(n+2),1}}, \cdots, \varphi_{e_{(n+2),(n+1)}}$. let $\sigma_i$ denote the largest initial segment of $\varphi_{e_i}$ constructed so far and $x_i$ denote the largest value in the domain of $\sigma_i$.

**Phase 0.** Initialize.
1. $x_1 = 0, \cdots, x_{n+2} = 0$.
2. $\sigma_1 = \emptyset, \cdots, \sigma_{n+2} = \emptyset$.
3. $M_1(\emptyset) = \emptyset, \cdots, M_{2n+1}(\emptyset) = \emptyset$.
4. $\sigma_1(x_1) = 2e_1 + 1$, $\sigma_1(x_1 + 1) = 2e_2 + 1 \cdots$, $\sigma_1(x_1 + n + 1) = 2e_{n+2} + 1$. (place special integers)
5. $\sigma_2 = \sigma_1$, $\sigma_3 = \sigma_1$, $\cdots$, $\sigma_{n+2} = \sigma_1$. ($n+2$ identical initial segments)

**End Phase 0.**

Now we will extend $\sigma_1, \cdots, \sigma_{n+2}$ simultaneously with more and more 0's until $n+1$ out of the $2n+1$ IIM's $(M_1, \cdots, M_{2n+1})$ converge on $\sigma_1$. Note that $\sigma_1, \cdots, \sigma_{n+1}$ are identical initial segments. If $n+1$ out of the $2n+1$ IIM's do not converge then $\sigma_1, \cdots, \sigma_{n+2}$ are total functions. Let $f = \sigma_1$, since $2e_1 + 1, \cdots, 2e_{n+2} + 1$ are in the range of $f$, and $\varphi_{e_1} = f, \cdots, \varphi_{e_{n+2}} = f$ implies that $f \in S$. Now $S \notin [n+1, 2n+1]EX_0^0$, since the IIMs $M_1, \cdots, M_{2n+1}$ have not output $n+1$ programs. With no loss of generality assume that $n+1$ out of the $2n+1$ IIMs have output $n+1$ programs on some finite initial segment $\sigma_1$.

**Phase 1.** Halt construction of segments $\sigma_1, \cdots, \sigma_{n+2}$ temporarily. Construct segments $\sigma_{i,1}, \cdots, \sigma_{i,(n+1)}$ for $1 \le i \le (n+2)$ such that $\sigma_i$ and $\sigma_{i,1}, \cdots, \sigma_{i,(n+1)}$ are identical for each $i$.

> *For $i := 1$ to $(n+2)$ do Begin*
> 1. Set $\sigma_i(x_i + 1) = 2e_{i,1} + 1, \cdots, \sigma_i(x_i + n + 1) = 2e_{i,n+1} + 1$.
> 2. Set $\sigma_{i,1} = \sigma_i, \cdots, \sigma_{i,(n+1)} = \sigma_i$.
> 3. Extend $\sigma_i, \sigma_{i,1}, \cdots, \sigma_{i,(n+1)}$ with more and more values of $2i$. (All the segments $\sigma_i, \sigma_{i,1}, \cdots, \sigma_{i,(n+1)}$ are identical.)
>
> *End For*

**End Phase 1.**

Now clearly you will have $(n+2)$ pairwise distinct functions and each one has $(n+1)$ other functions which are identical to it. The team has output $(n+1)$ programs and its allowed to output $n$ more programs. Hence one of the functions $\sigma_1$ and $\sigma_2, \cdots, \sigma_{(n+2)}$ will be the desired $f$ ⊠

## CONCLUSIONS AND OPEN PROBLEMS

For practical inference systems its is not possible to have unlimited resources. Hence solving Problem 11 and using small values for the parameters will help us better understand practical inference. This paper also proves that there does not exist a reasonable probability model which will capture the notion of inference with bounded number of mind changes.

Finally we would like to state the most general problem that is open.

PROBLEM 15. $(\forall a, b, c, d \in N)$, $(\forall n_1, m_1, n_2, m_2 \in N - \{0\})$ such that $(n_1 \leq m_1)$ and $(n_2 \leq m_2)$ find a predicate $P$ such that $[n_1, m_1] EX_b^a \subseteq [n_2, m_2] EX_d^c$ if and only if $P(a, b, c, d, n_1, m_1, n_2, m_2)$.

## ACKNOWLEDGEMENTS

I would like to thank Carl Smith for his invaluable advice in preparing this paper.

## REFERENCES

1. BARZDIN, J.A. AND FREIVALDS, R.V. On the prediction of general recursive functions. *Soviet Math Dokl. 13* (1972), 1224–1228.

2. BLUM, L. AND BLUM, M. Toward a mathematical theory of inductive inference. *Information and Control 28* (1975), 125–155.

3. CASE, J. Periodicity in generations of automata. *Mathematical Systems Theory 8* (1974), 15–32.

4. CASE, J. AND NGOMANGUELLE, S. Refinements of inductive inference by popperian machines. *Kybernetika* (198?). to appear.

5. CASE, J. AND SMITH, C. Comparison of identification criteria for machine inductive inference. *Theoretical Computer Science 25, 2* (1983), 193–220.

6. DALEY, R. P. AND SMITH, C. H. On the complexity of inductive inference. *Information and Control 69* (1986), 12–40.

7. FREIVALDS, R., SMITH, C., AND VELAUTHAPILLAI, M. Trade–offs amongst parameters effecting the inductive inferribility of classes of recursive functions. *Information and Computation* (1989). To appear.

8. FREIVALDS, R. V.  Finite identification of general recursive functions by probabilistic strategies.  In *Fundamentals of Computation Theory*, L. Budach, Ed., Akademie-Verlag, Berlin, 1979.

9. FREIVALDS, R. V.  On the principle capabilities of probabilistic algorithms in inductive inference. *Semiotika i informatika 12* (1979), 137–140. (in Russian).

10. GOLD, E. M.  Language identification in the limit. *Information and Control 10* (1967), 447–474.

11. JANTKE, K. P.  Natural properties of strategies identifying recursive functions. *Electronische Informationsverabeitung und Kybernetik 15,* 10 (1979), 487–496.

12. KINBER, E.B.  On a theory of inductive inference. *Lecture Notes in Computer Science 56* (1977), 435–440.

13. MACHTEY, M. AND YOUNG, P. *An Introduction to the General Theory of Algorithms.* North-Holland, New York, New York, 1978.

14. OSHERSON, D., STOB, M., AND WEINSTEIN, S. *Systems that Learn.* MIT Press, Cambridge, Mass., 1986.

15. OSHERSON, D. N., STOB, M., AND WEINSTEIN, S.  Aggregating inductive expertise. *Information and Control 70* (1986), 69–95.

16. PITT, L.  A Characterization of Probabilistic Inference. *Journal of the ACM*(1986). To appear.

17. PITT, L. AND SMITH, C.  Probability and plurality for aggregations of learning machines. *Information and Computation 77* (1988), 77–92.

18. PODNIEKS, K. M.  Probabilistic synthesis of enumerated classes of functions. *Soviet Math Dokl. 16* (1975), 1042–1045.

19. PODNIEKS, K. M.  Probabalistic program synthesis. In *Theory Of Algorithms and Programs*, Barzdin, Ed., Latvian State University, Riga, U.S.S.R., 1977. Russian.

20. SMITH, C. H.  The power of pluralism for automatic program synthesis. *Journal of the ACM 29,* 4 (1982), 1144–1165.

21. SMITH, C. H. AND VELAUTHAPILLAI, M.  On the inference of approximate explanations. *Theoretical Computer Science*(1982).  To appear.

22. VALIANT, L. G.  A theory of the learnable.  *Communications of the ACM 27,* 11 (1984), 1134–1142.

23. VELAUTHAPILLAI, M.  On the inductive inference of programs with anomalies. PhD Thesis, The University of Maryland, College Park, MD, 1986.

24. WIEHAGEN, R., FREIVALDS, R., AND KINBER, E. K.  On the power of probabilistic strategies in inductive inference. *Theoretical Computer Science 28* (1984), 111–133.

# LEARNING VIA QUERIES TO AN ORACLE

William I. Gasarch†
Department of Computer Science
Institute for Advanced Computer Studies
University of Maryland
College Park, MD 20742

Mark B. Pleszkoch‡
Department of Computer Science
University of Maryland
College Park, MD 20742

## ABSTRACT

We study the effect of additional computational power on passive inductive inference. Specifically, we investigate whether allowing IIM's (Inductive Inference Machines) access to an oracle $A$ extends the sets of functions which can be inferred. If we restrict the IIM's to make a finite number of queries to $A$, then it is the case that $A$ can be of help iff it is not recursive in the halting set (i.e. $A \not\leq_T K$). If an unrestricted number of queries to $A$ is allowed, then any oracle $A$ that is not low (i.e. $A' \not\leq_T K$) can be used to infer any set of functions which cannot be inferred by a non-oracle IIM. We also study the interaction between additional computational power and bounding the number of times that an IIM is allowed to change its mind. In this context, we have a strict double hierarchy: additional computational power always helps; increasing the number of mind changes allowed always helps; no amount of additional computational power can totally compensate for the extra benefit of one more mind change; and no increase in the number of mind changes allowed can overcome the extra benefit of additional computational power.

## 1. INTRODUCTION

Inductive inference is the study of machine learning in a theoretical framework. This paper is concerned with the inductive inference paradigm wherein one studies the ability of an IIM (Inductive Inference Machine, to be defined later) to learn a recursive function $f$, when presented with the function values $f(0), f(1), f(2), \ldots$, one value at a time [2,3,5,8]. At any time, the IIM may output a guess, that is, a program which is supposed to compute $f$. If the IIM converges on a single guess from some point on, and that guess is correct, then the IIM is said to infer $f$ in the limit. Given an IIM $M$, the set of all functions which $M$ can infer in the limit is denoted by $\text{EX}(M)$. The class of all sets of functions which can be inferred in the limit by any IIM, $\{C \mid \exists M \; C \subseteq \text{EX}(M)\}$, is called EX.

---

†Supported in part by NSF grant CCR 8803641.

‡Also with IBM Corporation, Systems Integration Division, Gaithersburg, MD 20879.

In this paper, we hope to discover which of the limitations of IIM's are recursion-theoretic in nature, and which are fundamental limitations inherent in the inference framework. We do this by studying the effect of increasing the computational power of the IIM's, by giving them access to an oracle. For example, the fact that an IIM cannot infer the set of all recursive functions is a recursion-theoretic limitation due to a lack of computational power. We can see this by observing that an IIM with access to an oracle for the halting set can infer the set of all recursive functions, and that a non-oracle IIM can infer the set of functions of less computational power, for example, the set of all primitive recursive functions. On the other hand, no IIM, regardless of what oracle it can access, can infer the set of all step functions if the IIM is required to make a bounded number of mind changes.

Adapting the definition of EX, we let $\text{EX}[A]$ be the class of sets of functions which can be inferred when the IIM's have access to the oracle $A$. If the IIM's can only query the oracle $A$ a finite number of times for each function, we call the resulting class $\text{EX}[A[*]]$. Clearly, we have $\text{EX} \subseteq \text{EX}[A[*]] \subseteq \text{EX}[A]$ for each oracle $A$. If, in addition, we require that the IIM's make at most $n$ mind changes, we obtain the classes $\text{EX}_n$, $\text{EX}_n[A]$, and $\text{EX}_n[A[*]]$.

In Section 3 we review and add to the results of Adleman and Blum [1] on when $\text{EX}[A]$ (and variations of it) contains the set of *all* recursive functions.

In Sections 4 and 5 we obtain a complete characterization of when $\text{EX} \subset \text{EX}[A[*]]$, and a partial characterization of when $\text{EX} \subset \text{EX}[A]$. In attempting to construct a set $S$ in $\text{EX}[A[*]] - \text{EX}$, one approach is to encode information about each function $f \in S$ into the value of $f(0)$, in such a manner that the oracle $A$ is required to decode the information. For a given set $A$, we define the following set of functions:

$$S_A = \{f \mid f(0) \in A \wedge \phi_{f(1)} = f\} \cup \{f \mid f(0) \notin A \wedge f =^* \lambda x[0]\}.$$

Intuitively, the value of $f(0)$ tells the IIM whether to guess $f(1)$ as an index, or to guess that $f$ is zero from some point on. Thus, we see that $S_A \in \text{EX}[A[*]]$. In fact, since only one query to $A$ is required, $S_A \in \text{EX}[A[1]]$. However, taking away the information contained in $f(0)$, we obtain the following set, which, using techniques of [3], is not in EX:

$$\{f \mid \phi_{f(1)} = f\} \cup \{f \mid f =^* \lambda x[0]\}.$$

From this fact, it seems that any IIM that is able to infer $S_A$ must have the ability to determine some information about $A$. We will show, in Sections 4 and 5, that this is so: $S_A \in \text{EX}$ iff $A \in \Sigma_2$. This tight constraint will enable us to deduce

$$A \not\leq_T K \text{ iff } \text{EX} \subset \text{EX}[A[*]] \text{ (Corollary 12)}$$

$$A' \not\leq_T K \text{ implies } \text{EX} \subset \text{EX}[A] \text{ (Corollary 13)}$$

In Section 6 we study the interaction between additional computational power and bounding the number of times that an IIM is allowed to change its mind. We have a strict double hierarchy (Theorem 19):

$$\text{EX}_m[A] \subseteq \text{EX}_n[B] \text{ iff } (A \leq_T B \text{ and } m \leq n).$$

In Section 7 we pose several open questions and introduce *degrees of inferability* which we believe are an interesting structure requiring further study. Many variations on the basic inference framework have been studied: bounding the number of times the IIM is allowed to change its guess (i.e. bounding mind changes) [5]; overlooking a finite number of anomalies in judging the correctness of a guess [5]; allowing teams of IIM's to simultaneously infer the function [11]; restricting or otherwise modifying the criteria for successful inference [6]; allowing the IIM to ask questions about the function using various query languages [7]. For each of the above variations, there are results concerning which sets of functions can or cannot be inferred.

## 2. NOTATION AND DEFINITIONS

Throughout this paper, $\{\phi_i\}_{i=0}^{\infty}$ will denote an acceptable programming system [10], and $\{\Phi_i\}_{i=0}^{\infty}$ will denote an associated Blum complexity measure [4]. The set of all (total) recursive functions is denoted by $REC$. The function $\phi_{i,s}$ is defined by

$$\phi_{i,s}(x) = \begin{cases} \phi_i(x) & \text{if } \Phi_i(x) \leq s, \\ \uparrow & \text{otherwise.} \end{cases}$$

For $i = 0, 1, 2, \ldots$ let $W_i = \{x \mid \phi_i(x) \downarrow\}$, the domain of $\phi_i$.

The halting set for this system is $K = \{i \mid \phi_i(i) \downarrow\}$. The set of indices of total functions is $TOT = \{i \mid W_i = \mathbb{N}\}$. The set of indices of functions with finite domain is $FIN = \{i \mid W_i \text{ is finite }\}$. Recall that $FIN$ is $\Sigma_2$-complete, $TOT$ is $\Pi_2$-complete, and that $A \leq_T K$ iff $A \in \Delta_2 = \Sigma_2 \cap \Pi_2$ [10].

The symbol $(\overset{\infty}{\forall} x)$ means for almost all $x$. If $A$ and $B$ are sets, then $A'$ is the halting set relative to $A$, and $A \oplus B$ is the set $\{2i \mid i \in A\} \cup \{2i + 1 \mid i \in B\}$. A set $A$ is *high* if $\emptyset'' \leq_T A'$, and *low* if $\emptyset' \equiv_T A'$. We will make use of the following lemma on several occasions:

*Lemma* 1: If $A \notin \Delta_2$, then $A \oplus \overline{A} \notin \Sigma_2$.

*Proof*:

We prove the contrapositive. If $A \oplus \overline{A} \in \Sigma_2$, then both $A \in \Sigma_2$ and $\overline{A} \in \Sigma_2$. Since $\overline{A} \in \Sigma_2$, we have $A \in \Pi_2$. Thus, $A \in \Sigma_2 \cap \Pi_2 = \Delta_2$.     $\boxtimes$

*Definition*: An *approximation sequence* to a set $A$ is a sequence of sets $A_0, A_1, A_2, \ldots$ such that $A = \lim_{i \to \infty} A_i$. The approximation sequence is *recursive* if the set $\{\langle i, x \rangle \mid x \in A_i\}$ is recursive.

In this paper, we only consider the inference of total recursive functions. Thus, without loss of generality, we can assume that the function values are presented in their natural order (i.e. $f(0), f(1), f(2), \ldots$). If $f$ and $g$ are functions, we say that $f =^* g$ iff $f$ and $g$ agree on all but a finite number of points, that is, iff $\exists x \forall y \geq x \; f(y) = g(y)$.

*Definition*: If $f$ is a function from $\mathbb{N}$ to $\mathbb{N}$ then $f_s$ is the string $f(0)f(1) \cdots f(s)$.

*Definition*: An *Inductive Inference Machine* (IIM) is a total algorithmic device with domain $\mathbb{N}^*$ and range $\mathbb{N} \cup \{\perp\}$. Let $M$ be an IIM and $f$ be a recursive function. *M infers* $f$ if there exists an $e$ such that $(\overset{\infty}{\forall} s)[M(f_s) = e]$, and $\phi_e$ computes $f$. $\mathrm{EX}(M)$ is the set of all functions that $M$ infers.

Intuitively, we can think of $M$ as taking input $f(0), f(1), \cdots$ and output (from time to time) programs intended to compute the function $f$ The guess $\perp$ means "no guess at this time."

The above definitions all relativize to an oracle $A$. Note that we are inferring recursive functions, not functions recursive in $A$.

*Definition*: Let $A$ be any set. An *Oracle Inductive Inference Machine (with oracle A)* ($\mathrm{IIM}^A$) is a total algorithmic device, with oracle $A$, with domain $\mathbb{N}^*$ and range $\mathbb{N} \cup \{\bot\}$. Let $M^A$ be an $\mathrm{IIM}^A$ and $f$ be a recursive function. $M^A$ *infers* $f$ if there exists an $e$ such that $(\overset{\infty}{\forall} s)[M^A(f_s) = e$, and $\phi_e$ computes $f$. $\mathrm{EX}(M^A)$ is the set of all functions that $M^A$ infers.

*Definition*: Let $M^A$ be an $\mathrm{IIM}^A$ and let $f$ be any function. The set of queries made by $M^A(f_s)$, denoted by $Queries(M^A(f_s))$, is defined to be the set of all values that are tested for membership in $A$ during the computation of $M^A(f_s)$. The set of queries made by $M^A(f)$, denoted by $Queries(M^A(f))$, is defined to be $\bigcup_{s \geq 0} Queries(M^A(f_s))$.

*Note*: Even if $f \in \mathrm{EX}(M^A)$, the set $Queries(M^A(f))$ can be infinite, since even after $M^A$ has converged it may keep asking questions to make sure that it does not want to change its mind. Consider, for example, the inference of $REC$ by a machine with oracle $K$ [7].

*Definition*: Let $M^A$ be an IIM which has access to an oracle $A$. The set of functions which $M^A$ infers in the limit is denoted by $\mathrm{EX}(M^A)$. The set of functions which $M^A$ infers in the limit with at most $n$ mind changes is denoted by $\mathrm{EX}_n(M^A)$. If $M$ is a (non-oracle) IIM, the definitions of $\mathrm{EX}(M)$ and $\mathrm{EX}_n(M)$ are analogous.

*Definition*: We have the following classes of sets of functions:

$$\mathrm{EX} = \{C \mid (\exists M)\, C \subseteq \mathrm{EX}(M)\}$$

$$\mathrm{EX}[A] = \{C \mid (\exists M^A)\, C \subseteq \mathrm{EX}(M^A)\}$$

$$\mathrm{EX}[A[m]] = \{C \mid (\exists M^A)\, C \subseteq \mathrm{EX}(M^A) \wedge \forall f \in C\, \big|Queries(M^A(f))\big| \leq m\}$$

$$\mathrm{EX}[A[*]] = \{C \mid (\exists M^A)\, C \subseteq \mathrm{EX}(M^A) \wedge \forall f \in C\, \big|Queries(M^A(f))\big| \text{ is finite }\}$$

Intuitively, $\mathrm{EX}[A]$ is the class of sets of functions which can be inferred by IIM's with access to the oracle $A$, $\mathrm{EX}[A[m]]$ is the class of sets of functions which can be inferred by IIM's with access to the oracle $A$ for at most $m$ queries per function. If we impose the additional restriction that $M$ or $M^A$ make at most $n$ mind changes, i.e.

$$|\{s \mid \perp \neq M(f_s) \neq M(f_{s+1})\}| \leq m,$$

then we obtain the classes $\mathrm{EX}_n$, $\mathrm{EX}_n[A]$, $\mathrm{EX}_n[A[m]]$, and $\mathrm{EX}_n[A[*]]$.

For the most part, inference with respect to an oracle is well behaved on Turing degrees.

*Lemma* 2: If $A \leq_T B$, then the following hold:

$$\mathrm{EX}[A] \subseteq \mathrm{EX}[B]$$

$$\mathrm{EX}[A[*]] \subseteq \mathrm{EX}[B[*]]$$

$$\mathrm{EX}_n[A] \subseteq \mathrm{EX}_n[B]$$

$$\mathrm{EX}_n[A[*]] \subseteq \mathrm{EX}_n[B[*]]$$

*Proof*:

Since $A \leq_T B$, we can modify $M^A$ so that all queries to $A$ are replaced by computations that make queries to $B$. If the number of queries to $A$ is finite, then the number of queries to $B$ will be finite as well. ⊠

*Corollary* 3: If $A \equiv_T B$, then the following hold:

$$\mathrm{EX}[A] = \mathrm{EX}[B]$$

$$\mathrm{EX}[A[*]] = \mathrm{EX}[B[*]]$$

$$\mathrm{EX}_n[A] = \mathrm{EX}_n[B]$$

$$\mathrm{EX}_n[A[*]] = \mathrm{EX}_n[B[*]].$$

We conjecture that $A \leq_T B$ does not imply $\mathrm{EX}[A[m]] \subseteq \mathrm{EX}[B[m]]$; the problem is still open. A related problem is whether $\mathrm{EX}[A[m]] \subset \mathrm{EX}[A[m+1]]$ for some oracle $A$.

## 3. INFERRING *REC*

Since the IIM's are required to output programs for their guesses, the best that we can hope for is to infer the class of all recursive functions. This section studies the circumstances where this is possible.

The next theorem is due to Adleman and Blum [1].

*Theorem* 4: $REC \in \text{EX}[A]$ iff $K' \leq_T A'$.

When the IIM's are only allowed to ask a bounded number of queries, we have the following results.

*Theorem* 5: $REC \in \text{EX}[TOT[*]]$

*Proof*:

We construct an oracle IIM $M^{TOT}$ that infers all recursive functions as follows. Upon receiving the first $s$ input values of $f$, $M^{TOT}$ outputs the smallest index $i$ such that $i \in TOT$ and $\phi_i$ agrees with $f$ on the given input values. It is easy to see that for any recursive function $f$, $M^{TOT}$ eventually converges to the smallest index $i$ such that $\phi_i = f$. Note that only $i$ queries to $TOT$ are made during this process. ⊠

*Theorem* 6: For all oracles $A$ and all $m \geq 0$, $REC \notin \text{EX}[A[m]]$.

*Proof*:

From [11], we consider $C(2^m, \text{EX})$, which is the set of classes of functions which can be inferred by a team of $2^m$ IIM's, where only one of the machines is required to correctly infer the function.

Since $m$ accesses to the oracle $A$ can only have $2^m$ different response patterns, we have $\text{EX}[A[m]] \subseteq C(2^m, \text{EX})$. Since $REC \notin C(2^m, \text{EX})$ (see [11]), the theorem follows. ⊠

## 4. WHEN ORACLES DO NOT HELP

In this section, we examine when the addition of an oracle to an IIM does not extend the sets of functions which can be inferred. We consider both bounded and unbounded queries to the oracle.

The following theorem indicates that allowing only finitely many queries to an oracle can help only if the oracle is very powerful.

*Theorem* 7: If $A \leq_T K$, then $\mathrm{EX}[A[*]] = \mathrm{EX}$.

*Proof*:

Let $M^A$ be an IIM with access to an oracle $A \leq_T K$, such that for each function $f \in \mathrm{EX}(M^A)$, $Queries(M^A(f))$ is finite. We will show that $\mathrm{EX}(M^A) \in \mathrm{EX}$.

Since $A \leq_T K$, by Shoenfield's Limit Lemma [12] there exists a recursive approximation sequence $A_0, A_1, A_2, \ldots$ for $A$. Using this approximation sequence, we construct a (non-oracle) IIM $N$ that recognizes every function in $\mathrm{EX}(M^A)$.

The output of $N$ upon receiving $f_s$, the first $s$ input points of function $f$, is defined to be that of $M^{A_i}(f_i)$, where $i$ is the largest number in the range $0 \leq i \leq s$ such that the computation of $M^{A_i}(f_i)$ halts within $s$ steps.

We now show that this construction works. Let $f$ be any function in $\mathrm{EX}(M^A)$. Let $t$ be the point beyond which the approximation sequence for $A$ has converged for all values that are queried in the computation of $M^A(f)$. Let $u$ be the first stage such that $M^A(f_u)$ converges upon the machine's final guess, which must be an index for $f$. Thus, $M^A(f)$ does not change its mind at any later stage. Let $v$ be the number of steps in the computation of $M^A(f_{\max(t,u)})$. Then it is easy to see that $N(f_s)$ converges to a correct index for $f$ for all stages $s \geq \max(t, u, v)$. ☒

Theorem 7 can be relativized as follows.

*Corollary* 8: If $A \leq_T B'$, then $\mathrm{EX}[A[*]] \subseteq \mathrm{EX}[B]$.

*Proof*:

Shoenfield's Limit Lemma gives us an approximation sequence for $A$ that is recursive in $B$. The construction and proof are the same from that point on. ☒

*Corollary* 9: If $A \leq_T K$, then $S_A \in \mathrm{EX}$.

*Proof*:

This follows from $S_A \in \mathrm{EX}[A[1]] \subseteq \mathrm{EX}[A[*]] = \mathrm{EX}$. ☒

We can improve upon this slightly by a direct construction.

*Theorem* 10:  If $A \in \Sigma_2$, then $S_A \in$ EX.

*Proof*:

Assume that $A \in \Sigma_2$. We construct an IIM $M$ that infers $S_A$. Since $A \in \Sigma_2$, there is a many-one reduction $r$ from $A$ to $FIN$.

Upon receiving the first $s$ values of a function $f$, machine $M$ will do the following. Let $i$ be the largest value such that $f(i) \neq 0$. Let $j$ be the largest value (less than or equal to $s$) such that $\phi_{r(f(0))}(j)$ halts within $s$ steps. If $i \leq j$, then $M$ guesses an index which gives a value of 0 to all points of $f$ not yet seen. If $i > j$, then $M$ guesses $f(1)$.

We now show that this construction works. If $f(0) \notin A$ and $f =^* \lambda x[0]$, then $\phi_{r(f(0))}$ has infinite domain, and $M$ will eventually only guess functions which are almost always zero. If $f(0) \in A$ and $\phi_{f(1)} = f$, then $M$ will eventually guess $f(1)$, unless $f$ is also almost always zero. In either case, $M$'s guess will be correct.      ⊠

## 5. WHEN ORACLES DO HELP

In this section, we examine when the addition of an oracle to the IIM's does extend the sets of functions which can be inferred. Again, we consider both bounded and unbounded queries to the oracle. Combined with the results from the previous section, we obtain rather tight characterizations of when EX$[A]$ and EX$[A[*]]$ are strictly more powerful than EX.

By a variation of the standard diagonalization technique, we show that $S_A$ is not in EX for suitably complex $A$.

*Theorem* 11:  If $S_A \in$ EX then $A \in \Sigma_2$.

*Proof*:

Assume that $S_A \in$ EX, say $S_A \subseteq$ EX$(M)$ for some (non-oracle) IIM $M$. As in [5], we seek to diagonalize against $M$'s current guess, while also checking whether $M$ changes its mind later on. By this method, we will obtain functions $f$ which $M$ does not correctly infer. However, instead of creating a contradiction, we conclude that $f \notin S_A$, thereby yielding information about the set $A$. In fact, what we will obtain is a many-one reduction from $A$ to $FIN$, showing that $A \in \Sigma_2$.

Specifically, for each $a \geq 0$, we construct a function $f_a$ such that $f_a(0) = a$, and $f_a(1)$ is an index for $f_a$. We do this by first constructing functions $h_{a,i}$, and then applying the recursion theorem to place the index of the desired function into the value of $i$.

Thus, for each $a, i \geq 0$, we construct a partial recursive function $h_{a,i}$ in effective stages of finite extension $h_{a,i}^0 \subseteq h_{a,i}^1 \subseteq h_{a,i}^2 \subseteq \cdots$ so that $h_{a,i} = \bigcup_{s \geq 0} h_{a,i}^s$.

At stage 0, we have $h_{a,i}^0 = \{(0,a), (1,i)\}$. At stage $s+1$, assume that $h_{a,i}^s$ has already been constructed, with domain $\{0, 1, 2, \ldots, x_s - 1\}$. Let $g_s = M(h_{a,i}^s)$ be $M$'s current guess. Perform the following computations simultaneously, until one computation terminates:

1) "Diagonalize against current guess."

   Run $\phi_{g_s}(x_s)$. If this computation terminates first, then we set

   $$h_{a,i}^{s+1} = h_{a,i}^s \cup \{(x_s, \phi_{g_s}(x_s) + 1)\}.$$

2) "Check for mind changes later on."

   For $n := 0, 1, 2, \ldots$, check if

   $$M(h_{a,i}^s \cup \{(x_s, 0), (x_s + 1, 0), \ldots, (x_s + n, 0)\}) \neq g_s.$$

If a value of $n$ that causes a mind change is found before the other computation terminates, then we set $h_{a,i}^{s+1} = h_{a,i}^s \cup \{(x_s, 0), (x_s + 1, 0), \ldots, (x_s + n, 0)\}$.

If neither computation terminates, then $h_{a,i}^s = h_{a,i}^{s+1} = h_{a,i}^{s+2} = \cdots = h_{a,i}$.

Note that $h_{a,i}(n)$ is actually a partial recursive function of $a$, $i$, and $n$. Thus, we can apply the recursion theorem to define a total recursive function $i(a)$ such that $h_{a,i(a)} = \phi_{i(a)}$. Define the $f_a = h_{a,i(a)} = \phi_{i(a)}$. Thus, as required, $f_a(0) = a$, and $f_a(1)$ is an index for $f_a$.

If each stage of the construction of $f_a = h_{a,i(a)}$ terminates, then $f_a$ will be a total function. However, by the construction process, either $M$ changes its mind on $f_a$ infinitely often (thus failing to converge), or $M$'s last guess is wrong infinitely often. In either case, we have $f_a \notin \mathrm{EX}(M)$, so $f_a \notin S_A$. By the definition of $S_A$, this means that $f_a(0) = a \notin A$.

On the other hand, if some stage $s + 1$ of the construction of $f_a$ runs forever, then $f_a$ will be a finite prefix. Let $f_a^*$ denote the total function obtained by extending $f_a$ to be zero on points $x_s$ and beyond. By the fact that sub-stage (2) failed to terminate, we know that $M$'s guess on $f_a^*$ must be $g_s$, which must be incorrect, since it is not total, failing to converge on $x_s$. Thus, we have $f_a^* \notin S_A \subset \text{EX}(M)$, and by the definition of $S_A$, this means that $f_a^*(0) = a \in A$.

Putting this together, we see that $f_a$ has finite domain iff $a \in A$. But this yields a many-one reduction from $A$ to $FIN$, given by the function which maps $a$ into an index for $f_a$. Thus, $A \in \Sigma_2$. ☒

We now have a complete characterization of when $\text{EX}[B[*]] = \text{EX}$:

*Corollary* 12: $B \not\leq_T K$ iff $\text{EX} \subset \text{EX}[B[*]]$.

*Proof*:

Assume $B \not\leq_T K$. Let $A = B \oplus \overline{B}$, so we have $A \notin \Sigma_2$ by Lemma 1 . By Theorem 11 , $S_A \notin \text{EX}$. However, $S_A \in \text{EX}[B[1]] \subseteq \text{EX}[B[*]]$, since $S_A$ can easily be inferred with one query to oracle $B$. Thus, $S_A \in \text{EX}[B[*]] - \text{EX}$.

The other direction follows from Theorem 7. ☒

When the number of queries to the oracle is not bounded, much weaker oracles provide additional inferencing capability.

*Corollary* 13: If $B' \not\leq_T K$ (i.e. $B$ is not low), then $\text{EX} \subset \text{EX}[B]$.

*Proof*:

Let $A = B' \oplus \overline{B'}$, so that $A \notin \Sigma_2$. By Theorem 11 , $S_A \notin \text{EX}$. However, since $A \leq_T B'$, by Corollary 8 from the previous section, $S_A \in \text{EX}[A[1]] \subseteq \text{EX}[A[*]] \subseteq \text{EX}[B]$. Thus, $S_A \in \text{EX}[B] - \text{EX}$. ☒

## 6. BOUNDING MIND CHANGES

In this section, we study the effect of additional computational power when the IIM's are restricted to make a bounded number of mind changes.

*Definition*: A function $f$ is said to be an *n-step function* if it is monotone non-decreasing with range $\{0, 1, 2, \ldots, n\}$. The set of all $n$-step functions is denoted by $STEP(n)$. Finally, we define $STEP = \bigcup_{n=0}^{\infty} STEP(n)$.

*Note*: A function in $STEP(n)$ will take on the $n + 1$ different values $\{0, 1, \ldots, n\}$.

It is known that $STEP \notin EX_n$ for any $n \geq 0$ [5]. We now show that this result is a fundamental limitation resulting from bounding mind changes.

*Theorem* 14: For any oracle $A$, $\bigcup\limits_{i=0}^{n+1} STEP(i) \notin EX_n[A]$.

*Proof*:

Suppose, by way of contradiction, that there is an IIM $M^A$ such that $\bigcup_{i=0}^{n+1} STEP(i) \subseteq EX(M^A)$, where $M^A$ makes at most $n$ mind changes for each function in this set.

In the following, we denote a function $f$ by the infinite string $f(0)f(1)f(2)\cdots$. Let $r_0 > 0$ be the stage where $M^A$ correctly infers the function $0^\omega$. Let $r_1 > r_0$ be the stage where $M^A$ correctly infers the function $0^{r_0}1^\omega$. In general, let $r_{i+1} > r_i$ be the stage where $M^A$ correctly infers the function $0^{r_0}1^{r_1-r_0}\cdots i^{r_i-r_{i-1}}(i+1)^\omega$. However, we then have that $M^A$ changes its mind $n + 1$ times on $0^{r_0}1^{r_1-r_0}\cdots n^{r_n-r_{n-1}}(n+1)^\omega$, a contradiction.    ☒

*Corollary* 15: For any oracle $A$, and any $n \geq 0$, $STEP \notin EX_n[A]$.

*Corollary* 16: For any oracle $A$ and any $n \geq 0$, we have $REC \notin EX_n[A]$.

The main result of this section is that the classes $EX_n[A]$ form a strict double hierarchy in terms of number of mind changes $n$ and oracle $A$. To prove this, we construct the following set:

$$U_{A,n} = \{f \mid \exists i < f(0) \; \lambda x[f(x + f(0) + 1)] \in STEP(i) \wedge f(i+1) \in A$$

$$\wedge \, |\{j : 0 < j \leq i \wedge f(j) \in A\}| \leq n\}.$$

We now describe the set $U_{A,n}$ intuitively. Except for the first $f(0) + 1$ values, a function $f \in U_{A,n}$ is a step function. The only possible values of $i$ such that $f$ (ignoring the first $f(0) + 1$ values) is in $STEP(i)$, are the first $n + 1$ values $j$ such that $f(j + 1) \in A$.

*Theorem* 17: $U_{A,m} \in EX_n[B]$ iff $m \leq n$ and $A$ is r.e. in $B$.

*Proof:*

The "if" part is easy. We construct an IIM $M^A$ that infers $U_{A,m}$ as follows. $M^A$ waits until the first $f(0) + 1$ values have been seen, and then guesses at the $n + 1$ spots indicated. Since there will be at most $n + 1$ guesses, there will be at most $n$ mind changes.

For the "only if" part, a technique similar to that used in the proof of Theorem 15 shows that $m \leq n$. Now, if we have an IIM $M^B$ that infers $U_{A,m}$, we can recursively enumerate $A$ as follows. Given a value $x$, construct $f$ to be $(n+1)xa^n0^\omega$, where $a$ is some value known to be in $A$. If $M^B(f)$ ever guesses a program, then $x \in A$. If not, then $x \notin A$. Thus, $A$ is r.e. in $B$.                                          ⊠

*Theorem* 18:  $\mathrm{EX}_m[A] \subseteq \mathrm{EX}_n[B]$ iff ($A \leq_T B$ and $m \leq n$).

*Proof:*

The "if" part is obvious. To show the "only if" part, consider the set $X = U_{A \oplus \overline{A}, m}$. Obviously, $X \in \mathrm{EX}_m[A]$, so by hypothesis we have $X \in \mathrm{EX}_n[B]$. By Theorem 18 , we have $m \leq n$, and $A \oplus \overline{A}$ is r.e. in $B$. However, this implies that $A$ is recursive in $B$, i.e. $A \leq_T B$.                                          ⊠

This result shows that there is a strict double hierarchy. In particular, we have the following corollaries.

*Corollary* 19:  If $A <_T B$ and $m \leq n$, then $\mathrm{EX}_m[A] \subset \mathrm{EX}_n[B]$.

*Proof:*

Since $B \not\leq_T A$, we have $\mathrm{EX}_n[B] \not\subseteq \mathrm{EX}_m[A]$ by Theorem 19.                                          ⊠

*Corollary* 20:  If $A \leq_T B$ and $m < n$, then $\mathrm{EX}_m[A] \subset \mathrm{EX}_n[B]$.

*Proof:*

By Theorem 19, we have $\mathrm{EX}_n[B] \not\subseteq \mathrm{EX}_m[A]$.                                          ⊠

Once we realize that a strict double hierarchy exists, we would like to determine if it is generated by two single hierarchies, that is, is it the case that $\mathrm{EX}_n[A] = \mathrm{EX}_n \cap \mathrm{EX}[A]$, for example? The next theorem shows that this is not the case.

**Theorem 21:** For any non-recursive oracle $A$ and any $n \geq 0$, we have

$$\mathrm{EX}_n \subset (\mathrm{EX}_n[A] \cap \mathrm{EX}_{n+1}).$$

*Proof:*

We use the set

$$X = \{f \mid \lambda x[f(x+1)] \in \bigcup_{i=0}^{n-1} STEP(i)\}$$
$$\cup \{f \mid f(0) \in (A \oplus \overline{A}) \wedge \lambda x[f(x+1)] \in STEP(n)\}$$
$$\cup \{f \mid f(0) \notin (A \oplus \overline{A}) \wedge \lambda x[f(x+1)] \in STEP(n+1)\}.$$

By ignoring the information contained in $f(0)$, we see that this is in $\mathrm{EX}_{n+1}$. By accessing oracle $A$, we can use the information in $f(0)$ to eliminate one mind change. The technique of Theorem 18 can be used to show that $X \in \mathrm{EX}_n$ implies that $A \oplus \overline{A}$ is r.e., that is, that $A$ is recursive. $\boxtimes$

We can relativize this construction to obtain the following theorem.

**Theorem 22:** If $B <_T A$, then $\mathrm{EX}_n[B] \subset (\mathrm{EX}_n[A] \cap \mathrm{EX}_{n+1}[B])$.

## 7. OPEN QUESTIONS AND THE DEGREE OF INFERABILITY

Is there an analogue for the Adleman and Blum result for bounded queries to an oracle?

*Conjecture:* For all oracles $A$, $REC \in \mathrm{EX}[A[*]]$ iff $TOT \leq_T A$.

For which sets $A$ is $EX = EX[A]$?

*Conjecture:* $EX = EX[A]$ iff $A$ is low.

This conjecture is motivated by the fact that low sets often behave like recursive sets (see [9] ).

*Definition:* Let $A$ and $B$ be any two sets. $A \leq_i B$ iff $EX[A] \subseteq EX[B]$. $A <_i B$ iff $EX[A] \subset EX[B]$. $A \equiv_i B$ iff $EX[A] = EX[B]$. If $\mathbf{a}$ and $\mathbf{b}$ are Turing degrees then $\mathbf{a} \leq_i \mathbf{b}$ iff there exists $A \in \mathbf{a}$ and $B \in \mathbf{b}$ such that $A \leq_i B$. The definitions of $<_i$ and $\equiv_i$ on Turing degrees are similar. It is easy to show that $\equiv_i$, defined on Turing degrees, is an equivalence relation. We call the equivalence classes *degrees of inferability*. Similar definitions could be made with $EX[A[*]]$ instead of $EX[A]$ and called the *degrees of \*-inferability*.

By Theorem 4 all the high degrees, and all degrees of Turing degree larger than $K$, are in the same inference degree. By Corollary 13 and the existence of a Turing degree below $K$ that is neither high nor low (see [9]) there exists an inference degree between that of $\emptyset$ and $K$. Nothing else is known about the inference degrees, though we believe them to be an interesting structure for future study.

*Conjecture*: There are an infinite number of incomparable inference degrees.

Many open questions can be obtained by combining the notions in this paper with variations of the notion of inference (see the last paragraph of the introduction for some of these variations). It is not clear which of the questions that could be raised are interesting.

## REFERENCES

1. ADLEMAN, L. AND BLUM, M. *Inductive Inference and Unsolvability*. Manuscript.

2. ANGLUIN, D. AND SMITH, C.H. Inductive Inference: Theory and Methods. *Computing Surveys 15, No. 3* (September 1983), 237-269.

3. BLUM, L. AND BLUM, M. Toward a mathematical theory of inductive inference. *Information and Computation 28* (1975), 125-155.

4. BLUM, M. A Machine Independent Theory of the Complexity of Recursive Functions. *J. Assoc. Comput. Mach. 18* (1967), 322-336.

5. CASE, J. AND SMITH, C. Comparison of Identification Criteria for Machine Inductive Inference. *Theoretical Computer Science 25* (1983), 193-220.

6. FULK, M.A. Saving the Phenomena: Requirements that Inductive Inference Machines Not Contradict Known Data. *Information and Computation 79* (1988), 193-209.

7. GASARCH, W. I. AND SMITH, C. H.  Learning via queries. In *Proceedings of the* 29<sup>th</sup> *Annual IEEE Symposium on Foundations of Computer Science*, White Plains, NY, 1988.

8. GOLD, E.M. Language Identification in the Limit. *Information and Control 10* (1967), 447-474.

9. LERMAN, M. *Degrees of Unsolvability*. Springer Verlag, 1983.

10. ROGERS, H. JR. *Theory of Recursive Functions and Effective Computability*. McGraw Hill, New York, 1967.

11. SMITH, C.H.  The Power of Pluralism for Automatic Program Synthesis. *Journal of the Association for Computing Machinery 29, No. 4* (October 1982), 1144-1165.

12. SOARE, R.I. *Recursively Enumerable Sets and Degrees*. Springer Verlag (Omega Series), Berlin, 1987.

# LEARNING STRUCTURE FROM DATA: A SURVEY [*]

Judea Pearl
Computer Science Dept.
University of California
Los Angeles, CA. 90024-1596

Rina Dechter
Dept. of Computer Sciences
Technion, I. I. T.
Haifa, Israel

## ABSTRACT

This paper summarizes several investigations into the prospects of identifying meaningful structures in empirical data. Starting with an early work on identifying probabilistic trees, we extend the method to polytrees (directed trees with arbitrary edge orientation) and show that, under certain conditions, the skeleton of the polytree as well as the orientation of some of the arrows, are identifiable. We next address the problem of identifying probabilistic trees in which some of the nodes are unobservable. It is shown that such trees can be effectively identified in cases where all variables are either bi-valued or normal, and where all correlation coefficients are known precisely. Finally, it is shown that an effective procedure exists for determining whether a given categorical relation is decomposable into a tree of binary relations and, if the answer is positive, identifying the topology of such a tree. Guided by these results, we then propose a general framework whereby the notion of *identifiability* is given a precise formal definition, similar to that of learnability.

## 1. INTRODUCTION

Discovering meaningful structures in empirical data has long been regarded as the hallmark of scientific activity. Formally, the task of finding "meaningful structures" can be stated as that of finding computationally attractive descriptions of the data whenever such descriptions exist. Invariably, the existence of useful descriptions rests on whether the dependencies among the data items are decomposable into a small number of more basic interactions. Given that the data was generated from a model where the dependencies are both sparse and local, one seeks a useful representation for these dependencies. A classical example would be to find a Markov model with the least number of states that accounts for observed dependencies among contingent symbols in a sequence. In more elaborate settings the dependencies can form a graph (as in the analysis of Markov fields) or a hypergraph (as in relational databases), and the task is to find the topology of these structures. Structure learning includes such tasks as finding effective representations for probability distributions, finding economical decompositions of database schema, or simplifying expressions of learned Boolean concepts to render subsequent processing tractable.

* This work was supported in part by National Science Foundation Grants #IRI-86-10155 and #IRI-8815522, and Naval Research Laboratory Grant #N00014-89-J-2007.

Despite the generality and importance of the task at hand, very few formal results have been established. In the economics literature the topic has been discussed under the heading of "latent structure analysis" [Lazarsfeld 1966; Glymour et. al. 1987], while in the pattern-recognition literature it became known as "unsupervised learning" [Duda and Hart 1973]. However, with the exception of the work of Chow and Liu [1968] the tasks were confined to learning very simple structures, such as those governing probability mixtures and hidden Markov models [Laird 1988].

This paper surveys several extensions of the Chow and Liu result (Section 2). These include identifying polytrees (Section 3), identifying trees with hidden variables (Section 4), and identifying tree decompositions of categorical relations (Section 5). A general formal framework for structure identification tasks and a comparison to Valiant's [1984] learning model are provided in Section 6.

## 2. IDENTIFYING TREES

**Definition:** A distribution $P^t(\mathbf{x})$ is said to be *tree-dependent* relative to the tree $t$; if it can be written as a product of pair-wise conditional probability distributions,

$$P^t(\mathbf{x}) = \prod_{i=1}^{n} P(x_i \mid x_{j(i)}),\qquad(1)$$

where $X_{j(i)}$ is the variable designated as the parent of $X_i$ in some orientation of the tree.

The root $X_1$ can be chosen arbitrarily, and having no parents, it is characterized by the prior probability $P(x_1 \mid x_0) = P(x_1)$. For example, the distribution corresponding to the tree oriented as in Figure 1 has the product form

$$P^t(\mathbf{x}) = P(x_1)P(x_2 \mid x_1)\,P(x_3 \mid x_2)\,P(x_4 \mid x_2)\,P(x_5 \mid x_2)\,P(x_6 \mid x_5).$$

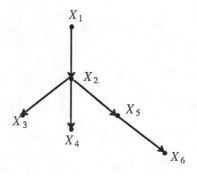

Figure 1.

Thus, the number of parameters needed for specifying a tree-dependent distribution is $(r-1)[r(n-1)+1]$, where $n$ is the number of variables and $r$ their arity. Tree-dependent distributions are unique in that they facilitate linear time query processing, as well as local unsupervised computations [Pearl 1988].

Chow and Liu asked the following question: Given a distribution $P$, what is the tree-dependent distribution $P^t$ that best approximates $P$, in the sense of minimizing the Kullback-Liebler measure

$$D(P,P') = \sum_{\mathbf{x}} P(\mathbf{x}) \log \frac{P(\mathbf{x})}{P'(\mathbf{x})} \ ? \tag{2}$$

This measure is nonnegative and attains the value 0 if and only if $P'$ coincides with $P$.

The minimization task can be performed in two surprisingly simple steps. First, we fix the structure of some tree $t$ and ask what conditional probabilities $P^t(x_i \mid x_j)$ would render $P^t$ the best approximation of $P$. We call this best approximation the *projection* of $P$ on $t$, $P_P^t$. Second, we vary the structure of $t$ over all possible spanning trees, and among all the projections of $P$ on these spanning trees we seek the one that is closest to $P$.

**Theorem 1:** *The projection of $P$ on $t$ is characterized by the equality*

$$P_P^t(x_i \mid x_{j(i)}) = P(x_i \mid x_{j(i)}) \ . \tag{3}$$

In other words, by forcing the conditional probabilities along the branches of the tree $t$ to coincide with those computed from $P$, we get the best $t$-dependent approximation to $P$. (see Pearl [1988], Appendix 8-A, for proof).

**Theorem 2** [Chow and Liu 1968]: *The distance measure of Eq. (2) is minimized by projecting $P$ on any maximum weight spanning tree (MWST), where the weight on the branch $(X_i, X_j)$ is defined by the mutual information measure*

$$I(X_i, X_j) = \sum_{x_i, x_j} P(x_i, x_j) \log \frac{P(x_i, x_j)}{P(x_i) P(x_j)} \geq 0 \ . \tag{4}$$

**Corollary 1:** *If the underlying distribution $P$ is itself tree-dependent, then its projection on every MWST must coincide with $P$.*

The merits of the MWST algorithm are several. First, it uses only second-order statistics, which are easily and reliably measured from sample data and are economical to store. The tree is developed in $O(n^2)$ steps using only weight comparisons, thereby avoiding expensive tests for conditional independence. Finally, it can be shown that if the branch weights are computed from sampled data, then $P_P^t$ will be a maximum likelihood estimate of $P$. The consequence of this is that if the underlying distribution is indeed one of tree-dependence, the approximating probability constructed by the MWST algorithm converges with probability 1 to the true underlying distribution [Chow and Wagner 1973].

These advantages are unique to tree structures and do not apply to general multiply connected graphs. Even if we could afford to enumerate all graphs in a given class, the task of finding the projection of $P$ on a product form that reflects any of these graphs might involve enormous computations, unless that graph could be embedded in a simple hyper-tree.

## 3. IDENTIFYING POLYTREES

A *polytree* is a directed tree with unrestricted edge orientation, thus allowing nodes to have multiple parents (see Figure 2). A polytree, though it allows us to describe higher-order interactions, enjoys many of the computational advantages of simple trees. In particular, it supports local computations, and its structure can sometimes be identified by second-order distributions using an MWST algorithm similar to that of Chow and Liu.

Assume we are given a distribution $P(\mathbf{x})$ of $n$ discrete-value variables, and we are told that $P(\mathbf{x})$ can be represented by some unknown polytree $F_0$, i.e., $P(\mathbf{x})$ has the form

$$P(\mathbf{x}) = \prod_{i=1}^{N} P(x_i \mid x_{j_1(i)}, x_{j_2(i)}, ..., x_{j_m(i)}) , \tag{5}$$

where $\{X_{j_1(i)}, X_{j_2(i)}, ..., X_{j_m(i)}\}$ is the (possibly empty) set of direct parents of variable $X_i$ in $F_0$, and the parents of each variable are mutually independent, i.e.,

$$P(x_{j_1(i)}, x_{j_2(i)}, ..., x_{j_m(i)}) = \prod_{k=1}^{m} P(x_{j_k(i)}) \quad \text{for all } i . \tag{6}$$

We seek to recover the structure of $F_0$, i.e., the set of branches and hopefully their directionality, by examining the properties of $P(\mathbf{x})$. That the structure of $F_0$ may not always be recoverable uniquely is apparent from examining the dependencies induced by the three possible types of adjacent triplets allowed in polytrees:

1.   $X \rightarrow Y \rightarrow Z$

2.   $X \leftarrow Y \rightarrow Z$

3.   $X \rightarrow Y \leftarrow Z$

Since type 1 and type 2 represent the same dependencies among $X$, $Y$ and $Z$, they are indistinguishable. Type 3, however, can be uniquely identified, since $X$ and $Z$ are marginally independent and all other pairs are dependent. Thus, while the *skeletons* (the graphs stripped of arrows) of these three triplets are identical, the directionality of the arrows is partially identifiable.

**Definition:** A distribution $P(\mathbf{x})$ is said to be ***nondegenerate*** if there exists a connected directed acyclic graph (DAG) that displays all the dependencies and independencies embedded in $P$.

**Theorem 3:** *If a nondegenerate $P(\mathbf{x})$ can be represented by a polytree $F_0$ (as in (5) and (6)), then the MWST algorithm of Chow and Liu unambiguously recovers the skeleton of $F_0$.*

**Definition:** A *causal basin* of a node $A$ in a DAG is a set of nodes consisting of $A$, the direct parents of $A$, all the descendants of $A$ and all of the direct parents of those descendants.

**Theorem 4** [Rebane and Pearl 1987]: *If a nondegenerate $P(\mathbf{x})$ is representable by a polytree $F_0$, then the directionality of a branch can be recovered if and only if it is contained within the causal basin of some multi-parent node in $F_0$.*

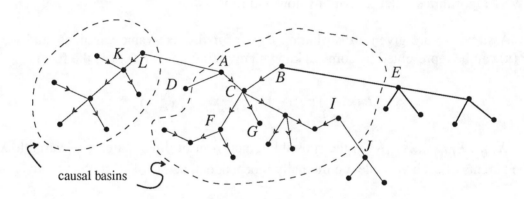

Figure 2.

Figure 2 depicts a polytree with two causal basins rooted as nodes $K$ and $C$. The arrows in each causal basin can be determined uniquely, while the directions of branches outside the basins are undetermined.

Under conditions of degeneracy, $P(\mathbf{x})$ can be represented by several polytrees, each having a different skeleton or a different branch orientation, or both. In general, while we are not guaranteed that every skeleton produced by the MWST algorithm will permit a faithful representation of $P$, we are guaranteed that at least one of these skeletons will do so. This is because if $P$ can be represented by a set of $k$ distinct skeletons $\mathbf{T} = (T_1,...,T_k)$, then each of these skeletons (and perhaps others) must have maximum weight.

## 4.  IDENTIFYING TREES WITH HIDDEN VARIABLES

The identification methods described in sections 2 and 3 assume that the interactions among the observed variables can be decomposed into the desired structures.  It is often the case that decomposition is hindered when some variables remain unobserved or *hidden,* in which case the task is to postulate the existence of such variables and identify their connections to the observables.  The task of learning mixture distributions [Duda and Hart 1973] has this flavor; we postulate the existence of a hidden variable $W$ such that observed distribution $P(\mathbf{x})$ can be written as sums of products

$$P(x_1, x_2, ..., x_n) = \sum_{j=1}^{\lambda} \prod_{i=1} P(x_i \mid w_j) P(w_j),$$

and attempt to find reasonable estimates of $\lambda$, $P(w_j)$ and $P(x_i \mid w_j)$.  Graphically, such decomposition corresponds to a *star* network, since the visible variables ( the $X_i$'s) are connected star-like to one central hidden variable $W$.

Lazarsfeld [1966] considered star-decomposable distributions where the visible variables are bi-valued and the hidden variable $W$ is permitted to range over $\lambda$ values, $\lambda > 2$.  The identification of $P(x_i \mid w_j)$ requires the solution of $\lambda n + \lambda - 1$ nonlinear equations to find the values of the $\lambda n + \lambda - 1$ independent parameters.  Letting $\lambda = 2^n - 1$ yields a trivial, unconstrained solution, where each value of $W$ corresponds to one entry of the joint distribution function.

To maintain uniformity in the tree, we can postulate several hidden binary variables but insist that they form a treelike structure, i.e., each triplet of leaves forms a star, but the central variables may differ from triplet to triplet.

**Definition:** We shall say that a distribution $P(x_1, x_2, ..., x_n)$ is *tree-decomposable* if it is the marginal probability of a tree-dependent distribution

$$P_T(x_1, x_2, ..., x_n, w_1, w_2, ..., w_m) \qquad m \leq n-2,$$

such that $W_1, W_2, ..., W_m$ correspond to the internal nodes of a tree $T$ and $X_1, X_2, ..., X_n$ correspond to its leaves.  We say that $P_T$ is a *tree-extension* of $P$, and $P$ is the *leaf-marginal* of $P_T$.  $P_T$ is said to be a *minimal* tree-extension of $P$ if no variable or link can be deleted from the tree $T$ without $P_T$ ceasing to be a tree-extension of $P$.  In the example of Figure 1, $P(x_1, x_3, x_4, x_6)$ is tree-decomposable, with $P(x_1, x_2, x_3, x_4, x_5, x_6)$ as its tree-extension.

Given a tree-decomposable distribution $P(x_1, ..., x_n)$, we ask if it is possible to find any minimal extension $P_T(x_1, ..., x_n, w_1, ..., w_m)$ of $P$.

**Theorem 5:** *If all variables are either bi-valued or normal, then (1) the minimal tree-extension $P_T$ is unique up to renaming of the variables or their values, (2) $P_T$ can be recovered from $P$ using $n \log n$ computations, and (3) the structure of $T$ is uniquely determined by the second-order* *probabilities of P .*

The method of constructing $P_T$ [Pearl and Tarsi 1986] is based on the observation that every four leaves in a tree are interconnected in one of four distinct topologies, depending on which pairs can be connected via non-intersecting paths (see Figure 3). Moreover, each of the

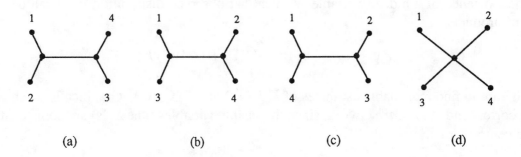

Figure 3.

four topologies is characterized by a unique equality among the leaves' correlation coefficients, which can be determined empirically. For example, the topology

is characterized by the equation $\rho_{ij}\rho_{kl} = \rho_{ik}\rho_{jl}$.

This method of constructing a tree-extension has two major shortcomings: it requires precise knowledge of the correlation coefficients, and it works only when the underlying model is tree-decomposable. In practice, we often have only sample estimates of the correlation coefficients; therefore, it is important to find a tree-structured *approximation* for a distribution that is not tree-decomposable. Unfortunately, no method is known which provides a guarantee on the quality of such an approximation.

## 5. IDENTIFYING TREE STRUCTURES IN CATEGORICAL RELATIONS

Let $\rho$ denote an n-ary relation over the set of attributes $U = \{X_1, \ldots, X_n\}$, i.e., a subset of the Cartesean product $Dom(X_1) \times, \ldots, \times Dom(X_n)$, where $Dom(X_i)$ is the set of values of attribute $X_i$. Let $\rho_S$ denote the projection of $\rho$ on a subset $S$ of attributes, namely, $\rho_S$ is obtained from $\rho$ by striking out columns corresponding to attributes $U - S$ and removing duplicate tuples in what remains. Given an attribute $A$ and an element of its domain $a$, the **restriction of** $\rho$ **to**

$A = a$, denoted by $\rho^{r\,(A=a)}$, is the n-ary relation containing all n-tuples in $\rho$ having value $a$ for $A$. Similarly, the restriction of $\rho$ to a subtuple $t = (X_{i1} = x_{i1}, \ldots, X_{ir} = x_{ir})$, denoted by $\rho^{r\,(t)}$ is all the n-tuples of $\rho$ that match $t$ for the corresponding attributes.

**Definition:** Let $S_1, S_2, S_3$ be subsets of $U$. $S_1$ and $S_2$ are *conditionally independent* given $S_3$, denoted by $<S_1 \mid S_3 \mid S_2>$, if for every combination of values for attributes in $S_3$, denoted by $S_3 = s_3$, we have

$$L^{r\,(S_3 = s_3)} = (L_{S_1 S_3})^{r\,(S_3 = s_3)} \times (L_{S_2 S_3})^{r\,(S_3 = s_3)},$$

where

$$L = \rho_{S_1 S_2 S_3}.$$

Conditional independence parallels the notion of Embedded-Multi-Valued-Dependencies (EMVDs) [Maier 1983]. That is, if $<S_1 \mid S_3 \mid S_2>$, holds in a relation $\rho$, and $S_1 = U - S_3 S_2$, then $\rho$ can be decomposed losslessly into the database scheme $S_1 S_3$ and $S_2 S_3$. A relation is said to be *tree-decomposable* if it can be decomposed losslessly into a tree of binary relations (also known as *constraint-tree*). For example, the constraint-tree shown in Figure 4 (together with the binary relations on its arcs) represents a lossless decomposition of the relation given in Figure 5. This can be verified by enumerating the 5-tuples that satisfy all the binary relations in Figure 4, and comparing to those listed in the table of Figure 5. The computational advantages of constraint-tree representations are that they permit queries of enumeration, extension and entailment to be answered in polynomial time.

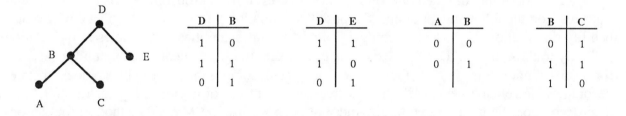

| D | B |
|---|---|
| 1 | 0 |
| 1 | 1 |
| 0 | 1 |

| D | E |
|---|---|
| 1 | 1 |
| 1 | 0 |
| 0 | 1 |

| A | B |
|---|---|
| 0 | 0 |
| 0 | 1 |

| B | C |
|---|---|
| 0 | 1 |
| 1 | 1 |
| 1 | 0 |

Figure 4.

| A | B | C | D | E |
|---|---|---|---|---|
| 0 | 0 | 1 | 1 | 1 |
| 0 | 0 | 1 | 1 | 0 |
| 0 | 1 | 1 | 1 | 1 |
| 0 | 1 | 1 | 1 | 0 |
| 0 | 1 | 1 | 0 | 1 |
| 0 | 1 | 0 | 1 | 1 |
| 0 | 1 | 0 | 1 | 0 |
| 0 | 1 | 0 | 0 | 1 |

Figure 5.

A constraint graph (or network), representing a relation, explicates some of its conditional independencies. In a graph, $S_2$ is said to **separate** $S_1$ from $S_3$ if by removing the nodes in $S_2$, nodes in $S_1$ are disconnected from nodes in $S_3$. Every **separation** in the constraint graph corresponds to a conditional independence, i.e., if a subset $S_1$ separates (in the constraint graph) subset $S_2$ from $S_3$ then $<S_2 \mid S_1 \mid S_3>$. However, there may be conditional independencies in the relation which are not manifested in the constraint graph. For a detailed discussion of conditional-independencies and their graphical representation see [Pearl and Paz 1986; Pearl 1988]. Constraint networks are discussed in [Montanari 1974] and [Dechter and Pearl 1987].

The possibility of extending Chow and Liu's result from probabilities to categorical relations rests on the following questions. Suppose that a relation $\rho$ is associated with a uniform probability distribution, $U_\rho$, which accords equal non-zero probabilities to all tuples in the relation and only to those tuples. Does the existence of an exact tree-dependent distribution for this uniform distribution imply that the relation is tree-decomposable? Moreover, does a tree-decomposable relation necessarily have a tree-dependent uniform probability distribution? Are they decomposable by the same tree? And if so, can we use the MWST method to find an optimal tree-decomposable approximation to a given relation? These questions were analyzed in [Dechter 1987]; the answers were shown to be in the affirmative for exact decompositions but remain unsettled for approximations.

**Theorem 6:** *If a probability distribution $P$ is tree-dependent along a tree $T$, then the relation defined by the possible tuples of $P$ ($P > 0$) has a lossless decomposition by the same tree.*

**Theorem 7:** *For any relation $\rho$, if $\rho$ can be decomposed losslessly into some tree $T$, then its associated uniform distribution, $U_\rho$, is tree-dependent along $T$.*

Thus, applying the MWST to $U_\rho$, we obtain the following theorem.

**Theorem 8:** *Let* $n(x_i)$ *be the number of n-tuples in* $\rho$ *for which* $X_i = x_i$, *and let* $n(x_i, x_j)$ *be the number of n-tuples in* $\rho$ *for which* $X_i = x_i$ *and* $X_j = x_j$. The MWST algorithm using the arc-weights:

$$m(X_i, X_j) = \frac{1}{|\rho|} \sum_{(x_i, x_j) \in \rho_{X_i X_j}} n(x_i, x_j) \log \frac{n(x_i, x_j)}{n(x_i) n(x_j)} \tag{7}$$

is guaranteed to produce a tree-decomposition to $\rho$ if such a decomposition exists.

The following algorithm takes a relation $\rho$ and returns a set of tree-structured binary relations, which are guaranteed to be lossless if the relation is tree-decomposable.

**Tree-generation-algorithm**

a. Compute the basic quantities: $n(x_i)$ and $n(x_i, x_j)$.

b. For every two attributes $X_i$, $X_j$ compute the weights $m(X_i, X_j)$ given in Eq. (7).

c. Find a **maximum weight spanning tree** of the complete graph w.r.t. the above arc-weights.

d. For each pair of attributes that corresponds to an arc in the selected tree find the associated relation by projecting the global relation on it.

The complexity of the algorithm is $O((l + \log n)n^2)$, where $n$ is the number of attributes and $l$ is the size of the relation. To verify that the generated tree represents the input relation, we compute (in linear time) the number of n-tuples represented by the tree-decomposition and compare it to the size of the given relation. If the two numbers are equal, the database losslessly represents the relation. Otherwise, we know that no tree representation exists.

When no tree-decomposition exists, the algorithm produces a decomposition which is not lossless but can be regarded as an approximation to $\rho$. The decomposition algorithm, when applied to $U_\rho$, finds $T$ such that the projection of $U_\rho$ on $T$ is the best approximation to $U_\rho$, with respect to the proximity measure of Eq. (2). However, it is not clear how this proximity measure translates into meaningful merit criteria for relations, such as the number of tuples in the approximating relation. Experiments show [Dechter 1987] that the MWST provides a very tight approximation whenever the relation $\rho$ is expressible as a network of binary constraints, tighter than any other known method of tree-decomposition. We also know that the tree produced by the MWST method is the smallest possible whenever the relation defined by joining all pair-wise projections of $\rho$ (so-called the *minimal network of* $\rho$ ) is tree-decomposable. However, whether this tree is the most specific one in the general case (i.e., whether it does not properly contain another tree-decomposable superset of $\rho$), remains an open problem. A non-numeric method of identifying tree-decompositions is developed in [Dechter, Meiri & Pearl 1989].

## 6. IDENTIFIABILITY VS. LEARNABILITY

The main difference between the problems described in this paper and those addressed by Valiant's model of learning is that in the latter we are given the concept class $C$ and our concern is to infer which individual member of $C$ is responsible for the observed instances. By contrast, in structure learning we are not given the concept class $C$. Rather, our main concern is to decide whether a fully observed concept, taken from some broad class $C'$ (e.g., all categorical relations), is also a member of a narrower class $C$ of concepts, one that possesses some desirable syntactical features (e.g., constraint-trees). Thus, the task is not to identify the semantic extension of a concept (this is assumed to be directly observed), but to identify its syntactical description.

It turns out that casting a concept in a convenient description requires more than clever syntactic manipulations. The feasibility of finding such a description rests heavily on the nature of the dependencies among the components of the concept (e.g., the attributes or the predicates), and these dependencies must be uncovered from the semantic extension of the concept. Moreover, finding a desirable description to a given concept, even when it is feasible and even when the concept is of small size, might require insurmountable computation; a problem not normally addressed in traditional models of learning.

To cast these considerations in a general formal framework, we define the notion of *Identifiability*, and contrast it with that of *Learnability*.

**Definition: (Identifiability)** A class of concepts $C$ is said to be identifiable relative to a background class $C'$, iff:

(1)    (Recognition) For every set $I$ of instances, representing a concept in $C'$, there is an algorithm $A$, polynomial in $|I|$, that determines if $I$ is a member of $C$, and

(2)    (Isolation) If the answer to (1) is positive, $A$ finds one member of $C$ that matches $I$.

**Definition: (Strong Identifiability)** Same as (1) and (2) above, with the addition of:

(3)    (Specificity) If the answer to (1) is negative, the algorithm finds a *minimal* concept $c_0$ in $C$ that contains $I$, i.e., $I \subset c_0$, and there is no $c \in C$ such that $I \subset c \subset c_0$.

By convention, a class in which the recognition or isolation tasks are NP-hard will be defined as non-identifiable. Moreover, the concept size $|I|$ should measure the overall code length used in the description of $I$, not merely the number of instances in $I$.

### EXAMPLES

1.    (**Constraint networks**) Let $C'$ be the set of all relations on $n$ attributes. The class

$C_N (\subset C')$ of relations expressible by *binary networks* of constraints is not identifiable. Although we have algorithms for meeting requirement (3) (and hence (2)) of constructing the most specific network (so called minimal network) for any given relation $I$, we do not have an effective way of testing whether the minimal network represents the relation $I$ exactly, or a superset thereof. Even generating a single instance of the minimal network might be an NP-complete problem, if the attributes are non-binary.

2. If the background class $C'$ is known in advance to consist of only relations that are expressible by binary constraint networks (i.e., $C' = C_N$), then it is possible to identify such a network in time linear in the number of instances. Thus, $C_N$ is strongly identifiable relative to itself. Under this condition it is also learnable, being a variant of $k-CNF$.

3. In general, if we set $C' = C$, then, if $C$ is learnable it must also be strongly identifiable, because condition (1) is satisfied automatically, and the learnability requirement of zero error on negative examples is equivalent to (3). (Note that since the learner is entitled to observe the entire concept, the second learnability requirement of limited generalization errors plays no role in identifiability tasks.) However, there are concept classes that are identifiable but not learnable under the condition $C' = C$, a trivial example of which is the set of subsets having size $|I| = k$. A more significant example is described next.

4. **(Constraint Trees)** The class $C_T (= C')$ of *constraint-trees* is identifiable but not learnable. The MWST algorithm (discussed in Section 5) correctly identifies a tree that represents the instances. Yet, $C_T$ is not learnable because it is not closed under intersection, i.e., there is no unique, most specific tree that captures every subset of instances drawn from a tree.

5. Section 5 shows that the class of constraint-trees is identifiable also relative to the background class of *all* relations. However, it is still an open question whether this class is strongly identifiable; we were not able to prove (or disprove) that, when the minimal network is not tree-decomposable, the MWST method still returns a minimal tree.

6. **(Constraint Chains)** The class $C_C (= C')$ of *constraint chains* is not learnable nor identifiable. The reason being that, since chains are not matroids, we do not have a greedy algorithm similar to the MWST for identifying the correct ordering of the variables.

7. **(Partial Orders)** Let $C (= C')$ be the class of all partial orders on $n$ objects. $C$ is known to be learnable (hence identifiable). However, if $C (= C')$ is the class of partial orders representable by a tree then it is not learnable but strongly identifiable (even if we

let $C'$ extend to the class of all partial orders). [*]

8.     **(Rooted Trees)** Let $C'$ be all subsets of ordered triples $(x, y, z)$ taken from a collection of $n$ objects, and let each member $c$ of $C$ be the set of triplets $(x, y, z)$ generated by a rooted tree with $n$ leaves, such that $(x, y, z)$ is in $c$ iff the deepest common ancestor of $x$ and $y$ is also the deepest common ancestor of $x$ and $z$. $C$ is strongly identifiable in $O(n \ logn)$ time (see Pearl and Tarsi, 1985).

## CONCLUSIONS

This paper summarizes several investigations into the prospects of identifying meaningful structures in empirical data. The central theme is to identify the topology of a tree of dependencies, in cases where the observed data possess such dependencies. Starting with an early work of Chow and Liu [1968] on identifying the best tree-dependent approximation to a given probability distribution, we extend the method to polytrees (directed trees with arbitrary edge orientation) and show that, under certain conditions, the skeleton of the polytree as well as the orientation of some of the arrows, are identifiable. We next address the problem of identifying probabilistic trees in which some of the nodes are unobservable. It is shown that such trees can be effectively identified in cases where all variables are either bi-valued or normal, and where all correlation coefficients are known precisely. Finding the best tree approximation to data that does not lend itself to precise tree representation (with hidden variables) remains an open problem. Finally, extending the task from probabilistic to categorical data, it is shown that an effective procedure exists for determining whether a given relation is decomposable into a tree of binary relations and, if the answer is positive, identifying the topology of such a tree. The procedure runs in time proportional to the size of the relation and can be used to provide an approximate, representation to a set of observed tuples, which is economical in both storage space and query processing time.

The task of finding a desirable description for a concept has been given a formal definition through the notion of identifiability, which is normally weaker (if $C' = C$) than that of learnability. Possibly due to their matroid properties, constraint-trees (as well as probabilistic trees) were found to be one of the very few useful structures which is identifiable yet not learnable.

### Acknowledgements

We thank Othar Hansson, Itay Meiri and Amir Weinshtain for useful discussions on the notion of identifiability.

---

(*) This example is due to Othar Hansson.

# References

C. K. Chow, & C.N. Liu. Approximating Discrete Probability Distributions with Dependence Trees. *IEEE Trans. on Info. Theory,* IT-l4:462-67 (1968)

C.K. Chow & T.J. Wagner. Consistency of an Estimate of Tree-dependent Probability Distributions. *IEEE Trans. on Info. Theory,* IT-l9:369-71 (1973)

R. Dechter. Decomposing a Relation into a Tree of Binary Relations. In *Proceedings,* 6th Conf. on Princ. of Database Systems, San Diego, CA., pp. 185-189 (March 1987). To appear in *Journal of Computer and System Science,* Special Issue on the Theory of Relational Databases.

R. Dechter & J. Pearl. Network-Based Heuristics for Constraint-Satisfaction Problems. *Artificial Intelligence,* Vol. 34(1), pp. 1-38 December (1987)

R. Dechter, I. Meiri & J. Pearl. On the Identifiability of Binary Relations. UCLA Cognitive Systems Laboratory, *Technical Report, (R-140).* In preparation (1989)

R.O. Duda & P.E. Hart. *Pattern Recognition and Scene Analysis.* New York: Wiley (1973)

C. Glymour, R. Scheines, P. Spirtes, & K. Kelly. *Discovering Causal Structure.* New York: Academic Press (1987)

P.D. Laird. Efficient Unsupervised Learning. In *Proceedings,* 1988 Workshop on Computational Learning Theory, Haussler and Pitt (eds), San Mateo: Morgan Kaufmann, pp. 297-311 (1988)

P.F. Lazarsfeld, P.F. Latent Structure Analysis. In *Measurement and Prediction,* ed. S.A. Stouffer, L. Guttman, E.A. Suchman, P.F. Lazarsfeld, S.A. Star, and J.A. Claussen. New York: Wiley (1966)

D. Maier. *The Theory of Relational Databases,* Rockville, Maryland: Computer Science Press (1983)

U. Montanari. Networks of Constraints, Fundamental Properties and Applications to Picture Processing. *Information Science* Vol 7:95-132 (1974)

J. Pearl. *Probabilistic Reasoning in Intelligent Systems: Networks of Plausible Inference,* San Mateo: Morgan Kaufmann Publishers (1988)

J. Pearl & A. Paz. On the Logic of Representing Dependencies by Graphs. In *Proceedings,* 1986 Canadian AI Conference, Montreal, Canada, pp. 94-98 (1986)

J. Pearl & M. Tarsi. Structuring Causal Trees. *Journal of Complexity* Vol. 2(1):60-77 (1986)

G. Rebane & J. Pearl.  The Recovery of Causal Poly-trees from Statistical Data. *Proceedings, 3rd Workshop on Uncertainty in AI,* Seattle, Washington, pp. 222-228 (1987)

L.G. Valiant.  A Theory of the Learnable.  *Communications of the ACM,* Vol. 27(11):1134-1142, November (1984)

# A Statistical Approach to Learning and Generalization

# in Layered Neural Networks

*Esther Levin  and  Naftali Tishby*

AT&T Bell Laboratories, Murray Hill, NJ 07974

*Sara A. Solla*

AT&T Bell Laboratories, Holmdel, NJ 07733

## Abstract

This paper presents a general statistical description of the problem of learning from examples. Our focus is learning in layered networks, which is posed as an optimization problem: a search in the network parameter space for a network that minimizes an additive error function of the statistically independent examples. By imposing the equivalence of the minimum error and maximum likelihood criteria for training the network, we arrive at the Gibbs distribution on the ensemble of networks with fixed architecture. The probability of correct prediction of a novel example is used as a measure of the generalization ability of the trained network. The entropy of the prediction distribution is shown to be the relevant measure of network's performance, and is derived directly from the statistical properties of the ensemble. This can be viewed as a link between the information-theoretic model-order-estimation techniques, particularly the predictive Minimum Description Length, and the statistical mechanical properties of neural networks. As important theoretical applications of the proposed formalism we discuss optimal training strategies and asymptotic learning curves, i.e the generalization ability as a function of the number of examples.

## 1.  Introduction

Layered neural networks are nonlinear parametric models that can approximate any continuous input-output relation.[1] [2] [3] The quality of the approximation depends on the architecture of the network used, as well as on the complexity of the modeled relation. The problem of finding a suitable set of parameters that approximate an unknown relation $F$ is usually solved using supervised learning algorithms. Supervised learning requires a training set: a finite set of examples, i.e. input-output pairs related through the relation $F$, as formalized by Valiant.[4] Learning the training set is often posed as an optimization problem by introducing an error function. This error is a function of the training set as well as of the network parameters, and it measures the quality of the network's approximation to the relation $F$ on the restricted domain covered by the training set. The minimization of this error function over the network's parameter space is called the learning process.

In this work we focus on a statistical description of the learning process. By imposing the consistency condition that the error minimization is equivalent to a likelihood maximization - a standard procedure in statistical modeling - we arrive at the Gibbs distribution on the configuration space for a canonical ensemble[5] of networks with fixed architecture. This distribution is interpreted as the post-training distribution, where the probability of arriving at a specific network decreases exponentially with the error of the network on the training set. The imposed consistency condition leaves only one free parameter for the training process: the error sensitivity, which determines the level of acceptable training error. The normalization constant of the Gibbs distribution (i.e. the partition function) measures the weighted volume of the configuration space of trained networks. Using the resulting statistical formulation we show the following: a) Training on an additional example reduces the weighted volume of configuration space. b) The average post-training error and the weighted volume of configuration space are both decreasing functions of the error sensitivity. c) The information gained by the training process, as measured by the Kullback- Leibler distance between the post-training and the prior probability distributions over the configuration space, is a function of the weighted volume and the value of the average post-training error.

This learning process selects network configurations that perform well on the restricted domain defined by the training set examples. Various authors[6] [7] [8] have shown that there is often little connection between the training error, restricted to the training set, and the network's ability to generalize outside of the training set. It is generally possible to get increasingly better performance on the training set by increasing the complexity of the model, but such procedure does not necessarily lead to a better generalization ability. Using the post-training distribution and the likelihood that results from the consistency condition, we are now able to express the probability of predicting a new independent example. We show that this prediction probability induces a consistent measure of generalization, which can be viewed as an application to layered networks of the predictive minimum description length method (PMDL) as proposed by Rissanen.[9]

The problem of estimating the sufficient training set size for learning with layered networks has been previously discussed[10] in a distribution free, worst case analysis. Our work is a step towards a typical case theory of generalization with layered networks. Though the general principles described in this work can be applied to a wider class of parametric models, they are of special interest in the context of statistical mechanics of 'neural networks'.

## 1.1 Layered networks

We would like to 'learn', or model, an input-output relation $F$ by a feed-forward layered network, consisting of $L$ layers of processing. The architecture is fixed and determined by the number $\{N_l, 0 \leq l \leq L\}$ of processing elements per layer. The elements of the $l+1$-th layer are connected to the previous layer and their state is determined through the recursion relation

$$
\begin{cases}
u_i^{(l+1)} = \displaystyle\sum_{j=1}^{N_l} w_{ij}^{(l+1)} \, v_j^{(l)} + w_i^{(l+1)} \\[2mm]
v_i^{(l+1)} = h\,(u_i^{(l+1)}) \quad , \quad 1 \leq i \leq N_{l+1} \ .
\end{cases}
\tag{1}
$$

The input to the the $i^{th}$ element of the $l^{th}$ layer $u_i^{(l)}$ determines the state $v_i^{(l)}$ of the element, through a sigmoid nonlinearity, such as $h(x) = 1/(1+\exp(-x))$. The parameters of the network are the connections $\{w_{ij}^{(l)}, 1 \leq j \leq N_{l-1}, 1 \leq i \leq N_l, 1 \leq l \leq L\}$ and the biases $\{w_i^{(l)}, 1 \leq i \leq N_l, 1 \leq l \leq L\}$, corresponding to a point $\omega$ in the $D = \displaystyle\sum_{l=1}^{L} N_l(N_{l-1}+1)$ dimensional Euclidean space, $R^D$. For every point $\omega$ in the *network configuration space*, $W \subset R^D$, the network (1) is a realization of a mapping from an input $x \in X \subset R^p$ and an output $y \in Y \subset R^q$, provided that $N_0 = p$ and $N_L = q$. We denote this mapping by $y = F_\omega(x)$, or by the set of pairs $F_\omega = \{\xi \mid \xi = (x, F_\omega(x))\}$. In what follows we discuss the ensemble of all networks in the configuration space $W$.

We focus on the problem of learning an unknown input-output relation $F$ from examples: a training set of $m$ input-output pairs, related through the unknown relation $F$, $\xi^{(m)} \equiv \{\xi_i, 1 \leq i \leq m\}$, where $\xi \equiv (x, y)$, $x \in X \subset R^p$, and $y \in Y \subset R^q$. The relation $F$ can be generally described by the probability density function defined over the space of input-output pairs $X \otimes Y \subset R^{p+q}$: $P_F(\xi) = P_F(x)P_F(y \mid x)$, where $P_F(x)$ defines the region of interest in the input space and $P_F(y \mid x)$ describes the functional or the statistical relation between the inputs and the outputs. The training set consists of examples drawn independently according to this probability density function. Learning the training set by a layered network is posed as an optimization problem by introducing a measure of quality of the approximation of the desired relation $F$ by the mapping $F_\omega$ realized by the network. The additive error function

$$
E^{(m)}(\omega) \equiv E(\xi^{(m)} \mid \omega) = \sum_{i=1}^{m} e(\xi_i \mid \omega) \ ,
\tag{2}
$$

measures the dissimilarity between $F$ and $F_\omega(x)$ on the restricted domain covered by the training set. The error function $e(\xi \mid \omega)$ is often a distance measure on $R^q$ between the target output $y$, and the output of the network on the given input $x$, i.e. $e(\xi \mid \omega) = d(y, F_\omega(x))$.

## 2.  Probability inference in the network space

### 2.1  Consistency between minimum error and maximum likelihood

Our first goal is to introduce a statistical description of the training process. The statistical modeling problem is usually posed as finding a model that maximize the likelihood of the training set:

$$\operatorname*{Max}_{\omega \in W} P(\xi^{(m)} \mid \omega) = \operatorname*{Max}_{\omega \in W} \prod_{i=1}^{m} p(\xi_i \mid \omega) \ . \tag{3}$$

Our primary requirement, which we consider as a consistency condition, is that this maximization of likelihood be equivalent to the minimization of the additive error (2), for *every* set of independent training points $\xi^{(m)}$.

To achieve this we need to infer probabilities on the events $\xi \mid \omega$, which should be multiplicative for independent examples. If such probabilities $p(\xi \mid \omega)$ exist,[11] we can alternatively train the network by maximizing the likelihood (3). The only way that these two optimization criteria can be equivalent, is if they are directly related through an arbitrary monotonic and smooth function $\phi$, namely,

$$\prod_{i=1}^{m} p(\xi_i \mid \omega) = \phi(\sum_{i=1}^{m} e(\xi_i \mid \omega)) \ , \tag{4}$$

assuming that the derivatives w.r.t $\omega$ vanish at the extremal points of both the likelihood and the error.

This equation, however, puts a strong constraint on the possible form of $p(\xi \mid \omega)$.[12] For a smooth positive error function $e(\xi \mid \omega)$, the only solution to the functional equation (4) is given by[13]

$$p(\xi \mid \omega) = \frac{1}{z(\beta)} \exp[-\beta e(\xi \mid \omega)] \tag{5}$$
$$z(\beta) = \int_{X \otimes Y} \exp[-\beta e(\xi \mid \omega)] d\xi \ ,$$

where $\beta$ is a positive constant which determines the sensitivity of the probability $p(\xi \mid \omega)$ to the error value. The mean error $\overline{e} = \int e(\xi \mid \omega) p(\xi \mid \omega) d\xi$, is a measure of the *acceptable error level,* and is related to $\beta$ through

$$\overline{e} = -\frac{\partial \log z}{\partial \beta} \ ; \ \frac{\partial \overline{e}}{\partial \beta} < 0 \ . \tag{6}$$

We assume that the normalization constant $z(\beta)$, or equivalently the mean error $\overline{e}$, is not an explicit function of the specific network $\omega$. This assumption is justified considering that the integration in (5) is performed over all possible input-output pairs, and is rigorously correct if the error is invariant under translations in the range $Y$.

An important example is the case of a quadratic error function in the range $Y$, $e(x,y \mid \omega) = (y - F_\omega(x))^2$. The resulting $p(y \mid x, \omega)$ is a Gaussian distribution,

$$p(y \mid x, \omega) = (2\pi\sigma^2)^{-\frac{1}{2}} \exp[-(y - F_\omega(x))^2 / (2\sigma^2)] \ ,$$

with $\beta = 1/(2\sigma^2)$. Then $z(\beta) = \sqrt{\dfrac{\pi}{\beta}}$, and $\bar{e} = \sigma^2$, both independent of the network $\omega$.

## 2.2  The Gibbs distribution

We henceforth consider the input-output examples to be random samples from the distribution $P_F(\xi)$. For a given network configuration $\omega$, the likelihood (3) that the set of examples $\xi^{(m)}$ are compatible with the network $\omega$, i.e. $\xi_i \in F_\omega$ , $1 \le i \le m$, is given by

$$P(\xi^{(m)} \mid \omega) = \prod_{i=1}^{m} p(\xi_i \mid \omega) = \frac{1}{z^m} \exp[-\beta \sum_{i=1}^{m} e(\xi_i \mid \omega)] \ , \tag{7}$$

as follows from (5).

The conditional distribution (7) can now be inverted using Bayes formula to induce a distribution on the network configuration space $W$ given the set of input-output pairs $\xi^{(m)}$,

$$\rho^{(m)}(\omega) \equiv P(\omega \mid \xi^{(m)}) = \frac{\rho^{(0)}(\omega)\, P(\xi^{(m)} \mid \omega)}{\int\limits_{W} \rho^{(0)}(\omega)\, P(\xi^{(m)} \mid \omega)\, d\omega} \ , \tag{8}$$

where $\rho^{(0)}$ is a nonsingular *prior* distribution on the configuration space.

By writing Eq. (8) directly in terms of the error function (2) on the training set, $E(\xi^{(m)} \mid \omega)$, we arrive at the "Gibbs canonical distribution" on the ensemble of networks

$$\rho^{(m)}(\omega) = \frac{1}{Z^{(m)}} \rho^{(0)}(\omega)\, \exp[-\beta E^{(m)}(\omega)] \ , \tag{9a}$$

where

$$Z^{(m)}(\beta) = \int\limits_{W} \rho^{(0)}(\omega)\, \exp[-\beta E^{(m)}(\omega)]\, d\omega, \tag{9b}$$

is the error moment generating function (known in statistical mechanics as the partition function) and measures the weighted accessible volume in configuration space. Equation (9) has a clear intuitive meaning as the *post–training* distribution in $W$: the probability of each point $\omega$ is reduced exponentially according to the error of the network on the $m$ examples $\xi^{(m)}$. Though this distribution may appear unlikely for some training processes, it is very natural for stochastic algorithms, such as simulated annealing,[14] which essentially implement the Gibbs distribution in configuration space. It is the only distribution on the configuration space $W$ that directly corresponds to the error minimization.

The reversed argument starting from Eq. (9) suggests the interpretation of $p(\xi \mid \omega)$ in Eq. (5) as the probability that the example $\xi$ was included in the training set leading to the network $\omega$.

In the Gibbs formulation, training on an additional independent example $\xi_{m+1}$, is equivalent to multiplying the distribution $\rho^{(m)}$ by the factor $\exp(-e(\xi_{m+1} \mid \omega))$ and renormalizing, i.e.

$$
\begin{aligned}
Z^{(m+1)} &= \int_{W} \rho^{(0)}(\omega) \exp\left[ -\beta E^{(m)}(\omega) - \beta e(\xi_{m+1} \mid \omega) \right] d\omega \\
&\leq \int_{W} \rho^{(0)}(\omega) \exp\left[ -\beta E^{(m)}(\omega) \right] d\omega = Z^{(m)} \quad .
\end{aligned}
\tag{10}
$$

Training thus results in a reduction of the weighted volume in configuration space, or equivalently, a monotonic increase of the *ensemble free energy* $\beta f \equiv -\log Z^{(m)}$ with the size $m$ of the training set. Note that the only parameter in the post-training distribution $\rho^{(m)}(\omega)$ is $\beta$, or equivalently the average training error

$$
<E^{(m)}> = \int_{W} \rho^{(m)}(\omega) \; E^{(m)}(\omega) \; d\omega = -\frac{\partial \log Z^{(m)}}{\partial \beta} \geq 0 ,
\tag{11}
$$

which we control directly in the training process. The ensemble-variance of the training error is determined from the error through

$$
\frac{\partial <E>}{\partial \beta} = -\frac{\partial^2 \log Z}{\partial \beta^2} = -<(E - <E>)^2> < 0 .
\tag{12}
$$

The average training error is a decreasing function of the sensitivity, as expected.


## 2.3  Information gain and Entropy

The natural measure of "information gain" during the training process is given by the relative-entropy of the ensemble with respect to the prior distribution (Kullback-Leibler distance[15] ), as

$$S^{(m)} \equiv D \left[ \rho^{(m)} \mid \rho^{(0)} \right] = \int_{W} \rho^{(m)}(\omega) \log \frac{\rho^{(m)}(\omega)}{\rho^{(0)}(\omega)} \, d\omega \geq 0 \; . \tag{13}$$

The familiar (thermodynamic) relation

$$S^{(m)} = -\log Z^{(m)} - \beta < E^{(m)} > , \tag{14}$$

indicates that information is gained by reducing the weighted configuration volume $Z^{(m)}$, as well as by reducing the training error $< E^{(m)} >$. In the extreme cases when the final training error vanishes or the sensitivity $\beta$ is zero, the entropy is just the logarithm of the weighted volume, i.e. the free energy. In this sense this formalism generalizes the work of Denker et al [16] to the case of finite average training error. Equation (14) provides another meaning for the parameter $\beta$ as the Lagrange multiplier for the constrained average training error $< E^{(m)} >$ during minimization of the relative-entropy (13). The Gibbs distribution (9) is therefore the minimal relative-entropy distribution subject to the average training error as a constraint, and the inverse of $\beta$ plays the same role as the ensemble temperature in statistical mechanics.[1]

The relative entropy of Eq. (13) is equal to the relative entropy defined in the function-space,[16] because the partitioning of configuration space $W$ into regions implementing specific functions is *sufficient*[15] in the statistical sense.

## 3.  Predictions and generalization

### 3.1  The prediction probability

The learning process selects network configurations that have small error on the restricted domain defined by the training examples. Whether the learning process leads to successful rule extraction, in that the resulting network configurations $\omega$ implement the desired relation $F$, can only be tested through performance on *novel* patterns not belonging to the training set. It is generally possible to get increasingly better performance of the models on the training set, but

---

1.  The usual entropy, $S = -\int_{W} \rho(\omega) \log \rho(\omega) \, d\omega$, is *maximized* by the Gibbs distribution, subject to the $< E^{(m)} >$ constraint.

such procedure does not necessarily lead to better generalization.

The generalization ability is measured by the probability that networks trained on $m$ examples will correctly predict another *independent* input-output pair, drawn from the same probability distribution $P_F(\xi)$. This probability can be calculated using Eqs. (9) and (5),

$$p^{(m)}(\xi) \equiv P(\xi \mid \xi^{(m)}) = \int_W \rho^{(m)}(\omega) p(\xi \mid \omega) d\omega = \frac{Z^{(m+1)}(\xi)}{Z^{(m)} z} , \qquad (15)$$

since $\rho^{(m)}(\omega) = P(\omega \mid \xi^{(m)})$ is the post-training probability of network $\omega$ and $p(\xi \mid \omega)$ is the probability that the new pair $\xi$ is compatible with the network $\omega$. Since $Z^{(m)}$ is a decreasing function of $m$, the *generalization error* $-\log p^{(m)}(\xi)$ follows from Eq. (15) and can be expressed as a free energy derivative

$$-\log p^{(m)} \approx -\frac{\partial \log Z^{(m)}}{\partial m} + \log z . \qquad (16)$$

A reliable estimate of the generalization error requires the prediction of a large number of independent points $\xi^{(T)}$, distributed according to the underlying probability function $P_F(\xi)$. The average generalization error can be shown to be a consistent measure of the generalization ability by using the Gibbs inequality:

$$\frac{-1}{N} \log \prod_{n=1}^{N} p^{(m)}(\xi_n) = \frac{-1}{N} \sum_{n=1}^{N} \log p^{(m)}(\xi_n) \underset{N \to \infty}{\to} <-\log p^{(m)}> \qquad (17)$$

$$\equiv -\int P_F(\xi) \log p^{(m)}(\xi) d\xi \geq -\int P_F(\xi) \log P_F(\xi) d\xi .$$

The maximal generalization ability, or minimal generalization error, is obtained if, and only if, the prediction probability $p^{(m)}(\xi)$ of the trained networks equals $P_F(\xi)$. In that case the trained networks implement the underlying relation $F$.

Another important property of the generalization error $-\log p^{(m)}$ is that it is bounded by the average pre-training and post-training errors on the novel example $\xi$,

$$\beta <e(\xi)>_{\rho^{(m+1)}} \leq -\log p^{(m)}(\xi) - \log z \leq \beta <e(\xi)>_{\rho^{(m)}} , \qquad (18)$$

with equalities iff the two errors are equal. Thus $-\log p^{(m)}$ can be approximated by a simpler and more natural measure of generalization: the average error on examples not in the training set.

The average generalization error $<-\log p^{(m)}>$ has an additional meaning as the average number of bits required to encode a novel example, given a system trained on the $m$ examples. This quantity is directly related to another important concept: the stochastic complexity of the training data.[9] The stochastic complexity is the minimal number of bits needed to describe the given sequence of examples using a particular family of models. The network with minimal generalization error is thus the one that provides maximal compression of the given data. Training networks that minimize the generalization error can be viewed as an application to layered networks of the principle of minimum stochastic complexity, also known as the MDL.[9] The utility of this method for selecting the network's architecture has been demonstrated numerically for the contiguity problem.[17]

## 3.2 Sample and ensemble averages

The partition function and all the quantities derived from it are functions of the random choice of a specific training set, and as such are also random variables. The typical performance of the network must be estimated by averaging these random variables over all possible training sets of fixed size $m$. This averaging often denoted by $\ll \quad \gg$ is done with the *external* measure $P_F(\xi)$ and is different from the ensemble average over the Gibbs measure. The important function from which most interesting quantities are derived is the free energy $-\log Z^{(m)}(\beta)$, as shown in Eqs. (11) and (16). Due to the external nature of $P_F(\xi)$, we can interchange partial derivatives with sample averaging, and the basic problem is reduced to the calculation of the *quenched* average $\ll \log Z(m, \beta) \gg$. This in general very difficult problem has been solved in special cases using the "replica method",[18] [19] a not entirely rigorous method which has become an almost standard tool in the study of random systems in statistical physics. The basic equations of our theoretical framework are thus summarized by

$$\ll \log Z(m, \beta) \gg = \int P_F(\xi^{(m)}) \log Z(\xi^{(m)}, \beta) \, d\xi^{(m)} , \tag{19a}$$

$$\ll <E^{(m)}> \gg = -\frac{\partial \ll \log Z(m, \beta) \gg}{\partial \beta} , \tag{19b}$$

$$\ll -\log p^{(m)} \gg \approx -\frac{\partial \ll \log Z(m, \beta) \gg}{\partial m} + \log z(\beta) , \tag{19c}$$

with $P_F(\xi^{(m)}) \, d\xi^{(m)} = \prod_{i=1}^{m} P_F(\xi_i) \, d\xi_i$.

## 3.2.1 Example: the noisy linear map

The ideas are now illustrated by analyzing a simple example: the linear learning problem. Consider a linear network: the output of the network is given by $F_\omega(x) = \omega^T x$, where $x$ and $\omega$ are $D$-dimensional real column vectors and $\omega^T$ denotes the transpose of $\omega$. The prior on the network configuration space is taken to be a $D$ dimensional symmetric Gaussian distribution, $\rho^{(0)}(\omega) = N(0, R_\omega)$, with $R_\omega = \sigma_\omega^2 \cdot I_D$ , $\sigma_\omega \gg 1$, and $I_D$ is the $D$-dimensional unit matrix.

The examples are generated by a similar linear map corrupted by additive white Gaussian noise: $y = \omega_0^T x + \eta$, where the noise $\eta \sim N(0, \sigma_\eta^2)$. The distribution over the domain $X$ is taken to be also a $D$ dimensional Gaussian, $x \sim N(0, R_x)$ ; $R_x = \sigma_x^2 \cdot I_D$. These two distributions determine the underlying probability distribution of the examples, $P_F(\xi)$.

Learning proceeds using a quadratic error function: $e(y \mid x, \omega) = (y - \omega^T x)^2 = ((\omega - \omega_0)^T x - \eta)^2$.

The average free energy can be calculated (see appendix) for $m > D$ and $\sigma_\omega \gg 1$, and is

$$\ll \log Z(m, \beta) \gg = -D \log \sigma_\omega - \frac{\omega_0^T \omega_0}{2\sigma_\omega^2} - \frac{1}{2} D \log (2\beta \sigma_x^2 m) - \beta m \sigma_\eta^2 + \beta D \sigma_\eta^2 + O(\frac{1}{m}) . (20)$$

The training and generalization errors follow from (19),

$$\ll <E^{(m)}> \gg = \frac{D}{2\beta} + (m - D) \sigma_\eta^2 , \tag{21a}$$

$$\ll -\log p^{(m)} \gg \approx \frac{D}{2m} + \beta \sigma_\eta^2 + \log \sqrt{\frac{\pi}{\beta}} + O(\frac{1}{m^2}) . \tag{21b}$$

It is interesting to note that the optimal $\beta$, i.e. the one that gives minimal generalization error, can be easily determined from Eq. (21b) to be $\beta_o = 1/2\sigma_\eta^2$ (see the quadratic example below Eq. (6)), and is just the $\beta$ corresponding to the level of noise in the examples. For this value of $\beta$ the average generalization error reachs asymptotically its lowest possible value (Eq. (17)), which is the entropy of the noise in the examples. The optimal value $\beta_o$ corresponds to a training error which is simply a constant per training example, Eq. (21a), but not minimal! Reducing the training error by increasing the value of $\beta$ beyond $\beta_o$ *increases* the generalization error, due to an *over fitting* of the model to the noisy data. The asymptotic $D/2m$ decrease of the generalization error is of the form obtained for other learning problems, by Haussler, Littlestone and Warmuth,[20] and Hansel and Sompolinsky.[21]

## 3.3  The role of $\beta$: Training strategies

We have so far treated the parameter $\beta$ as fixed during the training process, but such an assumption is by no means necessary. We can consider several different training strategies, the simplest being training at a constant $\beta$, a value chosen once for all $m$. In this case both the average training error and the generalization error are determined completely by $m$, through Eqs. (19). A more realistic possibility is training at a fixed error. In this case $\beta$ is determined as a Lagrange multiplier by the constrained error, and is now a function $\beta(m)$ of the number of examples. Equation (15) for the prediction probability is no longer exact: it should be modified to include the possible change in $\beta$. The optimal strategy is obtained by adjusting

$\beta(m)$ to minimize the generalization error for each $m$. In the linear example of the preceding section the optimal $\beta$ was found to be independent of $m$, yielding a constant training error per example. However, a variable $\beta$ strategy has been recently shown to give a superior generalization ability for the nonlinear single layer network.[21]

The *optimal* $\beta$ can be calculated solely from the training error, and is determined by the equation

$$-\frac{\partial \ll \log p^{(m)} \gg}{\partial \beta} = \frac{\partial \ll E^{(m)} \gg}{\partial m} + \frac{\partial \log z(\beta)}{\partial \beta} = 0 . \tag{22}$$

At fixed $\beta$, the optimal choice for learning thus corresponds to a constant average training error per example, given by $\bar{e}$ of Eq. (6).

# 4. Asymptotic learning curves in the self-averaging case

The calculation of the sample average free energy for the general layered network is a very hard problem. A useful approximation, introduced by Schwartz et al,[22] becomes valid when the partition function is a 'self-averaging' quantity, namely when the random $Z^{(m)}(\beta)$ converges for large $m$ to a deterministic function. In this case the partition function obeys a simple recursion relation, and the prediction probability can be written as a ratio of two successive moments of a well defined prior distribution. The dependence of the generalization error on the number of examples can be predicted within this approximation.

## 4.1 Generalization densities

The relation $F_\omega$ corresponding to the choice of a particular configuration $\omega$ is described by the probability density function $p(\xi \mid \omega)$ of Eq. (5) it induces in the space of the examples. The ability of this network configuration $\omega$ to represent the desired input-output relation $F$ can be measured by this probability, averaged over the examples distributed according to $P_F(\xi)$. The *average generalization ability* of a network $\omega$ is thus given by

$$g(\omega) \equiv \int P_F(\xi) p(\xi \mid \omega) d\xi . \tag{23}$$

The *generalization density* $\rho^{(m)}(g)$ is defined as the density of networks with generalization ability $g(\omega) = g$,

$$\rho^{(m)}(g) \equiv \int_W \rho^{(m)}(\omega) \, \delta(g(\omega) - g) \, d\omega , \tag{24}$$

where $\delta(x)$ is the Dirac delta function. It is easy to verify that $\rho^{(m)}(g)$ is normalized to 1 for $0 \leq g \leq 1$.

For sufficiently large $m$ the partition function becomes asymptotically independent of the specific sample, $\xi^{(m)}$, and can be replaced by its average,

$$\ll Z^{(m)}(\beta) \gg = \int P_F(\xi^{(m)}) \, Z(\xi^{(m)}, \beta) \, d\xi^{(m)} \,. \tag{25}$$

The corresponding average of the generalization density (24) results in

$$\bar{\rho}^{(m)}(g) \equiv \ll \rho^{(m)}(g) \gg = \frac{z^m}{\ll Z^{(m)}(\beta) \gg} \int_W \rho^{(0)}(\omega) \, [g(\omega)]^m \, \delta(g(\omega) - g) \, d\omega \,, \tag{26}$$

leading to the recursion relation

$$\bar{\rho}^{(m)}(g) = \frac{z}{\ll Z^{(m)}(\beta) \gg} \, g \, \bar{\rho}^{(m-1)}(g) = \frac{z^m}{\ll Z^{(m)}(\beta) \gg} \, g^m \, \rho^{(0)}(g) \,. \tag{27}$$

The density $\rho^{(0)}(g) \equiv \int \rho^{(0)}(\omega) \, \delta(g(\omega) - g) \, d\omega$ is the *prior generalization density*, and contains all the information about the configuration space through $\rho^{(0)}(\omega)$ and about the task (the desired relation $F$) through the definition of $g(\omega)$. The average generalization ability after training with $m$ examples,

$$\bar{g}^{(m)} \equiv \int_0^1 g \, \bar{\rho}^{(m)}(g) \, dg \tag{28}$$

is given by

$$\bar{g}^{(m)} = \frac{\ll Z^{(m+1)}(\beta) \gg}{\ll Z^{(m)}(\beta) \gg z} = p^{(m)} \,, \tag{29}$$

and is simply the average of the prediction probability, Eq. (15). The recursion relation (27) provides an expression for the average prediction probability after training on $m$ examples as a ratio of two successive moments of the prior generalization density $\rho^{(0)}(g)$,

$$p^{(m)} = \frac{<g^{m+1}>_{\rho^{(0)}}}{<g^m>_{\rho^{(0)}}} \,, \tag{30}$$

where

$$<g^m>_{\rho^{(0)}} \equiv \int_0^1 \rho^{(0)}(g) \, g^m \, dg \,. \tag{31}$$

Learning curves, $-\log p^{(m)}$ versus $m$, can thus be obtained simply by calculating the moments of possible prior densities.[17][22]

The asymptotic behavior of the moments ratio, (30), is determined solely by the functional form of $\rho^{(0)}(g)$ near $g=1$. If $\rho^{(0)}(g) \sim (1-g)^d$ as $g \to 1$, for some $d \geq 0$,

$$p^{(m)} \approx 1 - \frac{d+1}{m} \quad ; \quad -\log p^{(m)} \approx \frac{d+1}{m} \, , \tag{32}$$

for large $m$. The asymptotic form (32) is in agreement with the $1/m$ decrease of the generalization error found earlier.[20] This suggests an interesting possible relation between the value of the exponent $d$ and the VC-dimension[23] of the learning system.

### Acknowledgment

Special thanks are due to Neri Merhav for many illuminating discussions, for his help in the calculations of the linear example, and for critically reading the manuscript. Useful discussions with Géza György, Dan Schwartz, Andrew Ogielski, and John Denker are greatly appreciated.

### REFERENCES

1. R. P. Lippmann, "An Introduction to Computing with Neural Nets", ASSP Magazine, 4:2, (1987) 4.

2. G. Cybenko, "Continuous Valued Neural Networks with Two Hidden Layers are Sufficient", Tufts University preprint (1988).

3. B. Giraud, H. Axelrad, L.C. Liu, "Flexibility of One-Layer Neural Models". Saclay preprint, (1988).

4. L.G. Valiant, "A Theory of the Learnable", Comm. ACM 27 (1984) 1134.

5. See for example: L.D. Landau and E.M. Lifshitz, "Course of Theoretical Physics -Vol 5", 3-rd edition, Pergamon (1980).

6. T. Cover,"Geometrical and Statistical Properties of Systems of Linear Inequalities with Applications to Patterns Recognition", IEEE Trans. Elect. Comp., 14 (1965) 326.

7. E.B. Baum, "On the capabilities of multilayer perceptrons", preprint (1988).

8. D. Wolpert, "Alternative Generalization to Neural Nets", preprint (1988).

9. J. Rissanen, "Stochastic Complexity and Modeling", Annals of Statistics, 14:3, (1986) 1080.

10. E.B. Baum and D. Haussler, "What Size Net Gives Valid Generalization", Neural Computation, 1:1, (1989) 151.

11. This probability should be considered as 'reasonable expectation' rather than relative frequency in some sample space. See: R.T. Cox, "Probability, Frequency and Reasonable Expectation", Am. J. Phys., 14: 1 (1946) 1.

12. J. Aczél and Z. Daróczy, "On Measures of Information and Their Characterizations" Academic Press (1975) 16.

13. Y. Tikochinsky, N. Tishby, and R.D. Levine, "Alternative Approach to Maximum Entropy Inference", Phys. Rev. A 30 (1984) 2638.

14. S. Kirkpatrick, C.D. Gelatt, and M.P. Vecchi, "Optimization by Simulated Annealing", Science, 220 (1983) 671.

15. S. Kullback, "Information Theory and Statistics", Wiley, New York (1959).

16. J. Denker, D. Schwartz, B. Wittner, S. Solla, R. Howard, L. Jackel, and J. Hopfield "Large Automatic Learning, Rule Extraction, and Generalization", Complex Systems 1, (1987) 877.

17. N. Tishby, E. Levin, and S.A. Solla, "Consistent Inference of Probabilities in Layered Networks: Predictions and Generalization", in the Proc. of the International Joint Conference on Neural Networks, (IJCNN) 1989.

18. S. Edwards and P.W. Anderson, J. Phys. F 5 (1975) 965.

19. E. Gardner, J. Phys. A21 (1988) 257; E. Gardner and B. Derrida, J. Phys. A21, (1988) 271.

20. D. Haussler, N. Littlestone and M.K. Warmuth, "Predicting {0,1} Functions on Randomly Drawn Points", in the Proc. of COLT'88.

21. D. Hansel and H. Sompolinsky, "Learning from examples in a single layer neural network", Hebrew University preprint (1989).

22. D.B. Schwartz, V.K. Samalam, J.S. Denker, and S.A. Solla, "Exhaustive Learning", GTE - AT&T Bell Labs preprint (1989).

23. see for example: A. Blumer, A. Ehrenfeucht, D. Haussler, and M.K. Warmuth, "Learnability and the Vapnik-Chervonenkis Dimension", UCSC-CRL preprint (1988).

**Appendix:**

We derive Eq. (20), the average free energy for the linear network case. The partition function integral for this case is given by

$$Z^{(m)}(\beta) = \exp[-\beta \sum_{i=1}^{m} \eta_i^2] \int_W d\omega \, (2\pi\sigma_\omega^2)^{-\frac{D}{2}} \tag{A.1}$$

$$\cdot \exp[-\frac{1}{2\sigma_\omega^2}\omega^T\omega - \frac{1}{2}(\omega-\omega_0)^T\Lambda^{-1}(\omega-\omega_0) + 2\beta(\omega-\omega_0)^T(\sum_{i=1}^{m}\eta_i x^i)]$$

$$= \exp[-\beta\sum_{i=1}^{m}\eta_i^2 - \frac{\omega_0^T\omega_0}{2\sigma_\omega^2}] \int_W d\omega\,(2\pi\sigma_\omega^2)^{-\frac{D}{2}}$$

$$\cdot \exp[-\frac{1}{2}(\omega-\omega_0)^T(\Lambda^{-1} + \frac{1}{\sigma_\omega^2}I_D)(\omega-\omega_0) + (\omega-\omega_0)^T(2\beta\sum_{i=1}^{m}\eta_i x^i - \frac{1}{\sigma_\omega^2}\omega_0)] \, ,$$

where the sample covariance matrix, $\Lambda^{-1} \equiv 2\beta\sum_{i=1}^{m} x^i \cdot (x^i)^T$, is nonsingular for $m \geq D$ with probability 1. For $m > D$, and $\sigma_\omega \gg 1$, we can neglect the $1/\sigma_\omega$ terms compared to $O(m)$ terms, i.e. $I_D/\sigma_\omega^2 + \Lambda^{-1} \approx \Lambda^{-1}$ and $-\omega_0/\sigma_\omega^2 + 2\beta\sum_{i=1}^{m}\eta_i x^i \approx 2\beta\sum_{i=1}^{m}\eta_i x^i$, yielding

$$Z^{(m)}(\beta) = \sigma_\omega^{-D}(\det\Lambda)^{\frac{1}{2}} \exp[-\beta\sum_{i=1}^{m}\eta_i^2 - \frac{\omega_0^T\omega_0}{2\sigma_\omega^2} + 2\beta^2(\sum_{i}\eta_i(x^i)^T)\Lambda(\sum_{i}\eta_i x^i)] \tag{A.2}$$

or

$$\log Z^{(m)} = -D\log(\sigma_\omega) + \frac{1}{2}\log\det\Lambda - \beta\sum_{i=1}^{m}\eta_i^2 - \frac{\omega_0^T\omega_0}{2\sigma_\omega^2} + 2\beta^2(\sum_{i}\eta_i(x^i)^T)\Lambda(\sum_{i}\eta_i x^i) \, .$$

Averaging over the noise, $\eta_i$, $i=1, ..., m$, we obtain

$$<\log Z^{(m)}> = -D\log\sigma_\omega - \frac{\omega_0^T\omega_0}{2\sigma_\omega^2} + \frac{1}{2}\log\det\Lambda - \beta m <\eta^2> \tag{A.3}$$

$$+ 2\beta^2 < \sum_{k=1}^{D}\sum_{l=1}^{D}\Lambda_{kl}\sum_{i=1}^{m}\eta_i x_k^i \sum_{j=1}^{m}\eta_j x_l^j > \, ,$$

where $x_k^i$ denotes the $k$-th component of the input vector $x^i$, and $\Lambda_{kl}$ - the $k,l$-th entry of the matrix $\Lambda$. Using the fact that $\eta_i$ and $\eta_j$ are independent for $i\neq j$, the last term becomes

$$2\beta^2 < \sum_{k,l=1}^{D}\Lambda_{kl}\sum_{i=1}^{m}\eta_i x_k^i \sum_{j=1}^{m}\eta_j x_l^j > = 2\beta^2 <\eta^2> \sum_{k,l=1}^{D}\Lambda_{kl}\sum_{i=1}^{m}x_k^i x_l^i \tag{A.4}$$

$$= 2\beta^2\sigma_\eta^2 \sum_{k,l=1}^{D}\Lambda_{kl}\frac{1}{2\beta}\Lambda^{lk} = \beta\sigma_\eta^2 D \, ,$$

where $\Lambda^{lk} \equiv 2\beta\sum_{i=1}^{m}x_k^i x_l^i$ is the $lk$-th entry of the matrix $\Lambda^{-1}$.

Therefore,

$$< \log Z^{(m)} > = -D \log \sigma_\omega - \frac{\omega_0^T \omega_0}{2\sigma_\omega^2} + \frac{1}{2} \log \det \Lambda - \beta m \sigma_\eta^2 + \beta D \sigma_\eta^2 . \qquad (A.5)$$

Proceeding by averaging over the examples $x^i$, $i = 1, \cdots m$,

$$< \log \det \Lambda > = -< \log \det 2\beta \sum_{i=1}^{m} x^i (x^i)^T > = -\log(2\beta m \sigma_x^2) - < \log \det (I_D + \varepsilon^m) > , \qquad (A.6)$$

where $\varepsilon^m \equiv \frac{1}{m\sigma_x^2} \sum_{i=1}^{m} x^i (x^i)^T - I_D$ . The first two moments of $\varepsilon^m$ are given by

$$<\varepsilon_{kl}^m> = 0 ; \quad <\varepsilon_{kl}^m \varepsilon_{pr}^m> = \frac{1}{m} (\delta_{kp} \cdot \delta_{lr} + \delta_{kl} \cdot \delta_{pr}) ,$$

where $\delta_{kl}$ is the Kronecker delta. Expanding $\log \det \Lambda$ to second order in $\varepsilon$, gives

$$< \log \det \Lambda > = -\log(2\beta m \sigma_x^2)^D - \sum_{k,l=1}^{D} \frac{\partial \log \det (X)}{\partial \varepsilon_{kl}^m} \bigg|_{X=I_D} <\varepsilon_{kl}^m > \qquad (A.7)$$

$$+ \frac{1}{2} \sum_{k,l,p,r} \frac{\partial^2 \log \det (X)}{\partial \varepsilon_{kl}^m \partial \varepsilon_{pr}^m} \bigg|_{X=I_D} <\varepsilon_{kl}^m \varepsilon_{pr}^m> + o(\frac{1}{m}) ,$$

yielding the final sample average free energy, Eq. (20)

$$\ll \log Z^{(m)} \gg = -D \log \sigma_\omega - \frac{\omega_0^T \omega_0}{2\sigma_\omega^2} - \frac{1}{2} D \log(2\beta\sigma_x^2 m) - \beta m \sigma_\eta^2 + \beta D \sigma_\eta^2 + O(\frac{1}{m}). \qquad (A.8)$$

# THE LIGHT BULB PROBLEM

## (Extended Abstract)

**Ramamohan Paturi**[1]
Univ. of California, San Diego

**Sanguthevar Rajasekaran**[2]
Univ. of Pennsylvania

**John Reif**[2]
Duke University

## ABSTRACT

In this paper, we consider the problem of correlational learning and present efficient algorithms to determine correlated objects.

## INTRODUCTION

Correlational learning, a subclass of unsupervised learning, aims to identify statistically correlated groups of attributes. In this paper, we consider the following correlational learning problem due to L. G. Valiant [7,8]: We have a sequence of $n$ random light bulbs each of which is either on or off with equal probability at each time step. Further, we know that a certain pair of bulbs is positively correlated. The problem is to find efficient algorithms for recognizing the pair of light bulbs with the maximum correlation.

It is experimentally observed that humans can detect such a correlated pair *quickly* after being exposed to a 'small' number of samples. The motivation for the present problem is the desire to provide an algorithmic explanation for this phenomenon [6,7]. Some preliminary results are reported in Paturi [4].

In this paper, we consider a more general version of the basic light bulb problem. In the general version, we assume that the behavior of the bulbs is governed by some unknown probability distribution. Our goal would be to find the pair of bulbs with the largest pairwise correlation. We then consider the more general problem of $k$–way correlations.

[1] This work was done while the author was at Harvard University in 1985-86 and was supported by the NSF grant MCS-83-02385.

[2] Supported by NSF-DCR-85-03251 and ONR contract N00014-87-K-0310 and AFOSR-87-0386.

Mathematically, we can regard each light bulb $l_i$ at time step $t$ as a random variable $X_i^t$ which takes the values $\pm 1$. We call $(X_1^t, X_2^t, \ldots, X_n^t)$ the $t$-th *sample*. We also assume that the behavior of the light bulbs is independent of their past behavior. In other words, the samples are independent of each other. We would like to find the desired object ($k$–tuples with the maximum correlation) *with high probability*. The complexity measures of interest are sample size and the number of operations to determine the desired object.

Before we proceed further, we introduce some definitions and facts from probability theory.

We define the correlation of a pair of light bulbs $l_i$ and $l_j$ as $\mathbf{P}[X_i = X_j]$. In general, for any $k \geq 2$, the correlation coefficient of the $k$–tuple $(l_{i_1}, l_{i_2}, \ldots, l_{i_k})$ of light bulbs is defined as $\mathbf{P}[X_{i_1} = X_{i_2} = \cdots = X_{i_k}]$.

Let $Y$ be a random event with probability of success $p$. Consider the probability distribution of the number of successes in $k$ independent occurrences of the event $Y$. The following gives bounds for the probability of the tails of this distribution.

$$\mathbf{P}[\text{No. of Successes} < (1 - \delta)pk] \leq e^{-\delta^2 pk/2} \tag{1}$$

$$\mathbf{P}[\text{No. of Successes} > (1 + \delta)pk] \leq \left[\frac{e^\delta}{(1 + \delta)^{(1+\delta)}}\right]^{pk} \tag{2}$$

where $pk$ is the expected number of successes, and $\delta > 0$.

We say that a statement holds *with high probability*, if it holds with probability $1 - n^{-\alpha}$ for some $\alpha > 0$.


## A QUADRATIC–TIME ALGORITHM


We now a present an algorithm called algorithm Q which samples each pair of bulbs for $O(\ln n)$ time to determine the pair with the largest correlation.

Let $S_{ij}^t = |\{1 \leq u \leq t | X_i^u = X_j^u\}|$. In other words, $S_{ij}^t$ is the number of times the bulbs $l_i$ and $l_j$ have identical output when $t$ samples are considered. Let $p_1$ be the largest pairwise correlation and $p_2$ be the second largest correlation. Let $p_2 = p_1(1 - 1/\gamma)$ where $\gamma > 1$. We characterize the performance of our algorithms in terms of the parameter $\gamma$. We can see that the value of $S_{ij}^t$ tends to be larger if the pair $(i, j)$ is more correlated. Hence, if we take a sufficiently large $t$, we can guarantee that the pair $(i, j)$ with the largest $S_{ij}^t$ has the maximum correlation provided $p_1$ and

$p_2$ are sufficiently separated. It can easily be seen that the value of $t$ depends on the correlation $p_1$ and $p_2$ which we may not know *a priori*. To overcome this problem, we check if the largest $S_{ij}^t$ is greater than $O(\gamma^2 \alpha \ln n)$ for any $\alpha \geq 1$. If the largest $S_{ij}$ can be so separated, we declare $(i, j)$ as the correlated pair. Otherwise, we look at the random variables $X_i^{t+1}$ at step $t + 1$ and update $S_{ij}^{t+1}$ and repeat the above computation until we succeed.

Each step of this computation takes $O(n^2)$ operations. The following theorem gives us number of the iterations required.

**Theorem 1** *Algorithm $Q$ terminates when $t = O(\gamma^2 \alpha \ln n / p_1)$ and finds the pair with the maximum correlation with probability $1 - O(n^{-\alpha})$.*

It follows that the above algorithm takes $O(n^2 \ln n)$, where $n^2$ is the number of pairs considered. More generally, given $m$ pairs of random variables, the above algorithm finds the pair with the largest correlation in time $O(m \ln n)$. Can we do better? We now present two different algorithms which take only *subquadratic* time.

# ALGORITHM A

For each $i$ and $t$, we will consider the string $s_i^t = X_i^1 X_i^2 \ldots X_i^t$ as an element of the hypercube $\{-1, 1\}^t$. Consider the sphere of radius $\varepsilon t$ with center $s_i^t$. The volume $V(\varepsilon t)$ of this sphere is at most $\varepsilon t e^{h(\varepsilon)t}$ where $h(\varepsilon) = \varepsilon \ln(1/\varepsilon) + (1 - \varepsilon) \ln(1/(1 - \varepsilon))$ is the entropy function. If $\varepsilon$ and $t$ are selected appropriately, it is unlikely that the spheres corresponding to two different $i$ and $j$ would intersect if the light bulbs $l_i$ and $l_j$ do not have the maximum correlation. On the other hand, the spheres corresponding to the light bulbs with maximum correlation would intersect with high probability. This idea can be implemented as an algorithm with $O(nV(\varepsilon t))$ operations.

We consider the random variables $X_i^1, X_i^2, \ldots X_i^t$ for each $i$. We find a pair with the shortest distance in the $t$–dimensional hypercube by exploring the sphere around each $X_i^1 X_i^2 \ldots X_i^t$. Let $(i, j)$ be such a pair. We check if $S_{ij}^t > O(\ln n)$. If so, we declare $(i, j)$ as the pair with the maximum correlation. Otherwise, we consider the $t + 1$–dimensional hypercube and repeat.

If $p_2 = 1/2$ and $p_1 > 0.89$, we can select $\varepsilon$ to give a subquadratic time algorithm. The following theorem gives the precise condition under which we can get a subquadratic time algorithm.

**Theorem 2** *Let $p_2 = 1/2$. For any $p_1 > 0.89$, there exists an $\alpha > 0$ such that, with probability $1 - O(n^{-\alpha})$, Algorithm A finds the maximally correlated pair in time $O(n^{1+\mu} \ln n)$ for some $\mu < 1$.*

Algorithm A gives a subquadratic algorithm by looking at $O(\ln n)$ samples, only if the maximum correlation is sufficiently high. We now give an algorithm which does not suffer from this disadvantage but uses $O(n^{\varepsilon})$ $(\varepsilon < 1)$ samples. We later use bootstrap technique to reduce the number of samples to $O(\ln n)$.

## ALGORITHM B

To understand this algorithm, consider the special case with $p_1 = 1$. In this case, the problem is reduced to sorting. We want to determine the pair that produced identical outputs. This can be done by sorting the strings $s_i^t = X_i^1 X_i^2 \ldots X_i^t$. With $t = O(\ln n)$, we can identify the desired pair with high probability. The constant involved depends on $p_2$. The total number of operations in this special case is $O(n \ln n)$.

Even in the more general case, we can use the above idea to reduce the number of pairs to be considered. We classify the random variables based on their $s_i^t$. We say that two bulbs $i$ and $j$ fall into the same bucket if $s_i^t = s_j^t$. We consider all the pairs $(i, j)$ for $i$ and $j$ in the same bucket. We select $t$ such that no more than $c$ variables $X_i$ have the same $s_i^t$ for some large enough constant $c$. This ensures that number of pairs to be considered is $O(n)$. On the other hand, if $t$ is not too large, maximally correlated pair falls into same bucket with a sufficiently large probability. If this is repeated for a sufficient number of times, we can find the maximally correlated pair with high probability. In the following, we give the algorithm and a sketch of its analysis.

**Algorithm B:**

> Let $PAIRS$ be the empty list $\emptyset$;
> *for* $i = 1$ *to* $O(n^{\frac{\ln p_1}{\ln p_2}} \ln n)$ *do*
>
>> **(step1)** Take $t = c \ln n$ (for some constant $c$ to be determined later) and obtain the sample vectors $(X_1^j, X_2^j, \ldots, X_n^j)$ for $j = 1, 2, \ldots, t$.
>>
>> **(step2)** Sort the $n$ strings (of length $c \ln n$) $s_i^t = X_i^1 X_i^2 \cdots X_i^t$ for $i = 1, \ldots, n$.
>>
>> **(step3)** For each bucket of bulbs obtained in step 2, consider all possible pairs of bulbs from the bucket. (A bucket is a group of all bulbs with equal value in all the $t$ sample steps). Add any new pairs to the list $PAIRS$.
>
> Using the algorithm Q that checks for correlation of each of the pairs, output the pair with the maximum correlation from among the pairs in PAIRS.

The following theorem gives the time and sample complexity of algorithm B. Let $p_2 = (1 - 1/\gamma)p_1$.

**Theorem 3** *Algorithm B finds the pair with the largest correlation in expected time* $O(c'n^{1+\frac{\ln p_1}{\ln p_2}} \ln^2 n)$ *with probability* $1 - O(n^{-\alpha})$.

**Proof:** For any $i$, the probability that $s_i^t = s_j^t$ is at most $p_2^{(c \ln n)}$ if $(i, j)$ is not the pair with the maximum correlation. Hence, if we select $c = 1/\ln(1/p_2)$, the expected number of bulbs falling into any one bucket is $O(1)$. In each iteration of the outer loop, at most $O(n)$ pairs will be added to the list PAIRS.

With this value of $c$, the probability that the maximum correlated pair falls into the same bucket is $(p_1)^{\ln n / \ln(1/p_2)} = n^{\ln p_1 / \ln(1/p_2)}$. Therefore, if the outer loop of the algorithm B is executed $c'n^{\ln p_1 / \ln p_2} \ln n$ times, then the maximum correlated pair will be included in the list PAIRS with probability $1 - O(n^{-\alpha})$. The constant $c'$ depends on $\alpha$.

Since the expected length of list PAIRS is $O(n^{1+\ln p_1 / \ln p_2} \ln n)$, we find the correct pair with high probability in expected time $O(\gamma^2 \alpha n^{1+\ln p_1 / \ln p_2} \ln^2 n / p_1)$ using the algorithm Q.

## BOOTSTRAP TECHNIQUE

Algorithm B uses a large number ($O(n^{\ln p_1 / \ln p_2})$) of samples. We can reduce the sample size to $O(\log n)$ using the Bootstrap technique [1,2,3].

Assume that we are given a data set (i.e., a random sample of size $d$) $D = \{x_1, x_2, \ldots, x_d\}$ from an unknown distribution, and we want to estimate some statistic, say $\theta$. The idea of bootstrap is to generate a large number of new data sets from $D$ and estimate $\theta$ on each one of the generated data sets to obtain a better estimate of $\theta$. A data set is generated by drawing samples independently with replacement from $D$ with each element in $D$ being equally likely.

We can use this idea of bootstrap in algorithm B. We first make $d \log n$ observations (for some constant $d \geq \gamma$, where $p_2 = p_1(1 - 1/\gamma)$). This sample is then used to generate data sets for step 1 of the algorithm.

The reason why bootstrap works in our case can be explained as follows. The separation between the maximum correlated pair and the second largest correlated pair is preserved in the sample data (with high probability). More precisely, using Chernoff bounds, we can show that the **sample** correlation of the pair with the largest correlation is at least $(1 - \epsilon)p_1$ (for any $\epsilon > \sqrt{\frac{\alpha}{dp_1}}$) with probability $\geq (1 - n^{-\alpha})$ (for any $\alpha > 1$). Also the sample correlation of the pair with the second largest correlation is at the most $(1 + \delta)p_2$ (for any $\delta > \sqrt{\frac{(2+\alpha)}{dp_2}}$) with probability $\geq (1 - n^{-\alpha})$. Therefore the expected run time of the modified algorithm is $O(n^{1 + \frac{\log((1-\epsilon)p_1)}{\log((1+\delta)p_2)}} \ln^2 n)$. The constant will depend on $\gamma$ and $\alpha$.

# $k$–WAY CORRELATION

We can modify the algorithm B to detect a $k$–tuple with the largest $k$–way correlation. The run time of the algorithm would then be $O(n^{k\frac{\log p_1}{\log p_2}+1} \ln^2 n)$ where $p_1$ is the largest $k$–way correlation and $p_2$ is the second largest $k$–way correlation.

Let $t = c \log n$. Algorithm $B_k$ is the same as Algorithm B except that $c$ has to be chosen to equal $k/\ln(1/p_2)$. Also, instead of obtaining pairs in step3, we obtain $k$–tuples here.

Algorithm $B_k$:

$TUPLES = \emptyset$;
*for* $i = 1$ to $O(n^{k \log p_1 / \log p_2} \ln n)$ *do*

(**step1**) Observe the light bulbs for $t = c \log n$ time and obtain the sample vectors $(X_1^j, X_2^j, \ldots, X_n^j)$ for $j = 1, 2, \ldots, t$.

(**step2**) Sort the $n$ numbers ($c \log n$ bits each) $(X_1^1 X_1^2 \ldots X_1^t), (X_2^1 X_2^2 \ldots X_2^t), \ldots, (X_n^1 X_n^2 \ldots X_n^t)$ using radix sort.

(**step3**) Obtain all possible $k$-tuples from out of the bulbs in each bucket of step2. Add these $k$-tuples to $TUPLES$.

Find the $k$–tuple with the maximum correlation using a variant of Algorithm Q.

The analysis of this algorithm is similar to that of Algorithm B. For any $\alpha > 0$, we get that Algorithm $B_k$ finds the $k$–tuple with the largest correlation in $O(n^{k\frac{\log p_1}{\log p_2}+1} \ln^2 n)$ expected time with probability $\geq 1 - n^{-\alpha}$. The constant will depend on $\gamma$ and $\alpha$.

## $k$–WAY CORRELATION FOR ARBITRARY $k$

The algorithm in the previous section has a run time exponential in $k$. Is there a polynomial time algorithm for $k$-WAY CORRELATION for arbitrary $k$? The answer is yes if $O(\ln n)$ sample size suffices to solve the problem. This implies that $p_1$ and $p_2$ should be separated by a constant.

Given that $O(\log n)$ sample size suffices, the problem can be restated as follows. We define the observation matrix $M$ of size $n$ by $t$ to be $M_{ij} = X_i^j$. A row corresponds to a light bulb and a column corresponds to a sample time step. The correlation of any $k$ rows ($k$–tuple) is defined to be the number of identical columns in $M$ when restricted to these $k$ rows. The problem is to find the $k$ rows with the maximum correlation.

The maximum correlated $k$-tuple will have $i$ identical columns and no other $k$-tuple will have greater than $i$ identical columns for some $1 \leq i \leq t$. The algorithm for $k$–WAY CORRELATION for an arbitrary $k$ would exhaustively check if there is a $k$-tuple with $j$ identical columns for $j = 1, 2, \ldots, t$.

Algorithm ARBITRARY $k$-WAY;

> *for* $j = 1, 2, \ldots, t$ *do*
>> *for* each possible choice of $j$ columns (there are $\binom{t}{j}$ choices in all) *do*
>>> Find if there is a $k$-tuple with identical entries in these $j$ columns. This can be done using radix sort of the $n$ ($j$-bit) integers (one corresponding to each row).
>>>
>>> If there is a bucket with $\geq k$ bulbs then it means there are $k$ rows with $j$ identical columns. If so, set $MAXCORR = j$ and register the corresponding bucket in $BUCKET$.
>>
>> Output $MAXCORR$ and a $k$-tuple from $BUCKET$

If $t = c \log n$, clearly, the innerloop will be executed $\sum_{j=1}^{c \log n} \binom{c \log n}{j} = n^c - 1$ times and each execution takes $O(n)$ time. Observe the total run time is independent of $k$. If $t$ were polynomial in $n$, then this algorithm runs in exponential time.

The problem of $k$-WAY CORRELATION becomes harder for large observation lengths. In fact, given the observation matrix the problem of finding the maximum correlated $k$ rows is NP-Hard. We prove this by reducing the clique problem to this problem. Details will appear in the full paper.

OPEN PROBLEM: Can we find an $O(n \ln n)$ algorithm for determining the pair with the maximum correlation?

**Acknowledgments:** We would like to thank Prof. Les Valiant for suggesting this problem and for listening to our solutions.

# References

[1] P. Diaconis, and B. Efron. Computer-Intensive Methods in Statistics. <u>Annals of Statistics</u> (1980).

[2] B. Efron. Bootstrap Methods: Another Look at the Jackknife. <u>Annals of Statistics 7</u> (1979).

[3] B. Efron. The Jacknife, the Bootstrap and Other Resampling Plans. <u>SIAM</u>, Philadelphia, Pennsylvania (1982).

[4] R. Paturi. The Light Bulb Problem. <u>Technical Report CS88–129</u>, University of California, San Diego (1988).

[5] L.G. Valiant. A Theory of the Learnable. <u>CACM 27(11)</u> (1984).

[6] L.G. Valiant. Learning Disjunctions of Conjunctions. <u>Proc. 9th IJCAI</u>, Los Angeles, CA, (1985).

[7] L.G. Valiant. Private Communication (1985).

[8] L. G. Valiant. Functionality in Neural Nets. <u>First Work shop on COLT</u> (1988).

# From On-line to Batch Learning

Nick Littlestone *

Aiken Computation Laboratory, Harvard

Cambridge, MA 02138

### Abstract

We contrast on-line and batch settings for concept learning, and describe an on-line learning model in which no probabilistic assumptions are made. We briefly mention some of our recent results pertaining to on-line learning algorithms developed using this model. We then turn to the main topic, which is an analysis of a conversion to improve the performance of on-line learning algorithms in a batch setting. For the batch setting we use the PAC-learning model. The conversion is straightforward, consisting of running the given on-line algorithm, collecting the hypotheses it uses for making predictions, and then choosing the hypothesis among them that does the best in a subsequent hypothesis testing phase. We have developed an analysis, using a version of Chernoff bounds applied to supermartingales, that shows that for some target classes the converted algorithm will be asymptotically optimal.

## 1  Introduction

We consider the task of learning concepts from examples, which we take to be one of learning to classify instances into two categories, depending on whether or not they are examples of some target concept. Among settings in which this type of learning takes place one can distinguish two that we wish to focus on. We refer to these as *batch* and *on-line* settings. In the batch setting there are separate training and working phases. During the training phase the learner is given a sequence of instances together with their correct classifications. The learner is not required to produce any output until the end of the training phase, at which time the learner outputs a classification rule. This rule is used to classify instances during the working phase. During the working phase, correct classifications are not supplied to the learner, and no further learning takes place. This setting is natural if, for example, training takes place in a school or, for machines, in a factory, away from where the actual work will be performed. In the on-line setting, the learner is faced with a sequence of trials. In each trial, the learner observes an instance to be classified and must make a prediction of its correct classification. The learner then finds out whether or not the prediction was correct. In contrast to the batch setting, predictions are required of the learner from the time that the very first instance is seen. We take the goal of the learner to be to attempt to make use of regularities in the sequence of trials to minimize the number of mistaken predictions. In this setting we assume that the learner continues to be told the correct response after every prediction. Hence the training and the working phases coincide. We will summarize some recent results from [Lit88,Lit89] regarding on-line learning algorithms and then turn to our main topic here, which is a consideration of ways to convert on-line algorithms that make few mistakes to obtain algorithms that perform well in a batch setting. In the batch setting we use the PAC-learning model introduced by Valiant [Val84]. We are able to show that for some learning tasks a simple conversion

*Supported by ONR grant N00014-85-K-0445. A major part of this research was done while the author was at the University of Calif. at Santa Cruz with support from ONR grant N00014-86-K-0454.

that we describe produces PAC-learning algorithms that have sample-size bounds that are within a constant factor of optimal. Our proof uses a version of Chernoff bounds that applies to supermartingales.

In the on-line setting it is possible to obtain interesting bounds on the number of mistakes that will be made by the learner without invoking any probabilistic assumptions, for certain types of learning tasks. Our search for mistake-bounded algorithms has led to the development of efficient algorithms for learning certain concepts. In [Lit88] an algorithm, Winnow, is described that can be used for learning various types of Boolean concepts including, among others, conjunctions, $k$-DNF for small fixed $k$, and $r$-of-$k$ threshold functions. This algorithm is a linear-threshold algorithm, that is, it maintains a collection of weights and compares a weighted sum of the values of the Boolean attributes to a threshold in order to determine its response. Learning is carried out by modifying the weights. The algorithm is similar in form to the perceptron algorithm [Ros62,DH73], except that Winnow works with non-negative weights and makes multiplicative adjustments to them, instead of making the additive adjustments of the perceptron algorithm. Winnow is noteworthy for its performance when many of the Boolean attributes contained in the instances are irrelevant. If a successful prediction rule can be based on a small number of relevant attributes, then these can be mixed up among a large number of irrelevant attributes; the mistake bounds derived in [Lit88,Lit89] grow in proportion to the logarithm of the number of irrelevant attributes.

In [Lit89], the analysis of this algorithm is extended to cover the real domain $[0,1]^n$. In addition, an algorithm with similar form, the Weighted Majority Algorithm [LW89], is shown to have similar capabilities. It is also demonstrated that both of these algorithms can tolerate a limited number of anomalous trials. An anomalous trials is a trial that is not consistent with the function being learned. (The ability of the Weighted Majority Algorithm to tolerate anomalies is also central to the results of Littlestone and Warmuth [LW89].)

The derivations of the bounds for these algorithms are based on functions that measure the progress made by the learner. (These functions are not computable by the learner.) The measure of progress for the Weighted Majority Algorithm is particularly interesting, resembling the formula for relative entropy from information theory [Gal68,Kul59,Wat85]. In an information theoretic setting, relative entropy can be used as a measure of how much one probability distribution differs from another. In its use in [Lit89] as a measure of progress, it measures how much the weights maintained by the algorithm differ from the desired weights. Since the Weighted Majority Algorithm uses non-negative weights that can be normalized to sum to 1, the weights formally resemble probabilities; however, except in certain special cases, their interpretation is quite different.

In the remainder of the paper we will focus on methods for making use of mistake-bounded algorithms such as these in a batch learning setting. In the next section we introduce some terminology. Then in the following section we give a brief description of our method and compare it with other methods. In the two succeeding sections we describe the form of Chernoff bounds that we use and give the main part of the analysis of our method. In the final section, we compare the bounds we obtain with other PAC-learning bounds.

## 2   Description of Models and Terminology

In the on-line setting, in each trial the learner observes an *instance* $\mathbf{x}$ chosen from some space $X$ that we call the *domain* or *instance space*. The learner then makes a response that we will sometimes call the learner's *prediction*. We assume that this response is chosen from $\{0, 1\}$. Finally the learner receives a *reinforcement* whose value is the value of the correct response for the trial, either 0 or 1. In the batch setting the learner observes a sequence of examples. Each example consists of a pair $(\mathbf{x}, \rho)$ chosen from $X \times \{0, 1\}$. In keeping with the on-line terminology we call the first element of this pair the instance and the second the reinforcement. The output of a batch algorithm consists of a function from the instance space to $\{0, 1\}$. We call this function the *hypothesis* produced by the algorithm. For an on-line algorithm, we define the notion of *current hypothesis*. The current hypothesis of an on-line algorithm is defined before the first trial, between trials, and after the last trial. It is the function from $X$ to $\{0, 1\}$ that describes the prediction that the algorithm will make in the next trial (if it occurs) as a function of the instance of that trial.

We confine our attention to deterministic learning algorithms. We call an on-line algorithm *conservative* if its hypothesis changes only during a trial in which it makes a mistake. We call it *strongly conservative* if its entire state between trials (including the current hypothesis) is the same before and after each trial in which no mistake occurs.

We turn to a description of the PAC-learning model. We shall describe only enough aspects of this model to meet our needs. In the version of the model that we shall use, a PAC-learning algorithm has access to an oracle from which it can request examples of the concept to be learned. We shall assume that there is some *target function* $f$ such that every example $(\mathbf{x}, \rho)$ returned by the oracle is an example of $f$, that is, it satisfies $\rho = f(\mathbf{x})$. We also assume that there is a probability distribution $P$ on the instance space $X$, and that the instances returned by the oracle are selected independently at random from $P$. Among the parameters passed to the PAC-learning algorithm will be two parameters $\epsilon$ and $\delta$, called the *accuracy* and *confidence* parameters, respectively. The output of the algorithm will be a hypothesis. The goal of the algorithm is to use examples returned by the oracle to produce a hypothesis that is with high probability a good approximation of the target concept. Specifically, we define the *error of a hypothesis h* with respect to a distribution $P$ and a target concept $f$ to be $P(\{\mathbf{x} : h(\mathbf{x}) \neq f(\mathbf{x})\})$. We denote this $Error(h)$, with the target concept and distribution to be understood from the context. Given parameters $\epsilon$ and $\delta$, a PAC-learning algorithm must with probability at least $1 - \delta$ produce a hypothesis with error at most $\epsilon$. The probability $1 - \delta$ is with respect to the random choice of the sequence of examples that the algorithm sees, which are to be chosen independently from the same distribution, $P$, used to determine the error of the hypothesis. The model we are concerned with is a distribution-free model, in which the distribution is unknown to the algorithm, and results are given as worst-case bounds over all possible distributions on the instance space and over all target functions in some target class. For a more complete description of a variety of related PAC-learning models, see [HKLW88b,HKLW88a].

The distinction between on-line and batch settings that we make here is concerned with the circumstances under which learning occurs. Associated with the different circumstances are different ways of evaluating learning algorithms. We are not here making a distinction between measures of predictive performance and other measures. In both settings, we consider measures of predictive performance. In the on-line setting we measure the success of the learner at predicting the correct reinforcements in some sequence of trials. In the batch setting our interest in the final hypothesis produced by the learner is in its expected ability to make correct predictions during a subsequent working phase. By contrast, some other research using the PAC-learning model has, in addition to considering expected predictive performance, paid attention to the form that the final hypothesis takes (e.g. [PV86,KLPV87]).

The distinction that we make is also not a distinction between on-line and batch *algorithms*. It is easy to use algorithms designed for either setting in the other. However, some batch algorithms may become considerably less efficient if they must provide output at every trial, as required for the on-line setting. (It may be necessary to re-run them at each trial on the entire sequence of examples seen so far.) In the on-line setting it is desirable to use *incremental* algorithms that do not involve this overhead. We will not be concerned with this issue in this paper.

It is easy to conceive of interesting learning settings that do not fit the description of the on-line and batch settings that we consider. For example, one might want to consider a setting that is like the batch setting in that there is an initial training period during which predictions are not required, but that resembles the on-line setting during a subsequent working period, with reinforcements continuing to be available.

# 3    Converting from On-line to Batch

Given a mistake-bounded learning algorithm, there are several ways to proceed if one wants a PAC-learning algorithm. Haussler [Hau88], using the language of Markov processes, has shown that if a strongly conservative mistake-bounded algorithm is used directly as a PAC-learning algorithm then the number of examples that it requires is polynomial in $\epsilon$ and $\delta$. His results apply to deterministic algorithms receiving instances from finite domains.[1] As noted in [Lit88,Lit89], any mistake-bounded algorithm can be converted into a strongly conservative algorithm without changing the mistake bound. Haussler's result is valuable in showing that a single algorithm will perform well under both types of criteria; one is not required to settle upon one criterion or the other before choosing the algorithm. On the other hand, if one is willing to apply a transformation to the mistake-bounded algorithm, then one can obtain a transformed algorithm with better PAC-learning bounds. One method for performing such a conversion (assuming that one starts with a conservative mistake-bounded algorithm) chooses for the output hypothesis whatever hypothesis generated by the mistake-bounded algorithm survived the longest before a mistake caused it to be replaced. We call this the *longest-survivor* conversion. PAC-learning bounds for this conversion follow directly from results in [KLPV87]. An essentially equivalent conversion is considered by Angluin [Ang88]. The method of the longest-survivor conversion has been independently used by Gallant in his pocket algorithm [Gal86]. He analyzes the conversion from a different point of view.

We describe another conversion here. It uses a straightforward hypothesis testing technique and runs in two stages. We assume that we start with a conservative mistake-bounded algorithm. First the mistake-bounded algorithm is run for a while and the hypotheses that it uses for its responses are saved. Since the original algorithm is conservative, the number of distinct hypotheses that it uses will not exceed the mistake bound plus 1. In the second stage, these hypotheses are tested against a fresh batch of examples and the hypothesis that appears to be the best is chosen. Our contribution to PAC-learning theory is in the analysis of the results of the first stage. The second stage, and the analysis of it using Chernoff bounds, has been previously used in other types of conversions involving PAC-learning models, for example, in [HKLW88a]. It is also used as the second stage, with a slightly different analysis, of a general two-stage procedure described

---

[1]These final two restrictions are not mentioned in the relevant result of [Hau88]. However, some restrictions such as these appear to be needed to ensure that the resulting Markov process has a finite number of states, a requirement of the main lemma of that paper.

by Devroye [Dev88]. The conversion that we describe, at least in its current form, requires simultaneously remembering many more hypotheses than the single hypothesis required for longest-survivor conversion. We have not attempted to optimize the use of space by the transformation, and cannot presently say how space efficient this method could be made. Also, as our conversion is currently implemented, it requires the learner to know a mistake bound for the original on-line algorithm. We have not investigated removing this requirement. Our conversion has the advantage of needing asymptotically fewer examples than the longest survivor conversion, as a function of the mistake bound of the original algorithm. Unlike the longest survivor conversion, our conversion in some cases yields asymptotically optimal PAC-learning bounds. We will compare the number of examples needed by the various approaches later, following the presentation of our transformation.

# 4    Chernoff Bounds for Supermartingales

The primary tool that we use in our analysis of the first stage of our conversion is a generalization of Chernoff bounds. Roughly, Chernoff (and Hoeffding) bounds tell us that if we fix $\alpha > 0$ and conduct a sequence of independent Bernoulli trials with fixed probability of success, then the probability that the frequency of successes exceeds the expected frequency by more than $\alpha$ decreases exponentially with the number of trials. More generally, they tell us that if we sum $n$ independent random variables, each taking values in the range $[0, 1]$, then the probability decreases exponentially with $n$ that the actual sum exceeds the expected sum by more than $\alpha n$ (assuming that the expected sum grows in proportion to $n$). As pointed out by Hoeffding [Hoe63], the independence of the random variables is a stronger condition than is needed, and a weaker condition expressible in terms of martingales suffices. We describe such a condition. It is a necessary but not sufficient condition for a sequence of random variables $\xi_1, \ldots, \xi_n$ (with finite expectations) to be independent that for $i = 2, \ldots, n$ we have

$$\mathbf{E}(\xi_i | \xi_1, \ldots, \xi_{i-1}) = \mathbf{E}(\xi_i) \qquad \text{(a.s.)}$$

(The notation $\mathbf{E}(\xi_i | \xi_1, \ldots, \xi_{i-1})$ denotes the conditional expectation of $\xi_i$ with respect to the smallest $\sigma$-algebra making $\xi_1, \ldots, \xi_{i-1}$ measurable. Such a conditional expectation is a random variable that is measurable with respect to the described $\sigma$-algebra. Shiryayev [Shi84] and Billingsley [Bil86] provide good treatments of such conditional expectations.) If this condition holds then the sequence $\eta_1, \ldots, \eta_n$, where $\eta_i = \xi_i - \mathbf{E}(\xi_i)$, is a sequence of martingale differences. The sequence $S_1, \ldots, S_n$ given by $S_i = \sum_{j=1}^{i} \eta_j$ is a martingale. More generally, given random variables $S_1, \ldots, S_n$ and $\sigma$-algebras $\mathcal{G}_1, \ldots, \mathcal{G}_n$, a *martingale* is a sequence $(S_1, \mathcal{G}_1), \ldots, (S_n, \mathcal{G}_n)$ satisfying the properties: $S_i$ is $\mathcal{G}_i$ measurable and $\mathbf{E}(|S_i|) < \infty$ for $i = 1, \ldots, n$; $\mathcal{G}_1 \subseteq \ldots \subseteq \mathcal{G}_n$; and $\mathbf{E}(S_i | \mathcal{G}_{i-1}) = S_{i-1}$ (a.s.) for $i = 2, \ldots, n$. (Martingales are perhaps more typically defined to consist of infinite sequences, but finite sequences suffice here.) A sequence of random variables $S_1, \ldots, S_n$ is said to be a martingale if $(S_1, \mathcal{G}_1), \ldots, (S_n, \mathcal{G}_n)$ is a martingale for $\mathcal{G}_i = \sigma(S_1, \ldots, S_i)$ (the smallest $\sigma$-algebra with respect to which $S_1, \ldots, S_i$ are measurable). If we substitute for the condition $\mathbf{E}(S_i | \mathcal{G}_{i-1}) = S_{i-1}$ (a.s.) the condition $\mathbf{E}(S_i | \mathcal{G}_{i-1}) \leq S_{i-1}$ (a.s.) in the above definition, then the sequence $(S_1, \mathcal{G}_1), \ldots, (S_n, \mathcal{G}_n)$ is called a *supermartingale*. Note that $\mathbf{E}(S_i | \mathcal{G}_{i-1}) = \mathbf{E}(S_i - S_{i-1} | \mathcal{G}_{i-1}) + S_{i-1}$ (a.s.) and thus this condition from the definition of a supermartingale can also be expressed as the condition $\mathbf{E}(S_i - S_{i-1} | \mathcal{G}_{i-1}) \leq 0$ (a.s.). This is often a convenient way to think of this condition in the case where the $S_i$ are partial sums of a series of random variables.

Hoeffding [Hoe63] observed (without detailing the proof) that bounds of the Chernoff type hold for martingales. We state such bounds in the following theorem, and work out the details of their derivation. At the end of this section we give an example of the use of this theorem.

We use the notation $\overline{x} = 1 - x$.

**Theorem 1** *Let $(X, A, P)$ be a probability space and let $\mathcal{G} \subseteq \mathcal{G}_0 \subseteq \mathcal{G}_1 \subseteq \cdots \subseteq \mathcal{G}_t$ be $\sigma$-algebras contained in $A$. Let $\xi_1, \ldots, \xi_t$ be a sequence of random variables on this probability space such that $0 \leq \xi_i \leq 1$ for each $i$, and let $c_1, \ldots, c_t$ be $\mathcal{G}$-measurable random variables with $0 \leq c_i \leq 1$ for $i = 1, \ldots, t$. Let*

$$S_j = \sum_{i=1}^{j} (\xi_i - c_i)$$

*and let $S_0 = 0$. Let $\mu = \frac{1}{t} \sum_{j=1}^{t} c_j$. Let $\alpha$ be a $\mathcal{G}$-measurable random variable. Then if the sequence $((S_0, \mathcal{G}_0), \ldots, (S_t, \mathcal{G}_t))$ is a supermartingale, then the following statements hold at almost every point in $X$ for which $0 < \mu < 1$.*

**(a)** *If $0 < \alpha < \overline{\mu}$ then*

$$P(S_t \geq \alpha t | \mathcal{G}) \leq \left[ \left( \frac{\mu}{\mu + \alpha} \right)^{\mu + \alpha} \left( \frac{\overline{\mu}}{\overline{\mu + \alpha}} \right)^{\overline{\mu + \alpha}} \right]^t$$

**(b)** *If $0 \leq \alpha \leq \min(\mu, \overline{\mu})$ then*

$$P(S_t \geq \alpha t | \mathcal{G}) \leq e^{-\alpha^2 t / (3\mu)}$$

**(c)** *If $0 \leq \alpha \leq \overline{\mu}$ then*

$$P(S_t \geq \alpha t | \mathcal{G}) \leq e^{-\alpha^2 t / (2\overline{\mu})}$$

Note that the maximum possible value for $S_t$ is $\overline{\mu} t$, so the allowed range of $\alpha$ includes the entire range of interest (or its interior) except for the second of the three bounds. These bounds reduce to standard Chernoff bounds when $\mathcal{G}$ is the trivial $\sigma$-algebra, if each $c_i$ is taken to be the expected value of the corresponding $\xi_i$ and $\xi_1, \ldots, \xi_t$ are independent.

**Proof**     The proof that we give closely follows Hoeffding's derivation of bounds for sums of independent random variables [Hoe63] until the first bound of the theorem is derived, except for the modifications needed to handle the supermartingale hypothesis. The proof technique has apparently been frequently used, at least in the context of sums of independent random variables; Hoeffding mentions earlier use of the method by S. N. Bernstein. See also Chernoff [Che52].

Let

$$S_j' = \sum_{i=1}^{j} \xi_i$$

for $1 \leq j \leq t$ and let $S_0' = 0$. Note that $S_t = S_t' - t\mu$. We have

$$P(S_t \geq \alpha t | \mathcal{G}) \leq \mathbf{E}(e^{\beta(S_t - \alpha t)} | \mathcal{G}) = e^{-\beta \alpha t - \beta \mu t} \mathbf{E}(e^{\beta S_t'} | \mathcal{G}) \qquad \text{(a.s.)}$$

for any $\mathcal{G}$-measurable random variable $\beta > 0$.

We now argue that for $0 \leq j \leq t$,

$$\mathbf{E}(e^{\beta S_j'}|\mathcal{G}) \leq \prod_{i=1}^{j}(1 - c_i + c_i e^{\beta}) \qquad \text{(a.s.)}$$

taking the product to be 1 when $j = 0$. This clearly holds when $j = 0$. For $j > 0$ we argue by induction, assuming that the inequality holds for $j - 1$. We have

$$\mathbf{E}(e^{\beta S_j'}|\mathcal{G}) = \mathbf{E}(\mathbf{E}(e^{\beta S_j'}|\mathcal{G}_{j-1})|\mathcal{G}) \qquad \text{(a.s.)}.$$

Since $S_{j-1}'$ is measurable with respect to $\mathcal{G}_{j-1}$, so is $e^{\beta S_{j-1}'}$ and we have

$$\mathbf{E}(e^{\beta S_j'}|\mathcal{G}_{j-1}) = e^{\beta S_{j-1}'}\mathbf{E}(e^{\beta \xi_j}|\mathcal{G}_{j-1}) \qquad \text{(a.s.)}$$

The convexity of the exponential function gives us for $0 \leq x \leq 1$ the inequality $e^{\beta x} \leq 1 - x + x e^{\beta}$. Thus

$$\mathbf{E}(e^{\beta \xi_j}|\mathcal{G}_{j-1}) \leq \mathbf{E}(1 - \xi_j + \xi_j e^{\beta}|\mathcal{G}_{j-1})$$

$$= 1 + \mathbf{E}(\xi_j|\mathcal{G}_{j-1})(e^{\beta} - 1)$$

$$\leq 1 + c_j(e^{\beta} - 1) \qquad \text{(a.s.)}$$

The last inequality follows from the hypothesis that the sequence $(S_i, \mathcal{G}_i)$ is a supermartingale. Hence

$$\mathbf{E}(e^{\beta S_j'}|\mathcal{G}_{j-1}) \leq e^{\beta S_{j-1}'}(1 - c_j + c_j e^{\beta}) \qquad \text{(a.s.)}$$

giving

$$\mathbf{E}(e^{\beta S_j'}|\mathcal{G}) \leq (1 - c_j + c_j e^{\beta})\mathbf{E}(e^{\beta S_{j-1}'}|\mathcal{G})$$

$$\leq \prod_{i=1}^{j}(1 - c_i + c_i e^{\beta}) \qquad \text{(a.s.)}$$

by the induction hypothesis.

Next note that

$$\prod_{i=1}^{t}(1 - c_i + c_i e^{\beta}) \leq \left(\frac{1}{t}\sum_{i=1}^{t}(1 - c_i + c_i e^{\beta})\right)^t$$

$$= (1 - \mu + \mu e^{\beta})^t$$

At this point we obtain an inequality in exactly the form used by Hoeffding in the proof for the case of independent random variables, except for our extra conditioning on $\mathcal{G}$. We have

$$P(S_t \geq \alpha t|\mathcal{G}) \leq [e^{-\beta \alpha - \beta \mu}(1 - \mu + \mu e^{\beta})]^t \qquad \text{(a.s.)}$$

This bound holds for any positive $\beta$. Where $0 < \mu < 1$, it is minimized by choosing

$$\beta = \ln \frac{\overline{\mu}(\mu + \alpha)}{\mu(\overline{\mu + \alpha})}$$

and this choice of $\beta$ gives bound (a). (Set $\beta$ to an arbitrary constant on the set where $\mu = 0$ or 1.)

We now consider the remaining bounds. In the following argument we continue to assume that $0 < \alpha < \overline{\mu}$. To extend the bounds to the closed intervals for $\alpha$ given in the theorem, note that they are trivial for $\alpha = 0$. Extending bound (c) (and bound (b) when $\overline{\mu} \leq \mu$) to $\alpha = \overline{\mu}$ can be done by a straightforward argument based on the continuity of the bounding formulas.

To derive bound (b) note that the bound of part (a) can be written as

$$\exp\left(-t\left[(\mu + \alpha)\ln\frac{\mu + \alpha}{\mu} + \overline{\mu + \alpha}\ln\frac{\overline{\mu + \alpha}}{\overline{\mu}}\right]\right)$$

We now find a lower bound on the formula in brackets. Lemma 2, which appears following this proof, gives lower bounds for $x \ln x$ that have been derived from Taylor's formula. From this lemma we get

$$(\mu + \alpha)\ln\frac{\mu + \alpha}{\mu} = \mu\left(1 + \frac{\alpha}{\mu}\right)\ln\left(1 + \frac{\alpha}{\mu}\right)$$

$$\geq \alpha\left(1 + \frac{\alpha}{2\mu}\left(1 - \frac{\alpha}{3\mu}\right)\right)$$

Using these bounds we obtain, for $\alpha \leq \mu$,

$$(\mu + \alpha)\ln\frac{\mu + \alpha}{\mu} \geq \alpha\left(1 + \frac{\alpha}{3\mu}\right)$$

For any $x > 0$, $x \ln x \geq x - 1$ (Lemma 2). Thus

$$\overline{\mu + \alpha}\ln\frac{\overline{\mu + \alpha}}{\overline{\mu}} \geq \overline{\mu}\left(\frac{\overline{\mu + \alpha}}{\overline{\mu}} - 1\right) = -\alpha$$

Putting these two bounds together, we get

$$(\mu + \alpha)\ln\frac{\mu + \alpha}{\mu} + \overline{\mu + \alpha}\ln\frac{\overline{\mu + \alpha}}{\overline{\mu}} \geq \frac{\alpha^2}{3\mu}.$$

This gives bound (b).

We make a different approximation to get the final bound. Since $x \ln x \geq x - 1$ we have

$$(\mu + \alpha)\ln\frac{\mu + \alpha}{\mu} \geq \alpha$$

From Lemma 2 we obtain

$$\overline{\mu + \alpha}\ln\frac{\overline{\mu + \alpha}}{\overline{\mu}} \geq -\alpha + \frac{\alpha^2}{2\overline{\mu}}.$$

Putting these bounds together gives the final bound of the theorem.    □

**Lemma 2** *For all $x > 0$,*

**(a)**

$$x \ln x \geq x - 1$$

**(b)**

$$x \ln x \geq (x - 1) + \frac{1}{2}(x - 1)^2 - \frac{1}{6}(x - 1)^3$$

*Both inequalities are strict when $x \neq 1$.*

For $x < 1$, the final term of expression (b) is positive, and we can drop it to obtain

$$x \ln x > (x - 1) + \frac{1}{2}(x - 1)^2.$$

**Proof**    We use Taylor's formula with remainder, expanding about $x = 1$. Let $f(x) = x \ln x$. Then

$$f'(x) = 1 + \ln x$$

$$f''(x) = 1/x$$

$$f'''(x) = -1/x^2$$

$$f''''(x) = 2/x^3$$

For $x = 1$ the lemma is clear. For other $x$ there exist $u$ and $v$ strictly between $x$ and 1 such that

$$x \ln x = (x - 1) + \frac{(x - 1)^2}{2u}$$

and

$$x \ln x = (x - 1) + \frac{1}{2}(x - 1)^2 - \frac{1}{6}(x - 1)^3 + \frac{(x - 1)^4}{12v^3}$$

The terms involving $u$ and $v$ are both strictly positive (for $x \neq 1$), giving us the desired inequalities.    □

Standard Chernoff bounds can be obtained as a corollary of the above theorem. We state such bounds for later reference. For $t$ independent Bernoulli trials each of which has probability of success $p$, let $LE(p, t, r)$ denote the probability that there are at most $r$ successes in the $t$ trials, and let $GE(p, t, r)$ denote the probability that there are at least $r$ successes.

**Corollary 3 (Chernoff Bounds)**    *For $0 < p < 1$ and $p \leq q \leq \min(2p, 1)$,*

$$GE(p, t, qt) \leq e^{-(q-p)^2 t/(3p)}$$

*For $0 < p < 1$ and $0 \leq q \leq p$,*

$$LE(p, t, qt) \leq e^{-(p-q)^2 t/(2p)}$$

*We also have the following alternate forms for the bounds:*
*For $0 < p < 1$ and $p \leq q \leq 1$,*

$$GE(p, t, qt) \leq e^{-(q-p)^2 t/(2\overline{p})}$$

*For $0 < p < 1$ and $\max(0, p - \overline{p}) \leq q \leq p$,*

$$LE(p, t, qt) \leq e^{-(p-q)^2 t/(3\overline{p})}$$

As an example of the application of Theorem 1, suppose that a sequence of $\{0, 1\}$-valued random variables $\xi_1, \ldots, \xi_n$ has the property that for each $i$, $P(\xi_i = 1 | \xi_1, \ldots, \xi_{i-1}) \leq c_i$ for some constants $c_i$. Suppose that we are interested in the sum of some tail of this sequence. Theorem 1 yields the bound

$$P\left( \sum_{i=k}^{n} \xi_i \geq (\alpha + \mu)t \,\middle|\, \xi_1, \ldots, \xi_{k-1} \right) \leq e^{-\alpha^2 t/(3\mu)}$$

(for $\alpha$ in the appropriate range), where $t = n - k + 1$ and $\mu = \frac{1}{t} \sum_{i=k}^{n} c_i$. This bound also holds if the values of the $c_i$ are allowed to depend on the values of $\xi_1, \ldots, \xi_{k-1}$, that is, if they can be expressed as measurable functions of $\xi_1, \ldots, \xi_{k-1}$.

## 5    The Conversion

We next define the procedure used for the second stage of the transformation.

We say that a hypothesis $h$ is *consistent* with an example $(\mathbf{x}, \rho)$ if $\rho = h(\mathbf{x})$. We assume that all target functions and hypotheses are measurable.

**Procedure $MI(H, S)$**
**Minimize Inconsistencies**

**Parameters:**    $H$ is a finite set of hypotheses.
   $S = ((\mathbf{x}_1, \rho_1), \ldots, (\mathbf{x}_t, \rho_t))$ is a sample consisting of $t$ pairs chosen from $X \times \{0, 1\}$, for some $t$.

**Output:**    $h$, where $h$ is the hypothesis in $H$ that has the least number of inconsistencies with the sample; that is, the hypothesis $h \in H$ for which the cardinality of $\{j : \rho_j \neq h(\mathbf{x}_j)\}$ is the smallest. (If there is a tie, any scheme can be used to break the tie.)    □

We let $MI(H, S)$ denote the hypothesis produced by running $MI$ with the specified parameters.

**Lemma 4** *Fix a target function $f$ and a probability distribution $P$ on the instance space with respect to which the error of hypotheses is to be defined. Suppose that $0 < \epsilon < 1$ and let $H$ be a finite set of hypotheses containing at least one hypothesis with error at most $\frac{\epsilon}{2}$. Let $k$ be the number of hypotheses in $H$. Then if $\mathbf{x}_1, \ldots, \mathbf{x}_t$ are drawn independently from $P$ then with probability at least $1 - (k+1)e^{-\epsilon t/32}$,*

$$Error(MI(H, ((\mathbf{x}_1, f(\mathbf{x}_1)), \ldots, (\mathbf{x}_t, f(\mathbf{x}_t))))) \leq \epsilon$$

**Proof**   It will be convenient to think of using the $t$ examples to perform a test of each hypothesis in $H$. We say that a hypothesis $h$ passes the test if and only if it is consistent with at least a fraction $\left(1 - \frac{3\epsilon}{4}\right)$ of the $t$ examples. The probability that a particular hypothesis $h$ is inconsistent with a random example is $Error(h)$, so $h$ fails the test if and only if an event with probability $Error(h)$ occurs more than $\frac{3\epsilon t}{4}$ times in $t$ independent trials. Using standard Chernoff bounds, given in Corollary 3, the probability that a hypothesis with error at most $\frac{\epsilon}{2}$ fails the test is at most $GE(Error(h), t, \frac{3\epsilon t}{4}) \leq GE(\frac{\epsilon}{2}, t, \frac{3\epsilon t}{4}) \leq e^{-\epsilon t/24}$.

The probability that a hypothesis with error greater than $\epsilon$ passes the test is at most $LE(Error(h), t, \frac{3\epsilon t}{4}) \leq LE(\epsilon, t, \frac{3\epsilon t}{4}) \leq e^{-\epsilon t/32}$. Therefore the probability that any of the $k$ hypotheses has error exceeding $\epsilon$ and passes the test is bounded by $ke^{-\epsilon t/32}$.

For $MI$ to choose a hypothesis with error exceeding $\epsilon$, either every hypothesis with error less than or equal to $\frac{\epsilon}{2}$ must fail the test, or some hypothesis with error greater than $\epsilon$ must pass the test. Since there is at least one hypothesis with error at most $\frac{\epsilon}{2}$, the probability that either of these events occurs is bounded by $e^{-\epsilon t/24} + ke^{-\epsilon t/32} \leq (k+1)e^{-\epsilon t/32}$. This gives the lemma.

$\square$

We now give the conversion from a mistake-bounded on-line learning algorithm $A$ to a batch PAC-learning algorithm. This conversion assumes that we know a mistake bound for algorithm $A$ that suffices for whatever target function the oracle may return examples of. We assume that if one has fixed a target function $f$, then the responses of the algorithm to a sequence of trials are measurable functions of the instances observed in those trials.

## Algorithm Transformation $MPAC(A, Ran, m, \epsilon, \delta)$
## Mistake-bounded to PAC

**Parameters:**   $A$ is a conservative on-line learning algorithm.

$Ran$ is an oracle that returns independent random examples of some concept.

$m$ is a bound on the number of mistakes that $A$ will make on any sequence of random examples returned by the oracle $Ran$.

$\epsilon$ is the accuracy parameter.

$\delta$ is the confidence parameter.

**Description:**   The algorithm transformation operates in two stages. For the first stage, it sets $t = \left\lceil \max(\frac{16}{\epsilon} \ln \frac{2}{\delta}, \frac{4(m-1)}{\epsilon}) \right\rceil$. It then simulates the execution of $A$ for $t$ trials, using $t$ examples requested from $Ran$ as the source of the instances and reinforcements. It saves the set of hypotheses, $H = \{h_0, \ldots, h_t\}$ produced by $A$ for use in the second stage. (Since $A$ is conservative, many of these will be duplicates; $H$ is the set of distinct hypotheses.)

For the second stage, the algorithm transformation requests $\left\lceil \frac{32}{\epsilon} \ln \frac{2(m+2)}{\delta} \right\rceil$ examples from $Ran$ to create a sequence $S$ of examples. It then outputs the hypothesis $MI(H, S)$.

$\square$

**Theorem 5**   *If Ran returns independent random examples of some target function $f$, if $0 < \epsilon < 1$, $0 < \delta < 1$,* *and $m \geq 1$, and if $m$ is greater than or equal to the mistake bound for $A$ for the target function $f$, then with probability at least $1 - \delta$ the hypothesis output by $MPAC(A, Ran, m, \epsilon, \delta)$ will have error at most $\epsilon$ measured with respect to the target function and distribution used by Ran.*

*The number of examples used by $MPAC(A, Ran, m, \epsilon, \delta)$ will be bounded by*

$$\frac{1}{\epsilon}\left(48\ln\frac{2}{\delta} + 4m + 32\ln(m+2) - 2\right) = O\left(\frac{1}{\epsilon}\left(\ln\frac{1}{\delta} + m\right)\right).$$

To prove this theorem, we construct a sequence of $\{0,1\}$-valued random variables $\tilde{r}_1, \ldots, \tilde{r}_n$ to which we can apply Theorem 1. Given some sequence of trials, the random variable $\tilde{r}_j$ takes the value 1 if and only if the prediction of algorithm $A$ for the $j$th trial is correct and the hypothesis used to make that prediction has error at least $\frac{\epsilon}{2}$. We show that $\mathbf{E}(\tilde{r}_j | \tilde{r}_1, \ldots, \tilde{r}_{j-1}) \leq 1 - \frac{\epsilon}{2}$ (a.s.). The mistake bound for algorithm $A$ gives a limit to the number of trials for which the prediction is incorrect. If the number of trials for which $\tilde{r}_j = 0$ exceeds the mistake bound, then there must be some hypothesis with error less than $\frac{\epsilon}{2}$. We use Theorem 1 to show that this occurs with high probability. From this it follows that with high probability the second stage will choose a good hypothesis. The rest of this section is devoted to the details of this proof.

**Proof**  We first calculate the bound. Let $t$ be defined as in the description of $MPAC$. The total number of examples used is bounded by

$$t + \frac{32}{\epsilon}\left(\ln\frac{2}{\delta} + \ln(m+2)\right) + 1.$$

Since $t$ is bounded by $\frac{16}{\epsilon}\ln\frac{2}{\delta} + \frac{4(m-1)}{\epsilon} + 1$, the total number of examples used is bounded by

$$\frac{1}{\epsilon}\left(16\ln\frac{2}{\delta} + 4m - 4\right) + \frac{32}{\epsilon}\left(\ln\frac{2}{\delta} + \ln(m+2)\right) + 2$$

which gives the desired bound.

We now turn to the proof of the remainder of the theorem. Fix the target function $f$. With respect to $f$ the reinforcements received by the algorithm are determined by the instances, and thus the responses of the algorithm are a function of the sequence of instances. Let $\lambda_j(\mathbf{x}_1, \ldots, \mathbf{x}_j)$ be the response of algorithm $A$ in trial $j$ when the sequence of instances in the first $j$ trials is $\mathbf{x}_1, \ldots, \mathbf{x}_j$. Let

$$r_j(\mathbf{x}_1, \ldots, \mathbf{x}_j) = \begin{cases} 1 & \text{if } \lambda_j(\mathbf{x}_1, \ldots, \mathbf{x}_j) = f(x_j) \\ 0 & \text{otherwise} \end{cases}$$

i.e. $r_j$ is 1 if the algorithm responds correctly in the $j$th trial. Let $h_0$ denote the initial hypothesis of $A$ and let $h_j(\mathbf{x}_1, \ldots, \mathbf{x}_j)$ be the hypothesis produced by $A$ after the $j$th trial. Thus the value of $h_j(\mathbf{x}_1, \ldots, \mathbf{x}_j)$ for a particular $(\mathbf{x}_1, \ldots, \mathbf{x}_j)$ is the function $h: X \to \{0,1\}$ defined by $h(\mathbf{x}) = \lambda_{j+1}(\mathbf{x}_1, \ldots, \mathbf{x}_j, \mathbf{x})$. We have $Error(h_0) = P(\{\mathbf{x}: r_1(\mathbf{x}) = 0\})$ and for $j \geq 1$

$$Error(h_j(\mathbf{x}_1, \ldots, \mathbf{x}_j)) = P(\{\mathbf{x}: r_{j+1}(\mathbf{x}_1, \ldots, \mathbf{x}_j, \mathbf{x}) = 0\})$$

$$= 1 - \int r_{j+1}(\mathbf{x}_1, \ldots, \mathbf{x}_{j+1}) dP(\mathbf{x}_{j+1}).$$

For $j \geq 1$, let $B_j = \{(\mathbf{x}_1, \ldots, \mathbf{x}_j) : Error(h_j(\mathbf{x}_1, \ldots, \mathbf{x}_j)) \geq \frac{\epsilon}{2}\}$ and let $\tilde{r}_j : X^j \to \{0, 1\}$ be given by

$$\tilde{r}_1(\mathbf{x}_1) = \begin{cases} r_1(\mathbf{x}_1) & \text{if } Error(h_0) \geq \frac{\epsilon}{2} \\ 0 & \text{otherwise} \end{cases}$$

and for $j > 1$

$$\tilde{r}_j(\mathbf{x}_1, \ldots, \mathbf{x}_j) = \begin{cases} r_j(\mathbf{x}_1, \ldots, \mathbf{x}_j) & \text{if } (\mathbf{x}_1, \ldots, \mathbf{x}_{j-1}) \in B_{j-1} \\ 0 & \text{otherwise} \end{cases}$$

We next find bounds on $\mathbf{E}(\tilde{r}_1)$ and on $\mathbf{E}(\tilde{r}_j | \tilde{r}_1, \ldots, \tilde{r}_{j-1})$ for $j > 1$. If $Error(h_0) < \frac{\epsilon}{2}$ then $\mathbf{E}(\tilde{r}_1) = 0$. Otherwise, $\mathbf{E}(\tilde{r}_1) = \mathbf{E}(r_1) = 1 - Error(h_0) \leq 1 - \frac{\epsilon}{2}$. For $j \geq 2$, we wish to work with a function $\tilde{r}_j$ whose domain is $X^j$, and therefore in the following argument we will work with the probability space $X^j$. Let $\sigma(\tilde{r}_1, \ldots, \tilde{r}_{j-1})$ denote the $\sigma$-algebra of subsets of $X^j$ generated by the random variables $\tilde{r}_1, \ldots, \tilde{r}_{j-1}$. Since these functions depend only on $x_1, \ldots, x_{j-1}$, any set contained in $\sigma(\tilde{r}_1, \ldots, \tilde{r}_{j-1})$ can be written in the form $U \times X$ for some $U \subseteq X^{j-1}$. For any such set we have

$$\int_{U \times X} \mathbf{E}(\tilde{r}_j | \tilde{r}_1, \ldots, \tilde{r}_{j-1}) dP^j = \int_{U \times X} \tilde{r}_j dP^j$$

$$= \int_{(U \cap B_{j-1}) \times X} r_j dP^j = \int_{U \cap B_{j-1}} (1 - Error(h_{j-1})) dP^{j-1}$$

$$\leq \int_{U \cap B_{j-1}} (1 - \frac{\epsilon}{2}) dP^{j-1} \leq \int_{U \times X} (1 - \frac{\epsilon}{2}) dP^j$$

Since this holds for every set $U \times X \subseteq \sigma(\tilde{r}_1, \ldots, \tilde{r}_{j-1})$ and since $\mathbf{E}(\tilde{r}_j | \tilde{r}_1, \ldots, \tilde{r}_{j-1})$ is measurable with respect to $\sigma(\tilde{r}_1, \ldots, \tilde{r}_{j-1})$, this shows that $\mathbf{E}(\tilde{r}_j | \tilde{r}_1, \ldots, \tilde{r}_{j-1}) \leq 1 - \frac{\epsilon}{2}$ a.s. The sequence $\tilde{r}_1, \ldots, \tilde{r}_j$ thus satisfies the hypothesis of Theorem 1 with $\mu = c_1 = \cdots = c_j = 1 - \frac{\epsilon}{2}$. This theorem implies that for $t > \frac{16}{\epsilon} \ln \frac{2}{\delta}$ the probability that

$$\sum_{j=1}^{t} \tilde{r}_j \geq t(1 - \frac{\epsilon}{4})$$

is at most $e^{-\epsilon t/16} \leq \frac{\delta}{2}$. When $\tilde{r}_j = 0$ either a mistake was made at trial $j$ or $Error(h_{j-1}) < \frac{\epsilon}{2}$. Therefore when $\sum_{j=1}^{t} \tilde{r}_j \leq t - m$ then either at least one of the hypotheses $h_0, \ldots, h_{t-1}$ has error less than $\frac{\epsilon}{2}$ or at least $m$ mistakes were made during the $t$ trials. But we are assuming that at most $m$ mistakes will be made by the algorithm for any sequence of examples that can be returned by $Ran$. If $m$ mistakes were made in the first $t$ trials, then hypothesis $h_t$ must have error 0, for otherwise there would exist some sequence of $t + 1$ trials for which the algorithm would make more than $m$ mistakes. Therefore whenever $\sum_{j=1}^{t} \tilde{r}_j \leq t - m$ at least one of the $t + 1$ hypotheses $h_0, \ldots, h_t$ must have error less than $\frac{\epsilon}{2}$. We have chosen $t \geq \frac{4(m-1)}{\epsilon}$. Hence when $\sum_{j=1}^{t} \tilde{r}_j < t(1 - \frac{\epsilon}{4})$ we have $\sum_{j=1}^{t} \tilde{r}_j < t - m + 1$ implying $\sum_{j=1}^{t} \tilde{r}_j \leq t - m$. Therefore with probability at least $1 - \frac{\delta}{2}$ at least one of the $t + 1$ hypotheses produced by the first stage has error at most $\frac{\epsilon}{2}$. Let $H = \{h_0, \ldots, h_t\}$. Since $A$ is conservative and makes at most $m$ mistakes, the number of distinct hypotheses among $h_0, \ldots, h_t$ is bounded by $m + 1$; in other words $|H| \leq m + 1$.

Whenever the first stage results in a collection of hypotheses of which at least one has error at most $\frac{\epsilon}{2}$ then by Lemma 4 the probability that the second stage will produce a hypothesis with error at most $\epsilon$ is at least

$$1 - (|H| + 1)e^{-\frac{\epsilon}{32}\left\lceil \frac{32}{\epsilon} \ln \frac{2(m+2)}{\delta} \right\rceil} \geq 1 - (m + 2)e^{-\ln \frac{2(m+2)}{\delta}} = 1 - \frac{\delta}{2}.$$

The first stage will produce such a collection with probability at least $1 - \frac{\delta}{2}$. Since the second stage is independent of the first, the probability is at least $1 - \delta$ that this transformation will produce a hypothesis with error at most $\epsilon$, as desired. $\qquad\square$

## 6    Comparisons

We now compare the bound from the theorem that we have just proven with the bounds from the other approaches mentioned at the beginning of this section. If we start with a strongly conservative mistake-bounded algorithm $A$ with mistake bound $m$, then our bound on the number of examples needed by our conversion is

$$\frac{1}{\epsilon}\left(48\ln\frac{2}{\delta} + 4m + 32\ln(m + 2) - 2\right) = O\left(\frac{1}{\epsilon}\left(\ln\frac{1}{\delta} + m\right)\right).$$

The longest-survivor conversion gives a bound (from [KLPV87]) of

$$\frac{m + 1}{\epsilon}\left(\ln\frac{1}{\delta} + \ln m\right) = O\left(\frac{m}{\epsilon}\left(\ln\frac{1}{\delta} + \ln m\right)\right).$$

Finally, Haussler's bound [Hau88], obtainable without any conversion is

$$\frac{m^{3/2}}{\sqrt{2\pi}\epsilon\delta} + m = O\left(\frac{m^{3/2}}{\epsilon\delta}\right).$$

It is interesting to extend the comparison of upper and lower bounds given in [EHKV88]. We will ignore computational complexity; the algorithms mentioned in the bounds below are not necessarily efficient. We assume that the instance space is finite and that the target class is known to the algorithm in a form such that every function in the class can be evaluated by the algorithm on every point in the domain. (These assumptions are more restrictive than are needed for most of the results mentioned below.) Let $t_A(\epsilon, \delta)$ be the number of examples required by a PAC-learning algorithm $A$ to learn the target class $C$ with confidence $1 - \delta$ that the hypothesis output will have error no more than $\epsilon$. We let $opt(C)$ denote the best mistake bound that can be obtained for the target class $C$ by any algorithm, as in [Lit88,Lit89], and we let $VCdim(C)$ denote the Vapnik-Chervonenkis dimension of $C$ [VC71,BEHW88]. In comparing the following bounds, note that $VCdim(C) \leq opt(C) \leq \log_2|C|$ [Lit88,Lit89]. From [EHKV88] we have the following lower bound on

$t_A(\epsilon, \delta)$ for any algorithm $A$.

$$t_A(\epsilon, \delta) = \Omega\left(\frac{1}{\epsilon}\left(\log\frac{1}{\delta} + VCdim(C)\right)\right).$$

In [BEHW88] and [BEHW87] two different upper bounds are given for the value of $t_A$ for any algorithm $A$ that always produces a hypothesis chosen from the target class $C$ that is consistent with the examples it has seen. These bounds are

$$t_A(\epsilon, \delta) = O\left(\frac{1}{\epsilon}\left(\log\frac{1}{\delta} + VCdim(C)\log\frac{1}{\epsilon}\right)\right)$$

and

$$t_A(\epsilon, \delta) = O\left(\frac{1}{\epsilon}\left(\log\frac{1}{\delta} + \log|C|\right)\right).$$

In [HLW88] an algorithm $A$ is given for which

$$t_A(\epsilon, \delta) = O\left(\frac{1}{\epsilon}\left(\log\frac{1}{\delta}\right)VCdim(C)\right).$$

None of the above upper bounds is strictly better than any of the others for all choices of the parameters.

In Theorem 5 we show there exists an algorithm $A$ such that

$$t_A(\epsilon, \delta) = O\left(\frac{1}{\epsilon}\left(\log\frac{1}{\delta} + opt(C)\right)\right).$$

This bound is of the same form as the second upper bound given above, except that $opt(C)$ has been substituted for $\log|C|$. For some classes $C$, $opt(C)$ is significantly smaller than $\log_2|C|$. When $opt(C) = VCdim(C)$ then our conversion from mistake bounded algorithms provides an asymptotically optimal PAC-learning algorithm. Note that the bound obtainable from the longest survivor conversion

$$O\left(\frac{1}{\epsilon}\left(opt(C)\log\frac{1}{\delta} + opt(C)\log opt(C)\right)\right)$$

is worse than both our bound and the bound from [HLW88].

**Acknowledgment**   I would particularly like to thank David Haussler for careful reading of, and comments on, the first draft of the analysis of the conversion presented here, and Manfred Warmuth for suggesting an improvement to the bounds that resulted in bounds that are asymptotically optimal for certain target classes.

# References

[Ang88]    Dana Angluin. Queries and concept learning. *Machine Learning*, 2:319–342, 1988.

[BEHW87]    Anselm Blumer, Andrzej Ehrenfeucht, David Haussler, and Manfred K. Warmuth.  Occam's razor. *Information Processing Letters*, 24:377–380, 1987.

[BEHW88]    Anselm Blumer, Andrzej Ehrenfeucht, David Haussler, and Manfred K. Warmuth. *Learnability and the Vapnik-Chervonenkis Dimension*. Technical Report UCSC-CRL-87-20, University of California Computer Research Laboratory, Santa Cruz, CA, 1987, revised 1988. To appear in *JACM*.

[Bil86]     Patrick Billingsley. *Probability and Measure*. Wiley, New York, 1986.

[Che52]     Herman Chernoff. A measure of asymptotic efficiency for tests of a hypothesis based on the sum of observations. *Annals of Math. Stat.*, 23:493–507, 1952.

[Dev88]     Luc Devroye. Automatic pattern recognition: a study of the probability of error. *IEEE Trans. on Pattern Anal. and Mach. Intelligence*, 10(4):530–543, 1988.

[DH73]      R. O. Duda and P. E. Hart. *Pattern Classification and Scene Analysis*. Wiley, 1973.

[EHKV88]    Andrzej Ehrenfeucht, David Haussler, Michael Kearns, and Leslie Valiant. A general lower bound on the number of examples needed for learning. In *Proceedings of the 1988 Workshop on Computational Learning Theory*, pages 139–154, published by Morgan Kaufmann, San Mateo, CA, 1988.

[Gal68]     Robert G. Gallager. *Information Theory and Reliable Communication*. Wiley, New York, 1968.

[Gal86]     Stephen I. Gallant. Optimal linear discriminants. In *Eighth International Conference on Pattern Recognition*, pages 849–852, IEEE Computer Society, Paris, France, 1986.

[Hau88]     David Haussler. *Space Efficient Learning Algorithms*. Technical Report UCSC-CRL-88-2, University of Calif. Computer Research Laboratory, Santa Cruz, CA, 1985, revised 1988.

[HKLW88a]   David Haussler, Michael Kearns, Nick Littlestone, and Manfred K. Warmuth. *Equivalence of Models for Polynomial Learnability*. Technical Report UCSC-CRL-88-06, University of Calif. Computer Research Laboratory, Santa Cruz, CA, 1988.

[HKLW88b]   David Haussler, Michael Kearns, Nick Littlestone, and Manfred K. Warmuth. Equivalence of models for polynomial learnability. In *Proceedings of the 1988 Workshop on Computational Learning Theory*, pages 42–55, published by Morgan Kaufmann, San Mateo, CA, 1988.

[HLW88]     David Haussler, Nick Littlestone, and Manfred Warmuth. Predicting 0,1-functions on randomly drawn points. In *Proceedings of the 29th Annual Symposium on the Foundations of Computer Science*, pages 100–109, IEEE, 1988. (Also appears in Proceedings of the 1988 Workshop on Computational Learning Theory, published by Morgan Kaufmann, San Mateo, CA, 1988).

[Hoe63]     Wassily Hoeffding. Probability inequalities for sums of bounded random variables. *American Statistical Association Journal*, 58:13–30, 1963.

[KLPV87]    M. Kearns, M. Li, L. Pitt, and L. Valiant. Recent results on boolean concept learning. In Pat Langley, editor, *Proceedings of the Fourth International Workshop on Machine Learning*, pages 337–352, (published by Morgan Kaufmann, Los Altos California), Irvine, California, June 1987.

[Kul59]     Solomon Kullback. *Information Theory and Statistics*. Wiley, New York, 1959.

[Lit88]     Nick Littlestone. Learning quickly when irrelevant attributes abound: a new linear-threshold algorithm. *Machine Learning*, 2:285–318, 1988.

[Lit89]     Nick Littlestone. *Mistake Bounds and Logarithmic Linear-threshold Learning Algorithms*. PhD thesis, University of Calif., Santa Cruz, 1989.

[LW89]      Nick Littlestone and Manfred K. Warmuth. The weighted majority algorithm. 1989. To appear in the Proceedings of the 1989 Workshop on Computational Learning Theory.

[PV86]      Leonard Pitt and Leslie Valiant. *Computational Limitations on Learning from Examples*. Technical Report TR-05-86, Harvard Univ. Aiken Computation Lab., Cambridge, MA, 1986.

[Ros62]     F. Rosenblatt. *Principles of Neurodynamics: Perceptrons and the Theory of Brain Mechanisms*. Spartan Books, Washington, D. C., 1962.

[Shi84]     Albert Nikolaevich Shiryayev. *Probability*. Springer, New York, 1984.

[Val84]     L. G. Valiant. A theory of the learnable. *Comm. ACM*, 27(11):1134–42, 1984.

[VC71]      V. N. Vapnik and A. Ya. Chervonenkis. On the uniform convergence of relative frequencies of events to their probabilities. *Th. Prob. and its Appl.*, 16(2):264–80, 1971.

[Wat85]     Satosi Watanabe. *Pattern Recognition: Human and Mechanical*. Wiley, New York, 1985.

# A PARAMETRIZATION SCHEME FOR CLASSIFYING MODELS OF LEARNABILITY

*Shai Ben-David*

*Gyora M. Benedek*

and *Yishay Mansour*

Computer Science Department
Technion, Haifa, Israel

Computer Science Department
Technion, Haifa, Israel

Laboratory of Computer Science
MIT, Cambridge

## Abstract

We present a systematic framework for classifying, comparing and defining models of computational learnability. Apart from the obvious 'uniformity' parameters we present a novel 'solid learnability' notion that captures the difference between 'Guess and Test' learning algorithms and learnability notions for which consistency with the samples guarantees success.

We analyze known models in terms of our new parameterization scheme and investigate the relative strength of notions of learnability that correspond to different parameter values.

In the last section we consider 'proximity' between concept classes. We define notions of 'covering' one class by another and show that with respect to learnability they play a role similar to the role of reductions in computational complexity; If a class is coverable by a learnable one, then, the first class too is learnable.

We apply the covering technique to resolve some open questions raised in [BI2] and [LMR].

The discussion is carried out in the context of information-theoretic complexity rather than algorithmic complexity. For the sake of concreteness we have also limited the discussion to the setting of learning through randomly drawn samples. Nevertheless, our parameters, and consequently our analysis, are relevant to a much wider variety of learning situations.

## 1. INTRODUCTION

Modes of learning based on a probabilistic process of viewing examples are very appealing. In a sense such processes are the basis of our understanding of the world around us. Valiant [V1] has presented a computational model of such a learning. Valiant's model has invoked many investigations and by now there is a considerable body of results concerning this notion of computational learnability ([BEHW1], [BEHW2], [BI1], [BI2], [EHKV], [HKLW], [KLPV], [LMR], [N], [PV], [V2] and others).

In spite of (or maybe because of) the clear intuition behind Valiant's model, different researchers have formed different interpretations of it. The overall outcome seems a bit confusing, for an example [BEHW1] prove that a concept class is learnable if and only if it has a finite VC-dimension while [BI1] prove the learnability of a wider family of classes and [LMR] establish the learnability of classes that do not fit into any of the criteria presented elsewhere.

Of course some differences between the models are explicitly defined in the above-mentioned papers, yet we have found that substantial diversity is due to subtle variations in the notion of learnability, variations that have so far remained implicit.

The first objective of this paper is to provide parameters along which existing notions of computational learnability can be rigorously classified and new models systematically developed.

We begin our discussion by introducing *uniformity* parameters. A uniformity parameter applies to the size of the random sample upon which the learning function operates. It tells which variables (e.g. the concept being studied or the probability distribution) can affect the size of the sample that the student receives. This parameter is usually explicitly defined. The term 'non-uniform' is used in [BI1] to denote this meaning with respect to concepts, and [LMR] uses the term 'dynamic sampling' to denote a similar idea. This is the content of section 3.

In section 4 we introduce a new notion - *solid learnability*. This parameter comes to distinguish situations in which once you have seen sufficiently many examples, any guess consistent with them is a good enough answer. Blumer et al. [BEHW1] prove that in their model any learnable class is solidly learnable, this property, for somewhat different models, is implicitly assumed in [HKLW].

The last parameter we introduce concerns the communication between the student and the teacher. We suggest to separate models that allow an interactive learning process from those in which the student cannot affect (the size of) the sample provided by the teacher.

Once we define our parameters and show how they apply to previously defined models, we turn to a systematic analysis of the relative strength of the different models that emerge using the parameterization. We concentrate on the uniformity and solid learnability and show that different values of these parameters give rise to different families of learnable concept classes.

In the last section we consider 'proximity' between concept classes. We define notions of 'covering' one class by another and show that with respect to learnability they play a role similar to the role of reductions in computational complexity; If a class is coverable by a learnable one, then, the first class is guaranteed to be learnable.

As an application of the covering technique we can answer some questions from [LMR] and [BI2]. We prove that models of learnability defined in [LMR] and others of [BI2] are, on one hand, permissive enough so that any class of Lesbegue measurable sets in $\mathbb{R}^n$ is learnable (w.r.t. the uniform distribution), and on the other hand, there exist some non learnable classes.

We have chosen to focus on one branch of computational learning theory:

(1)    The notions we discuss are information-theoretic in the sense that we care about the amount of information the student requires and ignore (the complexity of) the computation he carries out.

(2)    We concentrate on the question of learnability rather than the complexity of the learning process. (I.e. the finiteness of the information rather than its precise size.)

(3)    The information passed to the student is of one type only - randomly chosen labeled samples.

Yet, our approach is easily adaptable to variations in the setting, and we hope that it will be adopted by researchers working in other branches of the field.

The second authors contribution is part of his Ph.D. dissertation under Professor A. Itai. A more detailed account of these results (and others) appear in [B].

## 2. BASIC DEFINITIONS

Following [V1] and others, we consider the problem of learning a class $C$ of *concepts* - subsets of a fixed domain $X$. Given a concept $c \in C$ an *example* of $c$ is a point $x \in X$, along with the value of the characteristic function $I_c$ of $c$ at $x$. A sequence of $l$ examples constitutes an *l-sample* of $c$. The problem of learning is the problem of recovering the *target concept $c$*, or at least a concept that approximates $c$, from a sample of $c$. We define a *learning function $F$* for $C$ as a function from the set of samples to subsets of $X$ (in most of the cases we discuss, the range of $F$ is $C$). The value of a learning function on a sample is called its *hypothesis*. (One may have preferred a learning *algorithm* rather than function, however, in this paper we are not concerned with the computability of the learning functions.)

We assume that the examples are chosen independently according to a probability distribution $D$ on $X$. Thus, an $l$-sample is chosen according to the product distribution $D^l$ on $X^l$. The *error* of a hypothesis $h$ for $c$ w.r.t. $D$ is the $D$-probability of $h \oplus c$ (the symmetric difference of $h$ and $c$). Given a distribution $D$ and a concept $c$, a learning function $F$ is $(l,\varepsilon,\delta)$-successful if, with probability exceeding $1-\delta$, when applied on an $l$-sample (chosen according to $D^l$) the error of the value of $F$ (as hypothesis for $c$) is less than $\varepsilon$.

$F$ is *successful* if for every $\varepsilon, \delta > 0$ there exists an $l = l(\varepsilon,\delta)$ such that $F$ is $(l,\varepsilon,\delta)$-successful. ($l$ may depend on other parameters too, as specified later.)

Some of the above definitions implicitly assume $D$-measurability of the appropriate sets (e.g. $h \oplus c$). Similar restrictions are relevant to most of the literature in this field and as far as we know, are nowhere fully discussed. We shall settle for noting these restrictions wherever they have a direct impact on our results. (See the appendix of [BEHW1] for more comments on this issue.) Another possible remedy to these problems is to assume that along with any domain set $X$ one also fixes a collection $K$ of concept classes and confine the discussion to the collection $P_K$ of all probability distributions under which every member of every class in $K$ is measurable. Subsequently all quantifications over concept classes (distributions) should be understood as quantifications over the members of $K$ (respectively $P_K$).

## 3. THE UNIFORMITY PARAMETER

In this section we present two uniformity parameters. A class is nonuniformly learnable w.r.t. concepts (distributions) if the size of the sample, upon which the student's conclusion is reached, may vary from one concept (distribution) to the other. It is uniform if there exists a bound on the sample sizes independent of the concept (distribution) in question.

**Definitions:** (the families $LU_cU_D$, $LN_cU_D$, $LU_cN_D$, $LN_cN_D$, $LU_c D$ and $LN_c D$ ) (i) A concept class $C$ over $X$ is in $LU_cU_D$ (*Learnable uniformly in $c \in C$ and uniformly in $D$* ) if there exists a learning function $F$ and an integer valued function $l=l(\varepsilon,\delta)$ such that for every $\varepsilon,\delta>0$, $c$ in $C$ and every distribution $D$ over $X$, $F$ is $(l,\varepsilon,\delta)$-successful.

(ii) $C$ is in $LN_cU_D$ (*Learnable nonuniformly in $c \in C$ and uniformly in $D$ learnable*) if the same holds except that $l(c,\varepsilon,\delta)$ is also a function of $c \in C$.

(iii) $C$ is in $LU_cN_D$ (*Learnable uniformly in $c \in C$ and nonuniformly in $D$ learnable*) if $l$ is a function of $D$, $\varepsilon$ and $\delta$.

(iv) $C$ is in $LN_cN_D$ (*Learnable nonuniformly in $c \in C$ and nonuniformly in $D$ learnable*) if $l$ is a function of $c \in C$, $D$, $\varepsilon$ and $\delta$.

(v) Let $D$ be a probability distribution on $X$, a concept class $C$ is in $LU_c D$ w.r.t. $D$ if there exists a learning function $F$ and an integer valued function $l=l(\varepsilon,\delta)$ such that for every $\varepsilon,\delta>0$ and $c$ in $C$, $F$ is $(l,\varepsilon,\delta)$-successful. We define $LN_c D$ similarly.

The definition of learnability in [BEHW1] is equivalent to our $LU_cU_D$, $LN_cN_D$ is the definition used by [LMR] (although, their main result applies to $LN_cU_D$), $LN_cU_D$ is the one used by [BI1], $LU_c D$ and $LN_c D$ were studied in [BI2]. [V1],[V2],[BEHW2] and others used definitions similar to $LN_cU_D$ on some fixed domain set. $LU_cN_D$ arises naturally when one considers the characterization of notions of learnability along the uniformity parameters above.

Trivially, every concept class in $LY_cN_D$ is also in $LY_c D$ for every distribution $D$ (where Y is U or N). Also, replacing uniformity by nonuniformity can only expand the family thus, for example, every concept class in $LU_cU_D$ is also in $LN_cU_D$ etc. The converse does not hold, as the following theorem shows:

**Theorem 1:**   a) $LN_cN_D$ strictly includes $LU_cN_D$, $LN_cU_D$ and their union.

                b) Each of $LU_cN_D$ and $LN_cU_D$ strictly include $LU_cU_D$.

The proof is deferred to section 4.3 where we show that $LU_cN_D$ is not a subfamily of $LN_cU_D$ and 4.2 where we prove that $LN_cU_D$ is not a subfamily of $LU_cN_D$. Furthermore, in section 5 we show that $LN_cN_D$ strictly includes the union of $LU_cN_D$ and $LN_cU_D$.

Diagram 1 in the appendix shows the relations between these four families.

Let us recall the definition of the Vapnik-Chervonenkis dimension of a class $C$:

**Definition:** [VC] (VC-dimension) Let $T$ be a subset of $X$. A concept class $C \subseteq 2^X$ *shatters* $T$ if for every subset $T'$ of $T$ there is a concept $c \in C$ such that $T \cap c = T'$. Let $\dim(C) = d$ if there is set of $d$ elements of $X$ shattered by $C$ and there is no set of $d+1$ elements shattered by $C$. If no such $d$ exists, $C$ has an *infinite dimension*.

Here are some relevant previous results stated in our terminology:

**P1:**    [BEHW1] A concept class is in $LU_cU_D$ if and only if it has finite VC-dimension.

**P2:**    [BI1] A concept class is in $LN_cU_D$ if and only if it equals the union of countably many subclasses all with finite VC-dimension.

**P3:**    [BI1] If a concept class shatters an infinite set then it is not in $LN_cU_D$.

## 4. SOLID LEARNABILITY

### 4.1 Definitions and discussion

**Definition:** (consistent learning function) Let us call a learning function *consistent* if for every sample its hypothesis is consistent with the sample (i.e. if $<x,0>$ is in the sample S then $x \notin F(S)$ and if $<x,1>$ is in S then $x \in F(S)$).

Blumer et al. [BEHW1] show that their notion of learnability enjoys the following nice property: Whenever there exists one successful learning function then every consistent function is successful. This property is implicitly (but justifiably) assumed in [HKLW] (for proving lemma 4.6), on the other hand, it fails in the models of Benedek-Itai ([BI1],[BI2]) and Linial et al. [LMR]. The distinction between these types of models gives rise to another parameter for classifying models of learnability. Let us call a class $C$ *solidly learnable* if every consistent learning function is successful. A precise definition depends upon the choice of the uniformity parameters. For an example:

**Definitions:** (the family $SU_cU_D$) A concept class $C$ over $X$ is in $SU_cU_D$ (*solidly, uniformly in $c \in C$ and uniformly in $D$ learnable*) if there exists an integer valued function $l(\varepsilon,\delta)$ such that for every consistent learning function $F$ and $\varepsilon,\delta>0$, $c$ in $C$ and every distribution $D$ over $X$, $F$ is $(l,\varepsilon,\delta)$-successful.

The definitions of $SN_cU_D$, $SU_cN_D$, $SN_cN_D$, $SU_c D$ and $SN_c D$ are similar to those of $LN_cU_D$, $LU_cN_D$, $LN_cN_D$, $LU_c D$ and $LN_c D$ respectively.

To learn a concept from a solidly learnable class "all you have to do" is to sort out hypotheses according to their consistency with the sample at hand.

Trivially, every $SY_cZ_D$ concept class is also $LY_cZ_D$ (where $Y \in \{N,U\}$ and $Z \in \{N,U,D\}$). We shall show in 4.2 that the converse may fail.

Analyzing known learning functions (e.g. in [BI1] and [LMR]) one can notice that learning functions, for non-solidly learnable classes, employ a scheme of 'guess and test'. On the basis of a part of the sample, they form (guess) some initial set of hypotheses and than test it against more instances supplied by the teacher. If non of the hypotheses in the initial set passes the test then the guess-and-test routine is re-applied. Such a scheme may succeed even when there are concepts consistent with the full sample and yet far from the target concept. The reason is, of course, that the statistical evidence gained by the agreement of a hypothesis with a sample that is independent of it, is much stronger than just the consistency of a hypothesis with the sample upon which it was formed.

A related issue that emerges from the examination of learning algorithms is the degree of interaction between the student and the teacher in the learning process. Learning is *non-interactive* if the teacher can retire as soon as he had started the learning process by presenting a sample. Another possible scenario is one in which the student, after viewing some sample, may ask for another sample, or may examine part of the sample before deciding upon the size of the full sample he needs. In this paper we do not investigate this interactiveness parameter, in [B] Benedek shows that the interactive families (defined by the uniformity parameters) are equal to the corresponding learnable families.

In the next two subsections we examine the interrelations among the various families. Diagram 2 in the appendix summarizes these results.

## 4.2. Learnability vs. solid learnability

Restated in our terminology, the main result of [BEHW1] is that if a class $C$ has finite dimension then it is in $SU_cU_D$, and on the other hand, every class in $LU_cU_D$ has finite dimension.

**Corollary 1:** A class $C$ is in $LU_cU_D$ if and only if it is in $SU_cU_D$.

The following theorem shows that the solid learnability notion is strictly weaker than learnability as soon as we consider nonuniformity in the concepts. The theorem states that allowing the size of the sample to depend upon the target concept does not add any classes to $SU_cU_D$. This should be contrasted with **P2** (at the end of section 3) that implies that the situation is different in the general (non-solidly learnable) case. First we need one more definition:

**Definition:** Let $Y_1, Y_2 \subseteq X$. $Y_1$ and $Y_2$ are *ε-close w.r.t. the distribution D* if $D(Y_1 \oplus Y_2) < \varepsilon$. (If $Y_1 \oplus Y_2$ is not measurable w.r.t. $D$ then we demand the existence of some measurable $A$ such that $Y_1 \oplus Y_2 \subseteq A$ and $D(A) < \varepsilon$.) Otherwise, $Y_1$ and $Y_2$ are *ε-far w.r.t. the distribution D*.

**Theorem 2:** If a class $C$ over $X$ is in $SN_cU_D$ then it has finite VC-dimension.

**Proof:** Assume $C$ is in $SN_cU_D$, i.e. for every concept $c \in C$ and every positive $\varepsilon, \delta$, there is some $l = l(c, \varepsilon, \delta)$ such that for every distribution $D$ with probability $\geq 1 - \delta$ given a random $l$-sample every concept $c' \in C$ consistent with it is $\varepsilon$-close to $c$.

Let us pick any $c \in C$, $\delta > 0$ and $\frac{1}{4} > \varepsilon > 0$. Let $l = l(c, \varepsilon, \delta)$. If, by way of contradiction, $\dim(C) = \infty$ then there exists a set $A$ of $2l$ elements that is shattered by $C$. Define a distribution $D$ by setting $D(Y) = |Y \cap A|/2l$ for every subset $Y$ of $X$. Given any $l$-sample S let $c'$ be a member of $C$ that agrees with the target concept $c$ on the elements picked by S in $A$ and disagrees with $c$ on every point in $A$ outside the domain of S. $c'$ is consistent with S but is $\frac{1}{2}$-far from $c$. ∎

**Corollary 2:** $SN_cU_D$ is strictly included in $LN_cU_D$.

**Theorem 3:**   (a) $SU_cN_D$ is strictly included in $LU_cN_D$.

(b) There exist distributions $D$ for which $LU_c D$ strictly includes $SU_c D$.

(c) $SN_cN_D$ does not include $LU_cN_D$.

(d) $LU_cU_D$ is strictly included in $(LU_cN_D \cap LN_cU_D)$.

**Proof:** Let $X = (0,1)$ and $C_{FN}$ be the set of all the finite subsets of $X$ and the set $X$ itself. It is easy to see that $C_{FN}$ is in $LU_cN_D$ and $LN_cU_D$ however, as we show, for the uniform distribution $D$ over $X$, $C_{FN}$ is not in $SU_c D$ moreover, $C_{FN}$ is not in $SN_cN_D$ (and thus not in $LU_cU_D$).

Let us pick $\delta > 0$, $1 > \varepsilon > 0$ and let $c = X$ be the target concept. Given any finite sample of $c$, there are finite sets that are consistent with the sample and yet 1-far from $c$ (which, of course, is also consistent with the sample). ∎

**Theorem 4:** $LN_cU_D$ is not a subfamily of $SN_cN_D$ or $LU_cN_D$.

**Proof:** Let $X$ be the open interval $(0,1)$, let $S$ be the set of its subintervals with rational endpoints. Let $C_{FO}$ be all the finite unions of $S$. $C_{FO}$ is countable and therefore, by **P2** is in $LN_cU_D$. (For $i>0$ $c_i \in C_{FO}$.) On the other hand let $D$ be the uniform distribution over $(0,1)$. Let $c_i = \{\alpha \in (0,1) : \text{the } i\text{'th bit of } \alpha = 1 \}$. This is an infinite set of pairwise ½-far concepts and every finite sample of some $c_i$, $S$, of irrational points is consistent with infinitely many $c_j$'s. Thus, since the probability of drawing a rational point is zero, $C_{FO}$ is not in $SN_cN_D$. (Using techniques of [BI2] one can also show that $C_{FO}$ is not in $LU_c D$ and therefore not in $LU_cN_D$.) ■

## 4.3 Relations among families of solidly learnable classes

**Definition:** ($X\sigma$-finite dimension) A concept class $C$ over a set $X$ has $X\sigma$-*finite dimension* if there are sets $\{A_i : i \in N\}$ such that (i) $X = \bigcup_{i \in N} A_i$, (ii) For every $i$, $C|A_i$ has finite VC-dimension (where $C|A \overset{\Delta}{=} \{c \cap A : c \in C\}$).

The following theorem resembles **P2** (from section 3).

**Theorem 5:** If $C$ has a $X\sigma$-finite dimension then $C$ is in $SU_cN_D$.

**Proof:** Let $C$ be a $X\sigma$-finite dimensional concept class and let $A_i$'s be as in the definition. For every probability distribution $D$ over $X$ and every positive $\alpha$ there exists a (finite) $k$ such that $D(\bigcup_{i \leq k} A_i) > 1 - \alpha$. Given $\varepsilon, \delta > 0$, let $\alpha < \varepsilon/2$ be such that for any set $A$ if $D(A) > 1 - \alpha$ then for every $l > 100$ with probability $\geq 1 - \delta/2$ at least half of a random $l$-sample meets $A$. Let $k$ be such that $D(\bigcup_{i \leq k} A_i) > 1 - \alpha$ and $l$ at least twice the needed sample size for learning $C|\bigcup_{i \leq k} A_i$. (As a finite union of finite dimensional classes $C|\bigcup_{i \leq k} A_i$ has finite VC-dimension.) ■

**Corollary 3:** If $X$ is a countable set then every concept class over $X$ is in $SU_cN_D$.

**Corollary 4:**

(1)          $SU_cU_D$ is a proper subfamily of $SU_cN_D$.

(2)          $SU_cN_D$ and thus $LU_cN_D$ are not subfamilies of $LN_cU_D$.

**Proof:** Let $X=N$ and let $C_{2^N}$ be all the subsets of $X$. $C_{2^N}$ is in $SU_cN_D$ by the previous corollary. By **P3** (section 3) $C_{2^N}$ is not in $LN_cU_D$ since it shatters the infinite set $X$. ∎

The question whether $SN_cN_D$ equals $SU_cN_D$ is still open. However, for a fixed distribution $D$ we can separate $SN_c D$ from $SU_c D$:

**Theorem 6:** There exist distributions $D$ such that $SN_c D$ strictly includes $SU_c D$.

**Proof:** For $i=2,3,\cdots$, let $S_i$ be the intervals $[\frac{1}{2}-(\frac{1}{2})^i, 1-(\frac{1}{2})^i]$. For any set $S$ let $P_i(S)$ denote the set of all the subsets of $S$ with exactly $i$ elements. Let $C_{DHS}=\{S_i : i=2,3,\cdots\}\cup(\underset{i}{\cup}P_i(S_i))$. Let $D$ be the uniform distribution over the interval $[0,1]$ then $C_{DHS}$ is not in $SU_c D$ but is in $SN_c D$.

To show that $C_{DHS}$ is in $SN_c D$ we show that for every target concept $c \in C_{DHS}$ and $\varepsilon,\delta>0$ there exists a number $l$ such that with probability $1-\delta$ any concept consistent with an $l$-sample of $c$ is $\varepsilon$-close to $c$ w.r.t. $D$. Let $c$ be in $P_i(S_i)$ for some $i>1$ then all the sets in $P_j(S_j)$ are 0-close to $c$ w.r.t. $D$. One example in $[\frac{1}{2},\frac{3}{4}]\oplus c$ suffices to rule out all the $S_j$'s. For target concept $c=S_i$ $(i>1)$ we need one example in $[(\frac{1}{2}-(\frac{1}{2})^{i-1}, \frac{1}{2}-(\frac{1}{2})^i]$ to rule out every $S_j$ for $j<i$ and $i+1$ examples in $[(\frac{1}{2}-(\frac{1}{2})^i, \frac{1}{2}-(\frac{1}{2})^{i+1}]$ to rule out every $S_j$ and $c'\in P_j(S_j)$ for $j>i$. The same examples will also rule out every $c'\in P_i(S_i)$. The claim follows from the observation that there exists an $l$ such that, in a random $l$-sample, all the above mentioned events happen with high probability.

On the other hand, for every $i>2$ if $c=S_i$ for every $i$-sample of $c$ there is a concept $c'\in P_i(S_i)$ consistent with the sample and $\frac{1}{2}$-far from $c$ w.r.t. $D$. Thus $C_{DHS}$ is not in $SU_c D$. ∎

Notice that $C_{DHS}$ is not in $SN_cN_D$.

## 5. COVERING RELATIONS BETWEEN CONCEPT CLASSES

We define three notions of approximating one concept class via another. As our relations are reflexive and transitive one can view them as an analogy of the reducibility relations of computational complexity theory, loosely speaking, if $K$ approximates $C$ and $K$ is learnable then so is $C$. Technically speaking, the above statement for a learnability family $W$ asserts that $W$ is closed under approximations. The major theme of this section is showing that certain learnability families are closed under appropriate approximation relations. We apply this results to resolve questions regarding the scope of some models of learnability.

**Definition:** (Covers) Let $A, B$ be two collections of subsets of a domain $X$, $(A, B \subseteq P(X))$.

(a) For an probability distribution $D$ over $X$, $Cov_D(A, B)$ holds ($A$ covers $B$ w.r.t. $D$) if for every $b \in B$ and every $\varepsilon > 0$ there exists some $a \in A$ which is $\varepsilon$-close to $b$ (w.r.t. $D$, of course).

(b) $Cov_{\forall D}(A, B)$ if for every distribution $D$ over $X$, $Cov_D(A, B)$ holds.

(c) $Cov_S(A, B)$ if for every $b \in B$ there exists a sequence $<a_i : i \in N>$ of elements of $A$ such that $\lim_{i \to \infty} a_i = b$.

($\lim_{i \to \infty} a_i = b$ if the characteristic function of $b$ is the pointwise limit of the characteristic functions of the $a_i$'s.

In other words, for every $x \in X$ there exists some $n_x$ s.t. for $j \geq n_x$, $x \in a_j$ if and only if $x \in b$.)

It is clear that for every $A, B$ $Cov_{\forall D}(A, B)$ implies for every $D$, $Cov_D(A, B)$. It is not difficult to construct classes $A, B$ and a distribution $D$ such that $Cov_D(A, B)$ but $Cov_{\forall D}(A, B)$ does not hold. Let us show that $Cov_S(A, B)$ is stronger than $Cov_{\forall D}(A, B)$.

**Lemma 1:** For every set $X$ and $A, B \subseteq P(X)$ if $Cov_S(A, B)$ then $Cov_{\forall D}(A, B)$.

**Proof:** Let $Cov_S(A, B)$, $b \in B$ and let $a_i \in A$ be such that $\lim_{i \to \infty} a_i = b$. For every $x \in X$ let $n_x$ be the smallest integer $n$ such that for every $m \geq n$, $x \in a_m$ if and only if $x \in b$. Consider the series of pairwise disjoint sets $g_j = \{x : n_x = j\}$. Let $D$ be some distribution over $X$ and $\varepsilon > 0$ then as $D$ is a $\sigma$-additive probability measure there exists some $j > 0$ such that $D(\underset{j < i}{\cup} g_i) < \varepsilon$. Thus for $i > j$ $a_i$ is $\varepsilon$-close to $b$. Notice that for all $i > 0$

$g_i = (a_{i-1} \oplus b) - \overset{\infty}{\underset{k=i}{\cup}} (a_k \oplus b)$ and therefore it is $D$-measurable. ∎

For countable $X$ we can show that for all $A, B \subseteq P(X)$, $Cov_{\forall D}(A, B)$ implies $Cov_S(A, B)$. We do not know whether this still holds over uncountable sets. This is one of those issues for which measurability considerations play a crucial role. It is shown in [B] that the $D$-measurability of the members of $A \cup B$ is a necessary condition for lemma 1.

It can be seen that all these relations are reflexive and transitive so they can be regarded as preorderings over the set $P(P(X))$ of concept classes over a domain $X$, $A \overset{*}{\leq} B$ if and only if $Cov_*(B, A)$.

**Lemma 2:** Let $C$ and $K$ be two concept classes. If $Cover_{\forall D}(K, C)$ then $\dim(C) \leq \dim(K)$.

**Proof:** Let $Y$ be a set of $d$ elements shattered by $C$. Let $D$ be the uniform distribution over the elements of $Y$ and 0 everywhere else. If $K$ does not shatter $Y$ then there is a subset of $Y$, $Y'$ $1/d$-far from any set $k$ in $K$. ∎

**Corollary 5:** $LU_cU_D$ (and therefore $SU_cU_D$ and $SU_cN_D$) is downwards closed under the relation $Cov_{\forall D}$.

Let us show that the same holds for $LU_cN_D$ and $LN_cN_D$, first we need the following definition and lemma.

**Definition:** (Derived sample) Let $S = <<x_1, b_1>, \cdots <x_l, b_l>>$ be an $l$-sample ($x_i \in X$ and $b_i \in \{0,1\}$). A *sample S' derived* from S is any sample $<<x_1, b_1'>, \cdots <x_l, b_l'>>$ for $b_i' \in \{0,1\}$. I.e. the sample derived from S has the same points with possibly different labelings.

**Lemma 3:** Let $X$ be a domain and $N \geq 1$. Let $H_N = \{h_1, \cdots, h_N\}$ be a finite hypothesis class over $X$, $D$ a distribution over $X$, $t \subseteq X$ and S an $l$-sample of $t$ drawn by $D$. If $t$ is $\varepsilon/2$-close to $h_N$ and $l \geq \frac{32}{\varepsilon} \ln \frac{N}{\delta}$ then with probability at least $1-\delta$ the most consistent hypothesis $h \in H_N$ will be $\varepsilon$-close to $t$.

**Proof:** The proof is analogous to the proof of lemma 4 in [BI2]. ∎

**Theorem 7:**

(a)         If $K$ is in $LU_cN_D$ and $Cover_{\forall D}(K,C)$ then $C$ is in $LU_cN_D$.

(b)         If $K$ is in $LN_cN_D$ and $Cover_{\forall D}(K,C)$ then $C$ is in $LN_cN_D$.

**Proof:** We shall prove only the first claim, the proof of the second is identical except that the number of examples may depend on the target concept too. Let $F$ be an $LU_cN_D$ learning function for $K$. The main idea is to use $F$ to find a hypothesis $h$ close to a set $k \in K$ which itself is close to the target concept $t \in C$. The problem is that an arbitrary sample **S** of $t$ might not be consistent with $h$, in this case there is no guarantee that $F$ will output a good approximation of $k$ and thus $t$. (In other words **S** as a sample of $h$ may contain errors.) We would like to supply $F$ with examples consistent with $k$ (i.e., change the labels of the erroneous examples). However, $k,t$ and $k \oplus t$ are not known. To solve this problem we pick an initial segment $S_1$ of **S** and apply $F$ on all the samples derived from $S_1$. Exactly one of these derived samples will be consistent with $k$, let us denote it $S'_1$. If $S'_1$ is long enough then, with high probability, $F(S'_1)$ is close to $k$ and $t$. By applying $F$ to all the samples derived from $S_1$, it will output at least one hypothesis close to $k$ and $t$. To select this one, we use the tail of **S** the subsample $S_2$. Hypotheses close to $t$ will be highly consistent with $S_2$ while those far from $t$ will not.

Here we give a formal description of the learning function $G$ represented as an algorithm that has access to the function $F$:

---

Given an $l$-sample **S**;
(1)         Let $S_1$ be the first $\sqrt{l}$ examples in **S** and let $S_2$ be the rest of **S**.
(2)         For every sample $S'_1$ derived from $S_1$ let $h_{S'_1}=F(S'_1)$. Let $H=\{h_{S'_1} : for S'_1\}$.
(3)         Let $h$ be the hypothesis in $H$ most consistent w.r.t. $S_2$.
(4)         Return $h$.

---

The proof that this algorithm is a successful learning function is along the intuitive lines we have sketched.

■

It can also be shown that for every distribution $D$ the families $LU_c D$ and $LN_c D$ are closed under the $Cov_D$ relation. On the other hand $SU_c D$ and $SN_c D$ are not.

**Definition:** (countably coverable) Let us say that $C$ is *countably coverable* (w.r.t. some parameters) if there exists a countable $K$ such that $Cov(K,C)$ (with the same parameters).

**Corollary 6:** If a concept class $C$ is countably $\forall D$-coverable then $C$ is in $LN_c N_D$. (Therefore, by lemma 1, every countably S-coverable $C$ is in $LN_c N_D$.)

**Corollary 7:** Every class of Borel sets in $\mathbb{R}^n$ (and even $\mathbb{R}^{\aleph_0}$) is in $LN_c N_D$. ($\mathbb{R}^n$ can be replaced by any countably generated topological space.)

As a corollary we can now separate $LN_c N_D$ from $(LN_c U_D) \cup (LU_c N_D)$:

**Corollary 8:** $(LN_c U_D) \cup (LU_c N_D)$ is a proper subfamily of $LN_c N_D$.

**Proof:** Let $C_O$ be the set of all the open sets over $X=(0,1)$. By corollary 8, $C_O$ is in $LN_c N_D$. On the other hand, $C_O$ shatters an infinite set thus, by **P3**, it is not in $LN_c U_D$. Moreover, $C_{FO}$ is a subclass of $C_O$ and is not in $LU_c N_D$ thus neither is $C_O$. ∎

**Corollary 9:** $LN_c U_D$ is not downward closed under the relations $Cov_S$ and $Cov_{\forall D}$.

**Theorem 8:** [BI2],[B] For any (fixed) distribution $D$ a class $C$ is in $LN_c D$ if and only if it is countably $D$-coverable.

It follows that if $C$ is in $LN_c N_D$ then for every distribution $D$, $C$ is countably $D$-coverable. We do not know whether the conclusion can be strengthened to "$C$ has a countable $\forall D$-cover".

**Corollary 10:** Let $D$ be the Lesbegue measure on $I=[0,1]$. Every class of Lesbegue measurable sets in $I^n$ (and even $I^{\aleph_0}$) is in $LN_c D$. (Again, Lesbegue measurability can be replaced by any completion of a measure on a countably generated $\sigma$-ring.)

The family $LN_c N_D$ is the learnability notion of [LMR], we now see that it is very wide; every 'natural' concept class in an Euclidean space is in it. On the other hand, we can show for the first time, that it is not a trivial notion, i.e. there exist non-$LN_c N_D$ classes. The question of the existence of such a class was stated open in [LMR].

Furthermore, we are now able to present an example of a concept class $C_A$ and a distribution $D$ such that $C_A$ is not in $LU_c D$. The question of the existence of such a class was left open in [BI2]. (As $C_A$ is not in $LU_c D$ for some fixed $D$, $C_A$ is not in $LN_cN_D$.)

**Example:** Let $D$ be the uniform distribution on the unit interval I=[0,1], let $A$ be an uncountable set.

The probability space $<I^A,B,D^A>$ is defined over the set $I^A$ of all functions from $A$ to $I$, $B$ is the $\sigma$-algebra generated by the set of all finite support cylinders (i.e. sets of the form $\prod_{\alpha \in A} B_\alpha$ where $B_\alpha=I$ for all but finitely many $\alpha$'s), the probability $D^A$ on this $\sigma$-algebra is the one generated by the product probability on the finite support cylinders. (For such a cylinder $G$, $D^A(G)=\Pi\{D(B_\alpha):B_\alpha{\neq}I\}$.) For details see e.g. [H ch. VII].

For every $\alpha{\in}A$ let $c_\alpha$ be $\Pi_{\beta \in A} B_\beta^\alpha$ where $B_\beta^\alpha$ is equal (½,1] for $\alpha=\beta$ and $I$ otherwise. In other words $c_\alpha$ has the interval (½,1] on its $\alpha$'s coordinate and the full unit interval on each of the other coordinates. Let $C_A=\{c_\alpha:\alpha{\in}A\}$.

**Lemma 4:** $C_A$ is not countably $D^A$-coverable.

**Proof:** Every $c_\alpha$ has probability ½ (w.r.t. $D^A$), on the other hand for every $\alpha{\neq}\beta$ $D^A(c_\alpha{\oplus}c_\beta)=¼$. As any two concepts are ¼-far no single set can be ⅛-close to more than one concept.

Now the lemma follows from the uncountability of $C_A$. ∎

## Acknowledgements:

It is a pleasure to thank Alon Itai for many stimulating discussions concerning this work. In particular, the authors wish to thank him for proving lemma 1 and improving the proof of theorem 7.

## REFERENCES

[B]      Benedek G.M., "Problems in computerized learnability" Ph.D. dissertation, Technion, Haifa, Israel (1989) TR 562.

[BEHW1] Blumer A., Ehrenfeucht A., Haussler D. and Warmuth M., "Classifying learnable geometric concepts with the Vapnik-Chervonenkis dimension", Proc. of $18^{th}$ Symp. Theory of Comp., 273-282., (1986).

[BEHW2] Blumer A., Ehrenfeucht A., Haussler D. and Warmuth M., "Occam's razor", Inf. Proc. Letters 24 (1987), 377-380, North-Holland.

[BI1]    Benedek G.M. and Itai A., "Nonuniform learnability", 15th ICALP, 82-92, (1988).

[BI2]    Benedek G.M. and Itai A., "Learnability by fixed distributions", COLT '88, Morgan Kaufmann, (1988).

[EHKV]   Ehrenfeucht A., Haussler D., Kearns M. and Valiant L., "A general lower bound on the number of examples needed for learning", COLT '88, Morgan Kaufmann, (1988).

[H]      Halmos P.R., "Measure theory", New York: Van Nostrand (1969).

[HKLW]   Haussler D., Kearns M., Littlestone N. and Warmuth M., "Equivalence of Models for Polynomial Learnability", COLT '88, Morgan Kaufmann, (1988).

[KLPV]   Kearns M., Ming Li, Pitt L., Valiant L.G., "On the learnability of Boolean formulae", Proc. of $19^{th}$ Symp. Theory of Comp., 285-295. ACM, New York, (1987).

[LMR]    Linial N., Mansour Y. and Rivest R.L., "Results on learnability and the Vapnik-Chervonenkis dimension" 29th FOCS, (1988).

[N]      Natarajan B. K., "On learning Boolean functions", In Proc. of $19^{th}$ Symp. Theory of Comp., 296-304. ACM, New York, (1987).

[PV]     Pitt L. and Valiant, L.G., "Computational limitations on learning from examples", Aiken Computation Laboratory, Harward University, Cambridge, MA 02138, (July 1986).

[VC]     Vapnik V.N. and Chervonenkis A.Ya., "On the uniform convergence of relative frequencies of events to their probabilities", Th. Prob. and its Appl., 16(2), 264-80, (1971).

[V1]     Valiant L.G., "A Theory of the Learnable", Comm. ACM, 27(11), 1134-42, (1984).

[V2]     Valiant L.G., "Learning disjunctions of conjunctions", Proceedings of the $9^{th}$ IJCAI, vol. 1, 560-566, Los Angeles, CA., (August 1985).

## Appendix: Diagrams of the learnability families:

In the following diagrams full arrows F1 $\rightarrow$ F2 denote F1 $\subseteq$ F2 and dotted arrows F1 $\cdots\cdots>$ F2 denote F1 $\not\subseteq$ F2. The trivial arrows (going from a family to one obtained by replacing a U by an N and going left to right from $LX_cY_D$ to a $SX_cY_D$ family) are omitted.

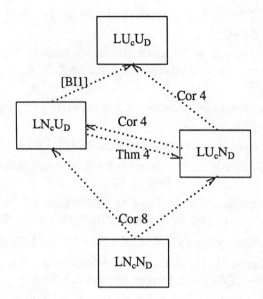

Diagram 1: The relations among the active learnability families.

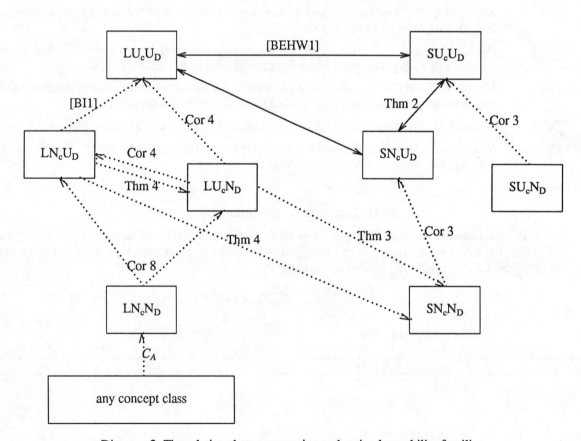

Diagram 2: The relations between passive and active learnability families.

# On the Role of Search for Learning

Stuart A. Kurtz*
Department of Computer Science
University of Chicago
stuart@tartarus.uchicago.edu

Carl H. Smith[†]
Department of Computer Science
Institute for Advanced Computer Studies
University of Maryland
smith@phisube.cs.umd.edu

## Abstract

Learning algorithms that input examples of some phenomenon and produce conjectured explanations of the phenomenon are examined. It is argued that there are two sources for the explanations that occur as outputs of the learning process:

1. use the input data to guide a search through some (possibly very complex) space of explanations, or

2. find the explanations in the data itself, e.g. search the data.

Using a suitable mathematical abstraction, it is proven that learning algorithms that only use the first source of explanations cannot possibly learn all that can be learned by machines.

## 1 Introduction

The role of search, for learning in the limit by examples, is examined in a theoretical setting. We show that it is possible to construct learning algorithms that search through complicated search spaces—so complicated that they are designed using an oracle for the halting problem. Furthermore, this more powerful search technique is not powerful enough, by itself, to account for all the learning that is possible by computer programs. This raises the tantalizing question as to where does a learning device obtain conjectures if *not* by searching some space of conjectures? We speculate that the only other possible source is the data itself. It follows then that some (powerful) mechanistic learning takes place by inputing some data and transforming it directly into an hypothesis. This is as if the learning device sees some data and recognizes it as the answer. Perhaps this is an analogue of serendipity for mechanised science.

*The first author was supported in part by NSF Grant CCR-8602562.
†The second author was supported in part by NSF Grant CCR-8701104.

Gold's seminal paper [Gol67] on inductive inference (learning in the limit) introduced a simple but powerful learning technique which became known as the *enumeration technique*. The enumeration technique begins with an infinite effective list $e_0$, $e_1$, $e_2$, $e_3$, ... of programs for total, computable functions. At stage $s$, the technique emits $e_i$ for the least $i < s$ such that $e_i$ correctly computes the mystery function $f$ for all inputs $i < s$. In essence, the enumeration technique is simply "innocent until proven guilty": each program is conjectured until it is proven "guilty" by failing to correctly predict a value of $f$, whereupon the next program not yet proven "guilty" becomes the conjecture.

The enumeration technique uses the data to guide a search through a space (in this case a list) of potential answers. This technique is embodied in many actual learning by example situations. See [Mit82] for a discussion of generalization techniques viewed as search and a taxonomy of existing search techniques. Consider any learning algorithm $\mathcal{A}$ such that

1. $\mathcal{A}$ learns by example,

2. $\mathcal{A}$ learns in the limit, and

3. $\mathcal{A}$ employs search as one of its components.

We claim that all such algorithms are, or can be effectively transformed into, examples of the enumeration technique. The enumeration technique calls for the searching of a linearly ordered set of alternatives. The algorithm $\mathcal{A}$ may search through a tree, or more complicated structure. The search space of $\mathcal{A}$ may be generated dynamically, as opposed to being specified in advance. In any event, algorithm $\mathcal{A}$ could be dissected and transformed into an effective procedure that generates all and only the items that could ever possibly be examined by $\mathcal{A}$. Thus, an effective linear order could, in principle, be placed on $\mathcal{A}$'s search space.

The enumeration technique also specifies that that *programs* are the object of the search while condition 3 above makes no mention of what is being searched for. We assume that the learning is not rote and that the result of the learning effort will be used to make predictions about examples that were not seen as input. The underlying phenomenon can then be viewed as a mapping from examples to predictions, i.e. a *function*. Using suitable, well known, encoding techniques, it is possible to use the natural numbers ($\omega$) to represent (name) all the possible examples and also the set of all possible predictions. This follows from the observation that it is possible to encode every string of ascii symbols in the natural numbers. These strings include arbitrarily long texts and are certainly sufficient to express both examples and predictions. The programs that are sought by the enumeration technique are viewed as computing the function that represents the phenomenon that is the subject of the learning activity. See [CS83] for a further discussion of the relationship between learning general phenomenon and the mathematical model suggested above.

The algorithm $\mathcal{A}$ alluded to above may search for something other than a program. Perhaps $\mathcal{A}$ is searching for a subprogram, or some vital parameters, or a predicate. From the above discussion, the output of $\mathcal{A}$ is a program. Whatever $\mathcal{A}$ is searching for, it must be incorporated into its output, as otherwise $\mathcal{A}$ could be rewritten as a functionally equivalent algorithm that uses no search, in violation of condition 3 above. Hence, any learning algorithm satisfying conditions 1, 2 and 3 will take the result of its search component and transform it into a program.

Suppose a learning algorithm takes as its examples points from the graph of some recursive function and outputs programs allegedly computing that function as its conjectures. Using the learning algorithm as a black box, we can feed it all possible input examples and record the outputs. The listing of all the possible outputs is close to the list required by the enumeration technique. This list is certainly r.e., but it may contain some programs for partial, not total, recursive functions. To circumvent this difficulty we will allow the black box enumerator an oracle for the halting problem [Rog67]. This will enable us not to list some of the bad programs and for others guarantee that the $i^{\text{th}}$ program listed is defined on inputs 0, ..., $i$. In this fashion, any learning algorithm can be replaced by one obstensibly as powerful that conforms to the paradigm of the enumeration technique. Unfortunately, as our result indicates, the problem with partial, not total, functions, will plague any such attempt.

The enumeration technique is used, explicitly or implicitly, in many learning systems [MCM83]. If the transformation is straightforward, we will say that $\mathcal{A}$ depends primarily on search to learn. In this note, we exhibit a fundamental deficiency in learning algorithms that depend on search as their main technique. Despite this limitation, the enumeration technique is quite powerful. This power comes from the following simple observation:

**Lemma 1** *The enumeration technique, given an effective list $\{e_i : i \in \omega\}$ of programs for total functions, will succeed in inferring a function $f$ if and only if some $e_i$ is a correct program for $f$.*

The enumeration technique also plays a central role in the theory of inductive inference [AS83]. Barzdins, in a series of lectures given at the Latvian Computing Centre in the mid 1970's, conjectured that all inferrible classes of total computable functions were simple encodings of classes inferrible via the enumeration technique. In this note, we disprove a formalization of Barzdins' conjecture by developing a more powerful enumeration technique. This more powerful technique allows for the inference of any class of total computable functions that is effectively enumerable using an oracle for the halting problem. Such classes all fall within a proper subset of the set of all inferrible classes.

## 2   Preliminaries

For a general background, we direct the reader to [Rog67, MY78, DW83] for the theory of computation, and to [AS83] for inductive inference.

Inductive inference machines (IIMs) are algorithmic devices that accept as input the graph of a recursive function and emit programs intended to compute the input function. Natural numbers will serve as names for programs. Program $i$ computes the (possibly partial) function denoted by $\varphi_i$. We assume that $\varphi_0, \varphi_1, ...,$ forms an acceptable programming system [Rog67] and that $\Phi_0, \Phi_1, ...,$ is an associated abstract measure of complexity [Blu67]. We use $\varphi_{i,k}(x) = y$ to denote $\varphi_i(x) = y$ and $\Phi(i, x) < k$.

An IIM $M$, on input from the graph of $f$, *converges* to $i$ if either $M$ outputs a *last* program which is $i$, or past some point, $M$ outputs only program $i$. If $M(f)$ converges, we may assume without loss of generality that it does so independently of the order in which $f$ is presented to $M$ [BB75]. An IIM $M$ *identifies* (or *explains*) $f$ (written: $f \in \mathbf{EX}(M)$) if $M(f)$ converges to $i$ and $f = \varphi_i$. The collection of sets $\{S : S \subseteq \mathbf{EX}(M)$ for $M$ an IIM$\}$ is denoted by $\mathbf{EX}$. We will primarily be concerned with the class of recursive functions, denoted by **Rec**.

There have been many proposed restrictions and enhancements of IIMs, as well as various notions of successful inference [AS83]. An IIM is called *popperian* if it only outputs programs that compute members of **Rec**. The class of families of languages inferrible by popperian IIMs is denoted by **PEX**. **PEX** is known to be a strict subset of **EX** and popperian inference machines are equivalent in power to a class of extrapolation mechanisms [CS83, Theorem 2.19].[1] Notice that any IIM using the enumeration technique is *a fortiori* popperian. Popperian inference machines have been studied extensively [CN98].

The remaining preliminaries are recursion theoretic in nature. Suppose $S \subset \mathbf{Rec}$. A *recursive operator* [Rog67] is a mapping ($\Theta$) from functions to functions such that there is a recursive $f$ with $\Theta(\varphi_i) = \varphi_{f(i)}$ for all programs $i$. The class $S$ is *recursively enumerable* (r.e.) if either $S = \emptyset$ or there is a recursive function $f$ such that $S = \{\varphi_{f(i)} : i \in \omega\}$. A $\mathbf{0}'$-*recursive* function is any total function that is computable using an oracle for the halting problem. A crucial result about $\mathbf{0}'$-recursive functions is

**Lemma 2 (The Limit Lemma [Sho71])** *A function $f$ is $\mathbf{0}'$-recursive if and only if there is a total recursive function $h$ such that*

$$(\forall x)[f(x) = \lim_{n \to \infty} h(x, n)].$$

A class $S$ is $\mathbf{0}'$-*enumerable* if either $S = \emptyset$ or there is a $\mathbf{0}'$-recursive function $f$ such that $S = \{\varphi_{f(i)} : i \in \omega\}$.

## 3    A More Powerful Enumeration Technique

In this section we show that any $\mathbf{0}'$-enumerable set of recursive functions is inferrible by an elimination technique. Furthermore, the witnessing IIM can be made popperian. A final definition will make the statement of our theorem easier.

**Definition 3** *A collection $S$ of partial recursive functions is **PEX**-stable if whenever $\Theta$ is a recursive operator such that $\Theta(S) \subseteq \mathbf{Rec}$, then $\Theta(S) \in \mathbf{PEX}$.*

Now we are ready for the main result.

**Theorem 4** *If $S$ is $\mathbf{0}'$-enumerable, then $S$ is **PEX**-stable.*

---

[1] Some complexity theoretic characterizations of these inference classes are given in [BB75]. The class **PEX** (called **NV**) is precisely the $h$-easy functions. The class **EX-R** (mentioned later) corresponds to the $\Theta$-honest functions.

**Proof:** Suppose $S$ is $\mathbf{0}'$-enumerable. Let $f$ be a $\mathbf{0}'$-recursive function such that $S = \{\varphi_{f(i)} : i \in \omega\}$. Choose $h$ by the limit lemma to be a total recursive function such that $f(x) = \lim_{s\to\infty} h(x,s)$, for all $x$. Suppose $\Theta$ is a recursive operator such that $\Theta(S) \subseteq \mathbf{Rec}$. Let $g$ be a recursive function witnessing the effectiveness of $\Theta$, i.e., $\varphi_{g(i)} = \Theta(\varphi_i)$ for all $i$.

We will construct an IIM $M$ such that $\Theta(S) \subseteq \mathbf{PEX}(M)$. In fact, we will do somewhat better, providing an $M$ such that $\Theta(S) = \mathbf{PEX}(M)$.

We first define the functions $\psi_y^n(x)$ as follows. Let $z > n$ be minimal such that either

1. $h(y,n) \neq h(y,z)$; or

2. $\varphi_{g(h(y,n)),z}(x)$ converges.

If condition 1 occurs, then $\psi_y^n(x) \overset{\text{def}}{=} 0$. If condition 2 occurs, then $\psi_y^n(x) \overset{\text{def}}{=} \varphi_{g(h(y,n))}(x)$. If no such $z$ exists, then $\psi_y^n(x)$ is undefined.

It is quite clear that the $\psi_y^n$'s form a uniformly recursive family of partial recursive functions. In fact, each $\psi_y^n$ is *total* recursive, as a $z$ satisfying condition 1 or 2 must always exist. There are two cases. If $h(y,n) = f(y)$, then $\varphi_{g(h(y,n))} = \varphi_{g(f(y))}$, which is total by choice of $g$, and so condition 2 must eventually apply. If $h(y,n) \neq f(y)$, then condition 1 must eventually occur by choice of $h$.

We define a predicate $\xi(y,\sigma)$ which is true if and only if there exists a $z > |\sigma|$ such that

3. $h(y,w) = h(y,|\sigma|)$ for all $w$ such that $|\sigma| \leq w \leq z$; and

4. $\varphi_{g(h(y,|\sigma|)),z}(k) = \sigma(k)$, for every $k < |\sigma|$.

The predicate $\xi$ is recursive, by the same proof as for the $\psi_y^n$'s.

We are now in a position to describe $M$. On input $\sigma$, let $y_0$ be the least $y < |\sigma|$ satisfying $\xi(y,\sigma)$. If no such $y_0$ exists, then $M(\sigma)$ is defined to be an index for the constant zero function. Let $n_0$ be the least $n$ such that $h(y_0,k) = h(y_0,|\sigma|)$ for all $k$ such that $n \leq k \leq |\sigma|$. Let $M(\sigma)$ be an index for $\psi_{y_0}^{n_0}$ in which $y_0$ is explicitly encoded.

By definition, $M$ can only produce indices for total recursive functions. Therefore, it remains only to show that $\Theta(S) = \mathbf{EX}(M)$.

First we show that $\Theta(S) \subseteq \mathbf{EX}(M)$.

Fix $\theta \in \Theta(S)$. Let $e$ be minimal such that $\theta = \varphi_{g(f(e))}$. Let $n > e$ be so large that

- if $m \geq n$, then $h(e',m) = f(e')$ for all $e' \leq e$; and

- if $e' < e$, then there is an $x < n$ such that $\varphi_{g(f(e'))}(x) \neq \theta(x)$.

Let $n_0$ be minimal such that $h(e,k) = f(e)$ for all $k \geq n_0$.

Let $\sigma$ be any initial segment of $\theta$ of length at least $n$. On input $\sigma$, $M$ must produce an index for $\psi_e^{n_0}$. To see this, notice that $\xi(e,\sigma)$ will be true for all initial segments $\sigma$ of $\theta$, we have chosen $\sigma$ to be so long that $\xi(e',\sigma)$ must be false for all $e' < e$, and we have required that $|\sigma| > e$, so $M$ will consider $e$. The choice of $n_0$ is similarly forced.

Moreover, $\psi_e^{n_0} = \theta$. To see this, note that $h(e,n) = f(e)$ for all $n \geq n_0$. Therefore $\theta = \varphi_{g(f(e))} = \varphi_{g(h(e,n_0))}$. By our definition, $\psi_e^{n_0}(x) = \varphi_{g(h(e,n_0))}(x)$ unless condition 1 occurs, but by choice of $n_0$, condition 1 cannot occur.

It remains only to show that $\mathbf{EX}(M) \subseteq \Theta(S)$. Assume $\theta$ is in $\mathbf{EX}(M)$. Then $M$ must, on sufficiently large initial segments $\sigma$ of $\theta$ produce a fixed index, say for $\psi_y^n$. If $\theta \neq \psi_y^n$, this will eventually be recognized (4 above) and $M$ will have to change its mind, contradicting the choice of $\psi_y^n$. If $\theta = \psi_y^n$, then we must have $\psi_y^n = \varphi_{g(f(y))}$, or else $M$ would eventually produce an index for $\psi_{y'}^k$, for some $y \neq y'$ (1 above). By the coding condition, the index $M$ produces for $\psi_{y'}^k$ must be different from the index it produced for $\psi_y^n$, contradicting the choice of $\phi_y^n$. Thus, $\theta = \psi_y^n = \varphi_{f(g(y))}$ and so $\theta \in \Theta(S)$.

$\square$

Suppose $S$ is a $\mathbf{0}'$-enumerable class of recursive functions and $\Theta$ is the identity recursive operator, whose effectiveness is witnessed by $\lambda x[x]$. By the above theorem, $\Theta(S) = S$ is inferrible, justifying the title of this section. The set of all possible outputs generated by $M$ of the above proof on all possible input sequences forms an r.e. set. Since $M$ was shown to be popperian, the set of all possible outputs of $M$ is an r.e. set of recursive functions that is also a superset of $S$, the $\mathbf{0}'$-enumerable class on which the theorem is based. Hence, every $\mathbf{0}'$-enumerable set of recursive functions is contained in some r.e. class of recursive functions. This was also noticed, in the context of inference, in [CS83].

# 4    Barzdins' Conjecture

There seem in general to be two types of learning algorithms: enumeration algorithms and what might be termed "self referential encoding" algorithms. The latter class of algorithms have thus far only found application by theoreticians who have used them to distinguish between various models of identification.

For example,

**Definition 5** ([BB75, CS83]) *A function $f$ is* self-describing *if $f = \varphi_{f(0)}$.*

The set of self-describing functions is a standard example of an element in $\mathbf{EX} - \mathbf{PEX}$. In fact, it is not difficult to show that no class containing the self-describing functions can be recursively enumerable.

On the other hand, the self-describing functions encode the class of all recursive functions, for if $\psi$ is a recursive function, one can use the recursion theorem to find an index $e$ such that

$$\varphi_e(x) = \begin{cases} e, & \text{if } x = 0; \\ \psi(x-1), & \text{otherwise.} \end{cases}$$

This sort of observation lead Barzdins to conjecture that whenever a class of functions cannot be inferred by the enumeration technique, it must be because it encodes some class that cannot be inferred at all. Barzdins' conjecture is stated formally below. The use of effective operators models the "encoding" part of the intuitive conjecture. In the above situation, we think of **Rec** as $\Theta$ applied to the self describing functions, where $\Theta$ erases the code.

**Conjecture 6 (Barzdins' Conjecture)** *Suppose $S \subseteq$ **Rec**. Then $S$ is r.e. if and only if for all effective operators $\Theta$ such that $\Theta(S) \subseteq$ **Rec**, $\Theta(S) \in EX$.*

To refute Barzdins' conjecture, by our theorem, we need only exhibit a $\mathbf{0}'$-enumerable class of recursive functions (and therefore **PEX**-stable by Theorem 4) that is not recursively enumerable. Let $\bar{K}$ denote the complement of the halting set. If the set $S' = \{\lambda x[c] : c \in \bar{K}\}$ were r.e., then $\bar{K}$ would be r.e., a contradiction. However, $S'$ is $\mathbf{0}'$-enumerable, by the following algorithm: on input $i$, enumerate an index for $\lambda x[c_i]$, where $c_i$ is the $i$-th member of $\bar{K}$.

Zeugmann considered a generalization of Barzdins' original conjecture [Zeu87]. His generalization was to replace the "**EX**" in the conjecture above by an arbitrary criterion of successful inference. Zeugmann showed that Barzdins' conjecture held for three different classes of inferrible functions [Zeu87]. These classes are now described. Consider IIMs constrained to automatically converge when they output the same conjecture twice in a row. The resulting class of inferrible sets is called **FIN** [TB73]. Let $S$ be a set of functions. An IIM $M$ is *reliable* on $S$ iff whenever $M$ is presented with input from the graph of some function in $S$, $M$ converges iff it successfully identifies [BB75]. Reliable inference machines have the nice property that any two may be combined into a third IIM that can infer all the functions inferred by either of the two original machines [Min76]. **EX-R** denotes the class of sets of functions inferrible by IIMs reliable on **Rec**. **EX-T** denotes the class of sets of functions inferrible by IIMs reliable on the set of total functions. Zeugmann showed that Barzdins' conjecture holds with "**EX**" replaced with either "**FIN**" or "**EX-R**" or "**EX-T**."

Even though Barzdins' conjecture does not hold for **EX**, perhaps a modified version does. The conjecture below is in the spirit of Barzdins original conjecture, but is not refuted by our results.

**Conjecture 7** *Suppose $S \subseteq$ **Rec**. If for all effective operators $\Theta$ such that $\Theta(S) \subseteq$ **Rec**, $\Theta(S) \in EX$ then $S$ is contained in some r.e. class of recursive functions.*

# 5   Implications for Systems that Learn

The enumeration technique is the basis of many learning algorithms used in artificial intelligence [MCM83]. Generally, a "solution search space" is defined and searched. To apply the enumeration technique in a specific context, one need only supply a subalgorithm which generates the elements of this solution search space: the rest of the learning algorithm is fixed.

The practical advantage of our technique is that it makes available a much more powerful language for expressing the generation subalgorithm: the language of the $\mathbf{0}'$-recursive functions. An important theoretical consequence is that enumeration techniques—no matter how clever—do not exhaust the potential of machine learning, because **PEX** is a *proper* subset of **EX**.

This raises the question of how to build learning strategies more powerful that ones that rely on searching a space of potential solutions. The mathematical answer is that the set of self describing functions is an example of something in **EX** but not in **PEX**. When viewed in the simple terms of an inductive inference machine, the only source of potential outputs is to search through some (perhaps dynamically generated) list *or* to search the data itself. To infer the set of self describing functions, it suffices to search the data itself. This suggests that to transcend the power of methodical learning (enumeration technique, **PEX**) some good fortune in discovering just the right datum, the one with the answer coded into it, is necessary. Even though the learnability of some function can be made independent of the order of the examples presented [BB75], the complexity of the inference may be radically altered [DS86]. We believe this to be an analogue of scientific serendipity.

## 6    Acknowledgments

Thomas Zeugmann communicated Barzdins' conjecture to the second author during the 1986 Workshop on Analogical and Inductive Inference in Wendisch-Rietz, DDR. The authors would like to thank Dianna Gordon and Jim Owings for reading and commenting on an earlier draft of this paper.

This work was initiated on the occasion of the first author's visit to the University of Maryland as part of the activities of the Capitol Area Theory Seminar, funded in part by NSF Grant CCR 8744916. Much of this work was done while the second author was on leave at the National Science Foundation. Any opinions, findings, and conclusions or recommendations expressed in this publication are those of the authors and do not necessarily reflect the views of the National Science Foundation.

## References

[AS83]    Dana Angluin and Carl H. Smith. Inductive inference: theory and methods. *Computing Surveys*, 15(3):237–269, September 1983.

[BB75]    Lenore Blum and Manuel Blum. Toward a mathematical theory of inductive inference. *Information and Control*, 28:125–155, 1975.

[Blu67]    Manuel Blum. A machine-independent theory of the complexity of recursive functions. *Journal of the Association for Computing Machinery*, 14(2):322–336, April 1967.

[CN98]    J. Case and S. Ngomanguelle. Refinements of inductive inference by popperian machines. *Kybernetica*, 198? To appear.

[CS83]    John Case and Carl H. Smith. Comparison of identification criteria for machine inductive inference. *Theoretical Computer Science*, 25(2):193–220, 1983.

[DS86]     Robert P. Daley and Carl H. Smith. On the complexity of inductive inference. *Information and Control*, 69:12–40, 1986.

[DW83]     Martin D. Davis and Elaine J. Weyuker. *Computability, Complexity, and Languages*. Academic Press, New York, 1983.

[Gol67]    E. M. Gold. Language identification in the limit. *Information and Control*, 10:447–474, 1967.

[MCM83]   R. Michalski, J. Carbonell, and T. Mitchell. *Machine Learning*. Tioga Publishing Co., Palo Alto, 1983.

[Min76]    E. Minicozzi. Some natural properties of strong-identification in inductive inference. *Theoretical Computer Science*, 2:345–360, 1976.

[Mit82]    Tom Mitchell. Generalization as search. *Artificial Intelligence*, 18(2):203–226, March 1982.

[MY78]     Michael Machtey and Paul Young. *An Introduction to the General Theory of Algorithms*. North-Holland, New York, 1978.

[Rog67]    Hartley Rogers, Jr. *Theory of Recursive Functions and Effective Computability*. McGraw-Hill, 1967.

[Sho71]    Joseph Shoenfield. *Degrees of Unsolvability*. North Holland, Amsterdam, 1971.

[TB73]     Boris Trakhtenbrot and Jan Barzdins. *Finite Automata: Behavior and Synthesis*. Springer-Verlag, 1973.

[Zeu87]    Thomas Zeugmann. On Barzdins' conjecture. In K. P. Jantke, editor, *Analogical and Inductive Inference*, volume 256, pages 220–227. Springer-Verlag, 1987.

# ELEMENTARY FORMAL SYSTEM AS A UNIFYING FRAMEWORK FOR LANGUAGE LEARNING

## Setsuo Arikawa
Research Institute of Fundamental Information Science
Kyushu University 33, Fukuoka 812, Japan

## Takeshi Shinohara
Department of Artificial Intelligence
Kyushu Institute of Technology, Iizuka 820

## Akihiro Yamamoto
Department of Information Systems
Kyushu University 39, Kasuga 816

## ABSTRACT

This paper presents a unifying framework for language learning, especially for inductive inference of various classes of languages. The elementary formal systems (EFS for short), Smullyan invented to develop his recursive function theory, are proved suitable to *generate* languages.

In this paper we first point out that EFS can also work as a logic programming language, and the resolution procedure for EFS can be used to *accept* languages. We give a theoretical foundation to EFS from the viewpoint of semantics of logic programs. Hence, Shapiro's theory of model inference can naturally be applied to our language learning by EFS.

We introduce some subclasses of EFS's which correspond to Chomsky hierarchy and other important classes of languages. We discuss computations of unifiers between two terms. Then we give, in a uniform way, inductive inference algorithms including refinement operators for these subclasses and show their completeness.

This paper was supported by Grant-in-Aid for Scientific Research on Priority Areas (No.63633011), The Ministry of Education, Science and Culture of Japan.

# 1   INTRODUCTION

In Computer Science and Artificial Intelligence, learning or inductive inference is attracting much attention. Many contributions have been made in this field for the last 25 years [4]. Theoretical studies of language learning, originated in the so called grammatical inference, are now laying a firm foundation for the other approaches to learning as the theory of languages and automata did for Computer Science in general [7, 1, 2, 4, 15]. However, most of such studies were developed in their own frameworks such as patterns, regular grammars, context-free and -sensitive grammars, phrase structure grammars, many kinds of automata, and so on. Hence they had to devise also their own procedures for generating hypotheses from examples so far given and for testing each hypothesis on them.

In this paper we introduce a new unifying framework called variable-bounded EFS to language learning, especially to inductive inference of languages. The EFS, elementary formal system [18, 6], that was invented by Smullyan to develop his recursive function theory is also a good framework for generating languages [5].

Recently some new approaches to learning are proposed [14, 19, 3, 8] and being studied extensively as seen, for example, in COLT'88. We here pay our attention to Shapiro's theory of model inference system (MIS for short) [14] that succeeded in unifying the various approaches to inductive inference such as program synthesis from examples, automatic knowledge acquisition, and automatic debugging. It has theoretical backgrounds in the first order logic and logic programming. His system also deals with language learning by using the so called difference-lists, which seems unnatural to develop the theory of language learning.

This paper combines EFS and MIS in order that we can take full advantage of theoretical results of them and extend our previous work [17]. First we give definitions of concepts necessary for our discussions. In Section 3 we show that the variable-bounded EFS has a good background in the theory of logic programming, and also it has an efficient derivation procedure for testing the guessed hypotheses on examples. In Section 4, we prove that the variable-bounded EFS's constitute a natural and proper subclass of the full EFS's, but they are powerful enough to define all the recursively enumerable sets of words. Then we describe in our framework many important subclasses of languages including Chomsky hierarchy and pattern languages. We also discuss the computations of unifiers which play a key role in the derivations for the above mentioned testing hypotheses. In Section 5 we give the inductive inference algorithms including contradiction backtracing and refinement operators for these subclasses in a uniform way, and prove their completeness. Thus we conclude that our variable-bounded EFS is an efficient unifying framework for language learning.

# 2   PRELIMINARIES

Let $\Sigma$, $X$, and $\Pi$ be mutually disjoint sets. We assume that $\Sigma$ and $\Pi$ are finite. We refer to $\Sigma$ as *alphabet*, and to each element of it as *symbol*, which will be denoted by $a, b, c, \ldots,$

to each element of $X$ as *variable*, denoted by $x, y, z, x_1, x_2, \ldots$ and to each element of $\Pi$ as *predicate symbol*, denoted by $p, q, q_1, q_2, \ldots$, where each of them has an *arity*. $A^+$ denotes the set of all nonempty words over a set $A$. Let $S$ be an EFS that is being defined below.

**Definition** A *term* of $S$ is an element of $(\Sigma \cup X)^+$. Each term is denoted by, $\pi, \tau, \pi_1, \pi_2, \ldots$, $\tau_1, \tau_2, \ldots$. A *ground term* of $S$ is an element of $\Sigma^+$. Terms are also called *patterns*.

**Definition** An *atomic formula* (or *atom* for short) of $S$ is an expression of the form $p(\tau_1, \ldots, \tau_n)$, where $p$ is a predicate symbol in $\Pi$ with arity $n$ and $\tau_1, \ldots, \tau_n$ are terms of $S$. The atom is *ground* if all $\tau_1, \ldots, \tau_n$ are ground.

*Well-formed formulas, clauses, empty clause* ($\square$), *ground clauses* and *substitutions* are defined in the ordinal ways [10].

**Definition** A *definite clause* is a clause of the form
$$A \leftarrow B_1, \ldots, B_n \qquad (n \geq 0).$$

**Definition (Smullyan [18])** An *elementary formal system* (*EFS* for short) $S$ is a triplet $(\Sigma, \Pi, \Gamma)$, where $\Gamma$ is a finite set of definite clauses. The definite clauses in $\Gamma$ are called *axioms* of $S$.

We denote a substitution by $\{x_1 := \tau_1, \ldots, x_n := \tau_n\}$, where $x_i$ are mutually distinct variables. We also define $p(\tau_1, \ldots, \tau_n)\theta = p(\tau_1\theta, \ldots, \tau_n\theta)$ and
$$(A \leftarrow B_1, \ldots, B_m)\theta = A\theta \leftarrow B_1\theta, \ldots, B_m\theta.$$
for a substitution $\theta$, an atom $p(\tau_1, \ldots, \tau_n)$ and a clause $A \leftarrow B_1, \ldots, B_m$.

**Definition** Let $S = (\Sigma, \Pi, \Gamma)$ be an EFS. We define the relation $\Gamma \vdash C$ for a clause $C$ of $S$ inductively as follows:

(2.1) If $\Gamma \ni C$, then $\Gamma \vdash C$.

(2.2) If $\Gamma \vdash C$, then $\Gamma \vdash C\theta$ for any substitution $\theta$.

(2.3) If $\Gamma \vdash A \leftarrow B_1, \ldots, B_{n+1}$ and $\Gamma \vdash B_{n+1}$, then $\Gamma \vdash A \leftarrow B_1, \ldots, B_n$.

$C$ is *provable from* $\Gamma$ if $\Gamma \vdash C$.

**Definition** For an EFS $S = (\Sigma, \Pi, \Gamma)$ and $p \in \Pi$ with arity $n$, we define
$$L(S, p) = \{(\alpha_1, \ldots, \alpha_n) \in (\Sigma^+)^n \mid \Gamma \vdash p(\alpha_1, \ldots, \alpha_n)\}.$$

In case $n = 1$, $L(S, p)$ is a language over $\Sigma$. A language $L \subseteq \Sigma^+$ is *definable by EFS* or an *EFS language* if such $S$ and $p$ exist.

Now we will give two interesting subclasses of EFS's. We need some notations. Let $v(A)$ be the set of all variables in an atom $A$. For a term $\pi$, $|\pi|$ denotes the length of $\pi$, that is, the number of all occurrences of symbols and variables in $\pi$, and $o(x, \pi)$ denotes the number of all occurrences of a variable $x$ in a term $\pi$. For an atom $p(\pi_1, \ldots, \pi_n)$, let
$$|p(\pi_1, \ldots, \pi_n)| = |\pi_1| + \cdots + |\pi_n|,$$
$$o(x, p(\pi_1, \ldots, \pi_n)) = o(x, \pi_1) + \cdots + o(x, \pi_n).$$

**Definition** A definite clause $A \leftarrow B_1, \ldots, B_n$ is *variable-bounded* if $v(A) \supseteq v(B_i)$ ($i = 1, \ldots, n$), and an EFS is *variable-bounded* if its axioms are all variable-bounded.

**Definition** A clause $A \leftarrow B_1, \ldots, B_n$ is *length-bounded* if
$$|A\theta| \geq |B_1\theta| + \cdots + |B_n\theta|$$
for any substitution $\theta$. An EFS $S = (\Sigma, \Pi, \Gamma)$ is *length-bounded* if axioms in $\Gamma$ are all length-bounded.

We can easily characterize the concept of length-boundness as follows.

**Lemma 2.1** *A clause $A \leftarrow B_1, \ldots, B_n$ is length-bounded if and only if*
$$|A| \geq |B_1| + \cdots + |B_n|,$$
$$o(x, A) \geq o(x, B_1) + \cdots + o(x, B_n)$$
*for any variable $x$.*

**Proof** Let $A \leftarrow B_1, \ldots, B_n$ be a length-bounded clause. Then $|A\theta| \geq |B_1\theta| + \ldots + |B_n\theta|$ for any substitution $\theta$. When $\theta = \{\ \}$, we have
$$|A| \geq |B_1| + \cdots + |B_n|.$$
Let $\theta = \{x := x^{k+1}\}$. Then
$$|A\theta| - \sum_{i=1}^{n} |B_i\theta| = |A| - \sum_{i=1}^{n} |B_i| + k \times \left(o(x, A) - \sum_{i=1}^{n} o(x, B_i)\right) \geq 0.$$
Therefore
$$o(x, A) - \sum_{i=1}^{n} o(x, B_i) \geq \frac{-\left(|A| - \sum_{i=1}^{n} |B_i|\right)}{k}.$$
If $k$ is large enough, for example, $k > A - \sum_{i=1}^{n} |B_i|$, we have
$$o(x, A) - \sum_{i=1}^{n} o(x, B_i) \geq 0.$$
Conversely let $A, B_1, \ldots, B_n$ be atoms such that
$$|A| \geq |B_1| + \cdots + |B_n|,$$
$$o(x, A) \geq o(x, B_1) + \cdots + o(x, B_n)$$
for any variable $x$, and let $\theta$ be any substitution. Then
$$|A\theta| - \sum_{i=1}^{n} |B_i\theta| = |A| + \sum_{x \in v(A)} ((|x\theta| - 1)o(x, A)) - \sum_{i=1}^{n}\left(|B_i| + \sum_{x \in v(A)} ((x|\theta| - 1)o(x, B_i))\right)$$
$$= |A| - \sum_{i=1}^{n} |B_i| + \sum_{x \in v(A)} \left((|x\theta| - 1)(o(x, A) - \sum_{i=1}^{n} o(x, B_i))\right) \geq 0$$

Here we should note that $|x\theta| \geq 1$ for any substitution. In case we allow an erasing substitution $\theta$ such that $|x\theta| = 0$, this lemma does not hold.

By this lemma, we know that length-bounded clauses are all variable-bounded and it is computable to test whether a given clause is length-bounded or not.

**Example 2.1** An EFS $S = (\{a, b, c\}, \{p, q\}, \Gamma)$ with

$$\Gamma = \left\{ \begin{array}{l} p(a, b, c) \leftarrow, \\ p(ax, by, cz) \leftarrow p(x, y, z), \\ q(xyz) \leftarrow p(x, y, z) \end{array} \right\}$$

is variable-bounded, and also length-bounded by Lemma 2.1. It defines a language $L(S, q) = \{a^n b^n c^n \mid n \geq 1\}$.

# 3    EFS AS A LOGIC PROGRAMMING LANGUAGE

In this section we show that EFS is a logic programming language. We give a refutation procedure for EFS and several kinds of semantics for EFS. Then we show the refutation is complete as a procedure to accept EFS languages. We also show that the negation as failure rule for variable-bounded EFS is complete and it is coincident with the Herbrand rule.

## Derivation Procedure for EFS

**Definition** Let $\alpha$ and $\beta$ be a pair of terms or atoms. Then a substitution $\theta$ is a *unifier* of $\alpha$ and $\beta$ if $\alpha\theta = \beta\theta$.

It is often the case that there are infinitely many maximally general unifiers.

**Example 3.1 (Plotkin[12])** Let $S = (\{a, b\}, \{p\}, \Gamma)$. Then $\{x := a^i\}$ for every $i$ is the unifier of $p(ax)$ and $p(xa)$. All the unifiers are maximally general. In case $\Sigma = \{a\}$, the empty substitution is the most general unifier of the two atoms.

We formalize the derivation for an EFS with no requirement that every unifier should be most general.

**Definition** A *goal clause* (or *goal* for short) of $S$ is a clause of the form

$$\leftarrow B_1, \ldots, B_n \qquad (n \geq 0).$$

**Definition** If clauses $C$ and $D$ are identical except renaming of variables, that is, $C = D\theta$ and $C\theta' = D$ for some substitutions $\theta$ and $\theta'$, we say $D$ is a *variant* of $C$ and write $C \equiv D$.

We assume a *computation rule $R$* to select an atom from every goal.

**Definition** Let $S$ be an EFS, and $G$ be a goal of $S$. A *derivation from $G$* is a (finite or infinite) sequence of triplets $(G_i, \theta_i, C_i)$ $(i = 0, 1, \ldots)$ which satisfies the following conditions:

(3.1)  $G_i$ is a goal, $\theta_i$ is a substitution, $C_i$ is a variant of an axiom of $S$, and $G_0 = G$.

(3.2)  $v(C_i) \cap v(C_j) = \phi$  $(i \neq j)$, and $v(C_j) \cap v(G) = \phi$ for every $i$.

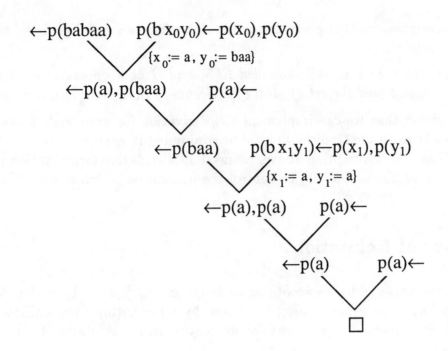

Figure 1: A refutation

(3.3) If $G_i$ is $\leftarrow A_1, \ldots, A_k$ and $A_m$ is the atom selected by $R$, then $C_i$ is $A \leftarrow B_1, \ldots, B_q$, and $\theta_i$ is a unifier of $A$ and $A_m$, and $G_{i+1}$ is

$$(\leftarrow A_1, \ldots, A_{m-1}, B_1, \ldots, B_q, A_{m+1}, \ldots, A_k)\theta_i.$$

$A_m$ is a *selected atom* of $G_i$, and $G_{i+1}$ is a *resolvent* of $G_i$ and $C_i$ by $\theta_i$.

**Definition** A *refutation* is a finite derivation ending with the empty goal $\square$.

**Example 3.2** Let EFS $S = (\{a, b\}, \{p\}, \Gamma)$ with

$$\Gamma = \left\{ \begin{array}{l} p(a) \leftarrow, \\ p(bxy) \leftarrow p(x), p(y) \end{array} \right\}.$$

Then a refutation from $\leftarrow p(babaa)$ is illustrated by Figure 1, where the computation rule selects the leftmost atom from every goal.

Now we give a property of unification. Makanin[11] showed that the existence of a unifier of two terms is decidable, but this fact is not suitable for constructing derivations. For ground patterns we have a good property.

**Lemma 3.1 (Yamamoto[21])** *Let $\alpha$ and $\beta$ be a pair of terms or atoms. If one of them is ground, then every unifier of $\alpha$ and $\beta$ is ground and the set of all unifiers is finite and computable.*

The aim of our formalization of derivation is to give a procedure accepting languages definable by EFS's. We will show in Section 4 that the variable-bounded EFS's are powerful enough. Thus we can assume that every derivation starts from a ground goal and that every EFS is variable-bounded.

**Proposition 3.1** *Let $S$ be a variable-bounded EFS, and $G$ be a ground goal. Then every resolvent of $G$ is ground, and the set of all the resolvents of $G$ is finite and computable.*

This lemma shows that we can implement the derivation for variable-bounded EFS in nearly the same way as in the traditional logic programming languages.

If we do not have the assumption above, we need an alternative formalization of derivation, such as given by Yamamoto[20], to control the unification which is not always terminating.

## Completeness of Refutation

We describe the semantics of EFS's according to Jaffar, et al.[9]. They have given a general framework of various logic programming languages by representing their unification algorithm as an equality theory. To represent the unification in the refutation for EFS we use the equality theory

$$E = \{cons(cons(x, y), z) = cons(x, cons(y, z))\},$$

where *cons* is to be interpreted as the catenation of terms.

The first semantics for an EFS $S = (\Sigma, \Pi, \Gamma)$ is its model. To interpret well-formed formulas of $S$ we can restrict the domains to the models of $E$. Then a model of $S$ is an interpretation which makes every axiom in $\Gamma$ true. We can use the set of all ground atoms as the *Herbrand base* denoted by $B(S)$. Every subset $I$ of $B(S)$ is called an *Herbrand interpretation* in the sense that $A \in I$ means $A$ is true and $A \notin I$ means $A$ is false for $A \in B(S)$. Then

$$M(S) = \cap\{M \subset B(S) \,|\, M \text{ is an Herbrand model of } S \}$$

is an Herbrand model of $S$, and every ground atom in $M(S)$ is true in any model of $S$. The second semantics is the least fixpoint $lfp(T_S)$ of the function $T_S : 2^{B(S)} \longrightarrow 2^{B(S)}$ defined by

$$T_S(I) = \left\{ A \in B(S) \,\middle|\, \begin{array}{l} \text{there is a ground instance of an axiom} \\ \qquad A \leftarrow B_1, \dots, B_n \\ \text{of } S \text{ such that } B_k \in I \text{ for } 1 \leq k \leq n \end{array} \right\}.$$

$lfp(T_S)$ is identical to $T_S \uparrow \omega$ defined as follows:

$$\begin{aligned} T_S \uparrow 0 &= \phi, \\ T_S \uparrow n &= T_S(T_S \uparrow (n-1)) \quad \text{for } n \geq 1, \\ T_S \uparrow \omega &= \bigcup_{n \geq 0} T_S \uparrow n. \end{aligned}$$

The third semantics using refutation is defined by

$$SS(S) = \{A \in B(S) \,|\, \text{there exists a refutation from } \leftarrow A \}.$$

These three semantics are shown to be identical by Jaffar, et al.[9] .

Now we give another semantics of EFS using the provability as the set

$$PS(S) = \{A \in B(S) \mid \Gamma \vdash A\}.$$

**Theorem 3.1 (Yamamoto[21])** *For every EFS $S$,*

$$M(S) = lfp(T_S) = T_S \uparrow \omega = SS(S) = PS(S).$$

Thus the refutation is complete as a procedure to accept EFS languages.

## Negation as Failure for EFS

Now we discuss the inference of negation. We prepare some definitions.

**Definition** A derivation is *finitely failed with length $n$* if its length is $n$ and there is no axiom which satisfies the condition (3.3) for the selected atom of the last goal.

**Example 3.3** Let $S$ be the EFS in Example 3.2. Then the derivation illustrated in Figure 2 is finitely failed with length 2.

**Definition** A derivation $(G_i, \theta_i, C_i)$ $(i = 0, 1, \ldots)$ is *fair* if it is finitely failed or, for each atom $A$ in $G_i$, there is a $k \geq i$ such that $A\theta_i \cdots \theta_{k-1}$ is the selected atom of $G_k$.

In the discussion of negation, we assume that any computation rule $R$ makes all derivations *fair*. We say such a computation rule to be *fair*.

The *negation as failure rule* is the rule that infers $\neg A$ when a ground atom $A$ is in the set

$$FF(S) = \left\{ A \in B(S) \;\middle|\; \begin{array}{l} \text{for any fair computation rule, there is an } n \text{ such that} \\ \text{all derivations from } \leftarrow A \text{ are finitely failed within length } n \end{array} \right\}.$$

Put $\overline{\theta} = (x_1 = \tau_1 \wedge \ldots \wedge x_n = \tau_n)$ for a substitution $\theta = \{x_1 := \tau_1, \ldots, x_n := \tau_n\}$, and for an empty $\theta$, $\overline{\theta} = true$. By Jaffar, et al. [9], negation as failure for EFS is complete if the following two are satisfied:

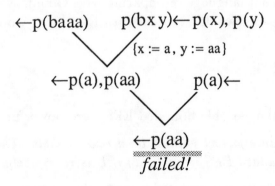

Figure 2: A derivation finitely failed with length 2

(3.4) There is a theory $E^*$ such that, for every two terms $\pi$ and $\tau$, $(\pi = \tau) \to \vee_{i=1}^{k} \overline{\theta_i}$ is a logical consequence, where $\theta_1, \ldots, \theta_k$ are all unifiers of $\pi$ and $\tau$, and the disjunction means $\square$ if $k = 0$.

(3.5) $FF(S)$ is the identical to the set

$$GF(S) = \left\{ A \in B(S) \,\middle|\, \begin{array}{l} \text{for any fair computation rule, all derivations} \\ \text{from} \leftarrow A \text{ are finitely failed} \end{array} \right\}.$$

In general, we can easily construct an $EFS$ such that $FF(S) \neq GF(S)$.

We show that negation as failure rule for variable-bounded EFS is complete. To prove the completeness, we need the set

$$GGF(S) = \left\{ A \in B(S) \,\middle|\, \begin{array}{l} \text{for any fair computation rule, all derivations from} \leftarrow A \\ \text{such that all goals in them are ground} \\ \text{are finitely failed} \end{array} \right\}.$$

The inference rule that infers $\neg A$ for a ground atom $A$ if $A$ is not in $GGF(S)$ is called the *Herbrand rule*[10].

**Theorem 3.2 (Yamamoto[21])** *For any variable-bounded EFS $S$,*
$$FF(S) = GF(S) = GGF(S).$$

By this theorem we can use the following equational theory instead of (3.4):

$$E^* = \left\{ \pi = \tau \to \vee_{i=1}^{k} \overline{\theta_i} \,\middle|\, \begin{array}{l} \pi \text{ is a ground term, } \tau \text{ is a term,} \\ \text{and } \theta_1, \ldots, \theta_k \text{ are all unifiers of } \pi \text{ and } \tau \end{array} \right\}.$$

Thus the negation as failure is complete and identical to the Herbrand rule for variable-bounded EFS's. Yamamoto[21] have discussed the closed world assumption for EFS.

# 4    THE CLASSES OF EFS LANGUAGES

We describe the classes of our languages comparing with Chomsky hierarchy and some other classes. Throughout the paper we do not deal with the empty word.

## The Power of EFS

The first theorem shows the variable-bounded EFS's are powerful enough.

**Theorem 4.1** *Let $\Sigma$ be an alphabet with at least two symbols. Then a language $L \subset \Sigma^+$ is definable by a variable-bounded EFS if and only if $L$ is recursively enumerable.*

**Proof** A Turing machine with left and right endmarkers to indicate the both ends of currently used tape can be simulated in a variable-bounded EFS by encoding tape symbols to words of $\Sigma^+$. The converse is clear from Smullyan [18].

The left to right part of Theorem 4.1 is still valid in case alphabet $\Sigma$ is singleton. However, to show the converse we need to weaken the statement slightly just as in Theorem 4.2(2) below.

Now we show relations between length-bounded EFS and CSG.

**Theorem 4.2** *(1) Any length-bounded EFS language is context-sensitive.*

*(2) For any context-sensitive language $L \subseteq \Sigma^+$, there exist a superset $\Sigma_0$ of $\Sigma$, a length-bounded EFS $S = (\Sigma_0, \Pi, \Gamma)$ and $p \in \Pi$ such that $L = L(S, p) \cap \Sigma^+$.*

**Proof** (1) Any derivation in a length-bounded EFS from a ground goal can be simulated by a nondeterministic linear bounded automaton, because all the goals in the derivation are kept ground and the total length of the newly added subgoals in each resolution step does not exceed the length of the selected atom by the definition.

(2) This can also be proved by a simulation.

The $\Sigma_0$ above corresponds to the auxiliary alphabet like tape symbols or non-terminal symbols. We can show another theorem related to the converse of Theorem 4.2(1).

**Definition** A function $\sigma$ from $\Sigma^+$ into itself is *length-bounded EFS realizable* if there exist a length-bounded EFS $S_0 = (\Sigma, \Pi_0, \Gamma_0)$ and a binary predicate symbol $p \in \Pi_0$ for which $\Gamma_0 \vdash p(u, w) \Leftrightarrow w = \sigma(u)$.

**Theorem 4.3** *Let $\Sigma$ be an alphabet with at least two symbols. Then for any context-sensitive language $L \subset \Sigma^+$, there exist a length-bounded EFS $S = (\Sigma, \Pi, \Gamma)$, a length-bounded EFS realizable function $\sigma$ and $p \in \Pi$ associated with $\sigma$ such that*

$$L = \{w \in \Sigma^+ \mid \Gamma \vdash p(w, \sigma(w))\}.$$

## Smaller Classes of EFS Languages

Now we compare EFS languages with some other smaller classes of languages.

**Definition** A length-bounded EFS $S = (\Sigma, \Pi, \Gamma)$ is *simple* if $\Pi$ consists of unary predicate symbols and for each axiom in $\Gamma$ is of the form

$$p(\pi) \leftarrow q_1(x_1), \ldots, q_n(x_n),$$

where $x_1, \ldots, x_n$ are mutually distinct variables.

**Example 4.1** An EFS $S = (\{a\}, \{p\}, \Gamma)$ with

$$\Gamma = \left\{ \begin{array}{l} p(a) \leftarrow, \\ p(xx) \leftarrow p(x) \end{array} \right\}$$

is simple and $L(S, p) = \{a^{2^n} \mid n \geq 0\}$.

It is known that simple EFS languages are context-sensitive [5].

**Definition** A pattern $\pi$ is *regular* if $o(x, \pi) \leq 1$ for any variable $x$. A simple EFS $S = (\Sigma, \Pi, \Gamma)$ is *regular* if the pattern in the head of each definite clause in $\Gamma$ is regular.

**Example 4.2** An EFS $S = (\{a, b\}, \{p\}, \Gamma)$ with

$$\Gamma = \left\{ \begin{array}{l} p(ab) \leftarrow, \\ p(axb) \leftarrow p(x) \end{array} \right\}$$

is regular and $L(S, p) = \{a^n b^n \mid n \geq 1\}$.

**Theorem 4.4** *A language is definable by a regular EFS if and only if it is context-free.*

**Definition** A regular EFS $S = (\Sigma, \Pi, \Gamma)$ is *right-linear* (*left-linear*) if each axiom in $\Gamma$ is one of the following forms:

$$p(\pi) \leftarrow,$$
$$p(ux) \leftarrow q(x) \qquad (p(ux) \leftarrow q(x)),$$

where $\pi$ is a regular pattern and $u \in \Sigma^+$.

A regular EFS is *one-sided linear* if it is right- or left-linear.

**Theorem 4.5** *A language is definable by a one-sided linear EFS if and only if it is regular.*

The pattern languages [1, 2, 15, 16] which are important in inductive inference of languages from positive data are also definable by special simple EFS's.

## Computations of Unifiers

As we have stated in Section 3, all the goals in the derivation from a ground goal are kept ground, because we deal with only the variable-bounded EFS's. Hence, every unification is made between a term and a ground term. To find a unifier is to get a solution of equation $w = \pi$, where $w$ is a ground term and $\pi$ is a term possibly with variables. In general, as is easily seen, the equation can be solved in $O(|w|^{|\pi|})$ time. Hence, for a fixed EFS, it can be solved in time polynomial in the length of the ground goal. However, if the EFS is not fixed, the problem is NP-complete, because it is equivalent to the membership problem of pattern languages [1].

As for the one-sided linear and regular EFS's, the problem can be proved to have good properties.

**Proposition 4.1** *The equation $w = \pi$ has at most one solution for every $w \in \Sigma^+$ if and only if $\pi$ contains at most one variable.*

**Proposition 4.2 (Shinohara [15])** *Let $w$ be a word in $\Sigma^+$ and $\pi$ be a regular pattern. Then each unifier of $w$ and $\pi$ is computed in $O(|w| + |\pi|)$ time.*

By these propositions, the unifier of $w$ and $\pi$ is at most unique in one-sided linear EFS, and each unifier of them can be computed in a linear time in regular EFS. However, in the worst case, there may exist unifiers in regular EFS as many as $|w|^{|\pi|}$.

# 5   INDUCTIVE INFERENCE OF EFS LANGUAGES

In this section, we show how EFS languages are inductively learned. To specify inductive inference problems we need to give five items, the set of rules, the representation of rules, the data presentation, the method of inference called the *inference machine*, and the criterion of successful inference [4].

In our problem, the class of rules are EFS languages. The examples are ground atoms $p(w)$ with sign + or − indicating whether $p(w)$ is provable from the target EFS or not. An example $+p(w)$ is said to be *positive*, $-p(w)$ *negative*. Our criterion of successful inference is the traditional *identification in the limit* [7].

The inference machine we consider here is based on Shapiro's MIS (Model Inference System) [14]. The following procedure MIEFS (Model Inference for EFS) describes the outline of our inference method, which uses a subprocedure CBA (Contradiction Backtracing Algorithm) and refinements of clauses. The hypothesis $H$ is *too strong*, if $H$ proves $p(w)$ for some negative example $-p(w)$. $H$ is *too weak*, if $H$ can not prove $p(w)$ for some positive example $+p(w)$.

When MIEFS finds the current hypothesis $H$ is not compatible with the examples read so far, it tries to modify $H$ as follows. If $H$ is too strong, then MIEFS searches $H$ for a false clause $C$ by using CBA and deletes $C$ from $H$. Otherwise MIEFS increases the power of $H$ by adding refinements of clauses deleted so far. A refinement $C'$ of a clause $C$ is a logical consequence of $C$. Therefore the hypothesis obtained by adding a refinement $C'$ is weaker than the hypothesis before deleting $C$.

**Procedure MIEFS;**
    **begin**
        $H := \{\square\}$;
        **repeat**
            read next example;
            **while** $H$ *is too strong or too weak* **do begin**
                **while** $H$ *is too strong* **do begin**
                    apply CBA to $H$ and detect a false clause $C$ in $H$;
                    delete $C$ from $H$;
                **end**
                **while** $H$ *is too weak* **do**
                    add a refinement of clause deleted so far to $H$;
            **end**
            output $H$;
        **forever**
    **end**

To guarantee our procedure MIEFS successfully identifies EFS languages, it is necessary to test whether CBA works for EFS's or not, and to devise refinement operator and show its completeness.

# Contradiction Backtracing Algorithm for EFS

Contradiction backtracing algorithm (CBA for short) devised by Shapiro[14] makes use of a refutation indicating a hypothesis $H$ is too strong. It traces selected atoms backward in the refutation. By using an oracle ASK, it tests their truth values to detect a false clause in $H$. When $A_i$ is not ground, CBA must select a ground instance of $A_i$. However, in variable-bounded EFS's, $A_i$ is always ground, and hence we can simplify CBA as follows.

**Procedure CBA_for_EFS;**
input:        $(G_0 = G, \theta_0, C_0), (G_1, \theta_1, C_1), \ldots, (G_k = \square, \theta_k, C_k);$
              {a refutation of a ground goal $G$ false in $M$}
output:     a clause $C_i$ false in $M$;
    **begin**
        **for** $i := k$ **downto** 1 **do begin**
            let $A_i$ be the selected atom of $G_{i-1}$;
            **if** $ASK(A_i)$ *is false* **then return** $C_{i-1}$;
        **end**
    **end**

The following lemma and theorem show our CBA procedure works correctly.

**Lemma 5.1** *Let $G'$ be the resolvent of a ground goal $G$ and a variable-bounded clause $C$ by a substitution $\theta$ and $A$ be the selected atom of $G$. Assume that $G'$ is false in a model $M$. If $A$ is true in $M$ then $G$ is false in $M$. Otherwise $C\theta$ is ground and false in $M$.*

**Proof** Let $G = \leftarrow A_1, \ldots, A_n$ be a ground goal and $C = A' \leftarrow B_1, \ldots, B_q$ be a variable-bounded clause, where $A = A_m$. Then

$$G' = \leftarrow A_1, \ldots, A_{m-1}, B_1\theta, \ldots, B_q\theta, A_{m+1}, \ldots, A_n$$

is a ground resolvent of $G$ and $C$. Since we assume $G'$ is false in a model $M$, all atoms in $A_1, \ldots, A_{m-1}, A_{m+1}, \ldots, A_n$ and $B_1\theta, \ldots, B_q\theta$ are ground and true in $M$. Therefore if $A$ is true in $M$, then $G = \leftarrow A_1, \ldots, A_{m-1}, A, A_{m+1}, \ldots, A_n$ is false in $M$, otherwise $C\theta = A \leftarrow B_1\theta, \ldots, B_q\theta$ is false in $M$.

**Theorem 5.1** *Let $M$ be a model of a variable-bounded EFS $S$, and $(G_0 = G, \theta_0, C_0)$, $(G_1, \theta_1, C_1), \ldots, (G_k = \square, \theta_k, C_k)$ be a refutation by $S$ of a ground goal $G$ false in $M$. If CBA is given the refutation, then it makes $i$ oracle calls and returns $C_{k-i}$ false in $M$ for some $i = 1, 2, \ldots, k$.*

**Proof** By Lemma 5.1 and an induction on $k - i$, the number of oracle calls made by CBA, we can easily prove that the clause returned by CBA is false in $M$.

We may assume that $G_0$ is not empty. Hence $k - i$ is positive. If CBA makes the $k$-th call to the oracle $ASK$, then the received truth value of $A_1$ upon which $G_1$ is resolved must be false because $A_1$ is identical to an atom in $G_0$. Therefore CBA always returns a clause $C_{k-i}$ after making at most $k$ oracle calls.

# Refinement Operator for EFS

We assume a structural complexity measure *size* of patterns and clauses such that the number of patterns or clauses whose sizes are equal to $n$ is finite (except renaming of variables) for any integer $n$. In what follows, we identify variants with each other.

**Definition** We define $\text{size}(\pi) = 2 \times |\pi| - |v(\pi)|$ for a pattern $\pi$, and $\text{size}(C) = \text{size}(\pi\tau_1 \ldots \tau_n)$ for a clause $C = p(\pi) \leftarrow q_1(\tau_1), \ldots, q_n(\tau_n)$.

For a binary relation $R$, $R(a)$ denotes the set $\{b \mid (a, b) \in R\}$ and $R^*$ denotes the reflexive transitive closure of $R$. A clause $D$ is a *refinement* of $C$ if $D$ is a logical consequence of $C$ and $\text{size}(C) < \text{size}(D)$. A *refinement operator* $\rho$ is a subrelation of refinement relation such that the set $\{D \in \rho(C) \mid \text{size}(D) \le n\}$ is finite and computable. A refinement operator $\rho$ is *complete for a set* $S$ if $\rho^*(\Box) = S$. A refinement operator $\rho$ is *locally finite* if $\rho(C)$ is finite for any clause $C$.

Now we introduce refinement operators for the subclasses of EFS's. All refinement operators defined below have a common feature. They are constructed by two types of operations, applying a substitution and adding a literal.

**Definition** A substitution $\theta$ is *basic for a clause* $C$ if

    (5.1) $\theta = \{x := y\}$, where $x \in v(C)$, $y \in v(C)$ and $x \ne y$,

    (5.2) $\theta = \{x := a\}$, where $x \in v(C)$ and $a \in \Sigma$, or

    (5.3) $\theta = \{x := yz\}$, where $x \in v(C)$, $y \notin v(C)$, $z \notin v(C)$ and $y \ne z$.

**Lemma 5.2** *Let $\theta$ be a basic substitution for a clause $C$. Then $\text{size}(C) < \text{size}(C\theta)$.*

**Proof** If $\theta$ is of the form $\{x := y\}$ or $\{x := a\}$, then $|v(C\theta)| = |v(C)| - 1$. Therefore $\text{size}(C\theta) = \text{size}(C) + 1$. If $\theta$ is of the form $\{x := yz\}$, then $|C\theta| = |C| + o(x, C)$ and $|v(C\theta)| = |v(C)| + 1$. Since $o(x, C) \ge 1$,

$$\text{size}(C\theta) = \text{size}(C) + 2 \times o(x, C) - 1 > \text{size}(C).$$

**Definition** Let $A$ be an atom. Then an atom $B$ is in $\rho_a(A)$ if and only if

    (5.4) $A = \Box$ and $B = p(x)$ for $p \in \Pi$, $x \in X$, or

    (5.5) $A\theta = B$ for a substitution $\theta$ basic for $A$.

**Lemma 5.3** *Let $C$ and $D$ be clauses such that $C\theta = D$ but $C \not\equiv D$ for some substitution $\theta$. Then there exists a sequence of substitutions $\theta_1, \theta_2, \ldots, \theta_n$ such that $\theta_i$ is basic for $C\theta_1 \ldots \theta_{i-1}$ $(i = 1, \ldots, n)$ and $C\theta_1 \ldots \theta_n = D$.*

**Theorem 5.2** $\rho_a$ *is a locally finite and complete refinement operator for atoms.*

Shinohara [15] discussed inductive inference of pattern languages from positive data. The method he called *tree search method* uses a special version of the refinement operator $\rho_a$. His method first tries to apply substitutions of type $\{x := yz\}$ to get the longest possible pattern, and then tries to apply substitutions of type $\{x := a\}$, and finally tries to unify variables by substitutions of type $\{x := y\}$.

**Definition** Let $C$ be a variable-bounded clause. Then a clause $D$ is in $\rho_{vb}(C)$ if and only if (5.4) or (5.5) holds, or

$$C = A \leftarrow B_1, \ldots, B_{n-1} \text{ and } D = A \leftarrow B_1, \ldots, B_{n-1}, B_n \text{ is variable-bounded.}$$

Similarly we define $\rho_{lb}$ for length-bounded clauses.

**Theorem 5.3** $\rho_{vb}$ *is a complete refinement operator for variable-bounded clauses.*

**Theorem 5.4** $\rho_{lb}$ *is a locally finite and complete refinement operator for length-bounded clauses.*

Note that $\rho_{vb}$ is not locally finite because the number of atoms $B_n$ possibly added by $\rho_{vb}$ is infinite, while $\rho_{lb}$ is locally finite. We can also define refinement operators for simple or regular clauses and prove they are locally finite and complete. For simple clauses, applications of basic substitutions should be restricted only to atoms. Further, for regular clauses, substitutions of the form $\{x := y\}$ should be inhibited.

# 6   CONCLUSION

We have introduced several important subclasses of EFS's by gradually imposing restrictions on the axioms, and given a theoretical foundation of EFS's from the viewpoint of logic programming. EFS's work for accepting languages as well as for generating them. This aspect of EFS's is particularly useful for inductive inference of languages. We have also shown inductive inference algorithms for some subclasses of EFS's in a uniform way and proved their completeness. Thus, EFS's are a good unifying framework for inductive inference of languages.

We can introduce pairs of parentheses to simple EFS's just like parenthesis grammars. Nearly the same approaches as [22, 13] will be applicable to our inductive inference of simple EFS languages. Thus, we can resolve the computational hardness of unifications.

There are many other problems in connection with computational complexity, the learning models such as [3, 19], and introduction of the empty word [16] which we will discuss elsewhere.

# References

[1] D. Angluin. Finding patterns common to a set of strings. In *Proc. 11th Annual ACM Symp. Theory of Computing*, 130–141, 1979.

[2] D. Angluin. Inductive inference of formal languages from positive data. *Inform. Contr.*, 45:117–135, 1980.

[3] D. Angluin. Learning regular sets from queries and counterexamples. *Inform. Comp.*, 75:87–106, 1987.

[4] D. Angluin and C. H. Smith. Inductive inference: Theory and methods. *Computing Surveys*, 15:237–269, 1983.

[5] S. Arikawa. Elementary formal systems and formal languages - simple formal systems. *Memoirs of Fac. Sci., Kyushu Univ. Ser. A.*, Math. 24:47–75, 1970.

[6] M. Fitting. *Computability Theory, Semantics, and Logic Programming.* Oxford Univ. Press, 1987.

[7] E. M. Gold. Language identification in the limit. *Inform. Contr.*, 10:447–474, 1967.

[8] H. Ishizaka. Inductive inference of regular languages based on model inference. *To appear in IJCM*, 1989.

[9] J. Jaffar, J.-L. Lassez, and M. J. Mahr. Logic programming scheme. In D. DeGroot and G. Lindstrom, editors, *Logic Programming: Functions, Relations, and Equations*, 211–233, 1986.

[10] J. W. Lloyd. *Foundations of Logic Programming, Second, Extended Edition.* Springer - Verlag, 1987.

[11] G. S. Makanin. The problem of solvability of equations in a free semigroup. *Soviet Math. Dokl.*, 18(2):330–334, 1977.

[12] G. D. Plotkin. Building in equational theories. In *Machine Intelligence 7*, 132–147, 1972.

[13] Y. Sakakibara. Learning context-free grammars from structural data in polynomial time. In *Proc. COLT'88*, 296–310, 1988.

[14] E. Y. Shapiro. Inductive inference of theories from facts. Research Report 192, Yale Univ., 1981.

[15] T. Shinohara. Polynomial time inference of pattern languages and its application. In *Proc. 7th IBM Symp. Math. Found. Comp. Sci.*, 191–209, 1982.

[16] T. Shinohara. Polynomial time inference of extended regular pattern languages. *LNCS*, 147:115–127, 1983.

[17] T. Shinohara. Inductive inference of formal systems from positive data. *Bull. Inform. Cyber.*, 22:9–18, 1986.

[18] R. M. Smullyan. *Theory of Formal Systems.* Princeton Univ. Press, 1961.

[19] L. G. Valiant. A theory of the learnable. *CACM*, 27(11):1134–1142, November 1984.

[20] A. Yamamoto. A theoretical combination of SLD-resolution and narrowing. In *Proc. 4th ICLP*, 470–487, 1987.

[21] A. Yamamoto. Elementary formal system as a logic programming language. Technical Report RIFIS-TR-CS-12, Research Institute of Fundamental Information Science, Kyushu University, 1989.

[22] T. Yokomori. Learning simple languages in polynomial time. In *SIG–FAI JSAI*, 21–30, 1988.

# IDENTIFICATION OF UNIONS OF LANGUAGES DRAWN FROM AN IDENTIFIABLE CLASS

Keith Wright
Department of Computer Science
University of Pittsburgh
Pittsburgh, PA 15213

## ABSTRACT

We follow a line of research begun by Gold and continued by Angluin. Gold defined a property of language classes: identifiability in the limit from positive examples (i.e. text). This means that given any stream of examples drawn from some language in the class it is possible to produce a stream of guesses that converges to the language from which the examples are drawn. Suppose we are given a class of languages that is identifiable from text, and a stream of examples drawn from *two* of those languages intermixed. Is it possible to converge in the limit to a pair of languages that together explain the examples? The answer is: in general, no. We define a property of language classes that ensures such bilingual identification is possible. We call this property of language classes <u>finite elasticity</u>. Finite elasticity is preserved by the operation of taking unions of pairs of languages. This generalizes a result due to Shinohara. Shinohara has shown that pairs of pattern languages are identifiable from text. It is easy to see that the class of pattern languages has finite elasticity. We now see that Shinohara's result holds for any language class with finite elasticity.

## INTRODUCTION

If $\mathfrak{X}$ is a language, a <u>text</u> for $\mathfrak{X}$ is an infinite sequence of strings containing all and only strings in $\mathfrak{X}$. We say a class of languages $\mathbb{C}$ is <u>identifiable from text</u> if there is an effective procedure (called an inference machine) such that for any language $\mathfrak{X} \in \mathbb{C}$ and any text for $\mathfrak{X}$, if the inference machine is given a sufficiently long initial segment of the text, it returns a name for $\mathfrak{X}$. The procedure may return incorrect answers when given short sequences of strings from $\mathfrak{X}$, and there need be no upper bound on the the amount of text required to produce a correct answer. These definitions are due to Gold[Go67]. Suppose $\mathbb{C}$ is identifiable from text, but an inference machine must be designed to work in a bilingual environment. We investigate conditions under which there is an inference machine able to produce a name for $\mathfrak{X} \cup \mathfrak{M}$ from text for $\mathfrak{X} \cup \mathfrak{M}$ for any $\mathfrak{X}, \mathfrak{M} \in \mathbb{C}$. Note that the text is not marked as to which strings are from $\mathfrak{X}$ and which from $\mathfrak{M}$, nor do we require that the inference machine produce names for $\mathfrak{X}$ and $\mathfrak{M}$ separately.

Angluin has investigated inductive identification of languages from text[An80]. She gave a simple sufficient condition for a class of languages to be identifiable from text, and a more complex necessary and sufficient condition. Even if a class satisfies one of these conditions, the class of unions of pairs of languages in the class need not satisfy the condition. We give an intermediate condition, implied by the sufficient condition and implying the necessary, that is closed under the operation of taking unions of pairs of languages. We call this property of language classes <u>finite elasticity</u>. Thus, if a class of languages has finite elasticity then so does the class of unions of pairs of languages in the class, and this class is therefore identifiable from text. This generalizes a result due to Shinohara[Sh83,Sh85]. Shinohara's Theorem 20 states that the class of unions of pairs of pattern languages is identifiable from text. We now see that the same is true of any language class that satisfies Angluin's sufficient condition, or the new weaker one.

## BASIC CONCEPTS

We use the usual logical symbols $\forall$, $\exists$, $\vee$, $\wedge$, $\neg$, $\rightarrow$, $\leftrightarrow$, and the set theory symbols $\in$, $\cup$ and $\cap$. The symbol $\subseteq$ means subset, while $\subset$ means proper subset. The cardinality of the set S is #(S). The direct image of S under the function f is $f``S = \{\ f(x) \mid x \in S\ \}$. The set of natural numbers is $\omega$.

The phrase "class of unions of pairs of languages in the class" is clumsy at best. The following definition explicates it.

**Definition 1**: For any classes of languages $\mathbb{C}$ and $\mathbb{D}$, let $\cup``(\mathbb{C} \times \mathbb{D}) = \{\ \mathcal{B} \cup \mathcal{M} \mid \mathcal{B} \in \mathbb{C} \wedge \mathcal{M} \in \mathbb{D}\ \}$ and $\mathbb{C}^2 = \cup``(\mathbb{C} \times \mathbb{C}) = \{\ \mathcal{B} \cup \mathcal{M} \mid \mathcal{B}, \mathcal{M} \in \mathbb{C}\ \}$. ∎

Do not confuse $\cup``(\mathbb{C} \times \mathbb{D})$ with $\mathbb{C} \cup \mathbb{D}$. The following example shows that it is possible to have $\mathbb{C}$ identifiable from text but $\mathbb{C}^2$ not identifiable. Therefore a sufficient condition for identifiability that is preserved by the operation $\cup``(\mathbb{C} \times \mathbb{D})$ can not also be necessary.

**Example 2**: Let $\mathbb{C} = \mathbb{E} \cup \mathbb{O} \cup \{\omega\}$, where $\omega$ is the set of natural numbers, $\mathbb{E}$ is the class of finite sets of even numbers, and $\mathbb{O}$ is the class of finite sets of odd numbers. An inference machine that conjectures the sample if the sample consists entirely of even numbers or entirely of odd numbers, and conjectures $\omega$ if the sample contains both even and odd numbers will successfully identify $\mathbb{C}$. On the other hand, $\mathbb{C}^2$ contains all finite sets and an infinite set, and so is not identifiable from text by Gold's theorem[Go67]. ∎

We review some definitions and results due to Angluin[An80].

**Definition 3:** An <u>indexed family of recursive languages</u> is a sequence of languages $\{\mathcal{B}_k\}_{k \in \omega}$ for which there is a total recursive function of two arguments, f(j,k), such that for all k, $\lambda j.f(j,k)$ is the characteristic function of $\mathcal{B}_k$. ∎

Soare[So87; Def II.2.5] calls this a <u>uniformly recursive sequence</u> of languages. Each language in a indexed family of recursive languages is a recursive language, and we are given a decision procedure.

The same class of languages may be a indexed family of recursive languages if indexed in one order, but not if indexed in a different order. On the other hand, the property of being a indexed family of recursive languages is preserved under any recursive permutation of the indices. Since we are usually not interested in the specific indexing of a sequence, we will often refer to an indexed family of recursive languages as simply a recursive family, and assume that some indexing is given.

**Definition 4:** Let $\mathbb{C} = \{\mathscr{B}_k\}_{k\in\omega}$ be a recursive family of languages. $\mathbb{C}$ has <u>finite thickness</u> iff for each string s the set $\{\mathscr{B}_k \mid s\in\mathscr{B}_k\in\mathbb{C}\}$ has finite cardinality. ∎

Angluin called this property Condition 3. The picture that inspired the revised terminology is a Venn diagram made of plywood. If over each point there is only a finite stack of ovals (languages), then the family has finite thickness. In terms of inductive inference, if the hypothesis space has finite thickness then there are only a finite number of possible conjectures to explain any given string.

Note that we require only that the set of languages in $\mathbb{C}$ containing s be finite, not that there be a finite number of indices of languages in $\mathbb{C}$ containing s. Thus the condition depends only upon the languages in $\mathbb{C}$, not on the way they are indexed.

**Definition 5:** A language $\mathscr{B}$ <u>describes</u> a finite set S <u>within</u> a class of languages $\mathbb{C}$ iff $S\subseteq\mathscr{B}$ and there is no $\mathscr{M}\in\mathbb{C}$ such that $S\subseteq\mathscr{M}\subset\mathscr{B}$. S is a <u>characteristic subset</u> of $\mathscr{B}$ <u>within</u> $\mathbb{C}$ iff S is finite and $\mathscr{B}$ describes S within $\mathbb{C}$. ∎

**Theorem 6**(Angluin): Any recursive family of languages of finite thickness is identifiable from text. A recursive family of languages $\{\mathscr{B}_k\}_{k\in\omega}$ is identifiable from text if and only if there is an effective procedure which, given k, enumerates a characteristic subset of $\mathscr{B}_k$. ∎

We next give our main new definition.

**Definition 7:** A class of languages $\mathbb{C}$ has <u>infinite elasticity</u> iff there is an infinite sequence of strings $s_0, s_1, s_2, \ldots$ and an infinite sequence of languages $\mathscr{B}_1, \mathscr{B}_2, \mathscr{B}_3, \ldots$ each in $\mathbb{C}$ such that for any n and k, $s_k\in\mathscr{B}_n$ if and only if $k<n$. A class has <u>finite elasticity</u> iff it does not have infinite elasticity. ∎

An equivalent definition is: $\mathbb{C}$ has infinite elasticity if there is a set of strings S such that $\cap``(\mathbb{C}\times\{S\})$, the class of intersections of sets in $\mathbb{C}$ with S, contains an infinite ascending chain, i.e. an infinite sequence of sets totally ordered by inclusion. Note that the class itself need not contain any ascending chain, but there is some S such the class restricted to S contains a chain.

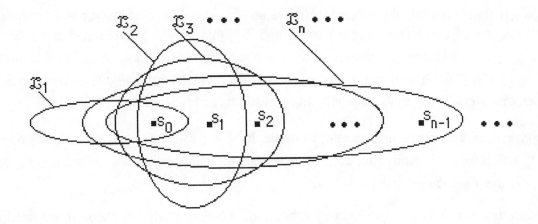

Figure 1: Infinite elasticity

The strings $s_0, s_1, s_2, \ldots$ must be pairwise distinct, because for all k, $s_k \in \mathcal{B}_{k+1}$ but $s_k \notin \mathcal{B}_k$. Similarly the languages $\mathcal{B}_1, \mathcal{B}_2, \mathcal{B}_3, \ldots$ must be pairwise distinct. Assuming $\mathbb{C} \subseteq \mathbb{D}$, $\mathbb{C}$ has infinite elasticity implies $\mathbb{D}$ has infinite elasticity, while $\mathbb{D}$ has finite elasticity implies $\mathbb{C}$ has finite elasticity.

## NEW RESULTS

The results can be summarized as: finite thickness implies finite elasticity, which implies identifiability from text. Neither of these implications can be reversed. If $\mathbb{C}$ has finite elasticity then $\mathbb{C}^2$ has finite elasticity.

If $\mathbb{C}$ has finite thickness then it has finite elasticity, because if $\mathbb{C}$ has infinite elasticity then $s_0$ is contained in an infinite sequence of distinct languages in $\mathbb{C}$. The converse is false. For example, let $\mathbb{C} = \{ \mathcal{B} \mid \#(\mathcal{B})=2 \}$; $\mathbb{C}$ has finite elasticity but infinite thickness.

**Theorem 8**: If $\mathbb{C}$ is an indexed family of recursive languages with finite elasticity then $\mathbb{C}$ is identifiable from text presentations.

Proof: We give an algorithm to enumerate a characteristic subset of $\mathcal{B}$ where $\mathcal{B}$ is any language in $\mathbb{C}$. The result then follows from Theorem 6. Angluin's proof is constructive, so there is a definite algorithm to identify a class with infinite elasticity which will be evident to anyone who reads her proof. That algorithm is a bother to describe directly, and the proof that it is correct would be repetition of her proof.

Stage 0: Let $s_0$ be any string in $\mathcal{B}$.

Stage k+1: Begin enumerating all languages in $\mathbb{C}$ that contain $\{s_0, \ldots, s_k\}$. For each such language $\mathfrak{M}$, begin a search for a string in $\mathcal{B}$ that is not in $\mathfrak{M}$. If such a string is found, let $s_{k+1}$ be that string, let $\mathcal{B}_{k+1}$ be $\mathfrak{M}$, halt the enumerations, and go on to stage k+2.

Since $\mathbb{C}$ has finite elasticity this process must eventually enter stage n and never leave it; otherwise it would construct two infinite sequences, $s_k$ and $\mathscr{B}_k$, that provide the counter example. Then $\{s_0, \ldots s_{n-1}\}$ is a characteristic subset of $\mathscr{B}$, for if not then there must be an $\mathfrak{M} \in \mathbb{C}$ such that $\{s_0, \ldots s_{n-1}\} \subseteq \mathfrak{M} \subset \mathscr{B}$. But then the procedure would eventually produce $\mathfrak{M}$ in its enumeration, and then discover a string in $\mathscr{B}$ but not in $\mathfrak{M}$, and so proceed to stage n+1. ∎

The converse of Theorem 8 is false. For example, let $\mathbb{C} = \{\ \mathscr{B}_k \mid k \in \omega\ \}$, where $\mathscr{B}_k = \{\ n \mid n \le k\ \}$. Then $\mathbb{C}$ has infinite elasticity, but an inference machine that guesses $\mathscr{B}_k$ where k is the largest number in the input sample will identify $\mathbb{C}$.

The main theorem follows from Ramsey's theorem. To state Ramsey's theorem we need a few definitions. A <u>complete</u> graph is a graph with an undirected edge between every pair of vertices; a <u>two-coloring</u> of a graph is a function f:E→{red, blue}, where E is the set of edges of the graph; a <u>monochromatic clique</u> for a two-coloring is a subset C of the vertices of the graph such that the restriction of the two-coloring to edges between vertices in C is a constant function.

**Theorem 9** (Ramsey): There is an infinite monochromatic clique for every two-coloring of a complete countably infinite graph.

**Theorem 10**: If $\mathbb{C}$ and $\mathbb{D}$ each have finite elasticity then $\mathbb{P} = \cup``(\mathbb{C} \times \mathbb{D})$ has finite elasticity.
Proof: We assume $\mathbb{P}$ has infinite elasticity and show (non-constructively) that either $\mathbb{C}$ has infinite elasticity or $\mathbb{D}$ has infinite elasticity.

Since $\mathbb{P}$ has infinite elasticity there is an infinite sequence of strings $s_0, s_1, s_2, \ldots$ and a sequence of languages $\mathscr{B}_1 \cup \mathfrak{M}_1, \mathscr{B}_2 \cup \mathfrak{M}_2, \mathscr{B}_3 \cup \mathfrak{M}_3, \ldots$ such that for any j, $\mathscr{B}_j \in \mathbb{C}$, $\mathfrak{M}_j \in \mathbb{D}$, and for any i, if i<j, $s_i \in \mathscr{B}_j \cup \mathfrak{M}_j$ but if i≥j then $s_i \notin \mathscr{B}_j \cup \mathfrak{M}_j$.

Although the languages $\mathscr{B}_j \cup \mathfrak{M}_j$ are distinct, it may be that $\mathscr{B}_j = \mathscr{B}_n$ or $\mathfrak{M}_j = \mathfrak{M}_n$ for some j≠n. Nevertheless, we can assume that for any given j there are only finitely many n such that $\mathscr{B}_j = \mathscr{B}_n$. For otherwise assume that $\mathscr{B}_{n_0} = \mathscr{B}_{n_1} = \mathscr{B}_{n_2} = \ldots$, where $n_0 < n_1 < n_2 \ldots$ . By infinite elasticity of $\mathbb{P}$, if k<j, then $s_{n_k} \in \mathfrak{M}_{n_j} \cup \mathscr{B}_{n_j} = \mathfrak{M}_{n_j} \cup \mathscr{B}_{n_0}$, but since $s_{n_k} \notin \mathfrak{M}_{n_0} \cup \mathscr{B}_{n_0}$ *a fortiori* $s_{n_k} \notin \mathscr{B}_{n_0}$, and hence $s_{n_k} \in \mathfrak{M}_{n_j}$. On the other hand, if k≥j then $s_{n_k} \notin \mathfrak{M}_{n_j} \cup \mathscr{B}_{n_j}$ and *a fortiori* $s_{n_k} \notin \mathfrak{M}_{n_j}$. Hence $\mathbb{D}$ has infinite elasticity. Similarly, if there are infinitely many n such that $\mathfrak{M}_j = \mathfrak{M}_n$ then $\mathbb{C}$ has infinite elasticity. Of course, if $\mathbb{C}$ or $\mathbb{D}$ has infinite elasticity we are done immediately.

Therefore, without loss of generality we can assume that the sequences $s_0, s_1, s_2, \ldots$, and $\mathscr{B}_1 \cup \mathfrak{M}_1, \mathscr{B}_2 \cup \mathfrak{M}_2, \mathscr{B}_3 \cup \mathfrak{M}_3, \ldots$ have been chosen so that if j≠k then $\mathscr{B}_j \neq \mathscr{B}_k$ and $\mathfrak{M}_j \neq \mathfrak{M}_k$, for if not, we simply remove the finitely many repetitions, keeping only the first occurrence of each language.

Now let G be the complete graph with $\omega$ as its set of vertices. For any k and j with k<j, we know $s_k \in \mathscr{B}_j \cup \mathfrak{M}_j$; color the edge between k and j red if $s_k \in \mathscr{B}_j$, otherwise note that $s_k \in \mathfrak{M}_j$

and color the edge blue. The edges of G are undirected, as they must be to apply Ramsey's theorem, but this causes no conflict in the coloring because if $k{\geq}j$ then $s_k \notin \mathscr{B}_j \cup \mathfrak{M}_j$.

By Ramsey's theorem G contains an infinite monochrome clique; without loss of generality assume it is red. Let $n_k$ be the k'th largest number in the clique. Define $t_k = s_{n_k}$, $\mathfrak{N}_k = \mathscr{B}_{n_k}$. Now if $k{<}j$, $s_{n_k} = t_k \in \mathfrak{N}_j = \mathscr{B}_{n_j}$, because the edge from $n_k$ to $n_j$ is red, but if $k{\geq}j$, then $s_{n_k} = t_k \notin \mathfrak{N}_j = \mathscr{B}_{n_j}$, because $s_{n_k} \notin \mathscr{B}_{n_j} \cup \mathfrak{M}_{n_j}$. Hence $\mathbb{C}$ has infinite elasticity, as witnessed by the $t_k$ and $\mathfrak{N}_k$. ∎

Note that, although the proof that the class of unions has finite elasticity is non-constructive, we possess a definite algorithm to solve the inductive inference problem for the class. The algorithm given by Theorem 8 works; it is only the proof that it works that is non-constructive.

**Corollary 11:** Let $\mathbb{C}^n = \cup``(\mathbb{C} \times \mathbb{C}^{n-1}) = \{ \mathscr{B}_1 \cup \mathscr{B}_2 \cup ... \mathscr{B}_n \mid \mathscr{B}_1, \mathscr{B}_2, ... \mathscr{B}_n \in \mathbb{C} \}$, for $n{>}2$. If $\mathbb{C}$ has finite elasticity then $\mathbb{C}^n$ has finite elasticity.
Proof: Induction on n, applying Theorem 10 at each step. ∎

**Corollary 12** (Shinohara): The class of unions of pattern languages is identifiable from text presentations.
Proof: The class of pattern languages has finite thickness and therefore finite elasticity. By Theorem 10 the class of unions has finite elasticity and therefore, by Theorem 8, is identifiable from text. ∎

On behalf of the reader, the author wishes to thank the anonymous referee who pointed out that several pages of nested induction and subscripted subscripts could be replaced by citation of Ramsey's theorem. On behalf of himself, he wishes to thank his dissertation advisor, Robert Daley, who introduced him to this subject.

## References

[An80] Angluin, Dana; Inductive Inference of Formal Languages from Positive Data, *Information & Control* **45**, 117-135 (1980)

[Go67] Gold, E. Mark; Language Identification in the Limit; *Information & Control* **10**, 447-474 (1967)

[GR80] Graham, Ronald; Rothschild, Bruce; Spencer, Joel; Ramsey Theory; *John Wiley & Sons* (1980)

[Ra30] Ramsey, Frank P.; On a Problem of Formal Logic; *Proc. London Math. Soc.* **30**, 264-286

[Sh83] Shinohara, Takeshi; Inferring Unions of Two Pattern Languages; *Bull. of Informatics and Cybernetics* **20**, 83-87 (1983)

[Sh85] Shinohara, Takeshi; Some Problems on Inductive Inference from Positive Data, *Computer Center, Kyushu University* (1985)

[So87] Soare, Robert; Recursively Enumerable Sets and Degrees; *Springer-Verlag* (1987)

# INDUCTION FROM THE GENERAL
# TO THE MORE GENERAL

Kevin T. Kelly

Department of Philosophy

Carnegie Mellon University

Pittsburgh, PA 15213

(KK3n@andrew.cmu.edu)

## ABSTRACT

Most learning-theoretic analyses of inductive problems assume that the evidence provided to the theorist is quantifier-free. But scientific methodologists and artificial intelligence programmers have long assumed that theorists receive universal claims as inputs. What are the limits on inductive inference from laws? How much more expressive can the language of a theory be than the language of the data it is reliably inferred from? This paper presents upper and lower bounds on the the relationship between quantifier complexity in the data and the quantifier complexity of the theory to be reliably inferred from this data. The lower bounds are established with the help of the Keisler n-sandwich theorem, a powerful model theoretic preservation theorem. This application suggests further fruitful applications of model theory to diagonal arguments in learning theory.

## 1. INTRODUCTION

Most theoretical analyses of learnability have assumed that the data provided to the learner is quantifier-free. But there are reasons to examine the solvability of inductive problems when the data includes quantifiers.

(1) Traditional methodologists (e.g. William Whewell) have proposed that theorists produce hypotheses on the basis of observational laws provided

to them by reliable experimental work.  So the theorist's data consists of universal generalizations.

(2) Bayesian conditionalization is an inductive method that is defined to work even when the evidence is quantified.  There is no reason why formal learning theory should be more limited in applicability.

(3) It is evident that even in ordinary tasks such as learning a foreign language, one relies both upon particular examples of the language to be learned, and upon some incomplete, general rules provided by a language textbook.

(4)  Well-known AI learning systems, such as Winston's concept learning system (1975), have long depended upon a kind of universal data.  The "closed world hypothesis" is an assurance that when a teacher shows you an object and points out its parts, there are no parts that have not been pointed out.  In logical notation, the closed world hypothesis amounts to the addition of a universal generalization to the evidence, which assures the learner that there are no parts other than the ones it has seen.  For example, Winston's system actually receives the following data concerning an arch:

Arch(a),
Part-of(a, b), Part-of(a, c),
Lintel(d), Post(b), Post(c),
On-top(d, b), On-top(d, c), - Touches(b, c),

$(\forall x) [x \neq b \;\&\; x \neq c \;\&\; x \neq d) \rightarrow$ - Part-of(x, a)]

So in order to analyze the performance of even the best known AI learning systems, learning theory must be extended to inductive problems with universal data.

Once we admit the possibility of universal laws in the data (e.g. "*All ravens are black*") it is natural to consider the possibility of more complex laws involving alternating quantifier prefixes (e.g. "*For each raven there is* a maximum velocity for that raven").    In general, any number of quantifier alternations in the data is possible ($\forall\exists$, $\forall\exists\exists\forall\forall$, $\exists\exists\forall\exists$). We can think of the number of alternations as a coarse measure of the *complexity* of the data.

In the usual case of induction, data with no quantifiers (e.g. complexity 0) is used to generate universal theories (quantifier complexity 1).  We may now ask a more general question:

> For data of a given quantifier complexity, how much more quantifier-complex can a theory be if the theory is to be reliably inferred from this data?

We can think of reliable inductive inference as "stretching" the quantifier complexity of the data into the quantifier complexity of the theory inferred.   To know the limitations of reliable inductive inference is to know just where the "breaking point" of this stretching occurs.

This paper establishes that a reliably  inferred theory can have one more quantifier alternation than the data, but may not have three more alternations.  The question about two alternations remains open.  These upper and lower bounds on evidential quantifier complexity yield an infinite hierarchy of ever more difficult inductive problems, requiring ever more quantifier complexity in the data for their solution.

Perhaps one reason why induction from laws is so little explored is that negative arguments are much harder to prove for such problems than for problems with quantifier-free data.  Negative results in formal learning theory are based upon a kind of "evil demon" or "diagonal" construction, in which the demon repeatedly misleads a given learner by making the world appear first one way and then another, even though in the end, a complete, consistent description of some world has been presented.  In standard learning theory this "demonic" construction is relatively simple, because any two literals are consistent unless the one is the negation of the other. So the demon's future lies can be added to his old lies without much trouble about consistency.

But when the demon must present some set of general laws to the scientist, the maintenance of consistency among these laws can be an unsolvable problem. Hence, the usual diagonal constructions, in which the next datum presented by the demon is a recursive function of the current output of the learner, are no longer applicable. To get a feel for the difficulty of the task, it is a good exercise to try to give a direct diagonal argument against a learner receiving data with three quantifier alternations.

The chief innovation of this paper is to apply the Keisler n-sandwich theorem to the construction of a very general demon that can fool learners who use quantified data. The Keisler n-sandwich theorem is a well-known preservation theorem in model theory. A *preservation theorem* states that any formula of a given class has its truth preserved under some operation defined on relational structures. The Keisler theorem's natural application here suggests the intriguing possibility that other model theoretic preservation theorems may have applications to negative results in the theory of learnability.

## 2. FORMAL PRELIMINARIES

### 2.1 LANGUAGES AND QUANTIFIER COMPLEXITY

A *block* of quantifiers is a list of quantifiers of the same type (e.g. $\forall x \forall y \forall z$). An *alternation* between blocks of quantifiers is a change between $\forall$ quantifiers and $\exists$ quantifiers. (e.g. $\exists y \forall x \forall y \exists z$ has two alternations). A list of quantifiers is $\Pi_n$ just in case it begins with $\forall$ and has at most $n-1$ alternations of blocks. A list of quantifiers is $\Sigma_n$ just in case it begins with $\exists$ and has at most $n-1$ alternations of blocks. A formula is $\Sigma_n$ just in case it is equivalent to a formula of form $Q_1, ..., Q_n \Phi$, where $\Phi$ is a quantifier-free formula and $Q_1, ..., Q_n$ is a $\Sigma_n$ list of quantifiers. A formula is $\Pi_n$ just in case it is equivalent to a formula of form $Q_1, ..., Q_n \Phi$, where $\Phi$ is a quantifier-free formula and $Q_1, ..., Q_n$ is a $\Pi_n$

list of quantifiers.    If L is a first-order language, then $\Pi_n(L)$ is the set of all $\Pi_n$ formulas of L and $\Sigma_n(L)$ is the set of all $\Sigma_n$ formulas of L.

## 2.2 WORLDS

Our "possible worlds of inquiry" will be relational structures for a first-order language L.    A relational structure for L interprets all the vocabulary of L and hence makes each sentence of L either true or false.    In this paper, we restrict our attention to relational structures with countable domains, for these are the structures that can be described completely in the limit. For all the theorist knows, the true structure may be any countable structure for his language.    To be reliable, he must succeed no matter which structure is actual.    We let gothic letters represent structures.

## 2.3 DATA PRESENTATIONS

The following concepts are the same as in (Osherson and Weinstein 88). Let $\mathfrak{A}$ be a countable structure for L.    Let the evidence language E be some arbitrary subset of L.    An *assignment* for E and $\mathfrak{A}$ is a map from the variables of E to the domain of $\mathfrak{A}$.    We write $\mathfrak{A} \models s[g]$ when structure $\mathfrak{A}$ makes formula s true under assignment g of values to the free variables of s (for details see Chang and Keisler 73).    An assignment is *complete* just in case it is onto $\mathfrak{A}$.    The E-*data of* $\mathfrak{A}$ with respect to assignment g is the set of all formulas satisfied by g in $\mathfrak{A}$ (i.e. $\{e \in E: A \models e[g]\}$).    An *E-environment* is an infinite sequence of E-formulas.    Let t be an E-environment.    Let *rng*(t) denote the set of all E-formulas occurring in t. Then we say that t is *for* A if and only if there exists a total assignment g such that rng(t) = the E-data of A with respect to g.    In the sequel, we let t[n] denote the initial segment of t of length n, and we let SEQ(E) denote the set of all finite sequences of E-formulas.

## 2.4 CONVERGENCE TO A THEORY

C. S. Peirce held that for *every* well formed question, *there is* a time at which science correctly settles it.   If we take this standard of scientific success seriously, we end up with the following notion of convergence to a theory:

> Theorist θ *AE-converges* to theory T on environment t ⇔
> ∀h ∃n ∀m > n, θ(t[m]) |= h ⇔ h ∈ T.

The "AE" reminds us that *each* question is settled at *some* time, but perhaps not all questions are settled at the same time.   The naturalness of this criterion is discussed in (Kelly and Glymour 89a).

## 2.5  THEORY IDENTIFICATION

Let H be some subset of L.   Let H($\mathfrak{A}$) denote the set of all H-formulas valid in structure L (i.e. true under all interpretations of free variables).   Then we define:

> Theorist θ *AE-identifies* the H-theory of structure $\mathfrak{A}$ from E-data ⇔
> for each E-environment t for $\mathfrak{A}$, θ AE-converges to H($\mathfrak{A}$).

## 2.6 INDUCTIVE SCOPE AND INDUCTIVE PROBLEMS

We are interested in theorists who are reliable, in the sense that they can converge to the truth over a wide range of possible worlds (relational structures).   So we define success over a collection of structures.

> θ AE-identifies the H-theories of collection K of worlds ⇔
> θ AE-identifies the H-theory of each world $\mathfrak{A}$ ∈ K.

The largest collection of structures that we hold θ responsible for is the set of all countable structures for the language E ∪ H. We denote this set by K(E ∪ H).

The following notation will simplify what follows:

AE(θ, H, E, K) ⇔
θ AE-identifies the H-theory of each structure in K from E-data.

AE(E, H, K) ⇔ ∃ a theorist θ such that AE(θ, E, H, K).

AE(E, H) ⇔ AE(E, H, K(E ∪ H))

# 3. RESULTS

## 3.1 BASIC RELATIONS

**L1:** $\forall n, E \subseteq L, AE(E, \Sigma_n) \Leftrightarrow AE(E, \Pi_{n+1})$

**L2:** $\forall n, H \subseteq L, AE(\Pi_n, H) \Leftrightarrow AE(\Sigma_{n+1}, H)$

*Proof sketch:* L1 follows from the fact that hypotheses must be valid in 𝔄, so free variables may be thought of as universally quantified. L2 follows from the fact that evidence formulas must be satisfied in A under some interpretation, so free variables may be thought of as existentially quantified.

## 3.2 THE AE HIERARCHY

### 3.2.1 Upper Bounds

**Proposition 1:** Let L be an arbitrary first-order language. Then

$$\forall n, AE(\Sigma_n(L), \Pi_n(L))$$

*Proof sketch:* Let $s \in \Pi_n(L)$. Define neg(s) = the result of binding all free variables of s with universal quantifiers, and then driving a negation through the resulting quantifier prefix. So for example, neg[$\exists$x P(x,y)] = $\exists$y$\forall$x$\neg$P(x,y). If s is false, then eventually neg(s) occurs in the data. Define theorist $\theta$ as follows. Let $\sigma$ be a finite evidence sequence of length n. Then $\theta$ examines the first n hypotheses in $\Pi_n(L)$ and crosses out any hypothesis s such that some variable renaming variant of neg(s) occurs in the data. Then $\theta$ conjectures the greatest initial segment of the remaining sequence that entails no crossed-out hypothesis. If s is false, then eventually a renaming variant of neg(s) occurs in the data, and s is crossed out and never again entailed by any conjecture. If s is true, then eventually every false hypothesis prior to s is crossed out. Moreover, a true hypothesis is never crossed out. So eventually, all and only the false hypotheses prior to s are crossed out, and since truth cannot entail falsehood, s is in the greatest initial segment of the non-crossed-out hypotheses that does not entail any crossed out hypothesis. So thereafter, s is entailed by each conjecture. ∎

The theorist constructed in the proof of Proposition 1 employs a non-computable consistency test. Hence the upper bound it provides does not necessarily hold for computable theorists. Proposition 1 has been extended to computable theorists over languages without function symbols, however (Kelly and Glymour 89a).

There exist languages for which the bound of Proposition 1 can be greatly improved. For example, consider the following, special class of languages.

L is *simple* $\Leftrightarrow$

1. L has no non-logical predicates of arity 2 or greater, no function symbols of arity 2 or greater, and no identity, or

2. L has no nonlogical predicates of arity 2 or greater and no function symbols of any arity.

Simple languages are common in the artificial intelligence literature. The first case covers Boolean concept learning and the second case covers the induction of "planning rules" of the form

$$\forall x \ [Glass(x) \rightarrow Concave(grind(x)))]$$

It turns out that the data quantifier complexity of theory discovery problems is trivial for simple languages, in the sense that no quantifiers at all are required in the data for the solution of the problem, regardless of the quantifier complexity of the theory to be inferred.

**Proposition 2:** Let L be simple. Then

$$AE(\Pi_0(L), L).$$

*Proof:* Case 1: L has no binary predicates or function symbols, so the result follows by Proposition 8 in (Kelly & Glymour 89a). Case 2: H has no binary non-logical predicates and no function symbols. The result follows by Proposition 7 in (Kelly & Glymour 89a). ∎

### 3.2.2 Lower Bounds

Proposition 2 shows that the upper bound of Proposition 1 cannot be met for all first-order languages. But we may still ask whether there exist languages that give rise to lower bounds that approach the upper bounds of Proposition 1. Consider the following class of languages:

L is *rich* $\Leftrightarrow \forall n \geq 0, \Pi_{n-1}(L) - \Pi_n(L) \neq \emptyset$ and $\Pi_n(L) - \Sigma_n(L) \neq \emptyset$.

Intuitively, a language is rich if more quantifier alternations can always say something more than fewer quantifier alternations. For example, any extension of the language of arithmetic is rich. The monadic predicate calculus is not rich.

The next theorem establishes an infinite hierarchy lower bounds for rich languages, and is the main result to be presented in this paper.

**Theorem 3:** Let L be rich.  Then

$$(\forall n \geq 0) \, (\forall s \in L) \, [s \notin \Sigma_{n+2} \Rightarrow \neg AE(\Sigma_n(L), \{s\})]$$

*Proof:*  The proof proceeds by three lemmas.

**Definitions:** Let $\mathfrak{A}$, $\mathfrak{B}$ be relational structures for L.  $\mathfrak{A}$ is a $\Sigma_n$-*substructure of B* $\Leftrightarrow$ A is a substructure of B and for each $s \in \Sigma_n(L)$ and for each assignment g into the domain of $\mathfrak{A}$, if $\mathfrak{A} \models s[g]$ then $\mathfrak{B} \models s[g]$. The indexed set $\{\mathfrak{A}_\alpha : \alpha < \beta\}$ is a $\Sigma_n$-*chain* $\Leftrightarrow \forall \gamma, \gamma' < \gamma$, $\mathfrak{A}_\gamma$ is a $\Sigma_n$-substructure of $\mathfrak{A}_{\gamma'}$.  A sentence s has its truth *preserved* under $\Sigma_n$-chains $\Leftrightarrow$ for each such chain, if s is true in each member of the chain, then s is true in the unique structure that results from taking the union of the chain.

**Lemma 1:**  If s has its truth preserved under unions of countable $\Sigma_n$-chains of countable structures then $s \in \Pi_{n+1}$.

*Proof:*  Apply the Lowenheim Skolem theorem (Chang and Keisler 73, theorem 3.1.6) at various stages in the proof of Keisler's n-sandwich theorem (Ibid., theorem 5.2.8). ∎

**Lemma 2:**  Let $\{\mathfrak{A}_i : i \in N\}$ be a $\Sigma_{n-1}$-chain and let $\mathfrak{A} = \bigcup_{i \in N} \mathfrak{A}_i$. Then for all i, $\mathfrak{A}_i$ is a $\Sigma_{n-1}$-substructure of $\mathfrak{A}$.

*Proof:*  A substitution instance of (Chang and Keisler 73, theorem 3.1.15). ∎

**Definition:**  E, s, K satisfy the Osherson-Weinstein condition $\Leftrightarrow$ for each $\mathfrak{A} \in K$ if $\mathfrak{A} \models s$ then there is a $\sigma \in SEQ(E)$ and a finite g: var($\sigma$) $\to$ Dom($\mathfrak{A}$) such that for each $\mathfrak{B}$ such that $\mathfrak{B} \not\models s$ and for each complete assignment f such that $\mathfrak{B} \models \sigma[f]$, there is a $\tau \in SEQ(E)$ such that $\mathfrak{B} \models t[f]$ and for all assignments g' such that $g \subseteq g'$, $\mathfrak{A} \not\models \tau[g']$.

**Lemma 3:**  If AE(E, H, K) then $\forall s \in H$, E, s, K satisfy the Osherson-Weinstein condition and E, $\neg s$, K satisfy the Osherson-Weinstein condition.

*Proof:*    Observe that the proof of Proposition 31 in (Osherson and Weinstein 88) works for data of arbitrary quantifier complexity. ∎

*Proof of theorem:* Pick s' $\notin \Sigma_{n+2}(L)$.    This is possible since L is rich. Let s = ¬s', so s $\notin \Pi_{n+2}(L)$.    Then by Lemma 1, there exists a countable $\Sigma_{n+1}$-chain of countable structures such that each structure $\mathfrak{A}_i$ in the chain satisfies s but the union $\mathfrak{A}$ does not.    Note that $\mathfrak{A}$ is a countable structure.    Let K be the chain together with its union.    So $\mathfrak{A} \models$ s'.

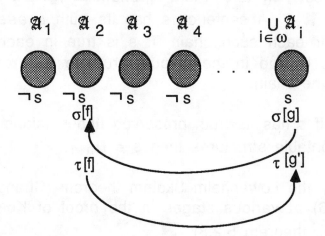

Let $\sigma \in$ SEQ($\Sigma_n(L)$).    Let $\mathfrak{A} \models \sigma[g]$ where g: var($\sigma$) → Dom($\mathfrak{A}$).    Find the first i such that rng(g) $\subseteq$ Dom($\mathfrak{A}_i$).    There is one, since rng(g) $\subseteq$ Dom($\mathfrak{A}$) and A = $\bigcup_{i \in N} \mathfrak{A}_i$. By lemma 2, $\mathfrak{A}_i$ is a $\Sigma_{n+1}$-substructure of $\mathfrak{A}$. So by the contrapositive of the definition of $S_{n+1}$-substructure  and by the fact that negated $\Sigma_n$ data is at worst $\Pi_n$ data, which is still $\Sigma_{n+1}$, we have that $\mathfrak{A}_i \models \sigma[g]$.    Pick surjection f: var → Dom(Ai) so that g $\subseteq$ f.    There is one since rng(g) $\subseteq$ Dom($\mathfrak{A}_i$).    Hence $\mathfrak{A}_i \models \sigma[f]$. Since $\mathfrak{A}_i$ is a $\Sigma_{n+1}$-substructure of $\mathfrak{A}$ and $\tau \in$ SEQ[$\Sigma_n$] and since rng(f) $\subseteq$ Dom($\mathfrak{A}_i$), we have that $\mathfrak{A} \models \tau[f]$.    But since g $\subseteq$ f, there is a g' such that g $\subseteq$ g' such that $\mathfrak{A} \models \tau[g']$.    So by Lemma 3, we have that not AE($\Sigma_n(L)$, {s'}, K). ∎

### 3.2.3 A System of Bounds

Proposition 1, together with basic relations L1 and L2, yields the following system of upper bounds:

Let L be a first-order language.  Then

**Cor. 1:** $\forall n \geq 0$, $AE(\Sigma_n(L), \Pi_n(L))$

**Cor. 2:** $\forall n \geq 0$, $AE(\Sigma_n(L), \Sigma_{n-1}(L))$

**Cor. 3:** $\forall n \geq 0$, $AE(\Pi_n(L), \Pi_{n+1}(L))$

**Cor. 4:** $\forall n \geq 0$, $AE(\Pi_n(L), \Sigma_n(L))$

Theorem 3, together with L1 and L2, yields the following system of lower bounds:

Let L be a rich first-order language.  Then

**Cor. 5:** $\forall n \geq 0$, $\neg AE(\Sigma_n(L), \Pi_{n+2}(L))$

**Cor. 6:** $\forall n \geq 0$, $\neg AE(\Sigma_n(L), \Sigma_{n+1}(L))$

**Cor. 7:** $\forall n \geq 0$, $\neg AE(\Pi_n(L), \Pi_{n+3}(L))$

**Cor. 8:** $\forall n \geq 0$, $\neg AE(\Pi_n(L), \Sigma_{n+2}(L))$

*Proof:* Cor. 6 follows from Theorem 3 and the fact that in a rich language, some $\Pi_{n+2}(L)$ formula is not $\Sigma_{n+2}(L)$.  Cor. 5 follows from Cor. 6 and L1.  Cor. 7 follows from Cor. 5 and L2.  Cor. 8 follows from Cor. 6 and L2. ∎

These consequences are summarized in the following diagram.

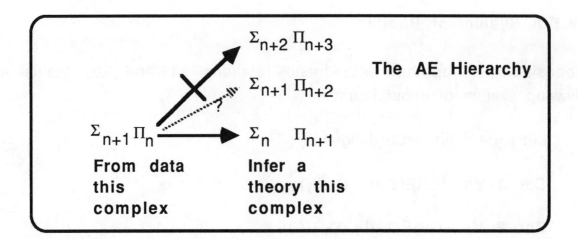

Notice that the AE hierarchy bounds leave a "gap" at $\Pi_{n+2}$. Intuitively, the gap results from the fact that we have to carry the data in two directions in the chain. To do this in a $\Sigma_n$ chain, we must make the data $\Sigma_{n-1}$, which is the same as $\Pi_{n-2}$ according to L2. The most plausible conjecture is that the open question will be settled in the negative, as it is in the base case of $n = 0$ (Kelly and Glymour 89a, Propositions 13, 14, and 15).

## 4. CONCLUSION

This paper presented a model-theoretic technique for proving impossibility theorems for reliable theory discovery from evidence consisting of laws of arbitrary quantifier complexity. The study of such evidence is motivated both by methodological considerations and by standard practice in machine learning. The analysis of such problems is harder than when the data is quantifier free. We have, in effect, established bounds on how far data of a given complexity can be "stretched" into theory of a higher complexity by means of reliable inductive inference in the limit. The result is an infinite hierarchy of inductive problems, of which the usual problems of formal learning theory constitute the first step.

The present study barely scratches the surface of the subject of induction from generalizations, which has been almost entirely neglected in the learning-theoretic literature. Obvious future topics include (a) computational limitations in solvable problems, (b) PAC learning from quantified data (Haussler 87), (c) further applications of model theoretic preservation theorems to negative results in learning theory, and (d) improving our technique to close the gap in the AE hierarchy theorem.

## Acknowledgments

Clark Glymour contributed substantially to the results in this paper. I would also like to thank Professor Stig Andur Pedersen for helpful comments on an early draft of the main theorem.

References

C. C. Chang and H. J. Keisler. <u>Model Theory</u>. Amsterdam: North Holland (1973).

D. Haussler. "Bias, Version Spaces, and Valiant's Learning Framework". <u>Proceedings of the Fourth International Workshop on Machine Learning</u>. San Mateo: Morgan Kaufmann (1987).

K. T. Kelly. <u>The Automated Induction of Universal Theories</u>. Ph. D. thesis, University of Pittsburgh (1986) .

K. T. Kelly. "Theory Discovery and the Hypothesis Language". <u>Proceedings of the Fifth International Conference on Machine Learning.</u> San Mateo: Morgan Kaufmann (1988).

K. T. Kelly and C. Glymour. "Convergence to the Truth and Nothing But the Truth", Forthcoming, <u>Philosophy of Science</u> (1989a).

K. T. Kelly and C. Glymour. "Theory Discovery from Data with Mixed Quantifiers". Forthcoming, <u>Journal of Philosophical Logic</u> (1989b).

D. Osherson and S. Weinstein  "Paradigms of Truth Detection", forthcoming, Journal of Philosophical Logic (1988).

P. H. Winston. "Learning Structural Descriptions from Examples", The Psychology of Computer Vision.  New York: McGraw-Hill (1975).

# SPACE-BOUNDED LEARNING
## AND THE VAPNIK-CHERVONENKIS DIMENSION

Sally Floyd*
Department of Computer Science
University of California, Berkeley CA 94720
E-mail: floyd@ernie.berkeley.edu

## ABSTRACT

This paper explores algorithms that learn a concept from a concept class of Vapnik-Chervonenkis (VC) dimension $d$ by saving at most $d$ examples at a time. The framework is the model of learning introduced by Valiant [V84]. A *maximum* concept class of VC dimension $d$ is defined. For a maximum class C of VC dimension $d$, we give an algorithm for representing a finite set of positive and negative examples of a concept by a subset of $d$ labeled examples of that set. This data compression scheme of size $d$ is used to construct a space-bounded algorithm that learns a concept from the class C by saving at most $d$ examples at a time. These $d$ examples represent the current hypothesis of the learning algorithm. A space-bounded learning algorithm is called *acyclic* if a hypothesis that has been rejected as incorrect is never reinstated. We give a sufficient condition for this algorithm to be acyclic on a maximum class C. Classes for which this algorithm is acyclic include positive half-spaces in Euclidean space $E^n$, balls in $E^n$, and arbitrary rectangles in the plane. This algorithm is also acyclic on positive sets in the plane where each positive set is defined by a polynomial of degree at most $n$. The algorithm can be thought of as learning a boundary between the positive and the negative examples.

## INTRODUCTION

This paper is an extended abstract of a longer paper [F89] examining algorithms that learn a concept from a class C of VC dimension $d$ by saving at most $d$ examples at a time. The longer paper contains a more complete explanation, along with the proofs for the results presented in this paper.

In [V84], Valiant introduced a model of learning concepts from examples drawn from an arbitrary distribution. In this model, a concept $c$ from a class C is a subset of the instance space X. Each example is drawn independently from a fixed but unknown distribution P on X. Each example is labeled either as a positive or as a negative example, consistently with some unknown target concept $c$.

The goal of the learning algorithm is to learn a good approximation of the target concept $c$, with high probability. The learning algorithm has the two inputs $\varepsilon$, the accuracy parameter, and $\delta$, the confidence parameter, along with an oracle for labeled examples of the target concept. The learning algorithm returns the hypothesis $h$. The error of the hypothesis is the total probability, with respect to the distribution P, of the symmetric difference of $c$ and $h$.

**Definitions:** A concept class C will be called *learnable* if there exists a learning algorithm such that, for any $\varepsilon$ and $\delta$, there exists a finite sample size such that, for any concept $c \in$ C and for any probability distribution on X, the algorithm produces a hypothesis that with probability at least $1-\delta$ has error at most

* Research supported by NSF Grant CCR-8411954, and by the International Computer Science Institute, Berkeley, California.

$\varepsilon$. The *sample complexity* is the smallest possible sample size. The concept class $\{C_n\}_{n \geq 1}$ is called *polynomially learnable* if the sample complexity and the time complexity of the learning algorithm are both polynomial in $1/\varepsilon$, $1/\delta$, and in the parameter $n$.

A general upper bound on the sample complexity for a learning algorithm for a concept class C is based on the Vapnik-Chervonenkis dimension of the class [BEHW87]. For a concept class C on X, and for $S \subset X$, let C(S) be the restriction of concept class C to the set S. Thus C(S) is the set of subsets T of S such that $T = S \cap c$ for some concept $c$ in C. If $C(S) = 2^S$, then the set S is *shattered* by C. The *Vapnik-Chervonenkis dimension* (VC dimension) of the class C is the largest integer $d$ such that some set $S \subset X$ of size $d$ is shattered. If arbitrarily large finite subsets of X are shattered by the class C, then the VC dimension of C is infinite. Note that a class C with one concept is of VC dimension 0. []

The following theorem from [BEHW87] gives an upper bound on the sample complexity of a learning algorithm with no space restrictions. This result is adapted from [VC71].

**Theorem 1 [BEHW87]:** Let C be a well-behaved* concept class. If the VC dimension of C is $d < \infty$, then for $0 < \varepsilon, \delta < 1$ and for sample size at least

$$s = \max\left[\frac{4}{\varepsilon}\log\frac{2}{\delta}, \frac{8d}{\varepsilon}\log\frac{13}{\varepsilon}\right],$$

any algorithm that finds a concept $c$ from C consistent with the sample set is a learning algorithm for C. []

A non-space-bounded learning algorithm for C might save $s$ examples in memory, for $s$ as defined above. In this paper, we explore algorithms that save at most $d$ examples in memory at one time.

Previous work on learning in the presence of space restrictions includes [H88], [BS88]. One of the simplest space-bounded learning algorithms is one for learning axis-parallel rectangles in $E^2$ [BEHW87]. In [H88], the sample complexity for space-bounded algorithms for learning a class of decision trees and for learning interval functions on the real line are analyzed. The analysis uses a general technique for establishing performance bounds for a class of space-efficient learning algorithms. In [BS88], it is shown that some classes of boolean functions on $n$ variables can be learned using O($log (n/\varepsilon)$) space. Communication complexity theory is used to show that, for certain classes, it is not possible to spare both examples and space. In contrast to previous work, in this paper we explore a general algorithm for space-bounded learning that is based on the VC dimension of the class.

**Definitions:** This paper uses the definitions from [W87] of *maximum* and *maximal* concept classes. A concept class is called *full* or *maximal* if adding any concept to the class increases the VC dimension of the class. From [VC71], [S72], for a class C of VC dimension $d$ on a finite set X of cardinality $m$, |C| is at most $\Phi_d(m)$, for $\Phi_d(m)$ defined as $\sum_{i=0}^{d}\binom{m}{i}$. A concept class C on X is called *complete* or *maximum* if, for every finite subset Y of X, the class C(Y) contains $\Phi_d(|Y|)$ concepts. A concept class that is maximum on a finite set X is also maximal on that set [WW87, pg. 53]. []

A concept $c$ in a class C can be thought of either as the subset B of positive examples from the set X, or as the characteristic function $\chi_B$ of B on X. We will refer to the characteristic function as a *0/1-*

---

*This is a measure-theoretic condition given in [BEHW87]. It is not likely to exclude any concept class considered in the context of machine learning applications.

*labeling* of the set X. Let X′ denote the set X along with some 0/1-labeling of the elements of X. Let $<x, 0>$ denote the element $x$ with the label 0, for example. This indicates that the element $x$ is a negative example.

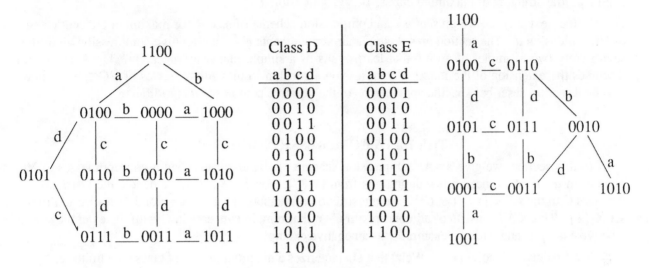

| Class D | Class E |
|---------|---------|
| a b c d | a b c d |
| 0 0 0 0 | 0 0 0 1 |
| 0 0 1 0 | 0 0 1 0 |
| 0 0 1 1 | 0 0 1 1 |
| 0 1 0 0 | 0 1 0 0 |
| 0 1 0 1 | 0 1 0 1 |
| 0 1 1 0 | 0 1 1 0 |
| 0 1 1 1 | 0 1 1 1 |
| 1 0 0 0 | 1 0 0 1 |
| 1 0 1 0 | 1 0 1 0 |
| 1 0 1 1 | 1 1 0 0 |
| 1 1 0 0 | |

Figure 1: Class D is maximum. Class E is maximal but not maximum.

**Example (maximum and maximal classes):** Figure 1 gives a chart of the concepts in the maximum class D, of VC dimension 2, on X={$a, b, c, d$}. Each row in the chart is a characteristic vector for a concept in the class D. Class D is maximum because it contains $\Phi_2(4)=11$ concepts. (See Theorem 2). The class E is maximal but not maximum, of VC dimension 2. No concepts can be added to the class E without increasing the VC dimension of the class. The *1-inclusion graph* for each class is also given. The 1-inclusion graph of a class C contains a node for each concept in C. Two nodes are connected by an edge if the corresponding concepts differ in the label for exactly one element $x$ of X. In this case, the edge is given the label $x$. [AHW87, D85]. []

The algorithms in this paper repeatedly use a data compression scheme to save $d$ out of $m$ examples, for $d$ the VC dimension of the class C. A *data compression scheme of size d* for a concept class C consists of two functions, a compression function and a reconstruction function [LW86]. The *compression function f* maps every set of $m$ labeled examples, for any $m \geq d$, to a subset of $d$ labeled examples, called the *compression set*. The *reconstruction function g* maps every possible subset of $d$ labeled examples to a hypothesis $c$ on X. This hypothesis is not required to be in the class C. The requirement for a data compression scheme is that, for any set $X_m'$ of labeled examples, the hypothesis $g(f(X_m'))$ is consistent with $X_m'$.

**Example (rectangles):** The compression function for the class of axis-parallel rectangles in $E^2$ takes the leftmost, rightmost, top, and bottom positive points from a sample set of $m$ positive and negative points in the plane. The reconstruction function has as a hypothesis the smallest axis-parallel rectangle consistent with these points. This hypothesis is guaranteed to be consistent with the original $m$ points. The class of axis-parallel rectangles in $E^2$ is a subset of a maximum class of VC dimension 4. []

The iterative compression algorithm presented in this paper saves $d$ examples at a time, using the data compression scheme described later in this paper. These $d$ examples represent the current hypothesis of the learning algorithm. When a new example is seen whose label is predicted incorrectly by the current hypothesis, the data compression scheme is used to decide which of the old examples to discard. The data compression scheme and the iterative compression algorithm are based on the elegant combinatorial structure of maximum classes of VC dimension $d$.

In the next section, we present a data compression scheme of size $d$ for maximum concept classes of VC dimension $d$. The section on simple planar arrangements gives an iterative compression algorithm saving only two examples at a time that learns cells of a simple planar arrangement. The next section discusses the extension of the iterative compression algorithm to maximum classes of VC dimension $d$. The final section describes specific applications of the iterative compression algorithm.

## THE DATA COMPRESSION SCHEME

In this section, we give a data compression scheme of size $d$ for maximum concept classes of VC dimension $d$. First we need a few definitions from [W87]. For $x \in X$, let $C - x$ denote the restriction of the class C to the set X-$\{x\}$. Let $C^{(x)}$ be the restriction of the class $\{c \in C \mid x \notin c$ and $c \cup \{x\} \in C\}$ to the set X-$\{x\}$. Thus $C^{(x)}$ consists of all concepts in $C - x$ that remain concepts in C with the example $x$ as a positive example, and with the example $x$ as a negative example.

We first give a theorem of E. Welzl that characterizes a maximum concept class on a finite set X.

**Theorem 2** [W87, p. 9]: A concept class C of VC dimension $d$ on a finite set X is maximum if and only if $|C| = \Phi_d(|X|)$.

**Proof:** By definition, if C is maximum, then $|C| = \Phi_d(|X|)$. We need to show if $|C| = \Phi_d(|X|)$, then, for every subset $Y$ of X, $|C(Y)| = \Phi_d(|Y|)$.

Assume that $|C| = \Phi_d(m)$, for X of cardinality $m$. Let $x \in X$. For every concept $c$ in $C^{(x)}$, the class C contains two concepts that are extensions of $c$, and for every concept $c$ in $C - x$ but not in $C^{(x)}$, the class C exactly contains one concept that is an extension of $c$. Thus $|C| = |C - x| + |C^{(x)}|$. The class $C - x$ is of VC dimension at most $d$ on X-$\{x\}$, so $|C - x| \leq \Phi_d(m-1)$.

The class $C^{(x)}$ is of VC dimension at most $d-1$ on X-$\{x\}$. If some set $X_d$ of cardinality $d$ was shattered by the class $C^{(x)}$, then the set $X_d \cup \{x\}$ would be shattered by the class C, contradicting the fact that C is of VC dimension $d$. Thus $|C^{(x)}| \leq \Phi_{d-1}(m-1)$.

Because $\Phi_d(m) = \Phi_d(m-1) + \Phi_{d-1}(m-1)$, it follows that $|C - x| = \Phi_d(m-1)$, and that $|C^{(x)}| = \Phi_{d-1}(m-1)$. By recursion, for any $Y \subset X$, $|C(Y)| = \Phi_d(|Y|)$. []

The following corollary of E. Welzl applies to maximum classes on a finite set X. Lemma 4 extends this corollary to a class that is both maximum and maximal on an infinite set X.

**Corollary 3** [W87, p. 10]: Let C be a maximum concept class of VC dimension $d$ on the finite set X, for $|X| = m > d$. Then for $x \in X$, $C - x$ is a maximum class of VC dimension $d$ on X-$\{x\}$, and $C^{(x)}$ is a maximum class of VC dimension $d-1$ on X-$\{x\}$. []

**Lemma 4:** Let C be a maximum and maximal concept class of VC dimension $d$ on the (possibly infinite) set X. Then for $x \in X$, $C - x$ is a maximum class of VC dimension $d$ on X-$\{x\}$, and $C^{(x)}$ is maximum and maximal of VC dimension $d-1$ on X-$\{x\}$. []

Let C be a maximum concept class C of VC dimension $d$ on the set X. For $A = \{x_1,...,x_k\}$, $A \subset X$, the class $C^A$ is defined as $((C^{(x_1)})...)^{(x_k)}$. For $|A| = d$, the class $C^A$ is maximum of VC dimension 0, and thus consists of a single concept. The class $C^A$ contains the single concept $c$ on X-A such that $c$ remains a concept in C for any labeling of the elements of A. For any set $A \subset X$, for $|A| = d$, let $c_A$ denote the unique concept in the class $C^A$.

**Example (at most two positive examples):** Consider the maximum class C of VC dimension two on X that consists of all concepts with at most two positive examples from the set X. Then, for $\{x_1, x_2\}$ $\subset$ X, $c_{\{x_1, x_2\}}$ denotes the concept on $X - \{x_1, x_2\}$ where every example is a negative example. This is the only concept on $X - \{x_1, x_2\}$ that remains a concept in C if both $x_1$ and $x_2$ are positive examples. []

**Example (intervals on the line):** Let $C_n$ be the class containing all unions of at most $n$ positive intervals on the line. This class is maximum of VC dimension $2n$. For $C_3$, let A be the set of 6 points $\{a, b, c, d, e, f\}$ shown below. Figure 2 shows the unique labeling of the line for the concept $c_A$. Positive examples are labeled "+", and negative examples are labeled "-". For any labeling of the points in A, the resulting labeling of the line corresponds to some concept in $C_3$. []

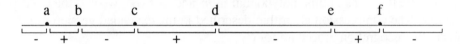

Figure 2: Union of three intervals on the line.

For a maximum concept class C of VC dimension $d$ on the finite set X, and for any $A \subset X$ of cardinality $d$, there is a corresponding concept $c_A$ on the set X-A. For the labeled set A', let $c_{A'}$ denote the concept with X-A labeled as in the concept $c_A$, and with A labeled as in A'. Thus for every set A' of cardinality $d$, for A $\subset$ X, there is a corresponding concept $c_{A'}$ on X. We say that the set A' *represents* the concept $c_{A'}$. Thus every set of $d$ labeled examples from the set X represents a unique concept from the maximum class C. Speaking loosely, we will say that a compression set A' *predicts labels* for the elements in X, according to the concept $c_{A'}$.

Theorem 5 states that for a maximum class C of VC dimension $d$ on a finite set X, every concept in C is represented by some labeled set A' of cardinality $d$. Theorem 6 states that, using this approach, there is a data compression scheme of size $d$ for any maximum and maximal class C of VC dimension $d$ on a (possibly infinite) set X.

**Theorem 5:** Let C be a maximum concept class of VC dimension $d$ on a finite set X, for $|X| = m \geq d$. Then for each concept $c \in$ C, there is a labeled set A' of exactly $d$ elements, for A' $\subset$ X, such that $c = c_{A'}$. (A somewhat different version of this theorem is presented, with a different approach, in [W87, p. 27]).

**Theorem 6:** Let C be a maximum and maximal class of VC dimension $d$ on the (possibly infinite) set X. Then there is a data compression scheme of size $d$ for C. Let Y be a finite subset of X. For $c$ a concept on Y, the compression function saves a labeled subset A' of cardinality $d$, for A $\subset$ Y, such that $c_{A'}$ in the class C(Y) is the concept $c$. The reconstruction function gives as a hypothesis the concept $c_{A'}$ on X.

**Proof sketch:** From Corollary 3, C(Y) is a maximum class of VC dimension $d$ on Y. From Theorem 5, for the concept $c$ on Y, there exists a subset A of Y such that $c_{A'}$ in the class C(Y) is the concept $c$.

The set A' is the compression set for some concept $c_{A'}$ on X. The concept $c_{A'}$ on X is consistent with the original concept $c$ on the set Y. Thus we have a data compression scheme of size $d$ for maximum classes of VC dimension d. []

Let $C_1$ be a proper subset of some maximum class C of VC dimension $d$ on the set X. That is, $C_1$ does not contain all of the concepts in the class C. The data compression scheme of size $d$ for C also gives a data compression scheme of size $d$ for $C_1$.

## AN ALGORITHM FOR THE COMPRESSION FUNCTION

This section gives a compression algorithm that implements the compression scheme defined above, for $C_n$ a maximum class of VC dimension $f(n)$ on the (possible infinite) set X. The input for the compression algorithm is a finite labeled sample set Y′ of cardinality $m \geq f(n)$. The examples in Y′ are assumed to be labeled consistently with some concept in $C_n$. The output is a labeled compression set $A' \subset Y'$ of cardinality $f(n)$ that represents some concept consistent with the labeled set Y′.

The compression algorithm is a greedy algorithm that considers the elements from Y′ one at a time. The initial compression set is empty, and for each element, the compression algorithm determines whether to add that element to the compression set. The simpliest version of the compression algorithm uses a procedure which, given a labeling of a finite sample set of cardinality $m$, determines whether there is a concept in C consistent with that labeling. We call this procedure the *recognition procedure*. If there exists such a procedure that runs in time polynomial in $m$ and in $f(n)$, we call the concept class *polynomially recognizable*. The compression algorithm described in the expanded version of this paper requires $O(m\, 2^{f(n)})$ calls to the recognition procedure for $C_n$.

A more efficient compression algorithm uses a more powerful recognition procedure. We define a *group recognition procedure* for the set A of cardinality at most $f(n)$, and for the maximum class $C_n$ of VC dimension $f(n)$, as a procedure that can determine whether a given set of examples is labeled consistently with some concept in the class $(C_n)^A$. We call a class $\{C_n\}_{n \geq 1}$ *polynomially group-recognizable* if there is a group recognition procedure for the class $C_n$ that runs in time polynomial in $m$ and in $f(n)$. The compression algorithm given in the expanded version of this paper requires at most $m$ calls to the group recognition procedure.

**Example (at most d positive examples):** The maximum class C of VC dimension $d$ on X which contains all concepts with at most $d$ positive examples is polynomially group-recognizable. Given $A \subset X$ of cardinality $k$, for $k \leq d$, the class $C^{(A)}$ consists of all concepts on X-A with at most $d-k$ positive examples. Therefore a group recognition procedure for $C^{(A)}$ simply needs to determine whether there are at most $d-k$ positive examples in the labeled sample set Y′-A′. []

The reconstruction algorithm is given a compression set A′ of cardinality $d$, and is asked to predict the label given by the concept $c_{A'}$ to some element $x$ from X. The reconstruction algorithm requires at most $2^{f(n)}$ calls to the recognition procedure, or one call to the group recognition procedure.

To summarize, if the maximum class $\{C_n\}_{n \geq 1}$ of VC dimension $f(n)$ is polynomially group-recognizable, then the data compression scheme can be implemented in time polynomial in $f(n)$ and in $m$.

## SIMPLE PLANAR ARRANGEMENTS

This section investigates an iterative compression algorithm that repeatedly applies the data compression scheme, always saving at most $d$ examples when learning a concept from a class of VC dimension $d$. We first describe this iterative compression algorithm for maximum classes of VC dimension 2 that can be represented as simple planar arrangements. Later sections of this paper discuss the application of the iterative compression algorithm to more general classes. The iterative compression algorithm is based on a partial order on the compression sets of size at most $d$. We discuss simple planar arrangements because these classes give a clear illustration of this partial order.

A *simple planar arrangement* G is the dissection of the plane into cells by a finite set of lines. No two lines are parallel, and no more than two lines intersect at a single point. A simple planar arrangement can be seen as a concept class C of VC dimension 2. The $m$ lines $x_1,..., x_m$ in the arrangement correspond to the $m$ elements $x_1,..., x_m$ in the set X, and each cell in the arrangement corresponds to a concept in the concept class C. Each line $x_i$ defines two half-spaces in the plane. For each cell in one of the half-spaces, the element $x_i$ is assigned the label "1", and $x_i$ is a positive example for the concept corresponding to that cell. For each cell in the opposite half-space, the element $x_i$ is assigned the label "0".

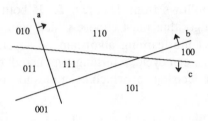
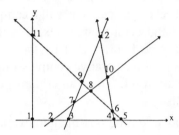

Figure 3.                    Figure 4.

**Example (simple arrangements):** The simple arrangement in Figure 3 corresponds to a concept class C with 7 concepts on a set X = $\{a, b, c\}$. The arrow at right angles to line $a$ indicates the half-plane containing cells for which $a$ is a positive example. For each cell, the labels for elements $a$, $b$ and $c$ are given. []

A concept class C that corresponds to a simple planar arrangement is maximum of VC dimension two. The proof uses the fact that a simple planar arrangement of $m$ lines has $\Phi_2(m)$ cells [E87, p. 7]. However, there are many maximum classes of VC dimension 2 that do not have a corresponding simple planar arrangement.

The unlabeled compression set A = $\{x_i, x_j\}$ in the class C corresponds to the vertex $\{x_i, x_j\}$ in G, where the vertex $\{x_i, x_j\}$ is defined as the intersection of the two lines $x_i$ and $x_j$. There are four concepts in C consistent with single concept $c_A$ on X-A. These four concepts have four different labels for the set A, and correspond to the four cells in G adjacent to the vertex $\{x_i, x_j\}$. In the class C, the labeled compression set A' = $\{<x_i,l_i>, <x_j,l_j>\}$ represents a specific concept $c_{A'}$, for $l_i,l_j \in \{0,1\}$. The concept $c_{A'}$ in C corresponds to that cell in G adjacent to the vertex $\{x_i, x_j\}$ for which $x_i$ and $x_j$ are labeled as in A'. For the sake of brevity, we refer to a labeled compression set as $\{x_i, x_j\}$, with the implicit assumption that $x_i$ and $x_j$ are labeled consistently with the target concept. If the compression set $\{x_i, x_j\}$ predicts the wrong label for $x_k$, then the vertex $\{x_i, x_j\}$ and the target concept must be on opposite sides of the line $x_k$.

**Example (compression sets in simple arrangements):** For the class C in Figure 3, let the compression set A' be $\{<a,1>, <b,1>\}$. Then the concept $c_{A'}$ is that cell adjacent to vertex $\{a, b\}$ in G for which $a$ has label "1", and $b$ has label "1". This cell "111" in G corresponds to concept "111" in C. []

We consider a learning algorithm for simple planar arrangements that saves at most two examples at a time, using the compression scheme presented earlier. The algorithm draws labeled examples, one at a time, and presents as a hypothesis a cell of the simple planar arrangement. The current compression set represents the current hypothesis of the learning algorithm. The current hypothesis is rejected if and only if it is inconsistent with the current example. In this case, the current example is saved, and one of the examples from the old compression set is discarded. An on-line learning algorithm is *acyclic* if a hypothesis that has been rejected as incorrect is never reinstated. We give an acyclic algorithm for learning cells of a simple planar arrangement.

The target concept $c$ to be learned corresponds to a cell $c$ in the simple arrangement. For each new example $x_k$ that is drawn, labeled as in the target, the learning algorithm uses the reconstruction algorithm to check if the current compression set $\{x_i, x_j\}$ predicts the correct label for that element. If so, the new example is discarded. If not, then the learning algorithm chooses a new compression set of size two from the set $\{x_i, x_j, x_k\}$. A compression set is called *valid* if it predicts the correct label for all of the saved examples. The existence of a valid compression set follows from Theorem 5. If both $\{x_i, x_k\}$ and $\{x_j, x_k\}$ are valid compression sets, then the learning algorithm must choose which compression set to save. This choice is motivated by the requirement that the learning algorithm be acyclic. There are several variants of the iterative compression algorithm that can cycle, returning over and over again to the same compression set. These algorithms make incorrect decisions of which examples to save, and which example to discard.

One way to ensure that the iterative learning algorithm is acyclic is to establish an appropriate partial order on the compression sets, and to construct an algorithm that is guaranteed to move to a compression set that is greater on the partial order than the current compression set when the current compression set is changed. That is what we do here. The learning algorithm and the partial order meet the condition that any time that the current compression set $\{x_i, x_j\}$ predicts the incorrect label for the new element $x_k$, and $\{x_i, x_k\}$ is a valid compression set, then $\{x_i, x_k\}$ is greater than $\{x_i, x_j\}$ in the partial order on compression sets.

In order to establish an appropriate partial order, the learning algorithm first adds two *distinguished lines* $x$ and $y$ to the simple arrangement, such that $x$ and $y$ are not parallel to any lines in the simple arrangement. This is shown in Figure 4. These lines can be considered as an $x$ and $y$ axis, added so that all vertices in the simple arrangement are in the upper right quadrant. The line $x$ divides the plane into a lower and an upper part. Lines $x$ and $y$ are given their natural orientation. Every other line crosses line $x$, and is directed toward the upper part of the plane. Thus lines $x$ and $y$ are used to assign a direction to each line in the simple arrangement. These directed lines are used by the learning algorithm to establish a partial order on the 2-element compression sets.

The learning algorithm starts with the compression set $\{x, y\}$. When the current compression set is $\{x_i, x_j\}$, and the new example is $x_k$, then the two compression sets $\{x_i, x_k\}$ and $\{x_j, x_k\}$ lie on the line $x_k$. Each directed line establishes an order on the compression sets that lie on that line. If the line $x_k$ is directed from $\{x_i, x_k\}$ to $\{x_j, x_k\}$, then we will define $\{x_i, x_k\} \leq \{x_j, x_k\}$ in the partial order. This defines the relation "$\leq$" on 2-element compression sets from the set X. Considering the transitive closure of the relation "$\leq$", Lemma 7 states that the relation "$\leq$" is a partial order on the compression sets.

**Lemma 7:** For a simple planar arrangement on the set X, the set of all two-element compression sets from the set $X \cup \{x, y\}$, along with the relation "$\leq$", is a partially ordered set. []

When the learning algorithm has a choice between two valid compression sets, the iterative compression algorithm chooses the compression set that is lower in the partial order. Oddly enough, this is the condition that ensures that future moves of the iterative compression algorithm are always to a compression set that is greater in the partial order.

Define the *target compression set* as the least compression set that exactly represents the target concept. Define a compression set $\{x_i, x_j\}$ as labeled *in standard form* if the labeling indicates that the target concept lies in the quadrant between the "positive" end of line $x_i$, with the arrow on the end, and the "positive" end of line $x_j$. The key to the correctness of the iterative compression algorithm is that the current compression set is always labeled in standard form.

Theorem 8 states that the iterative compression algorithm for simple planar arrangements is acyclic.

**Theorem 8:** The iterative compression algorithm for simple planar arrangements maintains the following invariants:

1. The current compression set is labeled in standard form.

2. When the current compression set is changed, the new compression set is greater in the partial order than the old compression set.

3. There is always a sequence of at most two examples that would cause the iterative compression algorithm to move to the target compression set.

**Proof sketch:** For part 1, the initial compression set $\{<x, 1>, <y, 1>\}$ is labeled in standard form. The proof shows that if the current compression set is labeled in standard form, then the subsequent compression set will also be labeled in standard form. There are two cases to consider. The first case occurs when the current compression set $\{x_i, x_j\}$ predicts the incorrect label for the new example $x_k$, and only one of the compression sets $\{x_i, x_k\}$ and $\{x_j, x_k\}$ is a valid compression set. The second case occurs when both $\{x_i, x_k\}$ and $\{x_j, x_k\}$ are valid compression sets.

For part 2, the proof shows that because the current compression set is labeled in standard form, and because the new compression set must predict the correct label for the elements in the old compression set, the new compression set must be greater in the partial order than the old compression set.

Let the target compression set be $\{x_p, x_q\}$. For part 3, the proof shows that if the two examples $x_p$ and $x_q$ are seen consecutively in the proper order, then the iterative compression algorithm will move to the target compression set. []

## MAXIMUM CLASSES OF VC DIMENSION TWO

In this section, we briefly discuss the iterative compression algorithm for an arbitrary maximum class of VC dimension 2. The application of this algorithm to maximum classes of VC dimension $d$ is an extension of this approach. As in the case of simple planar arrangements, a partial order on the 2-element compression sets is used to guide the algorithm when the algorithm must choose which examples to save, and which example to throw away. The iterative compression algorithm maintains the invariant that any change in the current compression set is always to to a compression set that is greater in the partial order.

In the case of simple planar arrangements, an orientation is assigned to each line $x_i$ in the arrangement. This orientation is determined by the intersection of that line with one of the distinguished elements. This orientation establishes an order on the two-element compression sets that contain the element $x_i$. For the general case of a maximum class of VC dimension 2, we add two distinguished examples $z_1$ and $z_2$ to the regular examples in the set X, and we enlarge the class C so that C is maximum of VC dimension 2 on $X \cup \{z_1, z_2\}$. The class C is enlarged so that the distinguished examples are labeled positive for every concept in the original class. For each $x_i \in X$, we use the distinguished elements to establish a partial order on the 2-element compression sets containing $x_i$. We say that the distinguished elements *determine* a partial order on the compression sets.

For each $x_i$, the partial order on the 2-element compression sets containing $x_i$ results from a partial order on the 1-element compression sets in $C^{(x_i)}$, a maximum class of VC dimension 1. To explain the partial order on compression sets on a maximum class of VC dimension 1, we need to consider the 1-inclusion graph for that class. The following theorem is due, in slightly different versions, to several different sources [D85, AHW87, WW87].

**Theorem 9** [WW87]: Let C be a maximum class of VC dimension 1 on the finite set X of cardinality $m$. Then the 1-inclusion graph of C is a tree, and every $x$ in X appears exactly once as a label on an edge. []

For each $x_i \neq z_1$, the distinguished example $z_1$ is used to establish directions on the edges in the 1-inclusion graph of $C^{(x_i)}$. The class $C^{(x_i)}$ is a maximum class of VC dimension 1. The label $z_1$ appears exactly once as the label for some edge in the 1-inclusion graph. The edge labeled $z_1$ is directed towards the adjacent node in which $z_1$ is labeled "1". The other edges in the 1-inclusion graph are then directed so that every path in the 1-inclusion graph is a directed path. The directed 1-inclusion graph is used to establish a partial order on the 1-element compression sets in C. If there is a directed path in the 1-inclusion graph from an edge labeled $x_j$ to an edge labeled $x_k$, then we define $x_j \leq x_k$ in the partial order on 1-element compression sets in $C^{(x_i)}$. This is explained in more detail in [F89].

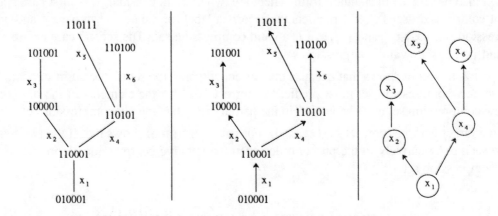

Figure 5. The 1-inclusion graph for a class of VC dimension 1.

**Example (a partial order on 1-element compression sets):** Part 1 of Figure 5 gives the 1-inclusion graph for a concept class C of VC dimension 1 on a finite set X of cardinality 6. Each node is labeled by the characteristic vector for the corresponding concept on the elements $x_1,.., x_6$. Part 2 of Figure 5 shows the directed 1-inclusion graph, with the edge directions determined by the distinguished example $x_1$. Part 3 of Figure 5 shows the partial order on the 1-element compression sets from C. Each 1-element compression set corresponds to an edge in the 1-inclusion graph. []

The partial order on the 1-element compression sets in $C^{(x_i)}$ is used to establish a partial order on the 2-element compression sets in C as follows. If $\{x_j\} \leq \{x_k\}$ in the partial order on 1-element compression sets from $C^{(x_i)}$, then define $\{x_i, x_j\} \leq \{x_i, x_k\}$ on the partial order "$\leq$" on 2-element compression sets from C. Define the relation "$\leq$" as a transitive relation.

**Theorem 10:** Let C be a maximum class of VC dimension 2 on the finite set X, with $z_1, z_2$ distinguished elements in X. The set of 2-element compression sets of C, along with the relation "$\leq$" defined above, is a partially ordered set. []

Theorem 11 states that the iterative compression algorithm for any maximum class of VC dimension 2 is acyclic.

**Theorem 11:** The iterative compression algorithm for a maximum class of VC dimension 2 maintains the following invariants:

1. When the current compression set is changed, the new compression set is greater in the partial order than the old compression set.

2. There is always a sequence of at most two examples that would cause the iterative compression algorithm to move from the current compression set to the target compression set.

**Proof sketch:** The proof of Theorem 11 is somewhat detailed, but the basic ideas are the similar to those in the proof of Theorem 8. The proof relies on a definition of a compression set labeled in standard form, and the proof first shows that the current compression set is always labeled in standard form. []

The iterative compression algorithm for certain maximum classes of VC dimension $d$ is similar to the algorithm for maximum classes of VC dimension 2. First, $d$ distinguished examples are added to the set X. These distinguished examples establish separate partial orders on compression sets from subsets of C of VC dimension 1. It is an open question whether, for all maximum classes of VC dimension $d$, these distinguished elements determine a partial order on the $d$-element compression sets. Theorem 12 states that for those maximum classes for which the distinguished examples determine a partial order on the d-element compression sets, the iterative compression algorithm can be shown to be acyclic.

**Theorem 12:** Let C be a maximum class of VC dimension $d$ on the set X. Let X contain the distinguished elements $z_1,.., z_d$, and assume that these distinguished elements determine a partial order on the compression sets. Then the iterative compression algorithm maintains the following invariants:

1. When the current compression set is changed, the new compression set is greater in the partial order than the old compression set.

2. There is always a sequence of at most $d$ examples that would cause the iterative compression algorithm to move from the current compression set to the target compression set. []

Let C be a maximum class of VC dimension $d$ for which the iterative compression algorithm is acyclic. Then the iterative compression algorithm is also acyclic on a class $C_1 \subset C$. In this case, each compression set is interpreted as representing a concept in the maximum class C.

One possible implementation of the iterative compression algorithm is to test the $i$th hypothesis with at most $\frac{1}{\varepsilon}\ln\frac{(i+1)^2}{\delta}$ examples [A88], [LMR88]. The algorithm halts and accepts the $i$th hypothesis only if that hypothesis has predicted the correct label for $\frac{1}{\varepsilon}\ln\frac{(i+1)^2}{\delta}$ consecutive examples. This implementation requires sufficient memory for a counter, to count the number of examples consistent with the current hypothesis. This algorithm outputs a hypothesis with error more that $\varepsilon$ with probability at most $\sum_{i=1}^{\infty}\frac{\delta}{(i+1)^2} \approx .65\delta$. With this implementation, the iterative compression algorithm does not draw a fixed number of examples. The analysis of the expected number of examples needed by this algorithm is an open problem. The next section presents experimental evidence of the average number of examples required by this algorithm when learning positive half-spaces in $E^n$. For these simulations, the examples were drawn from the uniform distribution on the unit hypercube.

## APPLICATIONS

In this section we give examples of classes for which the iterative compression algorithm is acyclic.

## SIMPLE ARRANGEMENTS

A *simple arrangement G in $E^d$* is the dissection of $E^d$ into cells by a finite set of $m$ hyperplanes. Any $d$ hyperplanes have a point in common, and no set of $d+1$ hyperplanes have a point in common. As with the simple planar arrangement, the cells of a simple arrangement in $E^d$ correspond the concepts of a maximum class C of VC dimension $d$ on a finite set X. Each hyperplane $y_i$ in G corresponds to an element of X, and each cell of the arrangement corresponds to a concept in the class C. Each hyperplane $y_i$ defines two half-spaces in $E^d$. For the cells in one half-space, $y_i$ has the label "1", and for the cells in the other half-space, $y_i$ has the label "0". There are $\Phi_d(m)$ cells in the simple arrangement [E87, p. 7]. The iterative compression algorithm for simple arrangements is acyclic.

## POSITIVE HALF-SPACES

Positive half-spaces in $E^n$, of VC dimension $n$, can be seen as a dual of the class of simple arrangements in $E^n$. An open positive half-space in $E^n$ consists of those points $(x_1,..,x_n)$ for which $x_j > a_{j-1}x_{j-1} +...+ a_1x_1 + a_0$, for $1 \leq j \leq n$. If $X \subset E^n$ contains at most $n$ points on any halfplane, then the class of positive half-spaces is maximum of VC dimension $n$ on X. The iterative compression algorithm for learning positive half-spaces in $E^n$ saves a set S of $j$ examples, for $j \leq n$, where each example is a labeled point from $E^n$. The examples in the set S satisfy an equation of the form $x_j = a_{j-1}x_{j-1} +...+ a_1x_1 + a_0$, and the hypothesis represented by the set S contains as positive examples those points for which $x_j > a_{j-1}x_{j-1} +...+ a_1x_1 + a_0$. Each example in the compression set S can be either a positive or a negative example, and therefore each hypothesis is a modified version of a positive half-space. In the most straightforward version of the algorithm, no prediction is made for the labels of other points for which $x_j = a_{j-1}x_{j-1} +...+ a_1x_1 + a_0$.

Each compression set corresponds to a modified version of a positive half-space of the form $x_j > a_{j-1}^-x_{j-1} +...+ a_1x_1 + a_0$, for $1 \leq j \leq n$. The partial order on the compression sets is consistent with the partial order on the positive half-spaces given by the lexicographic order on the coefficients $(a_{n-1},..., a_0)$. A coefficient $b_i$ is considered to be lexicographically greater than $a_i$ if $b_i \geq a_i$. This iterative compression algorithm for positive half-spaces is acyclic.

We have run simulations to explore the average number of examples needed by this algorithm. For each simulation, the target concept is a positive half-space in $E^n$, for some $n$. Each target halfspace is chosen by randomly drawing $n$ points from the unit hypercube, and computing the hyperplane through those $n$ points. Each example is drawn from the uniform distribution on the unit hypercube. For these simulations, the $i$ th hypothesis was tested with at most $\frac{1}{\varepsilon}\ln\frac{(i+1)^2}{\delta}$ examples. For $n=2$, the simulations were run with varying values for $\varepsilon$ and for $\delta$. For $\varepsilon$ and $\delta$ both equal to 0.01, the simulations were run for values of $n$ up to 40. For $n=2$ and for $\delta=0.01$, the average number of examples needed in these simulations can be roughly approximated by $27.73/\varepsilon$, and the average number of changes of hypothesis can be approximated by $3.29 \ln(1/\varepsilon)$. For $\varepsilon, \delta = 0.01$, the average number of changes of hypothesis needed in these simulations can be approximated by $1.69n^2$, and the average number of examples for these simulations can be roughly approximated by $75.35n^2 + 5193$. This experimental data is not sufficient to predict the expected number of examples needed by the iterative compression algorithm for these conditions. This is intended only to suggest that in this case, the expected number of examples is bounded above by some polynomial in $1/\varepsilon$ and in the dimension $n$. There is no experimental evidence on the average number of examples needed by the iterative compression algorithm for examples drawn from distributions other than the uniform distribution.

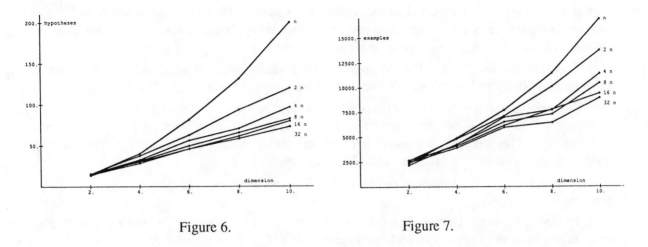

Figure 6.                    Figure 7.

Variants of the iterative compression algorithm can save more that $n$ examples at a time, for a maximum class of VC dimension $n$. Assume, for example, that the iterative compression algorithm saves $m$ examples at a time, for $m > n$. If there is more than one valid compression set of size $n$ from these $m$ examples, then the iterative compression algorithm chooses the valid compression set that is least in the partial order on compression sets. This compression set represents the current hypothesis for the iterative compression algorithm. For example, given a set of $m$ labeled points from some positive half-space in $E^n$, each valid compression set represents a positive halfspace. From the valid compression sets, the iterative compression algorithm chooses the compression set that is least in the partial order. For positive half-spaces, one way to find the least compression set is to use linear programming.

Figures 6 and 7 show the results of simulations exploring the space-time tradeoffs for the iterative compression algorithm for positive half-spaces. The expanded version of this paper describes the algorithm used in these simulations to decide which extra examples to save, in those cases where the iterative compression algorithm saves more than $n$ examples. For these simulations, the examples are drawn from the uniform distribution on the unit hypercube, as described earlier. Figure 6 shows the average number of changes of hypothesis for these simulations, and Figure 7 shows the average number of examples. Each point in the graph represents the average number of examples or of changes of hypothesis from more than 20 simulations. The $x$-axis is the dimension $n$. There are six curves in each figure. The top curve shows the results of simulations that saved $n$ examples, and the $i$th curve from the top shows the results of simulations that saved $2^{i-1}n$ examples. A more accurate idea of the average number of examples needed for each case would require more simulations. These results suggest that in this case, the average number of examples needed by the iterative compression algorithm can be significantly improved by a small increase in the number of examples saved by the algorithm.

Arbitrary rectangles and triangles can each be seen as the intersection of a finite number of half-spaces. For example, there is a noncyclic iterative compression algorithm for learning arbitrary rectangles in the plane that saves five examples at a time.

## VECTOR SPACES OF REAL FUNCTIONS

From [D84, P84], let H be an $n$-dimensional vector space of real functions on some set X. Therefore, for any $f$ in H, $f(x) = a_n f_n(x) + .. + a_1 f_1(x)$, for some fixed basis set of functions $f_1 ,..., f_n$, for $a_1,.., a_n \in \mathbf{R}$, and for $x \in X$. Let $f_0$ be an arbitrary real function on X. Let the concept $pos(f_0 - f)$ be defined as $\{x: f_0(x)-f(x) > 0\}$, and let the concept class $pos(f_0-H)$ be defined as $\{pos(f_0-f): f \in H\}$. This section investigates the iterative compression algorithm applied to classes of the form $pos(f_0-H)$. Theorem 13, from [WD81], also appears in [D84] and [P84].

**Theorem 13 [WD81]:** Let H be an $n$-dimensional vector space of real functions on the set X, and let $f_0$ be an arbitrary real function on X. Then the class $C = pos(f_0-H)$ is of VC dimension $n$.

**Example (polynomials):** Let X consist of the points $(x, y) \in E^2$. Let H be the $n$-dimensional vector space of functions of the form $f((x,y)) = a_{n-1}x^{n-1} + a_{n-2}x^{n-2} + \cdots + a_1 x + a_0$, and let $f_0((x,y)) = y$. Then the class $pos(y-H)$ is of VC dimension $n$. For $f \in H$, the concept $pos(y-f(x))$ consists of all the points in $E^2$ that lie "above" the polynomial $f$. []

Theorem 14 gives a sufficient condition for the class $pos(y-H)$ to be a maximum class of VC dimension $n$ on a set X.

**Theorem 14:** Let H be an $n$-dimensional vector space of real functions on the set X, such that H is an $n$-dimensional vector space of real functions on each $X_n \subset X$ of cardinality $n$. Further, for a given function $f_0$, assume that for each $f \in H$, there are at most $n$ elements of X such that $f_0(x) - f(x) = 0$. Then the class $C = pos(f_0-H)$ is a maximum class of VC dimension $n$ on X. []

**Corollary 15:** Let H be an $n$-dimensional vector space of real functions on X, and let $f_0$ be an arbitrary real function on X, with the conditions described in Theorem 14. Then for $A \subset X$ of cardinality $n$, the compression set A represents the concept $pos(f_0-f)$ on X-A, for $f$ the unique function in H such that $f_0(x)-f(x) = 0$ for each $x \in A$. []

The requirement that H be an $n$-dimensional vector space of functions on every $X_n \subset X$ of cardinality $n$ is a necessary condition for the class $pos(f_0-H)$ to be a maximum class of VC dimension $n$ on X.

**Example (circles):** Let X be a subset of $E^2$, let H be the three-dimensional vector space of functions of the form $f((x,y)) = a_3 y + a_2 x + a_1$, and let $f_0((x,y)) = -x^2 - y^2$. Then $f_0((x,y)) - f((x,y)) = -x^2 - y^2 - a_3 y - a_2 x - a_1$, and $pos(f_0-f)$ consists of all points for which $x^2 + y^2 + a_3 y + a_2 x + a_1 < 0$. There are the points contained in the circle with center $(-\frac{a_2}{2}, -\frac{a_3}{2})$, and with radius $\left[ (a_3/2)^2 + (a_2/2)^2 - a_1 \right]^{1/2}$. Restrict X to a subset of $E^2$ such that H is a 3-dimensional vector space on every $X_3 \subset X$ of cardinality 3. This is satisfied if, for every three points $(x_1, y_1)$, $(x_2, y_2)$, and $(x_3, y_3)$ in X, the three vectors $(x_1, x_2, x_3)$, $(y_1, y_2, y_3)$, and $(1, 1, 1)$ are linearly independent. Thus, X cannot contain three colinear points. Further restrict X to a subset of $E^2$ such that at most three points lie on the circumference of any circle. From Theorem 14, the class $pos(f_0-H)$ is maximum of VC dimension 3 on X. []

**Example (polynomials):** Let X be a subset of $E^2$, let H be the $n$-dimensional vector space of functions of the form $f((x,y)) = a_{n-1}x^{n-1} + a_{n-2}x^{n-2} + \cdots + a_1 x + a_0$, and let $f_0((x,y)) = y$. Restrict $X$ to a subset of $E^2$ such that no two points in X have the same $x$-coordinate. Then H is an $n$-dimensional vector space on every $X_n \subset X$ of cardinality $n$. Further assume that for every $f \in H$, there at most $n$ points in X for which $f(x) = y$. Then from Theorem 14 the class $pos(f_0-H)$ is maximum of VC dimension $n$ on X. []

Now consider the iterative compression algorithm on a maximum class $pos(f_0-H)$ of VC dimension $n$, where H has a fixed basis set $f_1,.., f_n$. Define $H_i$ as the class of functions of the form $a_i f_i + .. + a_1 f_1$. We assume that for each $f \in H_i$, there are at most $i$ examples in X for which $f_0(x)-f(x) = 0$. We add distinguished examples $z_1,.., z_n$ to the set X to ensure that a compression set $X_i$ of $i$ regular examples represents the concept $pos(f_0-f)$ on $X-X_i$, for $f$ the unique function in $H_i$ such that $f_0(x)-f(x)=0$ for each $x \in X_i$. This is explained further in [F89]. Theorem 16 states that the distinguished examples determine a partial order on the compression sets from $X \cup Z$.

**Theorem 16:** Let H be an $n$-dimensional real vector space of functions and let $f_0$ be an arbitrary real-valued function on the set X, with the conditions described in Theorem 14. Assume that for each $f \in H_i$, there are at most $i$ elements from X such that $f_0(x)-f(x)=0$. For the compression set $A_i$ with $i$ regular examples from X, for $1 \le i \le n$, let $f_{A_i}$ be the unique function in $H_i$ such that $f_0(x) - f_{A_i}(x)=0$ for each $x \in A_i$. Let the distinguished examples $z_1,.., z_n$ be added so that the compression set $A_i$ represents the concept $pos(f_0-f_{A_i})$ on $X-A_i$. Then the distinguished elements determine a partial order on the $n$-element compression sets from $X \cup Z$. This partial order is consistent with the partial order on the corresponding functions $f = a_n f_n +..+ a_1 f_1$ given by the lexicographic order on the absolute values of the coefficients $a_n,..,a_1$. []

**Corollary 17:** Let the vector space H, the function $f_0$, and the set X satisfy the conditions in Theorem 16. Then the iterative compression algorithm for the class $pos(f_0-H)$ is acyclic. []

**Example (polynomials):** Let X be $E^2$, let H be the $n$-dimensional vector space of functions of the form $f((x,y)) = a_{n-1}x^{n-1} + a_{n-2}x^{n-2} + \cdots + a_1 x + a_0$, and let $f_0((x,y))=y$. Then the iterative compression algorithm for the class $pos(f_0-H)$ is acyclic. In the $i$th stage, the algorithm saves $i$ examples, and the current hypothesis is of the form $pos(y-f(x))$ for $f$ a polynomial of degree at most $i-1$. The expanded version of this paper describes the extensions to the iterative compression algorithm so that the set X can contain all of the points in $E^2$. In this extension, for a current hypothesis $pos(y-f(x))$, the points for which $f(x)=y$ are labeled as intervals of alternating positive and negative points. The iterative compression algorithm for this class always saves alternating positive and negative examples, for a set of $i$ examples ordered from left to right. []

## CONCLUSIONS AND OPEN PROBLEMS

In this paper, we have presented a data compression scheme of size $d$ for maximum classes of VC dimension $d$, and we have used this data compression scheme to build an iterative compression algorithm. We have proved that this algorithm is acyclic for maximum classes of VC dimension 2, and we have given a sufficient condition for this algorithm to be acyclic for a maximum class of VC dimension $d$. We have discussed an implementation of the algorithm that tests the $i$th hypothesis with at most $\frac{1}{\varepsilon}\ln\frac{(i+1)^2}{\delta}$ examples. Applications of this algorithm include positive half-spaces in $E^n$, and classes of the form $pos(f_0-H)$, for H an $n$-dimensional vector space of real functions on X, and for $f_0$ a real-valued function on X.

There are many open questions. One open question is whether the iterative compression algorithm is acyclic for all maximum classes of VC dimension $d$. For the classes for which the iterative compression algorithm is acyclic, a theoretical analysis for the sample complexity of the algorithm is needed. Another open question is whether there is a data compression scheme of size $d$ for every maximal but not maximum class C of VC dimension $d$. The expanded version of this paper suggests an extension of the data compression scheme and of the iterative compression algorithm to classes that are maximal but not maximum. It is an open question whether this variant of the iterative compression algorithm behaves correctly and is acyclic for every maximal class of VC dimension $d$.

Acknowledgements

I am grateful for generous help from David Haussler, Richard Karp, and Manfred Warmuth. This work also benefitted from conversations with Steve Omohundro, Raimund Seidel, and others. The question of whether there is a data compression scheme of size $d$ for every class of VC dimension $d$ was communicated to me from Manfred Warmuth, and Theorem 5 is joint work with Warmuth. The suggestion to look at simple planar arrangements came from David Haussler. This work is based on the characterizations of maximum and maximal classes by Emo Welzl.

References

[AHW87]   Alon, N., Haussler, D., and Welzl, E., "Partitioning and Geometric Embedding of Range Spaces of Finite Vapnik-Chervonenkis Dimension", *Proc. 3rd Symp. on Computational Geometry*, Waterloo, June 87, pp. 331-340.

[A88]   Angluin, D., "Queries and Concept Learning", *Maching Learning 2*, pp. 319-342, 1988.

[BEHW87]   Blumer, A., Ehrenfeucht, A., Haussler, D., and Warmuth, M., "Learnability and the Vapnik-Chervonenkis Dimension," UC Santa Cruz Tech. Rep. UCSC-CRL-87-20, 1987, revised October 1988.

[BS88]   Boucheron, S., and Sallantin, J., "Some Remarks about Space-Complexity of Learning, and Circuit Complexity of Recognizing", *Proceedings of the 1988 Workshop on Computational Learning Theory*, Morgan Kaufmann, 1988.

[D84]   Dudley, R. M., "A Course on Empirical Processes", *Lecture Notes in Mathematics No. 1097*, Springer-Verlag, New York, 1984.

[D85]   Dudley, R. M., "The Structure of some Vapnik-Cervonenkis Classes", *Proc. Berkeley Conference in Honor of Jerzy Neyman and Jack Kiefer*, V. II, Wadsworth, Inc., 1985.

[E87]   Edelsbrunner, H., *Algorithms in Combinatorial Geometry*, Springer-Verlag, 1987.

[F89]   Floyd, S., On Space-bounded Learning and the Vapnik-Chervonenkis Dimension", unpublished manuscript available from the author, 1989.

[H88]   Haussler, D., Space Efficient Learning Algorithms, UC Santa Cruz Tech. Rep. UCSC-CRL-88-2, 1988.

[LMR88]   Linial, N., Mansour, Y., and Rivest, R., "Results on Learnability and the Vapnik-Chervonenkis Dimension", *Proceedings of the 1988 Workshop on Computational Learning Theory*, Morgan Kaufmann, 1988.

[LW86]   Littlestone, N, and Warmuth, M., "Relating Data Compression and Learnability", unpublished paper, 1987.

[P84]   Pollard, D., *Convergence of Stochastic Processes*, Springer-Verlag, New York, 1984.

[S72]   Sauer, N., "On the Density of Families of Sets", *Journal of Comb. Th.* (A) 13, p. 145-147.

[V84]   Valiant, L.G., "A Theory of the Learnable", *Comm. ACM*, 27(11), 1984, pp. 1134-42.

[VC71]   Vapnik, V.N. and Chervonenkis, A.Ya., "On the Uniform Convergence of Relative Frequencies of Events to their Probabilities", *Th. Prob. and its Appl.*, 16(2), 1971, pp. 264-280.

[WW87]   Welzl, E., and Woeginger, G., On Vapnik-Chervonenkis Dimension One, unpublished notes, 1987.

[W87]   Welzl, E., Complete Range Spaces, unpublished notes, 1987.

[WD81]   Wenocur, R.S., and Dudley, R.M., "Some special Vapnik-Chervonenkis classes", *Discrete Math.*, 33, 1981, pp. 313-318.

# Reliable and Useful Learning

Jyrki Kivinen

Department of Computer Science

University of Helsinki

Teollisuuskatu 23

SF-00510 Helsinki, Finland

e-mail: jkivinen@cs.helsinki.fi

## Abstract

Reliable and probably useful learning from examples, proposed by Rivest and Sloan, is a variant of Valiant's concept learning framework. We show that having different sources for positive and negative examples makes reliable learning easier than having just one source for labeled examples. We also show that the class of boolean monomials and the class of rectangles are not reliably learnable from a polynomial number of either kind of examples. This demonstrates that reliable learning is much more difficult than normal Valiant-style learning. On the positive side we prove that symmetric concepts can be learned reliably from a polynomial number of examples.

We also derive necessary and sufficient conditions for reliable learnability of a concept class. The conditions are stated in terms of the Vapnik-Chervonenkis dimension of certain related classes.

## 1 Introduction

Rivest and Sloan [9] have defined reliable and probably useful learning, a variation of Valiant's [11] probably approximately correct (pac) concept learning framework. A *concept* is a rule that partitions a given domain, the *instance space*, to positive and negative examples. The learner is given a sample of negative and positive examples of the *target* concept. The examples are drawn independently according to a fixed but otherwise arbitrary probability distribution on the instance space. The learner then outputs its *hypothesis*, a program that is supposed to classify further positive and negative examples, drawn according to the same probability distribution.

Learning is *reliable* if each time the hypothesis classifies an example positive (negative), the example indeed is positive (resp. negative). To give the learner some freedom the hypothesis is allowed to output also "I don't know." A learned hypothesis is said to be *useful* if the probability of answering "I don't know" is less that an *error parameter* $\epsilon$

defined by the user. Learning is said to be *probably* useful if the probability of samples resulting to a non-useful hypothesis is less than a user-defined *confidence parameter δ*.

We are interested in the number of examples needed for reliable and probably useful learning, when it is known that the target concept is a member of a given concept class. Especially, we wish to know whether this number is polynomial in $\frac{1}{\epsilon}$, $\frac{1}{\delta}$ and some parameter related to the complexity of the target concept (such as the number of variables in a boolean formula representing the target concept).

Rivest and Sloan proposed an algorithm that learns reliably and probably usefully any concept, when the instances can be represented by a sequence of boolean attributes and the target concept can be represented by a boolean formula of these attributes. The required number of examples and the amount of time needed to process these examples are polynomial in $\frac{1}{\epsilon}$, $\frac{1}{\delta}$, the number of the attributes and the length of the boolean formula.

When using this algorithm, the boolean formula is viewed as a program for computing the value of the formula. Each program line computes a value for a new boolean variable as a function of the values of the basic attributes and the values computed by the previous program lines. The function must be chosen from a class with a polynomial size, e.g., the class of conjunctions and disjunctions of two variables.

Each function computed by a program line defines a concept. These concepts are called *subconcepts* of the target concept. The algorithm requires examples of each subconcept. It then gradually builds up the target concept, using already learned subconcepts in learning new, more complicated ones.

In order to correctly generate examples of the subconcepts the teacher must know the subconcepts and thus the program for the boolean formula. In some potential applications even the teacher does not know the target concept. We are interested in this situation, in which only examples of the target concept are available.

Two different models are introduced in Section 2. In learning from *one source of examples* there is one probability distribution on the whole instance space. The learner gets a number of labeled examples from this distribution. There are no restrictions on the relative frequencies of positive and negative examples. In learning from *two sources of examples* there are separate probability distributions on negative and positive examples of the concept, and the learner gets a certain number of examples from both of these distributions. In pac-learning these two models are known to be equivalent [4]. Here it is shown that in reliable and probably useful learning, learnability from one source still implies learnability from two sources but the converse does not hold.

In Section 3 we introduce the canonical learning algorithm. The algorithm is based on Mitchell's candidate elimination approach [7] and is used also by Rivest and Sloan. The learner maintains a list of all concepts that are consistent with all the examples. Whenever two of these concepts classify an example differently, the learner does not classify it, but replies "I don't know." It is shown that of all reliable learning algorithms the canonical algorithm produces the least number of "I don't know" -answers.

In Section 4 we use the canonical algorithm to show that boolean monomials cannot be learned reliably and probably usefully from a polynomial number of examples. As Rivest and Sloan noticed, if the number of concepts in a class of boolean formulae over $n$ variables is polynomial in $n$, the class can be learned reliably and probably usefully in a polynomial time. We show that also the class of symmetric concepts can be learned polynomially. This class has size $2^n$. In Section 5 we show that rectangles in $\mathbb{R}^n$ can be learned reliably only for $n = 1$.

Much larger classes than monomials, for example decision trees of bounded rank [3], are known to be pac-learnable. Rectangles are known to be pac-learnable for all $n$ [1]. Our results show that reliable and probably useful learning is much more difficult than pac-learning.

In Section 6 we study general conditions for reliable and probably useful learnability. We make use of Natarajans results [8] of learning with one-sided error. These results are generalized to allow both positive and negative examples and, using the results of Blumer et. al. [1], infinite instance spaces. This gives a characterization of reliable and probably useful learnability of a concept class in terms of the *Vapnik-Chervonenkis dimension* [1] of certain related classes.

The results are to appear in a complete form in [6].

**Notation:** If $c \subseteq X$, then $\overline{c} = X - c$. ($X$ is clear from the context.) The cardinality of a set $S$ is denoted by $|S|$. For any infinite $S$ we simply write $|S| = \infty$. The symbol $\mathbb{N}_+$ is used for the set $\{1, 2, 3, \ldots\}$ of positive integers. The notations $[a, b]$ and $]a, b[$ are used for the closed and open interval of real numbers between $a$ and $b$. The respective half-closed intervals are denoted by $]a, b]$ and $[a, b[$. If $P$ is a probability distribution on $X$, probabilities of subsets of $X^m$ are measured by the product probability distribution; that is, we assume that the components of any sequence of events are independent.

## 2    Reliable and probably useful learning

Let $X$ be an arbitrary set, the *instance space*. Usually $X = \{0, 1\}^n$ or $X = \mathbb{R}^n$ for some $n$. We assume that there is a fixed family $\mathcal{F}$ of subsets of $X$ such that all probability distributions $P$ on $X$ are defined for the sets in $\mathcal{F}$. The sets in $\mathcal{F}$ are called *measurable*. For a finite $X$ we assume that $\mathcal{F} = 2^X$. For $X = \mathbb{R}^n$ we assume that $\mathcal{F}$ is the family of Borel sets.

Sometimes we use expressions like, "The probability of $S$ is at least $a$," although the set $S$ is not measurable. This is to be interpreted, "There is a measurable set $S' \subseteq S$ such that $P(S') \geq a$."

Elements of $\mathcal{F}$ are called *concepts* and subsets of $\mathcal{F}$ *concept classes* on $X$. If $X = \{0, 1\}^n$, we often represent concepts by boolean formulae of variables $x_i$. Here $x_i$ is interpreted as "the $i$th bit is 1." Examples of concept classes on $\{0, 1\}^n$ are $M_n$, the class of *monomials*, and $S_n$, the class of *symmetric concepts*. A monomial is a conjunction of variables and negated variables. A concept $c$ is symmetric if there is a set $S \subseteq \{0, \ldots, n\}$ such that $(x_1, \ldots, x_n) \in c$ iff $\sum x_i \in S$. For $X = \mathbb{R}^n$ we consider the class $R_n$ of closed $n$-dimensional rectangles: $R_n = \{[a_1, b_1] \times \cdots \times [a_n, b_n] \mid a_i, b_i \in \mathbb{R}\}$.

We use the symbol $I_c$ for the indicator function of a concept $c$:

$$I_c(x) = \begin{cases} 1 & \text{if } x \in c \\ 0 & \text{otherwise.} \end{cases}$$

If $\vec{x} = (x_1, \ldots, x_m)$ is a sequence of instances, then

$$\text{sam}_c(\vec{x}) = (\langle x_1, I_c(x_1) \rangle, \ldots, \langle x_m, I_c(x_m) \rangle)$$

is a labeled $m$-sample of $c$. We use $S_C$ to denote the set of all labeled $m$-samples of $c$ for all $m \in \mathbb{N}_+$ and all $c \in C$. Let $s = (\langle x_1, l_1 \rangle, \ldots, \langle x_m, l_m \rangle)$ be a sample. The instances $x_i$ are called examples in $s$. If $l_i = 1$, the example $x_i$ is a *positive* example, otherwise it is a *negative* example.

*Hypotheses* are functions from $X$ to $\{1, 0, *\}$. In addition we require that for a hypothesis $h$ the sets $\{x \mid h(x) = 1\}$, $\{x \mid h(x) = 0\}$ and $\{x \mid h(x) = *\}$ are measurable. If the learner outputs the hypothesis $h$ after seeing a sample of concept $c$, the intended interpretation is

$$h(x) = \begin{cases} 1 & \text{if certainly } x \in c \\ 0 & \text{if certainly } x \notin c \\ * & \text{if the learner is not certain.} \end{cases}$$

We use the symbol $H$ for the set of all hypotheses.

In the following definitions we view learning algorithms simply as some functions associating a hypothesis to each sample. The efficiency of an algorithm is measured only by the number of examples needed. Our main results imply that restricting the number of examples makes reliable and useful learning very difficult. Thus, additional restrictions coming from computational complexity do not seem interesting.

**Definition 1** *A function $A : S_C \to H$ is a reliable learning algorithm for $C$ from one source of examples if for all $m \in \mathbb{N}_+$, all $c \in C$ and all $\vec{x} \in X^m$ the following conditions hold:*

$$\text{if } A(\text{sam}_c(\vec{x}))(y) = 1 \quad \text{then } y \in c \quad \text{and}$$
$$\text{if } A(\text{sam}_c(\vec{x}))(y) = 0 \quad \text{then } y \notin c.$$

If the hypothesis answers "I don't know" all the time, the algorithm is trivially reliable but not very interesting. To restrict the number of "I don't know" -answers we introduce reliable and probably useful learning.

**Definition 2** *Let* $m$ *be a function* $]0,1] \times ]0,1] \to \mathbb{R}$. *A function* $A$ *learns* $C$ *probably usefully from* $m(\epsilon, \delta)$ *examples if for all probability distributions* $P$ *on* $X$, *all* $\epsilon', \delta' > 0$, *all* $m \geq m(\epsilon', \delta')$ *and all* $c \in C$ *the probability of getting* $\vec{x} \in X^m$ *such that*

$$P(A(\text{sam}_c(\vec{x}))(y) = *) \leq \epsilon'$$

*is at least* $1 - \delta'$.

*A concept class* $C$ *can be learned reliably and probably usefully from* $m(\epsilon, \delta)$ *examples if there is a reliable learning algorithm* $A$ *such that* $A$ *learns* $C$ *probably usefully from* $m(\epsilon, \delta)$ *examples.*

Reliability means that if the learner is given a sample of concept a $c$, the resulting hypothesis must always either agree with $c$ or not give a definitive answer. Usefulness means that for most samples the algorithm must produce a hypothesis that gives a definitive answer most of the time.

We call $(C_n)_{n \in \mathbb{N}_+}$ a *concept class sequence* if each $C_n$ is a concept class on some $X_n$. For example, $(M_n)_{n \in \mathbb{N}_+}$ is the concept class sequence of monomials. The following definition is based on the idea that a sample of a concept $c$ immediately reveals the index $n$ for which $c \in C_n$. For example, if monomials are to be learned, $n$ is the number of bits in each example.

**Definition 3** *A concept class sequence* $(C_n)_{n \in \mathbb{N}_+}$ *can be learned reliably and polynomially probably usefully from one source of examples if for all* $n \in \mathbb{N}_+$ *the concept class* $C_n$ *can be learned reliably and probably usefully from* $m_n(\epsilon, \delta)$ *examples and there is a polynomial* $p$ *such that* $m_n(\epsilon', \delta') \leq p(n, \frac{1}{\epsilon'}, \frac{1}{\delta'})$ *for all* $n$, $\epsilon'$ *and* $\delta'$.

Learning from one source of examples models a situation, in which the learner has a black box producing labeled examples according to a fixed probability distribution. We consider also the situation, in which the learner has two black boxes, one producing positive examples and one producing negative examples. This leads us to learning from two sources of examples.

When there are two sources of examples, the sample is not a sequence of labeled examples but two sequences of examples, one consisting of positive and the other of negative examples. For a concept $c$ the set $c^{m_+} \times \overline{c}^{m_-}$ is the set of all samples with $m_+$ positive and $m_-$ negative examples of $c$. We let

$$S_C^{\pm} = \bigcup_{c \in C} \bigcup_{m_+=1}^{\infty} \bigcup_{m_-=1}^{\infty} c^{m_+} \times \overline{c}^{m_-}.$$

We have assumed that the learner uses each black box at least once. Thus, a sample always contains at least one positive and one negative example. Let $s = (\vec{x}, \vec{y})$ be a sample. The instances $x_i$ are called *positive* examples in $s$ and the instances $y_i$ *negative* examples in $s$.

The definitions of learnability are similar to those for the model with one source of examples.

**Definition 4** *A function $A : S_C^{\pm} \to H$ is a reliable learning algorithm for $C$ from two sources of examples if for all $c \in C$, all $m_+, m_- \in \mathbb{N}_+$ and all $s \in c^{m_+} \times \overline{c}^{m_-}$ the following conditions hold:*

$$\text{if } A(s)(y) = 1 \quad \text{then } y \in c \quad \text{and}$$
$$\text{if } A(s)(y) = 0 \quad \text{then } y \notin c.$$

**Definition 5** *Let $m_+$ and $m_-$ be functions $]0,1] \times ]0,1] \to \mathbb{R}$. A function $A$ learns $C$ probably usefully from $m_+(\epsilon, \delta)$ positive and $m_-(\epsilon, \delta)$ negative examples if for all $c \in C$, all probability distributions $P_+$ on $c$ and $P_-$ on $\overline{c}$, all $\epsilon', \delta' > 0$, all $m_+ \geq m_+(\epsilon', \delta')$ and all $m_- \geq m_-(\epsilon', \delta')$, the probability of getting $s \in c^{m_+} \times \overline{c}^{m_-}$ such that*

$$P_+(A(s)(y) = *) \leq \epsilon' \text{ and } P_-(A(s)(y) = *) \leq \epsilon'$$

*is at least $1 - \delta'$.*

    *A concept class $C$ can be learned reliably and probably usefully from $m_+(\epsilon, \delta)$ positive and $m_-(\epsilon, \delta)$ negative examples if there is a reliable learning algorithm $A$ such that $A$ learns $C$ probably usefully from $m_+(\epsilon, \delta)$ positive and $m_-(\epsilon, \delta)$ negative examples.*

**Definition 6** *A concept class sequence $(C_n)_{n \in \mathbb{N}_+}$ can be learned reliably and polynomially probably usefully from two sources of examples if for all $n \in \mathbb{N}_+$ the concept class $C_n$ can be learned reliably and probably usefully from $m_{+_n}(\epsilon, \delta)$ positive and $m_{-_n}(\epsilon, \delta)$ negative examples and there is a polynomial $p$ such that $m_{+_n}(\epsilon', \delta') + m_{-_n}(\epsilon', \delta') \leq p(n, \frac{1}{\epsilon'}, \frac{1}{\delta'})$ for all $n$, $\epsilon'$ and $\delta'$.*

## 3   Basic results

Let $C$ be a concept class and $s \in S_C \cup S_C^{\pm}$ be a sample of a concept in $C$. A concept $c \in C$ is *consistent* with the sample $s$ if it includes all the positive examples of $s$ but none of the negative ones. The *version space* [7], denoted by $V_C(s)$, is the set of the consistent concepts:

$$V_C(s) = \{c \in C \mid c \text{ is consistent with } s\}.$$

If $s$ is a sample of a concept $c \in C$ then $c \in V_C(s)$. If $x \in X$ is an instance such that $x \in c'$ for all $c' \in V_C(s)$, we can safely deduce that $x \in c$. This leads us to the following canonical learning algorithm $A_C$ ($A_C^{\pm}$ for two sources of examples), based on Mitchell's candidate elimination approach [7] and used also by Rivest and Sloan [9]:

**Definition 7** *Let $C$ be a concept class on $X$ such that for all samples $s \in S_C$ the sets $\bigcap_{c \in V_C(s)} c$ and $\bigcup_{c \in V_C(s)} c$ are measurable. The canonical learning algorithm $A_C$ is the following function $S_C \to H$:*

$$A_C(s)(x) = \begin{cases} 1 & \text{if } x \in c \text{ for all } c \in V_C(s) \\ 0 & \text{if } x \notin c \text{ for all } c \in V_C(s) \\ * & \text{otherwise.} \end{cases}$$

*The canonical learning algorithm $A_C^{\pm}$ is the corresponding function from $S_C^{\pm}$ to $H$.*

It is easily seen that under the measurability assumptions stated in the definition the functions $A_C(s')$ and $A_C^{\pm}(s'')$ are always acceptable hypotheses. The assumptions are always true for a finite $X$. They are true also when $C$ is the class of $n$-dimensional rectangles, which is rather simple to prove.

The reliability of the canonical algorithms is obvious from the motivation we had for introducing them. On the other hand, if there are two concepts $c'$ and $c''$ in the version space such that $x \in c'$ and $x \notin c''$, no reliable learning algorithm $A$ can classify $x$. If $A(s)(x) = 1$, then $A$ is not reliable when learning the target concept $c''$, and if $A(s)(x) = 0$, then $A$ is not reliable when learning the target concept $c'$. We get the following result:

**Lemma 8** *The canonical learning algorithm $A_C$ is a reliable learning algorithm for $C$ from one source of examples. Let $A$ be any reliable learning algorithm for $C$ from one source of examples. If $A(s)(x) = 1$, then $A_C(s)(x) = 1$; if $A(s)(x) = 0$, then $A_C(s)(x) = 0$.*

*The canonical learning algorithm $A_C^{\pm}$ is a reliable learning algorithm for $C$ from two sources of examples. Let $A^{\pm}$ be any reliable learning algorithm for $C$ from two sources of examples. If $A^{\pm}(s)(x) = 1$, then $A_C^{\pm}(s)(x) = 1$; if $A^{\pm}(s)(x) = 0$, then $A_C^{\pm}(s)(x) = 0$.*

**Proof** The lemma follows from the preceding remarks. $\square$

Lemma 8 states that $A_C$ and $A_C^{\pm}$ are the most useful reliable learning algorithms. To prove a concept class $C$ non-learnable it suffices to show that algorithms $A_C$ and $A_C^{\pm}$ do not learn probably usefully. If a concept class can be learned, there usually are other learning algorithms as well. Some of these may be computationally easier or produce computationally easier hypotheses than the canonical ones.

It is well known [4] that a concept is pac-learnable from one source of examples iff it is pac-learnable from two sources of examples. The other direction of this equivalence holds for reliable and probably useful learning, as the following theorem shows.

**Theorem 9** *If $C$ can be learned reliably and probably usefully from $m(\epsilon, \delta)$ examples, it can be learned reliably and probably usefully from $m(\epsilon, \frac{\delta}{2})$ positive and $m(\epsilon, \frac{\delta}{2})$ negative examples.*

**Proof** Let $A$ be a reliable learning algorithm that learns $C$ probably usefully from $m(\epsilon, \delta)$ examples. For a sample $s \in S_C^{\pm}$ let the labeled sample $s_+$ consist of the positive examples in $s$ labeled positive and the labeled sample $s_-$ of the negative examples in $s$ labeled negative. Let $A^{\pm}$ be the following function:

$$A^{\pm}(s)(x) = \begin{cases} 1 & \text{if } A(s_+)(x) = 1 \\ 0 & \text{if } A(s_-)(x) = 0 \\ * & \text{otherwise.} \end{cases}$$

Let us assume that $A^{\pm}(s)(x) = 1$. By the reliability of $A$ this implies $x \in c'$ for all $c' \in V_C(s_+)$. Because $V_C(s) = V_C(s_+) \cap V_C(s_-)$, this further implies $x \in c'$ for all $c' \in V_C(s)$, so $x$ must be a positive instance of the target concept. The case $A^{\pm}(s)(x) = 0$ is similar. Thus $A^{\pm}$ is reliable.

To prove the usefulness of $A^{\pm}$, let $P_+$ be a probability distribution on the positive and $P_-$ on the negative instances of the target concept $c$. For a sample $s$ drawn according to these distributions, $s_+$ is a labeled sample drawn according to the distribution $P_+$. Therefore the usefulness of $A$ implies that $P_+(A(s_+)(x) = *) \leq \epsilon$ holds with probability at least $1 - \frac{\delta}{2}$. Similarly, $P_-(A(s_-)(x) = *) \leq \epsilon$ holds with probability at least $1 - \frac{\delta}{2}$. The probability that one of these conditions fails is less than $\delta$. □

In the proof we used the sources of negative and positive examples to simulate two sources of labeled examples, each with its own probability distribution. To get the converse of the theorem we should be able to use any source of labeled examples to simulate one source of positive examples and one source of negative examples. If the probability distribution for the labeled examples gives, for instance, probability 1 to the set of positive instances, a source for negative examples cannot be simulated. In Section 5 we see that the concept class $R_1$ of intervals of the real axis is learnable from two sources of examples but not from one source of examples.

# 4    Learnability of boolean concepts

The class of monomials was among the first to be shown pac-learnable [11]. Later, generalizations of monomials, such as decision trees of bounded rank [3], have been shown pac-learnable. This leads us to consider reliable and probably useful learning of monomials.

**Theorem 10** *The concept class sequence* $(M_n)_{n \in \mathbb{N}_+}$ *of monomials cannot be learned reliably and polynomially probably usefully from two sources of examples.*

**Proof** For $n \geq 2$, consider using the monomial $x_1 \ldots x_n$ as a target concept of the class $M_n$. The only possible positive example $(1, \ldots, 1)$ is consistent with all the monotone monomials (conjunctions of non-negated variables). Let $B_n \subseteq M_n$ be the set of monotone monomials with exactly $\lceil n/2 \rceil$ conjuncts and $D_n \subseteq \{0,1\}^n$ the set of vectors with exactly $\lceil n/2 \rceil$ 1-bits. Let $P_-$ be the uniform probability distribution on $D_n$.

For each instance $x \in D_n$ there is exactly one monomial $c_x \in B_n$ such that $x$ satisfies $c_x$. Thus, each negative example in a sample $s$ removes only one element of $B_n$ from $V_{M_n}(s)$. Let $p$ be any polynomial. Since $|B_n| = \binom{n}{\lceil n/2 \rceil} > 2^{\lceil n/2 \rceil}$ for large $n$, we can select $n$ such that $p(n, 2, 2) < \frac{1}{2}|B_n|$. If a sample $s$ contains at most $p(n, 2, 2)$ examples of the target concept, the monomial $c_x$ remains in $V_{M_n}(s)$ for more than half of the elements $x \in D_n$.

Setting $\epsilon = \delta = \frac{1}{2}$ we now have $P_-(A_{M_n}^{\pm}(s)(x) = *) > \epsilon$ with probability 1, when $s$ contains $p(n, \frac{1}{\epsilon}, \frac{1}{\delta})$ examples. The canonical algorithm $A_{M_n}^{\pm}$ does not learn probably usefully. $\quad\square$

It is possible to show that polynomially probably useful learning of monomials is impossible even if reliability is required only with probability $1 - \delta$. The proof, which resembles that of Theorem 15 in [5], is omitted.

Theorem 10 shows that reliable and probably useful learning is much more difficult than pac-learning. However, there are also some positive results. As Rivest and Sloan [9] notice, a concept class sequence $(C_n)_{n \in \mathbb{N}_+}$ can be learned reliably and polynomially probably usefully if $|C_n|$ is polynomial in $n$. This implies that the class of monomials with at most $k$ conjuncts is learnable, since there are at most $(3n)^k$ such conjunctions of at most $n$ variables. As an example of a learnable class with exponentially many concepts we have the class of symmetric concepts.

**Theorem 11** *The class $S_n$ of symmetric concepts can be learned reliably and probably usefully from $\frac{n+1}{\epsilon} \ln \frac{n+1}{\delta}$ examples.*

**Proof** For symmetric concepts the canonical learning algorithm can be represented as

$$A_{S_n}(s)(x) = \begin{cases} 1 & \text{if } \sum x_i = \sum y_i \text{ for some positive example } y \\ 0 & \text{if } \sum x_i = \sum y_i \text{ for some negative example } y \\ * & \text{otherwise.} \end{cases}$$

We apply the techniques of Blumer et. al. [2]. For any given $k \in \{0, \ldots, n\}$ there are two possibilities. If $P(\sum x_i = k) \leq \frac{\epsilon}{n+1}$ we can ignore $k$, since the probability of $\sum x_i$ hitting any such $k$ is at most $\epsilon$. Assume that $P(\sum x_i = k) > \frac{\epsilon}{n+1}$. A simple calculation shows that the probability of having $\sum y_i \neq k$ for all the examples $y$ is at most $\frac{\delta}{n+1}$. There are $n + 1$ possible values of $k$, so with at least probability $1 - \delta$ all these values of $k$ are covered by the examples. $\quad\square$

The easiness of learning the class of symmetric concepts is due to the fact that the class is closed under union and intersection. The results in Section 6 indicate that under this closure assumption reliable and probably useful learning is no more difficult than pac-learning.

# 5 Learnability of rectangles

The learnability of the class $R_1$ of closed subintervals of the real axis can be shown by the techniques of Blumer et. al. [1], if there are two sources of examples.

**Theorem 12** *The concept class $R_1$ of closed subintervals of the real axis can be learned reliably and probably usefully from $\frac{2}{\epsilon} \ln \frac{4}{\delta}$ positive and $\frac{2}{\epsilon} \ln \frac{4}{\delta}$ negative examples.*

**Proof** For a sample $s$ of a concept $[a, b] \in R_1$, let $a_+$ be the least and $b_+$ the greatest positive example. If there are negative examples larger than $b_+$, let $b_-$ be the least of them; otherwise let $b_- = \infty$. If there are negative examples less than $a_+$, let $a_-$ be the greatest of them; otherwise let $a_- = -\infty$. A concept $[a', b']$ is consistent with the sample $s$ iff $a_- < a' \leq a_+$ and $b_+ \leq a' < a_-$. Therefore,

$$A_{R_1}^{\pm}(s)(x) = \begin{cases} 1 & \text{if } a_+ \leq x \leq b_+ \\ 0 & \text{if } x \leq a_- \text{ or } b_- \leq x \\ * & \text{otherwise.} \end{cases}$$

It is easy to show that for $\frac{2}{\epsilon} \ln \frac{4}{\delta}$ positive examples the inequalities $P_+([a, a_+[) \leq \frac{\epsilon}{2}$ and $P_+(]b_+, b]) \leq \frac{\epsilon}{2}$ each hold with probability at least $1 - \frac{\delta}{4}$. Similarly, for $\frac{2}{\epsilon} \ln \frac{4}{\delta}$ negative examples the inequalities $P_-(]a_-, a[) \leq \frac{\epsilon}{2}$ and $P_-(]b, b_-[) \leq \frac{\epsilon}{2}$ each hold with probability at least $1 - \frac{\delta}{4}$. Therefore, the conditions

$$P_+(A_{R_1}^{\pm}(s)(x) = *) = P_+([a, a_+[ \cup ]b_+, b]) \leq \epsilon$$

and

$$P_-(A_{R_1}^{\pm}(s)(x) = *) = P_-(]a_-, a[ \cup ]b, b_-[) \leq \epsilon$$

hold with probability at least $1 - \delta$. $\qquad \square$

Having at least one positive example is necessary in learning subintervals:

**Theorem 13** *The concept class $R_1$ of closed subintervals of the real axis cannot be learned reliably and probably usefully from one source of examples with any number of examples.*

**Proof** Consider the one-element target concept $[0, 0]$ and the uniform probability distribution on the interval $[-1, 1]$. Let $m \in \mathbb{N}_+$ be arbitrary and let $s$ be a labeled $m$-sample of $[0, 0]$. With probability 1 all the examples are negative. Assume that this is the case.

Now let an instance $x$ be chosen according to $P$. Assume that $x \in [-1, 1]$ and $x$ is not one of the negative examples in $s$; this is true with probability 1. Now the concepts $[x, x]$ and $[2, 3]$ are both consistent with $s$. Because $x \in [x, x]$ and $x \notin [2, 3]$, we have $A_{R_1}(s)(x) = *$. This happens with probability 1, so $A_{R_1}$ does not learn probably usefully from $m$ examples. $\qquad \square$

Theorems 12 and 13 show that the converse of Theorem 9 does not hold.

More generally, $n$-dimensional rectangles can be pac-learned from $\frac{2n}{\epsilon} \ln \frac{2n}{\delta}$ examples [1]. In reliable and probably useful learning already two dimensions are too much, even with two sources of examples.

**Theorem 14** *The concept class $R_2$ of two-dimensional rectangles cannot be learned reliably and probably usefully from two sources of examples with any number of examples.*

**Proof** Let us consider the target concept $c_0 = [1,2] \times [1,2]$. Let the probability distribution $P_+$ be such that $P_+(\{(1,1)\}) = 1$. Let $P_-$ be the uniform probability distribution on the line segment $L = \{(r, 1 - r) \mid 0 \leq r \leq 1\}$ connecting the points $(0,1)$ and $(1,0)$. Let $m \in \mathbb{N}_+$ be arbitrary and let $s$ be a sample containing $m$ positive and $m$ negative examples.

With probability 1 all the negative examples in $s$ are from $L$ and the only positive example is $(1,1)$. When this is true, for any instance $x = (r, r - 1) \in L$ the rectangle $c_x = [r,1] \times [1-r, 1]$ is consistent with $s$ iff $x$ is not one of the negative examples in $s$. Let $x$ be an instance chosen according to the probability distribution $P_-$. With probability 1 the instance $x$ is not one of the negative examples in $s$, so both $c_0$ and $c_x$ are consistent with $s$. Because $x \in c_x$ and $x \notin c_0$ we have $A_{R_2}^{\pm}(s)(x) = *$. Thus, $A_{R_2}^{\pm}$ does not learn probably usefully from $m$ positive and $m$ negative examples. □

# 6   General conditions for learnability

To derive the necessary and sufficient conditions for reliable and polynomially probably useful learnability we consider *learning with one-sided error* [11, 8]. Learning with one-sided error is a sort of semi-reliable learning. Let $C$ be a concept class on the instance space $X$. First we consider only one source of examples.

**Definition 15** *A function $B : S_C \to \mathcal{F}$ learns $C$ with one-sided error from $m(\epsilon, \delta)$ examples if the following conditions hold:*

1. *For all concepts $c \in C$ and all samples $s$ of $c$, the hypothesis $B(s)$ is a subset of $c$.*

2. *For all concepts $c \in C$, all probability distributions $P$ on $X$, all $\epsilon', \delta' > 0$ and all $m > m(\epsilon', \delta')$, the probability of getting $\vec{x} \in X^m$ such that*

$$P(c - B(\text{sam}_c(\vec{x}))) \leq \epsilon'$$

   *is at least $1 - \delta'$.*

Polynomial learnability with one-sided error is defined like polynomially probably useful learnability.

To connect one-sided error and reliability we need some additional notation. Let $\tilde{C}$ be the class of complements of the concepts in $C$. That is,

$$\tilde{C} = \{\bar{c} \mid c \in C\}.$$

For a sample $s = \text{sam}_c(\vec{x})$ of a concept $c$, let $\tilde{s}$ be the sample $s$ with the labels changed:

$$\tilde{s} = \text{sam}_{\bar{c}}(\vec{x}).$$

Let us now assume that a function $B_+$ learns $C$ with one-sided error from $m(\epsilon, \delta)$ examples and a function $B_-$ learns $\widetilde{C}$ in the same way. Let $A : S_C \to H$ be the following function:

$$A(s)(x) = \begin{cases} 1 & \text{if } x \in B_+(s) \\ 0 & \text{if } x \in B_-(\tilde{s}) \\ * & \text{otherwise.} \end{cases}$$

It is easy to see that $A$ learns $C$ reliably and probably usefully from $m(\frac{\epsilon}{2}, \frac{\delta}{2})$ examples.

On the other hand, assume that $A$ learns $C$ reliably and probably usefully from $m(\epsilon, \delta)$ examples. Then, letting

$$B_+(s) = \{x \in X \mid A(s)(x) = 1\} \text{ and } B_-(\tilde{s}) = \{x \in X \mid A(s)(x) = 0\},$$

we get the algorithms $B_+$ and $B_-$ that learn the classes $C$ and $\widetilde{C}$, respectively, with one-sided error from $m(\epsilon, \delta)$ examples. Thus, we have the following result:

**Lemma 16** *A concept class sequence $(C_n)_{n \in \mathbb{N}_+}$ can be learned reliably and polynomially probably usefully from one source of examples iff the concept class sequences $(C_n)_{n \in \mathbb{N}_+}$ and $(\widetilde{C_n})_{n \in \mathbb{N}_+}$ can be learned polynomially with one-sided error.*

**Proof** The lemma follows from the preceding remarks. $\square$

Now we only need to consider learning with one-sided error. To state the general conditions for learnability we say that a concept class $C$ *shatters* a set $S \subseteq X$ if for each subset $s$ of $S$ there is a concept $c \in C$ such that $s = c \cap S$. The *Vapnik-Chervonenkis dimension* [1] of $C$, denoted by $\text{VCdim}(C)$, is the cardinality of the largest $S$ that is shattered by $C$, or $\infty$ if there are arbitrarily large shattered sets:

$$\text{VCdim}(C) = \sup\{|S| \mid S \text{ is shattered by } C\}.$$

Blumer et. al. [1] have shown that under certain measurability assumptions a concept class family $(C_n)_{n \in \mathbb{N}_+}$ is pac-learnable iff $\text{VCdim}(C_n)$ is polynomial in $n$. For reliable and probably useful learning we consider the Vapnik-Chervonenkis dimension of certain related concept classes. For a concept class $C$ on $X$, let

$$C^{\cap} = \left\{ \bigcap_{c \in V_C(s)} c \ \middle| \ s \in S_C \right\}.$$

To derive the necessary and sufficient conditions for learnability with one-sided error we must assume that the concept class sequence is *regular* in the sense of the following definition:

**Definition 17** *A concept class $C$ is regular if the following conditions are fulfilled:*

1. *The set $C^{\cap}$ is a well-behaved concept class. (See [1] for the definition of a well-behaved concept class.)*

2. *For all $\epsilon > 0$, all $c \in C$ and all probability distributions $P$ on $X$ there is a concept $c' \in C^{\cap}$ such that $c' \subseteq c$ and $P(c - c') < \epsilon$.*

*A concept class sequence $(C_n)_{n \in \mathbb{N}_+}$ is regular if the concept class $C_n$ is regular for all $n \in \mathbb{N}_+$.*

Condition 1 is a measurability assumption that is always met if the instance space $X$ is finite. For a finite $X$ always $C \subseteq C^{\cap}$, so condition 2 is also met. Therefore all boolean concept classes are regular. Also the classes $R_n$ of rectangles and $\widetilde{R_n}$ of the complements of rectangles can be shown to be regular. Condition 1 can be proved using the techniques of Blumer et. al. [1]. Condition 2 is straightforward.

Natarajan [8] and Shvaytser [10] have studied learning with one-sided error with only positive examples available. Generalizing their ideas gives us the following result:

**Lemma 18** *A regular concept class sequence $(C_n)_{n \in \mathbb{N}_+}$ can be learned polynomially with one-sided error iff there is a polynomial $p$ such that $\mathrm{VCdim}(C_n^{\cap}) < p(n)$ for all $n$.*

**Proof** (Sketch) First we show that a concept class sequence $(C_n)_{n \in \mathbb{N}_+}$ is polynomially learnable with one-sided error iff the concept class sequence $(C_n^{\cap})_{n \in \mathbb{N}_+}$ is. Condition 2 in definition 15 involves the probability of $c - B(s)$, a subset of $c$. Therefore it seems natural to assume that learning is most difficult when all the probability is concentrated to the set $c$. It can indeed be proved that if $B$ fulfills the conditions of definition 15 under the assumption that $P(c) = 1$, then $B$ learns $C$ with one-sided error from $\frac{8}{\epsilon} \ln \frac{2}{\delta} m(\epsilon, \frac{\delta}{2})$ examples. Thus, we may assume that the examples in a sample always are positive ones.

A sample with only positive examples of a concept $c \in C$ is also a sample of a concept $c' \in C^{\cap}$, and vice versa. Therefore, if $B$ learns $C_n$ with one-sided error from a polynomial number of examples, $B$ also learns $C_n^{\cap}$ from a polynomial number of examples. If $B$, on the other hand, learns $C_n^{\cap}$, then condition 2 in the definition of regularity guarantees that $B$ also learns $C_n$. Thus, $(C_n)_{n \in \mathbb{N}_+}$ can be learned polynomially with one-sided error iff $(C_n^{\cap})_{n \in \mathbb{N}_+}$ can be learned polynomially with one-sided error.

Finally, if $(C_n^{\cap})_{n \in \mathbb{N}_+}$ can be learned with one-sided error, it can also be pac-learned. By the results of Blumer et. al. [1] this implies that $\mathrm{VCdim}(C_n^{\cap})$ is polynomial. On the other hand, if $\mathrm{VCdim}(C_n^{\cap})$ is polynomial, then so is $\mathrm{VCdim}(C_n \cup C_n^{\cap})$. This, again by the results of Blumer et. al., implies that $(C_n \cup C_n^{\cap})_{n \in \mathbb{N}_+}$ can be pac-learned. Furthermore, pac-learning is achieved by any algorithm $B$ that always chooses the hypothesis $B(s)$ from the version space $V_{C_n \cup C_n^{\cap}}(s)$. If we select an algorithm $B$ such that $B(s) = \bigcap_{c \in V_{C_n}(s)} c$ for all the samples $s \in S_{C_n}$, then $B$ also learns $(C_n)_{n \in \mathbb{N}_+}$ with one-sided error from a polynomial number of examples. $\qquad \square$

Combining Lemmas 16 and 18 we now get the following result:

**Theorem 19** *Let $(C_n)_{n \in \mathbb{N}_+}$ be a regular concept class sequence such that also the concept class sequence $(\widetilde{C}_n)_{n \in \mathbb{N}_+}$ is regular. The concept class sequence $(C_n)_{n \in \mathbb{N}_+}$ can be learned reliably and polynomially probably usefully from one source of examples iff there is a polynomial $p$ such that $\mathrm{VCdim}(C_n^{\cap}) \le p(n)$ and $\mathrm{VCdim}(\widetilde{C}_n^{\cap}) \le p(n)$.*

**Proof** Lemmas 16 and 18. $\qquad\qquad\qquad\qquad\qquad\qquad\qquad\qquad\qquad\qquad\qquad$ $\square$

For two sources of examples we define

$$C^{\cap\pm} = \left\{ \bigcap_{c \in V_C(s)} c \;\middle|\; s \in S_C^{\pm} \right\}.$$

Applying the ideas of the proof of Theorem 19 we get the following result:

**Theorem 20** *Assume that $(C_n)_{n \in \mathbb{N}_+}$ is a concept class sequence such that the the following conditions are fulfilled for all $n \in \mathbb{N}_+$:*

1. *The sets $C_n^{\cap\pm}$ and $\widetilde{C}_n^{\cap\pm}$ are well-behaved concept classes.*

2. *For all $\epsilon > 0$, all $c \in C_n$ and all probability distributions $P$ on $X$ there is a concept $c' \in C_n^{\cap\pm}$ such that $c' \subseteq c$ and $P(c - c') < \epsilon$.*

3. *For all $\epsilon > 0$, all $c \in \widetilde{C}_n$ and all probability distributions $P$ on $X$ there is a concept $c' \in \widetilde{C}_n^{\cap\pm}$ such that $c' \subseteq c$ and $P(c - c') < \epsilon$.*

*The concept class sequence $(C_n)_{n \in \mathbb{N}_+}$ can be learned reliably and polynomially probably usefully from two sources of examples iff there is a polynomial $p$ such that $\mathrm{VCdim}(C_n^{\cap\pm}) < p(n)$ and $\mathrm{VCdim}(\widetilde{C}_n^{\cap\pm}) < p(n)$.*

**Proof** (Sketch) We use learning with one-sided error from two sources of examples in the same way we did with one source of examples. The main difference is that in learning from two sources of examples we cannot assume that all the examples are positive. Instead we can prove that the probability distribution $P_-$ on the negative instances of $c$ can be assumed to give probability 1 to some singleton $\{x\} \subseteq \bar{c}$. The motivation for this is the idea that two different negative examples provide more information than repetitions of one negative example, making it easier to find a good hypothesis.

The rest of the proof is similar to that of Lemmas 16 and 18. The details are omitted. $\square$

For any sample $s \in S_C^{\pm}$ there is a labeled sample $s' \in S_C$ such that $V_C(s') = V_C(s)$. Therefore always $C^{\cap\pm} \subseteq C^{\cap}$. By combining this fact with Theorems 19 and 20 we see that polynomial learnability from one source of examples implies polynomial learnability from two sources of examples. This is a special case of Theorem 9. If a labeled sample $s' \in S_C$ contains only positive or only negative examples, there are perhaps no samples $s' \in S_C^{\pm}$ such that $V_C(s) = V_C(s')$. Therefore we may have $C^{\cap} \not\subseteq C^{\cap\pm}$. This explains why the converse of Theorem 9 does not hold.

# 7   Summary and conclusions

We have considered reliable and probably useful learning, which was originally defined by Rivest and Sloan [9] with a hierarchical learning algorithm. Using Rivest and Sloan's algorithm requires the teacher to break the target concept into simple subconcepts. We noticed that this is not always possible. Thus we were led to search for concept classes that can be learned reliably and probably usefully from a polynomial number of examples without any additional information.

The results are mainly negative. In particular, we have shown that the class of boolean monomials cannot be learned reliably and probably usefully. Knowledge acquisition applications usually use concept classes, such as decicion trees, that include the class of boolean monomials as a special case. From the practical point of view our results thus imply that reliability cannot be achieved in such applications even if the examples are noiseless.

While we feel that breaking the concept into simple subconcepts is not always practical, our results show that many interesting concept classes cannot be learned reliably from examples without some additional information. This implies that we cannot generalize Rivest and Sloan's algorithm by allowing the subconcepts to be chosen from these more general classes.

Some modifications in the definitions are necessary, if we want to use reliable learning in applications. One possibility would be to allow the learner to output a non-reliable hypothesis with a probability less than $\delta$. The number of examples needed is usually polynomial in the *logarithm* of $\frac{1}{\delta}$, which allows the confidence parameter to be made quite small. Thus, learning would still be rather reliable. Unfortunately, even this modification does not allow monomials to be learned.

We have also derived a characterization of reliable and polynomially probably useful learnability using the Vapnik-Chervonenkis dimension. This characterization explains why learning from one source of examples is more difficult than learning from two sources of examples. It also explains why symmetric concepts are particularly easy to learn reliably and probably usefully.

# Acknowledgements

I am grateful to Esko Ukkonen for helpful discussions. This work has been supported by the Academy of Finland.

# References

[1]  Blumer, A., Ehrenfeucht, A., Haussler, D. and Warmuth, M.: Classifying Learnable Geometric Concepts with the Vapnik-Chervonenkis Dimension. *Proceedings of the*

*Eighteenth Annual ACM Symposium on Theory of Computing*, Berkeley, California, 1986, pp. 273–282.

[2] Blumer, A., Ehrenfeucht, A., Haussler, D. and Warmuth, M. K.: Occam's Razor. *Information Processing Letters*, 24(6), 1987, pp.377–380.

[3] Ehrenfeucht, A. and Haussler, D.: Learning Decision Trees From Random Examples. *First Workshop on Computational Learning Theory*, Cambridge, Massachusetts, 1988, pp. 238–250.

[4] Haussler, D., Kearns, M., Littlestone, N., Warmuth, M. K.: Equivalence of Models for Polynomial Learnability. *First Workshop on Computational Learning Theory*, Cambridge, Massachusetts, 1988, pp. 34–50.

[5] Kearns, M., Li, M., Pitt, L., Valiant, L.: On the Learnability of Boolean Formulae. *Proceedings of the Nineteenth Annual ACM Symposium on Theory of Computing*, New York City, 1987, pp. 285–295.

[6] Kivinen, J. Manuscript in preparation.

[7] Mitchell, T.M.: Version Spaces: a Candidate Elimination Approach to Rule Learning. *Proceedings of the 5th International Joint Conference on Artificial Intelligence*, Cambridge, Massachusetts, 1977, pp. 305–310.

[8] Natarajan, B. K.: On Learning Boolean Functions. *Proceedings of the Nineteenth Annual ACM Symposium on Theory of Computing*, New York City, 1987, pp. 296–304.

[9] Rivest, R. L. and Sloan, R.: Learning Complicated Concepts Reliably and Usefully. *First Workshop on Computational Learning Theory*, Cambridge, Massachusetts, 1988, pp. 61–71.

[10] Shvaytser, H.: Non-learnable Classes of Boolean Formulae That Are Closed Under Variable Permutation. *First Workshop on Computational Learning Theory*, Cambridge, Massachusetts, 1988, pp. 121–132.

[11] Valiant, L. G.: A Theory of the Learnable. *Communications of the acm*, 27(11), 1984, pp. 1134–1142.

# Short Abstracts

# The Strength of Weak Learnability

Robert E. Schapire

MIT Laboratory for Computer Science
Cambridge, MA   02139

The problem is considered of improving the accuracy of a hypothesis output by a learning algorithm in the distribution-free ("pac") learning model introduced by Valiant. In this model, the learner tries to identify an unknown concept based on randomly chosen examples of the concept. Examples are chosen according to a fixed but unknown and arbitrary distribution on the space of instances. The learner's task is to find a hypothesis or prediction rule of his own that correctly classifies new instances as positive or negative examples of the concept. With high probability, the hypothesis must be correct for all but an arbitrarily small fraction of the instances.

A class of concepts is *learnable* (or *strongly learnable*) if there exists a polynomial time algorithm that achieves low error with high confidence for all concepts in the class. A weaker model of learnability, called *weak learnability,* drops the requirement that the learner be able to achieve arbitrarily high accuracy; a weak learning algorithm need only output a hypothesis that performs slightly better (by an inverse polynomial) than random guessing. The notion of weak learnability was introduced by Kearns and Valiant who left open the question of whether the strong and weak learning models are equivalent. This question was termed the *hypothesis boosting problem* since the problem is to boost the low accuracy of a weak learning algorithm's hypotheses.

In this paper, the hypothesis boosting question is answered in the affirmative. The main result is a proof of the perhaps surprising equivalence of strong and weak learnability.

This result may have significant applications as a tool for proving that a concept class is learnable since, in the future, it will suffice to find an algorithm correct on only, say, 51% of the instances. Alternatively, in its negative contrapositive form, the result says that, if a concept class cannot be learned with accuracy 99.9%, then we cannot hope to do even slightly better than guessing on the class (for some distribution).

The proof presented is constructive; an explicit method is described for directly converting a weak learning algorithm into one that achieves arbitrary accuracy. The construction uses *filtering* to modify the distribution of examples and so forces the weak learning algorithm to focus on the harder to learn parts of the distribution. Thus, the distribution-free nature of the learning model is fully exploited.

Briefly, the construction uses filtering to simulate three new distributions, and runs an assumed weak learning algorithm on each of these distributions, combining the output hypotheses appropriately. In so doing, the error of the weak learning algorithm is reduced by a small but significant amount, and, applying this process recursively, the error can be made arbitrarily small.

An immediate corollary of the main result is the equivalence of strong and *group* learnability. A group learning algorithm need only output a hypothesis capable of classifying large groups of instances, all of which are either positive or negative. The notion of group learnability was shown to be equivalent to weak learnability by Kearns and Valiant.

Finally, an interesting and unexpected consequence of the construction is a proof that any strong learning algorithm that outputs hypotheses whose length (and thus whose time to evaluate) depends on the allowed error $\epsilon$ can be modified to output hypotheses whose length is only polynomial in $\log(1/\epsilon)$. Thus, any learning algorithm can be converted into one whose output hypotheses do not become significantly more complex as the error tolerance is lowered. The construction also yields general bounds on the dependence on $\epsilon$ of the time and sample size complexities of any strong learning algorithm.

This paper prepared with support from ARO Grant DAAL03-86-K-0171, and a grant from the Siemens Corporation. Author's net address: rs@theory.lcs.mit.edu.

# ON THE COMPLEXITY OF LEARNING FROM COUNTEREXAMPLES

WOLFGANG MAASS[*,**] AND GYÖRGY TURÁN[*,***]

## ABSTRACT

The complexity of learning concepts $C \in \mathcal{C}$ from various concrete concept classes $\mathcal{C} \subseteq 2^X$ over a finite domain $X$ is analyzed in terms of the number of counterexamples that are needed in the worst case (we consider the deterministic learning model of Angluin, where the learning algorithm produces a series of "equivalence queries"). It turns out that for many interesting concept classes $\mathcal{C}$ there exist exponential differences between the number of counterexamples that are required by a "naive" learning algorithm for $\mathcal{C}$ (e.g. one that always outputs the minimal consistent hypothesis) and a "smart" learning algorithm for $\mathcal{C}$ that attempts to make a more sophisticated prediction (this is in contrast to the situation for pac-learning, where every consistent learning algorithm requires about the same number of examples).

We give $\theta(\log n)$ bounds for the number of counterexamples that are required for learning boxes, balls, and halfspaces in a $d$-dimensional discrete space $X = \{1, \dots, n\}^d$ (for every finite dimension $d$). We also give an upper bound of $O(d^3)$ and a lower bound of $\Omega(d^2)$ for the complexity of learning a threshold function with $d$ input bits (i.e. $X = \{0,1\}^d$). For each of these concept classes one can give learning algorithms that are both optimal (resp. close to optimal in the case of threshold functions) with regard to the number of counterexamples which they require <u>and</u> computationally feasible (in the case of balls, halfspaces and threshold functions our learning algorithms use the method of the ellipsoid algorithm).

Finally, we determine the complexity of learning of the considered concept classes (as well as linear orders, perfect matchings, and some other concept classes that turn out to be useful for the separation of learning models) on several variations of the considered learning model (such as learning with arbitrary hypotheses, partial hypotheses, membership queries). We also clarify the relationship between these learning models and some related combinatorial invariants.

For an extended abstract of this paper we refer to the Proceedings of the IEEE FOCS Conference 1989.

---

[*]Department of Mathematics, Statistics, and Computer Science, University of Illinois at Chicago, Chicago, IL. 60680. E-mail: U45381 @ UICVM.BITNET.

[**]Written under partial support by NSF-Grant CCR 8703889.

[***]Automata Theory Research Group of the Hungarian Academy of Sciences, Szeged, Hungary. Partially supported by OTKA-433. E-mail: U11557 @ UICVM.BITNET.

# Generalizing the PAC Model:
## Sample Size Bounds From Metric Dimension-based Uniform Convergence Results

David Haussler

UC Santa Cruz, Computer Science, Santa Cruz, CA 95064

haussler@saturn.ucsc.edu

Summary:   We consider the problem of learning functions on a domain $X$ that take values in an arbitrary metric space $Y$. We assume only that the examples are generated by independent draws from an unknown distribution on $X \times Y$. The learner's goal is to find a function in a given hypothesis space $\mathcal{F}$ of functions from $X$ into $Y$ that on average gives $Y$-values that are close to those observed in random examples (i.e. that has small *error*). We give a theorem on the uniform convergence of empirical error estimates to true error rates for certain hypothesis spaces $\mathcal{F}$ (generalizing a result of Pollard's), and show how this implies learnability, disregarding computational complexity. We generalize the notion of VC dimension to classes of functions mapping into a metric space and show that small VC dimension gives rapid uniform convergence for any distribution. We do this by relating the VC dimension of $\mathcal{F}$ to the *metric dimension* of certain embeddings of $\mathcal{F}$, using results of Pollard and Dudley.

As an application, we give a distribution-free uniform convergence result for certain classes of functions computed by neural nets. Here we fix a multi-layer feedforward neural net architecture in which each computation node applies a smooth sigmoid function to a weighted sum of its inputs. We then consider the class of functions defined by varying the weights.

We also give uniform convergence results for classes of functions that are *uniformly continuous on average*, a new notion we introduce. These include classes of continuous functions with a uniform Lipschitz bound, and many classes of discontinuous functions, including indicator functions for regions of small boundary in the unit square. Our results are distribution-free in the former case, but distribution-specific in the latter case (we assume a "near uniform" distribution on the unit square). An extended abstract of this work is given in [1].

[1] Haussler, D., "Generalizing the PAC Model: Sample Size Bounds From Metric Dimension-based Uniform Convergence Results," Proc. 1989 IEEE Symp. on Foundations of Comp. Sci., to appear.

The author gratefully acknowledges the support of ONR grant N00014-86-K-0454.

# A Theory of Learning Simple Concepts
# Under Simple Distributions

*Ming Li**

Computer Science Department, York University
North York, Ontario M3J 1P3, Canada (li@yuyetti.bitnet)

*Paul M.B. Vitanyi*

Centrum voor Wiskunde en Informatica
Kruislaan 413, 1098 SJ Amsterdam (paulv@mcvax.bitnet)
and
Universiteit van Amsterdam
Faculteit Wiskunde en Informatica

## ABSTRACT

We aim at developing a learning theory where 'simple' concepts are easily learnable. In Valiant's learning model, many things appear to be hard to learn. Relatively few concept classes were shown to be learnable in polynomial time. In practice, almost nothing we care to learn appears to be not learnable. To model human learning more closely, we impose a reasonable restriction on Valiant model. We assume that learning happens under an *arbitrary simple* distribution, rather than an *arbitrary* distribution as assumed by Valiant [V]. A distribution is simple if it is dominated by a semi-computable distribution. Such an assumption appears to be not very restrictive in many practical cases. Most distributions we customarily deal with are computable or can be approximated or dominated by computable or semi-computable ones, hence they fit our assumption. However such an assumption, amazingly, allows us to exhibit a rich mathematical structure on learning. We systematically develop a general theory of learning under simple distributions. In particular we show that one can learn under all simple distributions, if one can learn under one fixed (universal) distribution. We present interesting learning algorithms and several quite general new learnable classes. These classes are more general than the classes known to be polynomial time learnable in Valiant's original model.

---

* The first author is supported by the NSERC operating grant OGP0036747. His current address is: Department of Computer Science, University of Waterloo, Waterloo, Ontario, Canada N2L 3G1.

# Learning Binary Relations and Total Orders
# (Abstract)

Sally A. Goldman          Ronald L. Rivest          Robert E. Schapire

Laboratory for Computer Science
Massachusetts Institute of Technology
Cambridge, Massachusetts 02139

We study the problem of designing polynomial prediction algorithms to learn a binary relation. We represent the relation as an $n \times m$ binary matrix. The learner is repeatedly given an element of the matrix and asked to predict its value. It is natural to consider learning scenarios in which a significant fraction of the matrix may be queried. So the natural dimension measure of the problem is not the size of an instance, but rather the size $nm$ of the entire instance space. As this problem demonstrates, there are interesting concept classes with polynomial sized instance spaces. Since the learner sees "most" of the instance space when presented with a polynomial number of instances, these concept classes are trivially pac-learnable.

It is natural for these concept classes to use a mistake bound model like that discussed by Littlestone. Clearly the mistake bound depends on the order in which instances are presented. We extend the basic mistake bound model to one in which a helpful teacher or the learner selects the query sequence, in addition to considering when instances are drawn by an adversary or according to a probability distribution on the instance space. Although helpful teachers have been considered before, they have been used only to provide counterexamples to conjectured concepts, or to break up the concept into smaller sub-concepts. In our framework, the teacher only selects the presentation order for the instances.

We apply this extension of the mistake bound model to the concept class of binary matrices that have at most $k$ distinct row types. (Two rows are of the same type if the agree in all columns.) The learner has no a priori knowledge about the predicate forming the relation. We present an algorithm that makes at most $mk + (n - k) \lg k$ mistakes for an unknown value of $k$ when the learner chooses the query sequence. We present an algorithm for $k = 2$ that makes at most $2m + n - 2$ mistakes when an adversary chooses the query sequence. For arbitrary $k$ we present an algorithm that makes at most $km + \frac{k-1}{2k}n^2$ mistakes against an adversary selected query sequence. We use the existence of projective geometries to prove an $\Omega(n^{3/2})$ lower bound on the worst case number of mistakes made by a large class of algorithms for a $2n \times n$ matrix when an adversary chooses the query sequence. Finally, we describe a simple prediction rule that achieves an expected mistake bound of $O(k(n\sqrt{m} + m))$ when the query sequence is chosen at random.

We also consider when the binary relation is constrained by the requirement that the predicate form a total order. For this problem of learning a total order the halving algorithm yields good mistake bounds. (The halving algorithm predicts according to the majority of the feasible concepts, and thus each mistake halves the number of concepts to consider.) We describe a general technique showing how a fully polynomial randomized approximation scheme (fpras) can be used to implement a randomized version of the halving algorithm. We then apply this technique using a fpras for counting the number extensions of a partial order to obtain a polynomial prediction algorithm for learning a total order that makes $n \lg n + o(n \lg n)$ mistakes with very high probability when an adversary selects the query sequence. (The small probability of making "too many" mistakes is taken over the coin flips of the learning algorithm and does not depend on the query sequence selected by the adversary.) We also consider when a teacher or the learner selects the query sequence. Finally, we discuss how the halving algorithm may be used to construct an efficient counting algorithm.

This paper prepared with support from NSF grant DCR-8607494, ARO Grant DAAL03-86-K-0171, and a grant from the Siemens Corporation. We thank Manfred Warmuth for suggesting the application of approximate and probabilistic counting to the problem of learning a total order. We also thank Nick Littlestone and Bob Sloan for their comments.

Authors' net addresses: sally@theory.lcs.mit.edu, rivest@theory.lcs.mit.edu, rs@theory.lcs.mit.edu.

# The Weighted Majority Algorithm

Nick Littlestone *

Aiken Computation Laboratory

Harvard Univ.

Manfred K. Warmuth †

Dep. of Computer Sc.

U. C. Santa Cruz

## Abstract

We study the construction of prediction algorithms in a situation in which a learner faces a sequence of trials, with a prediction to be made in each, and the goal of the learner is to make few mistakes. We are interested in the case that the learner has reason to believe that one of some pool of known algorithms will perform well, but the learner does not know which one. A simple and effective method, based on weighted voting, is introduced for constructing a compound algorithm in such a circumstance. We call this method the Weighted Majority Algorithm. We show that this algorithm is robust w.r.t. errors in the data. We discuss various versions of the Weighted Majority Algorithm and prove mistake bounds for them that are closely related to the mistake bounds of the best algorithms of the pool. For example, given a sequence of trials, if there is an algorithm in the pool $A$ that makes at most $m$ mistakes then the Weighted Majority Algorithm will make at most $c(\log n + m)$ mistakes on that sequence, where $c$ is fixed constant. One version of the Weighted Majority algorithm deals with pools that are countably infinite.

The Weighted Majority algorithm is:

an efficient and robust method for selecting good predictive performance from a pool algorithms;

a powerful tool getting upper bounds on learning problems while ignoring computational efficiency.

An extended abstract will appear in the *Proceedings of the 30th Annual Symposium on the Foundations of Computer Science*, Research Triangle, North Carolina, October 30 - November 1, 1989.

---

*Supported by ONR grant N00014-85-K-0445. Part of this research was done while this author was at the University of Calif. at Santa Cruz with support from ONR grant N00014-86-K-0454

†Supported by ONR grant N00014-86-K-0454. Part of this research was done while this author was on sabbatical at Aiken Computation Laboratory, Harvard, with partial support from the ONR grants N00014-85-K-0445 and N00014-86-K-0454

# Author Index